GRADE

9

Printed in the U.S.A.

ISBN 978-0-358-41642-5

10 11 12 13 14 15 16 0029 31 30 29 28 27 26 25 24 23

4500866833

r9.22

Program Consultants:
Kylene Beers
Martha Hougen
Tyrone C. Howard
Elena Izquierdo
Carol Jago
Weston Kieschnick
Erik Palmer
Robert E. Probst

GRADE
9

Program Consultants

Kylene Beers

Nationally known lecturer and author on reading and literacy; coauthor with Robert Probst of *Disrupting Thinking, Notice & Note: Strategies for Close Reading,* and *Reading Nonfiction;* former president of the National Council of Teachers of English. Dr. Beers is the author of *When Kids Can't Read: What Teachers Can Do* and coeditor of *Adolescent Literacy: Turning Promise into Practice,* as well as articles in the *Journal of Adolescent and Adult Literacy.* Former editor of *Voices from the Middle,* she is the 2001 recipient of NCTE's Richard W. Halle Award, given for outstanding contributions to middle school literacy.

Martha Hougen

National consultant, presenter, researcher, and author. Areas of expertise include differentiating instruction for students with learning difficulties, including those with learning disabilities and dyslexia; and teacher and leader preparation improvement. Dr. Hougen has taught at the middle school through graduate levels. Dr. Hougen has supported Educator Preparation Program reforms while working at the Meadows Center for Preventing Educational Risk at The University of Texas at Austin and at the CEEDAR Center, University of Florida.

Tyrone C. Howard

Veteran teacher, author, and professor in the Graduate School of Education and Information Studies at UCLA. Dr. Howard is the inaugural director of the UCLA Pritzker Center for Strengthening Children and Families, a campus-wide consortium examining academic, mental health, and social and emotional experiences and challenges for the most vulnerable youth populations. Dr. Howard has published over 75 peer-reviewed journal articles and several bestselling books, including, *Why Race & Culture Matters in Schools* and *Black Male(d): Peril and Promise in the Education of African American Males*. He is considered one of the premier experts on educational equity and access in the country.

Elena Izquierdo

Nationally recognized teacher educator and advocate for English language learners. Dr. Izquierdo is a linguist by training, with a Ph.D. in Applied Linguistics and Bilingual Education from Georgetown University. She has served on various state and national boards working to close the achievement gaps for bilingual students and English language learners. Dr. Izquierdo is a member of the Hispanic Leadership Council, which supports Hispanic students and educators at both the state and federal levels.

Carol Jago

Teacher of English with 32 years of experience at Santa Monica High School in California; author and nationally known lecturer; former president of the National Council of Teachers of English. Ms. Jago currently serves as Associate Director of the California Reading and Literature Project at UCLA. With expertise in standards assessment and secondary education, Ms. Jago is the author of numerous books on education, including *With Rigor for All* and *Papers, Papers, Papers*; and she is active with the California Association of Teachers of English, editing its scholarly journal *California English* since 1996. Ms. Jago also served on the planning committee for the 2009 NAEP Reading Framework and the 2011 NAEP Writing Framework.

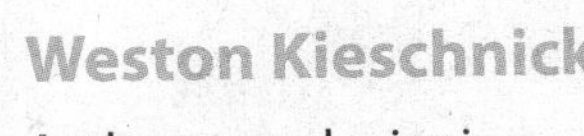

Weston Kieschnick

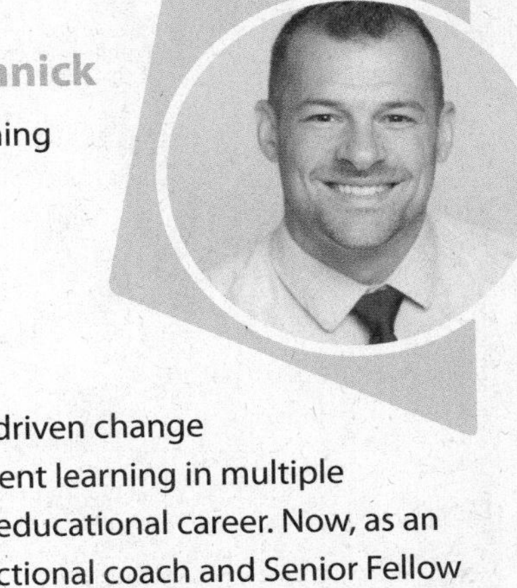

Author, award-winning teacher, principal, instructional development coordinator, and dean of education. Mr. Kieschnick has driven change and improved student learning in multiple capacities over his educational career. Now, as an experienced instructional coach and Senior Fellow with the International Center for Leadership in Education (ICLE), Mr. Kieschnick shares his expertise with teachers to transform learning through online and blended models. He is the author of *Bold School: Old School Wisdom + New School Innovation = Blended Learning that Works* and co-author of *The Learning Transformation: A Guide to Blended Learning for Administrators.*

Erik Palmer

Veteran teacher and education consultant based in Denver, Colorado. Author of *Well Spoken: Teaching Speaking to All Students* and *Digitally Speaking: How to Improve Student Presentations*. His areas of focus include improving oral communication, promoting technology in classroom presentations, and updating instruction through the use of digital tools. He holds a bachelor's degree from Oberlin College and a master's degree in curriculum and instruction from the University of Colorado.

Robert E. Probst

Nationally respected authority on the teaching of literature; Professor Emeritus of English Education at Georgia State University. Dr. Probst's publications include numerous articles in *English Journal* and *Voices from the Middle,* as well as professional texts including (as coeditor) *Adolescent Literacy: Turning Promise into Practice* and (as coauthor with Kylene Beers) *Disrupting Thinking, Notice & Note: Strategies for Close Reading,* and *Reading Nonfiction.* He has served NCTE in various leadership roles, including the Conference on English Leadership Board of Directors, the Commission on Reading, and column editor of the NCTE journal *Voices from the Middle.*

UNIT 1

Against All Odds

ESSENTIAL QUESTION: *What does it take to survive a crisis?*

KEY LEARNING OBJECTIVES

- Analyze text structures
- Analyze author's perspective
- Analyze arguments and rhetorical devices
- Analyze literary devices
- Make inferences
- Analyze poetic language and structure
- Analyze word choice

READER'S CHOICE

Available online

Ed

Recommendations

UNIT 1 TASKS

Ed

Go online for

- Unit and Selection Videos
- Interactive Annotation and Text Analysis
- Selection Audio Recordings
- Collaborative Writing — Writable

UNIT 2

Breaking Through Barriers

Page 98

ESSENTIAL QUESTION:
Are some differences too great to overcome?

KEY LEARNING OBJECTIVES

- Analyze central ideas and details
- Analyze text structures
- Analyze author's purpose, message, and rhetoric
- Analyze voice and tone
- Analyze setting and theme
- Analyze figurative language
- Analyze media representations

READER'S CHOICE

SHORT READS

Facing It
Poem by Yusef Komunyakaa

Making the Future Better, Together
Blog by Eboo Patel

Oklahoma Bombing Memorial Address
Speech by Bill Clinton

Night Calls
Short Story by Lisa Fugard

Available online Ed

LONG READS

To Kill a Mockingbird
Novel
Harper Lee

Love, Hate, and Other Filters
Novel
Samira Ahmed

Code Talker
Novel
Joseph Bruchac

Recommendations

UNIT 2 TASKS

Ed

Go online for	
Unit and Selection Videos	
Interactive Annotation and Text Analysis	
Selection Audio Recordings	
Collaborative Writing	Writable

UNIT 3

Crime Scenes

Page 194

ESSENTIAL QUESTION:
Who suffers when a crime is committed?

KEY LEARNING OBJECTIVES

- Analyze universal themes
- Analyze main idea and details
- Summarize and paraphrase texts
- Make inferences
- Analyze literary techniques
- Analyze media messages
- Build active listening skills

READER'S CHOICE

SHORT READS

Available online

LONG READS

In Cold Blood
Nonfiction
Truman Capote

Murder on the Orient Express
Mystery
Agatha Christie

We'll Fly Away
Novel
Bryan Bliss

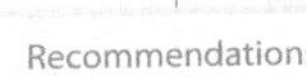

UNIT 3 TASKS

Go online for
Unit and Selection Videos
Interactive Annotation and Text Analysis
Selection Audio Recordings
Collaborative Writing — Writable

UNIT 4

Love and Loss

Page 292

ESSENTIAL QUESTION: *How can love bring both joy and pain?*

KEY LEARNING OBJECTIVES

- Analyze literary devices
- Analyze parallel plots
- Analyze source material
- Compare authors' claims
- Analyze rhetoric

READER'S CHOICE

SHORT READS

Available online

Ed

LONG READS

Romiette and Julio
Novel
Sharon Draper

The Fault in Our Stars
Novel
John Greene

Solo
Novel in Verse
Kwame Alexander

Recommendations

UNIT 4 TASKS

WRITING

Ed

Go online for

- Unit and Selection Videos
- Interactive Annotation and Text Analysis
- Selection Audio Recordings
- Collaborative Writing — Writable

UNIT 5

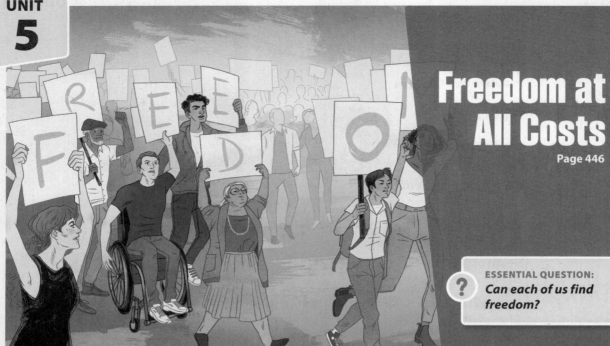

Freedom at All Costs

Page 446

ESSENTIAL QUESTION:
Can each of us find freedom?

KEY LEARNING OBJECTIVES

- Analyze irony and satire
- Analyze arguments and rhetorical devices
- Analyze author's purpose and point of view
- Analyze text structures
- Analyze word choice and poetic language
- Analyze narrator perspective
- Analyze accounts in different mediums

READER'S CHOICE

SHORT READS

We Wear the Mask
Poem by Paul Laurence Dunbar

The Prisoner Who Wore Glasses
Short Story by Bessie Head

Reforming the World *from* **America's Women**
History Writing by Gail Collins

from **Long Walk to Freedom**
Memoir by Nelson Mandela

Eulogy for Martin Luther King Jr.
Speech by Robert F. Kennedy

Available online

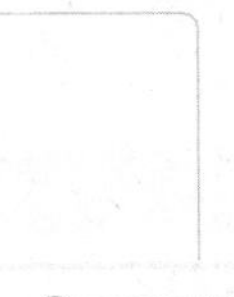

LONG READS

Long Walk to Freedom
Memoir
Nelson Mandela

Goodbye, Vietnam
Novel
Gloria Whelan

March
Graphic Memoir
John Lewis

Recommendations

UNIT 5 TASKS

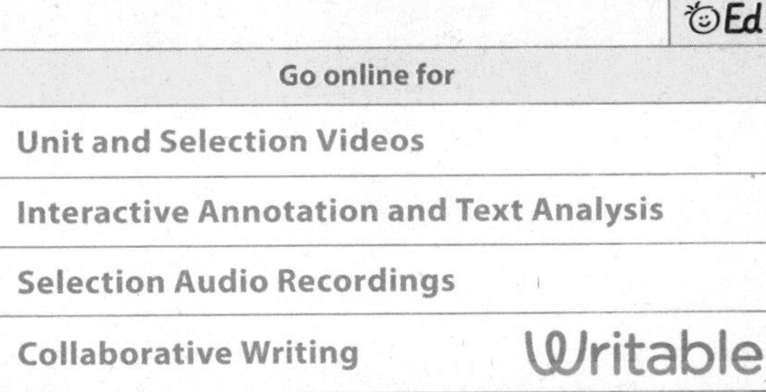

UNIT 6

Epic Journeys

Page 534

ESSENTIAL QUESTION: *What drives us to take on a challenge?*

KEY LEARNING OBJECTIVES

- Analyze epic hero and epic poetry
- Make predictions
- Analyze central ideas and events
- Evaluate graphic features
- Interpret figurative language

READER'S CHOICE

SHORT READS

Available online

Ed

LONG READS

The Thief
Novel
Megan Whalen Turner

Finding Miracles
Novel
Julia Alvarez

The Marrow Thieves
Science Fiction
Cheri Dimaline

Recommendations

UNIT 6 TASKS

Ed

Go online for	
Unit and Selection Videos	
Interactive Annotation and Text Analysis	
Selection Audio Recordings	
Collaborative Writing	Writable

Selections by Genre

FICTION

Short Story

NONFICTION

Argument

Autobiography/Memoir

Informational Text

POETRY

DRAMA

MEDIA STUDY

into Literature™ Online

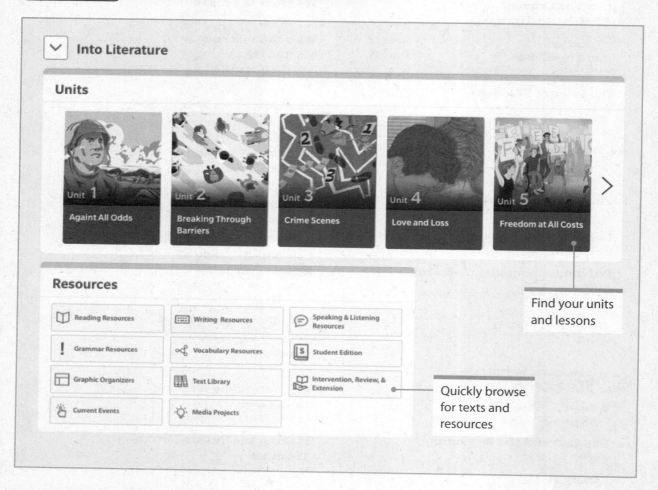

Experience the Power of *HMH Into Literature*

Into Literature

Units

Unit 1 Againt All Odds

Unit 2 Breaking Through Barriers

Unit 3 Crime Scenes

Unit 4 Love and Loss

Unit 5 Freedom at All Costs

Find your units and lessons

Resources

- Reading Resources
- Writing Resources
- Speaking & Listening Resources
- Grammar Resources
- Vocabulary Resources
- Student Edition
- Graphic Organizers
- Text Library
- Intervention, Review, & Extension
- Current Events
- Media Projects

Quickly browse for texts and resources

Tools for Today—All in One Place

Whether you're working alone or collaborating with others, it takes effort to analyze the complex texts and competing ideas that bombard us in this fast-paced world. What will help you succeed? Staying engaged and organized. The digital tools in this program will help you take charge of your learning.

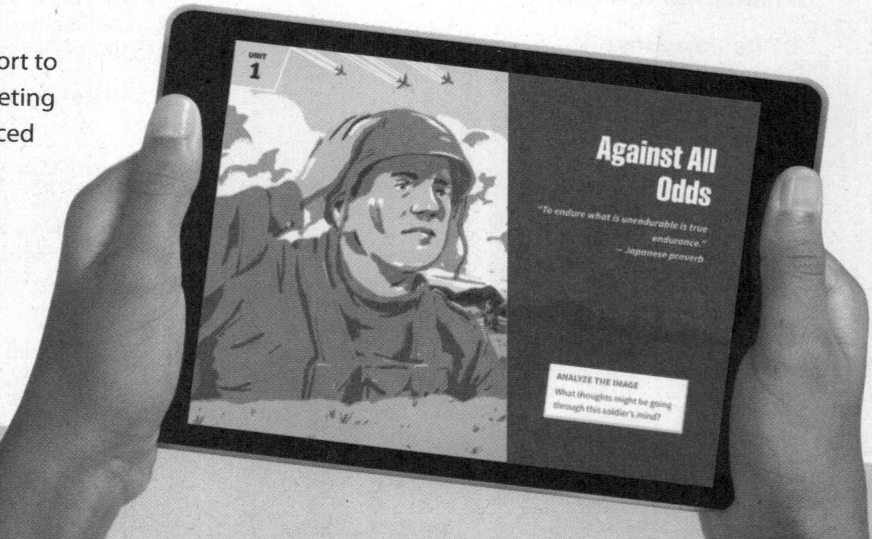

Engage!

Spark Your Learning

These activities kick-start the unit and help get you thinking about the unit theme.

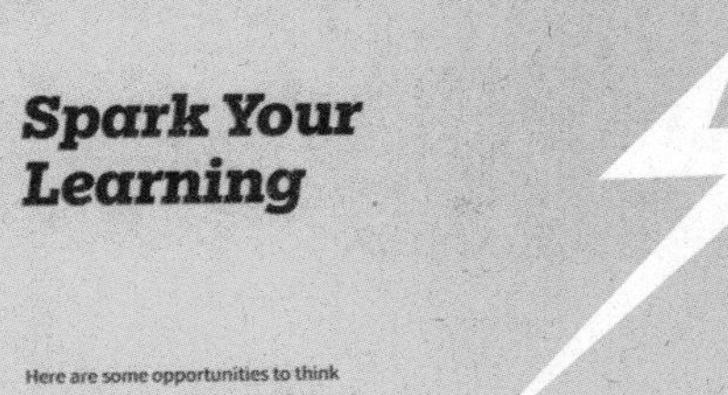

Engage Your Brain

Before you read, take some time to do a fun activity designed to rev up your brain and connect to the text.

Interact with the Texts

- As you read, highlight and take notes to mark the text in your own customized way.
- Use interactive graphic organizers to process, summarize, and track your thinking as you read.
- Play the audio to listen to the text read aloud. You can also turn on read-along highlighting.

Choices

Choose from engaging activities, such as writing an advice column, creating a podcast, or participating in a debate, to demonstrate what you've learned.

Stay Involved!

Collaborate with and Learn from Your Peers

- Watch brief **Peer Coach Videos** to learn more about a particular skill.
- Flex your creative muscles by digging into **Media Projects** tied to each unit theme.
- Bring your writing online with **Writable,** where you can share your work and give and receive valuable feedback.

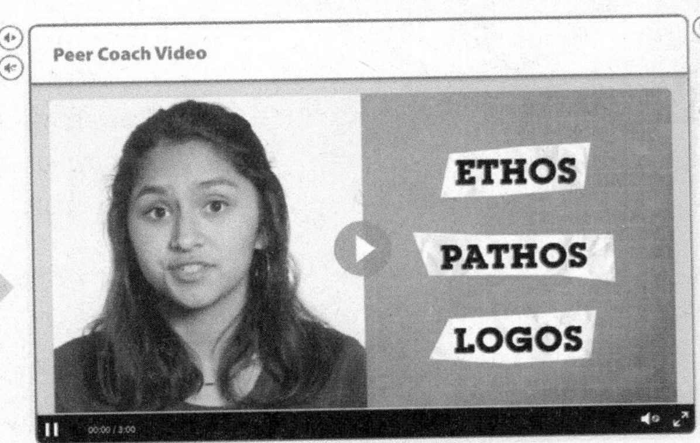

Writable

Read On!

Find helpful **Reader's Choice** suggestions with each unit, and access hundreds of texts online.

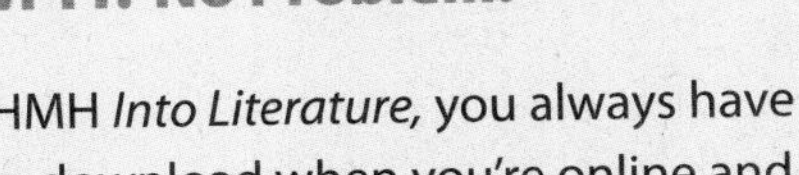

No Wi-Fi? No Problem!

With HMH *Into Literature,* you always have access; download when you're online and access what you need when you're offline.

NOTICE & NOTE

Becoming a Better Reader

Dr. Kylene Beers

Dr. Robert E. Probst

Reading is Change: Thoughts by Two Teachers

by **Dr. Kylene Beers** and **Dr. Robert E. Probst**

In reading, as in almost everything else, paying attention is essential.

You wouldn't stand in the batter's box, facing a hard-throwing pitcher, with your mind wandering to what you may have for dinner that evening. The prospect of a fastball coming toward you at 80 miles an hour tends to focus the mind. And you wouldn't attempt to sing a difficult song in front of a large crowd with your thoughts on what you're going to wear to the dance this weekend. The need to remember the words, keep the beat, move to the rhythm, and stay in tune keeps you focused. When something counts, you pay attention. Close attention.

It's the same with reading. Of course, if you don't concentrate while reading, you won't suffer the pain of being knocked down by the fastball or the embarrassment of failing to hit the notes in front of the crowd. But if you don't pay attention as you read, there is barely any purpose in picking up the text at all.

But there *is* a purpose in reading, and that purpose is change.

We may read just to pass the time, to entertain ourselves when we have nothing to do. Or we might read simply to get information that we need. Where is tonight's game? What are the instructions for making the brownies? What's happening on whatever new app tells you what your friends are doing? The changes that result in these cases might be small (hopefully the brownies turned out better!), but they're still changes.

Other reading might enable us to change in much more significant ways.

You might . . .

- read about child labor in foreign countries and change your mind about what you will buy and what you will boycott.
- read *The Hate U Give,* and change your thinking about race and the justice system.
- read about climate change and wonder what you can do to help preserve the earth.

It's important for us to keep in mind that it is we, the readers, who must do the changing.

We don't want to be molded, shaped, and directed entirely by others. We want to be in charge of our own lives. And so each reader has to take responsibility for noticing what's in the text, deciding what matters, paying attention to the thoughts and feelings it has awakened, and thinking about what to do next.

Not all books will be life-changing for you, and we can't tell you which ones they will be. A book about Harriet Tubman was life-changing for one of us, while Cousteau's *The Silent World* was as influential for the other. We can't know exactly what book will be powerful for which reader. But we know that for a book to be important to you, you have to notice what the text offers, think about it, and take what matters to you into your head and heart. We urge you to pay attention to three elements as you read:

- **The Book.** Or whatever text you have in your hand. Throughout this book, we're going to give you some strategies that we hope will make it easy for you to think critically about what the texts tell you.
- **Your Head.** If it's an article you're reading, then keep in mind what you thought about the topic before you began, and then think seriously about how you might have changed your thinking as a result of what you've read. If it's a story or a poem, then think about what thoughts or feelings it brought to mind and how they might have shaped your reaction to the text.
- **Your Heart.** Ask yourself what you want to carry away from the reading. What matters to you? How might you have shifted your attitudes about something, even if only slightly?

Book. Head. Heart. We call it **BHH** reading.

It all begins with noticing.

And that noticing will be easier to do if you keep in mind a few things that you will probably see in almost any text (unless it is very short). We call these elements **signposts** (see the chart on the next two pages) because they serve readers just as signposts or street signs serve drivers: they alert them to something significant. The careless driver who doesn't pay attention and misses a stop sign is likely to end up in trouble. Readers who don't notice the signposts won't end up in trouble, but they probably won't be able to follow what's going on in the text. They'll be limiting their ability to grow, learn, and change. Reading with purpose will get you so much further, and signposts can help. Reading with purpose can help you become the person you might not even know you want to be.

*For more about the signposts, see the **Notice & Note Handbook,** pp. R7–R19.*

COLLABORATIVE DISCUSSION

Share an example of something that has changed for you because of reading. Do you agree that the purpose of reading is to change?

NOTICE & NOTE

Signposts

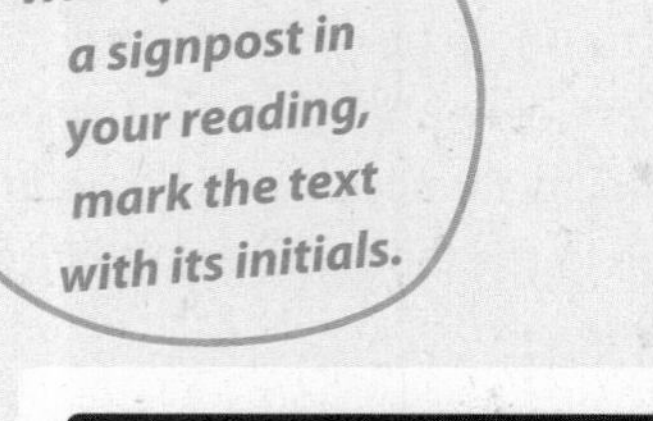

When you notice a signpost in your reading, mark the text with its initials.

LITERARY TEXTS

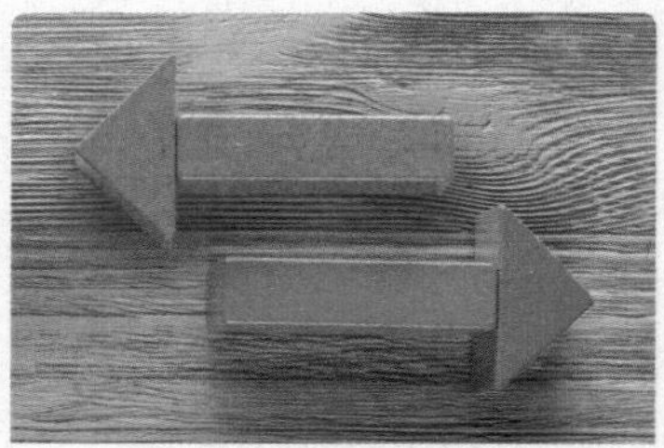

CONTRASTS AND CONTRADICTIONS CC

A sharp contrast between what we would expect and what we observe the character doing; behavior that contradicts previous behavior or well-established patterns

When you notice this signpost, ask:

Why would the character act (feel) this way?

p. **R8**

AHA MOMENT AM

A sudden realization of something that shifts a character's actions or understanding of self, others, or the world

When you notice this signpost, ask:

How might this change things?

p. **R9**

TOUGH QUESTIONS TQ

Questions characters raise that reveal their inner struggles

When you notice this signpost, ask:

What does this question make me wonder about?

p. **R10**

WORDS OF THE WISER WW

The advice or insight about life that a wiser character, who is usually older, offers to the main character

When you notice this signpost, ask:

What's the life lesson and how might this affect the character?

p. **R11**

AGAIN AND AGAIN AA

Events, images, or particular words that recur over a portion of the story

When you notice this signpost, ask:

Why might the author bring this up again and again?

p. **R12**

MEMORY MOMENT MM

A recollection by a character that interrupts the forward progress of the story

When you notice this signpost, ask:

Why might this memory moment be important?

p. **R13**

Ed

Peer Coach Videos

INFORMATIONAL TEXTS

BIG QUESTIONS

It's important to take a **Questioning Stance** or attitude when you read nonfiction.

- *What surprised me?*
- *What did the author think I already knew?*
- *What changed, challenged, or confirmed what I already knew?*

p. **R14**

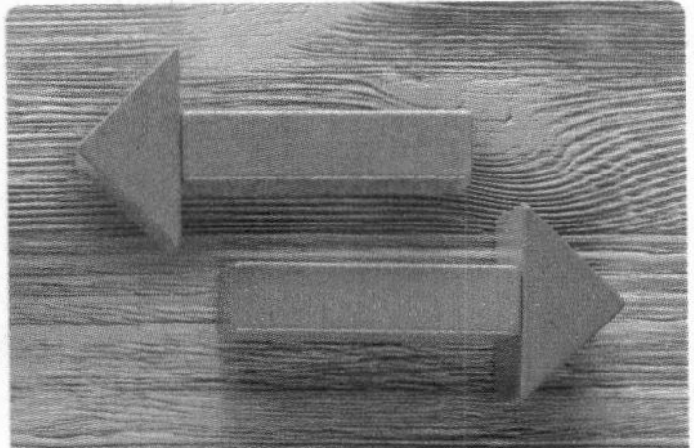

CONTRASTS AND CONTRADICTIONS

A sharp contrast between what we would expect and what we observe happening; a difference between two or more elements in the text

When you notice this signpost, ask:

What is the difference, and why does it matter?

p. **R15**

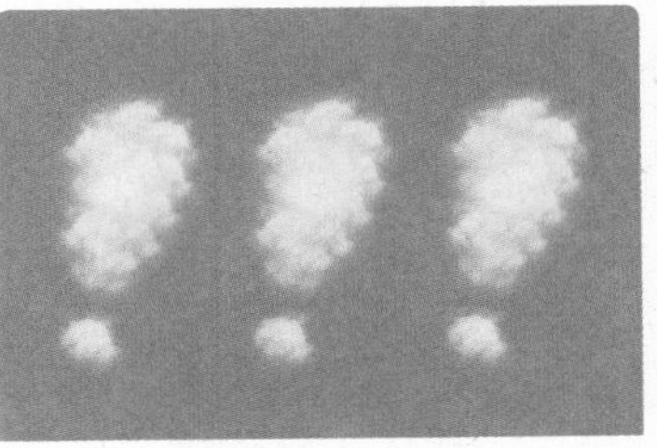

EXTREME OR ABSOLUTE LANGUAGE

Language that leaves no doubt about a situation or an event, allows no compromise, or seems to exaggerate or overstate a case

When you notice this signpost, ask:

Why did the author use this language?

p. **R16**

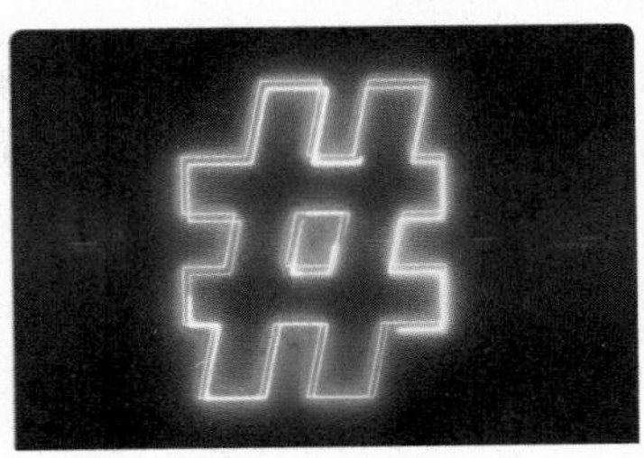

NUMBERS AND STATISTICS

Specific quantities or comparisons to depict the amount, size, or scale; or the writer is vague and imprecise about numbers when we would expect more precision

When you notice this signpost, ask:

Why did the author use these numbers or amounts?

p. **R17**

QUOTED WORDS

Opinions or conclusions of someone who is an expert on the subject or someone who might be a participant in or a witness to an event; or the author might cite other people to provide support for a point

When you notice this signpost, ask:

Why was this person quoted or cited and what did this add?

p. **R18**

WORD GAPS

Vocabulary that is unfamiliar to the reader—for example, a word with multiple meanings, a rare or technical word, a discipline-specific word, or one with a far-removed antecedent

When you notice this signpost, ask:

Do I know this word from someplace else? Does this seem like technical talk for experts on this topic? Can I find clues in the text to help me understand the word?

p. **R19**

Social & Emotional Learning

The Most Important Subject Is You!

by **Carol Jago**

You have essays to turn in. You have quizzes to take. You have group projects to complete. Your success in those areas depends on more than your understanding of the academic skills they cover. It also depends on how well you understand yourself, and how well you're able to extend that understanding to others. This might seem obvious, but there's an actual term for that type of learning—it's called **Social and Emotional Learning.**

Why It Matters

But doing well in school is not the only benefit to understanding yourself and others. When it comes to Social and Emotional Learning, the answer to the question, "When will I actually use this in my life?" is clear: every single day, forever. Whether you are with your family, your community, your friends, at a workplace, or by yourself on a deserted island, you will have a better chance of achieving satisfaction and making positive contributions if you're able to do things like the following:

- ✔ identify your emotions
- ✔ make smart choices
- ✔ set reasonable goals
- ✔ recognize your strengths
- ✔ have empathy
- ✔ manage your reactions
- ✔ evaluate problems and solutions
- ✔ show respect for others

Where Literature Comes In

English Language Arts classes can provide some of the best opportunities to develop these skills. That's because reading literature allows you to imagine yourself in different worlds and to understand what it's like to be in a wide range of situations. You can think through your own feelings and values as you read about various characters, conflicts, historical figures, and ideas, and you can become more aware of why others might act and feel as they do.

Throughout this book, you will find opportunities for Social and Emotional Learning in the Choices section of many lessons. But you don't need to wait for a special activity to practice and learn. Reading widely and discussing thoughtfully is a natural way to gain empathy and self-knowledge. The chart below shows the five main areas of Social and Emotional Learning and tells how reading can help you strengthen them.

Areas of Social and Emotional Learning	How Reading Can Help
If you have **self-awareness,** you're conscious of your own emotions, thoughts, and values, and you understand how they affect your behavior.	Understanding why characters act the way they do can increase your understanding of your own responses and motivations.
If you're good at **self-management,** you are able to control your emotions, thoughts, and behaviors in different situations.	Paying attention to why characters explode in tumultuous ways or how they keep calm under pressure can help you recognize what to do and not to do when faced with stressful situations in your own life.
If you have **social awareness,** you can empathize with others, including people who are different from you.	Reading about people with different life experiences can help you understand the perspectives of others.
If you have well-developed **relationship skills,** you can get along with different kinds of people and function well in groups.	Reflecting on the conflicts between characters can help you gain insight into what causes the conflicts in your life and how to reach mutual satisfaction.
If you are good at **responsible decision-making,** you make good choices that keep you and others safe and keep you moving toward your goals.	Evaluating the choices characters make and thinking about what you would do in their place can help you understand the consequences of your decisions.

Having the Hard Conversations

The more widely and deeply you read, the more you'll strengthen your social and emotional skills, and the more likely you are to encounter ideas that are different from your own. Some texts might bring up strong reactions from you, and you'll need to take a step back to understand how you're feeling. Or, your classmates might have responses that are dramatically different from yours, and you'll need to take a breath and decide how to engage with them. Remember: it's okay to disagree with a text or with a peer. In fact, discussing a difference of opinion can be one of the most powerful ways to learn.

Tips for Talking About Controversial Issues

So what I hear you saying is . . .

Did I get that right?

Listen actively.
Try your best to understand what the other person is saying, and why they might think or feel that way. If you don't understand, ask questions or rephrase what you thought you heard and ask them if you're getting it right.

The reason I think so is because I've noticed that I . . .

Communicate clearly.
Speak honestly and carefully, rather than for dramatic effect. Notice if the person listening seems confused and give them room to ask questions.

When you use that word I have a negative reaction because it sounds like you are saying you think that person isn't smart.

I'm sorry. That's not what I meant.

Take a stand against name-calling, belittling, stereotyping, and bias.
Always try exploring ideas further rather than making personal attacks. If someone feels hurt by something you said, listen to them with an open mind. Perhaps you expressed bias without realizing it. Apologize sincerely if that happens. And if you are hurt by a comment or hear something that could be interpreted as hurtful, calmly let the person who said it know why you feel that way.

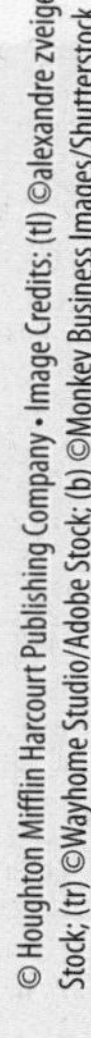

I need to take a break from this conversation now.

Pay attention to your feelings.
Recognize the topics or situations that make it hard for you to stay calm. Try to separate your strong feelings from what the person is saying. If you need to, excuse yourself from the conversation and find a place where you can help yourself relax.

We see this really differently, so let's move on for now.

Consider the relationship.
It's likely that the people you're in class with are people you will be seeing regularly for years. You don't have to be friends with them or agree with their point of view, but you do have to get an education alongside each other. Speaking respectfully even if you're on opposite sides of an issue will make it easier to work together if you ever have to collaborate. Try to assume the best about them rather than the worst. Acknowledge that our experiences affect our points of view.

Agree to disagree.
Even after listening carefully and being listened to, you still might not agree. That's okay. You can acknowledge your differences, remain respectful, and exit the conversation.

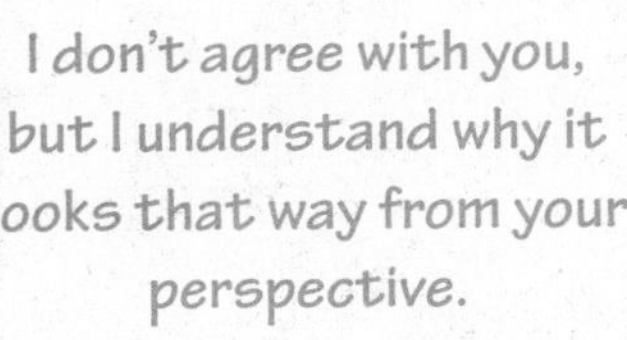

I don't agree with you, but I understand why it looks that way from your perspective.

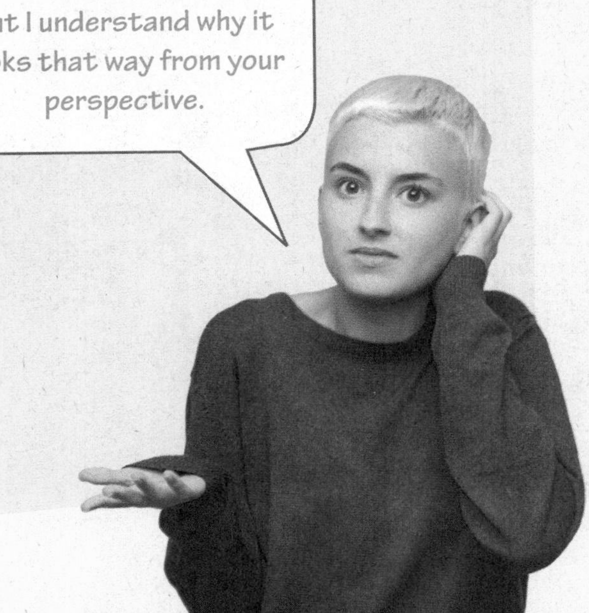

Learning, growing, and working with others isn't always easy. If you read widely and deeply and try your best to speak honestly, you're likely to gain the understanding and compassion that can help you manage the stresses, challenges, and opportunities that life brings your way.

Analyze the Image
What thoughts might be going through this soldier's mind?
Ed
Get hooked by the unit topic.
Stream to Start Video

UNIT 1

Against All Odds

"To endure what is unendurable is true endurance."
— Japanese proverb

ESSENTIAL QUESTION:
What does it take to survive a crisis?

Spark Your Learning

Here are some opportunities to think about the topics and themes of **Unit 1: Against All Odds.**

As you read, you can use the **Response Log** (page R1) to track your thinking about the Essential Question.

(page R1)

Think about the **Essential Question**

What does it take to survive a crisis?

Think about different kinds of extreme hardships people endure—for example, environmental (weather disasters), political (wars), or personal. What does it take to survive these crises?

Make the Connection

Think about the Japanese proverb on the unit introduction. The statement seems to be a contradiction. Is it? With a partner, discuss what the proverb might mean.

Build Academic Vocabulary

You can use these Academic Vocabulary words to write and talk about the topics and themes in the unit. Which of these words do you already feel comfortable using when speaking or writing?

	I can use it!	I understand it.	I'll look it up.
dimension			
external			
statistic			
sustain			
utilize			

Prove It!

Imagine you are stranded on a desert island. Use the vocabulary words you know to describe your circumstance or what you would do to survive.

Preview the Texts

Look over the images, titles, and descriptions of the texts in the unit. Mark the title of the text that interests you most.

from **A Chance in the World**

Literary Nonfiction by **Steve Pemberton**

A young boy in foster care seeks food for body and soul.

Is Survival Selfish?

Argument by **Lane Wallace**

If forced to choose, whose life would you save: Your own, or someone else's?

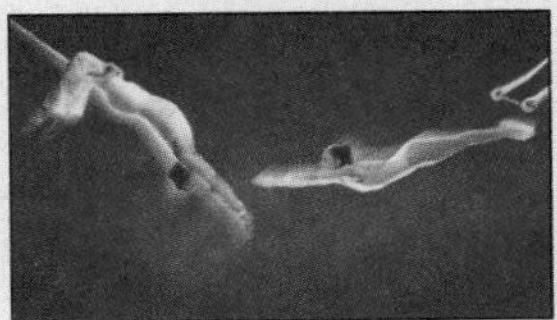

The Leap

Short Story by **Louise Erdrich**

A mother saves her daughter's life three times.

The End and the Beginning

Poem by **Wisława Szymborska**

What are the harsh realities of life after war?

from **Night**

Memoir by **Elie Wiesel**

A young man waits to hear whether he and his father will be selected to live another day or be killed.

from **Maus**

Graphic Memoir by **Art Spiegelman**

Cats and mice represent Nazis and Jews in this graphic novel about the Holocaust.

Think Outside the Box

Think of how crises affect people. How can a person change after enduring something difficult?

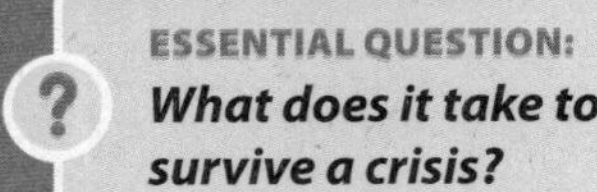
ESSENTIAL QUESTION:
What does it take to survive a crisis?

from
A Chance in the World

Literary Nonfiction by **Steve Pemberton**

Engage Your Brain

Choose one or more of these activities to start connecting with the text you're about to read.

Does Everyone Have a Chance?

Think about the title of this text. Does everyone have the same chances and opportunities to be successful in life?

1. In the appropriate column of the T-chart, list ways and reasons people do or do not have the same opportunities for success in life.
2. Discuss your conclusions with a partner.

Yes	No

Sources of Strength

We can draw on sources of strength and support when we find ourselves in a dangerous or painful situation. For example, we may turn to a trusted friend or adult. Make a list of ways people can cope with threatening or even perilous situations.

These Are a Few of My Favorite Things

Think back to when you were younger. What were your "comfort" items—things, activities, or places that made you happy or perhaps took you to another world? Sketch pictures or make a list.

Analyze Literary Nonfiction

Literary nonfiction conveys factual information, ideas, or experiences using literary techniques. Literary nonfiction can include memoirs such as *A Chance in the World* as well as autobiographies, biographies, and speeches. How can you tell the difference between literary nonfiction and other informational texts?

- Look for lyrical or even poetic descriptions that go beyond simple explanations.
- Notice **figurative language** (for example, similes and metaphors) and **sensory details** (words and phrases appealing to the senses).
- Take note of how the author interprets what he or she is describing or experiencing.
- Watch for the author's reflections on the meaning of experiences.

In this memoir, author Steve Pemberton recalls a traumatic time in his childhood—and shares where he found comfort and strength. As you read, notice the language the author uses to communicate the impact of his experiences. Also think about why he might have chosen to include particular events and details.

Focus on Genre
Literary Nonfiction

- conveys factual information, ideas, or experiences
- develops insights that go beyond the facts
- uses literary devices such as figurative and sensory language

Analyze Author's Perspective

An **author's perspective,** or point of view, is a unique combination of ideas, values, feelings, and beliefs that influences the way the writer looks at a topic. Authors reveal their perspectives in a variety of ways. One clue is the author's **diction,** or choice of words. Authors also communicate their perspective through the details they choose to focus on and direct statements about their feelings and beliefs.

As you read the text, fill out the chart to help you understand Steve Pemberton's perspective on this particular period in his childhood.

Clues to Author's Perspective	Examples from *A Chance in the World*
Language (diction)	"monsters" used to describe the Robinsons
Details the author includes	
Direct statements about the author's feelings and beliefs	

Annotation in Action

Here is an example of notes a student made about a passage from *A Chance in the World*. As you read, mark words and phrases that convey details about the author's situation.

One way I dealt with these monsters was to become a thief, and a very good one at that. My devious plots were elaborate, complete with escape routes and explanations if I were ever to get caught.

"Monsters!"—the Robinsons must be awful.

amazing what he does to cope

Expand Your Vocabulary

Put a check mark next to the vocabulary words that you feel comfortable using when speaking or writing.

fathom	☐
thwart	☐
cacophony	☐
sanctuary	☐
baffle	☐

Using the words you already know, work with a partner to write a paragraph about someone who is in a place that feels unsafe or threatening.

As you read the excerpt from *A Chance in the World*, use the definitions in the side column to help you learn the vocabulary words you don't already know.

Background

Steve Pemberton was born and raised in New Bedford, Massachusetts. After graduating from Boston College with degrees in political science and sociology, he worked as a college admissions officer and then embarked on a career as an executive at Monster.com, Walgreens, and Workhuman. Pemberton's memoir, *A Chance in the World*, was published in 2012. He says he wrote it in part because "I wanted to contribute to the universal story of family, faith, fortitude, and forgiveness."

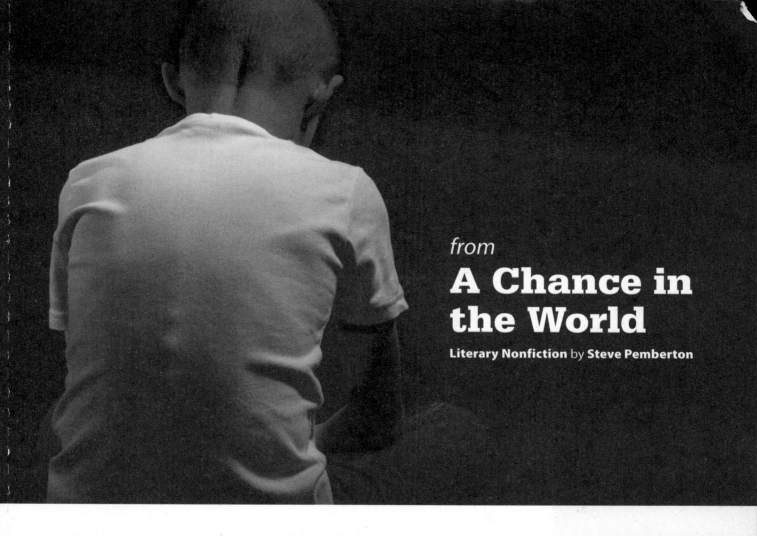

from

A Chance in the World

Literary Nonfiction by **Steve Pemberton**

A young boy in foster care seeks food for body and soul.

NOTICE & NOTE 
As you read, use the side margins to make notes about the text.

Steve Pemberton became an orphan at age three when it became clear that his birth parents could not care for him. After being moved through several foster homes, Steve was finally placed with the Robinson family in New Bedford, Massachusetts, which is the setting for this excerpt. The "Robinson Rules" refer to harsh regulations his foster parents imposed.

> *"All the world will be your enemy, Prince of a Thousand Enemies, and whenever they catch you, they will kill you. But first they must catch you, digger, listener, runner, prince with the swift warning. Be cunning and full of tricks . . ."*
> Richard Adams, *Watership Down*

1 I settled into a routine at the house on Arnold Street, to the degree one can ever become comfortable with monsters who disguise themselves as human beings. This is what they were to me: real-life boogeymen whose origins and intentions I could never **fathom**. Children rarely ask where monsters come from or how they came to be; children simply accept them as a fact of life, something to be dealt with, the way you deal with any other childhood fear.

fathom
(făth´əm) *v.* to comprehend.

2 One way I dealt with these monsters was to become a thief, and a very good one at that. My devious plots were elaborate, complete with escape routes and explanations if I were ever to get caught. I obsessed over the things I stole, and no matter how much I managed to get, I always tried to steal more. Once I stole something, I would stare at it, wondering how best I could hide it or preserve it. But I didn't steal just anything. I was fixated on one thing: food. At seven years old, I weighed just forty pounds, a fact the Robinsons explained away by saying I had tapeworms.

3 To avoid going hungry, I had to be creative—to outwit them. Nearly every morning of my days with the Robinsons, I would awake and immediately try to determine how I was going to get food to hide in the basement. It took me a while to learn what to steal. My first foray into the art of thievery was a huge block of government-rationed cheese that Willie had hustled. I hid it in the basement and sneaked away one afternoon ready to feast, only to find the mice that roamed the cellar had already beaten me to it. After that, I placed my thieving eye on the unlabeled silver cans of peanut butter Willie brought home; I was confident that the enterprising mice couldn't chew through the metal.

4 I wasn't usually that picky; I would eat whatever scraps I could get my hands on. If it wasn't moving, then it was fair game. Whenever they went grocery shopping, I had to unload the bags. I would scan the bags quickly to see what was in them and hide the one with the most goodies underneath the car. When the coast was clear, I would take the bag and dash to the cellar, where I would squirrel it away. From time to time, they would realize that they had come up a bag or two short and would fume at the person who had bagged their groceries. They never figured out it was me. The joy of outsmarting the Robinsons became almost as sweet as the food I stole. Almost.

ANALYZE LITERARY NONFICTION

Annotate: Mark the sensory language in paragraph 5.

Analyze: How does this language convey Steve's feelings about books?

5 Another very important way of coping was to immerse myself in books. When, precisely, I began reading, I cannot say. There was no signature moment, at least early on, but I imagine I discovered books as part of going to school. Books for me were what the ocean is to the fearless explorer—deep and mysterious, boundless and soothing. I loved the smell of books, the feel of their weight in my hands, the rustle of the pages as I turned them, the magnificent illustrations on the covers that promised hidden treasures within.

thwart
(thwôrt) *v.* to prevent the occurrence of.

6 Like food, books were hard for me to come by. The Robinsons never bought me any (Robinson Rule #10) and **thwarted** every attempt I made to get more. When I did bring home a book from the school library, I had to ask if I could read (Robinson Rule #11). If I were caught reading without permission, a merciless beating would follow (Robinson Rule #12). When permission was granted, it was granted begrudgingly and only under the condition that I read in the cellar. I was never allowed to keep books upstairs (Robinson Rule #13), nor could I read in their presence (Robinson Rule #14).

7 The cellar was cold, musty, and dank. Its walls tossed off long shadows in the dim light offered by a single swaying bulb. I frequently heard the mice clawing and scratching in the walls. The cellar was storage space for many of the home's utilities—washing machine, dryer, hot water and oil furnaces—but also for many of the things the Robinsons had no further use for, like broken furniture that didn't stand, ancient preserves no longer fit to be eaten, old clothes that had gone out of style. These abandoned items had served their purpose, but the Robinsons held on to them, believing that someday someone foolish enough to value them would come along and take them off their hands. To the Robinsons, the cellar was precisely where I belonged.

8 Amid all the clutter, I fashioned a makeshift reading space composed of mildewy clothes, torn pillows, and old box springs. I positioned this space directly under the stairs because, that way, I would be able to hear anyone coming down. And my hearing was finely tuned. I knew the stride pattern of each member of the family: Betty shuffled, Reggie had longer steps, and Willie's plodding was the easiest to detect, for he often walked with his oak cane. When they approached the cellar door, I would scramble to hide my book and stash of food. I kept a jug of water to wash away the peanut butter smell on my breath, a lesson I learned when Willie nearly caught me. If I had ever been caught reading down there with my moldy stash of hoarded food, I would have paid a dear price.

VOCABULARY

Patterns of Word Changes: Based on context clues in paragraph 6, what do you think *begrudgingly* means?

Analyze: What part of speech is *begrudgingly*? What other forms of the word can you make?

ANALYZE AUTHOR'S PERSPECTIVE

Annotate: Mark the sentence in paragraph 9 that reveals what Steve wonders about most.

Infer: What does this suggest about Steve's sense of identity?

9 I loved the cellar, finding it a welcome refuge from the Robinson Rules. Yet it was not my favorite place to read—at least not during the warmer months. Across from the Robinsons' house, right next to Fuller's paint store, was Mrs. Blake's house. Alongside her yard was a small retaining wall. A large oak tree hung over the area, so large that it kept half the block in shade. The wall itself was no more than a few feet high and craggy, as if hewn from the side of a mountain, except for a single, smooth, square piece of rock at the wall's northern end. Once my chores were done and I had received permission, I would take my favorite book, go to that shaded haven, and lose myself in my latest mystery, none of which seemed as great as the mystery of where I had come from.

10 Nearly every summer day, you would find me sitting on that wall, accompanied by squirrels playing in the trees, as well as the occasional ant that tried to make my sneaker its home. I was never more at peace during my childhood than when I sat there. I loved the sound of the wind rustling through the leaves of the large oak, the smell of freshly cut grass brought on by neighborhood lawn mowers, the **cacophony** of birds that twittered as they flew by, the bumblebees that hovered by my head before moving on to more interesting things. This was my **sanctuary**, the place where I felt the most alive—and the safest.

cacophony (kə-kŏf´ə-nē) *n.* jarring, discordant sound.

sanctuary (săngk´cho͞o-ĕr´ē) *n.* a sacred place.

11 One summer afternoon when I was about eight years old, I looked up from my perch atop my reading wall to see a woman strolling down Chancery Street toward me. It was a neighbor, Mrs. Levin. I had seen her on many occasions walking to Sunnybrook Farms, the neighborhood grocery store. She was a small woman with dark hair pulled away from her face, although now, looking at her up close for the first time, I noticed the first signs of gray. Mrs. Levin was plainly dressed as always and moved at a casual pace, thoroughly enjoying her walk.

12 She often waved and smiled at the Robinsons but nothing more than that. From time to time, her husband joined her. He was slightly taller, a balding man who wore red suspenders over a white T-shirt. They were Jewish, and the only reason I knew that was because as soon as they were out of earshot, Betty or Willie would fling anti-Semitic[1] remarks at their backs. For quite some time I thought they said "jewels" instead of "Jews." For the life of me, I couldn't figure out why the Robinsons thought something as precious as jewels would be such bad people.

[1] **anti-Semitic:** describing one who discriminates against or who is hostile toward or prejudiced against Jews.

Don't forget to **Notice & Note** as you read the text.

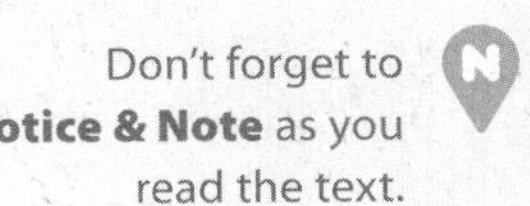

13 Now I looked down, careful not to make any eye contact that would initiate a conversation (Robinson Rule #15). The walkway alongside the Blake home was not paved, and I could hear the crunching of Mrs. Levin's footsteps on the gravel as she neared. As I so often did with strangers, I hoped that she would walk on by and pay me no attention. But that's not what happened. Her white tennis shoes, scuffed ever so lightly around the toe, stopped right in front of me. And though I was not afraid, I still swallowed hard. "What are you reading there?" she asked.

14 I looked up from the pages and showed her the cover of my Encyclopedia Brown mystery. Leroy Brown, "Encyclopedia" to his friends, was a boy detective who often sat at the dinner table helping his dad, the chief of police in the fictional town of Idaville, solve cases that had **baffled** the department.

baffle
(băf´əl) *v.* to confuse or perplex.

15 "You like mysteries?" she asked.

16 "Oh, yes, ma'am," I said, making the conversation far longer than the Robinson Rules dictated. "I really like how you get a chance to figure out the clues for yourself."

17 "Now, if I remember, weren't you reading this book last week?"

18 It puzzled me how she could have known that. "Yes, ma'am. But when I finish a book, I go back to the beginning and start all over again."

19 "I see." She said nothing more and ambled on toward the store, but I still remember the long look she sent in the direction of my house on Arnold Street.

20 Later that evening, there was a knock at the door. I was in the pantry washing dishes when Betty answered. A voice I immediately recognized asked, "Is Steve here? I have something I would like to give him." It was Mrs. Levin.

21 I grabbed for the dishrag, began drying my hands, and heard Betty say, "I can give them to him." But Mrs. Levin was insistent: "If it's okay, I would like to give him these myself."

22 There was a pause. "Stevie!" Betty said, the sweet, melodic voice, and use of a nickname, telling me that she was "onstage." I came around the corner much faster than I should have, but my eavesdropping[2] was either missed or ignored.

23 "You remember me?" Mrs. Levin asked. I nodded my head yes.

24 "Well, I thought you might like these." In her arms was a brown, open-ended box, but I could not see what was in it. She lowered it, and I could barely believe my eyes. Inside the box were stacks of books, of different thicknesses and colors, their covers bright and promising.

[2] **eavesdropping:** secretly listening to the private conversation of others.

25 "Whoa," I said.

26 "These," she said, "are for the boy who likes to read."

27 "Thank you, ma'am," I said, barely able to take my eyes off the box. "You're welcome," she said, smiling; and with that, she left. She was barely out of earshot before Betty's voice boomed, 'Take those books downstairs! I better never see them up here."

28 "Yes, ma'am, right now, ma'am," I stammered. I feared that she would make me throw them away.

29 Nothing I write can accurately capture the power and timeliness of the gift Mrs. Levin gave me that day. Though I did not know it at the time, several years earlier, when I was one and a half years old, a babysitter had written: "Dropped Steve off at the latest family his mother is boarding him out to . . . he cried his heart out . . . this little boy doesn't have a chance in the world." Others believed this as well, especially those to whose care I was entrusted. I sensed it in their sidelong glances and empathetic shakes of the head, their eyes saying what their tongues would not. *You are beyond repair.*

NOTICE & NOTE

MEMORY MOMENT

When you notice the narrator has interrupted the forward progress of a story by bringing up something from the past, you've found a **Memory Moment** signpost.

Notice & Note: Mark the lines in paragraph 29 that tell about something that happened in the past.

Analyze: Why might this memory be important?

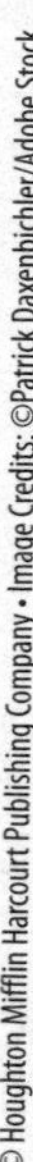

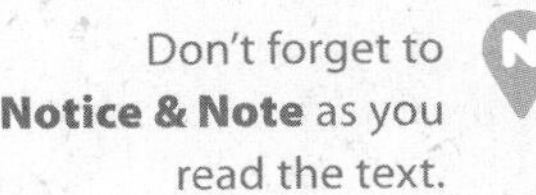
Don't forget to **Notice & Note** as you read the text.

30 I had beaten my fists against this fate as long as I could. Now, frequently starved and beaten almost daily, failed and abandoned by the institutions tasked with my care, and waiting for a family that was never going to come for me, I was beginning to lose my desperate battle with the Robinsons. Caseworkers at the time described me as tense, nervous, and anxious. What was really unfolding was something far more damaging, something they never looked hard enough to see: I had begun to resign myself to this fate, to accept I was to be the Robinsons' prisoner and that their world would be the only one I would ever know.

31 But the characters that unfolded in those books and the worlds they lived in showed me a different life, a future far beyond the pain of the house on Arnold Street. I learned that not everyone lived the way I did, that most people came from intact homes that offered joy and laughter, freedom and exploration, promise and possibility. And because of what I read, I developed the ridiculously absurd notion that one day I, too, could have a life like the ones I read about.

32 At every opportunity I would steal down to the cellar to dive into my cardboard chest of hidden treasures, planting myself right in the middle of those adventures. I became a fearless explorer, a brilliant scientist, and a master riddle solver. I went to the depths of the ocean with Captain Nemo and *20,000 Leagues Under the Sea*, stood right by Howard Carter's side as he discovered the tomb of King Tutankhamen, and landed on the moon with the crew of *Apollo 11*. I unlocked more riddles with boy detective Encyclopedia Brown and joined forces with Alfred Hitchcock and the Three Investigators to solve even greater mysteries. My books became my shelter, protecting me as the Robinsons' slings and arrows rained overhead. And I returned my books' protection by guarding them the way most children guard their teddy bears. As a little boy, I was mystified when bookworms burrowed into their pages and crushed when a basement flood destroyed several of them.

33 Mrs. Levin's books gave me something else that I did not fully appreciate until many years later: a model for dealing with the Robinsons. It came from my favorite book, *Watership Down*, a novel I would read over and over again. Published in 1972 and written by the British author Richard Adams, this book tells the tale of a band of resilient rabbits searching for a new home. Led by the small but exceedingly clever Hazel, these rabbits encounter many obstacles in their search. One of their first challenges was one I knew all too well: they encounter a warren of contented rabbits—a home that seems to be exactly what the group is looking for—yet they learn that this new home is not at all what it appears to be and that it is, in fact, a cleverly crafted rabbit farm intended to ensnare them.

ANALYZE AUTHOR'S PERSPECTIVE

Annotate: Mark the sentence in paragraph 30 that describes Steve's key realization about himself.

Analyze: How does his diction help you understand the change in Steve's state of mind?

ANALYZE LITERARY NONFICTION

Annotate: Mark the figurative language in paragraph 32. What types of figurative language are used here?

Analyze: What shelters the narrator? Who or what is threatening him?

ANALYZE AUTHOR'S PERSPECTIVE

Annotate: Mark the sentence in paragraph 34 where the author states a belief.

Interpret: What does this belief suggest about Steve's view of the world?

34 The rabbits escape the farm and often resort to trickery in their pursuit of a new home. Deception may seem unprincipled, but it is absolutely necessary if Hazel and his group of rabbits are to survive, especially when their very existence is threatened by another group of rabbits, the Efrafrans, and their evil leader, General Woundwort. There comes a time when deception is not enough, and the group must take a stand against General Woundwort, although they know it will likely cost them their lives.

35 I found kinship in the rabbits of *Watership Down*. They became my childhood friends, the only ones I was allowed to have, and I could cite their names at the drop of a hat: Fiver, Bigwig, Pipkin, and Blackberry. My friends were smart, fast, elusive, and resourceful—their very survival was predicated on their ability to sense danger. Though confronted by bigger foes, they outwitted them. Perhaps most important, I saw the rabbits as fighters, their combativeness driven by a certainty that they could create a different and better life for themselves. For Hazel and his followers, it was never a question of *if* they would find a home; it was simply a matter of *when*.

ANALYZE LITERARY NONFICTION

Annotate: Mark the sentences in paragraph 36 where the author is reflecting on Mrs. Levin.

Interpret: What does Steve mean by the metaphor that books would "sow the seeds of my rebellion"?

36 Over the years, Mrs. Levin stopped by many times to deliver a new box of books. In my quiet moments of reflection, I often wonder what might have become of me had not this kind woman lit a pathway for me through the suffocating darkness of the house on Arnold Street. The Robinsons never refused her request, perhaps because they knew that would raise suspicions. But had they known those books would sow the seeds of my rebellion, they would have torched them the minute Mrs. Levin was out of their sight.

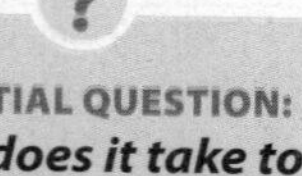

ESSENTIAL QUESTION:
What does it take to survive a crisis?

Review your notes and add your thoughts to your Response Log.

COLLABORATIVE DISCUSSION

Based on this excerpt, what is the single most important factor in making Steve feel like he has "a chance in the world"? Discuss your opinion with a partner.

Assessment Practice

Answer these questions before moving on to the **Analyze the Text** section on the following page.

1. Select **two** strategies Steve uses to cope with his situation.

- (A) sneaking food
- (B) running away
- (C) reading
- (D) taking walks
- (E) staying with the Levins

2. How does paragraph 32 contribute to the development of the author's ideas?

- (A) by emphasizing the importance of having a challenging reading list
- (B) by providing details of the author's escape into the world of books
- (C) by describing how his books were gradually destroyed
- (D) by describing his secret reading place in the cellar

3. This question has two parts. First, answer **Part A**. Then, answer **Part B**.

Part A

Which statement best describes the purpose of this text?

- (A) to demonstrate the cruelty of the Robinsons
- (B) to describe the books Steve read during this time
- (C) to describe how Steve confronted and overcame hardships
- (D) to show how the American foster system works

Part B

Select the sentence that best supports the answer to Part A.

- (A) "Children rarely ask where monsters come from or how they came to be . . ." (paragraph 1)
- (B) ". . . this little boy doesn't have a chance in the world." (paragraph 29)
- (C) "Caseworkers at the time described me as tense, nervous, and anxious." (paragraph 30)
- (D) "Mrs. Levin's books gave me . . . a model for dealing with the Robinsons." (paragraph 33)

Ed

Test-Taking Strategies

Analyze the Text

Support your responses with evidence from the text.

NOTICE & NOTE

Review what you **noticed and noted** as you read the text. Your annotations can help you answer these questions.

1. **INTERPRET** Review the chart you completed on the Get Ready page. How would you describe the author's perspective on this period of his life?

2. **ANALYZE** Identify two or three "Robinson Rules." How do you know there are many such rules? How does this fact add to the author's portrayal of this period in his life?

3. **INFER** The author describes a wall "as if hewn from the side of a mountain." Find other examples of figurative language. Why did the author not confine himself to a literal recounting of events?

4. **EVALUATE** Deception, cunning, trickery, thieving: Steve boasts about his abilities to deceive and outwit the Robinsons. Who or what is Steve's model? How does he justify his own deceptions?

5. **ANALYZE** What **sensory language**—descriptions that appeal to the senses—does the author use? Cite two or three examples. What does this language tell you about the narrator's perceptions?

6. **SYNTHESIZE** Review the **Memory Moment** in paragraph 29. How do Mrs. Levin's actions provide Steve with the "chance" the babysitter and others were sure he didn't have?

7. **CONNECT** How does this memoir excerpt address the unit's Essential Question, What does it take to survive a crisis? Use the graphic organizer to record strategies Steve uses to survive, physically and emotionally, in the Robinson household.

Essential Question: What does it take to survive a crisis?	
Coping Mechanism or Source of Support	**How It Helps Steve Endure His Situation**

Choices

Here are some other ways to demonstrate your understanding of the ideas in this lesson.

As you write and discuss, be sure to use the **Academic Vocabulary** words.

- dimension
- external
- statistic
- sustain
- utilize

Writing
Personal Reflection

Author Steve Pemberton describes several significant personal experiences in this excerpt from his memoir. These experiences, and his reactions to them, shaped the person he later became. Think about one experience you would be comfortable sharing that has shaped your life. Then freewrite about it. Include relevant information such as:

- a description of the experience
- who was involved besides you
- how it affected or changed you

Social & Emotional Learning
Tribute

Create a video or illustrated booklet describing a person, group, or organization that has had a positive effect on your life. Include the following information:

- background or description of the person(s) or organization
- how and why the connection occurred
- how your life has changed as a result

Speaking & Listening
Debate

Some schools require students to complete volunteer hours in addition to their regular class work. Those schools believe students are improving their communities and learning important life lessons. Others believe that to require volunteering makes it less meaningful. Research the topic, then organize a debate about whether schools should require students to volunteer.

1. Organize two groups: one in favor of mandatory volunteer work, the other opposed.
2. Each side will choose a representative to state the group's opinion.
3. Each side should argue their position using evidence and reasons.
4. Debaters should use appropriate register (degree of formality) and tone.
5. Group members should listen and respond to other arguments, identifying any faulty reasoning or distorted evidence.
6. Together, the two sides should review the ideas discussed and summarize conclusions.

Expand Your Vocabulary

PRACTICE AND APPLY

Answer the questions to show your understanding of the vocabulary words.

1. Are animals likely to be safe or threatened in a wildlife **sanctuary**?
2. If I do not understand something, am I able to **fathom** it? Why?
3. What might **baffle** you: A difficult puzzle or a cookbook recipe?
4. If a place is **cacophonous,** is it noisy or quiet?
5. If I **thwart** someone's plan, have I prevented it or helped the person achieve it?

Vocabulary Strategy

↳ Patterns of Word Changes

Interactive Vocabulary Lesson: Analyzing Word Structure

You have probably noticed that many words can change form to become new words with related meanings. When you learn the common patterns of word changes, you can recognize different forms of familiar words and figure out what they mean. Knowing the patterns will also help you spell different forms of a word correctly.

The word *precisely* in paragraphs 5 and 7 is an adverb meaning "exactly." Adding the suffix *-ion* to the root *precis* creates the noun *precision.* Removing *-ly* from *precisely* creates the adjective *precise*. Adding the prefix *im-* creates the word *imprecise,* meaning "not exact."

Verb	Noun	Adjective	Adverb
explain	explanation	explainable	explanatively
frequent	frequency	frequent	frequently
create	creation/creativity	creative	creatively

PRACTICE AND APPLY

- For each verb in the chart, identify one new verb that has the same ending (*-ain, -ent, -ate*).
- Create a chart with your words in the first column.
- Complete the chart with noun, adjective, and adverb forms of each word.
- Choose one word from each row of your chart and use it in a sentence.

Watch Your Language!

Colons and Semicolons

An author's use of punctuation not only can help readers understand the message but also can help create meaning and tone.

Read the following sentence from the memoir.

> This is what they were to me: real-life boogeymen whose origins and intentions I could never fathom.

The two-part sentence provides readers with a question (What were the Robinsons to Steve?) followed by its answer (monsters he cannot understand).

"I REALIZE THAT MOST OF YOU THINK THE FUNCTION OF THE SEMI-COLON IS TO MAKE A ***WINKING SMILEY FACE*** WHEN TEXTING . . ."

Uses of Colons	
Purpose	**Example**
illustrate or provide an example of what was just stated	I was fixated on one thing: food.
introduce a quotation or dialogue	But Mrs. Levin was insistent: "If it's okay, I would like to give him these myself."
introduce a list	And my hearing was finely tuned. I knew the stride pattern of each member of the family: Betty shuffled, Reggie had longer steps, and Willie's plodding was the easiest to detect. . . .

Author Steve Pemberton also uses semicolons effectively. Here is another sentence from *A Chance in the World:*

> For Hazel and his followers, it was never a question of *if* they would find a home; it was simply a matter of *when.*

The author's use of the semicolon shows the relationship between the two statements.

Ed
Interactive Grammar Lesson: Colons

PRACTICE AND APPLY

With a partner, write a paragraph about whether you think Steve's deceptions were justified given his living conditions at the Robinsons. Use colons and semicolons in at least three places. At least one colon should provide an example of the first part of the statement; and at least one semicolon should come before a conjunctive adverb (*however, nevertheless, also*).

Get Ready

MENTOR TEXT

Is Survival Selfish?

Argument by **Lane Wallace**

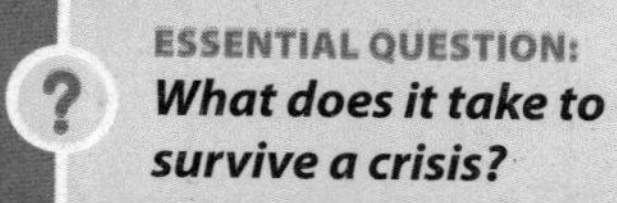

ESSENTIAL QUESTION: ***What does it take to survive a crisis?***

Engage Your Brain

Choose one or more of these activities to start connecting with the argument you're about to read.

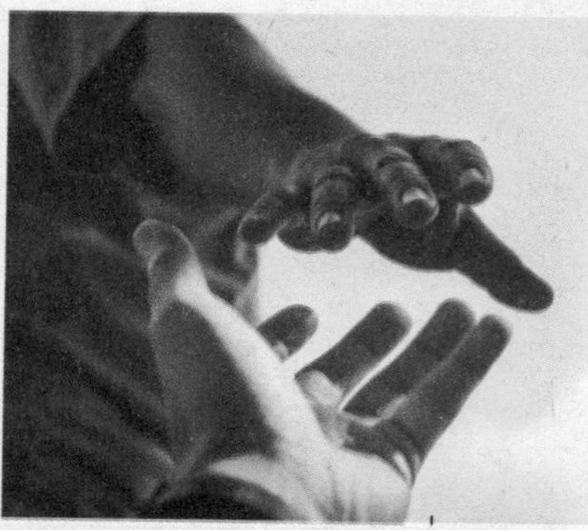

How Did They Survive?

Have you read any survival stories or watched shows or movies that have a character facing a life-or-death situation?

1. List stories or shows you remember.
2. Compare your list with a partner's.
3. Discuss whether and how each character survived.
4. Identify what factors helped the survivors.

Me, or You?

Imagine you and your friend are rock climbing and the line snaps. You're both in danger of plummeting to the ground far below. You're an experienced climber who might be able to reach the ledge and save yourself, but you know your friend won't be able to hang onto the side of the cliff much longer. Discuss the following in a small group:

- Do you save yourself and head toward safety, or risk your life in trying to save your friend?
- Why did you choose one action over the other?

Explore a Key Word

Survive means "to stay alive or carry on despite hardships."

- What kinds of images does the word *survive* suggest to you?
- Draw a picture or make some notes.

Analyze Arguments

In an **argument,** an author expresses a position on an issue and then attempts to support that position. A successful argument persuades readers to agree with the author's **claim,** or position. To analyze an argument, you must first outline its basic parts.

Parts of an Argument	
Claim	Author's position on the topic or issue; central idea of the argument
Reasons	Explanations that support the claim; should follow clear and logical organization
Evidence	Facts, statistics, personal experiences, statements by experts; supports the reasons and ultimately the claim
Conclusion	Revisits the claim with a persuasive closing statement

To be persuasive, an argument must include evidence that is valid, relevant, and sufficient. Facts must be true and provable through research. Opinions are beliefs but they do not support reasons and aren't evidence.

As you read "Is Survival Selfish?" mark the basic parts of the author's argument using the chart as reference.

Focus on Genre
↳ Argument

- presents a claim or position on an issue
- includes reasons or evidence that support the claim
- may include rhetorical devices or other persuasive strategies

Analyze Rhetorical Devices

Authors often use **rhetorical devices** when they write arguments. For example, the author of this article uses **rhetorical questions,** questions that do not call for an answer. They are intended to engage the audience and make a point. In other cases, an author may rely on faulty logic or rhetorical devices meant to deceive the audience. Always read arguments critically in order to assess the accuracy and validity of the author's argument. In particular, be on the lookout for false statements or **fallacious reasoning,** which are errors in reasoning.

As you read this argument, make a note where you notice the author using rhetorical devices.

Annotation in Action

Here are one reader's notes about a rhetorical device in "Is Survival Selfish?" As you read, take notes about rhetorical devices the author uses.

> The "women and children first" protocol of the *Titanic* may not be as strong a social stricture as it was a century ago. But we still tend to laud those who risk or sacrifice themselves to save others in moments of danger or crisis and look less kindly on those who focus on saving themselves, instead.
>
> But is survival really selfish and uncivilized? Or is it smart? And is going in to rescue others always heroic? Or is it sometimes just stupid?
>
> *rhetorical questions make me ask myself what I believe*

Expand Your Vocabulary

Put a check mark next to the vocabulary words that you feel comfortable using when speaking or writing.

laud	☐
transfix	☐
consume	☐
berate	☐
edict	☐

Turn to a partner and use one of the vocabulary words you know in a sentence about the ways people react in life-threatening situations.

As you read "Is Survival Selfish?" use the definitions in the side column to help you learn the vocabulary words you don't already know.

Background

Lane Wallace is a writer, adventurer, and career development coach. She has written for *The Atlantic,* the *New York Times,* and *Outside* magazine, and was the first woman columnist ever hired at *Flying* magazine, where she worked as an editor and columnist for 12 years. Her adventures have taken her to six different continents, and from 120 feet below sea level to 70,000 feet above the Earth. She has a blog on charting your own course in life (*No Map. No Guide. No Limits.*) and has written two books on the lessons of adventure (*Surviving Uncertainty* and *Unforgettable*). Her latest project is a book on the power of a woman's authentic self and voice.

Is Survival Selfish?

Argument by Lane Wallace

If forced to choose, whose life would you save: Your own, or someone else's?

NOTICE & NOTE
As you read, use the side margins to make notes about the text.

1 When the ocean liner *Titanic* sank in April of 1912, one of the few men to survive the tragedy was J. Bruce Ismay, the chairman and managing director of the company that owned the ship. After the disaster, however, Ismay was savaged by the media and the general public for climbing into a lifeboat and saving himself when there were other women and children still on board. Ismay said he'd already helped many women and children into lifeboats and had only climbed in one himself when there were no other women or children in the area and the boat was ready to release. But it didn't matter. His reputation was ruined. He was labeled an uncivilized coward and, a year after the disaster, he resigned his position at White Star.

ANALYZE ARGUMENTS

Annotate: In paragraph 1, mark the topic the author introduces with an anecdote.

Analyze: Consider the title of this selection. Why might the author have chosen to begin her argument with this example?

2 The "women and children first" protocol of the *Titanic* may not be as strong a social stricture[1] as it was a century ago. But we still tend to **laud** those who risk or sacrifice themselves to save others in moments of danger or crisis and look less kindly on those who focus on saving themselves, instead.

laud
(lôd) *v.* to praise.

[1] **social stricture:** behavioral restriction placed on society.

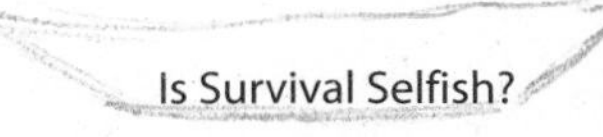

ANALYZE ARGUMENTS

Annotate: In paragraph 3, mark a statement the author can build on to create a full claim.

Analyze: How do the rhetorical questions in this paragraph set up the author's claim?

transfix
(trăns-fĭks´) *v.* to captivate or make motionless with awe.

NOTICE & NOTE
CONTRASTS AND CONTRADICTIONS

When you notice a sharp contrast between what you would expect and what you observe happening, you've found a **Contrasts and Contradictions** signpost.

Notice & Note: Mark details in paragraph 5 that indicate an unexpected event or situation.

Evaluate: Does this unexpected event support or refute the author's claim?

consume
(kən-so͞om´) *v.* to completely destroy or eradicate.

berate
(bĭ-rāt´) *v.* to criticize or scold.

3 But is survival really selfish and uncivilized? Or is it smart? And is going in to rescue others always heroic? Or is it sometimes just stupid? It's a complex question, because there are so many factors involved, and every survival situation is different.

4 Self-preservation is supposedly an instinct. So one would think that in life-and-death situations, we'd all be very focused on whatever was necessary to survive. But that's not always true. In July 2007, I was having a drink with a friend in Grand Central Station[2] when an underground steam pipe exploded just outside. From where we sat, we heard a dull "boom!" and then suddenly, people were running, streaming out of the tunnels and out the doors.

5 My friend and I walked quickly and calmly outside, but to get any further, we had to push our way through a crowd of people who were staring, **transfixed**, at the column of smoke rising from the front of the station. Some people were crying, others were screaming, others were on their cell phones . . . but the crowd, for the most part, was *not* doing the one thing that would increase everyone's chances of survival, if in fact a terrorist bomb with god knows what inside it had just gone off—namely, moving away from the area.

6 We may have an instinct for survival, but it clearly doesn't always kick in the way it should. A guy who provides survival training for pilots told me once that the number one determining factor for survival is simply whether people hold it together in a crisis or fall apart. And, he said, it's impossible to predict ahead of time who's going to hold it together, and who's going to fall apart.

7 So what is the responsibility of those who hold it together? I remember reading the account of one woman who was in an airliner that crashed on landing. People were frozen or screaming, but nobody was moving toward the emergency exits, even as smoke began to fill the cabin. After realizing that the people around her were too paralyzed to react, she took direct action, crawling over several rows of people to get to the exit. She got out of the plane and survived. Very few others in the plane, which was soon **consumed** by smoke and fire, did. And afterward, I remember she said she battled a lot of guilt for saving herself instead of trying to save the others.

8 Could she really have saved the others? Probably not, and certainly not from the back of the plane. If she'd tried, she probably would have perished with them. So why do survivors **berate** themselves for not adding to the loss by attempting the impossible? Perhaps it's because we get very mixed messages about survival ethics.

[2] **Grand Central Station:** a large commuter-rail and subway terminal in New York City.

9 On the one hand, we're told to put our own oxygen masks on first, and not to jump in the water with a drowning victim. But then the people who ignore those **edicts** and survive to tell the tale are lauded as heroes. And people who do the "smart" thing are sometimes criticized quite heavily after the fact.

edict
(ē´dĭkt) *n.* an official rule or proclamation.

10 In a famous mountain-climbing accident chronicled in the book and documentary *Touching the Void*, climber Simon Yates was attempting to rope his already-injured friend Joe Simpson down a mountain in bad weather when the belay[3] went awry. Simpson ended up hanging off a cliff, unable to climb up, and Yates, unable to lift him up and losing his own grip on the mountain, ended up cutting the rope to Simpson to save himself. Miraculously, Simpson survived the 100 foot fall and eventually made his way down the mountain. But Yates was criticized by some for his survival decision, even though the alternative would have almost certainly led to both of their deaths.

11 In Yates' case, he had time to think hard about the odds, and the possibilities he was facing, and to realize that he couldn't save anyone but himself. But what about people who have to make more instantaneous decisions? If, in fact, survivors are driven by instinct not civilization, how do you explain all those who choose otherwise? Who would dive into icy waters or onto subway tracks or disobey orders to make repeat trips onto a minefield to bring wounded to safety? Are they more civilized than the rest of us? More brave? More noble?

[3] **belay:** the securing of a rope to a cleat or another object.

ANALYZE RHETORICAL DEVICES

Annotate: In paragraph 12, mark the sentence that appears to contradict the author's argument about how people behave in a crisis.

Analyze: Why is this an example of fallacious reasoning as far as confirming the author's claim about bravery versus selfishness?

12 It sounds nice, but oddly enough, most of the people who perform such impulsive rescues say that they didn't really think before acting. Which means they weren't "choosing" civilization over instinct. If survival is an instinct, it seems to me that there must be something equally instinctive that drives us, sometimes, to run into danger instead of away from it.

13 Perhaps it comes down to the ancient "fight or flight" impulse. Animals confronted with danger will choose to attack it, or run from it, and it's hard to say which one they'll choose, or when. Or maybe humans are such social herd animals, dependent on the herd for survival, that we feel a pull toward others even as we feel a contrary pull toward our own preservation, and the two impulses battle it out within us . . . leading to the mixed messages we send each other on which impulse to follow.

14 Some people hold it together in a crisis and some people fall apart. Some people might run away from danger one day, and toward it the next. We pick up a thousand cues in an instant of crisis and respond in ways that even surprise ourselves, sometimes.

15 But while we laud those who sacrifice themselves in an attempt to save another, there is a fine line between brave and foolish. There can also be a fine line between smart and selfish. And as a friend who's served in the military for 27 years says, the truth is, sometimes there's no line at all between the two.

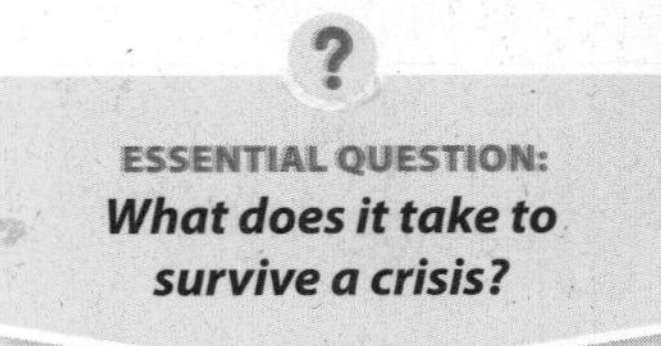
ESSENTIAL QUESTION:
What does it take to survive a crisis?

Review your notes and add your thoughts to your Response Log.

COLLABORATIVE DISCUSSION

With a partner, review the various stories of survivors. Discuss whether you would describe each person's actions as selfish. Is being selfish always bad?

Assessment Practice

Answer these questions before moving on to the **Analyze the Text** section on the following page.

1. Which sentence states a claim central to the author's argument?

- (A) Running away is the best way to survive a disaster.
- (B) Heroes have to fight their survival instinct to save others.
- (C) People who save themselves are cowards who lack courage.
- (D) People are sometimes criticized for saving themselves.

2. How do paragraphs 7 and 8 contribute to the development of the author's ideas?

- (A) by arguing that in some cases, selfish actions cost people their lives.
- (B) by demonstrating that in some cases, saving your life is the right action
- (C) by offering an example of what to do in an airplane fire or similar disaster
- (D) by criticizing the other passengers for not trying to save themselves

3. The author concludes her argument with —

- (A) recommendations for what to do in a live-or-die situation
- (B) another example that explains what being selfish in a crisis means
- (C) a story about a friend who says you have to be brave and foolish
- (D) a reflection that it can be hard to distinguish between smart and selfish action

Ed
Test-Taking Strategies

Analyze the Text

Support your responses with evidence from the text.

NOTICE & NOTE

Review what you **noticed and noted** as you read the text. Your annotations can help you answer these questions.

1. **INFER** In paragraph 3, Lane Wallace poses a series of questions to get her readers thinking about what is selfish and what is heroic. What is the effect of these questions?

2. **SYNTHESIZE** In your own words, state the claim Wallace expresses in paragraph 3. What reasons and evidence does she present to support her claim?

Author's Claim	Reasons and Evidence

3. **ANALYZE** Wallace writes that "the number one determining factor for survival is simply whether people hold it together in a crisis or fall apart." Is this an example of a claim, a reason, or evidence? Explain with an example from the text.

4. **CRITIQUE** Wallace writes that "Self-preservation is supposedly an instinct. So one would think that in life-and-death situations, we'd all be very focused on whatever was necessary to survive." Explain how she argues that as a generalization this reasoning is fallacious.

5. **EVALUATE** Reread paragraph 12. As evidence for Wallace's claim, is this paragraph valid and relevant? Explain.

6. **CONNECT** In the final paragraph, Wallace writes that there can be "a fine line between smart and selfish," and that "sometimes there's no line at all between the two." How do the **Contrasts and Contradictions** she presents throughout the text support this claim?

7. **DRAW CONCLUSIONS** Now that you've read the article, how would you define "survival instinct"? What, if any, Word Gaps did you fill that helped you understand the article?

Choices

Here are some other ways to demonstrate your understanding of the ideas in this lesson.

Social & Emotional Learning

↳ Selfish or Smart?

Reread the last paragraph of the text. How do the author's comments relate to how you make choices about your own behavior? Draft points to agree or disagree with the idea that there can be "a fine line between smart and selfish."

- Think about how you would balance your own well-being against that of others in a crisis situation.
- Consider your beliefs about ethical responsibility: In your mind, what constitutes right and wrong in an extreme situation?
- Decide on your claim—the position you will take.
- Express your claim in one sentence.
- Draft 3–4 reasons to support your claim.

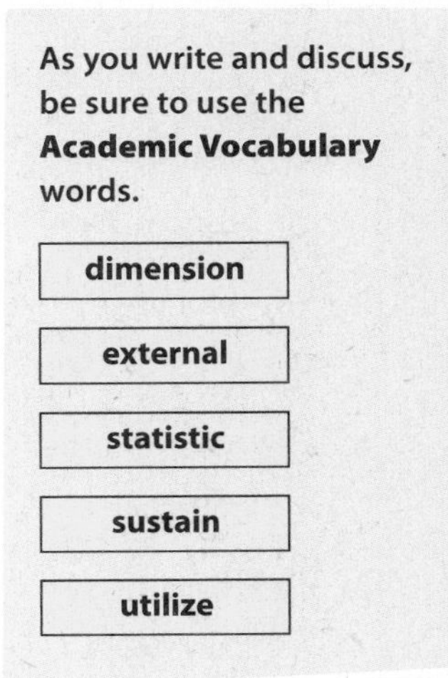

As you write and discuss, be sure to use the **Academic Vocabulary** words.
dimension
external
statistic
sustain
utilize

Media

↳ Survivor Tales

Research individuals who have survived life-threatening situations. Choose the experience that interests you the most, and create a social media profile for that individual.

Include:

- posts describing the person's everyday life before the life-threatening situation
- a detailed description of the danger the person faced and what he or she did to survive
- images or videos related to the events

Speaking & Listening

↳ Group Discussion

Hold a group discussion on the issues of survival discussed in the text.

- Before the discussion, review the author's claim, evidence, and reasoning.
- Establish rules for speaking as you decide on your group's goals; vote on key issues.
- During the discussion, state your ideas clearly. Listen, respond to, and build on others' ideas and opinions. Use appropriate content-area vocabulary.
- End the discussion by summarizing the main points.

Expand Your Vocabulary

PRACTICE AND APPLY

Mark the best answer to each question. Then, explain your response.

1. Which of the following would be something you might **laud**?
   - ◯ a supreme accomplishment
   - ◯ a failure to complete a task
2. If something were to **transfix** you, how would you react?
   - ◯ stand in awe
   - ◯ run in fear
3. Which of the following would be likely to **consume** something?
   - ◯ a cloud of fog
   - ◯ a forest fire
4. If I **berate** another person, how would that person feel?
   - ◯ humiliated
   - ◯ delighted
5. If a king issued an **edict,** what would it be like?
   - ◯ an opinion
   - ◯ a law

Vocabulary Strategy

↳ Synonyms

Interactive Vocabulary Lesson: Synonyms and Antonyms

Words that share the same or nearly the same meaning are called **synonyms**. Authors sometimes use synonyms to vary word choice and make their writing more interesting. For example, in paragraph 7 of "Is Survival Selfish?" the author uses the word *paralyzed*. The synonym *transfixed* might also have worked, but the author had already used it in paragraph 5.

If you come across an unfamiliar word in a text:

- Try to think of another word that would make sense in context.
- Check a dictionary or thesaurus to see if your word is truly a synonym.
- Note any differences between the synonyms and think about why the author chose that exact word.
- Ask if the sentence has the same or a slightly different meaning with the synonym as with the author's original word.

PRACTICE AND APPLY

Use a print or online thesaurus to complete this activity.

1. Create a two-column chart. In the first column, write the vocabulary words. In the second, write at least two synonyms for each word.
2. Write a sentence using each vocabulary word.
3. For each sentence you write, exchange the vocabulary word for a synonym. Work with a partner to choose the best synonym for each sentence.

Watch Your Language!

Commas

A writer's use of punctuation not only helps readers understand the writer's message, but it also signals how the writer wants the text to be read. In your writing, you can use commas to signal a break or a pause to the reader. Commas are also used to distinguish and divide phrases, as well as independent and dependent clauses.

Here are examples of comma use from "Is Survival Selfish?"

Purpose of Comma	Example from the Selection
to signal a break in thought	And afterward, I remember she said she battled a lot of guilt for saving herself instead of trying to save the others.
to signal the reader to pause; to set off a phrase	He was labeled an uncivilized coward and, a year after the disaster, he resigned his position at White Star.
to divide independent and dependent clauses	If survival is an instinct, it seems to me that there must be something equally instinctive that drives us . . . to run into danger instead of away from it.

PRACTICE AND APPLY

Rewrite the sentences, inserting the needed commas.

1. Yes I absolutely want to survive.
2. Beyond saving your own life people expect you to save others.
3. If you survive people think you should have saved others.
4. If she'd tried to help others she probably would have died with them.

Get Ready

The Leap

Short Story by Louise Erdrich

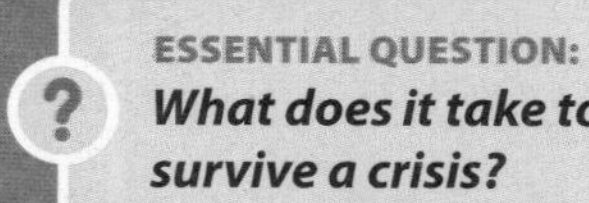

ESSENTIAL QUESTION:
What does it take to survive a crisis?

Engage Your Brain

Choose one or more of these activities to start connecting with the story you are about to read.

Speaking of Courage

In this story, a mother fearlessly enters a burning house to save her child. Think of a time when you or someone you know had to think fast and act courageously. What motivated the act?

Leap to Predictions!

Think of expressions you've heard that include the word "leap"—for example, "leap of faith." With a partner, make a list. Then, look at the illustrations in the story. Write a few sentences describing what you think the story will be about.

Trapeze Artists

Part of this story takes place at a traditional circus.

- Look for images and descriptions of modern-day or older circuses, such as Ringling Brothers or Barnum & Bailey.
- Draw pictures or makes notes of typical circus events or scenes.

Analyze Flashback and Tension

Authors create **tension,** or suspense, when they want to propel a story forward and keep the reader wondering what will happen next. One effective technique for creating tension is the **flashback**—a literary device used to manipulate time by inserting an earlier event into the present action. To identify a flashback, look for shifts in verb tense from present to past or past perfect tense. Also, watch for signal words, such as *once* ("Once upon a time") and *remember* ("I remember when").

The chart below tracks some shifts in time in "The Leap" that sustain or build tension. Fill out your own chart as you analyze the story.

Focus on Genre

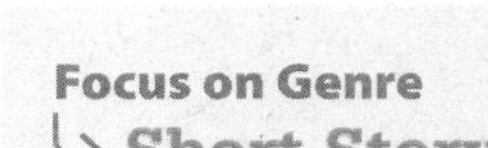

- **includes the basic elements of fiction—setting, characters, plot, conflict, and theme**
- **centers on a particular moment or event in life**
- **can be read in one sitting**

Tension Tracker		
Example	**Flashback Clues (Verb Tense or Signal Words)**	**Action Summary**
"I owe her my existence three times. The first was when . . ."	shift from present to past tense	narrator begins to explain her debt to her mother
"I have lived in the West . . ."	shift to past perfect tense	narrator provides information about her own adult life

Make Inferences

In a short story, the **theme,** or underlying message, usually emerges through inference. An **inference** is a logical conclusion based on the text and what you already know. To uncover themes in "The Leap," first examine the story's title. You might note, for example, that the speaker's mother would have made many leaps as a trapeze artist. But could *leap* also have more figurative meanings? Then, look for clues in the story that hint at its meaning. For example, character or plot developments may help reveal a story's themes. You can also make inferences about real-world life experiences: In fact, you probably do it all the time!

As you read, use a chart like the one below to track your ideas and inferences about the story's themes.

Story Elements or Clues	My Inferences	Possible Theme
1.		
2.		
3.		

Annotation in Action

Here is one writer's note about an inference based on the first paragraph of "The Leap." As you read, note your own inferences and questions.

> My mother is the surviving half of a blindfold trapeze act, not a fact I think about much even now that she is sightless, the result of encroaching and stubborn cataracts. She walks slowly through her house here in New Hampshire . . .
>
> *"Surviving" means the mother's partner is dead. Trapeze accident?*

Expand Your Vocabulary

Put a check mark next to the vocabulary words that you feel comfortable using when speaking or writing.

encroach	☐
extricate	☐
constrict	☐
comply	☐
tentative	☐

Turn to a partner and talk about the vocabulary words you already know. Then, write a few sentences about a circus, festival, or other event using as many vocabulary words as you can.

As you read "The Leap," use the definitions in the side column to learn the vocabulary words you don't already know.

Background

Louise Erdrich (b. 1954) is best known for exploring the Native American experience in her novels, poetry, and children's books. Born in Little Falls, Minnesota, she grew up in North Dakota. Of German American and Ojibwa (Chippewa) descent, her writing reflects a fascination with the influence of family and heritage on individuals and community. She lives in Minneapolis, Minnesota, where she owns a bookstore and continues to write. Her best-known works include the novels *Love Medicine, The Beet Queen*, and *The Round House*.

The Leap

Short Story by **Louise Erdrich**

A mother saves her daughter's life three times.

NOTICE & NOTE
As you read, use the side margins to make notes about the text.

1 My mother is the surviving half of a blindfold trapeze act, not a fact I think about much even now that she is sightless, the result of **encroaching** and stubborn cataracts. She walks slowly through her house here in New Hampshire, lightly touching her way along walls and running her hands over knickknacks, books, the drift of a grown child's belongings and castoffs. She has never upset an object or as much as brushed a magazine onto the floor. She has never lost her balance or bumped into a closet door left carelessly open.

encroach
(ĕn-krōch´) *v.* to gradually intrude upon or invade.

2 It has occurred to me that the catlike precision of her movements in old age might be the result of her early training, but she shows so little of the drama or flair one might expect from a performer that I tend to forget the Flying Avalons. She has kept no sequined costume, no photographs, no fliers or posters from that part of her youth. I would, in fact, tend to think that all memory of double somersaults and heartstopping catches had left her arms and legs were it not for the fact that sometimes, as I sit sewing in the room of the rebuilt

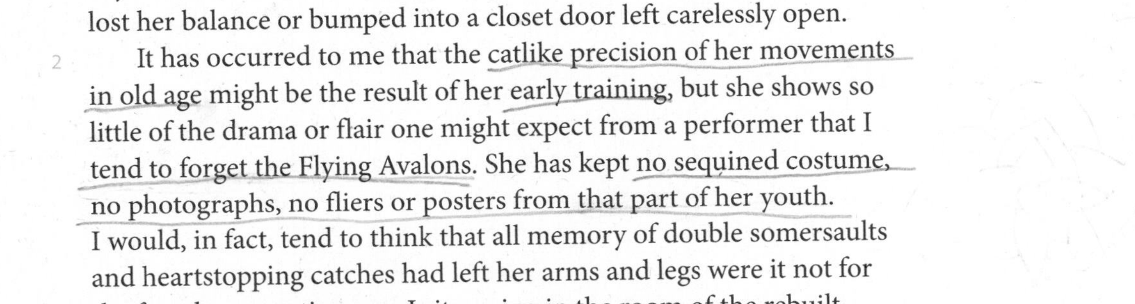

house in which I slept as a child, I hear the crackle, catch a whiff of smoke from the stove downstairs and suddenly the room goes dark, the stitches burn beneath my fingers, and I am sewing with a needle of hot silver, a thread of fire.

ANALYZE FLASHBACK AND TENSION

Annotate: Mark details in paragraph 3 that provide clues about what this flashback will reveal.

Analyze: How do these details build tension?

3 I owe her my existence three times. The first was when she saved herself. In the town square a replica tent pole, cracked and splintered, now stands cast in concrete. It commemorates the disaster that put our town smack on the front page of the Boston and New York tabloids. It is from those old newspapers, now historical records, that I get my information. Not from my mother, Anna of the Flying Avalons, nor from any of her in-laws, nor certainly from the other half of her particular act, Harold Avalon, her first husband. In one news account it says, "The day was mildly overcast, but nothing in the air or temperature gave any hint of the sudden force with which the deadly gale would strike."

4 I have lived in the West, where you can see the weather coming for miles, and it is true that out here we are at something of a disadvantage. When extremes of temperature collide, a hot and cold front, winds generate instantaneously behind a hill and crash upon you without warning. That, I think, was the likely situation on that day in June. People probably commented on the pleasant air, grateful that no hot sun beat upon the striped tent that stretched over the

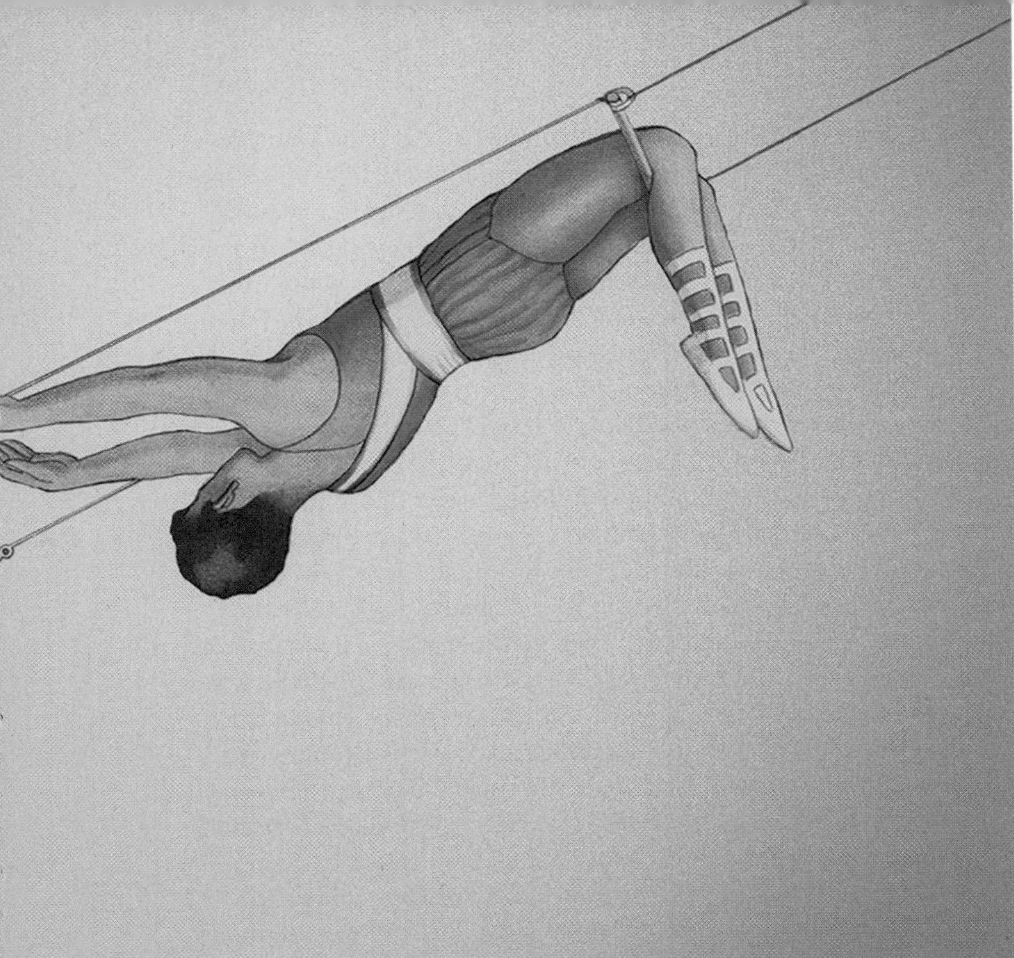

Don't forget to **Notice & Note** as you read the text.

entire center green. They bought their tickets and surrendered them in anticipation. They sat. They ate caramelized popcorn and roasted peanuts. There was time, before the storm, for three acts. The White Arabians of Ali-Khazar rose on their hind legs and waltzed. The Mysterious Bernie folded himself into a painted cracker tin, and the Lady of the Mists made herself appear and disappear in surprising places. As the clouds gathered outside, unnoticed, the ringmaster cracked his whip, shouted his introduction, and pointed to the ceiling of the tent, where the Flying Avalons were perched.

5 They loved to drop gracefully from nowhere, like two sparkling birds, and blow kisses as they threw off their plumed helmets and high-collared capes. They laughed and flirted openly as they beat their way up again on the trapeze bars. In the final vignette[1] of their act, they actually would kiss in midair, pausing, almost hovering as they swooped past one another. On the ground, between bows, Harry Avalon would skip quickly to the front rows and point out the smear of my mother's lipstick, just off the edge of his mouth. They made a romantic pair all right, especially in the blindfold sequence.

6 That afternoon, as the anticipation increased, as Mr. and Mrs. Avalon tied sparkling strips of cloth onto each other's face and as they puckered their lips in mock kisses, lips destined "never again to meet," as one long breathless article put it, the wind rose, miles

MAKE INFERENCES

Annotate: In paragraph 6, mark lines that reveal the daughter's feelings about her mother.

Infer: What does she admire about her mother?

[1] **vignette** (vĭn-yĕt´): a brief scene.

ANALYZE FLASHBACK AND TENSION

Annotate: Underline words in paragraph 6 that signal shifts in time.

Analyze: How do these shifts reveal the narrator's thinking as she tells the story?

off, wrapped itself into a cone, and howled. There came a rumble of electrical energy, drowned out by the sudden roll of drums. One detail not mentioned by the press, perhaps unknown—Anna was pregnant at the time, seven months and hardly showing, her stomach muscles were that strong. It seems incredible that she would work high above the ground when any fall could be so dangerous, but the explanation—I know from watching her go blind—is that my mother lives comfortably in extreme elements. She is one with the constant dark now, just as the air was her home, familiar to her, safe, before the storm that afternoon.

7 From opposite ends of the tent they waved, blind and smiling, to the crowd below. The ringmaster removed his hat and called for silence, so that the two above could concentrate. They rubbed their hands in chalky powder, then Harry launched himself and swung once, twice, in huge calibrated[2] beats across space. He hung from his knees and on the third swing stretched wide his arms, held his hand out to receive his pregnant wife as she dove from her shining bar.

8 It was while the two were in midair, their hands about to meet, that lightning struck the main pole and sizzled down the guy wires, filling the air with a blue radiance that Harry Avalon must certainly have seen through the cloth of his blindfold as the tent buckled and the edifice toppled him forward, the swing continuing and not returning in its sweep, and Harry going down, down into the crowd with his last thought, perhaps, just a prickle of surprise at his empty hands.

NOTICE & NOTE
MEMORY MOMENT

A **Memory Moment** occurs when the narrator interrupts the forward progress of the story to recall something from the past.

Notice & Note: Mark the Memory Moment the narrator shares in paragraph 9.

Analyze: Why might this memory be important?

9 My mother once said that I'd be amazed at how many things a person can do within the act of falling. Perhaps, at the time, she was teaching me to dive off a board at the town pool, for I associated the idea with midair somersaults. But I also think she meant that even in that awful doomed second one could think, for she certainly did. When her hands did not meet her husband's, my mother tore her blindfold away. As he swept past her on the wrong side, she could have grasped his ankle, the toe-end of his tights, and gone down clutching him. Instead, she changed direction. Her body twisted toward a heavy wire and she managed to hang on to the braided metal, still hot from the lightning strike. Her palms were burned so terribly that once healed they bore no lines, only the blank scar tissue of a quieter future. She was lowered, gently, to the sawdust ring just underneath the dome of the canvas roof, which did not entirely settle but was held up on one end and jabbed through, torn, and still on fire in places from the giant spark, though rain and men's jackets soon put that out.

10 Three people died, but except for her hands my mother was not seriously harmed until an overeager rescuer broke her arm in **extricating** her and also, in the process, collapsed a portion of the

extricate
(ĕk´strĭ-kāt) *v.* to release or disentangle from.

[2] **calibrated:** checked or determined by comparison with a standard.

tent bearing a huge buckle that knocked her unconscious. She was taken to the town hospital, and there she must have hemorrhaged,[3] for they kept her, confined to her bed, a month and a half before her baby was born without life.

11 Harry Avalon had wanted to be buried in the circus cemetery next to the original Avalon, his uncle, so she sent him back with his brothers. The child, however, is buried around the corner, beyond this house and just down the highway. Sometimes I used to walk there just to sit. She was a girl, but I rarely thought of her as a sister or even as a separate person really. I suppose you could call it the egocentrism[4] of a child, of all young children, but I considered her a less finished version of myself.

12 When the snow falls, throwing shadows among the stones, I can easily pick hers out from the road, for it is bigger than the others and in the shape of a lamb at rest, its legs curled beneath. The carved lamb looms larger as the years pass, though it is probably only my eyes, the visions shifting, as what is close to me blurs and distances sharpen. In odd moments, I think it is the edge drawing near, the edge of everything, the unseen horizon we do not really speak of in the eastern woods. And it also seems to me, although this is probably an idle fantasy, that the statue is growing more sharply etched, as if, instead of weathering itself into a porous mass, it is hardening on the hillside with each snowfall, perfecting itself.

13 It was during her confinement in the hospital that my mother met my father. He was called in to look at the set of her arm, which was complicated. He stayed, sitting at her bedside, for he was something of an armchair traveler and had spent his war quietly, at an air force training grounds, where he became a specialist in arms and legs broken during parachute training exercises. Anna Avalon had been to many of the places he longed to visit—Venice, Rome, Mexico, all through France and Spain. She had no family of her own and was taken in by the Avalons, trained to perform from a very young age. They toured Europe before the war, then based themselves in New York. She was illiterate.

14 It was in the hospital that she finally learned to read and write, as a way of overcoming the boredom and depression of those weeks, and it was my father who insisted on teaching her. In return for stories of her adventures, he graded her first exercises. He bought her her first book, and over her bold letters, which the pale guides of the penmanship pads could not contain, they fell in love.

15 I wonder if my father calculated the exchange he offered: one form of flight for another. For after that, and for as long as I can remember, my mother has never been without a book. Until now, that is, and it remains the greatest difficulty of her blindness. Since

[3] **hemorrhaged** (hĕm′ər-ĭjd): bled heavily.

[4] **egocentrism:** belief in the primary or sole importance of the self.

VOCABULARY

Use Prefixes: The word *unconscious* consists of the prefix *un-*, meaning "not," combined with the word *conscius,* meaning "knowing or aware." Recognizing prefixes can help you understand a word's meaning.

Analyze: What happened to the mother's awareness when the buckle hit her head?

my father's recent death, there is no one to read to her, which is why I returned, in fact, from my failed life where the land is flat. I came home to read to my mother, to read out loud, to read long into the dark if I must, to read all night.

16 Once my father and mother married, they moved onto the old farm he had inherited but didn't care much for. Though he'd been thinking of moving to a larger city, he settled down and broadened his practice in this valley. It still seems odd to me, when they could have gone anywhere else, that they chose to stay in the town where the disaster had occurred, and which my father in the first place had found so **constricting.** It was my mother who insisted upon it, after her child did not survive. And then, too, she loved the sagging farmhouse with its scrap of what was left of a vast acreage of woods and hidden hay fields that stretched to the game park.

constrict
(kən-strĭkt´) *v.* to limit or impede growth.

17 I owe my existence, the second time then, to the two of them and the hospital that brought them together. That is the debt we take for granted since none of us asks for life. It is only once we have it that we hang on so dearly.

NOTICE & NOTE
AGAIN AND AGAIN

When you notice a certain event, image, or word recurs over a portion of a story, you've spotted an **Again and Again** signpost.

Notice & Note: Mark the words and phrases in paragraph 17 that you've seen earlier in the story.

Evaluate: What might the author be trying to emphasize by using these phrases repeatedly?

18 I was seven the year the house caught fire, probably from standing ash. It can rekindle, and my father, forgetful around the house and perpetually exhausted from night hours on call, often emptied what he thought were ashes from cold stoves into wooden or cardboard containers. The fire could have started from a flaming box, or perhaps a buildup of creosote[5] inside the chimney was the culprit. It started right around the stove, and the heart of the house was gutted. The baby-sitter, fallen asleep in my father's den on the first floor, woke to find the stairway to my upstairs room cut off by flames. She used the phone, then ran outside to stand beneath my window.

19 When my parents arrived, the town volunteers had drawn water from the fire pond and were spraying the outside of the house, preparing to go inside after me, not knowing at the time that there was only one staircase and that it was lost. On the other side of the house, the superannuated[6] extension ladder broke in half. Perhaps the clatter of it falling against the walls woke me, for I'd been asleep up to that point.

20 As soon as I awakened, in the small room that I now use for sewing, I smelled the smoke. I followed things by the letter then, was good at memorizing instructions, and so I did exactly what was taught in the second-grade home fire drill. I got up, I touched the back of my door before opening it. Finding it hot, I left it closed and stuffed my rolled-up rug beneath the crack. I did not hide under my bed or crawl into my closet. I put on my flannel robe, and then I sat down to wait.

MAKE INFERENCES

Annotate: Mark lines in paragraph 20 that describe the daughter's reaction to the fire.

Infer: How is the narrator like her mother? What characteristics do they share?

[5] **creosote:** a flammable, oily byproduct of burning carbon-based fuels like coal, peat, and wood.

[6] **superannuated:** obsolete; ready for retirement.

Don't forget to **Notice & Note** as you read the text.

21 Outside, my mother stood below my dark window and saw clearly that there was no rescue. Flames had pierced one side wall, and the glare of the fire lighted the massive limbs and trunk of the vigorous old elm that had probably been planted the year the house was built, a hundred years ago at least. No leaf touched the wall, and just one thin branch scraped the roof. From below, it looked as though even a squirrel would have had trouble jumping from the tree onto the house, for the breadth of that small branch was no bigger than my mother's wrist.

22 Standing there, beside Father, who was preparing to rush back around to the front of the house, my mother asked him to unzip her dress. When he wouldn't be bothered, she made him understand. He couldn't make his hands work, so she finally tore it off and stood there in her pearls and stockings. She directed one of the men to lean the broken half of the extension ladder up against the trunk of the tree. In surprise, he **complied.** She ascended. She vanished. Then she could be seen among the leafless branches of late November as she made her way up and, along her stomach, inched the length of a bough that curved above the branch that brushed the roof.

comply
(kəm-plī´) *v.* to obey an instruction or command.

23 Once there, swaying, she stood and balanced. There were plenty of people in the crowd and many who still remember, or think they do, my mother's leap through the ice-dark air toward that thinnest extension, and how she broke the branch falling so that it cracked in her hands, cracked louder than the flames as she vaulted with

it toward the edge of the roof, and how it hurtled down end over end without her, and their eyes went up, again, to see where she had flown.

24 I didn't see her leap through air, only heard the sudden thump and looked out my window. She was hanging by the backs of her heels from the new gutter we had put in that year, and she was smiling. I was not surprised to see her, she was so matter-of-fact. She tapped on the window. I remember how she did it, too. It was the friendliest tap, a bit **tentative**, as if she was afraid she had arrived too early at a friend's house. Then she gestured at the latch, and when I opened the window she told me to raise it wider and prop it up with the stick so it wouldn't crush her fingers. She swung down, caught the ledge, and crawled through the opening. Once she was in my room, I realized she had on only underclothing, a bra of the heavy stitched cotton women used to wear and step-in, lace-trimmed drawers. I remember feeling light-headed, of course, terribly relieved, and then embarrassed for her to be seen by the crowd undressed.

tentative
(tĕn′tə-tĭv) *adj.* with caution and without confidence.

25 I was still embarrassed as we flew out the window, toward earth, me in her lap, her toes pointed as we skimmed toward the painted target of the fire fighter's net.

26 I know that she's right. I knew it even then. As you fall, there is time to think. Curled as I was, against her stomach, I was not startled by the cries of the crowd or the looming faces. The wind roared and beat its hot breath at our back, the flames whistled. I slowly wondered what would happen if we missed the circle or bounced out of it. Then I wrapped my hands around my mother's hands. I felt the brush of her lips and heard the beat of her heart in my ears, loud as thunder, long as the roll of drums.

COLLABORATIVE DISCUSSION

How does the narrator feel about her mother, and why?

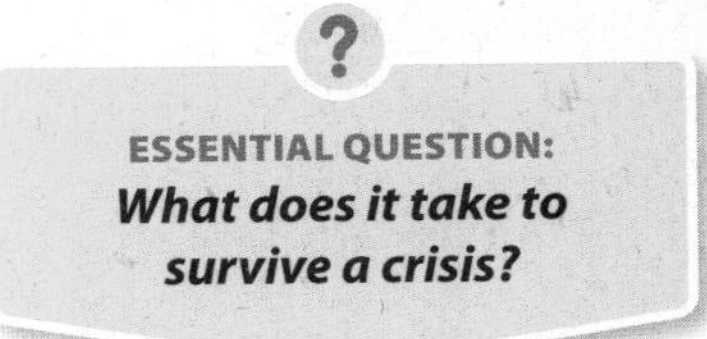
?
ESSENTIAL QUESTION:
What does it take to survive a crisis?

Review your notes and add to your Response Log.

Assessment Practice

Answer these questions before moving on to the **Analyze the Text** section on the following page.

1. Reread paragraph 9. What inference can be made from Anna's behavior as her husband falls past her?

(A) She had not really loved her husband that much.

(B) Her top priority was to die with her husband.

(C) Her first instinct was to survive with her child.

(D) She panicked in a life and death situation.

2. This question has two parts. First, answer **Part A**. Then, answer **Part B**.

Part A

Which of the below best explains Anna's act of bravery in saving her daughter?

(A) She has been traumatized by her husband's death.

(B) She feels guilty about not having saved her husband.

(C) She reacts calmly to dangerous or stressful situations.

(D) She still mourns the death of her unborn child.

Part B

Which passage from the story best supports the answer to Part A?

(A) "It seems incredible that she would work high above the ground . . . but the explanation—I know from watching her go blind—is that my mother lives comfortably in extreme elements." (paragraph 6)

(B) "As he swept past her on the wrong side, she could have grasped his ankle . . . and gone down clutching him. Instead, she changed direction." (paragraph 9)

(C) "She must have hemorrhaged, for they kept her . . . a month and a half before her baby was born without life." (paragraph 10)

(D) "For after that . . . my mother has never been without a book. Until now . . . and it remains the greatest difficulty of her blindness." (paragraph 15)

Ed

Test-Taking Strategies

Analyze the Text

Support your responses with evidence from the text.

NOTICE & NOTE

Review what you **noticed and noted** as you read the text. Your annotations can help you answer these questions.

1. **INTERPRET** How does paragraph 2 act as a flashback? What clues does it give about the rest of the story?

2. **DRAW CONCLUSIONS** In paragraph 9, Anna decides to reach for the hot braided metal rather than for her husband as he falls. What does this reveal about her character?

3. **IDENTIFY PATTERNS** Identify the leaps in the story. Which leaps are literal? Which are figurative?

The Leaps	Literal or Figurative?

4. **INFER** Review the chart you filled out to track your ideas and inferences as you read this story. Then, reread paragraph 26. What does the narrator learn from this **Memory Moment**? What inferences can you make about the story's theme or themes?

5. **COMPARE** Compare the description of the trapeze accident with the description of the house fire. What do these descriptions reveal about the mother's character?

6. **ANALYZE** The narrator speaks **Again and Again** of the ways that she owes her existence to her mother. Identify the three ways and describe how this repetition affects the mood of the story.

Choices

Here are some other ways to demonstrate your understanding of the ideas in this lesson.

Writing

Retell the Story

Imagine you were one of the firefighters on the scene when the narrator was saved from her burning house. You can't believe what you saw and can't wait to share it with friends and family. In a social media post, retell the story from your point of view as a firefighter.

- Reread the part of the story that describes the fire.
- Think about what you would have seen, and what you would have noticed as a professional firefighter.
- Describe events using vivid descriptions and concrete details. Remember—the people you're writing for weren't there!

As you write and discuss, be sure to use the **Academic Vocabulary** words.

dimension

external

statistic

sustain

utilize

Media

Build a Timeline

With a partner or in a small group, create an illustrated timeline of the story's key events.

- Make a list of story events in the order they occurred.
- Find images that depict each scene.
- Write captions for each image that tell the story.
- Publish your timeline for the rest of the class.

Speaking & Listening

Group Discussion

"The Leap" is a work of fiction. Though some events seem like they could have actually happened, others may seem unlikely. Discuss your opinions with a small group.

- Which events seem realistic?
- Which events seem unrealistic?
- Defend your opinions with additional examples.
- Respond to and build on others' arguments.

Expand Your Vocabulary

PRACTICE AND APPLY

Answer the questions to show your understanding of the vocabulary words. Use a dictionary or thesaurus as needed.

1. Should a rescue crew provide a **tentative** response to an **encroaching** forest fire? Why or why not?
2. Would it feel **constricting** to always **comply** with the wishes of others? Explain.
3. Why would you **extricate** yourself from a planned road trip upon learning of an approaching blizzard?

Vocabulary Strategy
Prefixes

Vocabulary Practice: Common Roots, Prefixes, and Suffixes

The vocabulary words *encroach*, *extricate*, *constrict*, and *comply* all contain a **prefix**, an affix added to the beginning of a base word. Knowing the meaning of common prefixes, such as *en-*, *ex-*, *con-*, and *com-*, will help you clarify the meaning of unknown words. Here are the meanings of some common prefixes and examples of other words that contain the prefixes:

Prefix	Meaning	Example
en-	to go into or onto	encapsulate, encircle
ex-	out of or away from	exchange, exterminate
con-	together, with, jointly	consensus, congenial

If a base word is unfamiliar, use your knowledge of the word's prefix and how the word is used in context to clarify its meaning. If necessary, consult a dictionary to determine the precise meaning of the word.

PRACTICE AND APPLY

For each prefix in the chart, identify one word that contains it. The word may be in the text, or it may be a word of your own choosing. For each word you choose, follow these steps:

1. Identify the base word, the main word part. For example, the base word of *exchange* is *change.*
2. Write a definition for each word that incorporates the prefix meaning and the base word meaning. Use a dictionary to check your definition.
3. Write a sample sentence for each word you choose.

Watch Your Language!

Relative Clauses

A **clause** is a group of words that contains a subject and a predicate. **Relative clauses** describe nouns and function as adjectives. Here are the characteristics of a relative clause:

- It begins with a signal word: a relative pronoun (*that, which, who, whom, whose*) or a relative adverb (*when, where,* or *why*).
- It follows a noun or a noun phrase.
- It provides extra information about a noun or a noun phrase, or it answers the questions *What kind? How many? Which one?*

Authors use relative clauses not only to convey specific meanings, but also to add interest and variety to their work. Read this sentence from "The Leap":

It commemorates the disaster that put our town smack on the front page of the Boston and New York tabloids.

The clause contains all the elements of a relative clause: it begins with a relative pronoun—*that*; it follows a noun—*disaster*; it answers the question *Which one*?—the disaster that put the town in the tabloids.

Here are other examples of relative clauses from the "The Leap":

Relative Clauses		
Signal Word	**Example from Story**	**Words Modified**
which	**He was called in to look at the set of her arm, which was complicated.**	"the set of her arm"
who	**. . . and it was my father who insisted on teaching her.**	"father"

PRACTICE AND APPLY

Work with a partner to identify three or four more relative clauses in "The Leap" that are not included as examples in this lesson.

The End and the Beginning

Poem by Wisława Szymborska

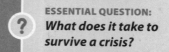

ESSENTIAL QUESTION:
What does it take to survive a crisis?

Engage Your Brain

Choose one or more of these activities to start connecting with the poem you are about to read.

Historical Backdrop

Wisława Szymborska was born in Poland in 1923. Research the experience of the Polish people during World War II. Then talk with a partner about how a young poet might have been affected by Poland's role in the war.

War Zones

With a partner, do some quick research on areas of the world with ongoing wars or conflicts.

1. Identify at least three regions or countries currently at war.
2. Explain the causes behind the conflicts.
3. Compare your findings with another pair.

What Does It Look Like?

Think about the aspects of daily life that are disrupted by war or mass violence. What kinds of challenges do people face in the aftermath of war? Make a list, or sketch your ideas.

Analyze Poetic Language

"The End and the Beginning" is a **lyric poem,** one in which a single speaker expresses his or her personal ideas and feelings. Lyric poetry can take many forms and can address all types of topics, from everyday experiences to complex ideas. Most poems—except narrative poems, which tell a story—are lyric poems.

Poetry is highly concentrated as far as language used, so poets must be precise and economical about the words they choose. As Szymborska said in her Nobel Prize acceptance speech, "every word is weighed." Analyzing an author's language choices—and the literary effect of those choices—can deepen your understanding of a poem. You can analyze Wisława Szymborska's poetic language in "The End and the Beginning" by looking at the elements outlined in the chart below.

Focus on Genre

Lyric Poetry

- usually short to convey strong emotions
- written using first-person point of view to express the speaker's thoughts and feelings
- often uses repetition and rhyme to create a melodic quality
- includes many forms, such as sonnets, odes, and elegies

Tone	Imagery	Diction/Syntax
Tone refers to the author's attitude toward the subject. Authors shape a work's tone through topics they choose to explore, word choices, and images those words create. Elements to consider when evaluating tone include: • words with positive or negative connotations • use of informal language, such as idioms or colloquial expressions • repetition of significant words or phrases	Poets often use **imagery,** or descriptive words and phrases that create sensory experiences for the reader. Imagery usually appeals to one or more of the five senses to help readers imagine exactly what is being described. For example, the striking image of "corpse-filled wagons" passing through rubble-lined roads calls to mind photographs that most readers will have seen of war-torn, bombed-out cities. Look for other images in the poem that engage your senses and evoke a strong emotional response.	Two closely related elements that affect the tone of a poem are diction and syntax. • **Diction** is the writer's choice of specific words. • **Syntax** is the way those words are arranged into phrases and sentences. Look for the specific words the author chose for the poem and how she chose to arrange them. What tone do those carefully chosen words create?

Analyze Poetic Structure

Poets use rhetorical devices such as repetition and parallelism to convey meaning. **Repetition** is the use of a word or phrase two or more times. **Parallelism** is the use of the same grammatical or metrical structure within and across lines and verses. Parallelism can provide rhythmic symmetry and balance to a piece, and often shows that two or more ideas are similar.

Below are the third and fourth stanzas of "The End and the Beginning." Find and underline examples of repetition and parallelism.

Someone has to get mired
in scum and ashes,
sofa springs,
splintered glass,
and bloody rags.

Someone has to drag in a girder
to prop up a wall.
Someone has to glaze a window,
rehang a door.

As you read the poem, look for the use of repetition and parallelism. Think about the effect of these and other elements of the author's style and how that style conveys information about the message and speaker.

Annotation in Action

Here is one reader's response to the second stanza of "The End and the Beginning." As you read, note your observations about the poem's tone, the use of sensory imagery, and the author's choice of diction and syntax.

Someone has to push the rubble
to the side of the road,
so the corpse-filled wagons
can pass.

Rubble = debris from bombed-out buildings? "corpse-filled"—strong image

Background

Wisława Szymborska (1923–2012) was born in Poland. Her first two published volumes of poetry, written in post-World War II Communist-dominated Poland, were written in the style of Socialist Realism. Szymborska later disowned these works. Her disillusionment with communism was reflected in *Calling Out to Yeti*, published in 1957. Her poems, noted for their unique, ironic tone, have been translated into many languages. Szymborska won the Nobel Prize in Literature in 1996.

The End and the Beginning

Poem by **Wisława Szymborska**

What are the harsh realities of life after war?

After every war
someone has to clean up.
Things won't
straighten themselves up, after all.

Someone has to push the rubble
to the side of the road,
so the corpse-filled wagons
can pass.

Someone has to get mired
in scum and ashes,
sofa springs,
splintered glass,
and bloody rags.

NOTICE & NOTE

As you read, use the side margins to make notes about the text.

ANALYZE POETIC LANGUAGE

Annotate: Underline words and phrases in lines 1–13 that appeal to the reader's senses.

Interpret: What general picture do these words or phrases create in your mind?

Close Read Screencast

Listen to a modeled close read of this text.

ANALYZE POETIC STRUCTURE

Annotate: Mark the use of repetition and parallelism in the first four stanzas of the poem.

Interpret: What is the effect of these devices?

Someone has to drag in a girder
to prop up a wall.
Someone has to glaze a window,
rehang a door.

Photogenic it's not,
and takes years.
All the cameras have left
for another war.

We'll need the bridges back,
and new railway stations.
Sleeves will go ragged
from rolling them up.

Someone, broom in hand,
still recalls the way it was.
Someone else listens
and nods with unsevered[1] head.
But already there are those nearby
starting to mill about[2]
who will find it dull.

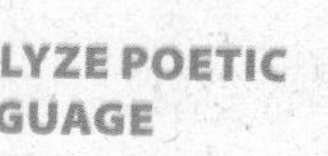

ANALYZE POETIC LANGUAGE

Annotate: Mark the use of figurative language in lines 33–36.

Interpret: What tone does this image convey?

From out of the bushes
sometimes someone still unearths
rusted-out arguments
and carries them to the garbage pile.

Those who knew
what was going on here
must make way for
those who know little.
And less than little.
And finally as little as nothing.

In the grass that has overgrown
causes and effects,
someone must be stretched out
blade of grass in his mouth
gazing at the clouds.

[1] **unsevered:** not cut off; not separated.
[2] **mill about:** move idly or aimlessly.

COLLABORATIVE DISCUSSION

Turn to a partner and discuss the last three lines of the poem. Do they surprise you? What message is the poet conveying through this image?

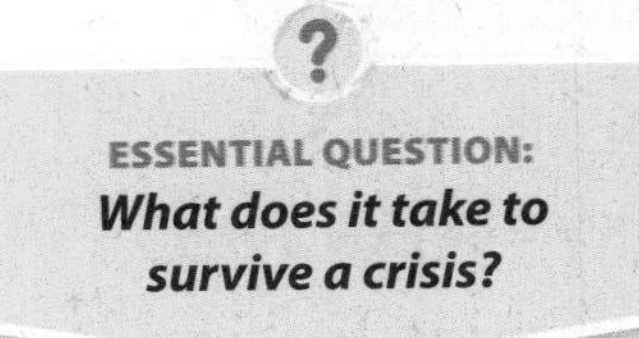
ESSENTIAL QUESTION:
What does it take to survive a crisis?

Review your notes and add your thoughts to your Response Log.

Assessment Practice

Answer these questions before moving on to the **Analyze the Text** section on the following page.

1. This question has two parts. First, answer **Part A**. Then, answer **Part B**.

Part A

What is a central idea of the poem?

- (A) Wars cause destruction that can never be repaired.
- (B) Wars seem logical to those who do not witness their horrors.
- (C) Wars and their effects are forgotten by future generations.
- (D) Wars are exciting to fight but destroy many communities.

Part B

How is the central idea developed throughout the poem?

- (A) by listing a sequence of events that occur after a war ends
- (B) by explaining why people don't want to clean up after a war
- (C) by reminding the reader that avoiding war avoids destruction
- (D) by describing the causes of wars and why they are repeated

2. Which word best describes the speaker's tone in the poem?

- (A) grateful—the speaker is happy to be alive
- (B) resolute—the speaker is ready to get on with the rebuilding
- (C) harsh—the speaker is bitter about what has happened
- (D) ironic—the speaker notices people tend to forget about war

Ed

Test-Taking Strategies

Analyze the Text

Support your responses with evidence from the text.

NOTICE & NOTE

Review what you **noticed and noted** as you read the text. Your annotations can help you answer these questions.

1. **ANALYZE** Answer the questions in the chart to explore how Szymborska creates the tone of the poem.

Question	Your Answer	Evidence from the Poem
Does the speaker use formal or informal language? What is the cumulative effect of Szymborska's word choice?		
What is the speaker's attitude toward the situation he or she is describing?		
How does the tone of the poem change beginning with line 30?		

2. **INFER** Notice the repetition of the word "someone" again and again in the poem. What statement is the speaker making by using an indefinite pronoun rather than referring to a specific person?

3. **IDENTIFY PATTERNS** In line 18, the speaker says that the aftermath of war is not "photogenic." What images in the poem reinforce this idea about war? How does the poet show the extent of the devastation?

4. **INTERPRET** Reread the last stanza of the poem. What does the grass symbolize, or represent? What does the speaker mean by describing this "someone" as being "stretched out / blade of grass in his mouth / gazing at the clouds"?

5. **EVALUATE** In lines 37–42, the speaker contrasts "those who knew" with those who know "as little as nothing." What is the contrast between these two groups of people?

6. **DRAW CONCLUSIONS** The poem's title—with "End" coming before "Beginning"—reverses the order in which we usually think about events. What theme might the author be suggesting about the cyclic, repetitive nature of human events?

Choices

Here are some other ways to demonstrate your understanding of the ideas in this lesson.

Writing

Write a Dialogue

Starting at line 30, the poem starts to reveal different attitudes between generations. Think about how different generations today tend to have different attitudes, beliefs, and priorities.

1. In a small group, script a dialogue between two or more individuals from different generations discussing their views about a certain idea or object: perhaps a digital device, or the role of technology.
2. Read your script to another group, and listen to theirs.
3. Compare your scripts: Did the characters agree, compromise, or hold fast to their views?

As you write and discuss, be sure to use the **Academic Vocabulary** words.

- dimension
- external
- statistic
- sustain
- utilize

Media

Blog

The poem's speaker says that war is not photogenic, meaning it's not attractive. However, photographs of war and conflict flood today's media. In a blog or social media page:

- Include at least three images showing people trying to recover from war or conflict.
- Write captions for each image. Describe each image in both literal and figurative terms.
- If the conflict is ongoing, suggest actions others can take to provide aid.

Speaking & Listening

Podcast

Working with a partner, record a podcast in which you are news reporters who have just visited a site of conflict or war. Your assignment is to report on what you both have seen, including the impact of violence on local people.

- Identify descriptions, thoughts, feelings, and experiences you want to share with listeners.
- Script the information as a conversation where you build on your news partner's points.
- Include vivid sensory details of sights, sounds, and smells.
- Ensure you both have equal speaking time and respond to each other's comments.

Collaborate & Compare

IIESSENTIAL QUESTION:
What does it take to survive a crisis?

Compare Accounts

You're about to read excerpts from two memoirs about the Holocaust. As you read, notice similarities and differences in the settings, characters, points of view, and author's purpose in these two texts.

A
from Night
Memoir by Elie Wiesel
pages 60–67
B
from Maus
Graphic Memoir by Art Spiegelman
Pages 74–79

After you have read both texts, you will collaborate with a small group on a final project. You will compare the two accounts by following these steps:

- Review your notes
- Plan your presentation
- Consider using media
- Practice and present your comparison

from Night

Memoir by **Elie Wiesel**

Engage Your Brain

Choose one or both of these activities to start connecting with the memoir you're about to read.

Background to *Night*

You probably know a lot about the general history of World War II through school, movies, and books. In the chart, take notes on what you know about the plight of Jewish communities in Europe shortly before and during the war. Share what you know in a group discussion, listening to what others know and what they would like to know. In the second column, note questions or topics sparked by the discussion that you would like to learn more about.

I know . . .	I wonder . . .

Images of the Holocaust

Examine the drawings and photograph accompanying the text of the memoir. What is the message of these carefully drawn portraits? What is the significance of the photograph of shoes? Express your thoughts by freewriting or through a poem, song, or video.

Analyze Memoirs

A **memoir** is an autobiographical account of a person's experiences and observations of an event. As you read this excerpt from Elie Wiesel's memoir, use these questions to help you think about Wiesel's purposes for writing:

- What is the historical context for the memoir? About what significant events and people does the author share memories?
- What perspective do you understand from reading a first-person account?
- Think about other nonfiction books or articles that you have read about Jews during World War II. How is this first-person account different?
- Who is the audience for the memoir?
- What do you learn about the impact on people of the historical events described?

Focus on Genre
Memoir

- records actual events based on the writer's observations
- reveals the writer's feelings
- provides historical context for the events described

Analyze Word Choice

The **tone** of a work is the author's attitude toward the subject. A writer's tone may be formal, informal, serious, angry, or lighthearted. The **mood** of a work is the emotional atmosphere the writer creates. Writers shape tone and mood through word choice. Words with particular connotations shape the overall meaning of a work. Similar words can describe both tone and mood—for example, *fear, dread, amusement*—but mood relates to how the author's words affect the reader. Which words in the examples in the chart help create the tone and mood?

Tone or Mood	Example from the Text
Tone: Fear and dread	One more hour. Then we would know the verdict: death or reprieve.
Tone: Despair	He felt time was running out. He was speaking rapidly, he wanted to tell me so many things. His speech became confused, his voice was choked.
Mood: Suspense	My father had remained near the block, leaning against the wall. Then he began to run, to try to catch up with us.

As you read the memoir, identify specific words that contribute to the text's tone and mood.

Annotation in Action

Here are one reader's notes about the excerpt from *Night.* As you read, highlight words that shape the tone and mood of the memoir.

The SS offered us a beautiful present for the new year. We had just returned from work. As soon as we passed the camp's entrance, we sensed something out of the ordinary in the air. The roll call was shorter than usual. The evening soup was distributed at great speed, swallowed as quickly. We were anxious.	"beautiful" = ironic or sarcastic Prisoners are nervous because something is different.

Expand Your Vocabulary

Put a check mark next to the vocabulary words that you feel comfortable using when speaking or writing.

reprieve	☐
emaciated	☐
execute	☐
decisive	☐
din	☐

Turn to a partner and use the vocabulary words you already know in a short discussion about what you think the text will be about.

As you read the excerpt from *Night,* use the definitions in the side column to learn the vocabulary words you don't already know.

Background

Elie Wiesel (1928–2016) was a teacher, writer, and Nobel Peace Prize winner. Born in Romania, Wiesel and his family were among millions of European Jews deported to concentration camps during the Holocaust. In 1944, Hungarian and German authorities sent the family to Auschwitz, where Wiesel's mother and sister were immediately killed in the gas chambers. Months later, when Wiesel and his father were moved to Buchenwald concentration camp, his father also died. Buchenwald was eventually liberated, and Wiesel went on to write about his experience. His many works include *Dawn* and *The Accident,* both sequels to *Night*.

NOTICE & NOTE

As you read, use the side margins to make notes about the text.

from Night

Memoir by **Elie Wiesel**

A young man waits to hear whether he and his father will be selected to live another day or be killed.

1 The SS[1] offered us a beautiful present for the new year. We had just returned from work. As soon as we passed the camp's entrance, we sensed something out of the ordinary in the air. The roll call was shorter than usual. The evening soup was distributed at great speed, swallowed as quickly. We were anxious.

2 I was no longer in the same block as my father. They had transferred me to another Kommando,[2] the construction one, where twelve hours a day I hauled heavy slabs of stone. The head of my new block was a German Jew, small with piercing eyes. That evening he announced to us that henceforth no one was allowed to leave the block after the evening soup. A terrible word began to circulate soon thereafter: selection.

---

[1] **SS:** abbreviation of *Schutzstaffel*, German for "defense force"; an armed unit of the Nazi Party that controlled concentration camps.

[2] **Kommando** (kə-măn´dō): German for "command," a small-group organization for laborers in the camps.

Don't forget to **Notice & Note** as you read the text.

3 We knew what it meant. An SS would examine us. Whenever he found someone extremely frail—a "Muselman" was what we called those inmates—he would write down his number: good for the crematorium.

4 After the soup, we gathered between the bunks. The veterans told us: "You're lucky to have been brought here so late. Today, this is paradise compared to what the camp was two years ago. Back then, Buna[3] was a veritable hell. No water, no blankets, less soup and bread. At night, we slept almost naked and the temperature was thirty below. We were collecting corpses by the hundreds every day. Work was very hard. Today, this is a little paradise. The Kapos[4] back then had orders to kill a certain number of prisoners every day. And every week, selection. A merciless selection . . . Yes, you are lucky."

5 "Enough! Be quiet!" I begged them. "Tell your stories tomorrow, or some other day."

6 They burst out laughing. They were not veterans for nothing.

7 "Are you scared? We too were scared. And, at that time, for good reason."

8 The old men stayed in their corner, silent, motionless, hunted-down creatures. Some were praying.

9 One more hour. Then we would know the verdict: death or **reprieve.**

10 And my father? I first thought of him now. How would he pass selection? He had aged so much. . . .

11 Our *Blockälteste*[5] had not been outside a concentration camp since 1933. He had already been through all the slaughterhouses, all the factories of death. Around nine o'clock, he came to stand in our midst:

12 *"Achtung!"*[6]

13 There was instant silence.

14 "Listen carefully to what I am about to tell you." For the first time, his voice quivered. "In a few moments, selection will take place. You will have to undress completely. Then you will go, one by one, before the SS doctors. I hope you will all pass. But you must try to increase your chances. Before you go into the next room, try to move your limbs, give yourself some color. Don't walk slowly, run! Run as if you had the devil at your heels! Don't look at the SS. Run, straight in front of you!"

15 He paused and then added:

16 "And most important, don't be afraid!"

17 That was a piece of advice we would have loved to be able to follow.

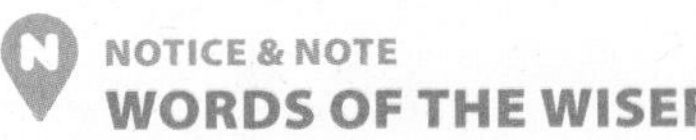

NOTICE & NOTE
WORDS OF THE WISER

When you notice older characters giving life advice to the main character, you've identified a **Words of the Wiser** signpost.

Notice & Note: Underline what the author learns from the veteran inmates.

Interpret: What's the life lesson and how might it affect Elie?

reprieve
(rĭ-prēv′) *n.* the cancellation or postponement of punishment.

Close Read Screencast

Listen to a modeled close read of this text.

[3] **Buna** (bo͞o′nə): a section of the concentration camp at Auschwitz.

[4] **Kapos** (kä′pōs): prisoners who performed certain duties for the guards.

[5] **Blockälteste** (blŏk ĕl′təs-tə): a rank of Kapos; a prisoner designated by the Nazis to be the leader or representative of a block, or group of barracks.

[6] **Achtung!** (ăk′to͝ong): German command for "Attention!"

18 I undressed, leaving my clothes on my cot. Tonight, there was no danger that they would be stolen.

19 Tibi and Yossi, who had changed Kommandos at the same time I did, came to urge me:

20 "Let's stay together. It will make us stronger."

21 Yossi was mumbling something. He probably was praying. I had never suspected that Yossi was religious. In fact, I had always believed the opposite. Tibi was silent and very pale. All the block inmates stood naked between the rows of bunks. This must be how one stands for the Last Judgment.

22 "They are coming!"

23 Three SS officers surrounded the notorious Dr. Mengele,[7] the very same who had received us in Birkenau. The *Blockälteste* attempted a smile. He asked us:

24 "Ready?"

25 Yes, we were ready. So were the SS doctors. Dr. Mengele was holding a list: our numbers. He nodded to the *Blockälteste:* we can begin! As if this were a game.

26 The first to go were the "notables" of the block, the *Stubenälteste,*[8] the Kapos, the foremen, all of whom were in perfect physical condition, of course! Then came the ordinary prisoners' turns. Dr. Mengele looked them over from head to toe. From time to time, he noted a number. I had but one thought: not to have my number taken down and not to show my left arm.

[7] **Dr. Mengele** (mĕn-gə´lə): Josef Mengele (1911–1979), Nazi physician at Auschwitz known for conducting cruel experiments on prisoners.

[8] **Stubenälteste** (shtyo͞o´bə-nĭl-tŭs -tə): a rank of Kapos; prisoners designated by the Nazis to be the leaders of their barracks, or rooms.

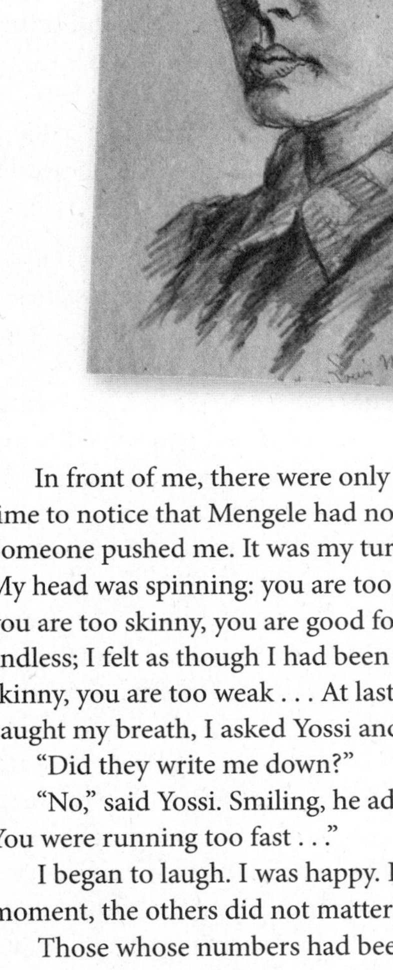

Don't forget to **Notice & Note** as you read the text.

27 In front of me, there were only Tibi and Yossi. They passed. I had time to notice that Mengele had not written down their numbers. Someone pushed me. It was my turn. I ran without looking back. My head was spinning: you are too skinny . . . you are too weak . . . you are too skinny, you are good for the ovens . . . The race seemed endless; I felt as though I had been running for years . . . You are too skinny, you are too weak . . . At last I arrived. Exhausted. When I had caught my breath, I asked Yossi and Tibi:

28 "Did they write me down?"

29 "No," said Yossi. Smiling, he added, "Anyway, they couldn't have. You were running too fast . . ."

30 I began to laugh. I was happy. I felt like kissing him. At that moment, the others did not matter! They had not written me down.

31 Those whose numbers had been noted were standing apart, abandoned by the whole world. Some were silently weeping.

ANALYZE MEMOIRS

Annotate: Mark details in paragraphs 27–31 that help you understand Wiesel's character at the time of the events.

Evaluate: How has the passage of time given Wiesel insight into what he experienced at the end of the "selection"?

32 THE SS OFFICERS left. The *Blockälteste* appeared, his face reflecting our collective weariness.

33 "It all went well. Don't worry. Nothing will happen to anyone. Not to anyone . . ."

34 He was still trying to smile. A poor **emaciated** Jew questioned him anxiously, his voice trembling:

35 "But . . . sir. They *did* write me down!"

36 At that, the *Blockälteste* vented his anger: What! Someone refused to take his word?

37 "What is it now? Perhaps you think I'm lying? I'm telling you, once and for all: nothing will happen to you! Nothing! You just like to wallow in your despair, you fools!"

emaciated
(ĭ-mā´shē-āt id) *adj.* made extremely thin and weak.

38 The bell rang, signaling that the selection had ended in the entire camp.

39 With all my strength I began to race toward Block 36; midway, I met my father. He came toward me:

40 "So? Did you pass?"

41 "Yes. And you?"

42 "Also."

43 We were able to breathe again. My father had a present for me: a half ration of bread, bartered for something he had found at the depot, a piece of rubber that could be used to repair a shoe.

44 The bell. It was already time to part, to go to bed. The bell regulated everything. It gave me orders and I **executed** them blindly. I hated that bell. Whenever I happened to dream of a better world, I imagined a universe without a bell.

execute
(ĕk´sĭ-kyōōt) *v.* to carry out, or accomplish.

45 A FEW DAYS passed. We were no longer thinking about the selection. We went to work as usual and loaded the heavy stones onto the freight cars. The rations had grown smaller; that was the only change.

46 We had risen at dawn, as we did every day. We had received our black coffee, our ration of bread. We were about to head to the work yard as always. The *Blockälteste* came running:

47 "Let's have a moment of quiet. I have here a list of numbers. I shall read them to you. All those called will not go to work this morning; they will stay in camp."

48 Softly, he read some ten numbers. We understood. These were the numbers from the selection. Dr. Mengele had not forgotten.

49 The *Blockälteste* turned to go to his room. The ten prisoners surrounded him, clinging to his clothes:

50 "Save us! You promised . . . We want to go to the depot, we are strong enough to work. We are good workers. We can . . . we want . . ."

51 He tried to calm them, to reassure them about their fate, to explain to them that staying in the camp did not mean much, had no tragic significance: "After all, I stay here every day . . ."

52 The argument was more than flimsy. He realized it and, without another word, locked himself in his room.

53 The bell had just rung.

54 "Form ranks!"

55 Now, it no longer mattered that the work was hard. All that mattered was to be far from the block, far from the crucible[9] of death, from the center of hell.

56 I saw my father running in my direction. Suddenly, I was afraid.

57 "What is happening?"

58 He was out of breath, hardly able to open his mouth.

59 "Me too, me too . . . They told me too to stay in the camp."

60 They had recorded his number without his noticing.

[9] **crucible:** a vessel used for melting materials at high temperatures.

61 "What are we going to do?" I said anxiously.

62 But it was he who tried to reassure me:

63 "It's not certain yet. There's still a chance. Today, they will do another selection . . . a **decisive** one . . ."

64 I said nothing.

65 He felt time was running out. He was speaking rapidly, he wanted to tell me so many things. His speech became confused, his voice was choked. He knew that I had to leave in a few moments. He was going to remain alone, so alone . . .

66 "Here, take this knife," he said. "I won't need it anymore. You may find it useful. Also take this spoon. Don't sell it. Quickly! Go ahead, take what I'm giving you!"

67 My inheritance . . .

68 "Don't talk like that, Father." I was on the verge of breaking into sobs. "I don't want you to say such things. Keep the spoon and knife. You will need them as much as I. We'll see each other tonight, after work."

69 He looked at me with his tired eyes, veiled by despair. He insisted:

70 "I am asking you . . . Take it, do as I ask you, my son. Time is running out. Do as your father asks you . . ."

71 Our Kapo shouted the order to march.

decisive
(dĭ-sī´sĭv) *adj.* final or concluding.

ANALYZE WORD CHOICE

Annotate: Mark words in paragraphs 65–70 that contribute to the tone of the text.

Analyze: How does the word *inheritance* in line 67 communicate the author's tone?

72 The Kommando headed toward the camp gate. Left, right! I was biting my lips. My father had remained near the block, leaning against the wall. Then he began to run, to try to catch up with us. Perhaps he had forgotten to tell me something . . . But we were marching too fast . . . Left, right!

din
(dĭn) *n.* loud noise.

73 We were at the gate. We were being counted. Around us, the **din** of military music. Then we were outside.

74 ALL DAY, I PLODDED AROUND like a sleepwalker. Tibi and Yossi would call out to me, from time to time, trying to reassure me. As did the Kapo who had given me easier tasks that day. I felt sick at heart. How kindly they treated me. Like an orphan. I thought:
Even now, my father is helping me.

VOCABULARY

Multiple-Meaning Words: The word *pass* has many meanings. Note all the possible meanings you can think of.

Analyze: What context clues help you know the meaning of *passed* in paragraph 77?

75 I myself didn't know whether I wanted the day to go by quickly or not. I was afraid of finding myself alone that evening. How good it would be to die right here!

76 At last, we began the return journey. How I longed for an order to run! The military march. The gate. The camp. I ran toward Block 36.

77 Were there still miracles on this earth? He was alive. He had passed the second selection. He had still proved his usefulness . . .
I gave him back his knife and spoon.

?

ESSENTIAL QUESTION:
What does it take to survive a crisis?

Review your notes and add your thoughts to your Response Log.

COLLABORATIVE DISCUSSION

What details from Elie Wiesel's experience at Auschwitz surprised you? With a partner, discuss two unexpected details.

Assessment Practice

Answer these questions before moving on to the **Analyze the Text** section on the following page.

1. After the first selection, why doesn't Wiesel mind his work?

   (A) It is easier than what he had been doing.

   (B) It gives him a chance to be with his father.

   (C) It keeps his mind occupied.

   (D) It means he has been spared.

2. This question has two parts. First answer **Part A**. Then, answer **Part B**.

   Part A

   Why does Wiesel not want to accept his inheritance?

   (A) He does not like anyone telling him what to do.

   (B) He refuses to accept the fact that his father may die.

   (C) He thinks his father is being too generous.

   (D) He does not have time to take the items back to his bunk.

   Part B

   Select **two** sentences that best support the answer to Part A.

   (A) "I said nothing." (paragraph 64)

   (B) "He knew that I had to leave in a few moments." (paragraph 65)

   (C) "I was on the verge of breaking into sobs." (paragraph 68)

   (D) "You will need them as much as I." (paragraph 68)

   (E) "We'll see each other tonight, after work." (paragraph 68)

Ed

Test-Taking Strategies

Analyze the Text

Support your responses with evidence from the text.

NOTICE & NOTE

Review what you **noticed and noted** as you read the text. Your annotations can help you answer these questions.

1. **INFER** In paragraph 8, Wiesel writes, "The old men stayed in their corner, silent, motionless, hunted-down creatures. Some were praying." Which words in this quotation have strong connotations? How do these words convey the tone and mood of Wiesel's narrative?

2. **INTERPRET** The veteran inmates tell new arrivals they are "lucky" to have arrived only recently. Why might these "wiser" inmates feel the need to stress that prison conditions have become less harsh?

3. **ANALYZE** Look back at the scene in which Wiesel must run before the SS doctors during selection. Why does Wiesel repeat his thoughts, "you are too skinny . . . you are too weak"? How do these words—repeated again and again—help the reader relate to Wiesel's experience?

4. **CITE EVIDENCE** What evidence does Wiesel provide to support the idea that though beaten down, the prisoners had creative ways of coping with their confinement and of sustaining themselves?

5. **ANALYZE** Wiesel includes statements and reactions from other prisoners, the head of the block, and the veterans of the camp that reveal different perspectives about life in the concentration camp. Identify examples of these different perspectives. Why do you think he includes these quoted words in his memoir?

Statement or Reaction	What It Reveals about the Prisoners' Situation

6. **DRAW CONCLUSIONS** Why do you think Wiesel chose to call his memoir *Night*? What might be the significance of this title?

Choices

Here are some other ways to demonstrate your understanding of the ideas in this lesson.

Writing

Create a Flyer

Search for the Eyewitness Testimony video in which Elie Wiesel talks about the importance of preventing holocausts and other atrocities. Create a flyer that conveys Wiesel's message.

1. Focus on an event such as the Holocaust, or another event or situation you care about.
2. Adapt Wiesel's points to state what people must do to resist destructive actions by others.
3. Include your own interpretation of "Never again."
4. Close by stressing the importance of individual action and responsibility.

As you write and discuss, be sure to use the Academic Vocabulary words.

- **dimension**
- **external**
- **statistic**
- **sustain**
- **utilize**

Social & Emotional Learning

A Life in Art

Review the Background paragraph on the Get Ready page as well as what you learned about Elie Wiesel from his memoir. Use your imagination to see the world from his perspective so that you can empathize, or feel compassion, for him in his situation. Then, create a piece of art that conveys Wiesel's perceptions and/or experiences. You can use words and phrases to create an image, draw a key scene from his memoir, design a collage, or create some other visual presentation.

Research

Multimedia Presentation

Night is set within the historical events of World War II and the Holocaust. Research a detail or event from the text that you would like to know more about. For ideas, review notes you took before and while reading the text. Then, create a presentation to share with the class.

- Compile your research in an easy-to-read format.
- Include images, videos, or graphics that will help your audience better understand the topic.
- Present your findings to the class and compare information.
- Cite referenced sources appropriately.

Expand Your Vocabulary

PRACTICE AND APPLY

Answer the questions to show your understanding of the vocabulary words.

1. Wiesel describes one of the prisoners as **emaciated.** What does the prisoner look like?
2. When Wiesel's father passes the second **decisive** selection, Wiesel is relieved. Explain why.
3. While a prisoner, Wiesel **executes** his work tasks. Do the guards likely have a complaint about his work? Explain.
4. The prisoners at the concentration camp hope for a **reprieve** from death. What do they hope will happen?
5. The narrator can hear the **din** of military music in the background. What does the music sound like?

Vocabulary Strategy

↳ Multiple-Meaning Words

Interactive Vocabulary Lesson: Words with Multiple Meanings

The vocabulary word *execute* means "to accomplish or carry out fully." *Execute* has another definition, "to put to death." Like *execute*, many words have **multiple meanings.** Use the strategies below to determine or clarify the meaning of a multiple-meaning word.

- Use context, or the way the word is used in a sentence or paragraph, to clarify its meaning. For example, look at the following sentence: *Mountain climbing was her passion, and she wanted to scale every peak.* The context tells you that *scale* refers to climbing.
- Consult general and specialized reference materials, particularly glossaries and dictionaries, to determine or clarify the precise meaning of a word. Dictionary entries provide all the definitions of a word, so select the definition that makes sense.

PRACTICE AND APPLY

Work in a group to locate these words: *present* (paragraph 1) and *block* (paragraph 2). Use context clues or reference materials to determine the precise meaning for each word.

Watch Your Language!

Clauses

A **clause** is a group of words with a subject and a verb. There are two types of clauses: an **independent clause** can stand alone as a sentence; a **dependent clause** cannot. Instead, dependent clauses act as modifiers, adding meaning to independent clauses. Dependent clauses often begin with these words: *as if, as, since, than, that, though, until, whenever, where, while, who, why*. These words are subordinating conjunctions that clarify the connection between the clauses.

Read the following sentence from *Night:*

> They had transferred me to another Kommando, the construction one, where twelve hours a day I hauled heavy slabs of stone.

This sentence contains one independent clause and one dependent clause. Notice how the independent clause *They had transferred me to another Kommando, the construction one* forms a complete thought and can stand alone as a sentence. The dependent clause, which is underlined, provides additional information about the independent clause, but it cannot stand alone. The two types of clauses function together to convey the author's meaning.

Interactive Grammar Lesson: The Clause

PRACTICE AND APPLY

Write three to four sentences, each with at least one independent and one dependent clause, about your reaction to the memoir. Try to use different subordinating conjunctions in your sentences.

from Maus

Graphic Memoir by **Art Spiegelman**

Engage Your Brain

Choose one or more of these activities to start connecting with the graphic novel you are about to read.

Make a Prediction

The graphic novel excerpt you are about to read flashes back to the same time period that Elie Wiesel's memoir covers.

Scan the images from *Maus*.

- What do you predict the excerpt focuses on?
- What do you predict the tone of the scene is?

Graphic Novels, Anyone?

Think about a comic book or graphic novel you recently read.

- What was it about?
- What were the images like?
- Was there a little bit of text, or a lot?
- Do you prefer to read a graphic novel or a conventional book? Or does it depend?

Share your answers with a partner.

Sketch a Scene

Imagine a character facing a dangerous situation or struggling to make a difficult decision. The character could be a human or an animal. In the space, draw a scene or short graphic story that shows what the character is going through.

Analyze Graphic Memoirs

A **graphic memoir** is a kind of autobiographical writing in which the author shares his or her personal experiences and observations in a comic-strip format. Like prose memoirs, a graphic memoir usually gives readers insight into the impact of historical events on people's lives. However, the author is able to use a range of graphic features to convey meaning and to propel the narrative.

As you read, use the following chart to note how Art Spiegelman uses features of the graphic novel genre to tell his story.

Focus on Genre
↳ Graphic Novel

- tells a book-length story in comic-strip style
- combines images, narrative text, and dialogue in frames or panels
- has a plot, characters, and themes
- may be fiction or nonfiction

How Does Spiegelman . . .	Details from *Maus*
show how events unfold in a particular sequence?	
make transitions between the story's present and flashback events?	
show what characters do and say?	
present narrative text (as opposed to dialogue)?	
reveal how characters feel about situations and events?	

Background

Art Spiegelman (b. 1948) is a political cartoonist and satirist, best known for his memoir *Maus*, a graphic novel. In it he recounts the struggles of his parents, Vladek and Anja, to survive the Holocaust. He uses animals to represent different groups involved in the war, portraying Europe's Jews as mice, Germans as cats, and Poles as pigs. Spiegelman was awarded the Pulitzer Prize for *Maus* in 1992, demonstrating that the graphic novel had earned its status as a serious literary genre. Spiegelman considers *Maus* to be a work of nonfiction because of the extensive research he did for historical scenes. The excerpt you will read begins in the United States, with the author speaking to his father, and flashes back to events his father remembers in Sosnowiec, a city in southern Poland.

from

Maus

Graphic Memoir by Art Spiegelman

NOTICE & NOTE

As you read, use the side margins to make notes about the text.

Cats and mice represent Germans and Jews in this graphic novel about the Holocaust.

AFTER WHAT HAPPENED TO THE GRANDPARENTS, IT WAS A FEW MONTHS QUIET. THEN IT CAME POSTERS EVERYWHERE AND SPEECHES FROM THE GEMEINDE...

ANALYZE GRAPHIC MEMOIRS

Annotate: Mark the narrative text (text that is not dialogue) on this page.

Infer: Who is speaking these words?

Don't forget to **Notice & Note** as you read the text.

NOTICE & NOTE

TOUGH QUESTIONS

When you notice characters asking questions that reveal their internal struggles, you've found a **Tough Questions** signpost.

Notice & Note: Mark the tough question Vladek's father asks in the second panel on this page.

Analyze: What does this question make you wonder about?

ANALYZE GRAPHIC MEMOIRS

Annotate: Mark details on this page that show the setting of this scene.

Analyze: Why do you think the author used different-size panels to depict this event?

WHEN WE WERE EVERYBODY INSIDE, GESTAPO WITH MACHINE GUNS SURROUNDED THE STADIUM.

THEN WAS A SELECTION, WITH PEOPLE SENT EITHER TO THE LEFT, EITHER TO THE RIGHT.

ME AND ANJA CAME TO THE TABLE WHERE MY COUSIN WAS SITTING...

Don't forget to **Notice & Note** as you read the text.

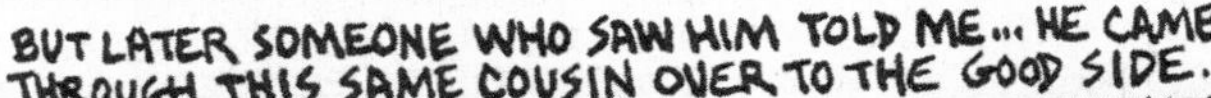

ANALYZE GRAPHIC MEMOIRS

Annotate: Mark different sizes and styles of text you see on this page.

Interpret: How do the various text treatments help you "hear" the way characters speak the dialogue?

ANALYZE GRAPHIC MEMOIRS

Annotate: Mark where another person's experience is described.

Analyze: What is the impact of this story on the memoir?

COLLABORATIVE DISCUSSION

With a partner, choose three or four words to describe community members' feelings as the Nazis classify and prepare to deport them.

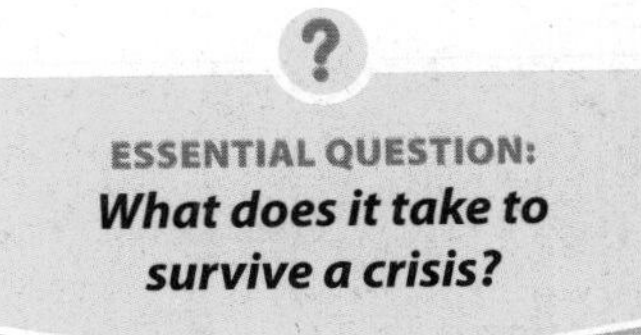
ESSENTIAL QUESTION:
What does it take to survive a crisis?

Review your notes and add your thoughts to your Response Log.

Assessment Practice

Answer these questions before moving on to the **Analyze the Text** section on the following page.

1. Why do the author's father and other Jews go to the Dienst stadium?

- (A) They are all being deported from Poland.
- (B) People who need jobs may apply for one there.
- (C) The Nazis require them to appear with their documents.
- (D) It is a place to look for missing friends and family members.

2. At the stadium, all the Jews —

- (A) get new documents
- (B) get a new stamp on their passports
- (C) are sorted into two groups
- (D) are sent to Auschwitz

3. Select **two** sentences that explain why Vladek never sees his father again.

- (A) He gives the wrong answers to the Nazis' questions.
- (B) He chooses to be with his daughter Fela and her children.
- (C) He is too old and sick to hold a job.
- (D) He gets lost in the stadium crowd.
- (E) He climbs over the fence onto the left side.

Ed

Test-Taking Strategies

Analyze the Text

Support your responses with evidence from the text.

NOTICE & NOTE

Review what you **noticed and noted** as you read the text. Your annotations can help you answer these questions.

1. **DRAW CONCLUSIONS** Why do you think families with many children were "sent to the left" in the selection process?

2. **INFER** Find the **Tough Question** Vladek's father asks himself after his daughter Fela is sorted to the left. What internal struggle does the question reveal, and how does Vladek's father resolve it?

3. **ANALYZE** Vladek's flashback ends with a drawing of Vladek that has no panel around it. Why do you think the author did this? What impact does it have on readers?

4. **SYNTHESIZE** In the last scene of the excerpt, the woman in the kitchen shares some of her Holocaust memories. How does this scene, combined with Vladek's memory from Sosnowiec, add depth to a memoir about the author's own life and experiences?

5. **EVALUATE** Do you think the graphic-novel format is effective for Spiegelman's memoir? Review the notes you took in the Analyze Graphic Memoirs chart on the second Get Ready page for *Maus*. Then use the following chart to evaluate elements of the excerpt.

Feature	Effective? Yes/No	Explain your response.
Mice represent Jews, and cats represent Germans.		
Vladek's memories are illustrated with images and dialogue.		
Spiegelman uses larger or bolder text for certain words.		

Choices

Here are some other ways to demonstrate your understanding of the ideas in this lesson.

Writing

Draft an Argument

Take a position about whether it is appropriate for an event like the Holocaust to be the subject of a graphic novel. Then, create an outline for an argumentative essay.

- Draft your opinion, or thesis statement.
- List examples and reasons.
- Make notes about how you will respond to opposing views.
- Draft a strong restatement of your opinion as a conclusion.

Use your outline to present an argument to your class or a small group. Invite responses, listening actively and responding respectfully to other points of view.

As you write and discuss, be sure to use the Academic Vocabulary words.

dimension

external

statistic

sustain

utilize

Media

Create a Comic Book

The focus of this unit is surviving in a crisis. Create a short comic book or graphic story depicting a character attempting to survive a difficult or dangerous situation. You can build on work you created earlier, or create something new.

- Brainstorm the elements of your story (for example, plot and characters).
- Create storyboards consisting of each panel image that will tell your story.
- Decide how to use captions and speech bubbles to convey the speech and thoughts of your characters.
- Share your comic by posting on a school site or blog.

Speaking & Listening

Produce an Oral History

Maus is based on what author Art Spiegelman learned about his father's experiences during the Holocaust. Interview one or more adult family members or trusted friends about their lives. Create a presentation to share with classmates describing what you learned about your family member or friend.

Compare Accounts

Elie Wiesel's *Night* and Art Spiegelman's *Maus* are both memoirs that focus on the experiences of European Jews during the Holocaust. Each person who witnesses or participates in any event will remember it slightly differently. Factors that may influence a person's experience include his or her age, values, beliefs, and background. Comparing these two memoirs about the Holocaust can reveal the different ways people experience the same devastating events.

In a small group, answer the questions in the chart for the excerpts from *Night* and *Maus*. Be sure to support your ideas with text evidence.

	A from *Night*	B from *Maus*
What specific events from the Holocaust are described?		
What genre features does the author use to share facts about the historical period?		
What details about the Holocaust experience does the author emphasize?		
How does the author convey his attitude or tone about the events described?		

Analyze the Texts

Discuss these questions in your group.

1. **CRITIQUE** What are some advantages and disadvantages of each genre (prose memoir, graphic memoir) in describing people's experiences of the Holocaust? Cite details from the selections to support your answers.

2. **COMPARE** What ideas or themes about human life are expressed in both Holocaust memoirs? Support your ideas with evidence from the text.

3. **SYNTHESIZE** In both selections, some Jews work for the Nazis. How do you explain this? Which selection gives you more insight into these characters?

Collaborate and Present

Your group can continue exploring the ideas in these texts by presenting a comparison of the two memoirs. Follow these steps:

1. **REVIEW NOTES** As a group, review the notes you took while discussing similarities and differences between the memoirs. Select several important points to cover in your presentation.
2. **PLAN YOUR PRESENTATION** Choose the best order in which to present your ideas. Decide how you will conclude your presentation. Assign part of the presentation to each group member.
3. **CONSIDER USING MEDIA** Presentation software can help engage your audience. If you decide to use such software, create slides that summarize your ideas clearly and succinctly.
4. **PRACTICE** Before facing your audience, take the time to practice your presentation at least once. If anything does not go smoothly, fix the problem now.
5. **PRESENT** Deliver your presentation to the rest of the class, and listen to the other presentations.
6. **DISCUSS** As a class, discuss whether you think the memoir is an appropriate genre for writers to explore the events of the Holocaust. Explain your thinking.

Reader's Choice

Continue your exploration of the Essential Question by doing some independent reading on facing and surviving challenges. Read the titles and descriptions shown. Then mark the texts that interest you.

ESSENTIAL QUESTION:
What does it take to survive a crisis?

Short Reads

Available on 

These texts are available in your ebook. Choose one to read and rate. Then defend your rating to the class.

Adventurers Change. Danger Does Not.

Article by **Alan Cowell**

Which is more important—to reach the summit of Mount Everest or to save the life of a fellow climber in trouble?

Rate It 

from An Ordinary Man

Memoir by **Paul Rusesabagina**

A Rwandan hotel owner of mixed Hutu and Tutsi descent saves more than a thousand refugees and survives the 1994 genocide.

Rate It 

Who Understands Me But Me

Poem by **Jimmy Santiago Baca**

When a young man is sentenced to prison, he loses a lot but gains even more.

Rate It 

Truth at All Costs

Speech by **Marie Colvin**

Is it worth the risk to report from a war zone? Do war correspondents make a difference?

Rate It 

from Deep Survival

Informational Text by **Laurence Gonzales**

Is a positive mental attitude really the key to survival? The author explores how disaster survivors manage to beat the odds.

Rate It 

Long Reads

Here are a few recommended books that connect to this unit topic. For additional options, ask your teacher, school librarian, or peers. Which titles spark your interest?

Night

Memoir by **Elie Wiesel**

Elie Wiesel recounts the horrors he faced as a teenager in the Nazi death camps. He reflects on his will to survive and man's capacity for inhumanity.

Enchanted Air: Two Cultures, Two Wings

Memoir by **Margarita Engle**

Margarita is a girl from two worlds. With hostility brewing between Cuba and the United States, she wonders if she can still belong to both.

Bad Boy

Memoir by **Walter Dean Myers**

Walter has a quick temper and is always ready for a fight. He also loves to read and write. How will the streets of Harlem shape him, and who will he become?

Extension

↳ Connect & Create

DEAR AUTHOR Write a letter to the author of one of the texts. Include:

- questions you noted as you read
- topics or events you wish the author had discussed
- your thoughts about how the writer addressed the Essential Question—how people survive and overcome challenges

CREATE A COLLAGE Make a collage to visually express your ideas about the text you read.

1. Decide what images you want to include.
2. Include photos and/or illustrations from magazines, newspapers, or online sources that represent settings, characters, events, or situations described in the text.
3. Write captions describing how each image connects to the text.

Share your finished product with the class.

NOTICE & NOTE

- Pick one of the texts and annotate the Notice & Note signposts you find.
- Then, use the **Notice & Note Writing Frames** to help you write about the significance of the signposts.
- Compare your findings with those of other students who read the same text.

Reader's Choice

Notice & Note Writing Frames

Write an Argument

Writing Prompt

Using ideas, information, and examples from multiple texts in this unit, write an argument that would serve as a newspaper editorial opinion stating your position on the question "Does survival require selfishness?"

Manage your time carefully so that you can

- review the texts in the unit;
- plan your essay;
- write your essay; and
- revise and edit your essay.

Be sure to

- clearly state the claim of your argument;
- address alternate or opposing claims;
- use and cite relevant and sufficient evidence; and
- avoid relying too much on one source.

Review the Mentor Text

For an example of a well-written argument you can use as a mentor text and as a source for your essay, review:

- **Is Survival Selfish?** (pages 23–27)

Make sure to carefully review your notes and annotations about this text. Think about the techniques the author used to make her argument persuasive.

Consider Your Sources

Review the list of Unit 1 texts and choose at least three that you may want to use as a sources of evidence for your argument.

As you review potential sources, consult the notes you made on your **Response Log** and make additional notes about any ideas that might be useful as you write your argument. Include source titles and page numbers in your notes so that you can provide accurate text evidence and citations when you include support from these texts.

UNIT 1 SOURCES

- ☐ *from* **A Chance in the World**
- ☐ **Is Survival Selfish?**
- ☐ **The Leap**
- ☐ **The End and the Beginning**
- ☐ *from* **Night**
- ☐ *from* **Maus**

Analyze the Prompt

Review the prompt to make sure you understand the assignment.

1. Mark the sentence in the prompt that identifies the topic of your argument. Rewrite the sentence in your own words.
2. Look for words that indicate the purpose and audience of your essay, and write a sentence describing each.

Find a Purpose

Two common purposes of an argument are

- to **persuade** others to agree with your position
- to **address** opposing claims

What is my topic? What is my writing task?

What is my purpose?

Who is my audience?

Review the Rubric

Your argument will be scored using a rubric. As you write, focus on the characteristics described in the chart. You will learn more about these characteristics as you work through the lesson.

Purpose, Focus, and Organization	Evidence and Elaboration	Conventions of Standard English
The response includes: • A strongly maintained claim • Effective responses to opposing claims • Use of transitions to connect ideas • Logical progression of ideas • Appropriate style and tone	The response includes: • Integrated, thorough, and credible relevant evidence • Precise references to sources • Effective use of a variety of elaboration techniques • Academic and domain-specific vocabulary • Varied sentence structure	The response may include: • Some minor errors in usage but no pattern of errors. • Correct punctuation, capitalization, sentence formation, and spelling • Command of basic conventions

PLAN YOUR ARGUMENT

Develop a Claim

In an argument, the **claim** is the writer's position on an issue. In the chart below, identify your position on whether survival requires selfishness. Then, draft your claim, making sure it is direct and specific.

Should teen's vote or not?

~~Does Survival Require Selfishness?~~	Claim
👍 👎	Teen's are more mature then you think

Ed Help with Planning

Consult **Interactive Writing Lesson: Writing Arguments**

Identify Support

To build a strong argument, you need solid support for your claim. Support consists of reasons and evidence.

- Logical **reasons** explain why you have taken a particular position on an issue.
- Credible **evidence**, such as facts, statistics, examples, or expert opinions, support your reasons.

Use the chart to outline your support. Draw on notes you took as you read. In the source column, be sure to record the title, author, and page number.

Focus on an Idea

Your claim should be direct and specific. It should focus on one idea. Revise your claim until you are confident that your readers will understand your position.

Reasons	Evidence	Source
Knowledgeable	Civic knowledge, political skills, political enfficacy, and tolerance	
Increases voter turnout	has a 13% turnout	
Teens should have a voice in the election	If teens don't a voice no one will hear them	

Address Opposing Claims

Your essay should include a response to an opposing claim in which you explain why your position is more valid. Review your notes on texts in this unit to find claims you can **refute,** or argue against.

Opposing Claim	My Response
People think teens aren't mature enough 18-29 age group has extremely low voter turnout 16 year olds should not be given the right to vote	

Organize Ideas

Organize your material in a way that will help you draft your argument. Keep in mind that a well-written argument has an organization that establishes clear relationships among claims, reasons, and evidence. Paragraph breaks and transitional words and phrases help create a logical progression of ideas and help readers understand how ideas are related to one another.

Create Structure

As you organize your argument, be sure to

- Clearly link ideas with supporting reasons and evidence
- Use transitions to link ideas
- Refute opposing claims soon after introducing them

INTRODUCTION	• Clearly introduce your claim. • Include an interesting question, quotation, or detail to grab the reader's attention.
BODY PARAGRAPHS	• Present logical reasons and credible evidence to support your claim, devoting a paragraph to each main idea. • Include a paragraph in which you address an opposing claim. • Use transitional phrases such as "First . . ." and "Another example . . ." to link your ideas.
CONCLUSION	• Restate your claim and its significance. • Summarize your ideas and leave readers with a thought-provoking idea closely related to your claim.

2 DEVELOP A DRAFT

Now it is time to draft your essay. Examine how professional authors craft effective arguments to use similar techniques in your own writing.

Ed

Drafting Online

Check your assignment list for a writing task from your teacher.

Write an Engaging Introduction

EXAMINE THE MENTOR TEXT

Notice how the opening lines of **"Is Survival Selfish?"** capture the reader's attention.

The author opens with a famous tragedy that many readers will be familiar with.

When the ocean liner *Titanic* sank in April of 1912, one of the few men to survive the tragedy was J. Bruce Ismay, the chairman and managing director of the company that owned the ship. After the disaster, however, Ismay was savaged by the media and the general public for climbing into a lifeboat and saving himself when there were other women and children still on board. Ismay said he'd already helped many women and children into lifeboats and had only climbed in one himself when there were no other women or children in the area and the boat was ready to release. But it didn't matter. His reputation was ruined. He was labeled an uncivilized coward and, a year after the disaster, he resigned his position at White Star.

She startles the reader with a surprising fact.

She concludes with the shocking fate of Ismay after the Titanic's sinking.

APPLY TO YOUR DRAFT

Use this web to generate ideas for creating an introduction that captures the reader's attention.

IDEAS FOR INTRODUCTION

Try These Suggestions

Consider using a variety of methods to engage your reader. You might:

- reference an event or an idea readers will be familiar with
- include a surprising fact
- reveal something important about your topic

Present Opposing Claims

EXAMINE THE MENTOR TEXT

Notice how the author of "**Is Survival Selfish?**" introduces opposing claims.

> But is survival really selfish and uncivilized? Or is it smart? And is going in to rescue others always heroic? Or is it sometimes just stupid? It's a complex question, because there are so many factors involved, and every survival situation is different.

The author poses a series of questions that introduce opposing claims, which she will address.

APPLY TO YOUR DRAFT

Consider how to introduce an opposing claim. Then include a response that addresses the opposing claim. Use the chart to guide you.

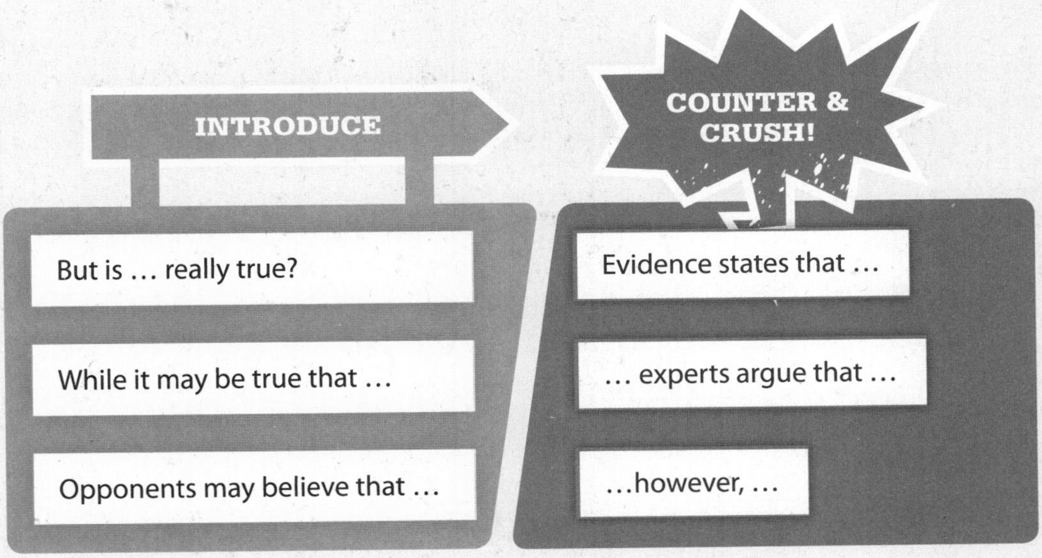

INTRODUCE	COUNTER & CRUSH!
But is … really true?	Evidence states that …
While it may be true that …	… experts argue that …
Opponents may believe that …	…however, …

3 REVISE YOUR ARGUMENT

Help with Revision

Find a **Peer Review Guide** and **Student Models**.

Even professional writers rework their ideas and language as they revise. No one gets it right the first time. Use the guide to help you revise your essay.

REVISION CHART		
Ask Yourself	**Prove It**	**Revise It**
Introduction Does my introduction contain a clear claim?	**Highlight** the introduction. **Underline** the claim your argument makes.	**Add to** or **revise** your claim to clarify or strengthen your position on the issue.
Body Are body paragraphs organized in a logical sequence?	**Number** the paragraphs and make sure the most important reason comes first or last.	**Rearrange** paragraphs in order of importance.
Transitions Do transitions connect ideas throughout the essay?	**Mark** transitions that connect ideas.	**Add** transitions to connect ideas.
Support for My Claim Do at least two reasons support my claim? Is each reason supported with well-elaborated evidence	**Mark** each reason. **Highlight** the supporting evidence for each reason. **Underline** elaboration that explains how evidence supports your claim.	**Add** reasons. **Add** elaboration to clarify how the evidence supports your claim.
Sources Do I identify my sources?	✔ **Put a check mark** next to references to your sources.	**Add** references to sources
Opposing Claims Do I address opposing claims?	**Underline** opposing claims. **Highlight** sentences that address them.	**Add** possible opposing claims and persuasive responses to refute them.
Conclusion Does my conclusion logically flow from the reasoning of my argument?	**Highlight** the parts of the conclusion that support your claim and reasons.	**Add** or **revise** the conclusion to sum up your ideas.

APPLY TO YOUR DRAFT

Consider the following as you look for opportunities to improve your writing.

- Make sure that your claim is clear and strongly stated.
- Check that your reasons are logical and backed by credible evidence.
- Correct any errors in grammar and punctuation.

Peer Review in Action

Once you have finished revising your argument, you will exchange papers with a partner in a peer review. During a peer review, you will give suggestions to improve your partner's draft.

Read the introduction from a student's draft and examine the comments made by his peer reviewer.

Draft

It's Human Nature to Want to Survive
By Javy Oliver, Lakeview High School

Most people want to save themselves. They might be willing to help a few other people along the way, but most people just want to survive a tragedy themselves. Surviving a tragedy sometimes requires people to be selfish, and society should not shame survivors for doing what comes naturally.

Add a stronger, more engaging first sentence to hook readers' interest and establish a tone for the essay.

Avoid simply repeating the claim.

Now read the revised introduction below. Notice how the writer has improved his draft by making revisions based on his peer reviewer's comments.

Revision

It's Human Nature to Want to Survive
By Javy Oliver, Lakeview High School

"Save yourselves!" It's a line that's been used as a joke in many movies. But it's true. Most people want to save themselves. They might be willing to help a few other people along the way, but most people will fight to survive a tragedy. Is that a bad thing? How would you really react in a tragedy? Would you really risk your life to save a stranger? Ten strangers? Are you selfish if you don't? Surviving a tragedy sometimes requires people to be selfish, and society should not shame survivors for doing what comes naturally.

This is an engaging hook for your argument.

These thought-provoking questions engage the reader.

APPLY TO YOUR DRAFT

During your peer review, give each other specific suggestions for how you could make your arguments more effective. Use your revision guide to help you.

When receiving feedback from your partner, listen attentively and ask questions to make sure you fully understand the revision suggestions.

4 EDIT YOUR ARGUMENT

Edit your final draft to make sure it conforms to standard English conventions and to correct any misspellings or grammatical errors.

Watch Your Language!

USE TRANSITIONAL WORDS AND PHRASES

Transitional words and phrases connect ideas and show how they are related. Skillful use of transitions will strengthen your argument by making it unified and cohesive.

Read the following sentences from "Is Survival Selfish?"

> **In July 2007**, I was having a drink with a friend in Grand Central Station **when** an underground steam pipe exploded just outside. From where we sat, we heard a dull "boom!" and **then** suddenly, people were running, streaming out of the tunnels and out the doors.

The phrase *In July 2007* transitions into the example anecdote. The transition words *when* and *then* connect the ideas in the anecdote to help the flow of the text.

Transitions

Here are some common transitional words and phrases:

Contrast: but, conversely, on the one hand, however, even so, nonetheless, in spite of, in contrast to

Sequence: then, when, first, second, next, last, finally

APPLY TO YOUR DRAFT

Now apply what you've learned about transitions to your own work. Look for places in your argument where you can use transition words to link ideas, events, or reasons.

1. **Read your paper aloud** and underline transitions you've used.
2. **Add transitional words and phrases** that will help connect ideas.
3. **Exchange drafts** with a peer and review transitions in each other's argument.

5 PUBLISH YOUR ARGUMENT

Share It!

Finalize your argument for your writing portfolio. You may also use your argument as inspiration for other projects.

Ways to Share

- **Submit your argument** to the school newspaper.
- **Engage in a debate** with someone who is on the opposite side of your argument.
- **Adapt your argument** for an oral presentation. See the next task for tips on how.

Speaking & Listening

Present and Respond to an Argument

You have written an argument about whether survival requires that a person be selfish. Now you will prepare to deliver your argument as an oral presentation.

Plan Your Presentation

Consider how your essay sounds when read aloud. Add, subtract, or revise any sections that may not translate well to a presentation. Use the chart to take notes and help plan your presentation.

	Ask Yourself	Answers and Notes
Title and Introduction	How will you revise your title and introductory paragraph to capture the listener's attention?	
Audience	What information will your audience already know? What opposing claims might they make?	
Effective Language and Organization	Which parts of your argument should be simplified? Consider clarifying your main points by adding connecting words such as *first, second,* and *third.*	
Visuals	What images could you use to illustrate your points or make your argument more persuasive?	

Practice with a Partner or Group

Practicing your presentation will help you improve both the argument and your delivery.

Practice	Ask Yourself	Fix It!
Pronunciation, Enunciation	Do you know how to pronounce all the words in your argument? Are there words you stumble over when you read them aloud?	Check the dictionary if you are not sure about a pronunciation. Replace difficult words with words you can easily enunciate.
Volume, Voice Modulation, and Pitch	Can you be heard by your audience? Are you using your voice to emphasize your points?	Make sure the overall volume of your voice is appropriate. Practice raising and lowering your voice to emphasize points.
Speaking Rate, or Pacing	Are you speaking too quickly or too slowly?	Practice speaking at a "just right" pace or rate, so that listeners can understand you and don't lose interest.

Deliver Your Presentation

Use the advice you received to make final changes to your argument. Then, making effective use of verbal and nonverbal techniques, present it to your classmates.

Productive Discussion

When you are discussing your project with your group, remember to:

- **Point out strengths as well as weaknesses.**
- **Contribute only information that is relevant to the discussion.**
- **Avoid generalizations such as, "It was good," or "It could be better."**
- **Include suggestions for improvement in a considerate and tactful manner.**

Rhetorical Appeals

Listen for **rhetorical appeals,** supports to a claim that appeal to the reader's logic, ethics, or emotions. Here are some techniques presenters may use to manipulate your emotions:

- **Bandwagon** (saying everyone is doing it)
- **Loaded language** (choosing words that elicit strong feelings)
- **Understatement** (deliberately saying less than you mean)
- **Overstatement** (purposefully exaggerating or hyping)
- **Ad Hominem** (an argument directed against a person rather than an issue)

Share It!

- **Record your presentation** and share it with family members and friends.
- **Have a partner discussion** about how your position may have changed after listening to other presentations.

Interactive Speaking & Listening Lesson: Giving a Presentations

Reflect & Extend

Here are some other ways to show you understand the ideas in Unit 1.

Reflect on the
Essential Question

What does it take to survive a crisis?

Has your answer to the question changed after reading the texts in the unit? Discuss your ideas.

You can use these sentence starters to help you reflect on your learning.

- **I think differently now because . . .**
- **I mostly feel the same because . . .**
- **I'm still wondering about . . .**

Project-Based Learning

Create a Documentary

You've read about different stories of survival. Now, with a group of classmates, create a documentary that tells how one person or group of people survived a crisis.

Here are some questions to get you started.

- Who do we want to be the subject of our documentary?
- What sources will we use?
- What messages do we want to express?

Media Project

To find more help with this task online, access **Create a Documentary**.

Writing

Author Interview

Script an interview with the author of one text in the unit. Fill in the chart; then draft an introduction, questions for the author, and a conclusion thanking the writer.

Ask Yourself	My Notes
What questions about the topic do you still have after reading the text?	
What do you want to know about the author's purpose or motivation for writing the text?	

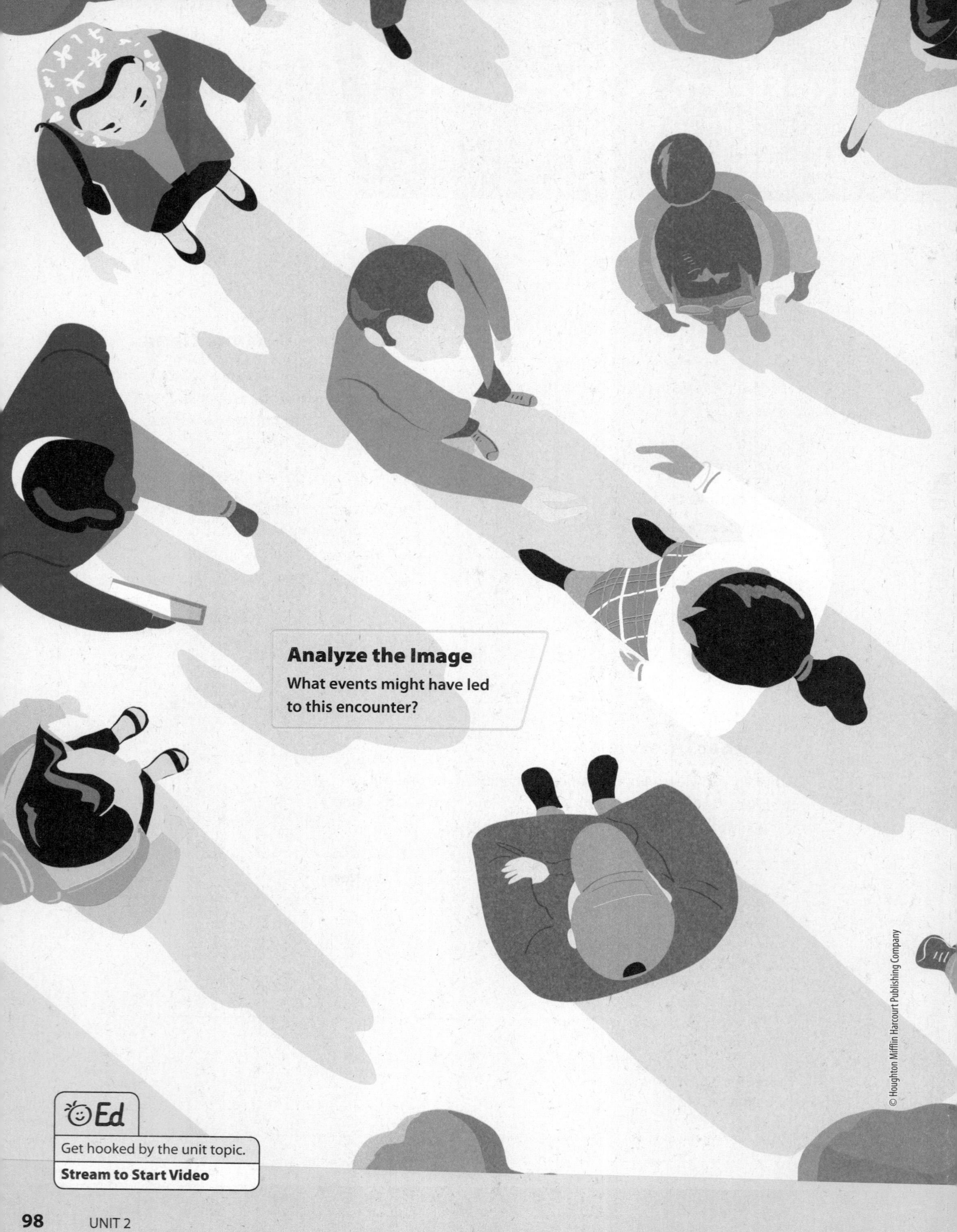

Analyze the Image

What events might have led to this encounter?

Ed

Get hooked by the unit topic.

Stream to Start Video

Breaking Through Barriers

"Sometimes perhaps you don't want to be a part of me.
Nor do I often want to be a part of you.
But we are, that's true!"
—Langston Hughes

ESSENTIAL QUESTION:
Are some differences too great to overcome?

Spark Your Learning

Here are some opportunities to think about the topics and themes of **Unit 2: Breaking Through Barriers.**

As you read, you can use the **Response Log** (page R2) to track your thinking about the Essential Question.

?

Think about the **Essential Question**

Are some differences too great to overcome?

How can people of different backgrounds and beliefs find common ground? What are the consequences when individuals or groups are not able to agree?

Make the Connection

Having a disagreement with someone can feel like a bad thing. But is it always? Discuss your thoughts with a partner.

Build Academic Vocabulary

You can use these Academic Vocabulary words to write and talk about people's differences described in this unit. Which of these words do you already feel comfortable using when speaking or writing?

	I can use it!	I understand it.	I'll look it up.
enforce			
entity			
internal			
presume			
resolve			

Prove It!

Think of a time you and a friend or family member had a difference of opinion. Were you able to compromise and work out your differences? What helped you accomplish that, or stood in your way? Use one or more academic vocabulary words in your response.

Preview the Texts

Look over the images, titles, and descriptions of the texts in the unit. Mark the title of the text that interests you most.

The Power of a Dinner Table

Editorial by **David Brooks**

A group of young people find compassion and acceptance at this couple's dinner table.

Unusual Normality

Personal Narrative by **Ishmael Beah**

A young man's traumatic past sets him apart from his classmates.

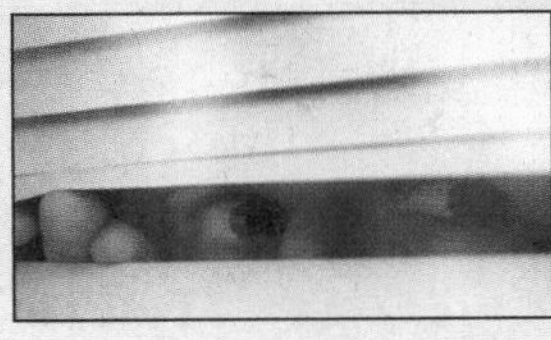

Once Upon a Time

Short Story by **Nadine Gordimer**

A family's isolation from its community leads to tragedy.

Theme for English B

Poem by **Langston Hughes**

Who are we, and what makes us different from other people?

The Vietnam Wall

Poem by **Alberto Ríos**

A poet describes his emotions confronting the Vietnam Veterans Memorial.

Views of the Wall

Visual Essay

See images of the Vietnam Veterans Memorial and its visitors.

The Gettysburg Address

Speech by **Abraham Lincoln**

President Lincoln emphasizes the importance of ending the Civil War and reuniting the country.

from Saving Lincoln

Film Clip

In this film clip, an actor recreates Lincoln's delivery of the Gettysburg Address.

Think Outside the Box

Why is empathy important when we encounter other views and beliefs?

Get Ready

The Power of a Dinner Table

Editorial by **David Brooks**

ESSENTIAL QUESTION:
Are some differences too great to overcome?

Engage Your Brain

Choose one or more of these activities to start connecting with the editorial you're about to read.

All Our Kids

The author of this editorial mentions a charitable organization called "All Our Kids." Visit their website and read about what they do for young adults. Record your impressions and any questions you have.

Dinner Time

Where do you typically eat dinner? Is it in the kitchen, in the living room, or on the go? With whom do you typically eat? Do you talk during dinner, watch TV, work on homework, or something else? Compare answers with a partner.

Feels Like Home

Where or who makes you feel welcome? Sketch that place or person.

Analyze Central Idea and Details

The **central idea** of a text is the most important idea the writer is trying to get across to the reader—the main idea.

- Sometimes, writers state their central idea directly.
- For most texts, readers must **infer,** or make an educated guess about, the central idea.
- Readers can determine the central idea by noticing key ideas and **text evidence**—the supporting details writers include in their work.
- **Supporting details** include facts, descriptions, examples, and quotations. This editorial contains all of these supporting details.

Read the entire editorial before identifying the central idea. As you read, use the chart to list supporting details to help you infer the central idea.

Focus on Genre
Editorial

- is an opinion piece that usually appears on a newspaper's editorial page or as part of a news broadcast
- presents a subjective viewpoint on an issue or topic, not an objective news report
- is often written by the publisher, the editorial board, or a commentator

Key Ideas	Supporting Details
Dinner at Kathy and David's is a special event.	Teens from all over come to the "big social occasion of the week."

Analyze Text Structure

Text structure refers to the way authors organize their writing. Text structures help writers show the relationship between information and themes or main ideas. They also help readers navigate through the text and grasp those ideas.

Authors may use a variety of text structures:

- **Compare-Contrast**—to analyze similarities and differences in two or more subjects
- **Cause-Effect**—to explore relationships between events or ideas
- **Problem-Solution**—to analyze problems and propose solutions
- **Argument**—to present a claim (position) and support it with reasons and evidence
- **Sequential/Chronological**—to arrange events or actions in the order in which they occur

As you read the editorial, look for text structure clues such as text features (such as headings), transitions, and supporting details.

Annotation in Action

Here is an example of notes a student made about a paragraph from "The Power of a Dinner Table." As you read, highlight key details that support how the author develops the central idea of the text.

> That friend had a friend and that friend had a friend, and now when you go to dinner at Kathy and David's house on Thursday night there might be 15 to 20 teenagers crammed around the table, and later there will be groups of them crashing in the basement or in the few small bedrooms upstairs.
>
> *Sounds like friends spread the word*
>
> *Lots of teens must want a safe space*

Expand Your Vocabulary

Put a check mark next to the vocabulary words that you feel comfortable using when speaking or writing.

- **sibling** ☐
- **anomalous** ☐
- **charismatic** ☐
- **intricate** ☐

Turn to a partner and talk about the vocabulary words you already know. Look up the words you don't know, then write a one- or two-sentence pitch for a TV episode or story using as many of the words as you can.

As you read "The Power of a Dinner Table," use the definitions in the side column to help you learn the vocabulary words you don't already know.

Background

David Brooks (b. 1961) is a regular columnist for *The New York Times,* a television and radio commentator, and a bestselling author. Many of his current writings focus on the extraordinary efforts that ordinary people are making to improve society, including the piece you are about to read and his most recent book, *The Second Mountain: The Quest for a Moral Life.*

The Power of a Dinner Table

Editorial by David Brooks

A group of young people find compassion and acceptance at this couple's dinner table.

NOTICE & NOTE
As you read, use the side margins to make notes about the text.

1 Kathy Fletcher and David Simpson have a son named Santi, who went to Washington, D.C., public schools. Santi had a friend who sometimes went to school hungry. So Santi invited him to occasionally eat and sleep at his house.

2 That friend had a friend and that friend had a friend, and now when you go to dinner at Kathy and David's house on Thursday night there might be 15 to 20 teenagers crammed around the table, and later there will be groups of them crashing in the basement or in the few small bedrooms upstairs.

3 The kids who show up at Kathy and David's have endured the ordeals of modern poverty: homelessness, hunger, abuse, sexual assault. Almost all have seen death firsthand—to a **sibling**, friend or parent.

4 It's **anomalous** for them to have a bed at home. One 21-year-old woman came to dinner last week and said this was the first time she'd been around a family table since she was 11.

5 And yet by some miracle, hostile soil has produced **charismatic** flowers. Thursday dinner is the big social occasion of the week. Kids come from around the city. Spicy chicken and black rice are served. Cellphones are banned ("Be in the now," Kathy says).

sibling
(sĭb´lĭng) *n.* a brother or a sister; a person with one or both parents in common with another person.

anomalous
(ə-nŏm´ə-ləs) *adj.* unusual or uncommon; out of the ordinary.

charismatic
(kăr´ĭz-măt´ĭk) *adj.* magnetic; captivating; having the qualities of a leader who is popular and enthusiastic.

NOTICE & NOTE
QUOTED WORDS

When you notice the author has quoted the opinions of participants in an event, you've found a **Quoted Words** signpost.

Notice & Note: Mark the quotations in paragraphs 8 and 10.

Infer: Why were these two people quoted? What key idea do these quoted words suggest?

intricate
(ĭn´trĭ-kĭt) *adj.* complicated or elaborate.

ANALYZE CENTRAL IDEA AND DETAILS

Annotate: In paragraph 14, mark words and phrases that identify gifts the teens present.

Synthesize: What are the adults doing that inspires the teens to present their gifts? Why is this significant?

6 The kids call Kathy and David "Momma" and "Dad," are unfailingly polite, clear the dishes, turn toward one another's love like plants toward the sun and burst with big glowing personalities. Birthdays and graduations are celebrated. Songs are performed.

7 I started going to dinner there about two years ago, hungry for something beyond food. Each meal we go around the table, and everybody has to say something nobody else knows about them.

8 Each meal we demonstrate our commitment to care for one another. I took my daughter once and on the way out she said, "That's the warmest place I can ever imagine."

9 Thursdays at Kathy and David's has been a weekly uplift, and their home a place to be reminded of what is beautiful about our country and what we can do to bring out its loveliness.

10 The kids need what all adolescents need: bikes, laptops and a listening heart. "Thank you for seeing the light in me," one young woman told Kathy after a cry on the couch. David and Kathy have set up a charitable organization called AOK, for All Our Kids, to help each of the kids come into his or her own fullness. Four started college this year, and one joined City Year, the national service organization.

11 Poverty up close is so much more **intricate** and unpredictable than the picture of poverty you get from the grand national debates. The kids can project total self-confidence one minute and then slide into utter lostness the next.

12 The college application process often seems like a shapeless fog to them; nobody's taught them the concrete steps to move along the way. One young woman lied on her financial aid forms because she didn't want to admit that her father was dead, her mother was on drugs—how messed up her home life actually was.

13 There's no margin for error for these kids, and she would have lost her college dreams if not for a squad of adults ready to mobilize around her.

14 The adults in this community give the kids the chance to present their gifts. At my first dinner, Edd read a poem from his cracked flip phone that I first thought was from Langston Hughes, but it turned out to be his own. Kesari has a voice that somehow emerged from New Orleans jazz from the 1920s. Madeline and Thalya practice friendship as if it were the highest art form. Jamel loses self-consciousness when he talks of engine repair.

15 They give us a gift—complete intolerance of social distance. When I first met Edd, I held out my hand to shake his. He looked at it and said, "We hug here," and we've been hugging and hanging off each other since.

16 Bill Milliken, a veteran youth activist, is often asked which programs turn around kids' lives. "I still haven't seen one program change one kid's life," he says. "What changes people is relationships. Somebody willing to walk through the shadow of the valley of adolescence with them."

17 Souls are not saved in bundles. Love is the necessary force.

18 The problems facing this country are deeper than the labor participation rate and ISIS. It's a crisis of solidarity, a crisis of segmentation, spiritual degradation, and intimacy.

19 AOK has been my visit to a better future, more powerful than any political tract about what we need next.

20 Sometimes Kathy and David are asked how they ended up with so many kids flowing through their house. They look at how many kids are out there, and respond, "How is it possible you don't?"

ANALYZE TEXT STRUCTURE

Annotate: Mark words and phrases in paragraphs 16–19 that identify social issues and how they might be addressed.

Analyze: What text structure has the author used? Do you think he has used it effectively? Why or why not?

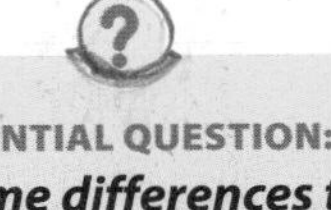

ESSENTIAL QUESTION:
Are some differences too great to overcome?

COLLABORATIVE DISCUSSION

Think about the title of this editorial, "The Power of a Dinner Table." What "power" does this dinner table have?

Assessment Practice

Answer these questions before moving on to the **Analyze the Text** section.

1. Which **two** sentences from the text best show the positive impact Thursday dinners have had on the young adults who go to Kathy and David's house?
   - (A) "It's anomalous for them to have a bed at home."
   - (B) "The kids . . . turn toward one another's love like plants toward the sun. . . ."
   - (C) "The kids need . . . bikes, laptops and a listening heart."
   - (D) "The kids can project total self-confidence one minute and slide into utter lostness the next."
   - (E) "They give us a gift—complete intolerance of social distance."

2. In paragraph 13, the phrase no margin for error means—
   - (A) Mistakes happen.
   - (B) Perfection always is the best goal.
   - (C) Mistakes always lead to new opportunities.
   - (D) Mistakes can be very hard to overcome.

3. Which solution is most likely to benefit teens who are struggling?
   - (A) new technology
   - (B) better programs
   - (C) positive relationships
   - (D) healthier food

Test-Taking Strategies

Analyze the Text

Support your responses with evidence from the text.

NOTICE & NOTE

Review what you **noticed and noted** as you read the text. Your annotations can help you answer these questions.

1. **ANALYZE** Reread paragraphs 1–3. What text structure is starting to emerge from details of the teens' lives? Explain whether the author used this text structure effectively.

2. **INFER** Why do the teens call Kathy "Momma" and David "Dad" (paragraph 6)? Why is the teens' use of these terms significant? Cite evidence from the text to support your response.

3. **CONNECT** Explain what "a listening heart" means as used in paragraph 10. How can "a listening heart" be part of the solution to the struggles many teens face?

4. **INTERPRET** Reread paragraph 16. In your own words, what insights does Bill Milliken's statement provide to readers? Explain how these and other **Quoted Words** help the author develop his central idea.

5. **CRITIQUE** In paragraph 18, the author states what he thinks the "problems facing this country are." Do you agree with him? Cite evidence from the text to support your response.

6. **SYNTHESIZE** Review the organizer you started on the Get Ready page. Mark the details you listed that you now think are the most important ones. Using the organizer below, state the central idea of the editorial and list key details that support that idea.

Central Idea of the Editorial:
Key Supporting Details:

7. **EVALUATE** Editorial writers try to persuade their audience to agree with their opinions and proposals. Did David Brooks achieve his purpose? Explain, considering your own response to the editorial.

Choices

Here are some other ways to demonstrate your understanding of the ideas in this lesson.

Social & Emotional Learning

Journal

Throughout this editorial, the author emphasizes the importance of relationships. Write about an event or situation that connects you to other people in a positive way. Include relevant information such as:

- a detailed description of the place, situation, or event
- the people involved
- your positive thoughts and emotions

As you write and discuss, be sure to use the **Academic Vocabulary** words.

- enforce
- entity
- internal
- presume
- resolve

Speaking & Listening

Research

We can learn a lot from people with different backgrounds and cultures from ours, but how can we connect with people unlike us? Research organizations or events in your community that would allow you to meet all kinds of people. Describe the purpose of one or two, and what you could potentially learn from them. Present your findings to a small group.

Media

Blog Posts

Imagine you regularly attend Kathy and David's Thursday night dinner. Write several blog posts describing your experiences. Include information about:

- people attending
- the food you eat
- conversation topics
- your own reflections and reactions

Expand Your Vocabulary

PRACTICE AND APPLY

Complete each sentence and answer the questions to show your understanding of the vocabulary words. Use a dictionary or thesaurus as needed.

1. Someone who spends a lot of time with one friend might feel like the friend is a **sibling.** Why?
2. If I received an A on a difficult test that I did not study for, that would be **anomalous.** Why?
3. A **charismatic** student council president is likely to get a lot of support for his or her proposals. Why?
4. In the computer lab, graphic design software would allow us to create some very **intricate** patterns for our posters. Why?

Vocabulary Strategy

Suffixes That Form Nouns

Interactive Vocabulary Lesson: Common Roots, Prefixes, and Suffixes

A **suffix** is a word part used at the end of a root or base word to create a new word. Suffixes can change the meaning of the word. They can also change a word to a different part of speech. For example, note how the verb *graduate* changes to the noun *graduations* (paragraph 6) by adding the suffix *-ions*.

Suffixes That Form Nouns	Meanings	Examples
-ance	act; process; quality; state of being	acceptance, alliance, guidance
-cy	fact or state of being	diplomacy, privacy, relevancy
-ion	act, condition, or result of	action, computation, degradation
-ity	condition; state of being	integrity, purity, sincerity

PRACTICE AND APPLY

Locate these words in the selection: *intolerance* (paragraph 15), *solidarity* (paragraph 18), *segmentation* (paragraph 18), and *intimacy* (paragraph 18).

Then, identify the suffixes used and write definitions for each word. Check your definitions in a dictionary.

Watch Your Language!

Noun Clauses

A **noun clause** is a subordinate clause that is used as a noun. Like other subordinate clauses, a noun clause has a subject and a verb, but it cannot stand alone as a sentence.

Noun clauses may be introduced by . . .	Examples from "The Power of a Dinner Table"	Function of the Noun Clause
Pronouns *that, what, which, who, whoever, whose*	The kids need what all adolescents need: bikes, laptops and a listening heart. (paragraph 10)	This noun clause serves as the direct object of the verb *need*. It tells what kids need.
Subordinating conjunctions *how, if, when, where, whether, why*	One young woman lied on her financial aid forms because she didn't want to admit . . . how messed up her home life actually was. (paragraph 12)	This noun clause serves as the direct object of the verb *admit*. It tells what the woman didn't want to admit.

Interactive Grammar Lesson: The Noun Clause

PRACTICE AND APPLY

With a partner, review "The Power of a Dinner Table" and identify additional examples of noun clauses. Discuss how these noun clauses add to readers' enjoyment and help them make sense of the text.

On your own, write two descriptive paragraphs about a meal or snack you especially enjoyed sharing with family or friends. Use noun clauses in both paragraphs and vary whether they start with a pronoun or with a subordinating conjunction.

Get Ready

MENTOR TEXT

Unusual Normality

Personal Narrative by **Ishmael Beah**

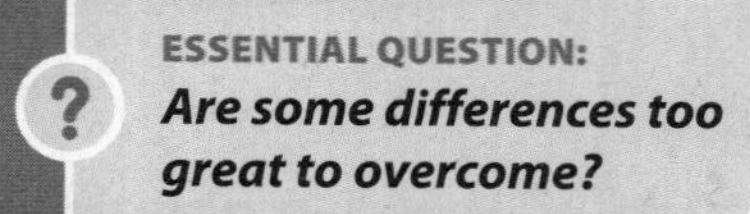
ESSENTIAL QUESTION:
Are some differences too great to overcome?

Engage Your Brain

Choose one or more of these activities to start connecting with the essay you're about to read.

It's not easy being a Jumbo Shrimp!

About Sierra Leone

Although Ishmael Beah's narrative is set in the United States, Beah writes about his earlier years as a child soldier. Find Sierra Leone on a map and briefly research the practice of children forced to become soldiers.

Do I Contradict Myself?

With a partner, discuss the title of the selection. What does each word mean? Why do you think the author put them together? Can you think of other oxymorons—words used together in a phrase that contradict each other?

We Usually . . .

List or draw activities you typically do with your friends. Are they team activities? Is there usually a winner? Do you always get along during these activities?

Analyze Purpose and Message

The **author's purpose** is the reason the writer has for writing a text. Authors may write to express thoughts or feelings, to persuade, to inform or explain, or to entertain. To determine the author's purpose in a personal essay:

- analyze the text structure. The author of this essay uses a chronological text structure to describe one period in his life.
- analyze language, including voice and tone
- make inferences based on the author's style and message

The **message** is the central idea of the work, or what the author is trying to communicate to the audience. To determine the central ideas and message in a personal essay:

- analyze the author's interpretations of events
- make inferences based on events and people the author describes

The **audience** is the people for whom the author is writing. To determine the audience of a personal essay:

- analyze evidence in the text, including voice and tone
- make inferences based on details in the text and the author's message

Focus on Genre

Personal Narrative

- similar to a memoir but shorter and more focused
- explores the writer's experiences
- includes the author's feelings and reactions at the time
- written after the events described

Analyze Voice and Tone

Voice and **tone** are elements of an author's style.

Literary Element	Example from "Unusual Normality"
Voice is a writer's unique use of language that allows a reader to "hear" a human personality in the writer's work. Elements of style that contribute to a writer's voice include sentence structure (or syntax), word choice (or diction), and tone.	And I thought to myself, *What a great omen. Fresh new start to everything.*
Tone is the writer's attitude toward his or her subject. A writer communicates tone through choice of words and details.	I learned a new American term for what they *did* find it. They were "weirded out" by the strange sense of humor that I had about this.

As you read, note the voice of the author and the tone of the text. Use them as clues to the author's purpose, message, and audience.

Annotation in Action

Here are one reader's notes about the beginning of the essay. As you read, note how the writer uses language to create a distinctive voice.

> I came to New York City in 1998. I was seventeen.
>
> I entered the United States with just a passport in my hand, because somehow the baggage that I'd checked when I boarded the flight from Ivory Coast (which was tattered in ways unimaginable) didn't make it.
>
> *unusual way to put this—writer has a unique personality*

Expand Your Vocabulary

Put a check mark next to the vocabulary words that you feel comfortable using when speaking or writing.

rehabilitation	☐
counterparts	☐
stereotype	☐
naïve	☐

Turn to a partner and talk about the vocabulary words you already know. Then, use as many vocabulary words as you can in a paragraph about playing a competitive game.

As you read "Unusual Normality," use the definitions in the side column to learn the vocabulary words you don't already know.

Background

Ishmael Beah (b. 1980) began to write about his experiences as a way of dealing with being forced to be a child soldier in Sierra Leone in Africa. After his family was killed when he was just 12 years old, Beah was threatened with death if he didn't fight with a rebel group that was trying to overthrow the country. An American working for UNICEF brought him to the United States. Today, he is a lawyer, an author, and a UN Goodwill Ambassador helping others like him.

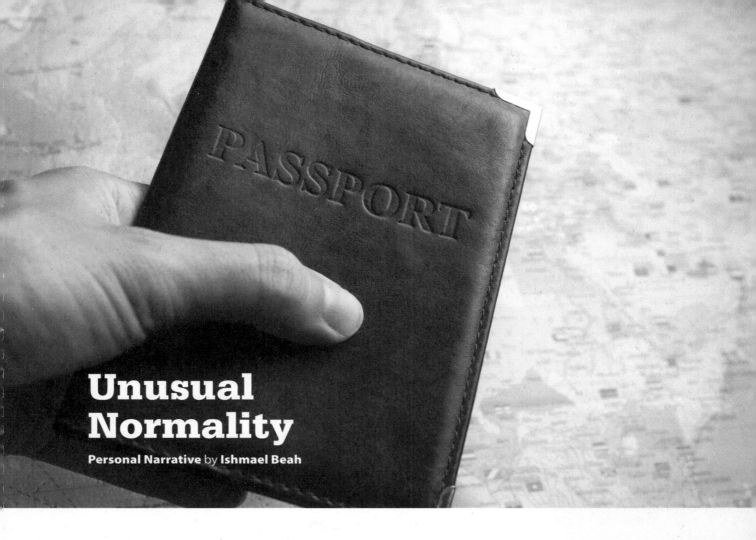

Unusual Normality

Personal Narrative by **Ishmael Beah**

A young man's traumatic past sets him apart from his classmates.

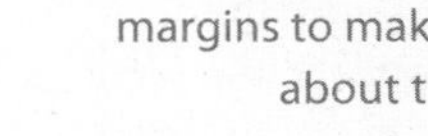

NOTICE & NOTE
As you read, use the side margins to make notes about the text.

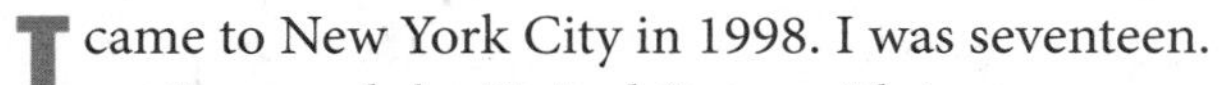

1 I came to New York City in 1998. I was seventeen.

2 I entered the United States with just a passport in my hand, because somehow the baggage that I'd checked when I boarded the flight from Ivory Coast (which was tattered in ways unimaginable) didn't make it.

3 I stood there at the luggage rack watching all these huge bags go by, and mine didn't come. This bag held all my possessions at this point: two pairs of pants and two shirts—one long-sleeved and one short. So I just started laughing, and I didn't even bother going to the lost-baggage section to claim it.

4 I just walked right out to meet my new adoptive mother, who was standing there with a beaming smile, waiting for me. And I explained to her what had happened, and we laughed some more.

5 We left and went into Manhattan, and that evening we went to Kmart. (After we had Chinese food and a fortune cookie that said, "You're about to have new clothes.")

6 And I thought to myself, *What a great omen. Fresh new start to everything.*

ANALYZE VOICE AND TONE

Annotate: Underline the author's thoughts, shown in italics. Mark two details in paragraphs 4–6 that caused these thoughts.

Analyze: How does the author's syntax and word choice reveal his attitude and outlook?

7 I was coming from a country called Sierra Leone. At age eleven, a war had started in my country. At twelve, I had become an orphan, because my mother, father, and two brothers had been killed in that war. At thirteen I was fighting as a soldier in that same war. At sixteen, after three years of war, I'd been removed from all that and had gone through **rehabilitation**, where I began learning how to deal with the memories of the war.

rehabilitation
(rē´hə-bĭl´ĭ-tā´shən) *n.* the act of being restored to good health or condition.

8 So from this experience, I had come to the United States. To have a new home, and to live with a mother who was willing to take me into her life when most people at the time were afraid of somebody like me.

9 It was a chance at living again, because all I had come to know, since I was eleven, was how to survive. I didn't know how to live. All I knew, really, up until this point in my life, was struggle. This was what I had come to expect from life, and I didn't trust in happiness or any kind of normality at all.

10 So here I was in New York, with my new mother. We needed to step into that normality.

NOTICE & NOTE
MEMORY MOMENT

When you notice the author has interrupted the forward progress of a narrative by bringing up something from the past, you've found a **Memory Moment** signpost.

Notice & Note: What words in paragraph 10 indicate that Beah is finished relating information about his earlier childhood? Mark these words.

Infer: Why might this information about the author's earlier childhood be important?

11 But we had a lot of things to deal with, and one of the most pressing ones was that I needed to get into school. You see, the visa that I had been given was a prospective-student visa. This meant that when I arrived in the United States, I had three months to get into a school. If I didn't, I would be returned to my war-torn country, Sierra Leone.

12 Now, when I arrived, it was in the summer, so all the schools were closed. But my mother got on the phone and called every school principal she could think of in Manhattan, and tried to get them to grant me an interview.

13 When I went to some of the interviews, I was immediately denied because of the following conversation:

14 "Do you have a report card to show that you had been in school?"

15 I would say, "No, but I know I have been in school."

16 And then my mother would interject to explain the context.

17 I would sit there thinking to myself, *What do these school principals think? Do they really think that when there's a war in your village or when your town is attacked, and people are gunned down in front of you, and you're running for your life, you're thinking to yourself, "You know, I must take my report card and put it in the back of my pocket."*

18 At some of these interviews, I was able to say some of these things, thinking that it would be funny. But the school principals didn't find it funny. I learned a new American term for what they *did* find it. They were "weirded out" by the strange sense of humor that I had about this.

19 So I decided that I was going to write an entrance essay about this, and the essay was simply titled "Why I Do Not Have a Report Card."

20 With this essay, along with exams that were given to me, I was accepted to the United Nations International School and placed in the eleventh grade.

21 Thus began my two years of high school and making other teenagers confused about who I was. You see, I didn't fit into any box. I didn't have the same worries about what shoes or clothes I wore. And so my teenage **counterparts** always wanted to find out why I was like that. Why I didn't worry about my essays or exams or things.

22 And of course I couldn't tell them, because I felt that they were not ready to hear the truth. What was I going to say?

23 During a break from class, "Hey, you know, I was a child soldier at thirteen. Let's go back to class now."

24 So I was silent, mostly. I didn't say much. I would just smile. And this made them more curious.

25 They would say to me, "You're such a weird kid."

26 And I would respond by saying, "No, no, no. I'm not weird. *Weird* has a negative connotation. I prefer the word *unusual*. It has a certain sophistication and gravitas[1] to it that suits my character."

27 And of course when I was finished saying this, they would look at me and say, "Why don't you speak like a normal person?"

28 The reason I spoke like this was because of my British-African English that I'd learned, which was the only formal English that I knew. So whenever I spoke, people felt ill at ease, particularly my fellow teenagers. They thought, *What is wrong with this fellow?*

29 Some of them, though, didn't find it as strange. They thought maybe my English was like this because I was from some royal African family.

30 So throughout my high-school years, I tried to make my English less formal, so that my friends would not feel disturbed by it. (However, I did not dispute the fact that I was from some royal African family or that I was a prince. Because, you see, sometimes some **stereotypes** have their benefits, and I certainly took advantage of that.)

31 But I needed to be silent about my background, because I also felt like I was being watched. When I got into the school, some of the other parents were not very happy that somebody with my background was in school with their children. And I realized that the way I conducted myself would determine whether they would ever let another child who had been through war into such a school.

Don't forget to **Notice & Note** as you read the text.

counterparts (koun´tər-pärts´) *n.* people or things that have the same characteristics and function as another.

ANALYZE VOICE AND TONE

Annotate: Mark the author's word choices and syntax that create the tone of paragraphs 21–27.

Draw Conclusions: What attitude does the author have toward his teenage counterparts?

stereotype (stĕr´ē-ə-tīp´) *n.* an oversimplified image or opinion.

[1] **gravitas** (grăv´ĭ-täs): seriousness, being solemn and respected.

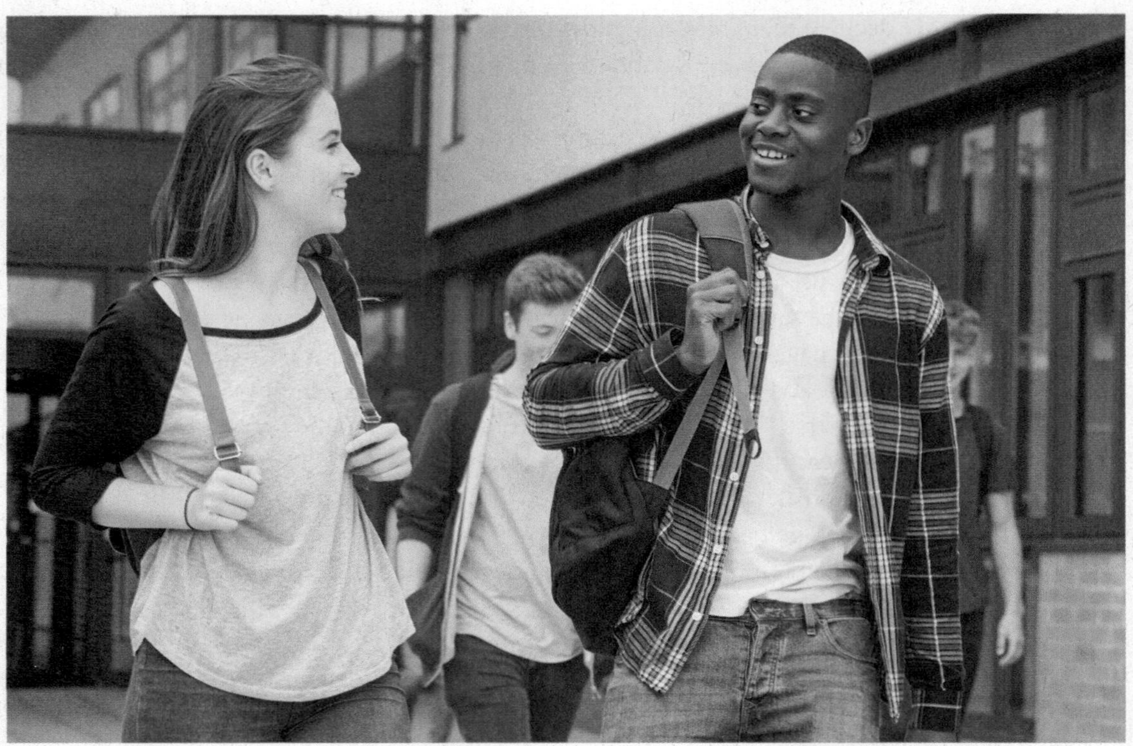

32 But even with all of these attitudes, and with my silence, I started making friends. To them it was sufficient that I was just some kid who lived in the East Village, who was from an African country.

33 And these kids were tough (they told me). Because they lived in a tough city, New York. And therefore *they* were tough.

34 They had been to the Bronx. They had been to Bed-Stuy. They had taken the train there. They had gotten into fights and won.

35 So they would say things to me like, "If you want to survive the streets of New York City, we need to teach you a few things."

36 And I'd be like, "Okay, sure. I'm open to learning."

37 And they would tell me things about how to be tough and stuff, and I would say, "Well, thank you very much. I truly appreciate this advice that you're giving me."

38 They were like, "No worries, our African brother. Anytime, anytime."

ANALYZE VOICE AND TONE

Annotate: In paragraphs 39–42, mark the words Beah uses to show the differences between himself and the "tough kids" of New York.

Compare: How does the violence of the "tough kids" differ from the violence the author has known?

39 Truth was, I'd been to some of these places that they spoke about, these neighborhoods, and I knew that the people who lived there didn't glorify violence the way they did. They didn't have time to pretend, because they lived in it, just like I had.

40 I noticed that these kids had a sort of *idea* of violence that they'd never really *lived*. They glorified it in a way, because they'd never actually experienced it at all.

41 When I walked with them, I observed that I paid more attention to the people who walked past us—how the person walked, which way they were coming from. I didn't take the same route twice, because I didn't want to develop a predictable path. These were all

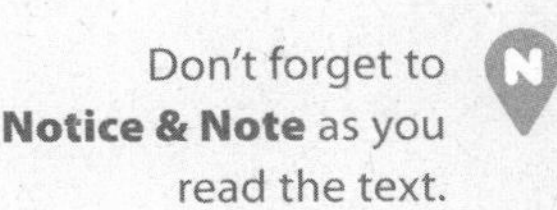

habits that were formed from my experiences, but I noticed that my new friends didn't do that at all. So I knew they were just saying these things to seem tough to me.

42 Now, I did enjoy listening to my new friends that I had made. I enjoyed listening to them tremendously, because I wished, when I listened to them, that the only violence I knew was the violence that I imagined.

43 And listening to them allowed me to experience childhood in a way that I hadn't known was possible. It let me be a normal kid.

44 So I listened to them, and we hung out all the time, and through that I participated in what was left of my childhood.

45 I got to be a child again with them; the only worries that we had were when we went rollerblading without any protective gear. We took our brakes off, and sometimes we would avoid hitting an old lady by falling into a trash can on the street, and we laughed about it.

46 These things meant a lot to me.

47 After about a year of being friends with these boys, one of them decided to invite a group of us, about ten of us, to upstate New York. His family had property up there, and he said we were going there for the weekend to play a game called paintball.

48 I said, "Well, what is that?"

49 And he said, "Oh, man, you've never played paintball? You're gonna love it. It's a great game. The fellows and I, we always play it. And don't worry, we'll teach it to you, and we'll protect you.

50 "You use these balls of paint, and you shoot people," and he explained the basics of the game to me.

51 I said, "Okay, that sounds interesting."

52 And I thought, *If these guys who only pretend about violence can play it, it must not be that difficult a game.*

53 But of course I didn't say this. I just thought these things. So I went with them upstate to a humongous property that had trees and creeks that ran into a bigger river—this beautiful open place.

54 But as soon as we arrived, I began to memorize the terrain immediately, and this was from habit. I knew how many paces it took to get to the house, how many paces it took to the first tree, to the first bush, to the shed. I learned the spaces between the trees.

55 Overnight, while everybody was sleeping, I tried to replay some of these things in my head—to memorize the terrain.

56 And this was all out of habit, because where I came from, in my previous life, this kind of skill set could determine whether you lived or died.

57 In the morning, at breakfast, they were pumped up.

58 Everyone was saying, "Yeah, the game is gonna be awesome today."

59 And so after we finished breakfast, I was introduced to the game of paintball. They showed me the weapon, how you can shoot it. And I allowed them to teach me to shoot things.

NOTICE & NOTE

AGAIN AND AGAIN

When you notice certain events, images, or words being repeated in a portion of the text, you've found an **Again and Again** signpost.

Notice & Note: In paragraph 52, mark a thought about his friends that the author revisits, this time in a paintball game.

Analyze: Why might the author bring this up again and again?

60 They were very macho about it.

61 They said to me, "This is how you shoot, you aim like this."

62 I said, "Okay." I tried it a few times. I deliberately missed.

63 Then they showed me the camouflage and the combat gear and everything.

64 And then everybody was ready to go, and they were amped up, and all like, "Yeah, we're gonna go out! We're gonna DO THIS!!"

65 They decided we were going to play one-on-one. And then, after, we would play team games.

66 So they started painting their faces, getting into this idea of war that they knew.

ANALYZE PURPOSE AND MESSAGE

Annotate: Mark words and phrases in paragraphs 67–71 that reveal Beah's actions during paintball.

Compare: Why does Beah fight the way he does during the paintball game? How does this help reveal the author's message?

67 I declined putting the face paint on, and I wanted to give them a hint about my past, but then I thought, *You know what? I'm going to have fun with this.*

68 So we went off into the bush, and when one of them shouted, "Yeah, let the war begin! I'm going to bring pain to all of you! I'm going to show you how it's done!" I thought to myself, *First rule of warfare, you never belittle your opponent.*

69 But I didn't say this. I went into the bushes. I already knew where to go, because I had memorized the layout of the place.

70 And so I would hide. I would wait for them. I would climb a tree here. I would hide under certain shrubs. And they would come rolling around, jumping, doing all kinds of things, things they'd probably seen in movies about how people act in war.

71 I would just wait for them. And after they were done exhausting themselves, I would come up behind them, and I would shoot the paintball at them.

72 This went on all day. And when we came back that night, during dinner, they talked about it.

73 You know: *How come you're so good? You're sure you've never played paintball before?*

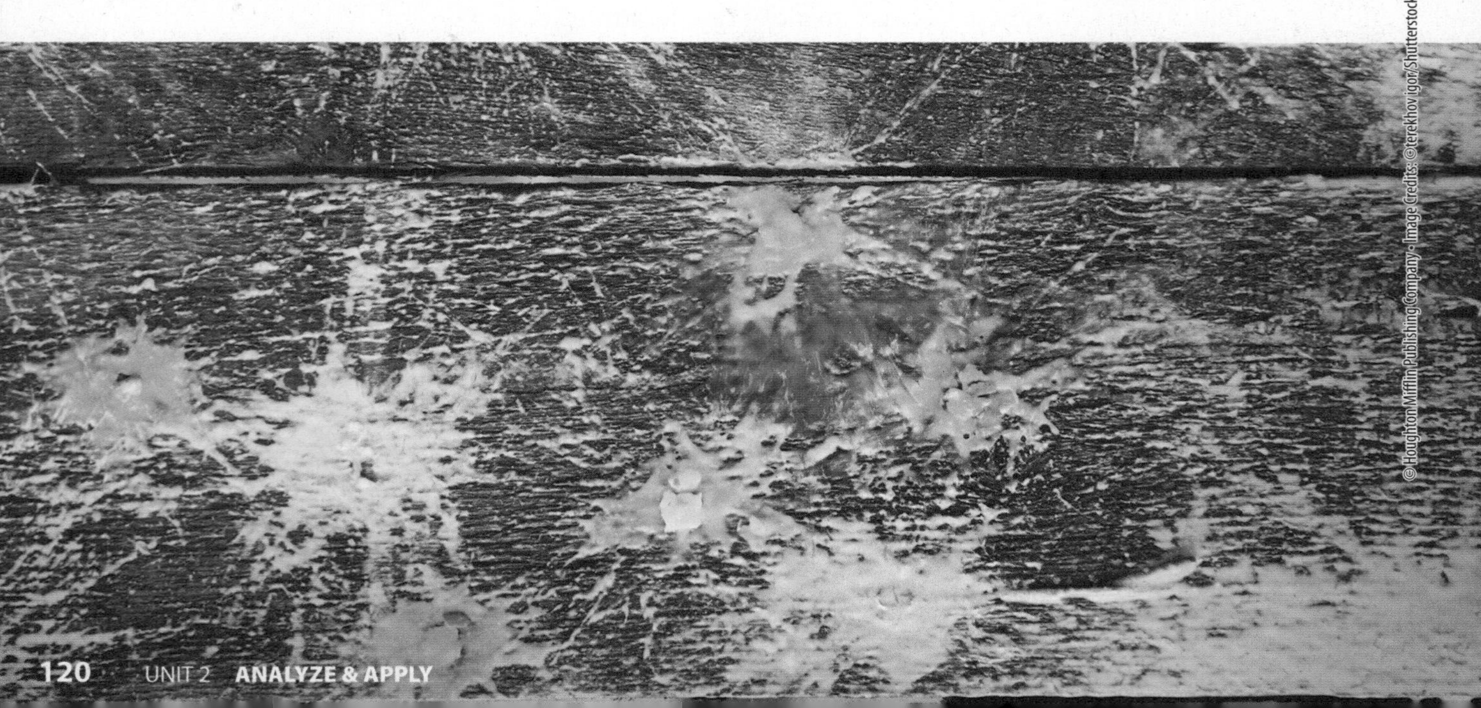

Don't forget to **Notice & Note** as you read the text.

74 I said, "No, I have never played paintball before. I'm just a quick learner, and you guys explained the game to me, and you are really great teachers. This is why I'm able to play so well."

75 But they said, "That can't be all."

76 Some of the kids' parents were there, and the kids said to them, "This guy, he comes up on you. You can't even hear him coming at all."

77 And I said, "Well, you know, I grew up in a village. And I used to be a hunter when I was a boy, so I know how to blend into the forest, like a chameleon.[2] I know how to adapt to my environment."

78 And they looked at me and said, "You're a very strange fellow, man. But you're *badass* at paintball."

79 I said, "Well, thank you. Thank you very, very much."

80 So this went on. We never got to play the group game. We played as individuals all throughout the weekend, because they wanted to beat me, and so they started to team up with each other. I would see them doing this, and then I would come up with a kind of watered-down version of another guerrilla tactic,[3] just to play with them.

81 For example, sometimes I would walk backwards and then stand where my footsteps "began" and hide. They would follow my footprints, and then I would come up behind them.

82 Anyway, at some point I decided that I was going to sit out the game, just so that they could enjoy it. And I saw a sense of relief on all of their faces.

83 They were like, *Oh, well, FINALLY!*

84 When I returned, I told my mother about this game. And my mother, being a mother, was immediately worried.

85 She said, "Oh, did that bring up something for you?"

86 And I said, "No, it didn't, absolutely."

[2] **chameleon** (kə-mēl´yən): a tropical lizard that can change color.

[3] **guerrilla tactic** (gə-rĭl´ə tăk´tĭk): a warfare technique practiced by small bands of native fighters harassing and surprising larger armies.

87 Because I know the difference between pretend war and real war.

88 But it was interesting for me to observe how my friends perceived what war is.

89 The next day at school, these friends of mine talked about the awesome weekend of paintball we'd had. But they never said how I'd won all the games. And I said nothing at all.

90 They never invited me back to play paintball with them. And I didn't ask to be invited back.

91 I so wanted to talk to them about the war while we were playing the game. I wanted to explain certain things, but I felt that if they knew about my background, they would no longer allow me to be a child. They would see me as an adult, and I was worried that they would fear me.

ANALYZE PURPOSE AND MESSAGE

Annotate: Mark the sentences in paragraphs 92–95 that reveal the author's message.

Interpret: What is the author's message, and what does it reveal about the author's purpose for writing and who he sees as his audience?

92 My silence allowed me to experience things, to participate in my childhood, to do things I hadn't been able to do as a child.

93 It was only years later that they learned why I had won the game.

94 But I wish I had been able to tell them early on, because I wanted them to understand how lucky they were to have a mother, a father, grandparents, siblings.[4] People who annoyed them by caring about them so much and calling them all the time to make sure they were okay.

[4] **siblings** (sĭb´lĭngs): brothers or sisters, individuals sharing one or more parents.

95 I wanted to tell them that they were so lucky to have this **naïve** innocence about the world. I wanted them to understand that it was extremely lucky for them to only play *pretend* war and never have to do the real thing. And that their naïve innocence about the world was something for which I no longer had the capacity.

naïve
(nī-ēv´) *adj.* lacking worldly experience or understanding.

COLLABORATIVE DISCUSSION

Ishmael Beah chooses not to reveal his traumatic past to his friends. What do you think about his decision? Discuss your opinion with a partner.

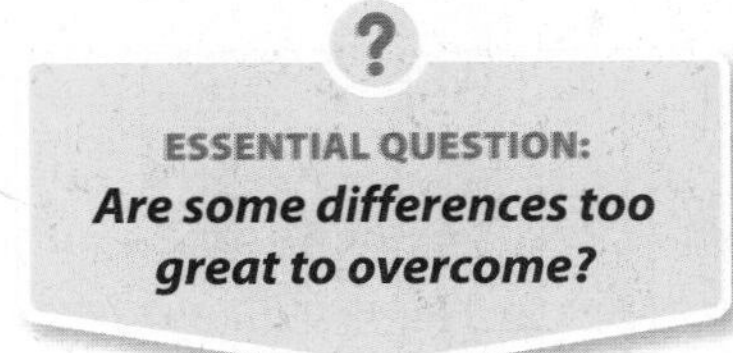
?
ESSENTIAL QUESTION:
Are some differences too great to overcome?

Assessment Practice

Answer these questions before moving on to the **Analyze the Text** section on the following page.

1. Which **two** sentences best illustrate the "naïve innocence" of the author's friends?

Ⓐ "They had gotten into fights and won." (paragraph 34)

Ⓑ "I noticed that these kids had a sort of *idea* of violence that they'd never really *lived*." (paragraph 40)

Ⓒ "We played as individuals all throughout the weekend, because they wanted to beat me, and so they started to team up with each other." (paragraph 80)

Ⓓ "They never invited me back to play paintball with them." (paragraph 90)

Ⓔ "I wanted them to understand that it was extremely lucky for them to only play *pretend* war and never have to do the real thing." (paragraph 95)

2. How does the author's story about the paintball game reflect the purpose of the personal essay?

Ⓐ It showcases the skills and abilities the author learned in Sierra Leone.

Ⓑ It emphasizes the differences between the author and his classmates.

Ⓒ It underlines the financial struggles faced by the author and his adoptive mom.

Ⓓ It reassures people that the author has been rehabilitated.

Analyze the Text

Support your responses with evidence from the text.

NOTICE & NOTE

Review what you **noticed and noted** as you read the text. Your annotations can help you answer these questions.

1. **INTERPRET** Ishmael Beah's use of language—his word choice and syntax—establishes an individual voice and tone. Describe the essay's voice and tone, citing examples from the selection.

2. **CITE EVIDENCE** What are some of the ways that the author differs from his classmates? What do they have in common?

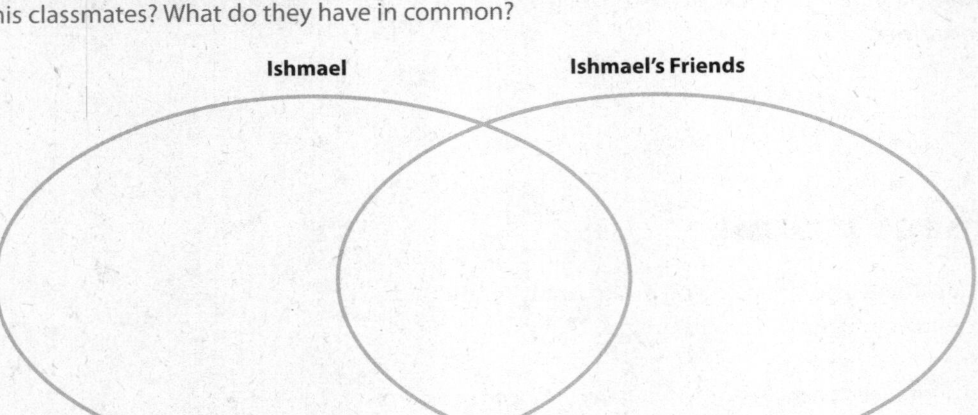

3. **INFER** **Again and Again,** Beah reflects on how his years as a child soldier have set him apart from his friends. Why does he choose to conceal his past? How do you think his friends would have reacted had he told them the truth?

4. **EVALUATE** Think about the **Memory Moments** you noticed during this story. What skills and habits did the author learn as a child soldier that helped him both in New York and in the paintball game?

5. **ANALYZE** Review the last sentence of paragraph 31. Use details in this sentence to help you infer a reason or purpose Beah might have had for writing this essay.

6. **SYNTHESIZE** How does the text structure—a personal essay—enable the author to deliver his message effectively? Explain your answer using examples from the text.

7. **PREDICT** Based on this text, how do you predict Beah's experience in the United States will unfold? Will he remain guarded? Or will his talent for making friends cause him to open up to others?

Choices

Here are some other ways to demonstrate your understanding of the ideas in this lesson.

Writing

↳ Film Review

Watch the documentary *The Lost Boys of Sudan* and write a review. Include information such as:

- persons involved
- summary of events
- analysis of the central message

Compare Ishmael Beah's experiences to those of the refugees in the documentary.

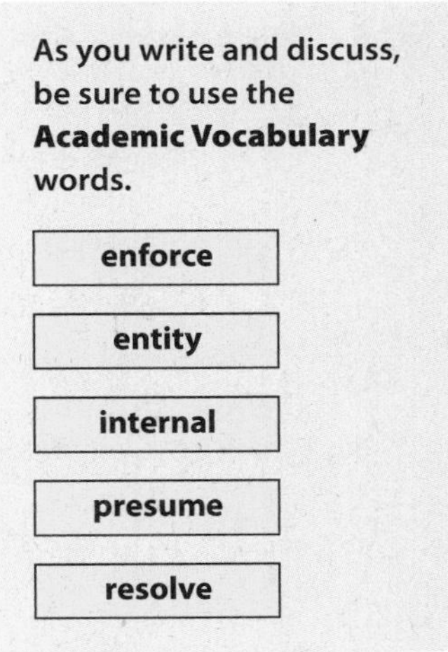
As you write and discuss, be sure to use the **Academic Vocabulary** words.
enforce
entity
internal
presume
resolve

Media

↳ Social Media Profile

Review the Background paragraph on the Get Ready page. Consider what you know about the author, Ishmael Beah, and his purpose for writing "Unusual Normality." Create a social media profile for him, including personal information and posts that raise social awareness or call others to action.

Speaking & Listening

↳ Debate a Solution

Research information about children forced to serve as soldiers in African nations such as Sierra Leone, Sudan, and the Democratic Republic of the Congo. Include specific stories or accounts, as well as information about the United States' efforts to resettle refugees. With a partner, propose a solution to the problem of child soldiers.

- Review the research with your partner. Take a stance.
- Debate best solutions with the whole class. Use appropriate register, vocabulary, and tone.
- Listen and respond to other proposed solutions, and adjust your stance accordingly.
- Summarize your conclusions, considering all arguments.

Expand Your Vocabulary

PRACTICE AND APPLY

To show your understanding of the vocabulary words, choose the best answer to each question. Then, explain your response.

1. Which of the following would be part of **rehabilitation**?
   - ○ constructing something from new parts
   - ○ nursing an injured animal
2. Which of the following are **counterparts**?
   - ○ the governors of two neighboring states
   - ○ the sky and the clouds floating through it
3. Which of the following is a **stereotype**?
   - ○ a tall person assumed to play basketball
   - ○ a teenager assumed to be between 13 and 19 years old
4. Which of the following is a **naïve** action?
   - ○ putting your money in a savings account
   - ○ trusting a stranger with all your money

Vocabulary Strategy

↳ Denotative and Connotative Meanings

Ed

Interactive Vocabulary Lesson: Denotation and Connotation

Some words have both a **denotative** and **connotative meaning.** A denotative meaning is the meaning that you would find in a dictionary. A word's connotative meaning includes the feelings and ideas that people may connect with the word. For example, someone may be described as *slender* or *skinny*. The denotative meanings of the words are similar. But *skinny* implies that someone is too thin. It has a negative connotation, while *slender* has a positive connotation.

PRACTICE AND APPLY

Read these sentences. Then, state the denotative and connotative meanings of the boldfaced words.

1. The man wore **tattered** clothes to the mall. She had **torn** the sleeve on her favorite shirt.
2. She **laughed** at the joke. He **cackled** when she finished telling the story.
3. She had a **weird** way of talking. His songs were **quirky.**

Watch Your Language!

Adverbial Clauses

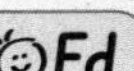

Interactive Grammar Lesson: The Adverb Clause

A **subordinate clause** has a subject and verb but cannot stand alone as a sentence. It is introduced by a subordinating conjunction, such as *how, when, where, why, because,* or *whether*.

An **adverbial clause** is a subordinate clause that functions as an adverb—that is, it modifies a verb, an adjective, or an adverb in a sentence. Authors use an adverbial clause to convey specific meaning and to add variety to their writing. In the following example from "Unusual Normality," an adverbial clause beginning with the subordinating conjunction *because* modifies the verb *tell:*

> And of course I couldn't tell them, because I felt that they were not ready to hear the truth.

The adverbial clause clarifies to readers the connection between the two ideas—that the author couldn't tell his friends and that he felt they were not ready to hear the truth.

Now read this sentence:

> When I got into the school, some of the other parents were not very happy that somebody with my background was in school with their children.

This sentence contains two adverbial clauses:

"When I got into the school"	Modifies the verb "were" by explaining when the action in the sentence happened.
"that somebody with my background was in school with their children"	Modifies the adjective phrase "not very happy" by explaining why the parents were not very happy.

PRACTICE AND APPLY

Review a paragraph or essay you recently wrote. Find two places where you can incorporate adverbial clauses into your writing. Then, have a partner review your work.

Get Ready

Once Upon a Time

Short Story by **Nadine Gordimer**

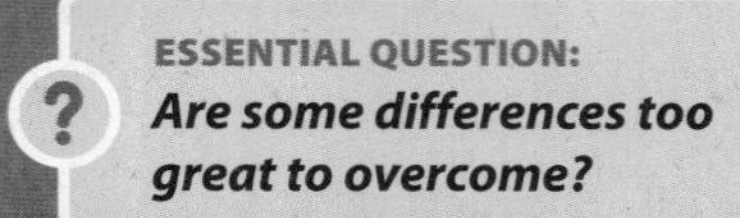
ESSENTIAL QUESTION:
Are some differences too great to overcome?

Engage Your Brain

Choose one or more of these activities to start connecting with the story you are about to read.

Apartheid Backstory

To better understand this short story, visit the "Apartheid" information page on History.com. Make notes below about major events.

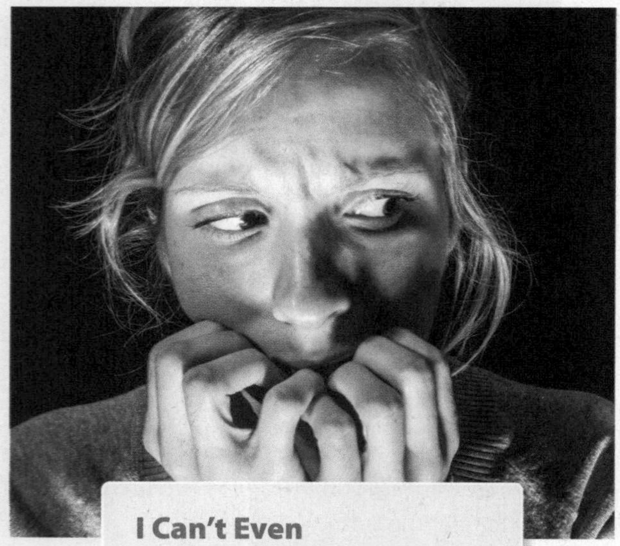

I Can't Even

What is something you fear? Do you know of friends or family members that share this fear? How does it affect your life?

Sanctuary

Draw a place where you feel most safe. What about it makes you feel that way?

Analyze Setting and Theme

The **setting** of a story is the time and place of the action of the story. The setting in this story includes a particular cultural and historical experience of the narrator and the characters she creates.

The main message of a story is the **theme,** which can be enhanced or advanced by the setting. As you analyze "Once Upon a Time," make **inferences,** or logical guesses, about the theme by considering the details and symbols Gordimer includes. Pay particular attention to the characters' actions and motivations, as well as the setting, to help you infer the theme. Also look for **universal themes,** which apply to people across cultures and time periods.

Focus on Genre
Short Story

- includes the basic elements of fiction—setting, characters, plot, conflict, and theme
- centers on one particular moment or event in life
- can be read in one sitting

Literary Element	Examples
A story's **setting** can shape the events of a story.	**In a house, in a suburb, in a city, there were a man and his wife . . .**
Look for clues to a story's **theme** throughout the story, such as changes in details of the setting.	**So from every window and door in the house . . . they now saw the trees and sky through bars . . .**

Analyze Text Structure

The **text structure** of a short story is the way an author organizes story elements to show connections between events and to develop ideas. In "Once Upon a Time," Gordimer uses several traditional elements of fairy tales, such as the title and the detail about "living happily ever after," to structure a story about South Africa's policy of apartheid in the 1980s. Her structural choices help create tension and surprise and reflect the fear and isolation that people felt. As you analyze the story's structure, look for the following fairy tale elements and notice how the story is similar to and different from other fairy tales.

Elements of a Fairy Tale
• The main characters are opposed by an evil force. • The story is used to teach a lesson. • Good characters have bad things happen to them. • The setting does not seem quite real. • Details in the story foreshadow that the problem, or conflict, will be resolved in a "happily ever after" ending.

Annotation in Action

Here are one reader's notes about the first part of the story. As you read, note how the writer uses the text structure of a fairy tale to tell the story.

I couldn't find a position in which my mind would let go of my body—release me to sleep again. So I began to tell myself a story; a bedtime story. In a house, in a suburb, in a city, there were a man and his wife who loved each other very much and were living happily ever after.	She's starting a second story within the first one

Expand Your Vocabulary

Put a check mark next to the vocabulary words that you feel comfortable using when speaking or writing.

distend	☐
intention	☐
audacious	☐
intrusion	☐
serrated	☐

With a partner, write a short description of a scary situation using as many of the vocabulary words as you can.

As you read "Once Upon a Time," use the definitions in the side column to learn the vocabulary words you don't already know.

Background

Nadine Gordimer (1923–2014) was born in South Africa. Her family was privileged and white in a country that practiced apartheid—an official policy of segregation of nonwhite South Africans. Gordimer became politically opposed to the policy. Her early works, such as *The Soft Voice of the Serpent* and *The Lying Days,* explore themes of exile and the effects of apartheid on life in South Africa. Before apartheid ended in 1994, some of Gordimer's writings were banned by the South African government. Gordimer was awarded many literary prizes, including the Nobel Prize for Literature in 1991.

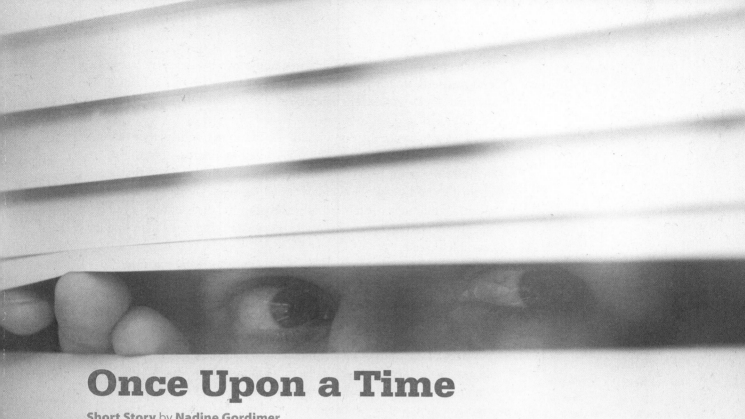

Once Upon a Time

Short Story by **Nadine Gordimer**

A family's isolation from its community leads to tragedy.

NOTICE & NOTE

As you read, use the side margins to make notes about the text.

1 Someone has written to ask me to contribute to an anthology of stories for children. I reply that I don't write children's stories; and he writes back that at a recent congress/book fair/seminar a certain novelist said every writer ought to write at least one story for children. I think of sending a postcard saying I don't accept that I "ought" to write anything.

Close Read Screencast

Listen to a modeled close read of this text.

2 And then last night I woke up—or rather was wakened without knowing what had roused me.

3 A voice in the echo chamber of the subconscious?

4 A sound.

5 A creaking of the kind made by the weight carried by one foot after another along a wooden floor. I listened. I felt the apertures of my ears **distend** with concentration. Again: the creaking. I was waiting for it; waiting to hear if it indicated that feet were moving from room to room, coming up the passage—to my door. I have no burglar bars, no gun under the pillow, but I have the same fears as people who do take these precautions, and my windowpanes are thin as rime,[1] could shatter like a wineglass. A woman was murdered (how

distend (dĭ-stĕnd´) *v.* to bulge or expand.

[1] **rime** (rīm): a coating of frost.

do they put it) in broad daylight in a house two blocks away, last year, and the fierce dogs who guarded an old widower and his collection of antique clocks were strangled before he was knifed by a casual laborer he had dismissed without pay.

6 I was staring at the door, making it out in my mind rather than seeing it, in the dark. I lay quite still—a victim already—but the arrhythmia[2] of my heart was fleeing, knocking this way and that against its body-cage. How finely tuned the senses are, just out of rest, sleep! I could never listen intently as that in the distractions of the day; I was reading every faintest sound, identifying and classifying its possible threat.

7 But I learned that I was to be neither threatened nor spared. There was no human weight pressing on the boards, the creaking was a buckling, an epicenter[3] of stress. I was in it. The house that surrounds me while I sleep is built on undermined ground; far beneath my bed, the floor, the house's foundations, the stopes[4] and passages of gold mines have hollowed the rock, and when some face trembles, detaches, and falls, three thousand feet below, the whole house shifts slightly, bringing uneasy strain to the balance and counterbalance of brick, cement, wood, and glass that hold it as a structure around me. The misbeats of my heart tailed off like the last muffled flourishes on one of the wooden xylophones made by the Chopi and Tsonga[5] migrant miners who might have been down there, under me in the earth at that moment. The stope where the fall was could have been disused, dripping water from its ruptured veins; or men might now be interred there in the most profound of tombs.

8 I couldn't find a position in which my mind would let go of my body—release me to sleep again. So I began to tell myself a story; a bedtime story.

9 In a house, in a suburb, in a city, there were a man and his wife who loved each other very much and were living happily ever after. They had a little boy, and they loved him very much. They had a cat and a dog that the little boy loved very much. They had a car and a caravan trailer for holidays, and a swimming pool which was fenced so that the little boy and his playmates would not fall in and drown. They had a housemaid who was absolutely trustworthy and an itinerant[6] gardener who was highly recommended by the neighbors. For when they began to live happily ever after, they were warned by that wise old witch, the husband's mother, not to take on anyone off the street. They were inscribed in a medical benefit society, their pet dog was licensed, they were insured against fire, flood damage, and theft, and subscribed to the local Neighborhood Watch, which supplied them with a plaque for their gates lettered YOU HAVE

NOTICE & NOTE
AHA MOMENT

An **Aha Moment** is a sudden realization of something that shifts a narrator's understanding of self, others, or the world.

Notice & Note: Mark the sentence in paragraph 8 where the narrator acts based on her realization.

Infer: Why does the author change her mind?

ANALYZE TEXT STRUCTURE

Annotate: Mark details in paragraph 9 that introduce elements of traditional fairy tales.

Compare: How does this bedtime story begin differently from other fairy tales? What might this text structure suggest?

---

[2] **arrhythmia** (ə-rĭth´mē-ə): an irregular heartbeat.
[3] **epicenter:** the focal point.
[4] **stopes:** step-like holes or trenches made by miners.
[5] **Chopi and Tsonga** (chō´pē and tsôn´ga): ethnic groups that live in Mozambique.
[6] **itinerant:** frequently traveling to different places.

BEEN WARNED over the silhouette of a would-be intruder. He was masked; it could not be said if he was black or white, and therefore proved the property owner was no racist.

Don't forget to **Notice & Note** as you read the text.

10 It was not possible to insure the house, the swimming pool, or the car against riot damage. There were riots, but these were outside the city, where people of another color were quartered. These people were not allowed into the suburb except as reliable housemaids and gardeners, so there was nothing to fear, the husband told the wife. Yet she was afraid that some day such people might come up the street and tear off the plaque YOU HAVE BEEN WARNED and open the gates and stream in. . . . Nonsense, my dear, said the husband, there are police and soldiers and tear gas and guns to keep them away. But to please her—for he loved her very much and buses were being burned, cars stoned, and schoolchildren shot by the police in those quarters out of sight and hearing of the suburb—he had electronically controlled gates fitted. Anyone who pulled off the sign YOU HAVE BEEN WARNED and tried to open the gates would have to announce his **intentions** by pressing a button and speaking into a receiver relayed to the house. The little boy was fascinated by the device and used it as a walkie-talkie in cops and robbers play with his small friends.

ANALYZE SETTING AND THEME

Annotate: What fear does the wife have? How does her husband reassure her that they are safe? Mark sentences in paragraph 10 that show the fear and the husband's reassurances.

Predict: What do you think will happen next?

intention
(ĭn-tĕn´shən) *n.* purpose or plan.

11 The riots were suppressed, but there were many burglaries in the suburb and somebody's trusted housemaid was tied up and shut in a cupboard by thieves while she was in charge of her employers' house. The trusted housemaid of the man and wife and little boy was so upset by this misfortune befalling a friend left, as she herself often was, with responsibility for the possessions of the man and his wife and the little boy, that she implored her employers to have burglar bars attached to the doors and windows of the house, and an alarm system installed. The wife said, she is right, let us take heed of her advice. So from every window and door in the house where they were living happily ever after they now saw the trees and sky through bars, and when the little boy's pet cat tried to climb in by the fanlight[7] to keep him company in his little bed at night, as it customarily had done, it set off the alarm keening[8] through the house.

12 The alarm was often answered—it seemed—by other burglar alarms, in other houses, that had been triggered by pet cats or nibbling mice. The alarms called to one another across the gardens in shrills and bleats and wails that everyone soon became accustomed to, so that the din roused the inhabitants of the suburb no more than the croak of frogs and musical grating of cicadas'[9] legs. Under cover of the electronic harpies'[10] discourse intruders sawed the iron bars and broke into homes, taking away hi-fi equipment, television sets, cassette players, cameras and radios, jewelry and clothing, and sometimes were hungry enough to devour everything in the

[7] **fanlight:** an arched window, usually over a door.
[8] **keening:** wailing or crying.
[9] **cicadas** (sĭ-kā´dəs)**:** large, loud insects.
[10] **harpies:** mythological creatures who were part woman and part bird.

audacious
(ô-dā´shəs) *adj.* bold, rebellious.

refrigerator or paused **audaciously** to drink the whiskey in the cabinets or patio bars. Insurance companies paid no compensation for single malt, a loss made keener by the property owner's knowledge that the thieves wouldn't even have been able to appreciate what it was they were drinking.

ANALYZE SETTING AND THEME

Annotate: Mark the phrases and sentences in paragraph 13 that suggest the wife's desire to help is in conflict with the family's fear.

Analyze: How might this conflict relate to the author's theme, or message?

Close Read Screencast

Listen to a modeled close read of this text.

13 Then the time came when many of the people who were not trusted housemaids and gardeners hung about the suburb because they were unemployed. Some importuned for a job: weeding or painting a roof; anything, *baas,*[11] madam. But the man and his wife remembered the warning about taking on anyone off the street. Some drank liquor and fouled the street with discarded bottles. Some begged, waiting for the man or his wife to drive the car out of the electronically operated gates. They sat about with their feet in the gutters, under the jacaranda trees that made a green tunnel of the street—for it was a beautiful suburb, spoiled only by their presence—and sometimes they fell asleep lying right before the gates in the midday sun. The wife could never see anyone go hungry. She sent the trusted housemaid out with bread and tea, but the trusted housemaid said these were loafers and *tsotsis,*[12] who would come and tie her up and shut her in a cupboard. The husband said, she's right. Take heed of her advice. You only encourage them with your bread and tea. They are looking for their chance. . . . And he brought the little boy's tricycle from the garden into the house every night, because if the house was surely secure, once locked and with the alarm set, someone might still be able to climb over the wall or the electronically closed gates into the garden.

14 You are right, said the wife, then the wall should be higher. And the wise old witch, the husband's mother, paid for the extra bricks as her Christmas present to her son and his wife—the little boy got a Space Man outfit and a book of fairy tales.

intrusion
(ĭn-trōō´ zhən) *n.* act of trespass or invasion.

15 But every week there were more reports of **intrusion:** in broad daylight and the dead of night, in the early hours of the morning, and even in the lovely summer twilight—a certain family was at dinner while the bedrooms were being ransacked upstairs. The man and his wife, talking of the latest armed robbery in the suburb, were distracted by the sight of the little boy's pet cat effortlessly arriving over the seven-foot wall, descending first with a rapid bracing of extended forepaws down on the sheer vertical surface, and then a graceful launch, landing with a swishing tail within the property. The whitewashed wall was marked with the cat's comings and goings; and on the street side of the wall there were larger red-earth smudges that could have been made by the kind of broken running shoes, seen on the feet of unemployed loiterers, that had no innocent destination.

[11] **baas** (bäs)**:** a white person in a position of authority in relation to nonwhites.
[12] **tsotsis** (tsō´tsēs)**:** dishonest, untrustworthy people.

16 When the man and wife and little boy took the pet dog for its walk round the neighborhood streets they no longer paused to admire this show of roses or that perfect lawn; these were hidden behind an array of different varieties of security fences, walls, and devices. The man, wife, little boy, and dog passed a remarkable choice: there was the low-cost option of pieces of broken glass embedded in cement along the top of walls, there were iron grilles ending in lance points, there were attempts at reconciling the aesthetics of prison architecture with the Spanish Villa style (spikes painted pink) and with the plastic urns of neoclassical facades (twelve-inch pikes finned like zigzags of lightning and painted pure white). Some walls had a small board affixed, giving the name and telephone number of the firm responsible for the installation of the devices. While the little boy and the pet dog raced ahead, the husband and wife found themselves comparing the possible effectiveness of each style against its appearance; and after several weeks when they paused before this barricade or that without needing to speak, both came out with the conclusion that only one was worth considering.

It was the ugliest but the most honest in its suggestion of the pure concentration-camp style, no frills, all evident efficacy. Placed the length of walls, it consisted of a continuous coil of stiff and shining metal **serrated** into jagged blades, so that there would be no way of climbing over it and no way through its tunnel without getting entangled in its fangs. There would be no way out, only a struggle getting bloodier and bloodier, a deeper and sharper hooking and tearing of flesh. The wife shuddered to look at it. You're right, said the husband, anyone would think twice. . . . And they took heed of the advice on a small board fixed to the wall: Consult DRAGON'S TEETH The People For Total Security.

serrated
(sĕr´ā´tĭd) *adj.* having a jagged, saw-toothed edge.

17 Next day, a gang of workmen came and stretched the razor-bladed coils all round the walls of the house where the husband and wife and little boy and pet dog and cat were living happily ever after. The sunlight flashed and slashed off the serrations, the cornice of razor thorns encircled the home, shining. The husband said, Never mind. It will weather. The wife said, You're wrong. They guarantee it's rustproof. And she waited until the little boy had run off to play before she said, I hope the cat will take heed. . . . The husband said, Don't worry, my dear, cats always look before they leap. And it was true that from that day on, the cat slept in the little boy's bed and kept to the garden, never risking a try at breaching security.

ANALYZE TEXT STRUCTURE

Annotate: Mark details in paragraph 18 that contrast with typical fairy-tale endings.

Connect: How does the fairy tale structure make the story's end especially shocking?

18 One evening, the mother read the little boy to sleep with a fairy story from the book the wise old witch had given him at Christmas. Next day, he pretended to be the prince who braves the terrible thicket of thorns to enter the palace and kiss the Sleeping Beauty back to life: he dragged a ladder to the wall, the shining coiled tunnel was just wide enough for his little body to creep in, and with the first fixing of its razor teeth in his knees and hands and head he screamed and struggled deeper into its tangle. The trusted housemaid and the itinerant gardener, whose "day" it was, came running, the first to see and to scream with him, and the itinerant gardener tore his hands trying to get at the little boy. Then the man and his wife burst wildly into the garden and for some reason (the cat, probably), the alarm set up wailing against the screams while the bleeding mass of the little boy was hacked out of the security coil with saws, wire cutters, choppers, and they carried it—the man, the wife, the hysterical trusted housemaid, and the weeping gardener—into the house.

ANALYZE SETTING AND THEME

Annotate: Mark the words that reveal the shocking ending of the story.

Connect: Think about the characters' actions and motivations that led to this ending. What can you infer about the theme, or message, of this story?

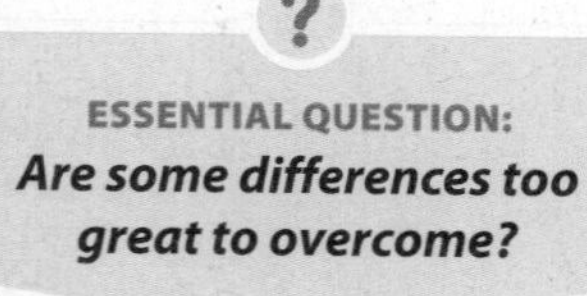
?
ESSENTIAL QUESTION:
Are some differences too great to overcome?

Review your notes and add your thoughts to your Response Log.

COLLABORATIVE DISCUSSION

Were you surprised by the story's ending? If so, what did you think was going to happen instead? If not, what clues did you notice in the text?

Assessment Practice

Answer these questions before moving on to the **Analyze the Text** section on the following page.

1. This question has two parts. First answer **Part A**. Then, answer **Part B**.

Part A

What is the author's purpose for writing this story?

(A) to warn about the dangers of intruders

(B) to examine techniques for staying safe

(C) to show the dangers of fear and paranoia

(D) to compare good and bad fairy-tale characters

Part B

Which detail from the story supports the answer to Part A?

(A) ". . . they were warned by that wise old witch, the husband's mother, not to take on anyone off the street." (paragraph 9)

(B) "But every week there were more reports of intrusion: in broad daylight and the dead of night . . ." (paragraph 15)

(C) ". . . the husband and wife found themselves comparing the possible effectiveness of each style against its appearance . . ." (paragraph 16)

(D) ". . . the bleeding mass of the little boy was hacked out of the security coil with saws, wire cutters, choppers . . ." (paragraph 18)

2. Which of the following is a central theme in the story?

(A) Sometimes people must suppress the majority population.

(B) Private security measures are important for people's safety.

(C) Racial prejudice and isolation are harmful to all people in a society.

(D) Police and law enforcement can control robberies and intrusions.

Test-Taking Strategies

Analyze the Text

Support your responses with evidence from the text.

NOTICE & NOTE

Review what you **noticed and noted** as you read the text. Your annotations can help you answer these questions.

1. **CONNECT** Nadine Gordimer wrote many stories about the injustices of apartheid. She was also active in bringing change to the political entities of South Africa. Even though her books were banned in South Africa for a time, she resolved to stay instead of living in exile. What do you learn about Gordimer's political and cultural point of view by reading this story? Explain your ideas using evidence from the story.

2. **ANALYZE** The narrator's **Aha Moment**—her decision to write a story for children—starts to take shape when she hears "a voice . . . of the subconscious." Reread paragraphs 3–7. What kinds of fears and memories is she confronting? How does her "bedtime story" reflect the experiences and fears that the culture of apartheid had created?

3. **SYNTHESIZE** What actions do the husband, wife, and their neighbors do again and again because of their fear of outsiders? How does this help to reveal the story's theme?

Similar actions repeated throughout the story	Theme that emerges from this pattern

4. **EVALUATE** How does Gordimer use the story's setting to develop the theme? Is it a universal theme? Cite specific examples to support your answer.

5. **INFER** Authors often leave things unstated in a story, leaving the reader with questions about the outcome. What can you infer about what Gordimer leaves unstated at the end of her story? How does it relate to her statements about the family living "happily ever after"?

6. **IDENTIFY PATTERNS** Reread the elements of fairy tales in the table on the Get Ready page. How is the structure of this story similar to a fairy tale? What elements do they share? Cite details from the text as support.

Choices

Here are some other ways to demonstrate your understanding of the ideas in this lesson.

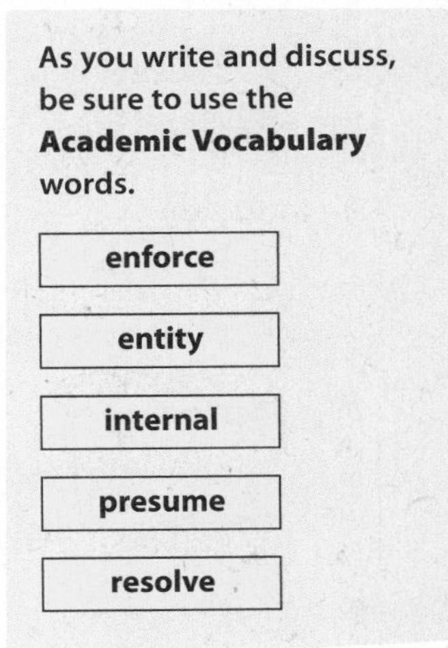
As you write and discuss, be sure to use the Academic Vocabulary words.
enforce
entity
internal
presume
resolve

Writing

↳ Fairy Tale

Many fairy tales have dark or disturbing aspects. With a partner, write a fairy tale that ends in a way other than "happily ever after."

- Introduce the setting and the characters.
- Include magical or made-up elements in creative settings.
- Have the tale demonstrate some truth about life or a central message.

Social & Emotional Learning

↳ Escape Room Challenge

Nadine Gordimer's story centers around the idea of keeping people out. With a small group, design an escape room meant to keep people *in*. For this puzzle game you will create clues to problems that must be solved in order to advance and, ultimately, escape.

1. Use Gordimer's story as inspiration for the setting and theme of your escape room.
2. Determine each person's skills or strengths within your group.
3. Incorporate a variety of clue types to appeal to different people's skills.
4. Communicate effectively to create clues.
5. If challenges, frustrations, or disagreements arise, determine how you plan to work through them.
6. When you finish your escape room design, swap with another group.

Speaking & Listening

↳ Radio Interview

Imagine you are a radio host in 1990, the year human rights activist Nelson Mandela was freed from prison in South Africa. You are interviewing a news reporter who has recently reported on apartheid in that country. With a partner, script a conversation that includes these elements:

- Introduction and explanation of the basics of apartheid
- General overview of the situation by the reporter, with examples and details
- Efforts being made (for example, by Nelson Mandela) to bring an end to apartheid
- A conclusion that gives readers something to think about

Record your interview to share, or perform it for the class.

Expand Your Vocabulary

PRACTICE AND APPLY

Choose which of the two situations best fits each word's meaning.

1. **distend**
   - ◯ After the Thanksgiving meal, our stomachs were uncomfortably full.
   - ◯ Platters of food completely covered the holiday table.
2. **intention**
   - ◯ The soccer player could not make a goal.
   - ◯ The soccer player's purpose was to play better in the next game.
3. **audacious**
   - ◯ The daring boy brought gum to the computer lab.
   - ◯ A teacher caught the mischievous boy.
4. **intrusion**
   - ◯ The newspaper talked about the girl's wrongful entrance into the clubhouse.
   - ◯ The girl's interruption of the conversation made the club members unhappy.
5. **serrated**
   - ◯ The edge of the paper was cut into a decorative pattern.
   - ◯ The notched edge of the paper looked like a set of teeth.

Vocabulary Strategy

Words from Latin

Etymologies show the origin and historical development of a word. For example, the vocabulary word *distend* comes from the Latin word *distendere,* which means "to stretch." Exploring the etymology of words can help you clarify their precise meanings and expand your vocabulary.

Ed

Vocabulary Practice: Understanding Word Origins

Word and Definition	Etymology
surround "to enclose on all sides"	from the Latin *super-* + *unda,* "to flow over in waves"

PRACTICE AND APPLY

Follow these steps for each vocabulary word.

- Find the etymology of each word in a dictionary.
- Compare the Latin roots of each word with the English definition. How does the English definition relate to the Latin meaning?

Watch Your Language!

Ed
Grammar Practice:
Prepositional Phrases

Prepositional Phrases

Prepositional phrases are phrases that consist of a preposition and an object of the preposition, such as a noun or a pronoun. Here are some common prepositions and phrases that can be created with them.

Preposition	Object of Preposition	Prepositional Phrase
from	the street	from the street
before	the rain	before the rain
during	the game	during the game
until	her test	until her test
outside	the gate	outside the gate

Read the following sentence from the story.

> **In a house, in a suburb, in a city, there were a man and his wife who loved each other very much and were living happily ever after.**

The prepositional phrases used one after another, *in a house, in a suburb, in a city,* help the author change gears from a story about something that happened to her to a story about another family. The phrases mimic the way a storyteller might use a steady beat or rhythm to start a story.

Notice that Gordimer used commas to emphasize each prepositional phrase.

Examine another sentence from "Once Upon a Time":

> **One evening, the mother read the little boy to sleep with a fairy story from the book the wise old witch had given him at Christmas.**

This series of prepositional phrases conveys the sense of a fairy tale. It also adds details to the sentence. Notice that here the prepositional phrases are not set off with commas.

PRACTICE AND APPLY

Write a few sentences describing the story's setting. Use prepositional phrases to add detail, and correct punctuation to set the phrases off.

Theme for English B

Poem by **Langston Hughes**

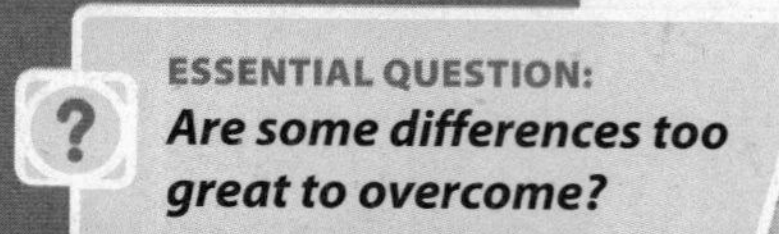
ESSENTIAL QUESTION:
Are some differences too great to overcome?

Engage Your Brain

Choose one or more activities to start connecting with the poem you're about to read.

Who Are You?

What experiences, people, or opportunities have shaped the person you are today? Fill in the outline with drawings or words to explain who you are.

True or False?

Has anyone ever thought the wrong thing about you? Maybe the person thought you were shy, but actually you love to sing! What do people already know about you that's true, and what might surprise them?

Harlem Back When

Find a partner to help research the Harlem Renaissance, an artistic and cultural movement that included Langston Hughes. Make notes about what you learn.

Analyze Theme and Details

A **theme** is a message about life or human nature that an author wants to convey. A theme can be specific to a poem or story, or it can be a **universal theme,** such as "Jealousy can ultimately destroy love." Writers rarely state a theme directly; instead, readers must make inferences, or logical guesses, about the themes expressed in a text.

As you determine themes in poetry, pay attention to the details the poet includes, and how the poet uses words to expresses tone, or attitude, toward a subject. As you read "Theme for English B," use these tips to help you analyze Langston Hughes's choices and make valid inferences about the poem's theme.

- A theme is different from the topic of a poem. A topic refers to general subjects that a poem is about—for example, nature. Theme refers to a message the author wants to convey about nature.
- Poets use their own experiences, as well as events in the outside world, to inspire their poetry and develop their themes.
- Understanding a poet's background can help you determine the messages and insights the poet wants to share.
- A poem may contain more than one theme. Analyzing the language, tone, and imagery will help you understand theme in a poem.
- Be alert for ideas or symbols that are repeated.

Focus on Genre

Lyric Poetry

- expresses the speaker's thoughts and feelings
- uses figurative language and imagery that appeals to the senses
- may include sound devices such as alliteration, assonance, repetition, and rhyme
- expresses a theme, or a message about life

Analyze Tone

Tone is the writer's attitude toward the subject of a poem. Authors create tone through their word choices and how those words evoke a sense of time and place. One way to classify tone is as formal or informal. A **formal** tone is more serious, while an **informal** tone is more lighthearted. A work's tone might be ominous, joyful, sad, or peaceful.

As you read, use the chart to help you track the poem's shifts in tone, and the details that convey tone.

Tone	Words/Details That Convey Tone
puzzled	line 6: "I wonder if it's that simple?"

Annotation in Action

Here is an example of notes a student made about lines from "Theme for English B." As you read, highlight words that reveal the poem's tone.

It's not easy to know what is true for you or me at twenty-two, my age.	Tone is direct—the speaker is thinking of himself and others.

Background

Langston Hughes (1902–1967) was a major American writer. An African American, he is identified with the Harlem Renaissance movement of the 1920s. During this period African Americans expressed thoughts and feelings through art, music, literature, and politics. Hughes, who was noted for using jazz rhythms and vivid imagery, wrote primarily in free verse. His writing reflects both pride in his culture and frustration with racial inequity.

Theme for English B

Poem by **Langston Hughes**

Who are we, and what makes us different from other people?

NOTICE & NOTE
As you read, use the side margins to make notes about the text.

The instructor said,

Go home and write
a page tonight.
And let that page come out of you—
Then, it will be true.

I wonder if it's that simple?
I am twenty-two, colored, born in Winston-Salem.
I went to school there, then Durham, then here
to this college on the hill above Harlem.
I am the only colored student in my class.
The steps from the hill lead down into Harlem,
through a park, then I cross St. Nicholas,
Eighth Avenue, Seventh, and I come to the Y,
the Harlem Branch Y, where I take the elevator
up to my room, sit down, and write this page:

ANALYZE TONE

Annotate: In lines 7–15, mark words and phrases that indicate the speaker's attitude toward the setting he is describing.

Interpret: How does the more formal tone of lines 7–15 affect your understanding of line 10?

It's not easy to know what is true for you or me
at twenty-two, my age. But I guess I'm what
I feel and see and hear, Harlem, I hear you.
hear you, hear me—we two—you, me, talk on this page.
(I hear New York, too.) Me—who?

Well, I like to eat, sleep, drink, and be in love.
I like to work, read, learn, and understand life.
I like a pipe for a Christmas present,
or records—Bessie, bop, or Bach.
I guess being colored doesn't make me *not* like
the same things other folks like who are other races.
So will my page be colored that I write?
Being me, it will not be white.
But it will be
a part of you, instructor.
You are white—
yet a part of me, as I am a part of you.
That's American.
Sometimes perhaps you don't want to be a part of me.
Nor do I often want to be a part of you.
But we are, that's true!
As I learn from you,
I guess you learn from me—
although you're older—and white—
and somewhat more free.

This is my page for English B.

ANALYZE THEME AND DETAILS

Annotate: Mark details in lines 25–36 that support a message about people in America.

Infer: What inference can you make about a universal message, or theme, expressed in lines 25–36?

?

ESSENTIAL QUESTION:
Are some differences too great to overcome?

Review your notes and add your thoughts to your Response Log.

COLLABORATIVE DISCUSSION

Reread lines 37–40. What could the speaker and his teacher learn from each other?

Assessment Practice

Answer these questions before moving on to the **Analyze the Text** section on the following page.

1. In the title, the word *theme* refers to —

(A) a course that is offered at the college

(B) an important idea or message in the poem

(C) an attitude the writer has toward the speaker

(D) the page the instructor asks the speaker to write

2. What is the speaker explaining in lines 29–38?

(A) He is explaining why the assignment is a problem.

(B) He is explaining how he and the instructor are connected.

(C) He is explaining how different he is from the instructor.

(D) He is explaining why it is important to write a certain way.

3. Select the **two** sentences that best describe themes developed in this poem.

(A) It takes time and experience to truly understand who we are.

(B) There is only one version of any truth.

(C) Race has little to do with opportunity.

(D) Being American is about having one joint identity.

(E) We can all learn something from one another.

Ed

Test-Taking Strategies

Analyze the Text

Support your responses with evidence from the text.

NOTICE & NOTE

Review what you **noticed and noted** as you read the text. Your annotations can help you answer these questions.

1. **INFER** Review the chart you filled out on the Get Ready page. What is the overall tone of the poem? Support your answer with text evidence.

2. **IDENTIFY PATTERNS** Reread the poem aloud. Notice the rhythms created by the words as well as **sound devices,** or the use of words for their auditory effect. Sound devices can convey meaning and mood in a poem. Record instances of the following sound devices and explain their effect:

- alliteration—the repetition of consonant sounds at the beginning of words
- assonance—the repetition of vowel sounds within words that do not rhyme
- repetition—a repeated sound, word, phrase, or line used for emphasis
- rhyme—similar or identical sounds at the end of two or more words

3. **INTERPRET** Reread lines 31–36. The speaker seems to be exploring a contradiction between racial difference and "being American." Is the contradiction resolved in lines 34–36?

4. **ANALYZE** Why do you think Hughes uses the word "somewhat" in line 40? Why might the white instructor not be as free as one might expect?

5. **EVALUATE** Hughes explores several topics in this poem. What are they, and how does he develop them into themes? List topics and the language Hughes uses to describe them; then write a theme statement describing the poem's overall meaning.

Topic	Details
Truth	"It's not easy to know what is true for you or me"
Theme Statement:	

Choices

Here are some other ways to demonstrate your understanding of the ideas in this lesson.

Writing

Found Poetry

Using this poem or another one by Langston Hughes, create found poetry: Black out words and phrases in an existing poem to create a new poem with new meaning. Look up examples of found poetry for inspiration and guidance.

As you write and discuss, be sure to use the **Academic Vocabulary** words.

- enforce
- entity
- internal
- presume
- resolve

Media

Poem and Song Comparison

Find a song that you think connects to "Theme for English B." Create a video in which you play the song while comparing each piece's

- theme
- use of literary devices
- tone

Include specific lines of text in your analysis. Publish your video and respond to comments and questions.

Social & Emotional Learning

Image Board

In his poem, Hughes says, "But I guess I'm what / I feel and see and hear. . . ." Think of what you feel and see and hear that makes up the experience of each day.

1. Create an image board that shows these feelings and experiences.
2. In front of a group that includes as many classmates from other backgrounds and cultures as possible, present your board.
3. As group members present their boards, see if you can step into their shoes to empathize with them and understand their perspective.
4. As a group, discuss the similarities and differences in your experiences.

Collaborate & Compare

ESSENTIAL QUESTION:
Are some differences too great to overcome?

Compare Across Genres

You're about to read a poem about and view images of the Vietnam Veterans Memorial in Washington, D.C. As you read and view, think about how both the poem and the images express the reactions of visitors to the Memorial.

A
The Vietnam Wall
Poem by Alberto Ríos
pages 154–157
B
Views of the Wall
Visual Essay
page 159

After you have read the poem and viewed the visual essay, you'll be asked to get creative in comparing the two selections. You will follow these steps:

- In a group, decide on similarities and differences you will focus on
- Identify details you will use to support your comparison
- Draft the presentation
- Present your work to the class
- Discuss and reflect on your work

The Vietnam Wall

Poem by **Alberto Ríos**

Engage Your Brain

Choose one or both of these activities to start connecting with the poem you're about to read.

Beyond Belief

Many visitors to the Vietnam Veterans Memorial experience strong emotional reactions. Others are inspired to reflect on the war and its legacy. Natural wonders, such as the Grand Canyon or a stunning waterfall, can inspire the same responses. Describe or draw an image of a human-made or natural object or place that moves you.

I Think, I Wonder

How much do you know about the Vietnam Veterans Memorial? List three things you think are true and three questions you have. Share your assumptions and questions with a small group.

I think . . .	I wonder . . .

Analyze Figurative Language

A writer using literal language states the facts. **Figurative language** makes a point by comparing two things that are dissimilar. Examples of figurative language include similes, metaphors, and personification.

Similes and metaphors are the basic elements of figurative language. A **simile** uses *like* or *as* to compare two unlike things. A **metaphor** directly compares two things by saying that one thing *is* another. Authors use **personification** to give human qualities to an object, animal, or idea. Figurative language creates mood, which helps the reader visualize what the poet is describing.

Focus on Genre
Poetry

- includes imagery that appeals to the senses
- includes sound devices such as rhyme, alliteration, assonance, consonance, and repetition
- creates a mood
- expresses a theme, or message about life

Type of Figurative Language	Example
Simile	Manute Bol loomed over opponents like a grown man in a crowd of toddlers.
Metaphor	To Bol, the opposing guards were the grass beneath his tremendous feet.
Personification	The ball danced and sang under Bol's hands.

As you read "The Vietnam Wall," watch for examples of figurative language. Notice what the author conveys through the use of language and the effect it has on you.

Analyze Representations in Different Mediums

A subject, such as the Vietnam Veterans Memorial, can be represented in different **artistic mediums,** such as poems, stories, paintings, or photographs. Each artistic medium can emphasize certain aspects of the subject. For example, an author might emphasize an emotion evoked by the subject and give a personal, internal reaction. A visual artist, on the other hand, might show intricate, physical details of the subject that a writer would not be able to express. Rather than using words to describe people's emotions, an artist shows them using visual images.

As you examine the photographs in the visual essay, pay attention to how they reveal the same details and themes as the poem.

Annotation in Action

Here are one reader's notes about lines 17–21 of the poem. As you read, note how the writer uses figurative language to develop his ideas.

One name. And then more
Names, long lines, lines of names until
They are the shape of the U.N. building
Taller than I am: I have walked
Into a grave.

Writer compares seeing the wall to walking into a grave

Background

The Vietnam Veterans Memorial was dedicated in 1982 to commemorate the 2.7 million military men and women who served in the Vietnam conflict. Approximately 58,272 names are inscribed in the wall in chronological order from the first death, injury, or missing-in-action date to the last. **Alberto Ríos** (b. 1952) grew up in the U.S.-Mexican border town of Nogales, Arizona. He has published numerous award-winning books of poetry, three books of short stories, and a memoir. In 2013, Ríos was named the first Poet Laureate of Arizona. He lives in Tempe and teaches at Arizona State University.

The Vietnam Wall

Poem by **Alberto Ríos**

A poet describes his emotions confronting the Vietnam Veterans Memorial.

I
Have seen it
And I like it: The magic,
The way like cutting onions
It brings water out of nowhere.
Invisible from one side, a scar
Into the skin of the ground
From the other, a black winding
Appendix line.
    A dig.
    An archaeologist can explain.
The walk is slow at first
Easy, a little black marble wall
Of a dollhouse,

ANALYZE FIGURATIVE LANGUAGE

Annotate: Mark the uses of figurative language in lines 3–5. What types of figurative language are used here?

Interpret: What does the speaker compare the "magic" of the memorial to in these lines? What does the speaker refer to in the line "It brings water out of nowhere"? Why is that "magic"?

NOTICE & NOTE

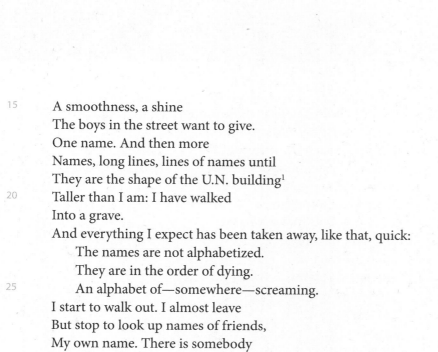

As you read, use the side margins to make notes about the text.

A smoothness, a shine
The boys in the street want to give.
One name. And then more
Names, long lines, lines of names until
They are the shape of the U.N. building[1]
Taller than I am: I have walked
Into a grave.
And everything I expect has been taken away, like that, quick:
    The names are not alphabetized.
    They are in the order of dying.
    An alphabet of—somewhere—screaming.
I start to walk out. I almost leave
But stop to look up names of friends,
My own name. There is somebody
Severiano Ríos.

ANALYZE FIGURATIVE LANGUAGE

Annotate: Mark the use of figurative language in lines 6–21. What type of figurative language is this?

Interpret: What does the speaker compare the wall to in these lines?

[1] **U. N. building:** headquarters of the United Nations in New York City.

ANALYZE REPRESENTATIONS IN DIFFERENT MEDIUMS

Annotate: Mark the details that describe possible actions in lines 30–33.

Interpret: What kind of action does the speaker refer to here? How could an artist depict such action in a story, painting, or photograph?

Little kids do not make the same noise
Here, junior high school boys don't run
Or hold each other in headlocks.
No rules, something just persists
Like pinching on St. Patrick's Day
Every year for no green.
    No one knows why.
Flowers are forced
Into the cracks
Between sections
Men have cried
At this wall.
I have
Seen them.

?

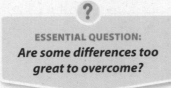

ESSENTIAL QUESTION:
Are some differences too great to overcome?

Assessment Practice

Answer these questions about "The Vietnam Wall" before moving on to the next selection.

1. This question has two parts. First, answer **Part A**. Then, answer **Part B**.

Part A

At one point, the speaker starts to leave the memorial. Why?

Ⓐ He thinks it is unimpressive, like the wall of a dollhouse.

Ⓑ He feels overwhelmed by its powerful evocation of death.

Ⓒ He thinks it is ugly, like a scar in the skin of the ground.

Ⓓ He feels it is cold and lifeless, like an archaeological dig.

Part B

Select the passage that best supports the answer to Part A.

Ⓐ "Invisible from one side, a scar / Into the skin of the ground / From the other, a black winding / Appendix line." (lines 6–9)

Ⓑ "A dig. / An archaeologist can explain." (lines 10–11)

Ⓒ "The walk is slow at first / Easy, a little black marble wall / Of a dollhouse, / A smoothness, a shine / The boys in the street want to give." (lines 12–16)

Ⓓ "And everything I expect has been taken away, like that, quick: / The names are not alphabetized. / They are in the order of dying." (lines 22–24)

2. Which metaphor does the author use to describe the structure of the memorial?

Ⓐ an appendectomy scar

Ⓑ the lines of names

Ⓒ an alphabet

Ⓓ the name Severiano Ríos

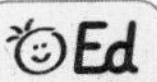

Test-Taking Strategies

MEDIA

Views of the Wall

Visual Essay

Engage Your Brain

Choose one or both of these activities to start connecting with the visual essay you're about to view.

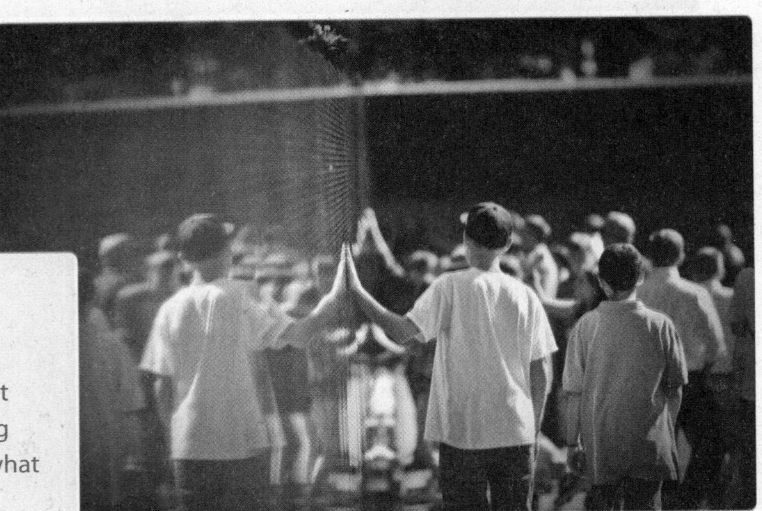

In Memoriam

Think back to a time when you witnessed or visited some kind of large memorial. Maybe it was at a museum on a class trip or something you saw on TV. Describe what you saw and what it made you think about.

Never Forget

You are about to look at photographs of the most famous memorial to the Vietnam War, the Wall. Two other memorials nearby also honor those who fought and died in the conflict. Find photos of The Three Soldiers memorial and the Vietnam Women's Memorial. Discuss your reactions to them with a partner.

Background

Among the nation's war memorials, the Vietnam Veterans Memorial is unique in its design and its commemoration of individual soldiers who died, were injured, or went missing in war. Traditionally, national memorials have been designed as monuments that include large representational sculptures, such as sculptures of people or national symbols, to honor leaders or soldiers who served their country in military conflicts. In contrast, the Vietnam Veterans Memorial is a stark V-shaped wall of polished black granite. The only adornment is the list of names that covers its dark surface. Each carved name serves as tribute to an individual soldier who died or was injured in the war, while the thousands of names together powerfully highlight the collective loss of American lives during the Vietnam War.

See images of the Vietnam Veterans Memorial and its visitors.
Views of the Wall
Ed
Video
View "Views of the Wall" in your ebook.

COLLABORATIVE DISCUSSION

How did seeing the collection of images help you better understand the poem?

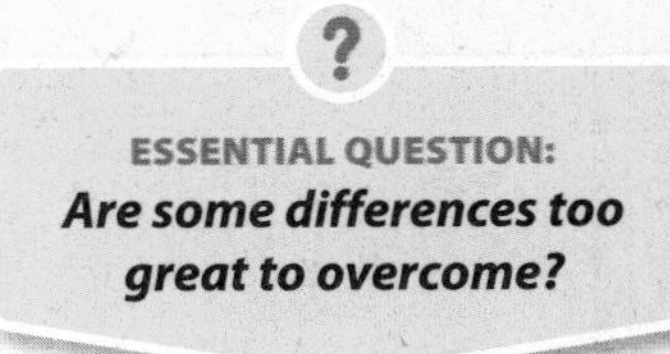

Review your notes and add your thoughts to your Response Log.

Analyze Text and Media

Support your responses with evidence from the text and the visual essay.

NOTICE & NOTE

Review what you **noticed and noted** as you read the text and viewed the visual essay. Your annotations can help you answer these questions.

1. **ANALYZE** A **simile** makes a comparison between two unlike things, using the word *like* or *as*. Explain the simile Ríos uses in lines 3–4.

2. **INTERPRET** Reread lines 20–25. What image is conveyed by the metaphor? What mood does the image create?

3. **EVALUATE** Over the course of the poem, the author describes several responses to the wall. What are they? Cite text evidence for each.

4. **DRAW CONCLUSIONS** What is the central idea of the poem? How does the poet use his subject—the Vietnam Veterans Memorial—to convey that central idea?

5. **CITE EVIDENCE** Which details of the memorial are emphasized in the images? How do these details contribute to the mood of the essay?

6. **CRITIQUE** Which image best conveys the experience of visiting the Vietnam Veterans Memorial? What reasons and details support your opinion?

7. **COMPARE** What are the similarities and differences between presenting ideas in photographs versus a poem? What does each emphasize or leave out?

Similarities	Differences
What does "The Vietnam Wall" emphasize? What does it leave out?	
What do the "Views of the Wall" images emphasize? What do they leave out?	

Choices

Here are some other ways to demonstrate your understanding of the ideas in this lesson.

Writing

Obituary

An obituary is a news article that reports the death of a person and includes information about that person's life. Write a fictitious obituary for a fallen soldier. Include the following:

- name
- place and date of birth
- place and date of death
- summary of the life, including major accomplishments
- list of close family members still alive

As you write and discuss, be sure to use the **Academic Vocabulary** words.

- enforce
- entity
- internal
- presume
- resolve

Media

Playlist

Create a playlist of songs that connect to the poem and the visual essay. Consider each song's message and tone. Present your playlist to a small group, and explain why you chose each song.

Speaking & Listening

Brochure

With a partner, create a brochure in which you promote visiting the Vietnam Veterans Memorial. Consider why people should visit and how you will call readers to action. Include the following in your brochure:

- compelling images
- contact information and address of the memorial
- times and dates to visit
- purpose for visiting

As you create your brochure, be sure to:

- consult authoritative and credible, or trustworthy, sources while researching
- cite your findings appropriately

When you have finished your brochure, present it to a large group. Explain why you chose certain images and designed your brochure the way you did. Allow follow-up questions and feedback. Listen to other presentations, and highlight similarities or differences from your own work.

Compare Across Genres

When you compare representations across genres in different mediums, you synthesize the information by making connections and extending your understanding of key ideas.

In a small group, complete the chart to identify similarities and differences in the poem and visual essay. Analyze the details in the text and images. Use the details to make inferences and draw conclusions about how each medium represents the subject. Discuss your inferences and conclusions with your group.

Details	A "The Vietnam Wall" (poem)	B "Views of the Wall" (visual essay)
Details about the Wall		
Details about visitors		
Details that convey emotion		

Analyze Text and Media

Discuss these questions in your group.

1. **ANALYZE** A **metaphor** directly compares two things by saying that one thing is another. Explain the metaphor Ríos uses in lines 20–21. Do the images in the visual essay support his metaphor? Explain.
2. **CRITIQUE** What is the central idea of both the visual essay and the poem? Which medium do you think most effectively communicates this central idea?
3. **SYNTHESIZE** How would you summarize the importance of the Vietnam Veterans Memorial using details from the poem and the visual essay?

Collaborate and Present

Within your group, discuss the information you recorded in your charts. Use the information to plan a presentation to the rest of the class that explains the similarities and differences in how the two mediums present information about the Vietnam Veterans Memorial.

1. **PLAN YOUR PRESENTATION** As a group, decide on the most important similarities and differences in the poem and visual essay. Identify details that support each similarity and difference. Use the following questions to help you plan and prepare your presentation:
   - In what order will you present the similarities and differences?
   - Would a visual help to communicate information in your presentation? If so, what type of visual will you create and what information will it include?
   - What will each group member say during the presentation?
   - How will you end your presentation?
2. **PRESENT** Deliver your presentation to the rest of the class. Remember the following tips as you present your information:
   - Speak clearly and loudly so that the audience can hear you.
   - Make eye contact with the audience as you speak.
   - After your group completes the presentation, ask your classmates in the audience whether they have any questions.
3. **DISCUSS AND REFLECT** After the presentation, discuss how the information in your presentation compares to the information presented by other groups. Share your ideas about which presentations were most effective and why. Use details and examples from the presentations to support your opinions.

Collaborate & Compare

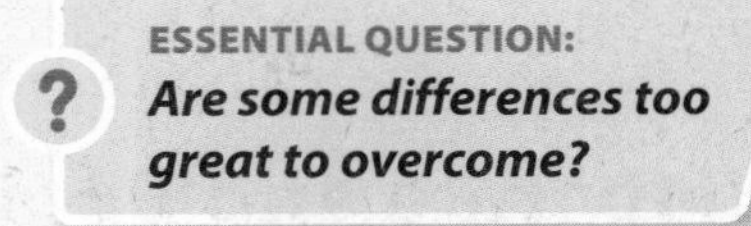

Compare Source and Interpretation

You're about to read one of the most famous speeches of all time—the Gettysburg Address—and then watch an actor delivering the speech on screen. How does comparing the written text with a film interpretation affect your understanding of Lincoln's message?

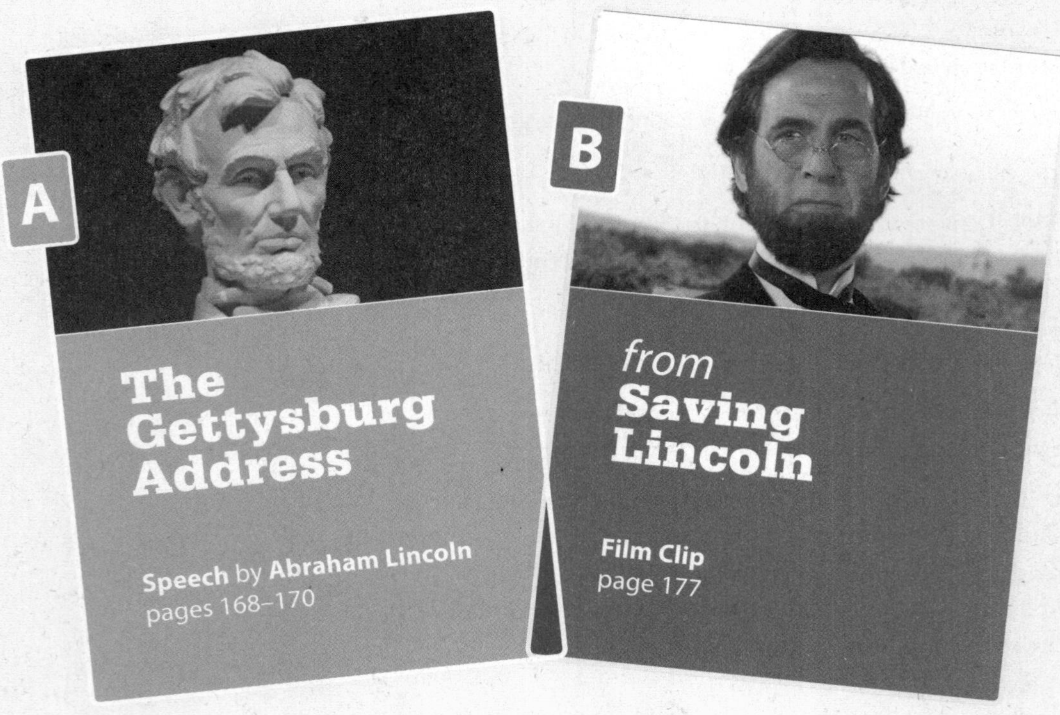

A
The Gettysburg Address
Speech by Abraham Lincoln
pages 168–170
B
from Saving Lincoln
Film Clip
page 177

After you read the speech and watch the clip, you'll put on your critic's hat to review different interpretations. You will follow these steps:

- Review the Address and at least one interpretation of it
- Analyze and record your thoughts about each
- Listen and share ideas with your group
- Come to a consensus about the speech and its effect on audiences

The Gettysburg Address

Speech by **Abraham Lincoln**

Engage Your Brain

Choose one or more of these activities to start connecting with the speech.

Strong Leaders

During difficult times, good leaders use words, images, and ideas that inspire and encourage people. What should a good leader say when things are going wrong? With a group, discuss what a strong leader has said to you when you have been discouraged. It could be a family member, teacher, coach, friend, or someone else.

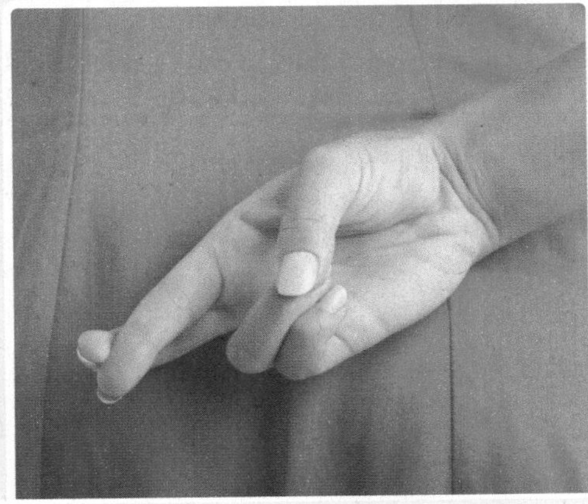

Two Truths and a Lie

Do some quick research on Abraham Lincoln. Write two truths and one lie about him. See if a partner can detect which two statements are true and which one is false.

List the Facts

What do you already know about the Civil War? List as many facts as you can. Compare your responses with a partner. Do some quick research to confirm or correct what you think you know.

Analyze Author's Purpose and Rhetoric

The reasons an author may write a speech are the **author's purpose.** An author's purpose might be to inform or explain, to persuade, to express thoughts or feelings, or to entertain.

To help advance a purpose, an author will often use **rhetoric,** or the art of using specific words and language structures, to make the message memorable. In the Gettysburg Address, Lincoln makes effective use of two rhetorical devices:

- **Repetition** is the use of the same word or words more than once. Repetition emphasizes key ideas.
- **Parallelism** is a form of repetition in which a grammatical pattern is repeated. Parallelism creates rhythm and evokes emotions.

Look at this example from President Ronald Reagan's remarks at Moscow State University. Notice how he uses repetition and parallelism for emphasis:

> The key is freedom—freedom of thought, freedom of information, freedom of communication.

As you analyze the Gettysburg Address, notice the relationship between the repeated words and parallelism. Think about how these techniques advance Lincoln's purpose.

Focus on Genre
Speech

- directly addresses and connects with audiences
- uses rhetorical devices to achieve specific purposes
- contains a clear message, stated near the beginning
- ends memorably

Analyze Seminal U.S. Documents

Speeches, essays, and other significant texts are called **seminal documents.** In the United States, the Gettysburg Address is a seminal document, as are George Washington's Farewell Address and Martin Luther King Jr.'s "Letter from Birmingham Jail." As you analyze Lincoln's speech, look for these characteristics that can help you recognize and analyze seminal documents:

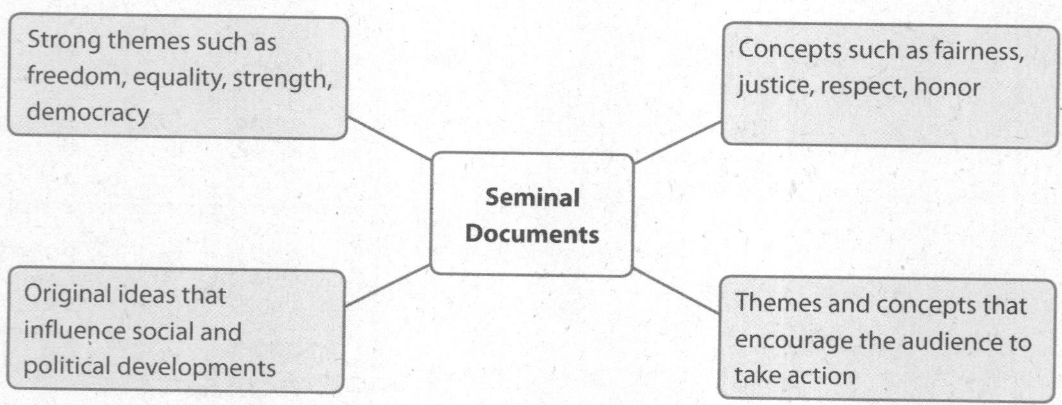
Strong themes such as freedom, equality, strength, democracy
Concepts such as fairness, justice, respect, honor
Seminal Documents
Original ideas that influence social and political developments
Themes and concepts that encourage the audience to take action

Annotation in Action

Here are one reader's notes about part of the Gettysburg Address. As you read, note how Lincoln uses rhetorical devices to develop his ideas.

> Now we are engaged in a great civil war, testing whether that nation, or any nation so conceived and so dedicated, can long endure.

parallel structure → "so conceived," "so dedicated"

Expand Your Vocabulary

Put a check mark next to the vocabulary words that you feel comfortable using when speaking or writing.

conceive	☐
detract	☐
resolve	☐
perish	☐

Turn to a partner and talk about the vocabulary words you already know. Then, use as many vocabulary words as you can in a few sentences telling what you know about the Gettysburg Address.

As you read Abraham Lincoln's speech, use the definitions in the side column to learn the vocabulary words you don't already know.

Background

President **Abraham Lincoln** (1809–1865) is considered an American hero for preserving the Union and abolishing slavery. He was a skillful politician, leader, and orator. One of his most famous speeches was delivered at the dedication of the National Cemetery at Gettysburg, Pennsylvania, in 1863, site of one of the most deadly battles of the Civil War. The victory for the Union forces marked a turning point in the Civil War, but losses on both sides at Gettysburg were staggering: 28,000 Confederate soldiers and 23,000 Union soldiers were killed or wounded. Lincoln was assassinated by John Wilkes Booth in 1865. Lincoln's dedication to the ideals of freedom and equality continue to inspire people around the world.

The Gettysburg Address

Speech by **Abraham Lincoln**

President Lincoln emphasizes the importance of ending the Civil War and reuniting the country.

1 Four score and seven[1] years ago our fathers brought forth on this continent a new nation, **conceived** in liberty and dedicated to the proposition that all men are created equal.

2 Now we are engaged in a great civil war, testing whether that nation, or any nation so conceived and so dedicated, can long endure. We are met on a great battlefield of that war. We have come to dedicate a portion of that field, as a final resting place for those who here gave their lives that that nation might live. It is altogether fitting and proper that we should do this.

conceive
(kən-sēv´) *v.* to form or develop in the mind; devise.

ANALYZE SEMINAL U.S. DOCUMENTS

Annotate: Mark details in paragraph 1 that introduce two themes often found in seminal U.S. documents.

Connect: The phrase "all men are created equal" is taken from the Declaration of Independence, a document written 87 years before Lincoln gave this speech. Why does Lincoln refer to it?

[1] **four score and seven:** eighty-seven.

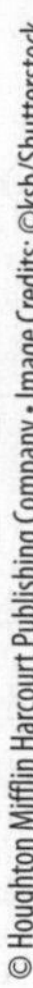

3 But in a larger sense, we cannot dedicate—we cannot consecrate[2]—we cannot hallow[3]—this ground. The brave men, living and dead, who struggled here have consecrated it, far above our poor power to add or **detract.** The world will little note, nor long remember what we say here, but it can never forget what they did here. It is for us, the living, rather to be dedicated here to the unfinished work which they who fought here have thus far so nobly advanced. It is rather for us to be here dedicated to the great task remaining before us—that from these honored dead we take increased devotion to that cause for which they gave the last full measure of devotion—that we here highly **resolve** that these dead shall not have died in vain—that this nation, under God, shall have a new birth of freedom—and that government of the people, by the people, for the people shall not **perish** from the earth.

[2] **consecrate:** to dedicate as sacred.
[3] **hallow:** to define as holy.

ANALYZE AUTHOR'S PURPOSE AND RHETORIC

Annotate: Mark the repetition and parallelism in the first sentence of paragraph 3.

Analyze: What is the effect of using these rhetorical devices in the same sentence? What point is Lincoln making?

detract
(dĭ-trăkt´) *v.* to take away from.

resolve
(rĭ-zŏlv´) *v.* to decide or become determined.

perish
(pĕr´ĭsh) *v.* to die or come to an end.

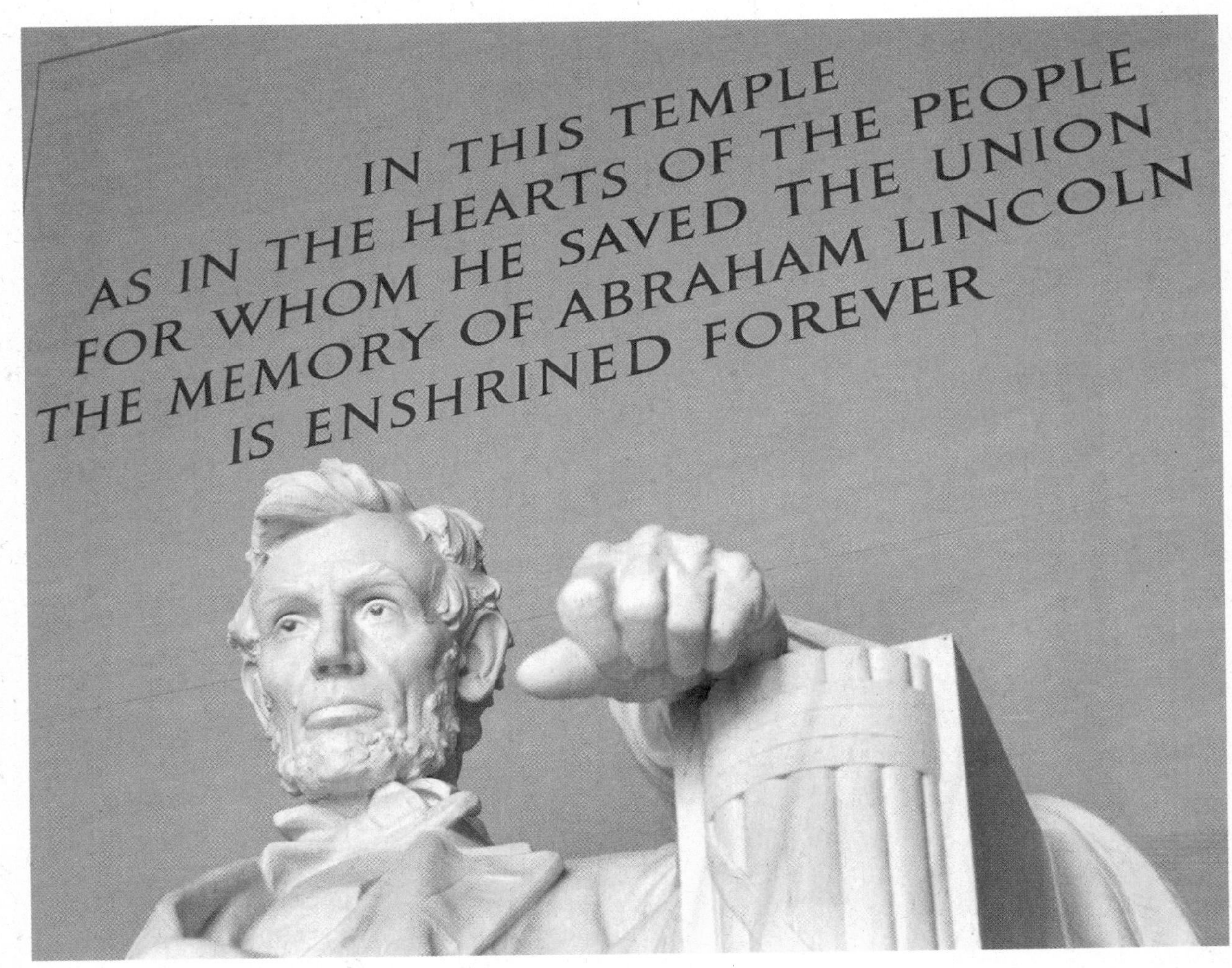

IN THIS TEMPLE
AS IN THE HEARTS OF THE PEOPLE
FOR WHOM HE SAVED THE UNION
THE MEMORY OF ABRAHAM LINCOLN
IS ENSHRINED FOREVER

COLLABORATIVE DISCUSSION

With a partner, discuss Lincoln's beliefs about reuniting the country.

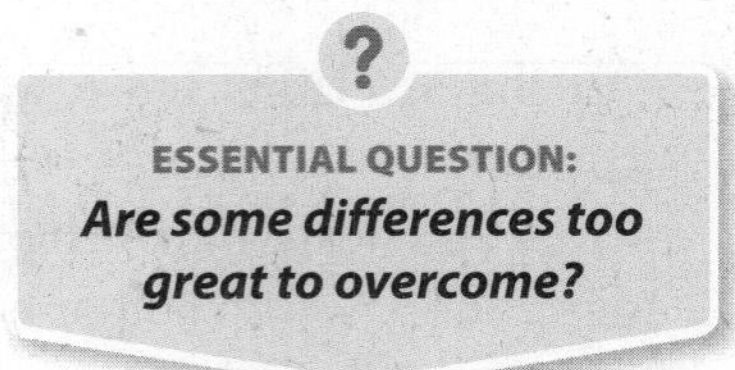
ESSENTIAL QUESTION:
Are some differences too great to overcome?

Review your notes and add your thoughts to your Response Log..

Assessment Practice

Answer these questions before moving on to the **Analyze the Text** section on the following page.

1. What is the main idea of the Gettysburg Address?

   (A) The soldiers died because of injustice.

   (B) The soldiers should not die in vain.

   (C) The Battle of Gettysburg was the most important battle of the war.

   (D) The causes of independence and freedom always require sacrifices.

2. This question has two parts. First, answer **Part A**. Then, answer **Part B**.

   Part A

   What does Lincoln try to persuade the audience to do?

   (A) continue supporting the war effort

   (B) reject the idea of war as a solution

   (C) enlist in the Union army and fight

   (D) help him create a new government

   Part B

   Select the quotation that best supports the answer to Part A.

   (A) "Now we are engaged in a great civil war, testing whether that nation . . . can long endure." (paragraph 2)

   (B) "We have come to dedicate a portion of that field, as a final resting place for those who here gave their lives that that nation might live." (paragraph 2)

   (C) "The brave men . . . have consecrated it, far above our poor power to add or detract." (paragraph 3)

   (D) "It is for us, the living, rather to be dedicated here to the unfinished work which they who fought here have thus far so nobly advanced." (paragraph 3)

Ed

Test-Taking Strategies

Analyze the Text

Support your responses with evidence from the text.

NOTICE & NOTE

Review what you **noticed and noted** as you read the text. Your annotations can help you answer these questions.

1. **ANALYZE** Why did Lincoln write and deliver the Gettysburg Address? What were his two main purposes? Explain using evidence from the speech.

2. **INFER** What is "the unfinished work" of those who died (paragraph 3)?

3. **INTERPRET** The word *dedicate* is repeated several times in the speech. What does *dedicate* mean? What idea does Lincoln emphasize with the repetition of this word?

4. **IDENTIFY PATTERNS** Identify two additional examples of parallel structure in paragraph 3, aside from the first sentence. How does Lincoln use parallel structure to persuade the audience to accept his message?

5. **INFER** Lincoln uses extreme language in this speech, such as "great battlefield" and "new birth of freedom." Find at least two other instances of extreme language. Why do you think Lincoln wanted his audience to believe Gettysburg was a major event in the country's history?

6. **DRAW CONCLUSIONS** Seminal U.S. documents often refer to themes and ideals that are important to the audience they address.
   - What is the **theme,** or underlying message, of the Gettysburg Address?
   - Is this theme still important today?
   - Explain the American ideals that the speech upholds.

7. **EVALUATE** Frederick Douglass spoke warmly of Lincoln's honesty and moral conviction. He said, "The image of the man went out with his words, and those who read them knew him." Based on your own reading, what impressions do you have of Lincoln's character?

Choices

Here are some other ways to demonstrate your understanding of the ideas in the speech.

Writing

Short-Film Screenplay

Script a film interpretation of Lincoln delivering the Gettysburg Address. Consider how you will convey the setting, the audience, and Lincoln's oral interpretation of the speech. Research images of screenplay templates for formatting examples and guidance.

As you write and discuss, be sure to use the **Academic Vocabulary** words.

- enforce
- entity
- internal
- presume
- resolve

Research

First-Person Reports

At the time of Lincoln's speech, only the people physically gathered with him at Gettysburg would have heard it. Everyone else would have been aware of it only through word of mouth or through newspaper reports. Find out more about the people and the news reporters who witnessed the event.

- Why had people gathered at the National Cemetery at Gettysburg?
- What were their reactions to Lincoln's speech?
- How did media reports describe the speech?

Cite the sources you used appropriately.

Social & Emotional Learning

Call to Action

In the Gettysburg Address, Lincoln aimed to unify the country and emphasize the importance of ending the Civil War. What about his speech was effective? How could it have been more effective?

Think of an issue you are passionate about and want others to engage with: For example, a war or conflict, world hunger, mistreatment of the environment, or equal rights. Draft a powerful speech that draws attention to the issue and calls others to action. Consider the following:

- your audience
- appeals and rhetorical devices you will use
- examples, evidence, and reasons that will persuade listeners

With a partner, read your speeches to one another and offer critiques and suggestions. Discuss similarities and differences in what you are each passionate about.

Expand Your Vocabulary

PRACTICE AND APPLY

Choose which vocabulary word is most closely associated with the underlined word or phrase in each sentence.

conceive	detract	resolve	perish

1. Additional details in a speech sometimes take away from the whole message.
2. A special election can be used to decide a tie in the vote for the student body president.
3. It takes a creative person to form an idea in his or her mind about an important issue and then convey that message to an audience.
4. Sometimes organizations such as clubs come to an end when the members are no longer interested.

Vocabulary Strategy

↳ Multiple-Meaning Words

Interactive Vocabulary Lesson: Words with Multiple Meanings

Words that have more than one definition are considered **multiple-meaning words.** To determine a word's appropriate meaning within a text, you need to look for context clues in the words, sentences, and paragraphs that surround it. Look at the word *fitting* in this sentence from the Gettysburg Address:

It is altogether fitting and proper that we should do this.

The word *fitting* can mean "the act of trying on clothes" or "a small part for a machine." However, the word *proper* is a context clue that tells you that the correct meaning of *fitting* in this sentence is "appropriate."

PRACTICE AND APPLY

Find the following multiple-meaning words in the speech: *engaged* (paragraph 2), *testing* (paragraph 2), *poor* (paragraph 3), *measure* (paragraph 3). Working with a partner, use context clues to determine each word's meaning as it is used in the speech.

1. Determine how the word functions in the sentence. Is it a noun, an adjective, a verb, or an adverb?
2. If the sentence does not provide enough information, read the paragraph in which the word appears and consider the larger context of the speech.
3. Write down your definition.

Watch Your Language!

Parallel Structure

As you read the Gettysburg Address, look for examples of **parallel structure** in Lincoln's words, phrases, and clauses. Then evaluate how this rhetorical device creates a poetic and rhythmic effect that helps make the words and ideas in this speech powerful and memorable.

Josefina likes to play music, wear hats, and ride horses.

Type of Structure	Example from the Gettysburg Address
parallel words	living and dead

Type of Structure	Example from the Gettysburg Address
parallel phrases	of the people, by the people, for the people

Type of Structure	Example from the Gettysburg Address
parallel clauses	we cannot dedicate—we cannot consecrate—we cannot hallow

PRACTICE AND APPLY

With a partner, look back at the Gettysburg Address and identify additional examples of parallel structure. Then imagine you were at Gettysburg on the day President Lincoln delivered his speech. Write a brief letter to Lincoln explaining how you were affected by his remarks. Use parallel structure at least twice in your letter. Exchange letters with a partner and discuss how effectively each of you used parallel structure to communicate your message to Lincoln.

MEDIA

from
Saving Lincoln

Film Clip

Engage Your Brain

Choose one or both of these activities to start connecting with the clip you're about to watch.

Comparing Films

Think of the different kinds of movies you have seen: animated, historical, documentary, fantasy, horror, etc. What do you like about certain kinds of films, and dislike about others? Make a list below.

Current Events

Nowadays, it seems like we have a video record of almost everything that happens. But actors on stage or on film can still retell events so that we see them in a new way. Think about a recent event in the news. What details from the event would have to be included in a film version? What could filmmakers do to emphasize the significance of the event? Discuss your ideas with a partner.

Background

Saving Lincoln is a biopic, released in 2013, that is partly about Abraham Lincoln. *Saving Lincoln* is told from the point of view of **Ward Hill Lamon** (1828–1893), who was Lincoln's law partner in Illinois and a longtime friend. When Lincoln became president, Lamon acted as his primary bodyguard, preventing several assassination attempts. *Saving Lincoln* ends up telling part of Lamon's life story as well. Film director Salvador Litvak researched Lincoln and Lamon's friendship by reading letters and diaries from both men. In this excerpt from the film, a voiceover describes what Lamon thinks is Lincoln's purpose for delivering the speech. Then we watch and hear the address delivered by the actor playing Lincoln.

Analyze Media Techniques

A film about the life of a real person, such as *Saving Lincoln*, is often called a *biopic* (biographical picture). Like biographies, biopics convey the story of a person's life and the time period in which he or she lived. Filmmakers research the subject's life to develop a central idea. They then use a combination of media techniques, including storytelling and production elements, to express this central idea in film.

Focus on Genre
Film

- created for a specific purpose or reason
- conveys a central idea or theme about the topic
- incorporates visuals and sound
- uses storytelling elements such as cast, setting, mood, and sequence
- uses production elements such as camera angles, music, and special effects

Storytelling Elements	What They Do
Cast: the actors portraying characters in a film	Actors' performances can add nuanced meanings to characters and events.
Setting: the locations on which a film is shot	Settings can be an integral part of how a filmmaker conveys the central idea.
Mood: the atmosphere created by visual and sound elements	Mood helps support the central idea by reinforcing what viewers see.
Sequence: the order in which images or scenes are presented	Images or scenes are presented in an order that helps viewers connect ideas.

In addition to these storytelling elements, the director of *Saving Lincoln* uses a variety of production elements.

Production Elements	Examples
Visual elements help the filmmaker convey connections among ideas.	• **camera angle:** the angle at which the camera is positioned during the recording of a shot or image
Sound elements may give additional information and set the mood for a scene.	• **music:** instrumental and vocal compositions • **sound effects:** sounds other than speech and music
Special effects are visual tricks created so the viewer "sees" something not happening naturally.	• **computer-generated imagery (CGI):** an image or animation created on a computer to show something that is not actually happening or that does not exist • **practical effect:** any effect created without a computer, such as water used to simulate rain

Analyze Media Representations

Historic events, such as speeches, can be represented in a variety of **mediums** to feature different aspects and details of the event. A printed copy of the text of a speech, for example, emphasizes the ideas contained in the words. A video recording of a speech might include audio of the speaker but images of only the audience to emphasize the speech's effect.

Analyzing how the same event is represented in different mediums can help you determine and analyze the central idea that is conveyed by a particular representation. As you watch the clip from the biopic *Saving Lincoln*, consider the various storytelling and production elements filmmakers can use to convey their messages. Use the chart to note details in the clip and their effect on your understanding of the event.

Time	Detail	Effect

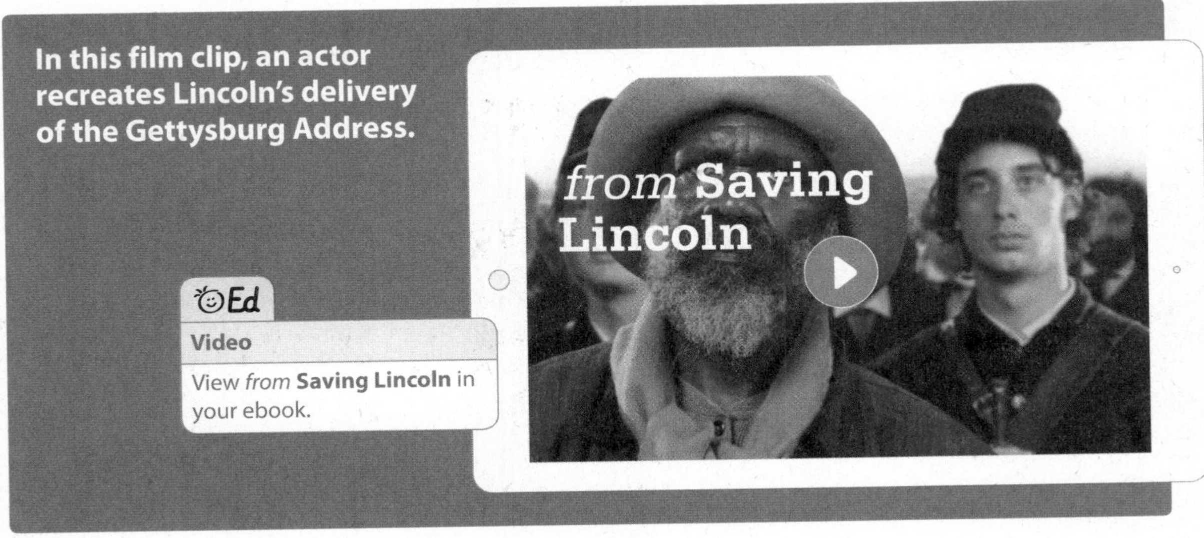

In this film clip, an actor recreates Lincoln's delivery of the Gettysburg Address.
from Saving Lincoln
Ed
Video
View *from* **Saving Lincoln** in your ebook.

COLLABORATIVE DISCUSSION

How would you describe the audience reaction to Lincoln's speech?

Analyze Media

Support your responses with evidence from the film clip.

1 **INFER** Based on the clip, how would you interpret the movie's title, *Saving Lincoln*? From whom or what did Lincoln need to be saved?

2 **SUMMARIZE** How does the narrator, Ward Hill Lamon, provide context for the presentation of the speech?

3 **ANALYZE** How would you describe Lincoln's audience, as shown in the film? What is their response to the speech?

4 **INTERPRET** The filmmakers use both close-up shots and distance or long shots in the scene you watched. What does each type of shot reveal—for example, about the physical setting and the impact of Lincoln's speech on his audience?

5 **SYNTHESIZE** Based on the title of the film and the background information you read, what do you think is the focus of *Saving Lincoln*?

6 **EVALUATE** How does the director use storytelling or production elements to add meaningful details? Describe at least two elements that you found particularly effective and what detail each one conveys or emphasizes.

Production Element	Detail It Conveys or Emphasizes

7 **DRAW CONCLUSIONS** Why do you think the director includes the scene in which Lamon reads newspaper reactions to the speech? Consider what biographical information this adds to the movie.

Choices

Here are some other ways to demonstrate your understanding of the ideas in this lesson.

Writing

Letter to Lincoln

Think about the ideals and values in the Gettysburg Address. Write a letter to Abraham Lincoln about how they are reflected today.

- In your own words, express the values and beliefs that are explicit or implied in the speech.
- Compare them to the values and beliefs Americans hold today.
- Provide specific examples and details.

Publish your letter on a blog or as a social media post for others to comment on or ask follow-up questions.

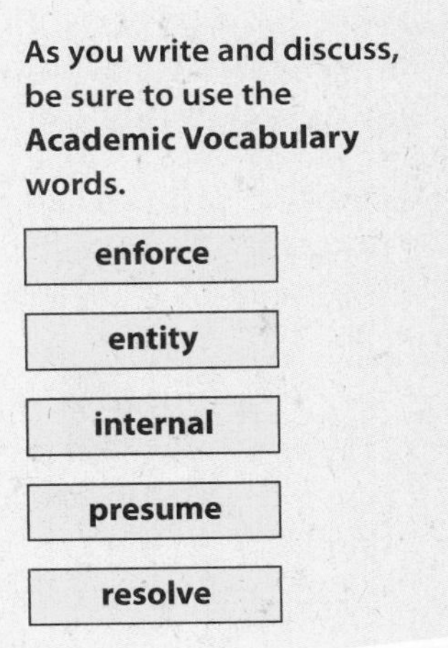
As you write and discuss, be sure to use the Academic Vocabulary words.
enforce
entity
internal
presume
resolve

Media

Film Analysis

You've seen a clip of *Saving Lincoln*; now watch the entire film. In the role of film reviewer, make notes as you watch. Include:

- a summary of events
- your impressions of the actors, costumes, and special effects
- how watching the film helped you understand historical events that shaped the Gettysburg Address

Research

Compare Interpretations

The Gettysburg Address has been recorded and filmed by many actors and narrators. Find other interpretations—video or audio—of the speech online. Take notes on how each version gives you a different insight, or enables you to understand the speech's message in a new way. Present your findings to the class, identifying the source of each version.

Compare Source and Interpretation

Interpretations of sources are all around us. For example, the Harry Potter movies are interpretations of J.K. Rowling's series of books, and countless illustrations interpret traditional and modern fairy tales. Interpretations help you notice different aspects, or even understand the source in a new way.

How did the film clip *Saving Lincoln* help you view the Gettysburg Address in a new or different way? In a small group, fill out the chart. One example is completed for you.

B Detail in *Saving Lincoln*	A How It Changed My Understanding of the Speech
Close-ups of audience members	Lincoln's words offered hope and inspiration to people of different backgrounds and races.

Analyze Text and Media

Discuss these questions in your group.

1. **CONTRAST** What do the introductory voiceover and the brief scene after Lincoln delivers his speech tell you about its purpose and the immediate response to it?

2. **EVALUATE** An audience member in the film reacts to the speech by saying that it was unusually short. Think about why Lincoln might have kept the speech so short.

3. **CONNECT** What did you visualize when you were reading the text of the speech? Compare that to how the director staged the speech.

4. **ANALYZE** How does the actor playing Lincoln use voice and body language to communicate the message of the speech?

Compare and Discuss

You have developed an understanding of the Gettysburg Address through a close read of the printed text and a film interpretation; you may also have evaluated other interpretations of the speech. Now, your group can discuss your overall understanding of the purpose and message of the Gettysburg Address. Follow these steps:

1. **SYNTHESIZE IDEAS** Review the different interpretations of the speech that you have studied—the excerpt from the film as well as any performances or recordings you found online. How was the speech presented? How did each interpretation add to your understanding of the speech's purpose, meaning, and impact, as well as its audience?

   Record your thoughts on the speech. You can use this framework to synthesize what you learn:

Information gained from written speech:	Information gained from film of speech:
Information gained from online source:	Information gained from class discussion:
My understanding of the speech's purpose:	
My understanding of the speech's meaning:	
My understanding of the speech's impact:	
My understanding of the speech's audience:	

2. **LISTEN AND SHARE IDEAS** In your group, state your understanding of the speech's purpose, meaning, and impact, as well as its actual audience. Use details from the source as well as interpretations of it to support your own interpretation of the speech. Ask questions about words or phrases you don't understand.

3. **COME TO A CONSENSUS** Based on the discussion, can the group construct a statement about the speech, telling its purpose, meaning, and impact? Together, write a summary statement about the Gettysburg Address and its effect on the audience.

Reader's Choice

Continue your exploration of the Essential Question by doing some independent reading on exploring and overcoming differences. Read the titles and descriptions shown. Then mark the texts that interest you.

ESSENTIAL QUESTION:
? ***Are some differences too great to overcome?***

Short Reads

Available on 

These texts are available in your ebook. Choose one to read and rate. Then defend your rating to the class.

Facing It

Poem by **Yusef Komunyakaa**

The speaker struggles with memories of fallen comrades as he contemplates the Vietnam Veterans Memorial.

Rate It 

Making the Future Better, Together

Blog by **Eboo Patel**

Could George Washington's views about unity and diversity be relevant today?

Rate It 

Oklahoma Bombing Memorial Address

Speech by **Bill Clinton**

President Bill Clinton takes a stand against the fear, hatred, and violence that can divide a nation.

Rate It 

Night Calls

Short Story by **Lisa Fugard**

A girl uses her gift of mimicking bird calls to create a bond with her emotionally distant father.

Rate It 

Long Reads

Here are three recommended books that connect to this unit topic. For additional options, ask your teacher, school librarian, or peers. Which titles spark your interest?

To Kill a Mockingbird

Novel by **Harper Lee**

When Scout's father defends a Black man accused of a crime against a white woman, Scout sees the prejudice —and the heroism—of those in her community.

Love, Hate, and Other Filters

Novel by **Samira Ahmed**

Maya is torn between becoming the traditional Indian daughter her parents want and fulfilling her own dreams.

Code Talker

Novel by **Joseph Bruchac**

Native Americans help the World War II Allied effort by transmitting messages in codes based on the Navajo language.

Extension

Connect & Create

BRIDGES BUILT OR BURNED? This unit is about people who try—and sometimes fail—to find a common understanding. With a partner or in a small group, choose one text and discuss these questions:

- What barriers or conflicts were involved?
- Were they overcome, or not?
- Either way, what were the reasons?

WRITE A HAIKU A haiku is a form of Japanese poetry in which 17 syllables are arranged in three lines of 5, 7, and 5 syllables each. Research online for more information about the form; then write a haiku that summarizes one text you read.

NOTICE & NOTE

- Pick one of the texts and annotate the Notice & Note signposts you find.
- Then, use the **Notice & Note Writing Frames** to help you write about the significance of the signposts.
- Compare your findings with those of other students who read the same text.

Reader's Choice

Notice & Note Writing Frames

Write a Personal Narrative

Writing Prompt

Using ideas, information, and examples from multiple texts in this unit, write a personal narrative about how differences between people can be opportunities rather than obstacles.

Manage your time carefully so that you can

- review the texts in the unit;
- plan your narrative;
- write your narrative; and
- revise and edit your narrative.

Be sure to

- establish a context and introduce a narrator
- develop the narrative with a logical sequence of events
- use narrative techniques such as dialogue and pacing
- include descriptive details and sensory language, and
- use transitions to clarify sequence and connect ideas.

Review the Mentor Text

For an example of a well-written personal narrative you can use as a mentor text, review:

- "Unusual Normality" (pages 115–123).

Review your notes and annotations about this text. Think about how the author expresses ideas about his experiences.

Consider Your Sources

Review the list of texts in the unit and choose at least three that you may want to use as sources of ideas or inspiration for your personal narrative.

As you review selections, consult the notes you made on your **Response Log** and make additional notes about any ideas that might be useful as you write your personal narrative. Especially consider how the writers establish a point of view and use narrative techniques to describe events or experiences.

UNIT 2 SOURCES

- ☐ **The Power of a Dinner Table**
- ☐ **Unusual Normality**
- ☐ **Once Upon a Time**
- ☐ **Theme for English B**
- ☐ **The Vietnam Wall**
- ☐ **Views of the Wall** MEDIA
- ☐ **The Gettysburg Address**
- ☐ *from* **Saving Lincoln** MEDIA

Analyze the Prompt

Review the prompt to make sure you understand the assignment.

1. Mark the phrase in the prompt that identifies the general topic of your personal narrative. Restate the topic in your own words.
2. Next, look for words that suggest the purpose and audience of your personal narrative, and write a sentence describing each.

Find a Purpose

Two common purposes of a personal narrative are

- to **entertain** readers
- to convey a **theme,** or a message about life or human nature

What is my topic? What is my writing task?

What is my purpose?

Who is my audience?

Review the Rubric

Your personal narrative will be scored using a rubric. As you write, focus on the characteristics described in the chart. You will learn more about these characteristics as you work through the lesson.

Purpose, Focus, and Organization	Narrative Techniques	Conventions of Standard English
The response includes: • An engaging introduction • A well-developed narrative structure • A clearly established point of view • Use of transitions to convey sequence and connect ideas • Logical sequence of events • A conclusion that follows from the narrated events	The response includes: • Use of descriptive details and sensory language • Effective use of narrative techniques • Varied sentence structure	The response may include: • Some minor errors in usage but no patterns of errors • Correct punctuation, capitalization, sentence formation, and spelling • Command of basic conventions

1 PLAN YOUR NARRATIVE

Choose a Topic

Use the chart to brainstorm ideas for your narrative. List your ideas about events or experiences that helped you understand something about the value of diversity. Then circle the event or experience that you would like to focus on for your narrative.

Brainstorm Topic Idea

Remember, an interesting **personal narrative** might explore

- how you faced a **problem** or challenge
- how a **realization** shaped your actions or understandings

Experience/Event	What I Thought and Felt About It

Brainstorm Details

Brainstorm **descriptive details** that will help bring your narrative to life. Jot down words and phrases that will help readers imagine events. Include **sensory language** that appeals to the senses of sight, hearing, touch, smell, or taste.

Help with Planning

Consult **Interactive Writing Lesson: Writing Narratives**

Event	Details

Organize Ideas

Think about the most logical and interesting way to structure your narrative. Use the chart to help you plan your draft.

Introduction (establish context and engage readers)

↓

Main Narrative (describe sequence of events)

↓

Conclusion (reflect on what happened)

Determine Narrative Techniques

Here are some **narrative techniques** that can add interest to your writing:

- use **flashback** to recall past events
- use **foreshadowing** to hint at events that occur later
- speed up or slow down the **pacing** by shortening or lengthening descriptions

2 DEVELOP A DRAFT

Now it is time to draft your essay. Examining the work of professional authors can help you develop your own writing skills. Read about techniques you might use as you draft your personal narrative.

Establish Point of View

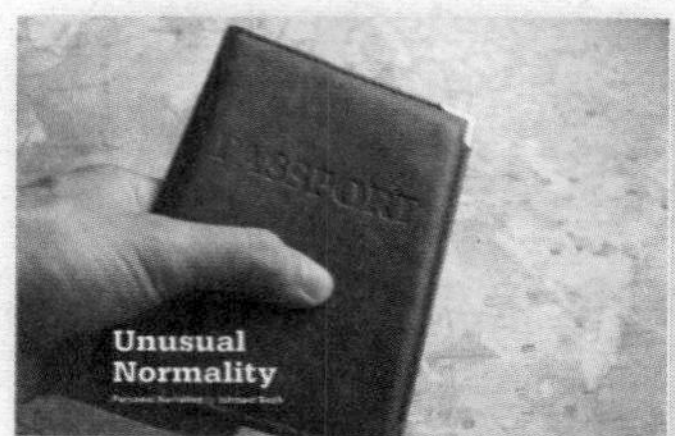

EXAMINE THE MENTOR TEXT

Notice how the author of "Unusual Normality" establishes himself as the first-person narrator and engages readers in his introduction.

The author establishes the context and first-person point of view by sharing key details about his background.

I came to New York City in 1998. I was seventeen.

I entered the United States with just a passport in my hand, because somehow the baggage that I'd checked when I boarded the flight from Ivory Coast (which was tattered in ways unimaginable) didn't make it.

I stood there at the luggage rack watching all these huge bags go by, and mine didn't come. This bag held all my possessions at this point: two pairs of pants and two shirts—one long-sleeved and one short. So I just started laughing, and I didn't even bother going to the lost-baggage section to claim it.

He reveals his personality through descriptions of his actions.

APPLY TO YOUR DRAFT

Use this chart to practice developing your point of view and engaging readers. Draft a few sentences that reveal your personality through description and dialogue. Then apply these techniques to your draft.

Try These Suggestions

Vary the way you develop your narrative voice. Try these out:

- **Refer to yourself as *I* or *me*.**
- **Share your own thoughts and feelings.**
- **Describe the action from your point of view.**
- **Use dialogue to draw in readers.**

Thoughts	
Actions	
Words	

Use Transitions

EXAMINE THE MENTOR TEXT

Transitions help create cohesion in narrative writing by conveying sequence and showing how ideas are related. Here, the author of "Unusual Normality" uses transitions to describe his response to his friend's invitation to play paintball in upstate New York.

Drafting Online

Check your assignment list for a writing task from your teacher.

I said, "Okay, that sounds interesting."

And I thought, *If these guys who only pretend about violence can play it, it must not be that difficult a game.*

But of course I didn't say this. I just thought these things. So I went with them upstate to a humongous property that had trees and creeks that ran into a bigger river—this beautiful open place.

The transition "But" highlights the contrast between what the author says and thinks.

"So" helps clarify what he did next.

APPLY TO YOUR DRAFT

Your personal narrative should include transitions that make the sequence of events clear and show the connections between ideas. Practice using the transitions in the chart below to describe your responses to events in your narrative. As you write, apply this technique to your draft.

Transition	Event → My Response
Before…	
After…	
Because of…	
As a result of…	

3 REVISE YOUR PERSONAL NARRATIVE

Even experienced writers rework their ideas and language during their writing process. Use the guide to help you revise your personal narrative.

Help with Revision

Find a **Peer Review Guide** and **Student Models** online.

REVISION GUIDE		
Ask Yourself	**Prove it**	**Revise it**
Introduction Does my introduction establish context and engage readers?	**Circle key** details that establish context. **Highlight** words and phrases that hint at what might happen.	**Add** key details to help readers understand the context of the narrative. **Reword** phrases to spark readers' curiosity about what happens next.
Point of View Do I establish and develop a first-person narrative voice?	**Put a star** (★) next to pronouns that show your point of view. **Underline** words and phrases that describe your thoughts and feelings.	**Change** third-person pronouns to first-person pronouns as necessary. **Add** descriptions to convey your thoughts and feelings.
Narrative Techniques Do I use narrative techniques to add interest and draw in readers?	**Put a check mark** (✔) next to dialogue. **Number** (1, 2, 3...) the sequence of events.	**Add** or **rearrange** details to vary the pacing or to convey a more natural or logical sequence.
Transitions Do I use transitions to clarify sequence and to show connections between ideas?	**Circle** transitions between sentences and paragraphs.	**Add** transitions as necessary.
Conclusion Does my conclusion reveal why the experience was significant?	**Underline** statements that tell why the experience was meaningful.	**Add** statements that explain the event's importance.

APPLY TO YOUR DRAFT

Consider the following as you look for opportunities to improve your writing.

- Make sure your narrative follows a logical sequence.
- Use dialogue and description to help readers imagine events.
- Correct any errors in grammar and punctuation.

Peer Review in Action

Once you have finished revising your personal narrative, you will exchange papers with a partner in a **peer review.** During a peer review, you will give suggestions to improve your partner's draft.

Read the introduction from a student's draft and examine the comments made by the peer reviewer to see how it's done.

Draft

Who Am I?

By Bao Manesis-Soares, Bartlett High School

I've always dreaded the first day at a new school. I've attended seven different schools in five states since I first arrived in this country as a baby. Some people might think that having to move a lot makes moving easier. For me, it definitely hasn't. In fact, it's felt harder each time because I've only grown more confused about how to answer the simple question, *Where are you from?* Trying to figure out how to answer this question often made me anxious, but I finally learned to let go of my worries.

I like how you share information that makes me curious, but it might sound more interesting if you vary your sentence structure.

Try giving a bigger hint about how you learned this, and consider adding more descriptive or vivid detail.

Now read the revised introduction below. Notice how the writer has improved the draft by making revisions based on the reviewer's comments.

Revision

Who Am I?

By Bao Manesis-Soares, Bartlett High School

Where are you from? This sounds like such a simple, friendly question, doesn't it? Until recently, hearing it would instantly cause beads of sweat to tickle my scalp as my cheeks lit up like fireballs. The trouble was, I never felt like I knew how to answer this question. I've attended seven different schools in five states since I first arrived in this country as a baby, and I've grown more confused about my answer every time I've moved. The welcoming experience on my first day at the Bartlett School finally changed that. Now I've traded my blushed cheeks for a beaming smile, and I embrace opportunities to show pride in my identity and build connections with others.

Great job! The questions you start with really get me thinking and make me want to keep reading!

Nice way to preview your main topic!

APPLY TO YOUR DRAFT

During your peer review, give each other specific suggestions for how you could make your personal narratives more vivid or engaging. Use the revision guide to help you.

When receiving feedback from your partner, listen attentively and ask questions to make sure you fully understand the revision suggestions.

4 EDIT YOUR PERSONAL NARRATIVE

Edit your final draft to check for proper use of standard English conventions and to correct any misspellings or grammatical errors.

Ed

Interactive Grammar Lesson: Colons

Watch Your Language!

USE COLONS AND SEMICOLONS

Varying your sentence structure—and using appropriate punctuation—adds interest to your narrative.

Read the following sentences from "Unusual Normality."

> This bag held all my possessions at this point: two pairs of pants and two shirts—one long-sleeved and one short.

The first clause is independent and introduces a list. Use of the colon helps draw attention to the narrator's surprisingly few belongings.

> I got to be a child again with them; the only worries that we had were when we went rollerblading without any protective gear.

The sentence contains two independent clauses. The semicolon helps show that the ideas are closely related—the second clause elaborates on the idea in the first clause.

Purposeful Punctuation

- Use a **colon** after an independent clause to introduce a list or a statement you want to emphasize.
- Use a **semicolon** to join independent clauses that are closely related.

APPLY TO YOUR DRAFT

Now apply what you've learned about punctuation to your own work.

1. Read your paper aloud and look for lists, statements you might want to emphasize, and short sentences that are closely related.
2. Use colons and semicolons to vary the structure of three or more of your sentences.
3. Exchange drafts with a peer and look for correct use of colons and semicolons in each other's work.

5 PUBLISH YOUR PERSONAL NARRATIVE

Share It!

Finalize your essay for your writing portfolio. You may also post your narrative as a blog on a classroom or school website.

Ways to Share

- Present your narrative as a **speech** to the class.
- **Record an interview** to answer a classmate's questions about your experience.
- **Create a video docudrama** based on your experience.

Reflect & Extend

Here are some other ways to show your understanding of the ideas in Unit 2.

Reflect on the **Essential Question**

Are some differences too great to overcome?

Has your answer to the question changed after reading the texts in the unit? Discuss your ideas.

You can use these sentence starters to help you reflect on your learning.

- **I think differently now because . . .**
- **Now that I've considered . . . , I realize . . .**
- **I still wonder about . . .**

Project-Based Learning

Create a Photo Essay

You've read about various ways in which people face differences. Now, create a photo essay to explore this topic.

Here are some questions to ask yourself as you get started.

- What is the purpose of my photo essay?
- What message do I want to convey?
- How will the composition and arrangement of my photos help tell my story?
- How can I use text to enhance my message?

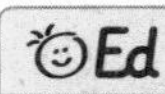

Media Project

To find help with this task online, access **Create a Photo Essay.**

Writing

Research and Report

Throughout history and up to the present day, individuals have inspired entire groups to overcome their differences. Research one person who has helped or is currently helping groups of people bridge their differences. Write a brief report about the individual, including the following information:

- Background of the person and the situation being addressed; goals the person has identified
- The person's methods for bringing groups together
- Results: successes, failures, and continuing efforts

Use a graphic organizer like this one to organize your work. Cite your sources appropriately. Publish your report online or present it to the class.

Inspiring Individual	Methods	Successes? Failures?

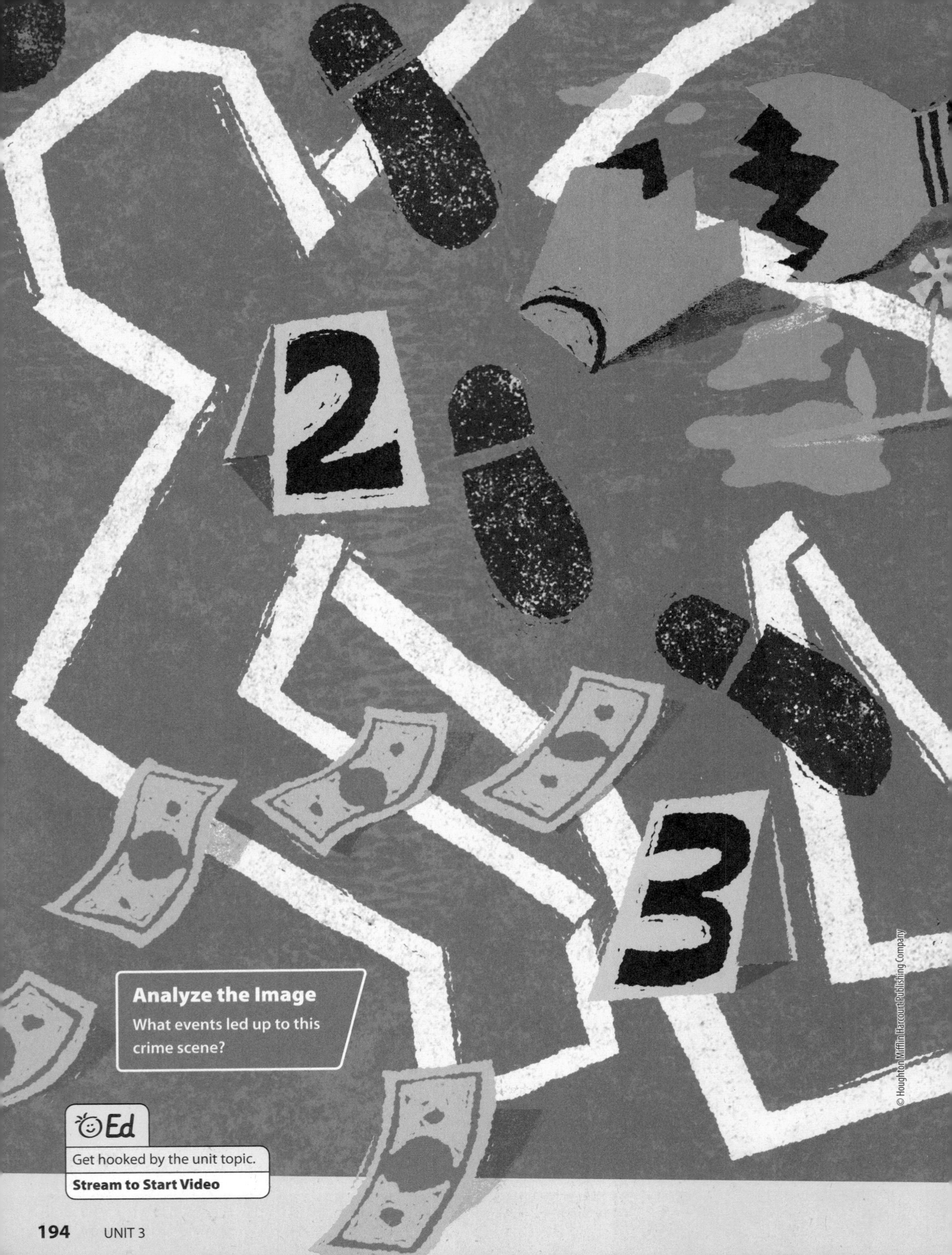

Analyze the Image

What events led up to this crime scene?

Ed

Get hooked by the unit topic.

Stream to Start Video

Crime Scenes

"Crime is terribly revealing . . . . Your tastes, your habits, your attitude of mind, and your soul is revealed by your actions."
— Agatha Christie

ESSENTIAL QUESTION:
Who suffers when a crime is committed?

Spark Your Learning

Here are some opportunities to think about the topics and themes of **Unit 3: Crime Scenes.**

As you read, you can use the **Response Log** (page R3) to track your thinking about the Essential Question.

?

Think About the **Essential Question**

Who suffers when a crime is committed?

List as many possibilities as you can.

Make the Connection

The word *crime* has a negative connotation, but many of us can't get enough of movies, podcasts and stories about true crime. Why do stories about crime capture our imagination? Discuss your ideas with a partner.

Build Academic Vocabulary

You can use these Academic Vocabulary words to write and talk about the topics and themes in the unit. Which of these words do you already feel comfortable using when speaking or writing?

	I can use it!	I understand it.	I'll look it up.
capacity			
confer			
emerge			
generate			
trace			

Prove It!

Imagine you had to defend someone accused of a crime. Use one of the Academic Vocabulary words in a statement arguing for the person's innocence.

Preview the Texts

Look over the images, titles, and descriptions of the texts in the unit. Mark the title of the text that most interests you

Entwined

Short Story by **Brian Tobin**

A fatal collision leads to shocking aftereffects for everyone involved.

Why Are We Obsessed with True Crime?

Informational Text by **Laura Hensley**

Find out why we can't resist true stories about wrongdoing.

from **The 57 Bus**

Literary Nonfiction by **Dashka Slater**

A bad decision shatters the lives of two teenagers.

Gift-Wrapped Fathers

Poem by **Eduardo (Echo) Martinez**

An imprisoned parent struggles to maintain a bond with his son.

Bully

Podcast from **Radiotopia/PRX**

A bully terrorizes a small town until citizens decide they've had enough.

Unsolved "Vigilante" Murder in the Heartland

News Article by **C.M. Frankie**

What are the consequences when someone is cruel to everyone he meets?

Think Outside the Box

Why is it important for someone accused of a crime to be considered innocent until proven guilty? Jot down some of your ideas.

Entwined

Short Story by **Brian Tobin**

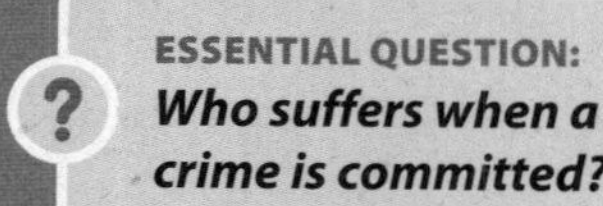

ESSENTIAL QUESTION:
Who suffers when a crime is committed?

Engage Your Brain

Choose one or more of these activities to start connecting with the story you're about to read.

Nothing but the Truth

Is not telling the whole truth ever justifiable?

- Write about a time when you felt that you had a good reason to *not* tell the whole truth.
- Include a description of how the situation turned out.

What Makes It a Crime Story?

Have you read any crime stories or watched shows or movies that focus on crime?

1. Make a list of stories or shows you remember.
2. Compare lists with a partner.
3. Discuss the common features of crime stories.

Crime stories usually have . . .

Exploring a Key Word

Entwine means "to wind or twist together."

- What kind of images does the word "entwined" suggest to you?
- Draw a picture or make some notes.

Analyze Universal Themes

Literature conveys lessons through **themes,** the messages about life or human nature that writers share with readers.

In some stories, the theme is explicit, or stated directly in the text. In most cases, the theme is implicit, or not stated directly. Readers must **infer,** or make an educated guess about, the theme based on clues in the text.

When the theme of the text applies to people across cultures and time periods, or comments on what it means to be human, it's a **universal theme.** For example, many literary works share the theme of an individual's struggle toward understanding.

The chart lists some clues to look for. As you read, fill it out so you can pin down the theme of "Entwined."

Focus on Genre

Short Story

- includes the basic elements of fiction—plot, character, setting, conflict
- creates suspense to maintain readers' interest
- expresses a theme, or message about life

Clues to a Story's Theme	Clues in "Entwined"
The work's title	
What characters say	
Interactions between characters	
Key events	

Analyze Characterization

The way a writer creates and develops characters' personalities is known as **characterization.** Authors develop complex yet believable characters by describing what they do, say, and think, as well as how they interact with other characters. Complex characters advance the plot and shape the story's themes. As you read "Entwined," use a chart to record text details that reveal the main character's personality. Then, make an inference or ask a question about each detail.

Text Evidence	Examples	Inferences and Questions
Character's words and actions		
Character's thoughts and observations		
What others say about the character		
Lessons the main character learns. (Pay close attention to wise words and advice given to the main character.)		

Annotation in Action

Here is an example of notes a student made about this paragraph from "Entwined." As you read, highlight words that reveal the narrator's character traits.

If only I could go back in time and slam the brake pedal, so that nothing more would have happened except Pearl Jam, the orange traffic cones, the young woman in white short shorts, the sound of kids playing.

Narrator takes responsibility for what happened

Expand Your Vocabulary

Put a check mark next to the vocabulary words that you feel comfortable using when speaking or listening.

- **negligent** ☐
- **condolence** ☐
- **empathy** ☐
- **irrevocably** ☐
- **ineffably** ☐
- **liability** ☐

With a partner, write a short description of a crime and its aftermath with as many of the words as you can.

As you read "Entwined," use the definitions in the side column to learn the vocabulary words you don't already know.

Background

Brian Tobin is the author of four novels: *The Ransom, The Missing Person, Below the Line,* and *A Victimless Crime*. In 2015, his short story "Teddy" was nominated for an Edgar Award. He lives in Los Angeles with his wife, Vickie. "Entwined" was inspired by an episode of *This American Life*. "Plotting is usually difficult for me," he said about the story, "involving many false starts and wrong turns. I was listening to *This American Life* during a morning walk. By the time I reached home, I had the story fully formed in my imagination."

Entwined

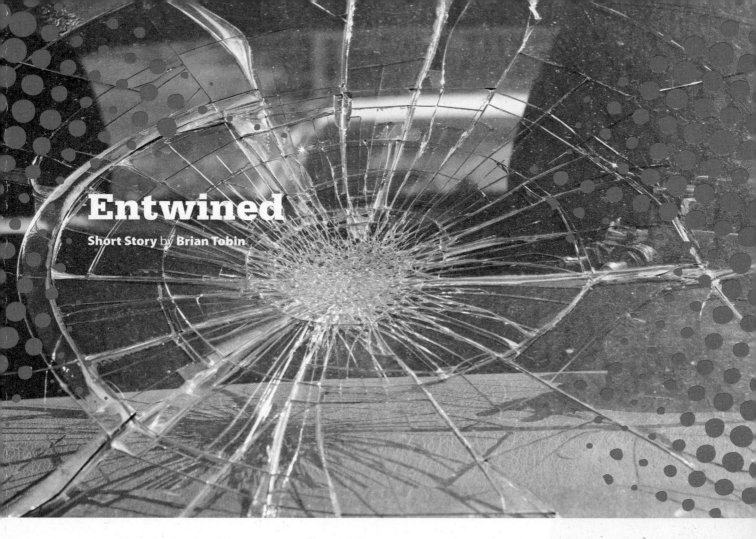

Short Story by Brian Tobin

A fatal collision leads to shocking aftereffects for everyone involved.

NOTICE & NOTE 
As you read, use the side margins to make notes about the text.

1 On September 12, 1994, in my second week of college, I killed Russell Gramercy.

2 In the last eighteen years, how often have I gone over it all? Pearl Jam, the orange traffic cones, the young woman in white short shorts, the sound of kids playing, and then…

3 I had been driving alone back to my dorm from the lake. Despite what people claimed later, I had not been drinking—not one drop. I want to be clear about that. Even though there were coolers full of beer at our blanket, I was not intoxicated. It was about five-thirty on a beautiful balmy afternoon, the last twinge of summer in upstate New York. I wasn't speeding, nor was I driving in a "careless, reckless, or **negligent** manner," which is the criteria for negligent homicide.

negligent
(nĕg´lĭ-jənt) *adj.* characterized by paying little attention to or failing to care for properly.

4 A song I loved, Pearl Jam's "Alive," came on the radio, and I took my hand off the two position of the ten-and-two driving stance I had so recently been taught in driver's ed. I reached down and turned the volume up from loud to *really* loud. I was barely aware of the pedestrians on the sidewalk; they were indistinct, background. Vaguely I registered the sign ROAD WORK AHEAD. However, my registering Daria Gramercy's figure was anything but vague. She was wearing white short shorts; seen from behind, she was breathtaking. This figure of lust (I can't describe it in any nicer way that reflects better on me) was walking with two males. All three had been forced to abandon the sidewalk that paralleled Beach Road because of construction—for fifty yards the sidewalk had been jackhammered and it was cordoned off with orange traffic cones and yellow caution tape. Later, when I went back to the scene, I saw the clearly marked signs that warned pedestrians to cross to the other side of the road, that clearly told them not to walk on the shoulder. Weren't those signs implicit—no, definite—warnings that to proceed was dangerous?

5 At the time, I have to admit, I didn't notice those signs. Even though the radio was blaring "Alive," I could also faintly hear children playing: a Pee Wee League soccer match was just beginning.

6 If only it could have stopped there. If only I could go back in time and slam the brake pedal, so that nothing more would have happened except Pearl Jam, the orange traffic cones, the young woman in white short shorts, the sound of kids playing. Then it all would have just faded, one of millions of trivial sense memories that disappeared.

7 But time didn't stand still.

ANALYZE CHARACTERIZATION

Annotate: In paragraphs 8 and 9, mark the details the narrator describes.

Infer: What can you infer about the narrator from his observations?

8 My car—actually, the 1979 Impala my father had handed down to me—was going around forty miles per hour. I know I lied about it later to the police, telling them that I was doing the posted thirty-five, but I can honestly say I was going about forty. At that speed, a car travels fifty-nine feet a second. (In my support group, *everyone*, every last person regardless of education, has done the calculations, the feet per second, the reaction times.) The three figures on the road outside the cones and caution tape, one with an extremely sexy sashay, were approaching rapidly. (I know they weren't approaching, that in fact I was overtaking them, but that's how it seemed to me.) And then the largest of them, a man in khaki shorts, a navy blue T-shirt, and Chuck Taylor Converse sneakers, stumbled beyond the white line into the road. Into the path of my thirty-five-hundred-pound lethal weapon going fifty-nine feet per second.

9 What happened took only milliseconds. There was a sickening jolt to the car; Russell Gramercy flew up over the hood. His shoulder and head shattered my windshield, then he disappeared over the roof of the Impala. I did not slam on the brakes until he had already landed on the highway behind me.

10 There was a faint whiff of something burnt—my tires on the asphalt—and Pearl Jam was still playing on the radio. Behind me someone was howling in pain and grief. "Oh, my God! Oh, my God!" Daria Gramercy.

Don't forget to **Notice & Note** as you read the text. 

11 Everything seemed in a heightened sense of unreality. I got out of the Impala, but immediately someone yelled, "Hey, put your car in gear." So I got back in the car, which was slowly rolling, and did so, also turning off the engine. I noticed glass on the passenger's side seat; in the next moment I realized that little shards of glass, almost festively decorative, covered my shirt as well.

12 The body lay in the road fifty yards away—I had traveled half a football field *after* hitting him. Another pedestrian stood in the middle of the road behind Daria and the victim, waving a hot-pink beach towel to stop oncoming traffic.

13 Racing back, I thought, He'll have some broken bones. He may have to go to the hospital. Daria was leaning over her father, whimpering.

14 Then I got a clear view of Russell Grammercy's body. This wasn't a case of some broken bones. His entire body was broken. One shoulder and arm were tilted at an impossible angle away from the rest of him. Blood was pooling behind his head, which also seemed . . . broken. Daria said, "Hold on, Dad. Hold on." But it was obvious to me that he could not hear, would never hear again.

15 And . . . I'm not proud of this, but I want to tell you exactly what it was like. Daria, in an attempt to stanch the ever-expanding pool of blood behind her father's head, took off her pale green sleeveless T-shirt and used it to compress the wound. She wore a white bikini top underneath. My eyes were drawn to her chest.

16 I had just killed a man, and I was ogling the daughter I had made an orphan.

17 There was probably a gap of time, but it seems to me now that the police cruiser arrived very quickly with short yelps of the siren and strobing of the Visibar. Walkie-talkies squawked, an ambulance came; someone shifted the cones from the sidewalk construction to the road. Daria was sobbing in the arms of her older brother, Chris. With a start, I realized I knew Chris; I had played baseball against him. Which meant I knew the victim as well.

18 Russell Gramercy was the coach of the Verplanck American Legion League baseball team of which his son, Chris, was the star pitcher. Russell Gramercy was also a chemistry professor at Howland College, the school I had just started two weeks earlier, though I wasn't in any of his classes. The previous year, the American Legion team I was on had played against Verplanck. Chris had been pitching, and he struck me out twice. He was by far the best player in our area, and scouts from the majors as well as LSU and Arizona State had shown interest in him. His father coached him that day, and I remembered Russell Gramercy putting his arm around Chris's shoulder with pride as he came off the field with another victory.

19 "Are you okay?" the paramedic asked me at one point. "Are you injured?"

20 "No, I'm fine," I replied, knowing even then that it was a lie, though there was nothing physically wrong.

21 Later, as the first ambulance took Russell Gramercy away, I asked the same paramedic, "He's going to be okay, isn't he?"

22 He stared back at me, then, masking his true feelings, said, "Well, we can only pray." After that, on instructions from one of the cops, he took my blood for a blood alcohol level test.

23 I gave my statement to three different police officers. The last one, a detective named Dave Pedrosian, interviewed me for a long time.

24 Pedrosian also questioned Chris and Daria. She had not seen the actual impact because she had been walking a few feet in front of her brother and father on the narrow shoulder. "I just heard this awful crunch, and by the time I turned around my dad was landing on the pavement," I overheard her say. And then she lost control and gave loud gasping sobs. Her brother put his arms around her.

25 At some point I also heard Chris being interviewed. "We were walking and my father sort of stumbled. I don't know if he twisted his ankle or what. But he veered into the road. I reached out to grab him, but then . . . just this unbelievable impact with that car . . ."

Don't forget to **Notice & Note** as you read the text.

26 What I remember most were his next words. "The car just slammed him. It was so fast. My dad never had a chance. And neither did the driver. It would have been impossible to react. It wasn't his fault."

27 Right after a cop gave me my second field sobriety test and first Breathalyzer, Chris came up to me. I was wary and I half expected him to take a swing at me. But in a dazed voice he told me, "There was nothing you could have done. Don't beat yourself up. It was just a horrible accident." He turned and walked back to his sister, who glared at me with eyes filled with anger and hate.

28 Detective Pedrosian came by in a while and said, "You're not going to be charged at this time. All the preliminary statements support yours. A collision-reconstruction unit will continue to investigate. If everything holds up, you will not be charged. Your father is here to drive you home."

29 On the ride home, back to my childhood bedroom, not my new dorm room, I kept saying, "It happened so fast. There was nothing I could do."

30 Russell Gramercy was declared DOA at Verplanck Hospital at about that same time.

31 The next few days I spent in my bedroom or, when my parents went to work, roaming the house. I couldn't eat, sleep, watch television. Both my parents kept telling me that it wasn't my fault, that it had been an accident. I shouldn't blame myself.

32 My father initially insisted that I go to the Gramercy family home.

33 "And do what? Upset them more? Apologize for killing their father?" I did not want to face them, in particular Daria.

34 "Just tell them how sorry you are for their loss," my mother replied.

35 I had already put on my suit and was waiting for my parents to drive me to a **condolence** visit that I wasn't sure I could endure when the phone rang. A few minutes later my father came into the living room and said, "We're not going."

condolence
(kən-dō´ləns) *n.* sympathy with a person who has experienced pain, grief, or misfortune.

36 The relief I felt was immense.

37 "Of course we are," my mother said.

38 "The insurance adjuster just called. He said we're not to have any contact with the victim's family."

39 *The victim.* His name was Russell Gramercy. He was a beloved father, a husband, a coach, a teacher. And we weren't using his name. He was the victim. And I was the person who had killed him.

40 "That's just not right," my mother complained.

41 "He's on our insurance policy," my father said, nodding toward me. "We could lose the house, our savings. Everything. Even a frivolous case could cost us hundreds of thousands of dollars."

42 So in the end we didn't go. And I did not apologize.

43 The funeral was private, so I didn't go to that either. But when I returned to Howland College two days later, one of the first things I noticed was a flier about a memorial service.

44 Howland College is a small liberal arts college in Verplanck, New York, twenty miles from my hometown. Its academic reputation is slight, its campus charmless—buildings of red brick and glass, dormitories that look like singles' apartments. In my area it was the ultimate backstop school, the place you wound up when your other scholastic plans didn't pan out.

45 That next weekend hundreds of students milled about in the quad. I was handed a slender white candle that reminded me of fencing foil. People kept glancing my way, it seemed to me with disgust or pity. Right before the service I overheard two students in front of me talking.

46 "I heard the kid who ran over Gramercy goes to school here."

47 "Yeah," his companion replied. "A freshman. Apparently some pathetic loser."

48 Hymns were sung. Speakers came up to a makeshift stage and talked about *Russ* or *Professor G.* It was heartfelt, moving, filled with the inadequate words we use when confronted with death. Some were amazingly articulate, others spoke badly, but their clichés and boilerplate emotions were overlooked because of a collective goodwill and understanding. One person read a poem that somehow felt familiar, and it was only years later that I realized he had cribbed the W. H. Auden work from the movie *Four Weddings and a Funeral.*

49 One speaker stood out for me. "I'm a doctor," he began. "And last week, on the day that Russell died, I saved a life." He went on to recount that if it hadn't been for the extraordinary work of Russell Gramercy, he would never have passed his organic chemistry course, the bane of all premed students. Gramercy had tutored him, made clear the obscure, gone way above and beyond for him. "It's a simple calculus for me. If it wasn't for Professor Gramercy, I wouldn't be a doctor. If I wasn't a doctor, that patient would not have been saved. That spared life, and everything good in it, can be toted up to Russ.

NOTICE & NOTE

WORDS OF THE WISER

When you notice a wiser character giving advice to the main character, you've found a **Words of the Wiser** signpost.

Notice & Note: Mark the insight offered in paragraph 50.

Infer: What life lesson is given here? How might it relate to the story's theme?

50 "There are connections in our lives that we're often not aware of. We're entwined. We intersect, like chains, or strands of DNA."

51 I did not speak at the service.

52 By November I had left college. I eventually moved to New York City; it is a place where not driving a car is the norm. My driver's license expired when I was twenty-one; I did not renew it, nor have I ever driven a car again after that day I killed Professor G.

53 Nightmares plagued me for a decade, though they diminished over time. For years I had to wear an orthodontic device because I ground my teeth in my sleep.

54 In my early twenties I aimlessly worked boring, dead-end jobs. Then, when it became clear that I was not going to resume my education, my father gave me the fifty thousand dollars he claimed he would have spent on tuition. So I started a small business, a frozen-yogurt shop in the West Village that I can walk to. It is a modest success.

55 I never married. Relationships never seemed to survive the moment I had to confess to the accident. The fault for these failed courtships, I'm sure, is mine. For the most part, the women I've been involved with were understanding, compassionate. (Though one woman got so angry that she slapped me.) But no matter the degree of their **empathy**, I always sensed in their eyes a change. In how they viewed me.

empathy
(ĕm´pə-thē) *n.* the ability to identify with or understand the perspective, experiences, or motivations of another individual and to comprehend and share another individual's emotional state.

56 Years ago, at one of my lousy, mind-shriveling jobs, a coworker asked all the people gathered around the break table, "What's the most memorable or important moment of your life?" The answers were predictable: *When I met my husband; When I gave birth to my daughter.* Or humorous: *When I felt up Gina Simmons in sixth grade,* or *It hasn't happened yet, but it will be when I get fired from this job.* When it was my turn, I was set to lie: *It was when the Giants won the Super Bowl.* Instead, I shocked myself by replying, "When I killed a man."

57 There was laughter around the table, and my questioner added, quoting Johnny Cash, "When you shot a man in Reno, just to watch him die?"

58 "Yeah," I answered, relieved. Although I knew that, unlike most people, I actually had a moment in my life that had **irrevocably** changed me.

irrevocably
(ĭ-rĕv´ə-kə-blē) *adv.* in a way that is impossible to retract or revoke.

59 So that was my existence. Constrained, nowhere near having fulfilled a potential. I always thought that there had been more than one victim that day, though I would never say that aloud. And certainly not to the family, not to the woman who had whimpered and sobbed by the side of Beach Road. Nor to her tall, athletic brother, who had once struck me out.

• • •

60 In April 2011 the first body was discovered.

61 Russell Gramercy's widow had sold the lakeside cabin months earlier. In upstate New York, the small vacation homes that dot the many lakes are called camps. The Gramercy camp, sheathed with cedar clapboards, was small, only sixteen by twenty-four, and had a half loft. It had been in the family for generations. Russell Gramercy winterized the structure himself early in his marriage. He liked to go there to unwind, he said, to write academic articles and prepare lessons and presentations. Except for a week or two in the summer when he was accompanied by his family, he went to the camp alone.

62 The new owners had no interest in rustic simplicity or outdoor showers. An architect drew up plans for some garish monstrosity. It was a backhoe operator digging trenches for the McMansion's new septic system that had uncovered the skeleton.

63 (A rumor went around that the new owners, with visions of construction delays and permit problems, tried to talk the construction workers out of reporting the discovery. I'm not sure I believe this. What is true is that they sued the Gramercy family.)

ineffably
(ĭn-ĕf´ə-blē) *adv.* in a way that cannot be expressed; indescribably or unutterably.

64 In the weeks after the grisly find, the police dug up eight other corpses. All but one were identified, and I can reel off the names by memory. I find it **ineffably** sad that the ninth victim could not be named. Had nobody in his short life felt connected enough to report him missing?

65 There were eight male victims and one female. Four of them were runaways. Two were thought to have been hitchhiking, a boyfriend and girlfriend, who had been on their way to a bluegrass festival. One was reported to have been a male hustler at truck stops, though his parents vehemently deny it. But one of the victims had also been a National Merit Scholarship winner. So there didn't really seem to be a pattern except the youth they had all shared.

66 Forensics teams found traces of dried blood inside the cabin. Most of it was too degraded, but one sample proved a DNA match with one of the victims. I've heard that incriminating and very disturbing photos were found, though I don't know for a fact that they exist. But other objects that had belonged to the victims were discovered in a hiding place in the cabin.

ANALYZE UNIVERSAL THEMES

Annotate: Mark the sentences that introduce a major plot event in paragraph 67.

Infer: Why is this discovery significant?

67 The conclusions were inescapable, and a grand jury agreed. The victims had all been murdered by Russell Gramercy. They had been murdered by *Russ*. By *Professor G*. By the man I had killed with my car.

68 On the hottest day of the following summer, my phone rang just as I was about to go to work. "Hi, this is Daria Gramercy. Do you remember me?"

69 Startled, I replied, "Yes, I remember."

70 Your parents gave me your number. I hope I'm not disturbing you," she said uncertainly.

71 "No you're not."

72 “I’d like to talk with you. About the accident and everything. If you don’t mind. I’d prefer in person, but if you’d rather we could do it over the phone.”

73 I had been hoping for and dreading this call for decades. We made plans to meet at a coffeehouse around the corner from her midtown hotel.

74 Daria had changed from the sexy teenager I had encountered briefly one fateful day. She had gained considerable weight, I saw as she entered the Starbucks. And her hair was cut in an unflattering style and frizzy from the equatorial humidity that day. Immediately I felt guilty and somehow disloyal for forming these unkind impressions. Given what she had been through, it was an achievement just to be walking around at all. I searched her eyes for anger or recrimination. My entire body seemed clenched with tension.

75 “Thanks for seeing me,” Daria said, shaking my hand and sitting down. She took a deep breath and seemed set to start a prepared talk.

76 “I want to apologize to you,” I interrupted. “I never did . . . back then.”

77 “You sent a sympathy card,” she replied noncommittally.

78 “I wanted to visit your family, but our legal advisers told us not to. They were afraid of **liability.**” *Legal advisers?* Some insurance company guy and my father’s fraternity brother who was the family lawyer?

79 She nodded. “I understand.”

80 “I wanted to,” I repeated, protesting too much. Then I blurted out, “Actually, that’s not accurate. I was dreading the visit; there was nothing I wanted to do less. When my father told me we couldn’t, it was like I had gotten a reprieve.”

81 Daria gave a knowing sigh. “Believe me, I understand how you felt.”

82 And then I let everything out. I told Daria exactly what I remembered. Everything: my inattention, the lies about my actual speed, my creepy, lascivious stares as she comforted her dying father. I’m not a Catholic, but I imagine it was like the sacrament of confession. “I’m just so very, very sorry,” I ended, and then, to my horror but yet relief, for the first time since the accident I broke down and cried.

83 She gave me a few moments, then said, “It wasn’t your fault. Even with everything you’ve told me, there was nothing you could have done to prevent it. You didn’t have time to react. I understand that.” Daria handed me a tissue.

84 When I had regained my composure, she gave me a rueful smile and said, “Well, you’ve sort of stolen my thunder. The reason I’m here is to apologize to you.”

85 Daria had been going to the families of all her father’s known victims and asking forgiveness. From how she described it, it sounded a bit like making amends in a twelve-step program. “After I had seen all the victims’ families, I knew I also needed to talk with you. My

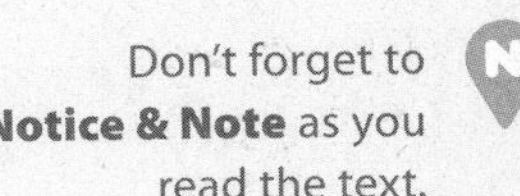

Don’t forget to **Notice & Note** as you read the text.

liability
(lī-ə-bĭl′ĭ-tē) *n.* the state of being legally obligated or responsible.

ANALYZE CHARACTERIZATION

Annotate: Mark what the narrator says to Daria in paragraph 80.

Infer: What does this tell you about the narrator’s character?

father caused so much pain and horror. If I can do anything to lessen that legacy, then I want to."

86 We talked for a while. For years I had imagined just this, I told her. In my daydreams I had talked with her: I had explained, I had been succored. And remarkably, something like those fantasies had just happened.

87 Near the end of our conversation, I asked, "How is your brother, Chris?"

88 She was momentarily taken aback. "Oh, I thought you knew," Daria said uncomfortably. "Chris died in 2004."

89 "I'm so sorry," I replied, mortified. "How?"

90 "A traffic accident."

91 I flinched.

92 "He was living in Arizona. It was a one-car accident, late at night. Alcohol was involved."

93 I must have seemed shaken.

94 "It had nothing to do with you," Daria said. "Believe me. If you're tempted to see this as some sort of delayed collateral damage from what you did, don't. My brother had his own demons."

95 We were silent a moment, then I said, "I went to the memorial service for your dad at Howland. The one speaker I remember most was a former student who your father helped become a doctor. And what he said was that our lives are inexplicably entwined. That many of the good things that the doctor had done could be added up in your father's column in this sort of cosmic ledger. I thought about that when I heard about the . . . incidents."

ANALYZE UNIVERSAL THEMES

Annotate: Mark the sentences in paragraphs 96–98 that describe how the actions of characters intersected or affected one another.

Interpret: How might these passages reveal the story's theme, or message about life?

96 "You thought that by killing my dad," she said gently, "even though inadvertently, you had saved other young people from being brutally slaughtered . . . Let's call it what it is."

97 "Once again, it's not something I'm real proud of. But yeah."

98 "I understand. More completely than you'll know. And I think you're right. I think what happened that day did spare others from my father's . . . evil."

99 We stared at one another for a moment, then she stood. There ensued one of the most awkward hugs in the history of farewells. Then she went out into the street and disappeared.

• • •

100 I discovered the tape by a fluke.

101 For the first time in years' I returned to Verplanck. A cousin was getting married. At the rehearsal party at my aunt's house, a bunch of my younger cousins were watching videos of their childhood in the family room. I was barely paying attention: the charms of children mugging for the camera is quickly lost if you're not the one doing the mugging.

102 "Oh, let me show you this one of Barry playing soccer," the brother of the groom said to the bride. "He falls right on his face."

103 Suddenly my aunt strode into the room from the kitchen and said, "Tim, that's enough of the videos." Her tone was brusque.

104 Tim seemed confused. "What?"

105 Flustered, my aunt said more insistently, "I asked you to do something. Turn off the TV. Not *all* our guests may be as enthralled as you."

106 Her last words seemed to have some special meaning, one that her son belatedly understood.

107 "Okay, Mom, sorry." He darted a glance my way, then looked away, embarrassed.

108 It was only an hour later that it clicked. I took my aunt aside and asked. "That videotape of Barry playing soccer. It was taken that day, wasn't it?"

109 Pained, she sighed. "I'm sorry. Tim just wasn't thinking. I could smack him sometimes."

110 "I'm not upset," I assured her. "But I'd like to see that tape. Not now, not this weekend."

111 I returned to New York with the DVD transfer of the VHS tape. It was in my DVD player even before I had taken off my coat.

112 Seven-year-olds are playing soccer. *Way to go, Kyle. Way to go*, some woman keeps calling out. Another faint but discernible conversation is a woman telling a friend about what a jerk her boss is. And then.

113 A small *thunk*. The tinny sound of screeching brakes. *Oh, my God, did you see that?*

114 The first time I watched the tape, I didn't really notice the accident at all. But on the second, I could see the tiny figures in the upper left corner of the frame. Pedestrians walking, a hazy blue car approaching. Then one of those figures flying high into the air, over the car. One detail, however, didn't quite fit.

115 Obsessively, I watched the tape over and over, at times my face just inches from the screen. And every time I thought I saw that troubling blur.

116 You can find almost anything on the Internet. Two days later I was in Irving Beckstein's workshop in Astoria, Queens. Beckstein is a forensic video analyst. He has worked for the Defense Department and often testifies as an expert witness at trials.

VOCABULARY

Context Clues: The word *brusque* in paragraph 103 is surrounded by other words in paragraphs 103–105 that can help you determine its meaning.

Analyze: Why does the narrator's aunt use this tone?

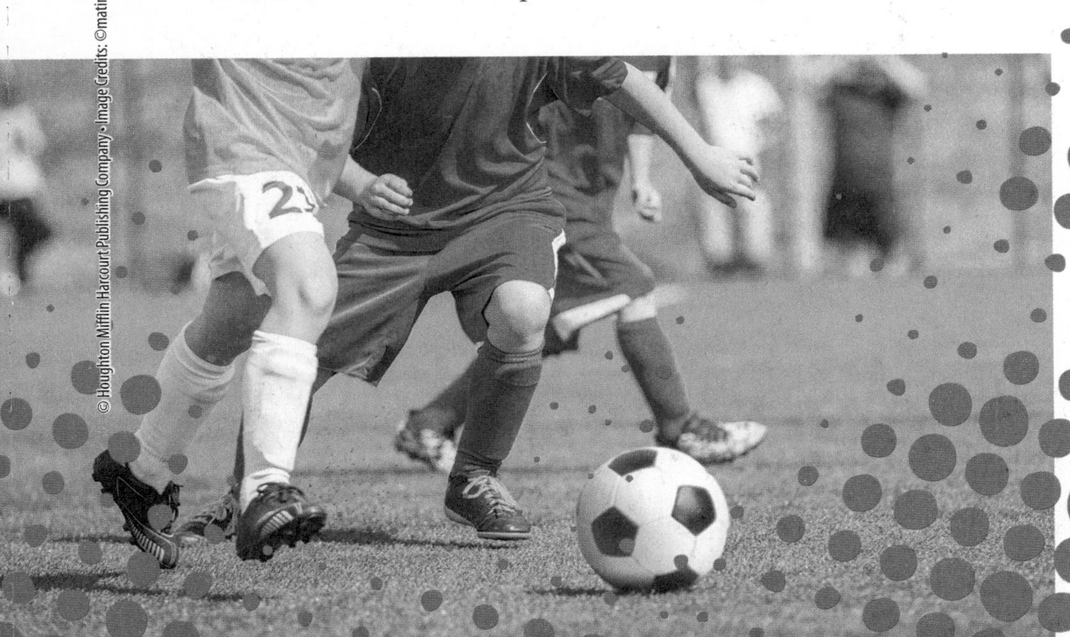

NOTICE & NOTE
AHA MOMENT

When you notice a sudden realization that shifts a character's actions or understanding, you've found an **Aha Moment** signpost.

Notice & Note: Mark text in paragraph 118 that describes an important realization by the narrator.

Infer: How might this realization change the narrator's feelings or behavior?

ANALYZE UNIVERSAL THEMES

Annotate: Mark what the police officer says about guilt in paragraph 119.

Analyze: How does his comment suggest a universal theme?

117 Beckstein had cropped and blown up the footage of the accident. "Forget what you see on TV. Our software can't miraculously sharpen an image so it looks like a thirty-five-millimeter movie. But we can do quite a bit." He went on to explain what he had done. His words seemed well burnished, as if he had given them many times in front of juries.

118 Then he played the images for me on a large, sixty-inch monitor. Though heavily pixilated, it showed Chris Gramercy shoving his father into the path of my oncoming car.

• • •

119 Over the years I've attended a number of support groups. Most of the people there are like me: someone who has caused a fatal accident. Most have not been charged because it was determined that they were not at fault. That it was all a tragic accident. A few of the group members had slightly different stories. One was a police officer who had been involved in a suicide-by-cop incident. Another was a train engineer who ran over and decapitated a suicidal man who had just been diagnosed with Alzheimer's who threw himself in front of his train. You would think that they would somehow feel less guilty. But they didn't. Maybe, the cop said, it was because it brought home how vulnerable, how much at the mercy of unseen forces, we all are.

120 As far as I know, no member of the groups ever was an unknowing instrument of a murderer. Except me.

121 I did nothing with the information I discovered from the tape. But a month ago Daria Gramercy called me late at night.

122 "I've been thinking about you," she said after apologizing for calling. "I somehow feel that we have unfinished business."

123 "And why is that?" I asked carefully.

124 "I have nothing definite to go on, but my brother may have been more involved in the accident."

125 "How?"

126 "I really don't know. It was just this impression . . . After the accident, Chris was never really the same."

127 "Were any of us?"

128 "I remember times when he was drunk—and he was drunk a lot near the end. He kept coming back to one theme. Was it ever justified to kill someone? Stupid stuff about would you go back in time to kill Hitler. Would I kill my husband to protect my children?" She sighed, then added plaintively, "My husband is the kindest, gentlest man in the world."

129 There was a long silence on the line, then I heard, "When everything came out about my father, Chris's words gained a different meaning."

130 "I'm not sure I follow," I said, though of course I did. "Are you saying that Chris somehow caused your father to fall in front of my car?"

131 "I don't know what I mean," she wailed. "I hope to God that's not what happened. But I thought you had the right to know."

132 I considered what she had told me, then said, "I really appreciate your calling me. And your contacting me has helped me in countless ways, so I'm grateful to you. But I can tell you definitely that your brother did not cause your father's death. I could clearly see them both, and Chris was a good two or three feet away from him. Your father stumbled. That image is etched in my mind permanently."

133 I heard her crying softly and then, "Thank you."

134 Did I do the right thing? I like to think I did, but who knows?

135 The nightmares and my obsessive thoughts about that day have lessened. I don't know. Maybe I'm getting better.

?

ESSENTIAL QUESTION:
Who suffers when a crime is committed?

Review your notes and add your thoughts to your Response Log.

COLLABORATIVE DISCUSSION

Get together with a partner and talk about whether the narrator did the right thing by not telling Daria what he knew about Chris.

Assessment Practice

Answer these questions before moving on to the **Analyze the Text** section on the following page.

1. What do we never learn about the narrator?

- (A) his name
- (B) whether the accident was his fault or not
- (C) why he didn't go to the funeral
- (D) whether he was speeding or not

2. What does the family video reveal?

- (A) the narrator not paying attention when he hits the professor
- (B) Chris Gramercy pushing his father in front of the car
- (C) the professor purposefully diving in front of the car
- (D) Daria warning her father before the narrator hits the professor

3. Which detail best expresses why Professor Gramercy's crimes are so shocking?

- (A) He was involved in community activities.
- (B) His students felt he went above and beyond for them.
- (C) He often went to his family's cabin alone.
- (D) His son was troubled.

Test-Taking Strategies

Analyze the Text

Support your responses with evidence from the text.

NOTICE & NOTE

Review what you **noticed and noted** as you read the text. Your annotations can help you answer these questions.

1. **ANALYZE** From what point of view is this story told? Why do you think the writer decided to tell it from this point of view?

2. **INFER** How would you characterize the narrator? Refer to the graphic organizer you filled out as you read the story. Mark the evidence you found that reveals the narrator's character traits. Then, summarize your inferences in the last box of this chart.

Text Evidence	Examples	Inferences and Questions
Character's words and actions		
Character's thoughts and observations		
What others say about the character		
My inferences about the narrator's character traits:		

3. **INTERPRET** Why does the author describe the lives of the Gramercys in great detail in paragraphs 18 and 49 before revealing the shocking truths later in the story?

4. **COMPARE** Reread paragraphs 53–56. Then, reread paragraphs 96–98. How do the narrator's feelings about the accident change throughout the story? Cite evidence from the text to support your answer.

5. **INTERPRET** Think about what the main character realizes during the **Aha Moment** in paragraphs 117–118. What does he do with this information when Daria calls him at the end of the story?

6. **CRITIQUE** Do you think the author has created a complex character in the narrator? Is he a believable character? Explain.

7. **EVALUATE** What is the theme of this story?

- Review the chart you filled out on the Get Ready page.
- Think about how the **Words of the Wiser** in paragraph 50 as well as the comments in paragraphs 96 and 119 help reveal the theme.
- Write a theme statement. Is the theme a universal one?

Choices

Here are some other ways to demonstrate your understanding of the ideas in this lesson.

Social & Emotional Learning

↳ Advice Column

Before the truth about Russell Gramercy comes out, the narrator of "Entwined" is unable to develop his career or relationships because he feels guilty about the car accident. Suppose you are an advice columnist, and you have received a letter from him. Write a column in which you offer suggestions for how he can better cope with this painful experience in his past. Consider

- the extent of the narrator's responsibility for causing the accident
- the narrator's thoughts about why he should feel guilty or ashamed
- how other characters view his role in the accident

As you write and discuss, be sure to use the **Academic Vocabulary** words.

capacity

confer

emerge

generate

trace

Writing

↳ Discussion: Good vs. Evil

In a small group, discuss whether good acts can offset, or cancel out, evil acts, and vice versa.

Before you meet:

- Decide what you think the story says about the question.
- Outline thoughts, feelings, and experiences you want to share.

During your discussion, listen and respond thoughtfully to others' opinions.

Speaking & Listening

↳ Debate

Participate in a small-group or whole-class debate in which you discuss whether the narrator was right to lie to Daria at the end of the story.

- Make notes about examples of cases in which it's either acceptable or unacceptable to lie.
- Establish rules for speaking. Will speakers go in order? When will the rest of the group be able to respond to a speaker's points?
- Hold the discussion with your panel. State your ideas, and listen and respond to the ideas and opinions of others.

Expand Your Vocabulary

PRACTICE AND APPLY

Answer the questions to show your understanding of the vocabulary words. Use a dictionary or thesaurus as needed.

negligent	empathy	ineffably
condolence	irrevocably	liability

1. If I am **negligent,** am I responsible or irresponsible? Why?
2. Which would be a **condolence:** laughing at someone or sending them flowers? Why?
3. If an action is taken **irrevocably,** can it be reversed, or is it permanent? Why?
4. Which would be more of a **liability:** buying a coffee or buying a phone? Why?
5. If I show **empathy,** am I being compassionate or rude? Why?
6. Which would show **ineffable** sadness: sitting in silence or crying loudly? Why?

Vocabulary Strategy

↳ Context Clues

When you read, you can use **context clues** to understand unfamiliar words. **Context** is how a word relates to the overall meaning of a sentence, paragraph, or piece of writing.

Ed

Interactive Vocabulary Lesson: Using Context Clues

Here are some types of context clues you may find in texts:

Synonyms or Definitions	Contrast	Examples
The text may provide a definition or a synonym.	The text may give an antonym, or contrasting information.	The text may list examples of the word.

PRACTICE AND APPLY

Locate these words in the story: *sobriety* (paragraph 27), *rueful* (paragraph 84), and *discernible* (paragraph 112).

Then use context clues to write definitions for each word. Check your definitions in a dictionary.

Watch Your Language!

Colons

Writers use colons to add clarity and structure to their writing. The primary function of a colon is to introduce an element or a series of elements that elaborate on what came before the colon.

"I'm having my colon checked."

Use of a Colon	Examples from "Entwined"
This example is one of the simpler uses of the colon: to provide an example of something.	Most of the people there are like me: someone who has caused a fatal accident.
In this passage, the writer uses three colons to do the same thing: to provide quotations or examples that elaborate on his statements.	The answers were predictable: *When I met my husband; When I gave birth to my daughter.* Or humorous: *When I felt up Gina Simmons in sixth grade,* or *It hasn't happened yet, but it will be when I get fired from this job.* When it was my turn, I was set to lie: *It was when the Giants won the Super Bowl.*
Colons can also be used like semicolons to connect two independent clauses. This is a stylistic choice. He could have made these separate sentences.	Even though the radio was blaring "Alive," I could also faintly hear children playing: *a Pee Wee League soccer match was just beginning.*

When an independent clause follows a colon, should that clause begin with a capital letter? Experts disagree. If your assignment is to follow a certain style (for example, APA, MLA, *The Chicago Manual of Style*), be sure to look up the rule in that style manual.

Interactive Grammar Lesson: Colons

PRACTICE AND APPLY

Write two paragraphs summarizing the main events in "Entwined." Use colons in at least three places. At least one colon should introduce a list, and one should introduce a quotation or an independent clause.

Get Ready

MENTOR TEXT

Why Are We Obsessed with True Crime?

Informational Text by **Laura Hensley**

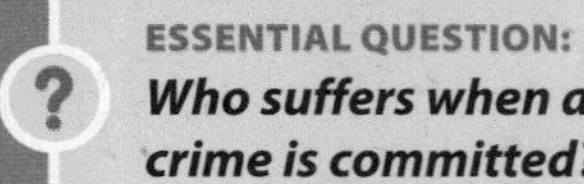

ESSENTIAL QUESTION:
Who suffers when a crime is committed?

Engage Your Brain

Choose one or more of these activities to start connecting with the text you're about to read.

I Couldn't Look Away

Sometimes we are fascinated by events that may trouble others. For example, media photos of organized-crime murders may rivet us. Make a list of other troubling events that may grip our attention.

NPR's *Serial*

Look up this popular podcast and scroll through the different seasons and episodes. Which one seems most interesting to you? Compare your ideas with a partner.

Crime—On Screen & In Print

Think of the games, shows, books, and movies dedicated to crime stories. With a partner, list or draw at least three examples you are familiar with.

Analyze Main Idea and Details

Writers of informational text often use main ideas and details to organize their writing. **Main ideas** are the most important concepts the writer wants readers to understand. **Details** are facts, reasons, and examples that support or explain the main ideas. The headings in a text often provide clues to the main ideas. Use the chart to note main ideas and details you identify in each section of "Why Are We Obsessed with True Crime?"

Focus on Genre
Informational Text

- conveys factual information about real people, places, and events
- supports ideas with evidence, such as quotations from experts
- must be evaluated for accuracy and completeness

Section Heading	Main Idea of Section	Key Details
Why are we obsessed with true crime?		
People feel like detectives		
But how does true crime affect our well-being?		
What about emotional health?		
When to tune out		

Summarize and Paraphrase Texts

When you **summarize** a text, you tell the writer's main ideas and leave out most of the details. When you **paraphrase** a text, you retell it using different words, but you include both the main ideas and the details from the writer's work. In both cases, you avoid adding your own opinions.

Summarizing and paraphrasing are good ways to check your understanding of what you have read. They are also useful when you want to cite another writer's facts or ideas in your own writing. However, you must be careful not to plagiarize, or use the other writer's phrasing as if it were your own. The chart below shows an example.

Original Sentence	"People have always been interested in true crime, but now that the genre is having a moment, public interest has soared."
Plagiarized Sentence	People have always liked true crime, but interest has soared in this time when the genre is having a moment.
Paraphrase	Hensley notes that since true crime is everywhere now—in TV series, podcasts, and books—more people are interested in the genre than ever before.

Annotation in Action

Here is an example of notes a student made about the opening paragraphs of "Why Are We Obsessed with True Crime?" As you read, mark main ideas in each section of the article and several details that support each one.

> If you're a fan of true crime, chances are you'll be binge-watching this year's latest series.
>
> But before you devour the latest crime shows, you might want to consider how consuming hours of disturbing content is affecting you—and why you can't stop watching it.
>
> *could be two main ideas of article*

Expand Your Vocabulary

Put a check mark next to the vocabulary words that you feel comfortable using when speaking or listening.

emulate	☐
reputable	☐
petition	☐
exonerate	☐
visceral	☐
normalize	☐

Turn to a partner and talk about the vocabulary words you already know. Then, write a brief news bulletin about a real or imaginary crime story, using as many of the vocabulary words as you can.

As you read the selection, use the definitions in the side column to learn the vocabulary words you don't already know.

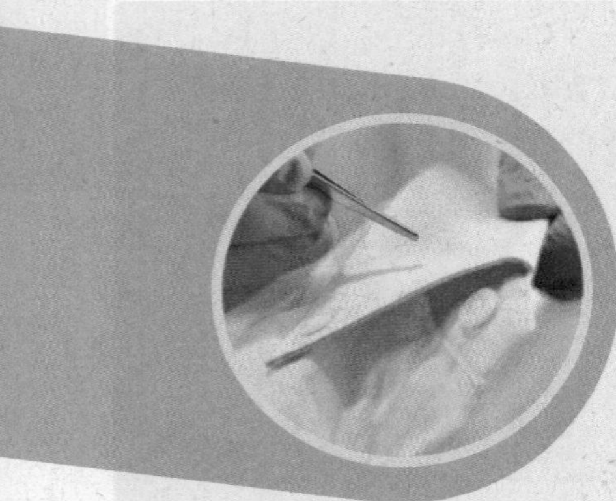

Background

Laura Hensley is a lifestyle reporter based in Toronto, Ontario, Canada. With degrees in fashion communication and journalism, she writes about a range of topics that include pop culture, health, and women's issues. She enjoys watching documentaries and traveling for both work and pleasure.

Why Are We Obsessed with True Crime?

Informational Text by **Laura Hensley**

Find out why we can't resist true stories about wrongdoing.

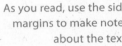

NOTICE & NOTE
As you read, use the side margins to make notes about the text.

1 If you're a fan of true crime, chances are you'll be binge-watching this year's latest series.

2 But before you devour the latest crime shows, you might want to consider how consuming hours of disturbing content is affecting you—and why you can't stop watching it.

3 "Bingeing true crime is not that much different from people watching a 24-hour news cycle covering a killing spree or a terrorist attack," said Jooyoung Lee, an associate professor of sociology at the University of Toronto.

4 "I think human beings, in general, are just drawn to extreme cases of violence. And when I say drawn to them, I don't mean that they watch something and hope to **emulate** it; there's just this fascination."

SUMMARIZE AND PARAPHRASE TEXTS

Annotate: Mark the exact words spoken by Jooyoung Lee in paragraph 4.

Interpret: Write a paraphrase of Lee's statement.

emulate
(ĕm´yə-lāt) *v.* to imitate in order to equal or to excel.

Why are we obsessed with true crime?

5 People have always been interested in true crime, but now that the genre is having a moment, public interest has soared.

6 Lee said that in the past, crime shows like *America's Most Wanted* and *Unsolved Mysteries* were seen as "tabloid television for crime junkies." Low-budget re-enactments and low production quality made the genre seem less **reputable**.

reputable
(rĕp´yə-tə-bəl) *adj.* having a good reputation; honorable.

7 But since the birth of NPR's wildly popular 2014 podcast *Serial*, the way people view true crime has changed.

8 "It was a flagship moment for the genre," Lee said of *Serial*'s success. "It sort of signalled to the larger world that you can do [true crime] in a smart way, in a way that conveyed lots of thought, and in a way that was captivating for an audience."

9 Since then, with the advent of on-demand TV options, viewers can watch an entire series in one go.

10 But why do we have this fascination with the dark side of humanity? One reason is that we're curious—especially when it comes to out-of-the-ordinary events.

11 "A good example would be a car accident," Lee said. "When you're driving on the [highway] and see a pile-up and a bunch of wreckage . . . you have this kind of curiosity as to what happened, even though you know in all likelihood, it's a really tragic story."

12 Another reason? Crime seems exciting—even if it's dark. The suspense when we don't know what's going to happen next, or being shocked by an unexpected turn, are tactics that hold our attention.

13 "The average viewer or the average reader is somebody who is intensely compelled and curious about what happened because, in a very [basic] way, it's exciting . . . and it's also entertaining," Lee said. "It's the same reason why we watch fights or tune into boxing matches."

ANALYZE MAIN IDEA AND DETAILS

Annotate: Mark the main idea of the section "People feel like detectives" (paragraphs 14–17). Then mark several details that support the main idea.

Evaluate: Has the writer provided enough details to support her main idea in this section? Explain.

People feel like detectives

14 Plus, Lee said that consuming real-life horror often makes people feel like they're part of the story. Looking for clues in a murder show or falling down an internet rabbit hole digging into a case gives people a sense of purpose outside of being a consumer.

15 After *Making a Murderer* came out, many viewers who believed convicted killers Steven Avery and Brendan Dassey were innocent formed support groups and began **petitioning** for their release.

petition
(pə-tĭsh´ən) *v.* to make a formal request, usually in writing.

16 "*Serial* and shows like *The Jinx* empower the audience in some way—even if it's not really empowering—but they give the illusion of empowerment because people at home are in this position where they feel like they can help crack the case, and are an active part of the investigation," Lee said.

17 "People think that they can help overturn a ruling, **exonerate** a person, or crack a cold case. That's exciting to people."

exonerate
(ĭg-zŏn´ə-rāt) *v.* to free from blame.

Don't forget to **Notice & Note** as you read the text. 

But how does true crime affect our well-being?

18 Even if you're a huge fan of the genre, you've likely experienced some side effects after watching a show or reading a scary book, like trouble falling asleep or nightmares. Disturbing content, after all, can affect your emotional well-being.

19 "Everybody is different," Lee explained. "Any time you're exposing yourself to extreme violence, you always run the risk of potentially traumatizing yourself. People have to be aware of that, and listen to their body's reactions to these kinds of series."

20 A 2014 study led by researchers at Mount Sinai in New York found that violent movies affect people's brains differently. The study found that people who are more aggressive were "less upset or nervous than non-aggressive participants" when watching violent content.

21 This could help explain why some people are more disturbed than others when it comes to true crime.

22 Still, Lee said many of us have a "**visceral** reaction to violence," which is why we are so captivated by the nature of true crime narratives.

visceral
(vĭs´ər-əl) *adj.* arising from sudden emotion rather than from thought.

23 "It signals the fight or flight response," he said. "Your heart rate quickens, [but] you feel compelled to keep watching."

What about our emotional health?

24 While we may have a hard time turning away, watching dark shows can also desensitize us, Lee said. He pointed out that over-consuming content that depicts violence—especially against women—runs the risk of **normalizing** crime.

normalize
(nôr´mə-līz) *v.* to cause something previously regarded as abnormal to be accepted as normal.

25 "It's this double-edged sword where on one hand, [true-crime shows] raise awareness about a serial killer like Ted Bundy[1] who

[1] **Ted Bundy:** American serial killer who murdered dozens of girls and young women in the 1970s.

SUMMARIZE AND PARAPHRASE TEXTS

Annotate: Mark words that indicate the main idea of paragraphs 24–25.

Summarize: Write a sentence that summarizes these two paragraphs.

targeted young women. But on the other hand . . . when we are so used to consuming these images, when lesser forms of violence occur, it doesn't bother us in the same way because we've seen the most extreme examples."

26 Lee said that some true-crime series also put an emphasis on the criminal, and pay less attention to victims or their families. This can cause people to "romanticize" a killer, for example, and not consider the communities affected by these crimes.

When to tune out

27 While there's nothing wrong with watching true-crime shows or reading books on gruesome events, it's important to know when to stop and take a break. If you're emotionally feeling unwell or having troubles functioning as usual, you may benefit from a breather.

28 "Now, you can go really deep into a series and consume seven, eight hours in a row on a topic that has a potentially negative impact on your mental health," he said.

29 "People have to understand their own limits, and know that if they're good after watching an episode or two, then that's how they should leave it."

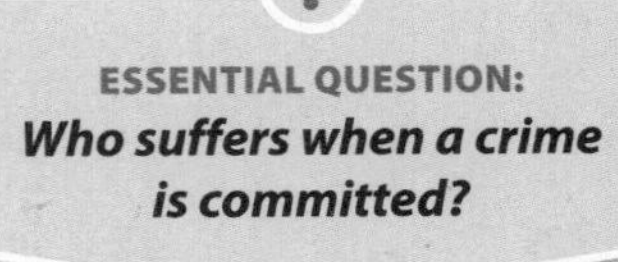

ESSENTIAL QUESTION:
Who suffers when a crime is committed?

Review your notes and add your thoughts to your Response Log.

COLLABORATIVE DISCUSSION

Why do people like to watch and listen to true crime stories?

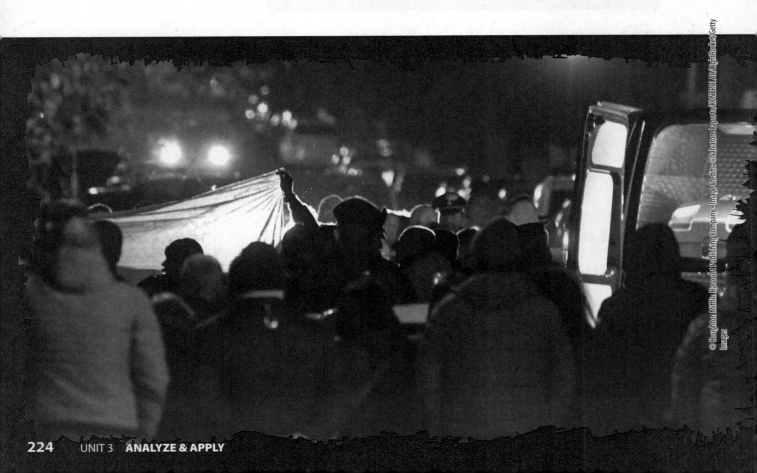

Assessment Practice

Answer these questions before moving on to the **Analyze the Text** section on the following page.

1. In what way are today's true-crime stories different from those of the past?

(A) They are produced more cheaply and sloppily.

(B) They are available in many forms and media.

(C) They focus on the dark side of human nature.

(D) They feature events that are out of the ordinary.

2. This question has two parts. First, answer **Part A**. Then, answer **Part B**.

Part A

What is one possible negative effect of true crime stories?

(A) People feel like part of the investigation and try to crack the case.

(B) People are fascinated with violence even if they don't imitate it.

(C) People can be traumatized physically and emotionally.

(D) People may binge-watch an entire true-crime series.

Part B

Select **two** sentences that provide relevant support for the answer in Part A.

(A) "'I think human beings, in general, are just drawn to extreme cases of violence.'" (paragraph 4)

(B) "The suspense when we don't know what's going to happen next, or being shocked by an unexpected turn, are tactics that hold our attention." (paragraph 12)

(C) "After *Making a Murderer* came out, many viewers who believed convicted killers Steven Avery and Brendan Dassey were innocent formed support groups and began petitioning for their release." (paragraph 15)

(D) "Even if you're a huge fan of the genre, you've likely experienced some side effects after watching a show or reading a scary book, like trouble falling asleep or nightmares." (paragraph 18)

(E) "'When we are so used to consuming these images, when lesser forms of violence occur, it doesn't bother us in the same way because we've seen the most extreme examples.'" (paragraph 25)

Ed

Test-Taking Strategies

Analyze the Text

Support your responses with evidence from the text.

NOTICE & NOTE

Review what you **noticed and noted** as you read the text. Your annotations can help you answer these questions.

1. **COMPARE** How is binge-watching a fictional true-crime series on TV similar to following news coverage of a real violent crime?

2. **CITE EVIDENCE** Review the notes you took in the chart on page 219. State the main idea of the section "Why are we obsessed with true crime?" What are two details that support this main idea?

3. **ANALYZE** An **analogy** is a comparison between two things that are alike in some way. How does the analogy of the car accident in paragraph 11 develop the main idea of this section (paragraphs 5–13)?

4. **INFER** Find the quoted words in paragraph 8. Why did the writer quote from this source, and what idea does the quotation support?

5. **INTERPRET** Read Jooyoung Lee's quotation in the chart below. Paraphrase his statement in your own words, and then write a one-sentence summary of his statement.

Quotation: "It's this double-edged sword where on one hand, [true-crime shows] raise awareness about a serial killer like Ted Bundy who targeted young women. But on the other hand . . . when we are so used to consuming these images, when lesser forms of violence occur, it doesn't bother us in the same way because we've seen the most extreme examples." (paragraph 25)	
Paraphrase	**Summary**

6. **EVALUATE** Is the entertainment value of true-crime stories worth the negative effects people may experience from consuming violent content? Explain your response.

Choices

Here are some other ways to demonstrate your understanding of the ideas in this lesson.

Writing

↳ Script a Scary Scene

The author of "Why Are We Obsessed with True Crime?" explains that people like to be in suspense when viewing or listening to something. Script a suspenseful short scene about a crime—imagined or real. It doesn't have to be violent or gruesome, but it should be mysterious and keep your audience at the edge of their seats!

As you write and discuss, be sure to use the **Academic Vocabulary** words.

- capacity
- confer
- emerge
- generate
- trace

Media

↳ Anatomy of a Crime Show

View or listen to a show or podcast about crime. Take notes about the episode and how it kept you engaged.

- What was the topic?
- What details were included?
- What techniques were used to create mystery or build suspense?
- Were other voices included—eyewitnesses, experts, victims?

Share your notes with a partner.

Speaking & Listening

↳ True-Crime Bingeing: Thumbs Up or Down?

Reread the paragraphs about how true crime affects our well-being. Do you think young adults should watch or listen to true crime? Draft an argument to share with a small group.

1. Outline your argument.
2. Include specific examples.
3. Acknowledge and address opposing points of view.

Expand Your Vocabulary

PRACTICE AND APPLY

To show your understanding of the boldfaced vocabulary words, answer each question. Then, explain your response.

1. Which of the following would you be more likely to **emulate:** a classmate who is always in trouble, or an athlete who shows good sportsmanship? Why?
2. Which of the following is more **reputable:** a tutor who helps you write a good essay, or a website that offers essays for sale? Why?
3. Which of the following might you **petition** to change: your relationship with a friend, or a school rule? Why?
4. Which kind of person might you try to **exonerate:** a famous serial killer, or a person wrongly convicted of a crime? Why?
5. Which of the following would cause a **visceral** response: being asked a complex question, or seeing an animal hit by a car? Why?
6. Which kinds of behaviors would most people want to **normalize:** kind and respectful, or dishonest and unreliable? Why?

Vocabulary Strategy

↳ Verify Word Meanings

When you encounter an unfamiliar word, you can use context clues and your own knowledge to guess what it means. Then you can verify its meaning in a dictionary or other reference source. Follow these steps:

- Examine the word. Is it a version of a word you know? Check to see if any parts of the word—prefix, base word, root, suffix—are familiar to you. Considering the etymology, or derivation of a word, can help you understand the word as well as the phrase it appears in.
- Look for context clues in the surrounding text.
- Guess what the word means. Then look it up in a dictionary.
- If the dictionary entry lists several definitions, select the one that fits the context.

PRACTICE AND APPLY

Locate each boldfaced word below in the text. Apply the steps above. Write both your definition and the one you verify in a dictionary.

Interactive Vocabulary Lesson: Using Reference Sources

1. "an associate professor of **sociology**" (paragraph 3)
2. "low-budget **re-enactments**" (paragraph 6)
3. "**captivating** for an audience" (paragraph 8)
4. "in all **likelihood**" (paragraph 11)

Watch Your Language!

Adjective and Adverb Phrases

A **phrase** is a group of related words that does not contain a subject and predicate but functions in a sentence as a single part of speech. An **adjective phrase** functions as an adjective by modifying a noun or pronoun. An **adverb phrase** functions as an adverb by modifying a verb, an adjective, or an adverb.

The examples in the chart show how Laura Hensley and Jooyoung Lee used both adjective and adverb phrases to add variety and detail in "Why Are We Obsessed with True Crime?"

Interactive Grammar Lesson: Adjective Phrases and Adverb Phrases

Examples	Explanations
"Bingeing true crime is not that much different from people watching a 24-hour news cycle covering a killing spree or a terrorist attack."	This participial phrase is an adjective phrase—it modifies the noun *news cycle*. The phrase explains exactly what kind of news cycle is similar to binge-watching a true-crime series.
Lee said that in the past, crime shows like *America's Most Wanted* and *Unsolved Mysteries* were seen as "tabloid television for crime junkies."	This prepositional phrase is an adjective phrase that modifies the noun *crime shows*. By giving specific examples, the writer connects with readers' prior knowledge of crime shows.
"*Serial* and shows like *The Jinx* empower the audience in some way—even if it's not really empowering—but they give the illusion of empowerment. . . ."	This prepositional phrase is an adverb phrase—it modifies the verb *empower*. The phrase helps emphasize the point that viewers are not literally empowered but feel as if they are.
"People have to understand their own limits, and know that if they're good after watching an episode or two, then that's how they should leave it."	This prepositional phrase is an adverb phrase that modifies the adjective *good*. It gives a concrete example of when a viewer might be ready to take a break from consuming true crime.

PRACTICE AND APPLY

Review the news bulletin about a real or imaginary crime story that you wrote for Expand Your Vocabulary on the Get Ready page, or another recent piece of writing. Look for places where you could insert phrases to add detail and interest to your writing. Include at least one adjective phrase and one adverb phrase. Then share your work with a partner to discuss how the added phrases affect the clarity or effectiveness of your writing.

ESSENTIAL QUESTION:
Who suffers when a crime is committed?

from
The 57 Bus

Literary Nonfiction by **Dashka Slater**

Engage Your Brain

Choose one or more of these activities to start connecting with the story you are about to read.

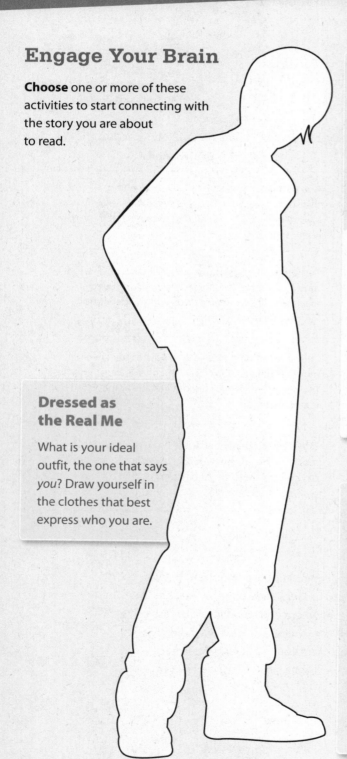

If You Didn't Know Me . . .

If someone didn't know you but looked at your social media accounts, what would they learn about you? What impression would your posts or likes on social media leave with someone? Make a T-chart listing what people might get right about who you are on one side and what they might get wrong on the other side.

Dressed as the Real Me

What is your ideal outfit, the one that says *you*? Draw yourself in the clothes that best express who you are.

What Did You Do?

Have you ever witnessed someone being bullied or otherwise mistreated? With a partner, discuss at least one incident you either witnessed or heard about.

- What was the situation?
- If you witnessed or saw it unfold on social media, did you intervene? Why or why not?
- What was the outcome?
- In retrospect, do you think witnesses should have acted differently, or brought in others to put a stop to the mistreatment?

Make Inferences About Characters

Although *The 57 Bus* is nonfiction, author Dashka Slater uses techniques of fiction to make individuals she writes about vivid and compelling. Readers can make **inferences,** or logical guesses, based on her descriptions of people. To make inferences, use details in the text along with your own experiences.

As you read, fill in the chart below. An example has been done for you.

Focus on Genre

Literary Nonfiction

- Conveys factual information, ideas, or experiences
- Develops insights based on factual evidence
- Uses literary techniques such as characterization and nonlinear narrative

Character Detail or Description	What I Already Know	My Inference
Sasha's Tumblr account: "I like parties/I dislike parties."	It's possible to feel more than one way about something.	Sasha is OK with complicated, conflicting feelings

Analyze Literary Techniques

Writers use **literary techniques,** or **devices,** to achieve their purposes. Dashka Slater borrows techniques from journalism, fiction, and other genres to create a fact-based narrative with the drama and pacing of a film or novel. Here are some techniques she uses:

Techniques from Journalism or Other Nonfiction

- The account consists of factual information supported by evidence.
- Descriptive details enhance factual information.

Techniques from Fiction

- Events may be presented out of chronological order.
- Narrative pacing varies from slow to fast-moving.
- Individuals at the story's center are developed like fiction characters.
- Dialogue is used to advance the narrative.

As you read, make notes where you see these techniques used. Ask yourself: How do these techniques influence my attitude toward the people the author describes?

Annotation in Action

Here is an example of an inference a student made based on a description in the text. As you read, highlight details that help you make inferences about the people in the excerpt.

> Today, like most days, Sasha wears a T-shirt, a black fleece jacket, a gray flat cap, and a gauzy white skirt.
>
> *Sasha likes to create an individual look—a personal style.*

Expand Your Vocabulary

Put a check mark next to the vocabulary words that you feel comfortable using when speaking or writing.

surreptitiously	☐
divert	☐
vantage point	☐
transpire	☐
callous	☐

With a partner, write a short description of a crime using at least one of the vocabulary words.

As you read the excerpt from *The 57 Bus*, use the definitions in the side column to learn the vocabulary words you don't already know.

Background

Dashka Slater is an award-winning journalist who has also written nine books of fiction and nonfiction. Slater's true-crime narrative, *The 57 Bus*, was based on an article she wrote for the *New York Times Magazine* in 2015. Slater says that while she was writing the article "it seemed clear to me that teenagers would find the characters compelling and I wanted them to have a chance to grapple with the complex issues the story raises: issues about either/or narratives, about race, gender, class, justice and forgiveness." You can read the article, "The Fire on the 57 Bus in Oakland," at nytimes.com.

from

The 57 Bus

Literary Nonfiction by **Dashka Slater**

A bad decision shatters the lives of two teenagers.

NOTICE & NOTE
As you read, use the side margins to make notes about the text.

Monday, November 4, 2013

1 By four-thirty in the afternoon, the first mad rush of after-school passengers has come and gone. What's left are stragglers and stay laters, swiping their bus passes as they climb onto the 57 bus and take seats among the coming-home workers, the shoppers and errand-doers, the other students from high schools and middle schools around the city. The bus is loud but not as loud as sometimes. A few clusters of kids are shouting and laughing and an older woman at the front keeps talking to the driver.

2 Dark is coming on. Daylight savings ended yesterday, and now evening rushes into the place where afternoon used to be. Everything is duskier, sleepier, wintrier now. Passengers look at their phones or stare through the scratched and grimy windows at the waning light.

3 Sasha sits near the back. For much of the journey, the teenager has been reading a paperback copy of *Anna Karenina* for a class in Russian literature. Today, like most days, Sasha wears a T-shirt, a black fleece jacket, a gray flat cap, and a gauzy white skirt. A senior

at a small private high school, the teenager identifies as agender—neither male nor female. As the bus lumbers through town, Sasha puts down the book and drifts into sleep, skirt draped over the edge of the seat.

4 A few feet away, three teenage boys are laughing and joking. One of them, Richard, wears a black hoodie and an orange-billed New York Knicks hat. A sixteen-year-old junior at Oakland High School, he's got hazel eyes and a slow, sweet grin. He stands with his back to Sasha, gripping a pole for balance.

5 Sasha sleeps as Richard and his companions goof around, play fighting. Sleeps as Richard's cousin Lloyd bounds up and down the aisle flirting with a girl up front. Sleeps as Richard **surreptitiously** flicks a lighter and touches it to the hem of that gauzy white skirt.

surreptitiously
(sûr-əp-tĭsh´əs-lē) *adv.* done by stealthy or secret means.

6 Wait.

7 In a moment, Sasha will wake inside a ball of flame and begin to scream.

8 In a moment, everything will be set in motion.

9 Taken by ambulance to a San Francisco burn unit, Sasha will spend the next three and a half weeks undergoing multiple surgeries to treat second- and third-degree burns running from calf to thigh.

10 Arrested at school the following day, Richard will be charged with two felonies, each with a hate-crime clause that will add time to his sentence if he is convicted. Citing the severity of the crime, the district attorney will charge him as an adult, stripping him of the protections normally given to juveniles. Before the week is out, he will be facing the possibility of life imprisonment.

ANALYZE LITERARY TECHNIQUES

Annotate: Mark the sentences in paragraphs 9–10 where the author reveals what happens to Sasha and Richard.

Analyze: Why do you think she flash forwards to the story's climax? What is the effect on the reader?

11 But none of that has happened yet. For now, both teenagers are just taking the bus home from school.

12 Surely it's not too late to stop things from going wrong. There must be some way to wake Sasha. **Divert** Richard. Get the driver to stop the bus.

divert
(dĭ-vûrt´) *v.* to turn aside from a course.

13 There must be something you can do.

Tumbling

14 (Adapted from Sasha's Tumblr page)

15 Favorite vegetable: bok choy
Favorite animals: cat and cuttlefish
Favorite type of movie: dream sequences

16 Three best qualities?
Navigation
My friends seem to like me
Purple

17 Of course I like hats
anyone who doesn't is wrong
18 I like compliments

I dislike compliments
19 I like my hair
I give good hugs

20 I'm good at finding potential puns.
21 If the whole world was listening, I might just
rant about a bunch of things like gender
wealth inequality
why school is important

22 I like parties
I dislike parties

23 I don't really keep track of disappointments.

24 Ideal vacation spot: prob'ly a city with a nice subway

25 Thinking of things to get me? Try this:
A brass airship
A transit map shower curtain
A medieval cloak
A corset with silver buttons
A chiseled chunk of gallium[1] that melts in your palm
A dress swirled with the image of a nebula[2]
A Victorian house on wheels
Tights painted like a mermaid tail

Don't forget to **Notice & Note** as you read the text.

MAKE INFERENCES ABOUT CHARACTERS

Annotate: Mark what Sasha would tell the "whole world."

Infer: What conclusions can you draw about Sasha's character and personality?

Book of Faces

26 (Pictures of Richard posted on Facebook)

27 Smiling beside his cousin's
slit-eyed hilarity.

28 Deadpan in ladies'
tortoiseshell sunglasses.

29 At fourteen, in a beanie:
round-faced, bright-eyed.

30 At sixteen: jaw slack, brows raised,
expression asking, *What?*

31 Soft-eyed on a sofa,
younger brother cuddled on his chest.

[1] **gallium:** a rare metallic element that is liquid near room temperature.
[2] **nebula:** a diffuse cloud of interstellar dust or gas.

32 Standing with Skeet, spines straight,
chins up, peas in a pod.

33 And later, beside Skeet's picture,
wearing a bandanna in tribute.

34 Mirror selfie: hand lodged
in his waistband, not even looking up.

35 None of it captures
how he looks in conversation

36 how his eyes hold your eyes,
seeing you see him.

37 His own secret power:
that paying attention.

ANALYZE LITERARY TECHNIQUES

Annotate: Mark the words in lines 27–36 that describe Richard.

Analyze: How does the author use this Facebook entry to convey Richard's personality?

4:52 P.M.

vantage point
(văn´tĭj point) *n.* a position that allows for a good view of something.

38 Every AC Transit bus is equipped with cameras that continuously record sound and video from multiple **vantage points**. The 57 bus was no exception. The cameras recorded Lloyd and Richard climbing on at the front a little before five p.m. and walking down the aisle toward the back—Lloyd chubby in a zipped-up black hoodie, Richard lean in a black hoodie over a white T-shirt and an orange-billed New York Knicks hat.

39 The bus was a double-length one, two buses fused together like conjoined twins by an accordion-pleated rubber seam. Most of the seats were taken. An older woman who wanted to talk to the bus driver about her route. A mom holding the hand of a little girl in a pink hoodie. A gaggle of laughing teenage boys.

40 "How's everything?" the driver asked a middle-aged man as he slid his bus pass into the machine.

41 "Long day," the man replied, shaking his head.

42 Richard recognized a boy named Jamal sitting at the back of the bus and greeted him with a dap.

43 "Mali B!" Lloyd shouted, following suit.

44 "What's up, dude?" Jamal was tall and lanky. He wore jeans and a white hoodie with a thick horizontal black stripe across the shoulders. His voice was low and thick, faded.

45 As the bus started up again, the two cousins gripped the silver pole in front of Jamal. Behind them, Sasha slept. A paperback copy of *Anna Karenina* lay closed in their[3] lap. Their skirt, gauzy and white, dangled over the edge of the seat.

[3] "Their," "they," and "them" are the pronouns Sasha identifies with.

Don't forget to **Notice & Note** as you read the text.

46 It couldn't have been easy to sleep with Lloyd nearby. He bounced up and down trying to make the bus shake, rapped a snippet of the song "Started from the Bottom" by Drake, screeched random words like "Chinchilla!" and "Obituary!" He shouted down the aisle to a girl he'd noticed when they climbed on board, "Hey! Girl! Excuse me!"

47 A girl in blue basketball shorts turned to look at him.

48 "No, your friend, the light-skinned one."

49 Jamal pointed at Sasha, whispered, "Look at this dude."

50 Lloyd turned and looked over his shoulder. He cackled.

51 On the video, you can't hear what Jamal says as he hands Richard the lighter. But you can see him take out his iPhone and point it toward Sasha as if planning to record. Later Richard would say that it was supposed to be funny, like that prank show on MTV with Ashton Kutcher, *Punk'd*. He thought the fabric would smolder for a minute and then Sasha would wake up and slap it out, startled.

52 "I *need* a good laugh," he'd said just after getting on the bus. Now he showed the lighter to Lloyd and then swung to the opposite side of the silver pole, closer to Sasha.

53 He flicked the lighter by the hem of Sasha's skirt. Nothing happened.

54 Lloyd was still shouting up to the front of the bus.

55 "Hey! Light-skinned girl!"

56 "Light-skinned girl." Jamal kept repeating what Lloyd said, his deep voice like an echo from the bottom of a well.

57 Lloyd bounced up the aisle to where the girls were sitting, perching on the edge of a nearby seat.

58 "Go ahead, you do it," Jamal said to Richard. Richard flicked the lighter again. Nothing.

59 Rebuffed by the girls, Lloyd returned to his companions, stopping in front of Sasha's sleeping form to shout an abrupt, parrotlike "Hey!"

60 Sasha stirred, but didn't wake.

61 "Whoa. You said, 'Hey!'" Jamal echoed. "Screamin."

62 Lloyd leaned close and screeched in Jamal's ear. Richard laughed and slapped Lloyd's head.

63 "Aw, you just broke my neck," Lloyd yelled.

64 Richard brandished the lighter, pretending to light Lloyd's sleeve. He looked at Jamal.

65 "Do it," Jamal urged.

66 Lloyd danced between them, landing half on Jamal's lap.

67 "Move! Get off me," Jamal grumbled. He kept his eyes on Richard, his phone poised. "You might as well do it," he said again.

68 Richard slunk back to Sasha, flicked the lighter. Nothing. He glanced at Jamal, grinned, and flicked the lighter a fourth time.

69 "Back door! Back door!" Lloyd called to the driver, ready for them to make their escape.

70 The doors opened. Richard leaped off the bus. Lloyd started to follow. Then he looked back and stopped, transfixed, as Sasha's skirt erupted into a sheet of flame. When the doors closed again, he hadn't moved.

Fire

71 The next few seconds of the surveillance video are hard to watch.

72 Sasha leaps up, slapping the flaming skirt. The skirt looks unearthly, impossible, a ball of white fire.

73 "Ow! *Ow!*" Sasha screams, voice high and terrified. "*I'm on fire! I'm on fire!*" Their hands snatch at the skirt, shaking it, waving it. Specks of flaming fabric swirl through the air. Sasha runs for the door and finds it closed. They turn, dance in place, screaming.

74 Jamal howls with laughter. Then, as Sasha careens toward him, he cringes and climbs onto his seat. "He's on fire!" he yells. "Put him out!"

75 Passengers sprint for the exits, shrieking and coughing. "It's a fire! It's a fire!" Some of the other kids on the bus are giggling. The bus is still moving, the driver just starting to register that something is going on way back at the far end of his vehicle.

76 "I ain't got time to be playin' with y'all, man," he calls over his shoulder.

77 Near the middle of the bus, two men leap from their seats and elbow through the press of people trying to escape. One man is short and balding; the other is taller, with a walrusy mustache and sad basset-hound eyes.

78 "Get down!" the mustached one yells. "Get on the ground!" The two men don't know each other, but they work in unison, shoving Sasha to the floor. The mustached man smothers Sasha's flaming skirt with his coat while the balding man stamps out the burning tatters that flame around them.

79 It's over in seconds. The driver pulls the bus to the curb. Sasha scrambles to a standing position, dazed and in shock. "Oh, Lord."

80 "That boy was on *fire*, wasn't he?" a man remarks as Sasha pushes through the back doors to the sidewalk. Behind him, Sasha's mustached rescuer paces the aisle. "Call an ambulance," he croaks.

ANALYZE LITERARY TECHNIQUES

Annotate: Mark the dialogue in paragraph 73, noticing the length of each sentence in the paragraph.

Analyze: What is the effect of these short, choppy sentences on the story's pace?

He goes to the door of the bus and calls to Sasha, who roams the sidewalk with a cell phone, charred legs. "You need to call an ambulance, man."

81 The girl in the blue basketball shorts calls to Sasha through the doors of the bus. "Are you okay?"

82 Sasha doesn't answer.

Don't forget to **Notice & Note** as you read the text.

Watching

83 After he jumped off the bus, Richard strode away with his hands in his pockets, trying to look casual. Then he heard Sasha's screams. He stopped, turned around, went back.

84 He stared at the bus, mouth open.

85 The bus had begun to move again. The driver, still unaware of the fire, was continuing along his route.

86 Richard ran after the bus. Suddenly, it lurched to the curb. Passengers spilled out, yelling and coughing. Another bus, the NL, had pulled up behind it, and after a moment, Richard turned around and climbed on. A few seconds later he got off again and walked back to where Sasha now paced the sidewalk on bare, charred legs.

87 He ambled past, snaking his head to stare at Sasha, then turned around and walked past Sasha again, still staring. Then Jamal and Lloyd got off the 57 and the three of them half walked, half ran to the other bus.

88 That night, Jasmine[4] noticed that Richard seemed sad.

89 "What's wrong?" she asked.

90 He wouldn't tell her.

NOTICE & NOTE

CONTRASTS AND CONTRADICTIONS

When you notice a contrast between what you would expect and what the character actually does, you've found a **Contrasts and Contradictions** signpost.

Notice & Note: Mark what Richard does in paragraph 86.

Interpret: What is unexpected about this? Why would he act this way?

Phone Call

91 The school day was long over at five o'clock, but Karl was still in his classroom when Sasha called him on his cell phone.

92 "Dad. I need you to come over here right now. I was on the bus and I got set on fire."

93 "What?" Karl said. The reception was terrible. "Say it again."

94 "You have to pick me up and take me to the hospital because someone set me on fire."

95 Karl was sure he wasn't hearing right. He walked around his classroom closing windows and gathering his things. "Wait. Say it again. You were on the bus and *what* happened?"

96 "I need to go to the hospital. Now."

97 And then Karl was running, still on the phone with Sasha, still asking the same question over and over as his feet carried him block after block, down one street and up another until he reached the place

[4] **Jasmine:** Richard's mother.

where Sasha lay on the sidewalk in their underwear, shivering and hyperventilating. "Tell me again. What happened?"

98 Most of the passengers had dispersed by now, but a few lingered with the driver on the sidewalk beside the empty bus. One of them, a teenage girl, had called her mother, who had called 911. The girl's mother arrived before the ambulance did. She stood with her arm around her daughter as Karl called Debbie and told her there had been an accident.

99 When Debbie got there, she thought Sasha must have fallen in mud, because why else would their legs have those black splotches? And then she understood and began to sob.

100 "Well," Sasha said. "It came true. What you were always worried about."

101 The ambulance took a long time to arrive. The police, on the other hand, came right away.

102 "Do you know who did this to you?" the officers kept asking Sasha.

103 "No." Sasha's teeth were chattering. "I was asleep."

104 They had never been so cold. Their legs were naked to the November chill. More than naked—skinless, exposed. Karl took off the outback hat he always wore and used it to shield Sasha's crotch from the eyes of passersby.

105 "Don't you have anything to keep him warm?" Debbie asked the cops, forgetting all about Sasha's pronouns. A police officer brought a sheet of yellow plastic from the squad car—the kind usually used for covering corpses. Debbie didn't want to put it over the open wounds on Sasha's legs, so she wrapped it around their shoulders.

106 At last, after maybe forty-five minutes, the ambulance arrived. Paramedics loaded Sasha onto a gurney and hooked up an IV. Warm fluids flowed into Sasha's veins. Morphine. The pain and cold receded. They were safe. Alive. Everything would be okay.

107 Karl climbed in the front of the ambulance that took Sasha to the hospital. There wasn't room for Debbie. She stood on the sidewalk and wept as they drove away. Everyone had left except the teenage girl and her mother.

108 "They did it because he was wearing a skirt!" Debbie sobbed.

109 Together, the girl and her mother wrapped Debbie in their arms. "That's no reason," they said.

The Interview, Part 1

110 When Richard arrived at the police station on the day of his arrest, the officers placed him in interview room 202 and instructed him to remove his shoelaces, belt, bandanna, and the cord from his hoodie. Then they left him there.

111 The room was small and shabby, containing only a rectangular table and three chairs with blue plastic seats. The plaster was pitted and peeling—pieces littered the floor as if someone had recently

VOCABULARY

Use Affixes: The word *hyperventilating* contains the Latin root *ventilate*, meaning "to inhale or exhale." The prefix *hyper-* means "over." The suffix *-ing* means "action or process."

Analyze: Why would Sasha be hyperventilating at this moment?

MAKE INFERENCES ABOUT CHARACTERS

Analyze: Mark what Sasha says in paragraph 100 when Debbie arrives.

Infer: What have Sasha's parents been worried about?

punched the wall and no one had bothered sweeping up afterward. Richard leaned forward and rested his forehead on the edge of the table. Minutes ticked by. He sat up and rubbed his eyes with two fingers. Leaned back in the chair and stared at the floor. Leaned forward with his chin resting on his arms. Cradled his head in his hand. Sat up and rested his chin in his palms. Ten minutes went by. Then twenty. Thirty.

112 After an hour an officer peeked in to hand him a bag lunch. He unpacked it: a soda, a turkey sandwich, a bag of SunChips. He smoothed the paper bag flat and placed the sandwich on top. Then he folded his hands and bowed his head. He crossed himself three times. Then he ate the sandwich.

113 He had his head down on the table when Officers Anwawn Jones and Jason Anderson came in, two hours and nineteen minutes after he'd first been placed in the room. They moved him into the center seat and settled themselves on either side of him.

114 "You didn't eat all your chips, man?" Officer Jones asked. He was tall and African American, with a shaved head, glasses, and an easy, sympathetic manner.

115 "I was getting a little stomachache," Richard said.

116 The officers assured him that they wanted to keep things relaxed. They asked about Richard's life—where he lived, what sports he played. "How are you doing in school?" Officer Jones asked.

117 "I was doing okay," Richard admitted. "But then it started falling off. The school's not good for me. There's too many distractions. I need to go to a smaller environment where I can focus."

118 "A lot of kids wouldn't understand that," Officer Jones said, nodding. "I had the same issue when I was younger."

119 "Any girlfriend right now?" asked Officer Anderson. He was white and heavyset, and though he smiled a lot, his friendliness seemed forced.

120 "I've been looking," Richard said.

121 "Looking?" Anderson grinned. "On the prowl?"

122 "It's not looking too good," Richard said.

123 "Were there girls up in Redding?" Anderson asked. "They cool?"

124 Richard looked puzzled. He'd been in a group home[5] up there, he explained, and hadn't been allowed to mix with girls.

125 Jones sat with one hand resting on his knee, the other on his writing pad. "Did you learn something in the group home? Did you learn some important lessons, being away from your family?"

126 "It was hard," Richard admitted. "It took me actually a while. And then I was doing good. And then my best friend since forever, my best friend ever, he passed. And then I had a little breakdown."

127 "What happened to your friend?" Jones asked.

128 "He was murdered."

129 As the conversation continued, Richard was candid, almost confiding. He told them about getting robbed, about how he'd been

Don't forget to **Notice & Note** as you read the text.

MAKE INFERENCES ABOUT CHARACTERS

Annotate: Mark details in paragraphs 117–129 that describe Richard's recent experiences and his reaction to them.

Draw Conclusions: What new inferences can we make about Richard based on these details?

[5] **group home:** a small supervised residential facility.

set up by someone he'd called a friend. "I have trust issues right now," he told the officers.

130 "Well, here's the deal," Officer Jones said at last. "I'm going to explain to you why you're in here. We have some questions we wanted to ask you. So we can get your side of the story, your version of what **transpired**. But before we get into that, I need to read you your rights."

transpire
(trăn-spīr´) *v.* to come about or happen.

The Interview, Part 2

131 "You have a pretty good memory, right?" Officer Jones asked when he finished reading Richard his rights. "Give me the rundown of what you were doing, say, yesterday, after, say, school. From the time school got out till, say, about eight to nine o'clock at night." Richard told him about Lloyd meeting him at the gate at the end of the school day and about going with him to get a phone from someone, a process that had taken close to two hours. Then he described getting on the bus and how there was a man on the bus wearing a skirt. He'd just gotten off the 57 bus to get the express bus, he said, when he heard screams and ran back. When they opened the door to the bus, he saw that the man's skirt was on fire.

132 "What do you think about dudes who dress up in skirts?" Jones asked.

133 "I'm not with that," Richard said. "I wouldn't say that I hate gay people, but I'm very homophobic."

134 Jones nodded. "Okay. Why would you call yourself homophobic?"

135 "I don't have no problem with somebody if they like men. But like if you do too much? Nobody cares, really."

136 "Do too much?"

137 "Taking it to the next level," Richard explained.

138 Jones asked for an example of the next level.

139 "Cross-dressing and like—some people, like they try to make everybody know that they are that and they try to do too much and—it's just a lot."

140 Jones spun his pencil in circles on his notepad, like the spinner for a board game. "A lot of people share the same views," he said. "People who display stuff outwardly for everybody to see."

141 Then he asked Richard to go through the events on the bus again.

142 "I think there's a couple parts where you haven't been completely honest with us," he said when Richard finished. "You're a good kid. I like people to be honest with me. We're going to be honest with you. I expect people to be honest with me."

143 He asked Richard to describe what he and Lloyd and Jamal had been wearing on the bus the day before. Then he slid some photographs across the table.

144 Richard. Lloyd. Jamal.

145 Richard picked them up. Looked them over.

146 “It’s pretty obvious we have some pictures,” Jones said, tucking the pictures under his notebook. “And mind you, these are not still pictures. These are pictures from video.”

147 “Both of the buses you were on, they have audio and video cameras,” Anderson added. “With that in mind, I want you to take a quick second and I want you to rethink the story that you told us. And I want you to tell us what *really* happened.

148 “You’re not a bad kid,” Anderson said. “Sometimes we make decisions that are not the best decisions. Keeping in mind that you know we have video, and the video shows everything that happened on that bus. Everything. Right now is a time in your life when you’ve got to decide, am I going to take responsibility for my actions? Am I going to be honest? Because that dude on the bus whose skirt caught on fire got burned pretty good.”

149 “Can I see the video?” Richard asked.

NOTICE & NOTE
WORDS OF THE WISER

Words of the Wiser are insights or advice about life offered to the narrator.

Notice & Note: Mark Officer Anderson’s advice to Richard.

Predict: How might this advice affect what happens to Richard in the coming weeks?

The Interview, Part 3

150 They only showed him a short snippet of the video, but it was enough. Richard slumped in his chair, one hand shoved in his pocket.

151 “Why would you set that dress on fire?” Officer Anderson asked.

152 “Being stupid.” Richard’s voice was low.

153 “What was going through your mind?”

154 “Nothin.”

155 “Have you done this before?”

156 “No.”

157 “What would even remotely make you think about setting something on fire like that—someone’s clothing?” Anderson persisted. “That dude got seriously burned. It’s not like he went home. He’s awaiting surgery at a San Francisco burn center right now. He got burned real bad. What was going through your mind when you decided to light that dress on fire?”

158 “Nothing.” It was a whisper now.

159 “Was it because the dude was wearing a dress? Did you have a problem with him?”

160 “I don’t know.”

161 “People do things for a reason,” the officer said. “We’ve all made decisions in life that may not have been the best choice to make at a given time. What we’re trying to figure out is why this happened.”

162 “I’m homophobic,” Richard said at last. “I don’t like gay people.”

163 “Really? And you had a problem seeing him on the bus?”

164 “I don’t know what was going through my head,” Richard said. “I just reacted.”

165 “Did Jamal or your cousin Lloyd tell you to do it?”

166 “No.”

167 “I know you said you didn’t know what was going through your mind,” Officer Jones said. “But did you get angry because he’s a gay dude in a skirt, not just being gay but ‘doing too much’?”

ANALYZE LITERARY TECHNIQUES

Annotate: Mark the sentence in paragraph 168 where Richard seems to change his reason for setting Sasha's skirt on fire.

Analyze: How do the officers' questions lead Richard to change his story?

168 "Actually, I really didn't know that his skirt was going to do that, I didn't know that it was going to catch like that," Richard blurted. "It was, like, a little flame. I thought it was just going to go out."

169 But it was too late to backpedal. On the charging documents, Officer Jones wrote in block capitals, *DURING SUSP INTERVIEW, THE SUSP STATED HE DID IT BECAUSE HE WAS HOMOPHOBIC.*

Charges

170 Two days after Richard's arrest, the district attorney's office released his name to the media. He was being charged as an adult, which meant he no longer had the protections given to juveniles, one of which is anonymity. They charged him with two felonies: "aggravated mayhem" and "assault with intent to cause great bodily injury." Each charge also contained a hate-crime clause that would increase Richard's sentence by an additional one to three years in state prison. If convicted, he faced a maximum sentence of life in prison, a punishment he would never have faced if he had been charged as a juvenile.

171 "[Richard ——'s] violent and senseless criminal conduct resulted in severe and traumatic injuries to a young and entirely innocent victim," Alameda County district attorney Nancy O'Malley said. "The intentional and **callous** nature of the crime is shocking and will not be tolerated in our community."

callous
(kăl´əs) *adj.* emotionally hardened; unfeeling.

172 Lloyd and Jamal were never interviewed, arrested, or charged.

COLLABORATIVE DISCUSSION

How do the events in this narrative relate to the unit's Essential Question: Who suffers when a crime is committed?

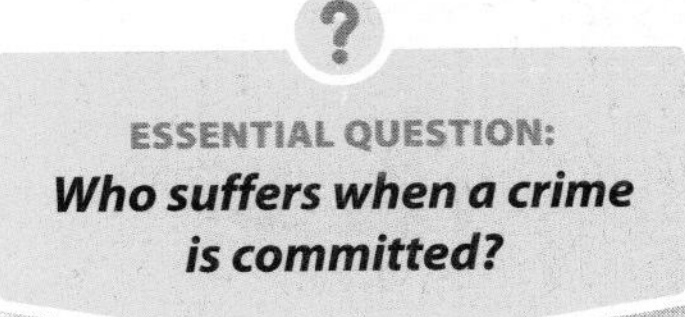
?
ESSENTIAL QUESTION:
Who suffers when a crime is committed?

Review your notes and add your thoughts to your Response Log.

Assessment Practice

Answer these questions before moving on to the **Analyze the Text** section on the following page.

1. How do the officers determine who set Sasha's skirt on fire?

- (A) The bus driver tells them.
- (B) Sasha identifies the attacker.
- (C) They have a video recording.
- (D) Other passengers identify Richard.

2. Why is Richard charged with hate crimes?

- (A) He committed the offense with two other young men.
- (B) He told the police officers he was homophobic.
- (C) He hoped Sasha would be severely injured.
- (D) He had a prior criminal record.

3. Which **two** events does Richard mention to explain his "trust issues"?

- (A) He has been in a group home.
- (B) His mother abandoned him as a child.
- (C) He was recently robbed.
- (D) He had been falsely arrested.
- (E) His best friend was murdered.

Ed

Test-Taking Strategies

Analyze the Text

Support your responses with evidence from the text.

NOTICE & NOTE

Review what you **noticed and noted** as you read the text. Your annotations can help you answer these questions.

1. **DRAW CONCLUSIONS** Review the chart you filled out on the Get Ready page. Based on details the author provides and your inferences, write character summaries of Sasha and Richard. Which one do you think you "know" better? Why?

2. **ANALYZE** Identify a **Contrast and Contradiction** you noticed for each of the main characters, Sasha and Richard. Why do you think each character acted or felt in a way that was different from what you expected?

3. **ANALYZE** Identify three examples of the author's use of literary techniques, and explain how each supports Dashka Slater's purposes for writing.

4. **EVALUATE** Richard is charged with hate crimes, although he claims he was just trying to pull a funny prank. Yet either way, Sasha is seriously injured. Should Richard's motivation make a difference in how his actions are judged? Explain the reasons for your opinion.

5. **INFER** Reread paragraph 162, then paragraphs 164–168. What differences do you notice between the explanations Richard gives for the attack on Sasha? How do you explain these different statements?

6. **SYNTHESIZE** Days after the incident on the 57 bus, Richard wrote two letters to Sasha. Here is part of the second letter:

   > I am not a thug, gangster, hoodlum, nor monster. Im a young African American male who's made a terrible mistake. Not only did I hurt you but I hurt your family & friends and also my family & friends for I have brought shame to them and our country and I shall be punished which is going to be hard for me because I'm not made to be incarcerated.

   How do Richard's comments relate to the Essential Question, Who suffers when a crime is committed?

Choices

Here are some other ways to demonstrate your understanding of the ideas in this lesson.

Writing

↳ Hate-Crime Factsheet

Richard is charged with two felonies, each of which contains a hate-crime clause. What is a hate crime? Research information about hate crimes on the U.S. Department of Justice website. Then review two or three instances where individuals were convicted of hate crimes. Prepare a factsheet based on your findings and your own observations. Include the following information:

- Legal definition
- Summary of one hate crime you read about: What was the incident and who was involved? What were the legal consequences for the person(s) convicted?
- Was there any kind of restitution for victims or families?
- Your thoughts and impressions, including why hate crimes are seen as especially vicious

Be sure to cite your sources. Present your factsheet to the class, or publish it in the form of a blog.

As you write and discuss, be sure to use the Academic Vocabulary words.

- capacity
- confer
- emerge
- generate
- trace

Media

↳ Graphic Adaptation

Reread paragraphs 150–169, where Richard is questioned by the police. What does the author want you to know that she doesn't explicitly say? Create a graphic adaptation of the scene. Focus on facial expressions and body language to accurately portray the subtleties the author alludes to.

Social & Emotional Learning

↳ Small-Group Discussion

How can we, as a society, better ensure that no one is attacked or mistreated because of prejudice, stereotypes, or bias? What needs to change so that everyone's rights are respected and protected?

With a small group, brainstorm ideas and propose solutions.

- If disagreements arise, determine how they will be handled.
- Ensure everyone's voice is heard.
- Summarize your group's conclusions.
- Reflect on how your group was able to work together.

Expand Your Vocabulary

PRACTICE AND APPLY

Use your understanding of the vocabulary words to answer each question.

surreptitiously | **divert** | **vantage point** | **transpire** | **callous**

1. If an action is **callous,** is it sensitive or heartless? Why?
2. Which action would a person do **surreptitiously:** Give a gift, or steal from a tip jar? Explain.
3. If I **divert** the conversation, do we stay on the same topic, or move to another?
4. When the friends discuss what will **transpire** after school today, what will they talk about?
5. If I can see the whole soccer field from my seat, do I have a good **vantage point**? Explain.

Vocabulary Strategy

Affixes

Interactive Vocabulary Lesson: Common Roots, Prefixes, and Suffixes

Affixes, or word parts that attach to a word before or after the root, include prefixes and suffixes. Knowing the meaning of affixes helps to understand technical or discipline-based vocabulary. The word *inequality* contains the Latin prefix *in-*, which means "not." Here are other examples:

Affix	Meaning	Example
a-	Greek prefix meaning "without"	*agender*
-ion	Latin suffix meaning "action" or "process"	*reception*
para-	Greek prefix meaning "beside"	*paramedic*

PRACTICE AND APPLY

Follow these steps for each example word in the chart.

1. Define the word using the meaning of the affix.
2. Use a print or online resource, such as a technical dictionary or a glossary, to clarify or validate the definition.
3. Use the word in a sentence that accurately reflects its meaning.

Watch Your Language!

Sentence Variety

Author Dashka Slater varies her style by using long sentences, short sentences, and even sentence fragments. Notice how this long sentence contains several facts in one clear statement.

> When Richard arrived at the police station on the day of his arrest, the officers placed him in interview room 202 and instructed him to remove his shoelaces, belt, bandanna, and the cord from his hoodie.

Short sentences can add drama by highlighting a fast-moving sequence of events.

> *"Ow! Ow!"* Sasha screams, voice high and terrified. *"I'm on fire! I'm on fire!"* Their hands snatch at the skirt, shaking it, waving it. Specks of flaming fabric swirl through the air. Sasha runs for the door and finds it closed. They turn, dance in place, screaming.

Fragments are complete thoughts but often lack subjects or predicates. Notice how the short sentences and fragments in this passage convey both the drama of the situation and the relief Sasha feels:

> Warm fluids flowed into Sasha's veins. Morphine. The pain and cold receded. They were safe. Alive. Everything would be okay.

Interactive Grammar Practice: Sentence Structure

PRACTICE AND APPLY

Write a short passage about a part of *The 57 Bus* excerpt that interests you. Vary the length of your sentences; try adding a fragment.

Share your writing with a partner and discuss how you incorporated variety into your writing by varying sentence length.

Get Ready

Gift-Wrapped Fathers

Poem by Eduardo (Echo) Martinez

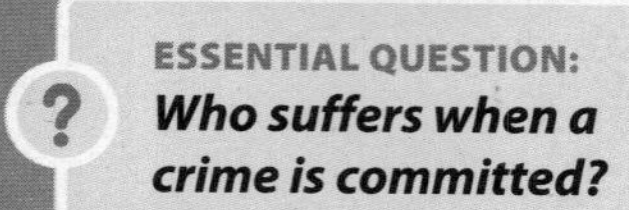
?
ESSENTIAL QUESTION:
Who suffers when a crime is committed?

Engage Your Brain

Choose one or more of these activities to start connecting with the poem you're about to read.

As Seen on TV

How are interactions between prison inmates and their visitors typically depicted on television or in movies? In a small group, discuss aspects such as

- who visits
- how visits take place (telephone, in person) and for how long
- degree of physical separation
- conversation topics
- typical mood or tone

Bonds Between Us

Our relationships with family members and friends often change over time. Freewrite about how your relationship with one friend or relative has evolved since you were younger. What changed—and why?

Like One, Unlike Another

Think of the important adults in your life. To whom are you most similar? From whom are you most different? Make a list of similarities and differences.

Make Inferences About Theme

Woven into almost any work of literature, including poetry, is **theme**—an important message about life experience, human nature, and the world. Themes are rarely stated outright. Instead, readers must find clues about theme within the text. Such clues can be used to make **inferences,** or logical guesses supported by evidence. Making inferences about theme will help you understand the texts you read.

Here are some other tips to help you infer theme:

- Pay attention to **figurative language,** or language that conveys meaning beyond the literal meaning of words.
- Identify **imagery**—descriptive words and phrases that appeal to one or more of the five senses (sight, hearing, smell, taste, and touch). Imagery may also suggest theme.
- Note recurring images or ideas, as they may point to a theme. Remember that a poem may have one or more themes.

Focus on Genre
Poetry

- uses figurative language, including personification, simile, and metaphor
- creates rhythm using line breaks, rhyme, and alliteration
- includes imagery that appeals to the senses and expresses emotions
- expresses a theme, or the author's message about life

As you read, use the chart to record words, phrases, and lines from the poem that may indicate theme. Use these details combined with what you already know to make inferences about theme. An example has been provided.

Evidence from the Poem	What I Already Know	Inference About Theme
"you were there . . . / but gone . . ." (lines 1–2)	Separation from a loved child is painful	loss, abandonment

Paraphrase Texts

Poems and other texts often present complex ideas or events. Paraphrasing is a skill that can help you better understand a text.

When you **paraphrase** a text, you restate each key idea and detail in your own words. Paraphrasing helps you clarify the author's meaning because you must understand it before you can rephrase it. An effective paraphrase maintains both the author's meaning and the logical order in which the ideas are presented.

As you read the poem:

- Paraphrase every few lines.
- Pay special attention to imagery.
- Review your paraphrases for key ideas and details.
- Write a theme statement based on your paraphrases.

Annotation in Action

Here is an example of notes a student made about several lines in "Gift-Wrapped Fathers." As you read, mark details that suggest a theme.

you know, the scene you always view in jail house flicks
palm pressed to palm is true
what they don't show you is the Plexi-glass aftermath
your reflection on the opposite side

Prison seems lonely and sad.

Background

In 2019, **Eduardo (Echo) Martinez** became the Inaugural Luiz A. Hernandez Florida Prison Poet Laureate. The honorary position is awarded to a prisoner poet by the organizations Exchange for Change, which teaches writing to prisoners in South Florida, and the O, Miami Poetry Festival, which offers the people of Miami-Dade County opportunities to engage with poetry. Martinez's mission involves "increasing visibility of Florida's prison population; promoting rehabilitation through the arts; and asserting the basic humanity of all living beings."

In an interview with the advocacy organization PEN America, Martinez said of his position as prison poet laureate, "My success is my words escaping this place."

Gift-Wrapped Fathers

Poem by **Eduardo (Echo) Martinez**

An imprisoned parent struggles to maintain a bond with his son.

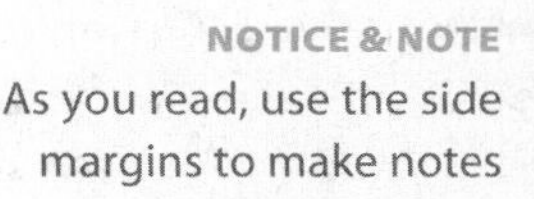

NOTICE & NOTE
As you read, use the side margins to make notes about the text.

you were there for his cute banana Gerber gibberish
but gone before words cartwheeled off his tongue
you held him up in your arms
and showed him off to the world like Simba
Hakuna Matata days
before you fell like timber
he made a convenience store out of your heart
open all night eyes
baby monitor ears by the bedside
alert and on patrol to any sound
one minute microwave milk runs
wrist drop temperature checks
proud diaper changes
then baby wiped your own tears when the chains came
while he was being potty-trained
you paced in pain inside a cemented port-a-potty
two syllables of a baby's vocab
"PAPI"
traveling through a sour tapped phone line
you know, the scene you always view in jail house flicks
palm pressed to palm is true
what they don't show you is the Plexi-glass aftermath
your reflection on the opposite side
place a hand on a mirror's glass

Close Read Screencast
Listen to a modeled close read of this text.

PARAPHRASE TEXTS

Annotate: Read lines 26–30. Mark the words that suggest the father in prison is thinking about his own childhood and father.

Analyze: Paraphrase lines 26–30. Why is the speaker mentioning his father at this point in the poem?

MAKE INFERENCES ABOUT THEME

Annotate: Mark the words in lines 45–50 that refer to the passage of time.

Infer: What is the significance of these references to time?

pretend it's skin and try not to cry
by the time you're convicted and sentenced to prison
you've missed his first step and birthdays
he's a toddler now
and you're still studying
to be a better father than the one you had
scared to answer your own questions
while piggy backin' a mocking Orangutan
one wearing a loud black market Rolex with a bootleg tick[1]
like a backpack bomb biting your shoulders
you become a terrorist to your emotions
terrorized by self-inflicted "what-if's"
praying to one day
see your son rise
then your son set
but these cell blocks pull pieces from your soul
like Lego blocks every time your visit finishes
playing chicken with a dim light through tunnel vision
as you sway your way back towards a cage
where you'll lay and replay every detail
you've captured during the 5 hours
you've waited 6 months for
as the only people that really love you
make a quiet 7 hour ride back home to a house
that once was alive with your potential, now it's haunted
by each visit he's grown inches
"Papi" is now *"Dad"*
yet you still talk to him in lullaby
the natural life kind
where good-bye is a common thing
some will portray a portrait of you as a bad guy
so you try not to be the bad guy
as you build a bond over a 15 minute collect call
while another man pretends to be his father
not cause he loves your son
but out of spite cause he looks like you
even down talks to you
so baby boy doesn't look up to you
for birthdays and holidays
he receives your gifts of apologies
so many of them that he no longer opens them
sometimes, he hugs you like a *homeboy*
maybe cause he's tired of you saying
that one day, you'll be *home boy*
another Lego block removed

[1] **black market Rolex with a bootleg tick:** *Black market* refers to an illegal trade of goods, such as items that have been stolen; Rolex is a brand of expensive wristwatch, usually of the analog type that makes a ticking sound. *Bootleg* refers to illegally produced goods, in this case, perhaps a fake Rolex.

another tick terrorizing emotion
another Simba grown without his Mufasa
Father's day hurts
so you write in second person
cause you feel like that's the kind of father you've been
cause you never should have been here in the first place
but with him
just another father gift-wrapped in sorry
hoping
his son opens up to him

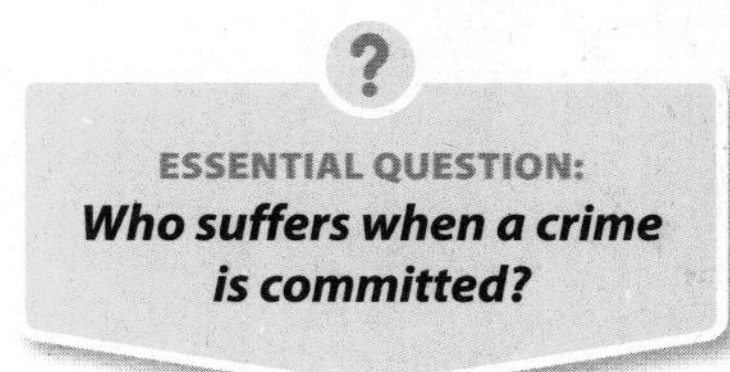
?
ESSENTIAL QUESTION:
Who suffers when a crime is committed?

Review your notes and add your thoughts to your Response Log.

COLLABORATIVE DISCUSSION

When did you figure out the speaker is a father in prison? With a partner, go back and find the clues in the poem.

Assessment Practice

Answer these questions before moving on the **Analyze the Text** section on the following page.

1. Which description best expresses the father's attitude toward his infant son in lines 1–13?

- (A) fearful, wary, ashamed
- (B) delighted, proud, attentive
- (C) distant, cold, threatening
- (D) curious, confident, calm

2. Select **two** sentences that show how the imprisoned father tries to connect with his son.

- (A) He has prison visits with his son.
- (B) He asks for advice about raising a son.
- (C) He attends his son's birthday parties.
- (D) He calls his son and sends him gifts.
- (E) He tells his son to call him "Papi."

3. By the end of the poem, the father expresses hope that —

- (A) his son will visit him more often
- (B) his son will learn to love his stepfather
- (C) he can raise another child someday
- (D) his son will learn to trust him

Ed

Test-Taking Strategies

Analyze the Text

Support your responses with evidence from the text.

1. **INTERPRET** Reread lines 1–6. How does the poet use imagery to describe the father's attitude toward his baby?

2. **EVALUATE** What does the poet achieve by introducing and developing the image of a convenience store in lines 7–13?

3. **COMPARE** Reread lines 14–19. How does this section compare to lines 7–13? What shift has occurred in the father's relationship to his son?

4. **INFER** Paraphrase lines 1–19 of the poem. What details in the passage help you understand the father's emotions?

My Paraphrase	Details that Reveal the Father's Emotions

5. **DRAW CONCLUSIONS** Reread lines 55–65. What do the unopened "gifts of apologies" (line 64) say about the relationship between father and son?

6. **SYNTHESIZE** Review the notes you took in the chart on the Get Ready page. Use your inferences to create two or more theme statements—messages from the poem about life or human nature. Write at least one theme statement in the chart.

Theme Statements

NOTICE & NOTE

Review what you **noticed and noted** as you read the text. Your annotations can help you answer these questions.

Choices

Here are some other ways to demonstrate your understanding of the ideas in this lesson.

Writing

↳ Future-Tense Letter

Imagine you are the imprisoned father writing a letter to your son, who is now a teenager. What do you want and need to say to him? Possible topics:

- the challenges and disappointments of fatherhood behind bars
- lessons learned in prison
- hopes for the future
- expectations for your son

Think about the tone you want your letter to convey, and its overall message. Exchange letters with a classmate and discuss each letter's effectiveness.

As you write and discuss, be sure to use the Academic Vocabulary words.

capacity

confer

emerge

generate

trace

Media

↳ Create a Playlist

Find songs that you think connect to the themes in "Gift-Wrapped Fathers." Create a playlist and publish the list online with links others can use to listen to the songs. Explain why you chose each song and how it connects to the poem.

Research

↳ White Paper: Prison Reforms

Do research on the prison reform movement in the United States and around the world. Choose one innovation—for example, programs that pair inmates with animals, or that teach barista skills for post-prison work in coffee shops. Summarize your findings in a multimedia presentation to share with the prison's board of directors (or your classmates).

- Describe the program and where it has been tested.
- Report results: In what ways has the program been a success? Are changes planned?
- Present charts and statistics if you have them, along with photos of inmate participants.
- Like a good researcher, cite your sources.

Collaborate & Compare

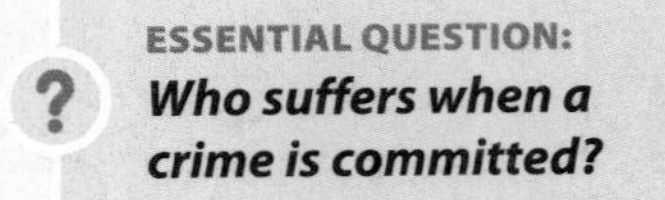

Compare Accounts

You are about to listen to a podcast and read a news article about tragic events in one small town. As you explore the two media accounts, notice the perspectives—points of view—each account presents. Then, think about how these media accounts help us picture the people and events by explaining what took place and why.

35
CITY LIMIT
SKIDMORE
POP. 342
SKIDMORE
COMMUNITY BETTERMENT
A
Bully
Podcast from Radiotopia/PRX
page 261
B
Unsolved "Vigilante" Murder in the Heartland
News Article by C.M. Frankie
pages 267–271

After you have compared the two media accounts, you will collaborate with a small group to create and present your own podcast or news article about the events described. You will follow these steps:

- Plan your podcast or news article
- Create a draft
- Prepare for sharing
- Share and discuss

MEDIA

Bully

Podcast from **Radiotopia/PRX**

Engage Your Brain

Choose one or both of these activities to start connecting with the podcast you're about to listen to.

Mob Mentality

In the podcast you are about to listen to, a crime is committed in broad daylight with multiple witnesses. Yet no one was charged with the crime. With a partner, talk about other instances reported in the media where a group of people denied knowledge of an event they must have witnessed. What might motivate people to keep quiet, or not get involved?

Word Association

What do you think of when you hear the word *bully*? Draw or describe your thoughts below.

Background

Radiotopia/PRX is a network of podcasts; that is, a collection of audio shows that people can listen to on electronic devices. The podcast you are about to hear, "Bully," was produced for the podcast series *Criminal*, which Radiotopia/PRX makes available for listeners. *Criminal* is created by a team of media professionals who make podcasts about true crimes—"stories of people who've done wrong, been wronged, or gotten caught somewhere in the middle."

The events in "Bully" took place in the small town of Skidmore, Missouri, during the 1970s. The central figure in these events is Ken McElroy. The podcast describes the confirmed facts and poses questions that are unanswered to this day.

Analyze Media Messages

Media refers to the many different methods or materials used to present information—paintings, books, plays, magazines, movies, videoblogs, podcasts, and many more. Each medium differs in how it treats, or presents, a subject or topic. For example, podcasts may use sound devices such as music, sound effects, pacing, and tone.

To analyze media messages, ask:

- What details and other information are included?
- What information is omitted?
- How is the information presented?
- How does the particular treatment shape the message for the audience?

As you listen to the podcast, use the chart to help you analyze the podcast and its main messages.

Focus on Genre
↳ Podcast

- **an audio file that can be listened to on a computer, smartphone, or other electronic device**
- **usually made up of a series of episodes, shows, or stories about one subject or issue**
- **may be fiction, such as a short story, or nonfiction, such as an interview or fact-based account**
- **often presents a specific point of view, or perspective, that is more subjective than news reporting**

Techniques Used
• *Narration consists of male and female voices*
Key Details in Podcast
• *Ken McElroy had a tough childhood.*
Messages to Listener
• *McElroy's actions as an adult can be considered in light of details about his childhood.*

Build Active Listening Skills

If you're _not_ an active listener, you may be missing out on a lot of what you hear! To truly understand what you hear requires a set of listening skills. Active listeners use techniques such as these:

- **Focusing**—They put aside distractions so they can focus on listening, whether to a live speaker or electronic audio.
- **Note-Taking**—They jot down important information, memorable phrases, and questions. For podcasts and other audio files, active listeners hit pause to jot down a note or question.
- **Repeated Listening**—Active listeners listen to an audio file more than one time. This helps them grasp information they may have missed and deepen their understanding.
- **Sharing**—Active listeners paraphrase and summarize what they heard. Then, they share notes with a partner or group.

As you listen to the podcast, fill out the chart.

What I Did to Focus	What I Learned from My Notes	What I Had Missed When I Listened Again	What I Shared/What Others Shared with Me

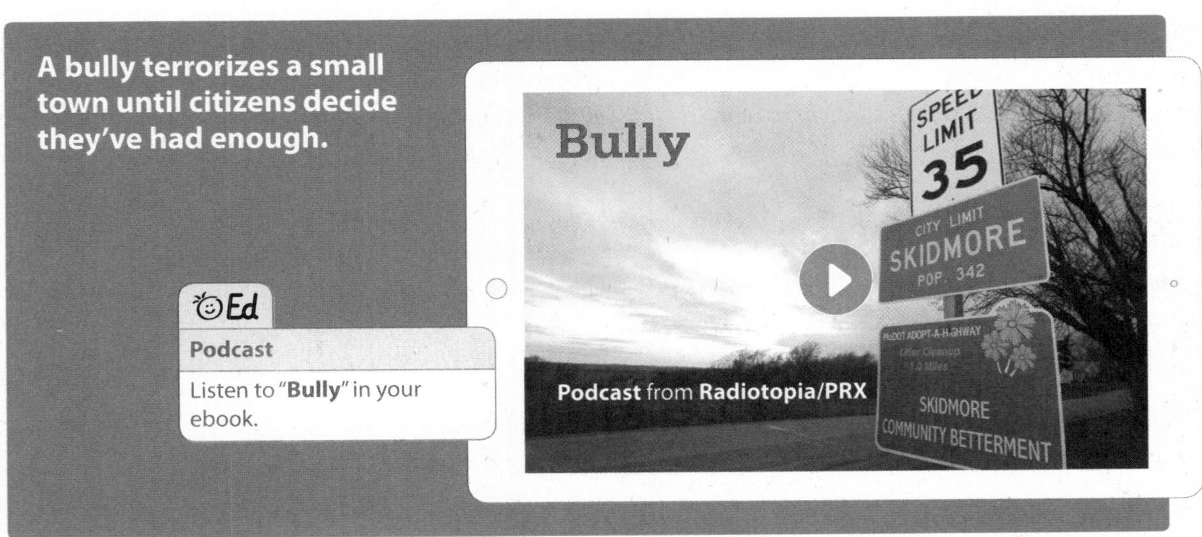

A bully terrorizes a small town until citizens decide they've had enough.
Ed
Podcast
Listen to "Bully" in your ebook.
Bully
SPEED LIMIT 35
CITY LIMIT SKIDMORE POP. 342
Podcast from Radiotopia/PRX
SKIDMORE COMMUNITY BETTERMENT

COLLABORATIVE DISCUSSION

Share your first impressions of this story with a partner.

Analyze the Podcast

Support your responses with evidence from the podcast.

NOTICE & NOTE

Review the notes you took as you listened to the podcast. Your notes can help you answer these questions.

1. **PREDICT** Based on the podcast, how would you summarize Ken McElroy's childhood? What circumstances from his childhood might have shaped him as an adult?

2. **INFER** Early in the podcast, the narrator says that there was a "myth of . . . invincibility" around Ken McElroy. What is the meaning of this description? Why is it significant?

3. **SYNTHESIZE** Some women and children who knew Ken McElroy said he was "not a monster" and was a "caring father." How can a person be loved by some people and feared by others? Why can people have such differing perspectives on the same person? Use the chart to help organize your ideas and response.

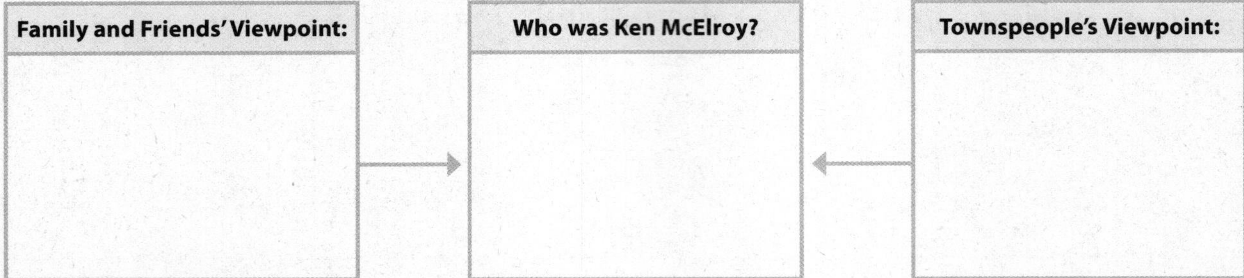

4. **ANALYZE** After Ken McElroy was convicted, he was released on bond. According to the narrator, the townspeople "lost complete confidence" in being protected by the law. Was this lack of trust in the legal system an expected result? Why or why not?

5. **EXPLAIN** According to the podcast, there were 40 witnesses to the murder of Ken McElroy. What most likely explains why "no one saw anything"? Include the perspective of the prosecutor, David Baird, in your response.

6. **DRAW CONCLUSIONS** Review the first chart you filled out on the Get Ready page. What do you think the main messages, or central ideas, of the podcast are?

7. **EVALUATE** The podcast quotes a number of individuals who witnessed the events in Skidmore as they unfolded. Why might the podcast producers have chosen to interview so many people? Do the different points of view result in a balanced, or objective, perspective? Why or why not?

Choices

Here are some other ways to demonstrate your understanding of the ideas in this lesson.

Writing

↳ Movie Treatment

Three decades ago, a movie based on the events described in "Bully" was released. Imagine that now a film studio thinks you have the talents to create a new mega-hit version. Outline your ideas for a pitch meeting, including

- a title (make it compelling!)
- actors for major roles
- aspects of the story you'll film (McElroy's early life? other characters' stories?)
- how you will order the events
- how you will film the climax

In a small group, compare your proposals. Revise your pitch based on suggestions and new ideas.

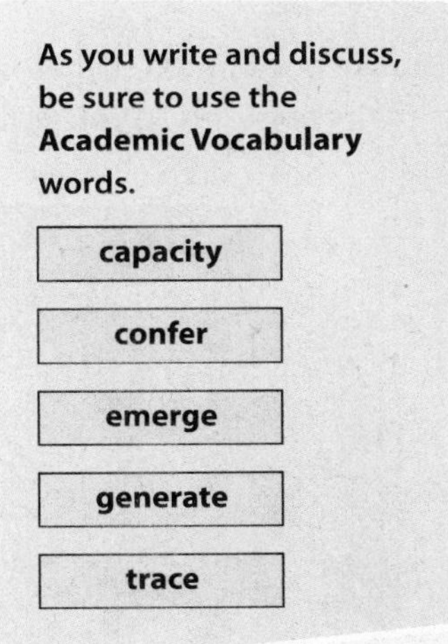
As you write and discuss, be sure to use the Academic Vocabulary words.

- capacity
- confer
- emerge
- generate
- trace

Social & Emotional Learning

↳ Panel Discussion

Organize a panel to discuss practical, moral, and ethical aspects of the action Skidmore's citizens took.

Consider these questions:

- Is it ever justifiable for individuals to take the law in their own hands? If so, under what conditions?
- What lawful options could the townspeople have considered?
- Was there an early incident which, if handled differently, could have ended Ken McElroy's crime spree without bloodshed?

During the discussion:

- Cite evidence from the podcast as support.
- Listen and respond respectfully to other opinions.
- Ask clarifying questions.
- As a group, review your discussion.

Media

↳ Breaking News

Imagine it is July 11, 1981—the day after Ken McElroy was killed in downtown Skidmore, Missouri. What would the newspaper coverage have been? Mock up a fictitious front page of the local Skidmore newspaper. Include the following:

- newspaper name and other front-page elements
- attention-grabbing headline
- image(s) that a family newspaper would print
- brief article summarizing the events
- other brief news items that might have appeared in July 1981, covering local, national, and world events

Present your front-page mockup to the class.

Unsolved "Vigilante" Murder in the Heartland

News Article by **C.M. Frankie**

Engage Your Brain

Choose one or both of these activities to start connecting with the news article you're about to read.

Zipped Lips

How good are you at keeping secrets? Have you ever had to keep a secret with a group of people—for example, a surprise event for someone? With a partner, discuss whether the group was able to prevent leaking the secret to others.

Still Wondering

If you listened to the podcast "Bully," what questions do you still have about the story? Make a list of what you'd like to learn—for example, about Ken McElroy, the facts of the case, or McElroy's murder.

Make Inferences

Making inferences means making logical guesses based on facts and other details, as well as your own knowledge and experiences. Making inferences is essential for understanding. As you read:

- Pause frequently. Think about what you just read.
- Focus on the information presented: What is it telling you? Why is it important or significant?
- Consider what else you know. Then, make your inferences and write them down (or make a mental note).

Use the chart to help you make inferences as you read the article.

Focus on Genre
News Article

- provides factual information
- includes evidence to support ideas
- may contain text features to organize ideas
- delivered in a variety of formats—for example, in paper or online newspapers, in magazines, or through online blogs or other media sites

What I Read	What I Know	What I Think (My Inferences)
There were a lot of witnesses, but no one said they saw anything. (paragraph 5)	Someone must have seen what took place but doesn't want to say anything.	They must be scared of someone or afraid of getting into some kind of trouble.

Compare Accounts of a Subject

The podcast "Bully" and this news article each presents its own account, or version, of the same set of events. Think about how each account gives you

- **Multiple points of view:** What is the same about the points of view they present? What is different?
- **Certain facts and other information:** What facts and other details are similar in both accounts? What is different?
- **A particular experience based on format:** For example, the podcast includes a narrator and eyewitness interviews. The article includes visual imagery and text features such as headings.

As you read the news article, compare and contrast its account to the podcast using a Venn diagram or other organizer.

Annotation in Action

Here is an example of an inference a student made based on a passage in the news article. As you read, mark information you can use to make inferences about the people and events in the article.

Despite the efforts of police, prosecutors and McElroy's family, no one has been charged in the murder. And it's likely to stay that way.

Why? No suspects or not enough evidence? Another reason it can't be solved?

Expand Your Vocabulary

Put a check mark next to the vocabulary words that you feel comfortable using when speaking or writing.

retribution	☐
taciturn	☐
ire	☐
macabre	☐
vigilante	☐

Turn to a partner and talk about the vocabulary words you already know. Then, use as many of the vocabulary words as you can to write a paragraph or two about your first thoughts on how a murder in a small town could stay unsolved.

As you read "Unsolved 'Vigilante' Murder in the Heartland," use the definitions in the side column to help you learn the vocabulary words you don't already know.

Background

The Heartland—geographically speaking—is the central region of the United States. It is generally considered to be made up of these states: Alabama, Arkansas, Illinois, Indiana, Iowa, Kansas, Kentucky, Louisiana, Michigan, Minnesota, Mississippi, Missouri, Nebraska, North Dakota, Ohio, Oklahoma, South Dakota, Tennessee, and Wisconsin.

America's heartland has long been viewed as the symbolic heart of the country. Many Americans, no matter what state they live in, think of the heartland as a reflection of the country's shared values and ideals.

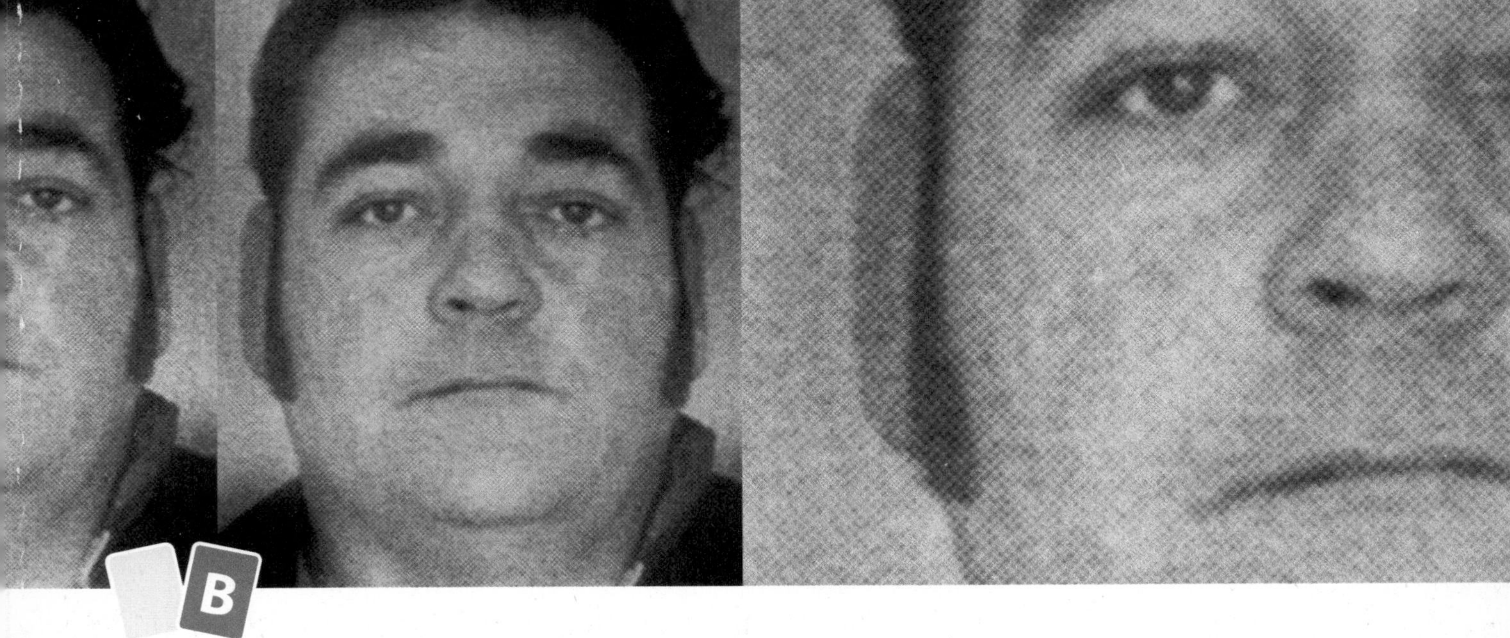

B

Unsolved "Vigilante" Murder in the Heartland

News Article by **C.M. Frankie**

NOTICE & NOTE
As you read, use the side margins to make notes about the text.

What are the consequences when someone is cruel to everyone he meets?

1 **Retribution** was slow coming to Ken McElroy—but lightning fast when it happened. On a steamy Missouri morning of July 10, 1981, a gunman took aim at the 47-year-old as he sat smoking in his Silverado pickup truck outside the local bar. The larger-than-life bully who menaced the farming community of Skidmore died in seconds. Witnessing the murder were McElroy's wife, Trena, screaming in the passenger seat and dozens of local residents.

retribution
(rĕt-rə-byo͞o′shən) *n.* punishment given in response to a wrongdoing.

MAKE INFERENCES

Annotate: Mark the main idea in paragraph 3.

Infer: Based on details in the first three paragraphs, why do you think no one has been charged with McElroy's murder?

2 Yet the identity of McElroy's killer is a public secret Skidmore has kept for 38 years.

3 Despite the efforts of police, prosecutors and McElroy's family, no one has been charged in the murder. And it's likely to stay that way.

4 "Nobody wanted to talk to us," retired Missouri State Highway Patrol Trooper Dan Boyer tells *A&E Real Crime.* Boyer was among the first responders to arrive outside the D&G tavern where McElroy was ambushed.

5 A reported crowd of up to 60 men had largely dispersed, but some onlookers remained, staring at the pickup. Those who spoke out were **taciturn**. "'I didn't see anything. I don't know what happened,'" Boyer recalls witnesses saying.

taciturn
(tăs′ĭ-tûrn) *adj.* untalkative; reserved.

Hog rustler, sweet talker

6 Ken McElroy was born in 1934, one of 16 children, author Harry MacLean explains in his book *In Broad Daylight,* an account of the case. His father was a tenant farmer,[1] his mother a housewife swamped with feeding and caring for the sprawling family.

7 There wasn't much parental supervision, but McElroy had a knack for taking care of himself. He never finished high school but knew how to hunt, drive fast and navigate the back roads of Nodaway County by his early teens. He put those skills to work rustling hogs and cattle,[2] MacLean recounts.

8 Charismatic, with jet-black hair and piercing eyes, McElroy could sweet-talk his way around women and had been married three times by his early 40s.

9 Police had charged him with various alleged crimes from stealing hogs to assault, but nothing stuck. One reason was McElroy's lawyer Richard "Gene" McFadin, a skilled defense attorney who ran rings around inexperienced prosecutors. Another was McElroy's intimidation tactics, MacLean writes. Once, a farmer who caught Ken red-handed stealing two horses filed charges but "withdrew them after McElroy smashed him across the face with a rifle."

VOCABULARY

Words from Greek and Latin The word *charismatic* is derived from the Greek word *kharisma*, which means "grace or divine favor." Knowing its Greek derivation helps readers understand that someone who is charismatic has rare or special qualities.

Analyze: The word *charismatic* is often used to describe someone who is "magnetic, captivating, and charming." Why do you think the author used *charismatic* to describe Ken McElroy?

Stalked going to church

10 Police also felt McElroy's **ire**. One night after he pulled a speeding pickup truck over, Boyer came face to face with McElroy. "I had my service weapon drawn, and I wouldn't have been the least bit surprised if he tried to do something," Boyer recalls. "His eyes just really put you in defense mode—he really looked like a mean person."

ire.
(īr) *n.* anger; fury; wrath.

11 A few days later, a pickup truck showed up in the wee hours outside Boyer's remote country house. It cruised up the street, came back and "just sat there for 20 seconds," says Boyer, adding he couldn't prove it was McElroy but waited behind a tree with his shotgun just in case.

12 In 1980, after a misunderstanding about a candy purchase from a Skidmore grocery store involving McElroy's daughters, McElroy shot popular owner "Bo" Bowenkamp in the neck.

13 When the call went out, State Police Cpl. Richard Stratton was ready. Stratton knew McElroy from a previous stop when he threatened the trooper with a shotgun. Anticipating McElroy's typical moves, Stratton waited on a back road near the Kansas border. His hunch paid off, and McElroy found himself handcuffed and charged with assault.

14 Shortly after, Stratton's wife Margaret was headed to church when she saw a strange truck in the driveway.

[1] **tenant farmer:** a person who rents the land they farm; they often have to give the landlord a share of what they grow.
[2] **rustling hogs and cattle:** stealing pigs and cows.

15 A man who turned out to be McElroy "pointed a shotgun at me," Margaret tells *A&E Real Crime*. "I didn't know what to do. I got in the car and was shaking so bad."

16 She gathered her strength and put the car in reverse. McElroy began backing out too, then tailed Margaret until she radioed Richard and squad cars showed up.

17 "I think he treated the whole town of Skidmore that way," the 78-year-old said, adding she "didn't feel brave." But "it got to the point it made me mad."

Don't forget to **Notice & Note** as you read the text.

COMPARE ACCOUNTS OF A SUBJECT

Annotate: In paragraphs 15–17, mark what Margaret Stratton tells *A&E Real Crime.*

Evaluate: The "Bully" podcast includes recorded comments from witnesses and others. What is the effect of hearing individuals' taped voices as opposed to reading their words in a print article?

Breaking point

18 Tensions in Skidmore soared as McElroy's trial neared. McElroy mounted a daily vigil outside Bowenkamp's house, his daughter Cheryl Brown recounts in *In Broad Daylight:*

19 "The town emptied out every time he came to town. Everyone was so uncomfortable and scared."

20 In court, Bowenkamp testified about how McElroy confronted him in the loading dock of the grocery while he was cutting up boxes and shot him in the neck. Then McElroy, described by veteran journalist Phil Conger as "a big brute of a guy with slicked-back hair like Elvis," took the stand. He testified that Bowenkamp attacked him with a knife and he acted in self-defense, MacLean writes.

21 The verdict was second-degree assault and two years.

22 The "final straw for Skidmore was when he was let out on bond. He went back home and was shot within a couple of days," explains Conger, editor of the *Bethany Republican-Clipper.*

Branded as vigilantes

23 The morning of July 10, 1981, a group of frustrated and angry men gathered at the Legion Hall in Skidmore, MacLean writes. The meeting broke up after participants learned McElroy and Trena were at the D&G Tavern.

24 Boyer was out showing a trainee the ropes when he got the call of a shooting in Skidmore. He found a **macabre** scene. McElroy's "rear window was shot out and the front window as well. Part of his teeth were lying on the dashboard," Boyer recalls.

25 Trena McElroy fingered a local rancher as one of the gunmen, but he denied the claim.

26 Local police, state investigators and FBI agents tried to break the town's silence, without success. Meanwhile, major media outlets descended onto Skidmore and reports of its "**vigilantes**" became water-cooler talk across the U.S.

macabre
(mə-kä´brə) *adj.* upsetting or horrifying in connection with death or injury; gruesome; ghastly.

vigilante
(vĭj-ə-lăn´tē) *n.* a person who is not a law officer, but who pursues and punishes people suspected of wrongdoing.

"You know what he was like"

27 For some residents, resentment against McElroy was projected onto the police.

28 Boyer was taking trajectory measurements[3] at the crime scene when a town official chided him.

29 The man asked, "what are you doing here?" Boyer remembers. "Why are you doing this? You know what he was like. You know how he oppressed and threatened us. I don't believe you're coming now—after we needed your help all this time."

30 Trena McElroy accused Skidmore residents of turning her husband into a scapegoat.

31 "He was a goodhearted person. He'd help anyone that needed to be helped," she said in an interview recounted in *In Broad Daylight*.

32 As of 2019, many of the main players in McElroy's story have died, including McFadin, Trena McElroy, Bowenkamp and the rancher accused of pulling the trigger, MacLean writes in his blog.

33 "Theoretically, [the murder] could be re-investigated," veteran Kansas City criminal defense attorney J.R. Hobbs tells *A&E Real Crime*. "But unless a very credible witness came forward, it's not likely to happen."

NOTICE & NOTE
QUOTED WORDS

When an author has quoted the opinion of a witness to an event, you've found a **Quoted Words** signpost.

Notice & Note: Mark the words of the official quoted in paragraph 29.

Analyze: Why was this person quoted? What did his comment add to the story?

[3] **trajectory measurements:** the path and distance a bullet or other projectile traveled.

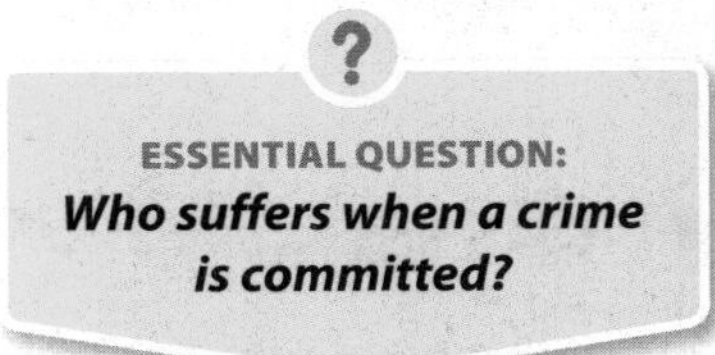
?
ESSENTIAL QUESTION:
Who suffers when a crime is committed?

COLLABORATIVE DISCUSSION

Get together with a partner and discuss what surprised you most about the events in Skidmore.

Review your notes and add your thoughts to your Response Log.

Assessment Practice

Answer these questions before moving on to the **Analyze the Text** section on the next page.

1. This question has two parts. First, answer Part A. Then, answer Part B.

Part A

What inference can you make about Ken McElroy?

(A) He had a balance of positive and negative qualities.

(B) He was liked by most townspeople but not his family.

(C) He enjoyed causing trouble and breaking the law.

(D) He tried to help the townspeople, but they did not want it.

Part B

Select **two** sentences that provide relevant support for the answer in Part A.

(A) "Despite the efforts of police . . . no one has been charged in the murder." (paragraph 3)

(B) "Ken McElroy was born in 1934, one of 16 children. . . ." (paragraph 6)

(C) "Police also felt McElroy's ire." (paragraph 10)

(D) "'You know how he oppressed and threatened us. . . .'" (paragraph 29)

(E) "'He was a goodhearted person. He'd help anyone. . . .'" (paragraph 31)

2. What conclusion is most likely shared by the podcast creators of "Bully" and the author of "Unsolved 'Vigilante' Murder in the Heartland"?

(A) An eyewitness will come forward and explain what really happened.

(B) The murder will be solved once all the investigations are completed.

(C) The murderer(s) will never be tried and convicted.

(D) The murderer(s) will soon be tried and convicted.

Ed
Test-Taking Strategies

Analyze the Text

Support your responses with evidence from the text.

NOTICE & NOTE

Review what you **noticed and noted** as you read the text. Your annotations can help you answer these questions.

1. **INFER** Reread paragraphs 1–3. Why would the author claim so early in the news article that the murder is likely to stay unsolved?

2. **SUMMARIZE** Review the section "Hog rustler, sweet talker," which is about the early years of Ken McElroy's life. Write a summary of this section; then state the main idea.

3. **SYNTHESIZE** Reread the **Quoted Words** in paragraphs 14–17. How do Margaret Stratton's words make both her and the event vivid and believable?

4. **ANALYZE** Reread paragraph 27. Why do you think some townspeople felt resentment, or bitterness, toward the police? Cite evidence from the text to support your answer.

5. **COMPARE** Think about the news article as a whole. How do the townspeople's reactions to McElroy change over time? How are they the same?

6. **DRAW CONCLUSIONS** After reading this news article, what do you think took place in the heartland town of Skidmore, and why? Review the notes you took on the Get Ready page about your inferences. Then use the chart below to explain what you think took place and why, and the text evidence that supports your explanation.

What I Think Took Place	Why I Think This	My Evidence from the Text

7. **COMPARE** Review the diagram you created to compare the podcast "Bully" with the article "Unsolved 'Vigilante' Murder in the Heartland." Briefly summarize your reactions to the differences in the two accounts: Which did you find easier to understand? Which was more engaging? Why?

Choices

Here are some other ways to demonstrate your understanding of the ideas in this lesson.

Writing

↳ Support for Trauma Survivors

Citizens of Skidmore described daily trauma they experienced during what some called Ken McElroy's "reign of terror." Many people don't know how to cope with traumatic experiences or where to seek help. With a group, create an information sheet to help people suffering from them.

Assign group members to these tasks:

- Research about types of trauma
- Help available for people experiencing traumatic disorders
- Resources and support available in your own community

Group members will also collaborate to build a website, blog, or social media page with useful information, links, and other citations for people who want to learn more.

Throughout the task, remind one another to take the perspective of people suffering from a trauma disorder: You want your final product to reflect empathy and sensitivity to their needs.

As you write and discuss, be sure to use the Academic Vocabulary words.

capacity
confer
emerge
generate
trace

Media

↳ Timeline of Events

Create a visual timeline of the events leading up to Ken McElroy's murder in Skidmore. Begin your timeline when McElroy's bullying first started. Include names of people he encountered and dates of when events took place. Present your timeline to the class.

Social & Emotional Learning

↳ Emergency Council Meeting

With classmates, convene a special meeting of the Skidmore City Council to discuss how to manage the situation with Ken McElroy. As a ground rule, the Council has agreed that any action must avoid violence. Follow these steps:

1. Decide on rules for discussion and decision-making.
2. Analyze the situation by reviewing the facts.
3. Brainstorm possible solutions.
4. Listen respectfully and build on others' ideas.
5. After the Council agrees on a solution, decide on a plan for incorporating citizen feedback before adopting the plan.

Expand Your Vocabulary

PRACTICE AND APPLY

In each item, mark the phrase that has a connection to each vocabulary word. Use a dictionary or thesaurus as needed.

1. **retribution**
   - ◯ asking for favors
   - ◯ acting with kindness
   - ◯ taking revenge

2. **taciturn**
   - ◯ someone who talks a lot
   - ◯ someone who is quiet
   - ◯ someone who rents farmland

3. **ire**
   - ◯ an angry person
   - ◯ a curious person
   - ◯ a farm tool

4. **macabre**
   - ◯ a horrifying scene
   - ◯ an unusual costume
   - ◯ a type of string art

5. **vigilante**
   - ◯ rustles cattle
   - ◯ acts within the law
   - ◯ acts outside the law

Vocabulary Strategy

Words from Greek and Latin

Interactive Vocabulary Lesson: Understanding Word Origins

Studying the **etymology** of words means that you look at word origins and the ways that words have changed over time. Many words in the English language come from Greek and Latin roots.

Knowing the meaning of **roots,** or basic word elements, can help you determine the meaning of unfamiliar words. For example, the word *theoretically* contains the Greek root *theoretos* that means "observable." In English, *theoretically* means "based on theory." A theory is a statement that is generally accepted as true because it explains something that took place and is based on facts. Knowing the meanings of roots can also help you determine the meanings of **derivations,** new words made from existing words by adding affixes. For example, the word *vigil* is the same as its Latin root, which means "to be watchful." *Vigilante* is a derivation of *vigil*.

PRACTICE AND APPLY

Look up these words from the selection in a dictionary. Write the meaning of the Latin or Greek root word, and then write a sentence using another word with that same root.

Word	Root	Word	Root
identity (paragraph 2)	*ident-*	intimidation (paragraph 9)	*timid-*
prosecutor (paragraph 3)	*prosecut-*	veteran (paragraph 20)	*veter-*
navigate (paragraph 7)	*navigat-*	credible (paragraph 33)	*cred-*

Watch Your Language!

Active and Passive Voice

Writers may express an idea in either the active or the passive voice. The subject of a sentence may either perform or receive the action expressed in a verb.

Active voice ↳ when the subject does the action	**Example** She gathered her strength and put the car in reverse.
Passive voice ↳ when the subject is the receiver of the action (or has the action performed on them)	**Example** Witnessing the murder were McElroy's wife . . . and dozens of local residents.

The active voice is most commonly used. Active voice:

- enables writers to be more direct, concise, and precise in their use of language, making their writing more effective and powerful
- helps readers feel a greater sense of immediacy—as if actually witnessing or experiencing the events

The passive voice:

- emphasizes the receiver of the action—"McElroy was ambushed."
- is used when the doer of the action is unknown—"The hogs and cattle were rustled."

Interactive Grammar Lesson: Active and Passive Voice

PRACTICE AND APPLY

With a partner, write two paragraphs of a news article, reporting on an event you observed recently such as a basketball game, musical performance, or family activity. Use the passive and the active voice at least once. Exchange papers with a partner and discuss how active and passive voice create different effects.

Compare Accounts

Every medium differs in how it treats, or presents, a subject or topic. Think about how a person's life might be depicted in a painting, a documentary, or a book.

Both "Bully" and "Unsolved 'Vigilante' Murder in the Heartland" provide fact-based accounts of the same events. However, the "Bully" podcast and "Unsolved" news article differ in the information provided and how it is presented. By comparing these two accounts in different media, you can gain a deeper understanding of the events surrounding McElroy's murder.

In a small group, complete the chart below. Be sure to support your ideas with evidence from both selections.

	A Bully	B Unsolved "Vigilante" Murder in the Heartland
What information is emphasized?		
How is this information emphasized?		
What perspectives, or points of view, are being presented?		
What messages are being conveyed?		
What techniques are used to engage the audience?		

Analyze Media and Text

Discuss these questions in your group.

1. **COMPARE** How is each account organized, or structured? What techniques does each use to connect people and events? Cite specific examples from the podcast and the article.
2. **DRAW CONCLUSIONS** Consider the information each article presents about Ken McElroy's childhood. Was it his fate, or destiny, to become a bully? Why or why not?
3. **SYNTHESIZE** Both selections describe how the legal system responded to McElroy's misdeeds. How do the podcast and news article together give you greater insight into these responses—and into the legal system in general?
4. **EVALUATE** Which account provides a more objective, or balanced, perspective on the events surrounding McElroy's murder? Support your ideas with evidence from each account.

Collaborate and Present

Your group can continue exploring the ideas in these media accounts by collaborating on your own podcast or news article. Follow these steps:

1. **DECIDE ON THE MESSAGE** First, review your notes on both selections as a group. Next, discuss what message you most want to convey about McElroy's murder.
2. **CHOOSE THE MEDIUM** Decide which medium—podcast or news article—will best convey your message. Think about how you will use the strengths of the medium to convey your message effectively.
3. **DEVELOP A PLAN** Plan how to use both selections as your sources. What information will you include—or omit—to best support your message? How will you grab and hold onto your audience's interest?
4. **MAKE AN OUTLINE** Organize your podcast or news article to ensure a logical structure, or flow, for your audience. Think about how to use transitions to connect events.
5. **CREATE A DRAFT** Assign sections of your outline to each group member. Work together to review, revise, and edit each section.
6. **PRACTICE AND PRESENT** For the podcast, practice it before you record and share it. For the news article, consider adding text-and-graphic features. Then proofread it before sharing it.
7. **DISCUSS AS A CLASS** Based on everyone's podcasts and news articles, has your perspective on this murder changed? Why or why not?

Reader's Choice

Continue your exploration of the Essential Question by doing some independent reading about crime and its consequences. Read the titles and descriptions shown. Then mark the texts that interest you.

? **ESSENTIAL QUESTION:**
Who suffers when a crime is committed?

Short Reads

Available on 

These texts are available in your ebook. Choose one to read and rate. Then defend your rating to the class.

Lamb to the Slaughter

Short Story by **Roald Dahl**

A loving, resourceful wife uses materials at hand when her husband comes home with news.

Rate It 

My Afterlife on the Body Farm

Informational Text by **Fawn Fitter**

Want to help fight crime long after you're gone? Donate your remains to a body farm!

Rate It 

The Crime of My Life

Short Story by **Gregg Olsen**

When the narrator, a true-crime writer, confronts a horrific crime in his own life, readers are taken along for the bizarre and shocking ride.

Rate It 

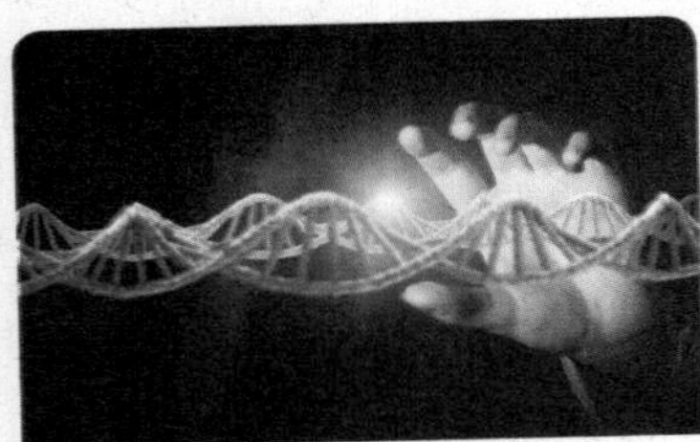

Why Aren't Police Solving More Murders with Genealogy Websites?

Science Writing by **Adam Janos**

DNA databases have become wildly popular with the general public. Why aren't crime investigators using them more?

Rate It 

Prometheus Bound

Graphic Story adapted from **Aeschylus** by **Ellis Rosen**

Meet the Greek hero Prometheus—mythological Titan and world's first lawbreaker.

Rate It ☆☆☆☆☆

Long Reads

Here are three recommended books that connect to this unit topic. For additional options, ask your teacher, school librarian, or peers. Which titles spark your interest?

In Cold Blood

Nonfiction by **Truman Capote**

Four members of the Clutter family are murdered in a seemingly random crime. Capote reconstructs the crime and the investigation that led to the murderers' capture.

Murder on the Orient Express

Mystery by **Agatha Christie**

On a three-day train ride, a detective must interrogate an array of international suspects to find the passenger who murdered a gangster on the Orient Express.

We'll Fly Away

Novel by **Bryan Bliss**

Luke and Toby are best friends who want to get away from their abusive and complicated families. It almost happens, until Luke is convicted of murder.

Extension

↳ Connect & Create

CRIME COVER With others or on your own, design a book cover for one of the texts you read. Decisions to make:

- Do you want to attract hardcore crime and true-crime fans, or do you want your cover to appeal to a broader audience? Think about an overall look that will persuade your target audience to click on or pick up the book.
- Consider the theme, ideas, and/or atmosphere you want to capture.
- What graphics will you use? Photographs, drawings, abstract shapes, a collage—or just the title and author?
- Assemble the elements into a design, and create a final version to share with the class.

CRIMINAL PREOCCUPATIONS In different ways, this unit asks the question, What is it about crime and its consequences that fascinates us? Write a response based on the text you read. Then share your ideas with others who read the same or different texts, recording your conclusions.

NOTICE & NOTE

- Pick one of the texts and annotate the Notice & Note signposts you find.
- Then, use the **Notice & Note Writing Frames** to help you write about the significance of the signposts.
- Compare your findings with those of other students who read the same text.

Notice & Note Writing Frames

Write an Informative Essay

Writing Prompt

Using ideas, information, and examples from multiple texts in this unit, write an informative essay that examines the impact and effects of crime.

Manage your time carefully so that you can

- review the texts in the unit;
- plan your informative essay;
- write your informative essay; and
- revise and edit your informative essay.

Be sure to

- include an introduction with a clear controlling idea, or thesis statement;
- organize ideas logically;
- support ideas with evidence; and
- sum up the central idea in a logical conclusion.

Review the Mentor Text

For an example of a well-written informative text you can use as a mentor text for your informative essay, review:

- **"Why Are We Obsessed with True Crime?"** (pages 221–225).

Review your notes and annotations about this text. Think about how the author uses evidence to develop ideas.

Consider Your Sources

Review the list of texts in the unit and choose at least three that you may want to use as sources of support for your informative essay.

As you review potential sources, review the notes you made on your **Response Log** and make additional notes about ideas that might be useful as you write. Include titles and page numbers so that you can easily find information later. Accurate text evidence and citations will support the presentation of your ideas.

UNIT 3 SOURCES

- [ ] **Entwined**
- [ ] **Why Are We Obsessed with True Crime?**
- [ ] *from* **The 57 Bus**
- [ ] **Gift-Wrapped Fathers**
- [ ] **Bully** MEDIA
- [ ] **Unsolved "Vigilante" Murder in the Heartland**

Analyze the Prompt

Review the prompt to make sure you understand the assignment.

1. Mark the phrase in the prompt that identifies the general topic of your informative essay. Restate the topic in your own words.
2. Look for words that suggest the purpose and audience of your informative essay, and write a sentence describing each.

Consider Your Audience

Ask yourself:

- Who will read my essay?
- What do my readers already know about my topic?
- What supporting evidence should I provide in my essay?

What is my topic? What is my writing task?

What is my purpose?

Who is my audience?

Review the Rubric

Your informative essay will be scored using a rubric. As you write, focus on the characteristics described in the chart. You will learn more about these characteristics as you work through the lesson.

Purpose, Focus, and Organization	Evidence and Elaboration	Conventions of Standard English
The response includes: • A strongly maintained controlling idea • Use of transitions to connect ideas • Logical progression of ideas • Appropriate style and tone	The response includes: • Effective use of evidence and sources • Effective use of elaboration • Clear and effective expression of ideas • Appropriate vocabulary • Varied sentence structure	The response may include: • Some minor errors in usage but no patterns of errors • Correct punctuation, capitalization, sentence formation, and spelling • Command of basic conventions

1 PLAN YOUR INFORMATIVE ESSAY

Develop a Controlling Idea

Think about the many ways crime has been examined and portrayed in this unit. List possible topics for your essay and the different points of view you might explore. Then circle the topic of your main focus.

Ed

Help with Planning

Consult **Interactive Writing Lesson: Writing Informative Texts**

Possible Topics	Points of View

Develop Your Key Ideas

Consider what you want to say about your topic. Write a thesis statement that expresses the controlling idea your informative essay will explore. Then, jot down key ideas that will help you develop this controlling idea.

Thesis	
Key Idea 1	
Key Idea 2	
Key Idea 3	

Identify Evidence

Your evidence should include facts, examples, and concrete details that support your key ideas. Review the notes in your Response Log and consider other sources that might help you develop your ideas. Record your evidence and source information in the chart.

Evidence	Source

Organize Ideas

Think about the most logical and engaging way to structure your informative essay. Use the chart to help you plan your draft.

INTRODUCTION	• Introduce your topic. • Clearly state your thesis. • Express your purpose.
BODY PARAGRAPHS	• Devote a paragraph to each key idea. • Support each idea with evidence. • Use transitions to connect ideas.
CONCLUSION	• Restate your thesis and its significance. • End with a final thought for readers to consider.

Use an Effective Structure

Here are some patterns of organization:

- **Cause and Effect:** explains reasons for and results of an issue
- **Comparison-Contrast:** examines similarities and differences related to an issue
- **Main Idea and Details:** presents important ideas and develops them with details, fact, and examples

2 DEVELOP A DRAFT

Now it is time to draft your essay. Examining how professional writers craft their informational writing can help you develop your own writing skills. Read about techniques you might use in your writing.

Drafting Online

Check your assignment list for a writing task from your teacher.

Use Evidence

EXAMINE THE MENTOR TEXT

Notice how the author of **"Why Are We Obsessed with True Crime?"** uses evidence to develop ideas about how audiences view the nonfiction crime genre.

Lee said that in the past, crime shows like *America's Most Wanted* and *Unsolved Mysteries* were seen as "tabloid television for crime junkies." Low-budget re-enactments and low production quality made the genre seem less reputable.

But since the birth of NPR's wildly popular 2014 podcast *Serial,* the way people view true crime has changed.

"It was a flagship moment for the genre," Lee said of *Serial's* success. "It sort of signaled to the larger world that you can do [true crime] in a smart way, in a way that conveyed lots of thought, and in a way that was captivating for an audience."

The author cites specific examples of the crime genre.

She uses concrete details and quotations to explain how the true-crime genre has changed.

APPLY TO YOUR DRAFT

Use this chart to practice developing one of your key ideas. Draft sentences that illustrate a key point, explain it, and elaborate on it. Then apply these techniques to your draft.

Illustrate
Explain
Elaborate

Try These Suggestions

Vary the way you develop your key ideas. Try these out:

- use **extended definitions** to explain complex ideas
- use **concrete details** to share specific information
- include **quotations** to show a perspective
- use **examples** to help clarify ideas

Organize Ideas

EXAMINE THE MENTOR TEXT

In informative texts, it is important to clarify connections and distinctions among complex ideas. Notice how the author of **"Why Are We Obsessed with True Crime?"** uses evidence and a heading to help show how ideas are organized.

The author explores reasons why people watch true crime.

"*Serial* and shows like *The Jinx* empower the audience in some way—even if it's not really empowering—but they give the illusion of empowerment because people at home are in this position where they feel like they can help crack the case, and are an active part of the investigation," Lee said.

"People think that they can help overturn a ruling, exonerate a person, or crack a cold case. That's exciting to people."

But how does true crime affect our well-being?

She uses a heading to signal a shift in ideas.

Even if you're a huge fan of the genre, you've likely experienced some side effects after watching a show or reading a scary book, like trouble falling asleep or nightmares. Disturbing content, after all, can affect your emotional well-being.

She provides examples to answer the question in her heading.

APPLY TO YOUR DRAFT

Use the chart to explore ways in which you might use formatting such as headings or graphics to help clarify key ideas in your essay. As you write, incorporate these features in your draft.

Complex Idea	Use of Formatting

Organize Information

Try these strategies to organize complex ideas in your essay:

- use headings to guide readers
- use a table to show cause/effect or comparison/contrast
- use bullets to emphasize key points
- use a chart or graph to show data

3 REVISE YOUR INFORMATIVE ESSAY

Professional writers rework their language as they write to make sure they are communicating their ideas effectively. Use the guide to help you as you revise your informative essay.

Help with Revision

Find a **Peer Review Guide** and **Student Models** online.

REVISION GUIDE		
Ask Yourself	**Prove it**	**Revise it**
Introduction Does my introduction clearly state my controlling idea, or thesis?	**Underline** your thesis statement.	**Reword** your thesis statement so that your purpose for writing is clear.
Supporting Evidence Do I develop my key ideas with supporting evidence?	**Put a star** (★) next to each key idea. **Put a check mark** (✓) next to supporting evidence.	**Add** facts, details, and examples to support key ideas.
Organization Is the structure of my informative essay clear?	**Underline** transitional words and phrases.	**Rearrange** paragraphs, if needed, to clarify your organizational structure. **Add** transitions to show connections between ideas.
Style Have I used a formal style?	**Cross out** (X) any informal words and phrases.	**Reword** to avoid informal language.
Conclusion Does my conclusion follow logically from the ideas I present?	**Highlight** your concluding statement.	**Add** a closing statement, if needed, to sum up the ideas that your informative essay presents.

APPLY TO YOUR DRAFT

Reread your informative essay and look for opportunities to improve your writing.

- Check that all evidence clearly relates to your controlling idea.
- Make sure the informative essay flows logically from one idea to the next.
- Be sure your conclusion sums up your key points in a memorable way.

Peer Review in Action

Once you have finished revising your informative essay, you will exchange papers with a partner in a **peer review**. During a peer review, you will give suggestions to improve your partner's draft.

Read the introduction from a student's draft and examine the comments made by the peer reviewer to see how it's done.

Draft

Lasting Impacts of Crime
By Eugenia Wilkinson, Sherman High School

When you think about it, a violent crime involving a single perpetrator and victim can actually impact a lot of people. You have emergency responders, witnesses, lawyers, judges, juries, and even people like family and friends of those involved. As you can see, crimes can have far-reaching effects on communities and society. And these impacts can last a really long time after you stop hearing the sirens and seeing the lights flashing.

This sounds a little wordy. Try deleting any unnecessary details.

Your language is a little informal. I think you should avoid using the pronoun "you" and words like "really."

Now read the revised introduction below. Notice how the writer has improved the draft by making revisions based on the reviewer's comments.

Revision

Lasting Impacts of Crime
By Eugenia Wilkinson, Sherman High School

Every crime has its victims and its perpetrators. In addition, crimes may involve countless others from witnesses to emergency responders. However, crimes also have far-reaching effects on communities and society. The impact of violent crime reverberates long after the lights and sirens stop flashing and wailing.

Nice! This is more concise and easier to read.

Great job. This language sounds more appropriate for an essay.

APPLY TO YOUR DRAFT

During your peer review, give each other specific suggestions for how you could make your informative essay more clear or engaging. Use your revision guide to help you.

When receiving feedback from your partner, listen attentively and ask questions to make sure you fully understand the revision suggestions.

4 EDIT YOUR INFORMATIVE ESSAY

Edit your final draft to check for proper use of standard English conventions and to correct any misspellings or grammatical errors.

Ed
Interactive Grammar Lesson: Spelling

Watch Your Language!

SPELL PLURAL NOUNS CORRECTLY

Misspelled plural nouns in your informative essay could confuse your readers. Most plural nouns are formed by adding either *-s* or *-es.*

Read the sentences from **"Why Are We Obsessed with True Crime?"**

> Lee said that in the past, crime shows like *America's Most Wanted* and *Unsolved Mysteries* were seen as "tabloid television for crime junkies." Low-budget re-enactments and low production quality made the genre seem less reputable.

The plural forms of the words *show* and *enactment* are formed by adding *-s.* For the words *mystery* and *junky,* plurals are formed by changing the *y* to an *i* and adding *-es.*

Spelling Plural Nouns

Here are some additional rules for spelling plural nouns:

- Add *-es* to form a plural of certain nouns that end in *o,* such as *hero, tomato, potato,* and *echo,* and all nouns that end in *s, sh, ch, x,* or *z.*
- When a singular noun ends in *y* with a consonant before it, change the *y* to *i* and add *-es.*
- When a singular noun ends in y with a vowel *(a, e, i, o, u)* before it, just add *-s.*

APPLY TO YOUR DRAFT

Now apply what you've learned about spelling to your own work.

1. Read your paper aloud and circle plural nouns.
2. Correct any errors in spelling.
3. Exchange drafts with a peer and edit each other's work, looking for spelling errors.

5 PUBLISH YOUR INFORMATIVE ESSAY

Share It!

The prompt asks you to write an informative essay. You may also adapt your informative essay to other formats.

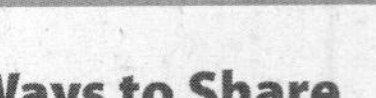

Ways to Share

- Conduct a **panel discussion** about your topic with other classmates or invited guests.
- **Design an infographic** that summarizes your key ideas and evidence.
- **Create a podcast.** See the next task for tips on how.

Speaking & Listening

Create a Podcast

With a group of 3–5 classmates, plan and present a ten- to twenty-minute podcast, or audio recording, in which you discuss the Essential Question: Who suffers when a crime is committed?

Plan Your Podcast

Your group's podcast will center on a thoughtful discussion of the question: Who suffers when a crime is committed? The discussion can focus on the texts in this unit, or on other aspects or topics related to the Essential Question. Engage your listeners by conducting your podcast discussion like a conversation among friends or colleagues. Tone and voice should be informal, but participants should avoid nonstandard English and slang.

Use the chart to guide you as you plan your podcast.

Engage Your Audience

- **Consider a variety of angles from which you might examine the topic.**
- **Try to discuss ideas you know will hold your listeners' attention.**

Speaking and Listening: Using Media in a Presentation

Ask	Answers and Notes
How will we introduce the podcast in a way that captures listeners' attention?	
What should our podcast format be? Should we have a moderator or other defined roles? Or a more casual exchange?	
Should we create a tight script, or just agree on key ideas or topics to explore?	
Will music or other sound effects help convey our ideas?	

Practice with Your Group

Once you've created a plan, rehearse it as a group.

Goal	Notes for Final Recording
Make sure your presentation has a clear focus or perspective based on the Essential Question.	
Rehearse a brief introduction and conclusion. Talk through the main points you plan to discuss.	
As you rehearse, make sure all participants speak at an appropriate volume and rate, or pace. Remind participants not to interrupt or speak over one another.	
If you are using sound effects, assign a group member to play them on cue.	

Record Your Podcast

With your teacher's help, plan how to record and share your podcast. Use these tips:

- Find a quiet place to record.
- Adjust the positioning of your recording device as needed so all voices are picked up.
- Review the recording in segments and edit it as needed.

Share It!

Listen to other classmates' podcasts. Then:

- **Create a concept map** showing the most interesting or surprising facts that you've learned from the podcasts.
- **Have a group discussion** about the effectiveness of any music and sound effects used in the podcasts.
- **Post your podcast** on a class or school website.

Reflect & Extend

Here are some other ways to show your understanding of the ideas in Unit 3.

Reflect on the
Essential Question

Who suffers when a crime is committed?

Has your answer to the question changed after reading the texts in the unit? Discuss your ideas.

You can use these sentence starters to help you reflect on your learning.

- **My thoughts on the question changed because . . .**
- **Now that I've considered . . . , I realize . . .**
- **I also gained insight about . . .**

Project-Based Learning

Create a Sketchnote

You've explored different ideas about crime and its impact. Now, create a sketchnote to help you understand a complicated passage or concept from one of the selections. A sketchnote is a form of note-taking that combines text with visuals such as doodles, arrows, numbers, and boxes to represent your thought processes.

Here are some questions to ask yourself as you get started.

- What do I want to understand about the passage or concept?
- What words, doodles, and markings can I use to show my thinking?
- How will I show connections between ideas?

Media Projects

To find more help with this task online, access **Create a Sketchnote.**

Writing

Write an Argument

Write an argument to support a claim about nonfiction crime stories. What impact do these stories have on audiences and the people involved in the crimes?

- Make a claim about positive or negative aspects of true-crime stories.
- Develop the claim with reasons and evidence from "Why Are We Obsessed with True Crime?" and other sources.
- Address counterclaims with effective responses.
- End with a conclusion that reinforces the claim and support.

Analyze the Image
What might be the thoughts going through the minds of these two people?
Ed
Get hooked by the unit topic.
Stream to Start Video

Love and Loss

"Love is the great intangible."
—Diane Ackerman

ESSENTIAL QUESTION:
How can love bring both joy and pain?

Spark Your Learning

Here are some opportunities to think about the topics and themes of **Unit 4: Love and Loss.**

As you read, you can use the **Response Log** (page R4) to track your thinking about the Essential Question.

Think about the **Essential Question**

How can love bring both joy and pain?

With a partner, brainstorm a list of examples.

Make the Connection

The drama of romantic love has probably captivated humans since the beginning of time: Two people fall in love, then a complication arises that threatens their bond. The resolution can bring joy, despair, or emotions in between. This story has been told thousands of times, yet we never seem to tire of it. Why? Discuss your thoughts and examples with a partner.

Build Academic Vocabulary

You can use these Academic Vocabulary words to write and talk about the topics and themes in the unit. Which of these words do you already feel comfortable using when speaking or writing?

	I can use it!	I understand it.	I'll look it up.
attribute			
commit			
expose			
initiate			
underlie			

Prove It!

How would you define the ideal love between two people? Use one or more Academic Vocabulary words in a one- or two-sentence definition. Then share with a partner.

Preview the Texts

Look over the images, titles, and descriptions of the texts in the unit. Mark the title of the text that interests you most.

The Tragedy of Romeo and Juliet

Drama by **William Shakespeare**

Rapturous passion ends tragically in this great story of love crossed and families divided.

My Shakespeare

Video and Poem by **Kae Tempest**

A rapper describes how Shakespeare's work is still relevant today.

More than Reckless Teenagers

Literary Analysis by **Caitlin Smith**

Are Romeo and Juliet foolish teenagers, or complex and self-aware characters?

Romeo Is a Dirtbag

Literary Analysis by **Lois Leveen**

The author argues that Shakespeare's Romeo and Juliet *isn't about romantic love at all.*

Think Outside the Box

Consider the quotation that opens this unit, "Love is the great intangible." Something that is *intangible* has no physical presence and cannot be touched. Do you think love is intangible? Freewrite your thoughts.

Shakespearean Drama

Shakespeare's 38 plays may be more popular today than they were in Elizabethan times. While Shakespeare's comedies and histories remain crowd-pleasing classics, his tragedies are perhaps his most powerful works. One of the most famous, *The Tragedy of Romeo and Juliet*, relates the tale of two love-struck teens caught in the tensions between their feuding families.

Characteristics of Shakespearean Tragedy

A **tragedy** is a drama that results in a catastrophe for the main characters. Shakespearean tragedies offer more than just despair; they provide comic moments that counter the underlying tension of the plot. Before you read, familiarize yourself with some character types and dramatic conventions of Shakespearean tragedy.

Characters	Dramatic Conventions
Tragic Hero • the protagonist, or central character • usually fails or dies because of a character flaw or a cruel twist of fate	**Soliloquy** • a speech given by a character alone • exposes a character's thoughts and feelings to the audience
Antagonist • the adversary or hostile force opposing the protagonist • can be a character, a group of characters, or a nonhuman entity	**Aside** • a character's remark that others on stage do not hear • reveals the character's private thoughts
Foil • a character whose personality and attitude contrast sharply with those of another character • emphasizes another character's attributes and traits	**Dramatic Irony** • when the audience knows more than the characters; helps build suspense **Comic Relief** • a humorous scene or speech meant to relieve tension; the contrast can heighten the seriousness of the action

The Language of Shakespeare

Blank Verse Shakespeare wrote his plays primarily in blank verse: unrhymed lines of **iambic pentameter**, a meter that contains five unstressed syllables (˘), each followed by a stressed syllable (´). Read the following line aloud, emphasizing each stressed syllable:

Hĕre's múch tŏ dó wĭth háte bŭt móre wĭth lóve.

While this pattern forms the general rule, variations in the rhythm prevent the play from sounding monotonous. As you read, pay close attention to places where characters speak in rhyming poetry instead of unrhymed verse.

Allusion An allusion is a reference to a literary or historical person or event that the audience is expected to know. Shakespeare's audience was familiar with Greek and Roman mythology and the Bible, so his plays include many references to these works. For example, Mercutio refers to the mythological god of love when he says, "Borrow Cupid's wings and soar with them . . ." (Act I, Scene 4).

Elizabethan Theater

A Wide Audience Though acting companies toured throughout England, London was the center of the Elizabethan stage. One reason that London's theaters did so well was that they attracted an avid audience of rich and poor alike. In fact, Elizabethan theaters were among the few forms of entertainment available to working class people, and one of the only places where people of all classes could mix.

The Globe In 1599, Shakespeare and other shareholders of The Lord Chamberlain's Men built the Globe Theatre, a three-story wooden structure with an open courtyard at its center where the actors performed on an elevated platform. The theater held 3,000 people, with most of them standing near the courtyard stage in an area known as the pit. The pit audience paid the lowest admission fee—usually just one penny. Theater-goers willing and able to pay more sat in the covered inner balconies that surrounded the courtyard.

Staging Elizabethan theater relied heavily on the audience's imagination. Most theaters had no curtains, no lighting, and very little scenery. Instead, props, sound effects, and certain lines of dialogue defined the setting of a scene. While the staging was simple, the scenes were hardly dull. Flashing swords, brightly colored banners, and elegant costumes contributed to the spectacle. The costumes also helped audience members imagine that women appeared in the female roles, which were actually performed by young men. In Shakespeare's time, women could not belong to theater companies in England—Elizabethan society considered it highly improper for a woman to appear on stage.

Get Ready

The Tragedy of Romeo and Juliet

Drama by **William Shakespeare**

ESSENTIAL QUESTION:
How can love bring both joy and pain?

Engage Your Brain

Choose one or more of these activities to start connecting with the drama you're about to read.

Lovestruck

Do you believe in love at first sight? Or do people feel an initial attraction that develops into love over time? Freewrite your thoughts; then share with the class or a small group.

"He's a Real Romeo!"

The influence of *Romeo and Juliet* is still huge, whether it's the plot of star-crossed lovers, lines from the play ("parting is such sweet sorrow"), or the star characters. Make a list of versions or adaptations you are familiar with: songs, movies, TV shows, poems, books, or graphic versions. Combine your list with those of other classmates into a physical or virtual poster.

Foolish Feuds

Sometimes feuds between two people or groups never seem to end: between siblings, rival schools, or former friends. Think of a time you witnessed or were in a fight that seemed to last forever. What caused it to continue? Did it get resolved? Why or why not? Discuss with a partner.

Analyze Literary Devices

Shakespeare uses a variety of literary devices in *The Tragedy of Romeo and Juliet* to create complex and believable characters, establish mood and setting, and develop suspense. As you read the play, start a word wall of any terms or phrases you find interesting or challenging. Add to this word wall as you continue to read.

Characters In creating his characters, Shakespeare often uses a **foil,** a character who contrasts with one of his major characters. Mercutio is one of the most famous foils in literature, his ironic wit contrasting with Romeo's romanticism and his fierce family pride contrasting with Romeo's desire for peace between the Montagues and the Capulets.

Setting Since Shakespearean theaters did not have stage sets with false trees and painted walls, the playwright had to create a sense of where the characters were by using **descriptive dialogue.** It's difficult to make that dialogue sound natural, but Shakespeare does it in this line from Act I, Scene 5: "More light, you knaves! and turn the tables up, / And quench the fire, the room is grown too hot."

Mood Shakespeare is brilliant at varying moods and building tension. Then he breaks that tension with such devices as **comic relief,** in which he uses word play. For example, Shakespeare's **puns** make use of a word's multiple meanings, or they play on its sound. One of Shakespeare's most powerful literary devices for mood building is the **soliloquy,** in which a character who is alone—or thinks he or she is alone—speaks his or her innermost thoughts and feelings. The overlapping soliloquies in the balcony scene of *The Tragedy of Romeo and Juliet* (Act II, Scene 2), which gradually become a dialogue, create a mood of romance and longing. Other literary devices Shakespeare uses include **oxymorons,** expressions containing an apparent contradiction ("parting is such sweet sorrow"); and **similes** ("My bounty is as boundless as the sea, / My love as deep; the more I give to thee, / The more I have, for both are infinite").

Suspense Shakespeare builds suspense even when the audience is so familiar with a story that it knows how the play ends. One device he uses is **dramatic irony,** in which the audience knows what one or more of the people on stage does not know. For example, Juliet pours out her heart in the balcony scene, not knowing that Romeo is listening. Another important device for building suspense is **foreshadowing.** At several points in the play characters refer, often unknowingly, to what will happen in the future.

Focus on Genre
↳ Drama

- written to be performed by actors in front of an audience
- tells a story through characters' words and actions
- includes stage directions with important details that explain what's happening
- may be divided into acts, which are in turn divided into scenes
- may show that the time or place of the action has changed by starting a new act or scene

Analyze Parallel Plots

Romeo and Juliet is not a simple love story with a **linear,** or straightforward, plot. It is a complex drama featuring **parallel plots,** separate story lines that happen at the same time and are linked by common characters and themes. The chart can help you identify the parallel plots in the play.

Plot	Purpose
The love story of Romeo and Juliet	How does this main plot intertwine with the other parallel plots?
The feud between the Capulets and the Montagues	How does this plot contribute to the drama of the play?
Romeo's unrequited love for Rosaline	What does this show us about Romeo?
Juliet's marriage proposal from Paris	What do we learn about Juliet and her relationship with her family?

Annotation in Action

Here are one reader's notes about the Act I Prologue to *The Tragedy of Romeo and Juliet*. As you read, note clues about the play's setting, plot, and characters.

Two households, both alike in dignity,
In fair Verona, where we lay our scene,
From ancient grudge break to new mutiny,
Where civil blood makes civil hands unclean.
From forth the fatal loins of these two foes,
A pair of star-crossed lovers take their life,
Whose misadventured piteous overthrows
Doth with their death bury their parents' strife.

Foreshadowing — we already know how the play ends.

The Tragedy of Romeo and Juliet

Drama by **William Shakespeare**

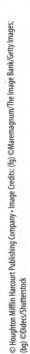

William Shakespeare (1564–1616)

Shakespeare has long been considered the greatest writer in the English language—and perhaps the greatest playwright of all time. Four hundred years after their first performances, his plays remain more popular than ever, and they have been produced more often and in more countries than those of any other author. Despite Shakespeare's worldwide fame, we have relatively few details about his life and career as an actor, poet, and playwright. He came from Stratford-upon-Avon, a small village about 90 miles northwest of London, and was probably born in 1564. Though no records exist, we assume that he attended the local grammar school. In 1582, he married Anne Hathaway, the daughter of a farmer. The couple's first child arrived in 1583, and twins, a boy and a girl, followed two years later.

We know nothing about the next seven years of Shakespeare's life, but he likely left his family behind and joined a traveling theater troupe. His trail resurfaces in London, where he had become a successful poet and playwright. He wrote for and acted with The Lord Chamberlain's Men, a popular theater troupe. By 1597, the year that *The Tragedy of Romeo and Juliet* was published, he had become a shareholder of the theater company. As his popularity grew, Shakespeare also became part owner of London's Globe Theatre. In 1603, King James I became a patron of the Globe Theatre, and the theater troupe became known as The King's Men.

In 1609, Shakespeare published his sonnets, a series of poems that received wide popular acclaim. Shakespeare then began to take advantage of his wealth and fame, spending more time in Stratford-upon-Avon and retiring there permanently around 1612. He would write no more plays after that year. No records confirm the cause or date of his death; a monument marking his gravesite indicates that he died on April 23, 1616. Although we have little data documenting his life, more pages have been written about Shakespeare than about any author in the history of Western civilization.

Rapturous passion ends tragically in this great story of lovers crossed and families divided.

THE TIME: The 14th century
THE PLACE: Verona (və-rō´nə) and Mantua (măn´cho͞o-ə) in northern Italy

Characters

The Montagues
Lord Montague (mŏn´tə-gyo͞o)
Lady Montague
Romeo, son of Montague
Benvolio (bĕn-vō´lē-ō), nephew of Montague and friend of Romeo
Balthasar (bäl´thə-sär), servant to Romeo
Abram, servant to Montague

The Capulets
Lord Capulet (kăp´yo͞o-lĕt)
Lady Capulet
Juliet, daughter of Capulet
Tybalt (tĭb´əlt), nephew of Lady Capulet
Nurse to Juliet
Peter, servant to Juliet's nurse
Sampson, servant to Capulet
Gregory, servant to Capulet
An Old Man of the Capulet family

Others
Prince Escalus (ĕs´kə-ləs), ruler of Verona
Mercutio (mĕr-kyo͞o´shē-ō), kinsman of the prince and friend of Romeo
Friar Laurence, a Franciscan priest
Friar John, another Franciscan priest
Count Paris, a young nobleman, kinsman of the prince
Apothecary (ə-pŏth´ĭ-kĕr-ē)
Page to Paris
Chief Watchman
Three Musicians
An Officer
Chorus
Citizens of Verona, **Gentlemen** and **Gentlewomen** of both houses, **Maskers, Torchbearers, Pages, Guards, Watchmen, Servants,** and **Attendants**

Prologue

[*Enter* Chorus.]

Chorus. Two households, both alike in dignity,
In fair Verona, where we lay our scene,
From ancient grudge break to new mutiny,
Where civil blood makes civil hands unclean.
From forth the fatal loins of these two foes,
A pair of star-crossed lovers take their life,
Whose misadventured piteous overthrows
Doth with their death bury their parents' strife.
The fearful passage of their death-marked love,
And the continuance of their parents' rage,
Which, but their children's end, naught could remove,
Is now the two hours' traffic of our stage,
The which if you with patient ears attend,
What here shall miss, our toil shall strive to mend.

[*Exit.*]

NOTICE & NOTE
As you read, use the side margins to make notes about the text.

Ed
Close Read Screencast
Listen to a modeled close read of this text.

3–4 **ancient . . . unclean:** A new outbreak of fighting (**mutiny**) between families has caused the citizens of Verona to have one another's blood on their hands.

6 **star-crossed:** doomed. The position of the stars when the lovers were born was not favorable. In Shakespeare's day, people took astrology very seriously.

7 **misadventured:** unlucky.

11 **but:** except for; **naught:** nothing.

14 **what . . . mend:** The play will fill in the details not mentioned in the prologue.

Act I

Scene 1 *A public square in Verona.*

[*Enter* Sampson *and* Gregory, *servants of the house of Capulet, armed with swords and bucklers (shields).*]

Sampson. Gregory, on my word, we'll not carry coals.

Gregory. No, for then we should be colliers.

Sampson. I mean, an we be in choler, we'll draw.

Gregory. Ay, while you live, draw your neck out of collar.

Sampson. I strike quickly, being moved.

Gregory. But thou art not quickly moved to strike.

Sampson. A dog of that house of Montague moves me.

Gregory. To move is to stir, and to be valiant is to stand. Therefore, if thou art moved, thou runnest away.

Sampson. A dog of that house shall move me to stand. I will take the wall of any man or maid of Montague's.

Gregory. That shows thee a weak slave, for the weakest goes to the wall.

1–2 **we'll not carry coals:** we won't stand to be insulted; **colliers:** those involved in the dirty work of hauling coal, who were often the butt of jokes.

3–4 **in choler:** angry; **collar:** a hangman's noose.

11 **take the wall:** walk. People of higher rank had the privilege of walking closer to the wall, to avoid any water or garbage in the street.

Sampson. 'Tis true; and therefore women, being the weaker vessels, are ever thrust to the wall. Therefore push I will Montague's men from the wall and thrust his maids to the wall.

Gregory. The quarrel is between our masters and us their men.

14–24 Sampson's tough talk includes boasts about his ability to overpower women.

Sampson. 'Tis all one. I will show myself a tyrant. When I have fought with the men, I will be cruel with the maids: I will cut off their heads.

Gregory. The heads of the maids?

Sampson. Ay, the heads of the maids, or their maidenheads. Take it in what sense thou wilt.

Gregory. They must take it in sense that feel it.

Sampson. Me they shall feel while I am able to stand; and 'tis known I am a pretty piece of flesh.

28 **poor-John:** a salted fish, considered fit only for poor people to eat.

Gregory. 'Tis well thou art not fish; if thou hadst, thou hadst been poor-John. Draw thy tool! Here comes two of the house of Montagues.

[*Enter* Abram *and* Balthasar, *servants to the Montagues.*]

Sampson. My naked weapon is out. Quarrel! I will back thee.

Gregory. How? turn thy back and run?

Sampson. Fear me not.

33 **marry:** a short form of "by the Virgin Mary" and so a mild exclamation.

Gregory. No, marry. I fear thee!

Sampson. Let us take the law of our sides; let them begin.

Gregory. I will frown as I pass by, and let them take it as they list.

34–44 Gregory and Sampson decide to pick a fight by insulting the Montague servants with a rude gesture (**bite my thumb**).

Sampson. Nay, as they dare. I will bite my thumb at them; which is disgrace to them, if they bear it.

Abram. Do you bite your thumb at us, sir?

Sampson. I do bite my thumb, sir.

Abram. Do you bite your thumb at us, sir?

Sampson. [*aside* to Gregory]. Is the law of our side if I say ay?

Gregory. [*aside* to Sampson]. No.

Sampson. No, sir, I do not bite my thumb at you, sir; but I bite my thumb, sir.

Gregory. Do you quarrel, sir?

Abram. Quarrel, sir? No, sir.

Sampson. But if you do, sir, I am for you. I serve as good a man as you.

ANALYZE PARALLEL PLOTS

Annotate: The storyline of the feud between the Capulets and Montagues runs parallel to the storyline of Romeo and Juliet. Mark the line(s) where the argument between the servants of the two households begins.

Predict: How might this parallel plot affect the main plot of the "star-crossed lovers"?

Abram. No better.

Sampson. Well, sir.

[*Enter* Benvolio, *nephew of Montague and first cousin of Romeo.*]

Gregory [*aside to Sampson*]. Say "better." Here comes one of my master's kinsmen.

Sampson. Yes, better, sir.

Abram. You lie.

Sampson. Draw, if you be men. Gregory, remember thy swashing blow.

[*They fight.*]

Benvolio. Part, fools!
Put up your swords. You know not what you do.
[*beats down their swords*]

[*Enter* Tybalt, *hot-headed nephew of Lady Capulet and first cousin of Juliet.*]

Tybalt. What, art thou drawn among these heartless hinds?
Turn thee, Benvolio! look upon thy death.

Benvolio. I do but keep the peace. Put up thy sword,
Or manage it to part these men with me.

Tybalt. What, drawn, and talk of peace? I hate the word
As I hate hell, all Montagues, and thee.
Have at thee, coward!

[*They fight.*]

[*Enter several of both houses, who join the fray; then enter* Citizens *and* Peace Officers, *with clubs.*]

Officer. Clubs, bills, and partisans! Strike! beat them down!

Citizens. Down with the Capulets! Down with the Montagues!

[*Enter old* Capulet *and* Lady Capulet.]

Capulet. What noise is this? Give me my long sword, ho!

Lady Capulet. A crutch, a crutch! Why call you for a sword?

Capulet. My sword, I say! Old Montague is come
And flourishes his blade in spite of me.

[*Enter old* Montague *and* Lady Montague.]

Montague. Thou villain Capulet!—Hold me not, let me go.

Lady Montague. Thou shalt not stir one foot to seek a foe.

[*Enter* Prince Escalus, *with attendants. At first no one hears him.*]

Don't forget to **Notice & Note** as you read the text.

59 **heartless hinds:** cowardly servants.

63 **drawn:** with your sword out.

65 **Have at thee:** Defend yourself.

66 **bills, and partisans:** spears.

69 **A crutch . . . sword:** You need a crutch more than a sword.

74–81 The prince is furious about the street fighting caused by the feud. He orders the men to drop their weapons and pay attention.

77 **pernicious:** destructive.

82–90 **Three . . . peace:** The prince holds Capulet and Montague responsible for three recent street fights, each probably started by an offhand remark or insult (**airy word**). He warns that they will be put to death if any more fights occur.

Exeunt: the plural form of *exit,* indicating that more than one person is leaving the stage.

97 **Who . . . abroach:** Who reopened this old argument?

99 **adversary:** enemy.

100 **ere:** before.

107 **on part and part:** some on one side, some on the other.

110 **fray:** fight.

113 **drave:** drove.

115 **rooteth:** grows.

Prince. Rebellious subjects, enemies to peace,
Profaners of this neighbor-stained steel—
Will they not hear? What, ho! you men, you beasts,
That quench the fire of your pernicious rage
With purple fountains issuing from your veins!
On pain of torture, from those bloody hands
Throw your mistempered weapons to the ground
And hear the sentence of your moved prince.
Three civil brawls, bred of an airy word
By thee, old Capulet, and Montague,
Have thrice disturbed the quiet of our streets
And made Verona's ancient citizens
Cast by their grave beseeming ornaments
To wield old partisans, in hands as old,
Cankered with peace, to part your cankered hate.
If ever you disturb our streets again,
Your lives shall pay the forfeit of the peace.
For this time all the rest depart away.
You, Capulet, shall go along with me;
And, Montague, come you this afternoon,
To know our farther pleasure in this case,
To old Freetown, our common judgment place.
Once more, on pain of death, all men depart.

[*Exeunt all but* Montague, Lady Montague, *and* Benvolio.]

Montague. Who set this ancient quarrel new abroach?
Speak, nephew, were you by when it began?

Benvolio. Here were the servants of your adversary
And yours, close fighting ere I did approach.
I drew to part them. In the instant came
The fiery Tybalt, with his sword prepared;
Which, as he breathed defiance to my ears,
He swung about his head and cut the winds,
Who, nothing hurt withal, hissed him in scorn.
While we were interchanging thrusts and blows,
Came more and more, and fought on part and part,
Till the Prince came, who parted either part.

Lady Montague. O, where is Romeo? Saw you him today?
Right glad I am he was not at this fray.

Benvolio. Madam, an hour before the worshiped sun
Peered forth the golden window of the East,
A troubled mind drave me to walk abroad,
Where, underneath the grove of sycamore
That westward rooteth from the city's side,

Don't forget to **Notice & Note** as you read the text.

So early walking did I see your son.
Towards him I made, but he was ware of me
And stole into the covert of the wood.
I—measuring his affections by my own,
Which then most sought where most might not be found,
Being one too many by my weary self—
Pursued my humor, not pursuing his,
And gladly shunned who gladly fled from me.

Montague. Many a morning hath he there been seen,
With tears augmenting the fresh morning's dew,
Adding to clouds more clouds with his deep sighs;
But all so soon as the all-cheering sun
Should in the farthest East begin to draw
The shady curtains from Aurora's bed,
Away from light steals home my heavy son
And private in his chamber pens himself,
Shuts up his windows, locks fair daylight out,
And makes himself an artificial night.
Black and portentous must this humor prove
Unless good counsel may the cause remove.

Benvolio. My noble uncle, do you know the cause?

Montague. I neither know it nor can learn of him.

Benvolio. Have you importuned him by any means?

Montague. Both by myself and many other friends;
But he, his own affections' counselor,
Is to himself—I will not say how true—
But to himself so secret and so close,
So far from sounding and discovery,
As is the bud bit with an envious worm
Ere he can spread his sweet leaves to the air
Or dedicate his beauty to the sun.
Could we but learn from whence his sorrows grow,
We would as willingly give cure as know.

[*Enter* Romeo *lost in thought.*]

Benvolio. See, where he comes. So please you step aside,
I'll know his grievance, or be much denied.

Montague. I would thou wert so happy by thy stay
To hear true shrift. Come, madam, let's away.

[*Exeunt* Montague *and* Lady.]

Benvolio. Good morrow, cousin.

Romeo. Is the day so young?

Benvolio. But new struck nine.

117–123 **made:** moved; **covert:** covering. Romeo saw Benvolio coming and hid in the woods. Benvolio himself was seeking solitude and did not go after him.

124–135 Romeo has been seen wandering through the woods at night, crying. At dawn he returns home and locks himself in his room. Montague feels that his son needs guidance.

129 **Aurora's bed:** Aurora was the goddess of the dawn.

134 **portentous:** indicating evil to come; threatening.

138 **importuned:** asked in an urgent way.

140 **his own affections' counselor:** Romeo keeps to himself.

143–148 **so far from . . . know:** Finding out what Romeo is thinking is almost impossible. Montague compares his son to a young bud destroyed by the bite of a worm before it has a chance to open its leaves. Montague wants to find out what is bothering Romeo so he can help him.

152 **shrift:** confession.

153 **cousin:** any relative or close friend. The informal version is *coz.*

Romeo. Ay me! sad hours seem long.
Was that my father that went hence so fast?

Benvolio. It was. What sadness lengthens Romeo's hours?

Romeo. Not having that which having makes them short.

Benvolio. In love?

Romeo. Out—

Benvolio. Of love?

Romeo. Out of her favor where I am in love.

Benvolio. Alas that love, so gentle in his view,
Should be so tyrannous and rough in proof!

Romeo. Alas that love, whose view is muffled still,
Should without eyes see pathways to his will!
Where shall we dine?—O me! What fray was here?—
Yet tell me not, for I have heard it all.

162–165 **love:** references to Cupid, the god of love, typically pictured as a blind boy with wings and a bow and arrow. Anyone hit by one of his arrows falls in love instantly.

Here's much to do with hate, but more with love.
Why then, O brawling love! O loving hate!
O anything, of nothing first create!
O heavy lightness! serious vanity!
Misshapen chaos of well-seeming forms!
Feather of lead, bright smoke, cold fire, sick health!
Still-waking sleep, that is not what it is!
This love feel I, that feel no love in this.
Dost thou not laugh?

Benvolio. No, coz, I rather weep.

Romeo. Good heart, at what?

Benvolio. At thy good heart's oppression.

Romeo. Why, such is love's transgression.
Griefs of mine own lie heavy in my breast,
Which thou wilt propagate, to have it prest
With more of thine. This love that thou hast shown
Doth add more grief to too much of mine own.
Love is a smoke raised with the fume of sighs;
Being purged, a fire sparkling in lovers' eyes;
Being vexed, a sea nourished with lovers' tears.
What is it else? A madness most discreet,
A choking gall, and a preserving sweet.
Farewell, my coz.

Benvolio. Soft! I will go along.
An if you leave me so, you do me wrong.

Romeo. Tut! I have lost myself; I am not here:
This is not Romeo, he's some other where.

Benvolio. Tell me in sadness, who is that you love?

Romeo. What, shall I groan and tell thee?

Benvolio. Groan? Why, no;
But sadly tell me who.

Romeo. Bid a sick man in sadness make his will.
Ah, word ill urged to one that is so ill!
In sadness, cousin, I do love a woman.

Benvolio. I aimed so near when I supposed you loved.

Romeo. A right good markman! And she's fair I love.

Benvolio. A right fair mark, fair coz, is soonest hit.

Romeo. Well, in that hit you miss. She'll not be hit
With Cupid's arrow. She hath Dian's wit,
And, in strong proof of chastity well armed,
From Love's weak childish bow she lives unharmed.

ANALYZE LITERARY DEVICES

Annotate: Romeo, confused and upset about love, describes his feelings using oxymorons, or contradictory expressions. Mark some of these expressions in lines 168–176.

Analyze: How do these oxymorons reveal the complexity of Romeo's feelings?

176–182 Benvolio expresses his sympathy for Romeo. Romeo replies that this is one more problem caused by love. He now feels worse than before because he must carry the weight of Benvolio's sympathy along with his own grief.

184 **purged:** cleansed (of the smoke).

185 **vexed:** troubled.

187 **gall:** something causing bitterness or hate.

188 **soft:** Wait a minute.

192 **sadness:** seriousness.

201–204 **She'll . . . unharmed:** The girl isn't interested in falling in love. She is like Diana, the goddess of chastity.

205–207 **She will not . . . gold:** She is not swayed by Romeo's love or his wealth.

She will not stay the siege of loving terms,
Nor bide the encounter of assailing eyes,
Nor ope her lap to saint-seducing gold.
O, she is rich in beauty; only poor
That, when she dies, with beauty dies her store.

Benvolio. Then she hath sworn that she will still live chaste?

212–213 **for beauty . . . posterity:** She wastes her beauty, which will not be passed on to future generations.

215–216 **to merit . . . despair:** The girl will reach heaven (**bliss**) by being so virtuous, which causes Romeo to feel despair; **forsworn to:** sworn not to.

Romeo. She hath, and in that sparing makes huge waste;
For beauty, starved with her severity,
Cuts beauty off from all posterity.
She is too fair, too wise, wisely too fair
To merit bliss by making me despair.
She hath forsworn to love, and in that vow
Do I live dead that live to tell it now.

Benvolio. Be ruled by me: forget to think of her.

Romeo. O, teach me how I should forget to think!

Benvolio. By giving liberty unto thine eyes:
Examine other beauties.

221–222 **'Tis . . . more:** That would only make me appreciate my own love's beauty more.

223 Masks were worn by Elizabethan women to protect their faces from the sun.

227–229 **Show me . . . fair:** A woman who is exceedingly (passing) beautiful will only remind me of my love, who is even prettier.

Romeo. 'Tis the way
To call hers, exquisite, in question more.
These happy masks that kiss fair ladies' brows,
Being black, puts us in mind they hide the fair.
He that is strucken blind cannot forget
The precious treasure of his eyesight lost.
Show me a mistress that is passing fair,
What doth her beauty serve but as a note
Where I may read who passed that passing fair?
Farewell. Thou canst not teach me to forget.

231 **I'll pay . . . debt:** I'll convince you you're wrong, or die trying.

Benvolio. I'll pay that doctrine, or else die in debt.

[*Exeunt.*]

Scene 2 *A street near the Capulet house.*

[*Enter* Capulet *with* Paris, *a kinsman of the Prince, and* Servant.]

1 **bound:** obligated.

4 **reckoning:** reputation.

6 **what say . . . suit:** Paris is asking for Capulet's response to his proposal to marry Juliet.

Capulet. But Montague is bound as well as I,
In penalty alike; and 'tis not hard, I think,
For men so old as we to keep the peace.

Paris. Of honorable reckoning are you both,
And pity 'tis you lived at odds so long.
But now, my lord, what say you to my suit?

Capulet. But saying o' er what I have said before:
My child is yet a stranger in the world,
She hath not seen the change of fourteen years;

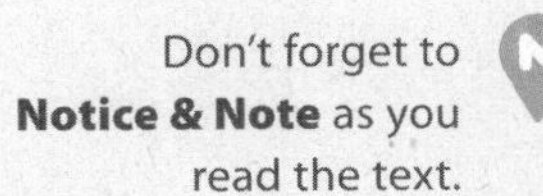
Don't forget to **Notice & Note** as you read the text.

Let two more summers wither in their pride
Ere we may think her ripe to be a bride.

Paris. Younger than she are happy mothers made.

Capulet. And too soon marred are those so early made.
The earth hath swallowed all my hopes but she;
She is the hopeful lady of my earth.
But woo her, gentle Paris, get her heart;
My will to her consent is but a part.
An she agree, within her scope of choice
Lies my consent and fair according voice.
This night I hold an old accustomed feast,
Whereto I have invited many a guest,
Such as I love, and you among the store,
One more, most welcome, makes my number more.
At my poor house look to behold this night
Earth-treading stars that make dark heaven light.
Such comfort as do lusty young men feel
When well-appareled April on the heel
Of limping Winter treads, even such delight
Among fresh female buds shall you this night
Inherit at my house. Hear all, all see,
And like her most whose merit most shall be;
Which, on more view of many, mine, being one,
May stand in number, though in reck'ning none.
Come, go with me. [*to* Servant, *giving him a paper*]
Go, sirrah, trudge about
Through fair Verona; find those persons out
Whose names are written there, and to them say,
My house and welcome on their pleasure stay.

[*Exeunt* Capulet *and* Paris.]

Servant. Find them out whose names are written here! It is written that the shoemaker should meddle with his yard and the tailor with his last, the fisher with his pencil and the painter with his nets; but I am sent to find those persons whose names are here writ, and can never find what names the writing person hath here writ. I must to the learned. In good time!

[*Enter* Benvolio *and* Romeo.]

Benvolio. Tut, man, one fire burns out another's burning;
One pain is lessened by another's anguish;
Turn giddy, and be holp by backward turning;
One desperate grief cures with another's languish.
Take thou some new infection to thy eye,
And the rank poison of the old will die.

10 **Let two more summers . . . pride:** let two more years pass.

14 **The earth . . . she:** All my children are dead except Juliet.

16 **woo her:** try to win her heart.

18–19 **An . . . voice:** I will give my approval to the one she chooses.

20 **old accustomed feast:** a traditional or annual party.

29–33 **among . . . none:** Tonight at the party you will see the loveliest girls in Verona, including Juliet. When you see all of them together, your opinion of Juliet may change.

34 **sirrah:** a term used to address a servant.

38–43 The servant cannot read. He confuses the craftsmen and their tools, tapping a typical source of humor for Elizabethan comic characters.

44–49 **Tut, man . . . die:** Benvolio says Romeo should find a new love—that a "new infection" will cure the old one.

Romeo. Your plantain leaf is excellent for that.

Benvolio. For what, I pray thee?

Romeo. For your broken shin.

Benvolio. Why, Romeo, art thou mad?

55 **God-den:** good evening. Romeo interrupts his lament to talk to the servant.

56 **God gi' go-den:** God give you a good evening.

Romeo. Not mad, but bound more than a madman is;
Shut up in prison, kept without my food,
Whipped and tormented and—God-den, good fellow.

Servant. God gi' go-den. I pray, sir, can you read?

Romeo. Ay, mine own fortune in my misery.

Servant. Perhaps you have learned it without book. But
I pray, can you read anything you see?

Romeo. Ay, if I know the letters and the language.

Servant. Ye say honestly. Rest you merry!

[Romeo's *joking goes over the clown's head. He concludes that* Romeo *cannot read and prepares to seek someone who can.*]

69 **Rosaline:** This is the woman that Romeo is in love with. Mercutio, a friend of both Romeo and the Capulets, is also invited to the party.

72 **whither:** where.

Romeo. Stay, fellow; I can read. [*He reads.*]
"Signior Martino and his wife and daughters;
County Anselmo and his beauteous sisters;
The lady widow of Vitruvio;
Signior Placentio and his lovely nieces;
Mercutio and his brother Valentine;
Mine uncle Capulet, his wife, and daughters;
My fair niece Rosaline and Livia;
Signior Valentio and his cousin Tybalt;
Lucio and the lively Helena."
[*gives back the paper*]
A fair assembly. Whither should they come?

Servant. Up.

Romeo. Whither?

Servant. To supper, to our house.

Romeo. Whose house?

Servant. My master's.

Romeo. Indeed I should have asked you that before.

81 **crush a cup of wine:** slang for "drink some wine."

Servant. Now I'll tell you without asking. My master is the great rich Capulet; and if you be not of the house of Montagues, I pray come and crush a cup of wine. Rest you merry!

[*Exit.*]

Benvolio. At this same ancient feast of Capulet's
Sups the fair Rosaline whom thou so lovest,
With all the admired beauties of Verona.

Go thither, and with unattainted eye
Compare her face with some that I shall show,
And I will make thee think thy swan a crow.

Romeo. When the devout religion of mine eye
Maintains such falsehood, then turn tears to fires;
And these, who, often drowned, could never die,
Transparent heretics, be burnt for liars!
One fairer than my love? The all-seeing sun
Ne'er saw her match since first the world begun.

Benvolio. Tut! you saw her fair, none else being by,
Herself poised with herself in either eye;
But in that crystal scales let there be weighed
Your lady's love against some other maid
That I will show you shining at this feast,
And she shall scant show well that now shows best.

Romeo. I'll go along, no such sight to be shown,
But to rejoice in splendor of mine own.

[*Exeunt.*]

85 **unattainted:** unbiased; unprejudiced.

88–91 **When . . . liars:** If the love I have for Rosaline, which is like a religion, changes because of such a lie (that others may be more beautiful), let my tears be turned to fire and my eyes be burned.

94–99 **Tut . . . best:** You've seen Rosaline alone; now compare her with some other women.

100–101 Romeo agrees to go to the party, but only to see Rosaline.

Scene 3 *Capulet's house.*

[*Enter* Lady Capulet *and* Nurse.]

Lady Capulet. Nurse, where's my daughter? Call her forth to me.

Nurse. Now, by my maidenhead at twelve year old,
I bade her come. What, lamb! what, ladybird!
God forbid! Where's this girl? What, Juliet!

[*Enter* Juliet.]

Juliet. How now? Who calls?

Nurse. Your mother.

Juliet. Madam, I am here. What is your will?

Lady Capulet. This is the matter—Nurse, give leave awhile,
We must talk in secret. Nurse, come back again;
I have remembered me, thou's hear our counsel.
Thou knowest my daughter's of a pretty age.

Nurse. Faith, I can tell her age unto an hour.

Lady Capulet. She's not fourteen.

Nurse. I'll lay fourteen of my teeth—
And yet, to my teen be it spoken, I have but four—
She's not fourteen. How long is it now
To Lammastide?

Lady Capulet. A fortnight and odd days.

8–11 **give leave . . . counsel:** Lady Capulet seems nervous, not sure whether she wants the nurse to stay or leave; of **a pretty age:** of an attractive age, ready for marriage.

14 **teen:** sorrow.

16 **Lammastide:** August 1, a religious feast day. It is two weeks (**a fortnight**) away.

17–49 The nurse babbles about Juliet's childhood. Her own daughter, Susan, was the same age as Juliet, and died in infancy, leaving the nurse available to become a wet nurse to Juliet. An earthquake happened on the day she stopped breastfeeding Juliet (**she was weaned**).

27 **laid wormwood to my dug:** applied a plant with a bitter taste to her breast to discourage the child from breastfeeding.

33 **tetchy:** cranky.

34–35 **Shake . . . trudge:** When the dove house shook, I knew enough to leave.

37 **by the rood:** by the cross of Christ (a mild oath).

39 **broke her brow:** cut her forehead.

42–49 **"Yea," . . . "Ay":** The nurse's husband made a crude joke, asking the baby whether she'd fall the other way (on her back) when she was older. Although Juliet didn't understand the question, she stopped crying (**stinted**) and answered "Yes." The nurse finds the story so funny that she can't stop retelling it.

Nurse. Even or odd, of all days in the year,
Come Lammas Eve at night shall she be fourteen.
Susan and she (*God rest all Christian souls!*)
Were of an age. Well, Susan is with God;
She was too good for me. But, as I said,
On Lammas Eve at night shall she be fourteen;
That shall she, marry; I remember it well.
'Tis since the earthquake now eleven years;
And she was weaned (*I never shall forget it*),
Of all the days of the year, upon that day.
For I had then laid wormwood to my dug,
Sitting in the sun under the dovehouse wall.
My lord and you were then at Mantua—
Nay, I do bear a brain—But, as I said,
When it did taste the wormwood on the nipple
Of my dug and felt it bitter, pretty fool,
To see it tetchy and fall out with the dug!
Shake, quoth the dovehouse! 'Twas no need, I trow,
To bid me trudge.
And since that time it is eleven years,
For then she could stand alone; nay, by the rood,
She could have run and waddled all about;
For even the day before, she broke her brow;
And then my husband (God be with his soul!
'A was a merry man) took up the child.
"Yea," quoth he, "dost thou fall upon thy face?
Thou wilt fall backward when thou has more wit,
Wilt thou not, Jule?" And, by my holidam,
The pretty wretch left crying, and said "Ay."
To see now how a jest shall come about!
I warrant, an I should live a thousand years,
I never should forget it. "Wilt thou not, Jule?" quoth he,
And, pretty fool, it stinted, and said "Ay."

Lady Capulet. Enough of this. I pray thee hold thy peace.

Nurse. Yes, madam. Yet I cannot choose but laugh
To think it should leave crying and say "Ay."
And yet, I warrant, it had upon its brow
A bump as big as a young cock'rel's stone;
A perilous knock; and it cried bitterly.
"Yea," quoth my husband, "fallst upon thy face?
Thou wilt fall backward when thou comest to age,
Wilt thou not, Jule?" It stinted, and said "Ay."

Juliet. And stint thou too, I pray thee, nurse, say I.

Don't forget to **Notice & Note** as you read the text.

Nurse. Peace, I have done. God mark thee to his grace!
Thou wast the prettiest babe that e'er I nursed.
An I might live to see thee married once,
I have my wish.

Lady Capulet. Marry, that "marry" is the very theme
I came to talk of. Tell me, daughter Juliet,
How stands your disposition to be married?

64 **Marry . . . "marry":** two different usages of the same word—the first meaning "by the Virgin Mary" and the second meaning "to wed."

Juliet. It is an honor that I dream not of.

Nurse. An honor? Were not I thine only nurse,
I would say thou hadst sucked wisdom from thy teat.

Lady Capulet. Well, think of marriage now. Younger than you,
Here in Verona, ladies of esteem,
Are made already mothers. By my count,
I was your mother much upon these years
That you are now a maid. Thus then in brief:
The valiant Paris seeks you for his love.

73–74 **I was . . . maid:** I was your mother at about your age, yet you are still unmarried.

Nurse. A man, young lady! lady, such a man
As all the world—why he's a man of wax.

77 **a man of wax:** a man so perfect he could be a wax statue, of the type sculptors once used as models for their works.

Lady Capulet. Verona's summer hath not such a flower.

Nurse. Nay, he's a flower, in faith—a very flower.

Lady Capulet. What say you? Can you love the gentleman?
This night you shall behold him at our feast.
Read o'er the volume of young Paris' face,

82–89 **Read . . . cover:** Lady Capulet uses an extended metaphor that compares Paris to a book that Juliet should read.

And find delight writ there with beauty's pen;
Examine every several lineament,
And see how one another lends content;
And what obscured in this fair volume lies
Find written in the margent of his eyes.
This precious book of love, this unbound lover,
To beautify him only lacks a cover.
The fish lives in the sea, and 'tis much pride
For fair without the fair within to hide.
That book in many's eyes doth share the glory,
That in gold clasps locks in the golden story;
So shall you share all that he doth possess,
By having him making yourself no less.

84 **every several lineament:** each separate feature (of Paris's face).

87 **margent . . . eyes:** She compares Paris's eyes to the margin of a page, where notes are written to explain the content.

88–91 **This . . . hide:** This beautiful book (Paris) needs only a cover (wife) to become even better. He may be hiding even more wonderful qualities inside.

Nurse. No less? Nay, bigger! Women grow by men.

96 Women get bigger (pregnant) when they marry.

Lady Capulet. Speak briefly, can you like of Paris' love?

Juliet. I'll look to like, if looking liking move;
But no more deep will I endart mine eye
Than your consent gives strength to make it fly.

98–100 **I'll look . . . fly:** I'll look at him with the intention of liking him, if simply looking can make me like him; **endart**: look deeply, as if penetrating with a dart.

[*Enter* a Servingman.]

Servingman. Madam, the guests are come, supper served up, you called, my young lady asked for, the nurse cursed in the pantry, and everything in extremity. I must hence to wait. I beseech you follow straight.

103–104 **extremity:** great confusion; **straight**: immediately.

Lady Capulet. We follow thee. [*Exit* Servingman.] Juliet, the County stays.

105 **the County stays:** Count Paris is waiting for you.

Nurse. Go, girl, seek happy nights to happy days.

[*Exeunt.*]

Scene 4 *A street near the Capulet house.*

[*Enter* Romeo, Mercutio, Benvolio, *with five or six other* Maskers; Torchbearers.]

Romeo. What, shall this speech be spoke for our excuse?
Or shall we on without apology?

Benvolio. The date is out of such prolixity.
We'll have no Cupid hoodwinked with a scarf,
Bearing a Tartar's painted bow of lath,
Scaring the ladies like a crowkeeper;
Nor no without-book prologue, faintly spoke
After the prompter, for our entrance;
But let them measure us by what they will,
We'll measure them a measure, and be gone.

1–10 **What, shall this . . . be gone:** Romeo asks whether they should send a messenger announcing their arrival at the party. Benvolio says that they'll dance one dance (**measure them a measure**) and then leave.

Don't forget to **Notice & Note** as you read the text. 

Romeo. Give me a torch. I am not for this ambling;
Being but heavy, I will bear the light.

Mercutio. Nay, gentle Romeo, we must have you dance.

Romeo. Not I, believe me. You have dancing shoes
With nimble soles; I have a soul of lead
So stakes me to the ground I cannot move.

Mercutio. You are a lover. Borrow Cupid's wings
And soar with them above a common bound.

Romeo. I am too sore enpierced with his shaft
To soar with his light feathers, and so bound
I cannot bound a pitch above dull woe.
Under love's heavy burden do I sink.

Mercutio. And, to sink in it, should you burden love—
Too great oppression for a tender thing.

Romeo. Is love a tender thing? It is too rough,
Too rude, too boist'rous, and it pricks like thorn.

Mercutio. If love be rough with you, be rough with love.
Prick love for pricking, and you beat love down.
Give me a case to put my visage in.
A visor for a visor! What care I
What curious eye doth quote deformities?
Here are the beetle brows shall blush for me.

Benvolio. Come, knock and enter, and no sooner in
But every man betake him to his legs.

Romeo. A torch for me! Let wantons light of heart
Tickle the senseless rushes with their heels;
For I am proverbed with a grandsire phrase,
I'll be a candle-holder and look on;
The game was ne'er so fair, and I am done.

Mercutio. Tut, dun's the mouse, the constable's own word!
If thou art Dun, we'll draw thee from the mire
Of, save your reverence, love, wherein thou stickst
Up to the ears. Come, we burn daylight, ho!

Romeo. Nay, that's not so.

Mercutio. I mean, sir, in delay
We waste our lights in vain, like lamps by day.
Take our good meaning, for our judgment sits
Five times in that ere once in our five wits.

Romeo. And we mean well in going to this masque;
But 'tis no wit to go.

12 **heavy:** sad. Romeo makes a joke based on the meanings of *heavy* and *light*.

14–32 Romeo continues to talk about his sadness, while Mercutio jokingly makes fun of him to try to cheer him up.

29–32 **Give . . . for me:** Give me a mask for an ugly face. I don't care if people notice my appearance. Here, look at my bushy eyebrows.

34 **betake . . . legs:** dance.

35–38 **Let . . . look on:** Let playful people tickle the grass (**rushes**) on the floor with their dancing. I'll follow the old saying (**grandsire phrase**) and just be a spectator.

40–43 **Tut . . . daylight:** Mercutio jokes, using various meanings of the word dun, which sounds like Romeo's last word, done. He concludes by saying they should not waste time (**burn daylight**).

Mercutio. Why, may one ask?

Romeo. I dreamt a dream tonight.

Mercutio. And so did I.

Romeo. Well, what was yours?

Mercutio. That dreamers often lie.

Romeo. In bed asleep, while they do dream things true.

Mercutio. O, then I see Queen Mab hath been with you.
She is the fairies' midwife, and she comes
In shape no bigger than an agate stone
On the forefinger of an alderman,
Drawn with a team of little atomies
Athwart men's noses as they lie asleep;
Her wagon spokes made of long spinners' legs,
The cover, of the wings of grasshoppers;
Her traces, of the smallest spider's web;

53–95 Mercutio talks of Mab, queen of the fairies, a folktale character well-known to Shakespeare's audience. His language includes vivid descriptions, puns, and satires of people; and ultimately he gets caught up in his own wild imaginings.

55 **agate stone:** jewel for a ring.

57 **atomies:** tiny creatures.

59 **spinners' legs:** spiders' legs.

61 **traces:** harness.

Her collars, of the moonshine's wat'ry beams;
Her whip, of cricket's bone; the lash, of film;
Her wagoner, a small grey-coated gnat,
Not half so big as a round little worm
Pricked from the lazy finger of a maid;
Her chariot is an empty hazelnut,
Made by the joiner squirrel or old grub,
Time out o' mind the fairies' coachmakers.
And in this state she gallops night by night
Through lovers' brains, and then they dream of love;
O'er courtiers' knees, that dream on curtsies straight;
O'er lawyers' fingers, who straight dream on fees;
O'er ladies' lips, who straight on kisses dream,
Which oft the angry Mab with blisters plagues,
Because their breaths with sweetmeats tainted are.
Sometime she gallops o'er a courtier's nose,
And then dreams he of smelling out a suit,
And sometime comes she with a tithe-pig's tail
Tickling a parson's nose as 'a lies asleep,
Then dreams he of another benefice.
Sometime she driveth o'er a soldier's neck,
And then dreams he of cutting foreign throats,
Of breaches, ambuscadoes, Spanish blades,
Of healths five fathom deep; and then anon
Drums in his ear, at which he starts and wakes,
And being thus frighted, swears a prayer or two
And sleeps again. This is that very Mab
That plaits the manes of horses in the night
And bakes the elflocks in foul sluttish hairs,
Which once untangled much misfortune bodes.
This is the hag, when maids lie on their backs,
That presses them and learns them first to bear,
Making them women of good carriage.
This is she—

Romeo. Peace, peace, Mercutio, peace!
Thou talkst of nothing.

Mercutio. True, I talk of dreams;
Which are the children of an idle brain,
Begot of nothing but vain fantasy;
Which is as thin of substance as the air,
And more inconstant than the wind, who woos
Even now the frozen bosom of the North
And, being angered, puffs away from thence,
Turning his face to the dew-dropping South.

Don't forget to **Notice & Note** as you read the text.

68 **joiner:** carpenter.

77–78 **Sometimes she . . . suit:** Sometimes Mab makes a member of the king's court dream of receiving special favors.

81 **benefice:** a well-paying position for a clergyman.

84 **ambuscadoes:** ambushes; **Spanish blades:** high-quality Spanish swords.

89 **plaits:** braids.

96–103 **True . . . South:** Mercutio is trying to keep Romeo from taking his dreams too seriously.

Benvolio. This wind you talk of blows us from ourselves.
Supper is done, and we shall come too late.

106–111 Romeo, still depressed, fears that some terrible event caused by the stars will begin at the party. Remember the phrase "star-crossed lovers" from the prologue.

Romeo. I fear, too early; for my mind misgives
Some consequence, yet hanging in the stars,
Shall bitterly begin his fearful date
With this night's revels and expire the term
Of a despised life, closed in my breast,
By some vile forfeit of untimely death.
But he that hath the steerage of my course
Direct my sail! On, lusty gentlemen!

Benvolio. Strike, drum.

[*Exeunt.*]

Scene 5 *A hall in Capulet's house; the scene of the party.*

[Servingmen *come forth with napkins.*]

1–13 These opening lines are a comic conversation among three servants as they work.

2 **trencher:** wooden plate.

6–7 **plate:** silverware and silver plates; **marchpane**: marzipan, a sweet made from almond paste.

First Servingman. Where's Potpan, that he helps not to take way? He shift a trencher! he scrape a trencher!

Second Servingman. When good manners shall lie all in one or two men's hands, and they unwashed too, 'tis a foul thing.

First Servingman. Away with the joint-stools, remove the court-cupboard, look to the plate. Good thou, save me a piece of marchpane and, as thou lovest me, let the porter let in Susan Grindstone and Nell. [*Exit Second Servant.*] Anthony, and Potpan!

[*Enter* Anthony *and* Potpan.]

Second Servingman. Ay, boy, ready.

First Servingman. You are looked for and called for, asked for and sought for, in the great chamber.

Third Servingman. We cannot be here and there too. Cheerly, boys! Be brisk awhile, and the longer liver take all.

[*Exeunt.*]

14–27 Capulet welcomes his guests and invites them all to dance. He alternates talking with his guests and telling the servants what to do.

17–18 **She that . . . corns:** Any woman too shy to dance will be assumed to have corns, ugly and painful growths on the toes.

20 **visor:** mask.

[Maskers *appear with* Capulet, Lady Capulet, Juliet, *all the* Guests, *and* Servants.]

Capulet. Welcome, gentlemen! Ladies that have their toes
Unplagued with corns will have a bout with you.
Ah ha, my mistresses! which of you all
Will now deny to dance? She that makes dainty,
She I'll swear hath corns. Am I come near ye now?
Welcome, gentlemen! I have seen the day
That I have worn a visor and could tell
A whispering tale in a fair lady's ear,
Such as would please. 'Tis gone, 'tis gone, 'tis gone!

You are welcome, gentlemen! Come, musicians, play.
A hall, a hall! give room! and foot it, girls.

[*Music plays and they dance.*]

More light, you knaves! and turn the tables up,
And quench the fire, the room is grown too hot.
Ah, sirrah, this unlooked-for sport comes well.
Nay, sit, nay, sit, good cousin Capulet,
For you and I are past our dancing days.
How long is't now since last yourself and I
Were in a mask?

Second Capulet. By'r Lady, thirty years.

Capulet. What, man? 'Tis not so much, 'tis not so much!
'Tis since the nuptial of Lucentio,
Come Pentecost as quickly as it will,
Some five-and-twenty years, and then we masked.

Second Capulet. 'Tis more, 'tis more! His son is elder, sir;
His son is thirty.

Capulet. Will you tell me that?
His son was but a ward two years ago.

Romeo [*to a* Servingman]. What lady's that, which doth enrich the hand
Of yonder knight?

Servant. I know not, sir.

Romeo. O, she doth teach the torches to burn bright!
It seems she hangs upon the cheek of night
Like a rich jewel in an Ethiop's ear—
Beauty too rich for use, for earth too dear!
So shows a snowy dove trooping with crows
As yonder lady o'er her fellows shows.
The measure done, I'll watch her place of stand
And, touching hers, make blessed my rude hand.
Did my heart love till now? Forswear it, sight!
For I ne'er saw true beauty till this night.

Tybalt. This, by his voice, should be a Montague.
Fetch me my rapier, boy. What, dares the slave
Come hither, covered with an antic face
To fleer and scorn at our solemnity?
Now, by the stock and honor of my kin,
To strike him dead I hold it not a sin.

Capulet. Why, how now, kinsman? Wherefore storm you so?

Tybalt. Uncle, this is a Montague, our foe;

Don't forget to **Notice & Note** as you read the text.

28–38 Capulet and his relative watch the dancing as they talk of days gone by.

33 **nuptial:** marriage.

44–45 **Ethiop's ear:** the ear of an Ethiopian (African); **for earth too dear:** too precious for this world.

52–57 Tybalt recognizes Romeo's voice and tells his servant to get his sword (**rapier**). He thinks Romeo has come to make fun of (**fleer**) their party.

A villain, that is hither come in spite
To scorn at our solemnity this night.

Capulet. Young Romeo is it?

Tybalt. 'Tis he, that villain Romeo.

Capulet. Content thee, gentle coz, let him alone.
'A bears him like a portly gentleman,
And, to say truth, Verona brags of him
To be a virtuous and well-governed youth.
I would not for the wealth of all this town
Here in my house do him disparagement.
Therefore be patient, take no note of him.
It is my will; the which if thou respect,
Show a fair presence and put off these frowns,
An ill-beseeming semblance for a feast.

Tybalt. It fits when such a villain is a guest.
I'll not endure him.

Capulet. He shall be endured.
What, goodman boy? I say he shall. Go to!
Am I the master here, or you? Go to!

64 **portly:** dignified.

68 **do him disparagement:** speak critically or insultingly to him.

72 **semblance:** outward appearance.

75 **goodman boy:** a term used to address an inferior; **Go to:** Stop, that's enough!

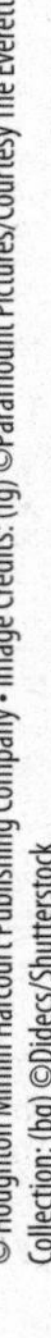

You'll not endure him? God shall mend my soul!
You'll make a mutiny among my guests!
You will set cock-a-hoop! You'll be the man.

Tybalt. Why, uncle, 'tis a shame.

Capulet. Go to, go to!
You are a saucy boy. Is't so, indeed?
This trick may chance to scathe you. I know what.
You must contrary me! Marry, 'tis time.—
Well said, my hearts!—You are a princox—go!
Be quiet, or—More light, more light!—For shame!
I'll make you quiet; what!—Cheerly, my hearts!

Tybalt. Patience perforce with willful choler meeting
Makes my flesh tremble in their different greeting.
I will withdraw; but this intrusion shall,
Now seeming sweet, convert to bitter gall.

[*Exit.*]

Romeo. If I profane with my unworthiest hand
This holy shrine, the gentle fine is this:
My lips, two blushing pilgrims, ready stand
To smooth that rough touch with a tender kiss.

Juliet. Good pilgrim, you do wrong your hand too much,
Which mannerly devotion shows in this;
For saints have hands that pilgrims' hands do touch,
And palm to palm is holy palmers' kiss.

Romeo. Have not saints lips, and holy palmers too?

Juliet. Ay, pilgrim, lips that they must use in prayer.

Romeo. O, then, dear saint, let lips do what hands do!
They pray; grant thou, lest faith turn to despair.

Juliet. Saints do not move, though grant for prayers' sake.

Romeo. Then move not while my prayer's effect I take.
Thus from my lips, by thine my sin is purged.

[*kisses her*]

Juliet. Then have my lips the sin that they have took.

Romeo. Sin from my lips? O trespass sweetly urged!
Give me my sin again.

[*kisses her*]

Juliet. You kiss by the book.

Nurse. Madam, your mother craves a word with you.

Romeo. What is her mother?

Nurse. Marry, bachelor,
Her mother is the lady of the house.
And a good lady, and a wise and virtuous.

Don't forget to **Notice & Note** as you read the text.

79 **set cock-a-hoop:** cause everything to be upset.

82–83 **scathe:** harm; **I know . . . contrary me:** I know what I'm doing! Don't you dare challenge my authority.

84–86 Capulet intersperses his angry speech to Tybalt with comments to his guests and servants.

87–90 **Patience . . . gall:** Tybalt says he will restrain himself, but his suppressed anger (**choler**) makes his body shake.

91–108 Romeo and Juliet are in the middle of the dance floor, with eyes only for each other. They touch the palms of their hands. Their conversation revolves around Romeo's comparison of his lips to pilgrims who have traveled to a holy shrine. Juliet goes along with the comparison.

105 **purged:** washed away.

108 **kiss by the book:** Juliet could mean "You kiss like someone who has practiced." Or she could be teasing Romeo, meaning "You kiss coldly, as though you had learned how by reading a book."

109 At the nurse's message, Juliet walks to her mother.

115 **shall have the chinks:** shall become rich.

116 **my life . . . debt:** my life belongs to my enemy.

120 **towards:** coming up.

I nursed her daughter that you talked withal.
I tell you, he that can lay hold of her
Shall have the chinks.

Romeo. Is she a Capulet?
O dear account! my life is my foe's debt.

Benvolio. Away, be gone, the sport is at the best.

Romeo. Ay, so I fear; the more is my unrest.

Capulet. Nay, gentlemen, prepare not to be gone;
We have a trifling foolish banquet towards.

[*They whisper in his ear.*]

Is it e'en so? Why then, I thank you all.
I thank you, honest gentlemen. Good night.
More torches here! [*Exeunt Maskers.*] Come on then, let's to bed.
Ah, sirrah, by my fay, it waxes late;
I'll to my rest.

[*Exeunt all but* Juliet *and* Nurse.]

Juliet. Come hither, nurse. What is yond gentleman?

Nurse. The son and heir of old Tiberio.

Juliet. What's he that now is going out of door?

Nurse. Marry, that, I think, be young Petruchio.

Juliet. What's he that follows there, that would not dance?

Nurse. I know not.

Juliet. Go ask his name.—If he be married,
My grave is like to be my wedding bed.

Nurse. His name is Romeo, and a Montague,
The only son of your great enemy.

Juliet. My only love, sprung from my only hate!
Too early seen unknown, and known too late!
Prodigious birth of love it is to me
That I must love a loathed enemy.

Nurse. What's this? what's this?

Juliet. A rhyme I learnt even now
Of one I danced withal.

[*One calls within, "Juliet."*]

Nurse. Anon, anon!
Come, let's away; the strangers all are gone.

[*Exeunt.*]

ANALYZE LITERARY DEVICES

Annotate: Foreshadowing is the use of hints or clues to suggest events that will happen later in the story. Mark the line(s) where Juliet's words foreshadow what will come later in the play.

Analyze: What do these lines suggest about Juliet's fate?

137–138 **Too early . . . too late:** I fell in love with him before I learned who he is; **prodigious:** abnormal; unlucky.

COLLABORATIVE DISCUSSION

With a partner, discuss your first impressions of Romeo and Juliet. What actions or lines of dialogue reveal their personalities?

Assessment Practice

Answer these questions before moving on to the **Analyze the Text** section on the following page.

1. Read the excerpt from the Prologue. Then, answer the question.

> From forth the fatal loins of these two foes,
> A pair of star-crossed lovers take their life, . . .
> Doth with their death bury their parents' strife. (lines 5–6, 8)

Based on the excerpt, what is the author's primary purpose for including a Prologue in the structure of the drama?

- (A) to identify the diverse settings of the drama
- (B) to introduce the main characters of the drama
- (C) to establish the fanciful mood of the drama
- (D) to summarize the plot of the drama

2. This question has two parts. First, answer **Part A**. Then, answer **Part B**.

Part A

Why does Benvolio encourage Romeo to attend Capulet's feast in Scene 2?

- (A) He hopes Romeo will start a fight with Lord Capulet at the feast.
- (B) He wants Romeo to compare Rosaline to other ladies of Verona.
- (C) He is pleased to receive an invitation and thinks they should accept.
- (D) He has conspired with Juliet, who does not wish to marry Paris.

Part B

Which detail supports the answer to Part A?

- (A) "My will to her consent is but a part" (Scene 2, line 17)
- (B) "And like her most whose merit most shall be" (Scene 2, line 31)
- (C) "Compare her face with some that I will show" (Scene 2, line 86)
- (D) "Ne'er saw her match since first the world begun" (Scene 2, line 93)

Test-Taking Strategies

Analyze the Text

Support your responses with evidence from the text.

1. **INTERPRET** An important **theme,** or message, in *Romeo and Juliet* is the struggle against fate, or forces that determine how a person's life will turn out. Explain how Act I's Prologue establishes the fate of the main characters. Why do you think Shakespeare gives away the ending before the play begins?

2. **PREDICT** Review the foreshadowing in Scene 5, line 133, where Juliet says: "My grave is like to be my wedding bed." Paraphrase this line, and then predict what event it foreshadows.

3. **ANALYZE** A **foil** is a character who highlights, through sharp contrast, the qualities of another character. Identify two sets of characters in Act I who are foils for each other. What do you learn about the characters by seeing them contrasted to one another?

4. **IDENTIFY** *Romeo and Juliet* is a play that deals with serious and tragic events, yet Shakespeare weaves in jokes and comical situations throughout Act I. One example is the conversation among the servants at the beginning of Scene 5. Identify other examples of **comic relief** in Act I.

5. **INFER** In Act I, Scene 5, there is an **Aha Moment** when Romeo realizes that Juliet is a Capulet (lines 116–117). How might this shape the plot?

NOTICE & NOTE

Review what you **noticed and noted** as you read the text. Your annotations can help you answer these questions.

Choices

Here are some other ways to demonstrate your understanding of Act I.

Writing

↳ Text Message Exchange

Romeo and Juliet have just met—and are instantly drawn to one another—at Lord Capulet's party. Each is devastated to learn that the other is from a rival family. Script a series of text messages the two teens, equipped with smartphones, might have sent each other after the party. Try to match Shakespeare's language.

Speaking & Listening

↳ Discussion

Throughout Act I, Shakespeare contrasts themes of love and hate through his characters.

Work with a partner to identify passages that express love or hate.

- Read the passages aloud with your partner. Read with feeling to express emotions.
- Discuss the dramatic effect Shakespeare creates by pairing these two emotions in Act I.
- Write a summary of your discussion.

Prologue

Don't forget to **Notice & Note** as you read the text.

[*Enter* Chorus.]

Chorus. Now old desire doth in his deathbed lie,
And young affection gapes to be his heir.
That fair for which love groaned for and would die,
With tender Juliet matched, is now not fair.
Now Romeo is beloved, and loves again,
Alike bewitched by the charm of looks;
But to his foe supposed he must complain,
And she steal love's sweet bait from fearful hooks.
Being held a foe, he may not have access
To breathe such vows as lovers use to swear,
And she as much in love, her means much less
To meet her new beloved anywhere;
But passion lends them power, time means, to meet,
Temp'ring extremities with extreme sweet.

[*Exit.*]

1–4 **Now . . . fair:** Romeo's love for Rosaline (**old desire**) is now dead. His new love for Juliet (**young affection**) replaces the old.

7 **but . . . complain:** Juliet, a Capulet, is Romeo's supposed enemy, yet she is the one to whom he must plead (**complain**) his love.

14 **Temp'ring . . . sweet:** moderating great difficulties with extreme delights.

Act II

Scene 1 *A lane by the wall of Capulet's orchard.*

[*Enter* Romeo *alone.*]

Romeo. Can I go forward when my heart is here?
Turn back, dull earth, and find thy center out.

[*climbs the wall and leaps down within it*]

[*Enter* Benvolio *with* Mercutio.]

Benvolio. Romeo! my cousin Romeo! Romeo!

Mercutio. He is wise,
And, on my life, hath stol'n him home to bed.

Benvolio. He ran this way, and leapt this orchard wall.
Call, good Mercutio.

1–2 **Can . . . out:** How can I leave when Juliet is still here? My body (**dull earth**) has to find its heart (**center**).

6 **conjure:** use magic to call him.

8–21 **Appear . . . us:** Mercutio jokes about Romeo's lovesickness.

ANALYZE LITERARY DEVICES

Annotate: Character foils have contrasting traits. Read the exchange between Mercutio and Benvolio in lines 16–42 and mark Benvolio's responses.

Analyze: How does Benvolio act as a foil to Mercutio in this scene?

23–29 **'Twould . . . raise up him:** It would anger him if I called a stranger to join his beloved (**mistress**), but I'm only calling Romeo to join her.

31 **To be . . . night:** to keep company with the night, which is as gloomy as Romeo is.

34 **medlar:** a fruit that looks like a small brown apple.

39 **truckle bed:** trundle bed, a small bed that fits beneath a bigger one.

Mercutio. Nay, I'll conjure too.
Romeo! humors! madman! passion! lover!
Appear thou in the likeness of a sigh;
Speak but one rhyme, and I am satisfied!
Cry but "Ay me!" pronounce but "love" and "dove";
Speak to my gossip Venus one fair word,
One nickname for her purblind son and heir,
Young Adam Cupid, he that shot so trim
When King Cophetua loved the beggar maid!
He heareth not, he stirreth not, he moveth not;
The ape is dead, and I must conjure him.
I conjure thee by Rosaline's bright eyes,
By her high forehead and her scarlet lip,
By her fine foot, straight leg, and quivering thigh,
And the demesnes that there adjacent lie,
That in thy likeness thou appear to us!

Benvolio. An if he hear thee, thou wilt anger him.

Mercutio. This cannot anger him. 'Twould anger him
To raise a spirit in his mistress' circle
Of some strange nature, letting it there stand
Till she had laid it and conjured it down.
That were some spite; my invocation
Is fair and honest and in his mistress' name
I conjure only but to raise up him.

Benvolio. Come, he hath hid himself among these trees
To be consorted with the humorous night.
Blind is his love, and best befits the dark.

Mercutio. If love be blind, love cannot hit the mark.
Now will he sit under a medlar tree
And wish his mistress were that kind of fruit
As maids call medlars when they laugh alone.
Oh, Romeo, that she were, O, that she were
An open et cetera, thou a pop'rin pear!
Romeo, good night. I'll to my truckle bed;
This field-bed is too cold for me to sleep.
Come, shall we go?

Benvolio. Go then, for 'tis in vain
To seek him here that means not to be found.

[*Exeunt.*]

Scene 2 *Capulet's orchard.*

Don't forget to **Notice & Note** as you read the text.

[*Enter* Romeo.]

Romeo. He jests at scars that never felt a wound.

[*Enter* Juliet *above at a window.*]

But soft! What light through yonder window breaks?
It is the East, and Juliet is the sun!
Arise, fair sun, and kill the envious moon,
Who is already sick and pale with grief
That thou her maid art far more fair than she.
Be not her maid, since she is envious;
Her vestal livery is but sick and green,
And none but fools do wear it; cast it off.
It is my lady; O, it is my love!
O that she knew she were!
She speaks, yet she says nothing. What of that?
Her eye discourses; I will answer it.
I am too bold; 'tis not to me she speaks.
Two of the fairest stars in all the heaven,
Having some business, do entreat her eyes
To twinkle in their spheres till they return.
What if her eyes were there, they in her head?
The brightness of her cheek would shame those stars
As daylight doth a lamp; her eyes in heaven
Would through the airy region stream so bright
That birds would sing and think it were not night.
See how she leans her cheek upon her hand!
O that I were a glove upon that hand,
That I might touch that cheek!

Juliet. Ay me!

Romeo. She speaks.
O, speak again, bright angel! for thou art
As glorious to this night, being o'er my head,
As is a winged messenger of heaven
Unto the white-upturned wond'ring eyes
Of mortals that fall back to gaze on him
When he bestrides the lazy-pacing clouds
And sails upon the bosom of the air.

Juliet. O Romeo, Romeo! wherefore art thou Romeo?
Deny thy father and refuse thy name!

1 **He jests . . . wound:** Romeo has overheard Mercutio and comments that Mercutio makes fun of love because he has never been wounded by it.

13–14 **Her eye . . . speaks:** Romeo shifts back and forth between wanting to speak to Juliet and being afraid.

15–22 **Two of . . . not night:** Romeo compares Juliet's eyes to stars in the sky.

25 Juliet begins to speak, not knowing that Romeo is nearby.

26–32 **thou art . . . of the air:** He compares Juliet to an angel (**winged messenger of heaven**) who stands on (**bestrides**) the clouds.

33 **wherefore:** why. Juliet asks why Romeo is who he is—someone from her enemy's family.

Or, if thou wilt not, be but sworn my love,
And I'll no longer be a Capulet.

Romeo. [*aside*]. Shall I hear more, or shall I speak at this?

Juliet. 'Tis but thy name that is my enemy.
Thou art thyself, though not a Montague.
What's Montague? It is nor hand, nor foot,
Nor arm, nor face, nor any other part
Belonging to a man. O, be some other name!
What's in a name? That which we call a rose
By any other name would smell as sweet.
So Romeo would, were he not Romeo called,
Retain that dear perfection which he owes
Without that title. Romeo, doff thy name;
And for that name, which is no part of thee,
Take all myself.

43–47 Juliet tries to convince herself that a name is just a meaningless word that has nothing to do with the person. She asks Romeo to get rid of (**doff**) his name.

Romeo. I take thee at thy word.
Call me but love, and I'll be new baptized;
Henceforth I never will be Romeo.

Juliet. What man art thou that, thus bescreened in night,
So stumblest on my counsel?

52–53 Juliet is startled that someone hiding (**bescreened**) nearby hears her private thoughts (**counsel**).

Romeo. By a name
I know not how to tell thee who I am.
My name, dear saint, is hateful to myself,
Because it is an enemy to thee.
Had I it written, I would tear the word.

Juliet. My ears have yet not drunk a hundred words
Of that tongue's utterance, yet I know the sound.
Art thou not Romeo, and a Montague?

Romeo. Neither, fair saint, if either thee dislike.

Juliet. How camest thou hither, tell me, and wherefore?
The orchard walls are high and hard to climb,
And the place death, considering who thou art,
If any of my kinsmen find thee here.

ANALYZE PARALLEL PLOTS

Annotate: Mark the words in lines 62–67 that refer to the feud between the Capulets and Montagues.

Analyze: How does the parallel plot of the feud affect the romance between Romeo and Juliet?

Romeo. With love's light wings did I o'erperch these walls;
For stony limits cannot hold love out,
And what love can do, that dares love attempt.
Therefore thy kinsmen are no let to me.

66–69 **With . . . me:** Love helped me climb (**o'erperch**) the walls. Neither walls nor your relatives are a hindrance (**let**) to me.

Juliet. If they do see thee, they will murder thee.

Romeo. Alack, there lies more peril in thine eye
Than twenty of their swords! Look thou but sweet,
And I am proof against their enmity.

Juliet. I would not for the world they saw thee here.

Romeo. I have night's cloak to hide me from their sight;
And but thou love me, let them find me here.
My life were better ended by their hate
Than death prorogued, wanting of thy love.

Juliet. By whose direction foundst thou out this place?

72–73 **Look . . . enmity:** Smile on me, and I will be defended against my enemies' hatred (**enmity**).

78 **than death . . . love:** than my death postponed (**prorogued**) if you don't love me.

Romeo. By love, that first did prompt me to enquire.
He lent me counsel, and I lent him eyes.
I am no pilot, yet, wert thou as far
As that vast shore washed with the farthest sea,
I would adventure for such merchandise.

85–89 **Thou . . . compliment:** Had I known you were listening, I would have gladly (**fain**) behaved more properly, but now it's too late for good manners (**farewell compliment**).

Juliet. Thou knowest the mask of night is on my face;
Else would a maiden blush bepaint my cheek
For that which thou hast heard me speak tonight.
Fain would I dwell on form—fain, fain deny
What I have spoke; but farewell compliment!
Dost thou love me? I know thou wilt say "Ay";
And I will take thy word. Yet, if thou swearst,
Thou mayst prove false. At lovers' perjuries,
They say Jove laughs. O gentle Romeo,
If thou dost love, pronounce it faithfully.
Or if thou thinkst I am too quickly won,
I'll frown, and be perverse, and say thee nay,
So thou wilt woo; but else, not for the world.
In truth, fair Montague, I am too fond,
And therefore thou mayst think my 'havior light;
But trust me, gentleman, I'll prove more true
Than those that have more cunning to be strange.
I should have been more strange, I must confess,
But that thou overheardst, ere I was ware,
My true love's passion. Therefore pardon me,
And not impute this yielding to light love,
Which the dark night hath so discovered.

92–93 **At . . . laughs:** Jove, the king of the gods, laughs at lovers who lie to each other.

95–101 **Or if . . . strange:** You might think I've fallen in love too easily and that I'm too outspoken. But I'll be truer to you than those who play games to hide their real feelings (**be strange**).

Romeo. Lady, by yonder blessed moon I swear,
That tips with silver all these fruit-tree tops—

Juliet. O, swear not by the moon, the inconstant moon,
That monthly changes in her circled orb,
Lest that thy love prove likewise variable.

Romeo. What shall I swear by?

Juliet. Do not swear at all;
Or if thou wilt, swear by thy gracious self,
Which is the god of my idolatry,
And I'll believe thee.

Romeo. If my heart's dear love—

117 **I have . . . contract:** I am concerned about this declaration of love (**contract**).

Juliet. Well, do not swear. Although I joy in thee,
I have no joy of this contract tonight.
It is too rash, too unadvised, too sudden;
Too like the lightning, which doth cease to be
Ere one can say "It lightens." Sweet, good night!

This bud of love, by summer's ripening breath,
May prove a beauteous flow'r when next we meet.

Good night, good night! As sweet repose and rest
Come to thy heart as that within my breast!

Romeo. O, wilt thou leave me so unsatisfied?

Juliet. What satisfaction canst thou have tonight?

Romeo. The exchange of thy love's faithful vow for mine.

Juliet. I gave thee mine before thou didst request it;
And yet I would it were to give again.

Romeo. Wouldst thou withdraw it? For what purpose, love?

Juliet. But to be frank and give it thee again.
And yet I wish but for the thing I have.
My bounty is as boundless as the sea,
My love as deep; the more I give to thee,
The more I have, for both are infinite.
I hear some noise within. Dear love, adieu!

[Nurse *calls within.*]

Anon, good nurse! Sweet Montague, be true.
Stay but a little, I will come again.

[*Exit.*]

Romeo. O blessed, blessed night! I am afeard,
Being in night, all this is but a dream,
Too flattering-sweet to be substantial.

[*Re-enter* Juliet, *above.*]

Juliet. Three words, dear Romeo, and good night indeed.
If that thy bent of love be honorable,
Thy purpose marriage, send me word tomorrow,
By one that I'll procure to come to thee,
Where and what time thou wilt perform the rite;
And all my fortunes at thy foot I'll lay
And follow thee my lord throughout the world.

Nurse [*within*]. Madam!

Juliet. I come, anon.—But if thou meanst not well,
I do beseech thee—

Nurse [*within*]. Madam!

Juliet. By-and-by I come.—
To cease thy suit and leave me to my grief.
Tomorrow will I send.

Romeo. So thrive my soul—

Juliet. A thousand times good night! [*Exit.*]

Don't forget to **Notice & Note** as you read the text.

ANALYZE LITERARY DEVICES

Annotate: Mark the lines Romeo speaks that contain foreshadowing.

Analyze: How do these lines foreshadow what may come later?

150–151 **But if . . . thee:** Juliet is still worried that Romeo is not serious.

ANALYZE LITERARY DEVICES

Annotate: Underline the simile in lines 156–157.

Interpret: What is being compared?

158–163 **Hist . . . name:** I wish I could speak your name as loudly as a falconer calls his falcon (**tassel-gentle**), but because of my parents I must whisper. **Echo** was a nymph in Greek mythology whose unreturned love for Narcissus caused her to waste away till only her voice was left.

Romeo. A thousand times the worse, to want thy light!
Love goes toward love as schoolboys from their books;
But love from love, towards school with heavy looks.

[*Enter* Juliet *again, above.*]

Juliet. Hist! Romeo, hist! O for a falc'ner's voice
To lure this tassel-gentle back again!
Bondage is hoarse and may not speak aloud;
Else would I tear the cave where Echo lies,
And make her airy tongue more hoarse than mine
With repetition of my Romeo's name.
Romeo!

Romeo. It is my soul that calls upon my name.
How silver-sweet sound lovers' tongues by night,
Like softest music to attending ears!

Juliet. Romeo!

Romeo. My sweet?

Juliet. What o'clock tomorrow
Shall I send to thee?

Romeo. By the hour of nine.

Juliet. I will not fail. 'Tis twenty years till then.
I have forgot why I did call thee back.

Romeo. Let me stand here till thou remember it.

Juliet. I shall forget, to have thee still stand there,
Rememb'ring how I love thy company.

Romeo. And I'll still stay, to have thee still forget,
Forgetting any other home but this.

177–182 **I would . . . liberty:** I know you must go, but I want you close to me like a pet bird that a thoughtless child (**wanton**) keeps on a string.

Juliet. 'Tis almost morning. I would have thee gone—
And yet no farther than a wanton's bird,
That lets it hop a little from her hand,
Like a poor prisoner in his twisted gyves,
And with a silk thread plucks it back again,
So loving-jealous of his liberty.

ANALYZE LITERARY DEVICES

Annotate: Mark the expression in lines 183–186 that is an oxymoron.

Analyze: How does this oxymoron foreshadow the fates of both Romeo and Juliet?

Romeo. I would I were thy bird.

Juliet. Sweet, so would I.
Yet I should kill thee with much cherishing.
Good night, good night! Parting is such sweet sorrow,
That I shall say good night till it be morrow.

[*Exit.*]

Romeo. Sleep dwell upon thine eyes, peace in thy breast!
Would I were sleep and peace, so sweet to rest!
Hence will I to my ghostly father's cell,
His help to crave and my dear hap to tell.

[*Exit.*]

189 **ghostly father:** spiritual adviser or priest.

190 **dear hap:** good fortune.

Scene 3 *Friar Laurence's cell in the monastery.*

[*Enter* Friar Laurence *alone, with a basket.]*

Friar Laurence. The grey-eyed morn smiles on the frowning night,
Chequ'ring the Eastern clouds with streaks of light;
And flecked darkness like a drunkard reels
From forth day's path and Titan's fiery wheels.
Now, ere the sun advance his burning eye
The day to cheer and night's dank dew to dry,
I must upfill this osier cage of ours
With baleful weeds and precious-juiced flowers.
The earth that's nature's mother is her tomb,
What is her burying grave, that is her womb;
And from her womb children of divers kind
We sucking on her natural bosom find;
Many for many virtues excellent,
None but for some, and yet all different.
O, mickle is the powerful grace that lies
In plants, herbs, stones, and their true qualities;
For naught so vile that on the earth doth live
But to the earth some special good doth give;
Nor aught so good but, strained from that fair use,
Revolts from true birth, stumbling on abuse.
Virtue itself turns vice, being misapplied,
And vice sometimes by action dignified.
Within the infant rind of this small flower
Poison hath residence, and medicine power;
For this, being smelt, with that part cheers each part;
Being tasted, slays all senses with the heart.
Two such opposed kings encamp them still
In man as well as herbs—grace and rude will;
And where the worser is predominant,
Full soon the canker death eats up that plant.

4 **Titan** is the god whose chariot pulls the sun into the sky each morning.

7 **osier cage:** willow basket.

9–12 **The earth . . . find:** The same earth that acts as a tomb is also the womb, or birthplace, of various useful plants that people can harvest.

15–18 **mickle:** great. The friar says that nothing from the earth is so evil that it doesn't do some good.

28 **grace and rude will:** good and evil. Both exist in people as well as in plants.

[*Enter* Romeo.]

Romeo. Good morrow, father.

Friar Laurence. Benedicite!
What early tongue so sweet saluteth me?

31 **Benedicite** (bĕ-nĕ-dī´sĭ-tē): God bless you.

33–42 **it argues . . . tonight:** Only a disturbed (**distempered**) mind could make you get up so early. Old people may have trouble sleeping, but it is not normal for someone as young as you. Or were you up all night?

Young son, it argues a distempered head
So soon to bid good morrow to thy bed.
Care keeps his watch in every old man's eye,
And where care lodges sleep will never lie;

But where unbruised youth with unstuffed brain
Doth couch his limbs, there golden sleep doth reign.
Therefore thy earliness doth me assure
Thou art uproused with some distemp'rature;
Or if not so, then here I hit it right—
Our Romeo hath not been in bed tonight.

Romeo. That last is true, the sweeter rest was mine.

Friar Laurence. God pardon sin! Wast thou with Rosaline?

Romeo. With Rosaline, my ghostly father? No.
I have forgot that name, and that name's woe.

Friar Laurence. That's my good son! But where hast thou been then?

Romeo. I'll tell thee ere thou ask it me again.
I have been feasting with mine enemy,
Where on a sudden one hath wounded me
That's by me wounded. Both our remedies
Within thy help and holy physic lies.
I bear no hatred, blessed man, for, lo,
My intercession likewise steads my foe.

49–56 Romeo tries to explain the situation, asking for help both for himself and his "foe" (Juliet). The friar does not understand Romeo's convoluted language and asks him to speak clearly so that he can help.

Friar Laurence. Be plain, good son, and homely in thy drift.
Riddling confession finds but riddling shrift.

Romeo. Then plainly know my heart's dear love is set
On the fair daughter of rich Capulet;
As mine on hers, so hers is set on mine,
And all combined, save what thou must combine
By holy marriage. When, and where, and how
We met, we wooed, and made exchange of vow,
I'll tell thee as we pass; but this I pray,
That thou consent to marry us today.

Friar Laurence. Holy Saint Francis! What a change is here!
Is Rosaline, that thou didst love so dear,
So soon forsaken? Young men's love then lies
Not truly in their hearts, but in their eyes.
Jesu Maria! What a deal of brine
Hath washed thy sallow cheeks for Rosaline!
How much salt water thrown away in waste,
To season love, that of it doth not taste!
The sun not yet thy sighs from heaven clears,
Thy old groans ring yet in mine ancient ears.
Lo, here upon thy cheek the stain doth sit
Of an old tear that is not washed off yet.
If e'er thou wast thyself, and these woes thine,
Thou and these woes were all for Rosaline.
And art thou changed? Pronounce this sentence then:
Women may fall when there's no strength in men.

69 **brine:** salt water—that is, the tears that Romeo has been shedding for Rosaline.

Romeo. Thou chidst me oft for loving Rosaline.

Friar Laurence. For doting, not for loving, pupil mine.

Romeo. And badest me bury love.

Friar Laurence. Not in a grave
To lay one in, another ought to have.

80 **Women . . . men:** If men are so weak, women may be forgiven for sinning.

81–82 **chidst:** scolded. The friar replies that he scolded Romeo for being lovesick, not for loving.

85–88 **She whom . . . spell:** Romeo says that the woman he loves feels the same way about him. That wasn't true of Rosaline. The friar replies that Rosaline knew that Romeo didn't know what real love is.

Romeo. I pray thee chide not. She whom I love now
Doth grace for grace and love for love allow.
The other did not so.

Friar Laurence. O, she knew well
Thy love did read by rote, that could not spell.
But come, young waverer, come go with me.
In one respect I'll thy assistant be;
For this alliance may so happy prove
To turn your households' rancor to pure love.

91–92 **For this . . . prove:** this marriage may work out so well; **rancor**: bitter hate.

Romeo. O, let us hence! I stand on sudden haste.

Friar Laurence. Wisely, and slow. They stumble that run fast.

[*Exeunt.*]

NOTICE & NOTE
WORDS OF THE WISER

When you notice a wiser character giving advice about life to a main character, you've found a **Words of the Wiser** signpost.

Notice & Note: Mark Friar Laurence's advice to Romeo in the last line of Scene 3.

Infer: What is Friar Laurence trying to make Romeo understand?

Scene 4 *A street.*

[*Enter* Benvolio *and* Mercutio.]

Mercutio. Where the devil should this Romeo be?
Came he not home tonight?

Benvolio. Not to his father's. I spoke with his man.

3 **man:** servant.

Mercutio. Why, that same pale hard-hearted wench, that Rosaline,
Torments him so that he will sure run mad.

Benvolio. Tybalt, the kinsman to old Capulet,
Hath sent a letter to his father's house.

6–12 **Tybalt . . . dared:** Tybalt, still angry with Romeo, has sent a letter challenging Romeo to a duel. Benvolio says that Romeo will accept Tybalt's challenge and fight him.

Mercutio. A challenge, on my life.

Benvolio. Romeo will answer it.

Mercutio. Any man that can write may answer a letter.

Benvolio. Nay, he will answer the letter's master, how he dares, being dared.

Mercutio. Alas, poor Romeo, he is already dead! stabbed with a white wench's black eye; shot through the ear with a love song; the very pin of his heart cleft with the blind bow-boy's butt-shaft; and is he a man to encounter Tybalt?

15 **blind bow-boy's butt-shaft:** Cupid's dull practice arrow. Mercutio suggests that Romeo fell in love with very little work on Cupid's part.

Benvolio. Why, what is Tybalt?

Mercutio. More than Prince of Cats, I can tell you. O, he's the courageous captain of compliments. He fights as you sing pricksong—keeps time, distance, and proportion; rests me his minim rest, one, two, and the third in your bosom! the very butcher of a silk button, a duelist, a duelist! a gentleman of the very first house, of the first and second cause. Ah, the immortal *passado*! the *punto reverso*! the *hay*!

18–24 **More than . . . *hay*: Prince of Cats** refers to a cat in a fable, named Tybalt. Mercutio makes fun of Tybalt's new style of dueling, comparing it to singing (**pricksong**). ***Passado, punto reverso***, and ***hay*** were terms used in the new dueling style.

Benvolio. The what?

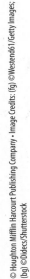

Mercutio. The pox of such antic, lisping, affecting fantasticoes—these new tuners of accent! "By Jesu, a very good blade! a very tall man! a very good whore!" Why, is not this a lamentable thing, grandsire, that we should be thus afflicted with these strange flies, these fashion-mongers, these perdona-mi's, who stand so much on the new form that they cannot sit at ease on the old bench? O, their bones, their bones!

[*Enter* Romeo, *no longer moody.*]

Benvolio. Here comes Romeo! here comes Romeo!

Mercutio. Without his roe, like a dried herring. O, flesh, flesh, how art thou fishified! Now is he for the numbers that Petrarch flowed in. Laura, to his lady, was but a kitchen wench (marry, she had a better love to berhyme her), Dido a dowdy, Cleopatra a gypsy, Helen and Hero hildings and harlots, Thisbe a grey eye or so, but not to the purpose. Signior Romeo, *bon jour*! There's a French salutation to your French slop. You gave us the counterfeit fairly last night.

Romeo. Good morrow to you both. What counterfeit did I give you?

Mercutio. The slip, sir, the slip. Can you not conceive?

Romeo. Pardon, good Mercutio. My business was great, and in such a case as mine a man may strain courtesy.

Mercutio. That's as much as to say, such a case as yours constrains a man to bow in the hams.

26–32 **The pox . . . their bones:** Mercutio continues to make fun of people who embrace new styles and new manners of speaking.

ANALYZE LITERARY DEVICES

Annotate: Mercutio refers to Petrarch, a poet, and uses literary and classical allusions to make fun of Romeo's lovesickness. Mark the allusions in Mercutio's speech.

Analyze: What is Mercutio's point in using these comparisons to mock Romeo's love?

39–44 ***bon jour:*** "Good day" in French; **There's . . . last night:** Here's a greeting to match your fancy French trousers (**slop**). You did a good job of getting away from us last night. (A piece of counterfeit money was called a **slip**.)

Romeo. Meaning, to curtsy.

Mercutio. Thou hast most kindly hit it.

Romeo. A most courteous exposition.

Mercutio. Nay, I am the very pink of courtesy.

Romeo. Pink for flower.

Mercutio. Right.

55 **pump:** shoe; **well-flowered:** Shoes with flowerlike designs.

Romeo. Why, then is my pump well-flowered.

Mercutio. Well said! Follow me this jest now till thou hast worn out thy pump, that, when the single sole of it is worn, the jest may remain, after the wearing, solely singular.

Romeo. Oh, single-soled jest, solely singular for the singleness!

Mercutio. Come between us, good Benvolio! My wits faint.

61 **Switch . . . match:** Keep going, or I'll claim victory.

Romeo. Switch and spurs, switch and spurs! or I'll cry a match.

64–65 **Was . . . goose:** Have I proved that you are a foolish person?

Mercutio. Nay, if our wits run the wild-goose chase, I am done; for thou hast more of the wild goose in one of thy wits than, I am sure, I have in my whole five. Was I with you there for the goose?

Romeo. Thou wast never with me for anything when thou wast not there for the goose.

Mercutio. I will bite thee by the ear for that jest.

Romeo. Nay, good goose, bite not!

Mercutio. Thy wit is a very bitter sweeting; it is a most sharp sauce.

Romeo. And is it not, then, well served in to a sweet goose?

73 **cheveril:** kidskin, which is flexible. Mercutio means that a little wit stretches a long way.

Mercutio. O, here's a wit of cheveril, that stretches from an inch narrow to an ell broad!

Romeo. I stretch it out for that word "broad," which, added to the goose, proves thee far and wide a broad goose.

80–81 **great natural:** an idiot, like a jester or clown who carries a fool's stick (**bauble**).

Mercutio. Why, is not this better now than groaning for love? Now art thou sociable, now art thou Romeo; now art thou what thou art, by art as well as by nature. For this driveling love is like a great natural that runs lolling up and down to hide his bauble in a hole.

Benvolio. Stop there, stop there!

Mercutio. Thou desirest me to stop in my tale against the hair.

Benvolio. Thou wouldst else have made thy tale large.

Mercutio. O, thou art deceived! I would have made it short; for I was come to the whole depth of my tale, and meant indeed to occupy the argument no longer.

[*Enter* Nurse *and* Peter, *her servant. He is carrying a large fan.*]

Romeo. Here's goodly gear!

Mercutio. A sail, a sail!

Benvolio. Two, two! a shirt and a smock.

Nurse. Peter!

Peter. Anon.

Nurse. My fan, Peter.

Mercutio. Good Peter, to hide her face; for her fan's the fairer of the two.

Nurse. God ye good morrow, gentlemen.

Mercutio. God ye good-den, fair gentlewoman.

Nurse. Is it good-den?

Mercutio. 'Tis no less, I tell ye, for the bawdy hand of the dial is now upon the prick of noon.

Nurse. Out upon you! What a man are you!

Romeo. One, gentlewoman, that God hath made himself to mar.

Nurse. By my troth, it is well said. "For himself to mar," quoth'a? Gentlemen, can any of you tell me where I may find the young Romeo?

Romeo. I can tell you; but young Romeo will be older when you have found him than he was when you sought him. I am the youngest of that name, for fault of a worse.

Nurse. You say well.

Mercutio. Yea, is the worst well? Very well took, i' faith! wisely, wisely.

Nurse. If you be he, sir, I desire some confidence with you.

Benvolio. She will endite him to some supper.

Mercutio. A bawd, a bawd, a bawd! So ho!

Romeo. What hast thou found?

Mercutio. No hare, sir; unless a hare, sir, in a lenten pie, that is something stale and hoar ere it be spent.

[*sings*]

"An old hare hoar,
And an old hare hoar,
Is very good meat in Lent.
But a hare that is hoar,
Is too much for a score
When it hoars ere it be spent."

Romeo, will you come to your father's? We'll to dinner thither.

Romeo. I will follow you.

Mercutio. Farewell, ancient lady. Farewell, [*sings*] lady, lady, lady.

88–89 **goodly gear:** something fine to joke about; **a sail:** Mercutio likens the nurse in all her petticoats to a huge ship coming toward them.

93 Fans were usually carried only by fine ladies. The nurse is trying to pretend that she is more than a servant.

112–113 **confidence:** The nurse means *conference*; she uses big words without understanding their meaning; **endite:** Benvolio makes fun of the nurse by using this word rather than *invite*.

114–124 Mercutio calls the nurse a **bawd,** or woman who runs a house of prostitution. His song uses the insulting puns **hare,** a rabbit or prostitute, and **hoar,** old.

[*Exeunt* Mercutio *and* Benvolio.]

Nurse. Marry, farewell! I pray you, sir, what saucy merchant was this that was so full of his ropery?

128 **ropery:** roguery, or jokes.

Romeo. A gentleman, nurse, that loves to hear himself talk and will speak more in a minute than he will stand to in a month.

Nurse. An 'a speak anything against me, I'll take him down, an 'a were lustier than he is, and twenty such Jacks; and if I cannot, I'll find those that shall. Scurvy knave! I am none of his flirt-gills; I am none of his skainsmates. [*turning* to Peter] And thou must stand by too, and suffer every knave to use me at his pleasure?

133–134 The nurse is angry that Mercutio treated her like one of his loose women (**flirt-gills**) or his gangsterlike friends (**skainsmates**).

Peter. I saw no man use you at his pleasure. If I had, my weapon should quickly have been out, I warrant you. I dare draw as soon as another man, if I see occasion in a good quarrel, and the law on my side.

Nurse. Now, afore God, I am so vexed that every part about me quivers. Scurvy knave! Pray you, sir, a word; and as I told you, my young lady bade me enquire you out. What she bid me say, I will keep to myself; but first let me tell ye, if ye should lead her into a fool's paradise, as they say, it were a very gross kind of behavior, as they say; for the gentlewoman is young; and therefore, if you should deal double with her, truly it were an ill thing to be offered to any gentlewoman, and very weak dealing.

142–147 The nurse warns Romeo that he'd better mean what he said about marrying Juliet.

Romeo. Nurse, commend me to thy lady and mistress. I protest unto thee—

148 **commend me:** give my respectful greetings.

Nurse. Good heart, and i' faith I will tell her as much. Lord, Lord! she will be a joyful woman.

Romeo. What wilt thou tell her, nurse? Thou dost not mark me.

Nurse. I will tell her, sir, that you do protest, which, as I take it, is a gentlemanlike offer.

Romeo. Bid her devise
Some means to come to shrift this afternoon;
And there she shall at Friar Laurence' cell
Be shrived and married. Here is for thy pains.

155–159 Romeo tells the nurse to have Juliet come to Friar Laurence's cell this afternoon, using the excuse that she is going to confess her sins (**shrift**). There she will receive forgiveness for her sins (**be shrived**) and be married.

Nurse. No, truly, sir; not a penny.

Romeo. Go to! I say you shall.

Nurse. This afternoon, sir? Well, she shall be there.

Romeo. And stay, good nurse, behind the abbey wall.
Within this hour my man shall be with thee
And bring thee cords made like a tackled stair,
Which to the high topgallant of my joy
Must be my convoy in the secret night.
Farewell. Be trusty, and I'll quit thy pains.
Farewell. Commend me to thy mistress.

164–165 **tackled stair:** rope ladder; **topgallant:** highest point.

167 **quit thy pains:** reward you.

Don't forget to **Notice & Note** as you read the text.

Nurse. Now God in heaven bless thee! Hark you, sir.

Romeo. What sayst thou, my dear nurse?

Nurse. Is your man secret? Did you ne'er hear say,
Two may keep counsel, putting one away?

Romeo. I warrant thee my man's as true as steel.

Nurse. Well, sir, my mistress is the sweetest lady. Lord, Lord! when 'twas a little prating thing—O, there is a nobleman in town, one Paris, that would fain lay knife aboard; but she, good soul, had as lief see a toad, a very toad, as see him. I anger her sometimes, and tell her that Paris is the properer man; but I'll warrant you, when I say so, she looks as pale as any clout in the versal world. Doth not rosemary and Romeo begin both with a letter?

174–177 The nurse begins to babble about Paris's proposal but says that Juliet would rather look at a toad than at Paris.

179–186 **clout:** old cloth; **the versal world:** the entire world; **Doth not . . . hear it:** The nurse tries to recall a clever saying that Juliet made up about Romeo and rosemary, the herb, but cannot remember it. She is sure that the two words couldn't begin with *R* because this letter sounds like a snarling dog; **sententious:** The nurse means *sentences*.

Romeo. Ay, nurse, what of that? Both with an R.

Nurse. Ah, mocker! that's the dog's name. R is for the—No; I know it begins with some other letter; and she hath the prettiest sententious of it, of you and rosemary, that it would do you good to hear it.

Romeo. Commend me to thy lady.

Nurse. Ay, a thousand times. [*Exit* Romeo.] Peter!

Peter. Anon.

Nurse. Peter, take my fan, and go before, and apace.

190 **apace:** quickly.

[*Exeunt.*]

Scene 5 *Capulet's orchard.*

[*Enter* Juliet.]

Juliet. The clock struck nine when I did send the nurse;
In half an hour she promised to return.
Perchance she cannot meet him. That's not so.
O, she is lame! Love's heralds should be thoughts,
Which ten times faster glide than the sun's beams
Driving back shadows over lowering hills.
Therefore do nimble-pinioned doves draw Love,
And therefore hath the wind-swift Cupid wings.
Now is the sun upon the highmost hill
Of this day's journey, and from nine till twelve
Is three long hours; yet she is not come.
Had she affections and warm youthful blood,
She would be as swift in motion as a ball;
My words would bandy her to my sweet love,
And his to me.
But old folks, many feign as they were dead—
Unwieldy, slow, heavy, and pale as lead.

4–6 **Love's . . . hills:** Love's messengers should be thoughts, which travel ten times faster than sunbeams.

7 **nimble-pinioned . . . Love:** Swift-winged doves pull the chariot of Venus, goddess of love.

14 **bandy:** toss.

16 **feign as:** act as if.

[*Enter* Nurse *and* Peter.] O God, she comes! O honey nurse, what news?
Hast thou met with him? Send thy man away.

Nurse. Peter, stay at the gate.

[*Exit* Peter.]

21–22 The nurse teases Juliet by putting on a sad face as if the news were bad.

Juliet. Now, good sweet nurse—O Lord, why lookst thou sad?
Though news be sad, yet tell them merrily;
If good, thou shamest the music of sweet news
By playing it to me with so sour a face.

25–26 **give me . . . I had:** Leave me alone for a while. I ache all over because of the running back and forth I've been doing.

Nurse. I am aweary, give me leave awhile.
Fie, how my bones ache! What a jaunce have I had!

Juliet. I would thou hadst my bones, and I thy news.
Nay, come, I pray thee speak. Good, good nurse, speak.

Nurse. Jesu, what haste! Can you not stay awhile?
Do you not see that I am out of breath?

Juliet. How art thou out of breath when thou hast breath
To say to me that thou art out of breath?
The excuse that thou dost make in this delay
Is longer than the tale thou dost excuse.
Is thy news good or bad? Answer to that.
Say either, and I'll stay the circumstance.
Let me be satisfied, is't good or bad?

36 **I'll . . . circumstance:** I'll wait for the details.

38 **simple:** foolish.

Nurse. Well, you have made a simple choice; you know not how to choose a man. Romeo? No, not he. Though his face be better than any man's, yet his leg excels all men's; and for a hand and a foot, and a body, though they be not to be talked on, yet they are past compare. He is not the flower of courtesy, but, I'll warrant him, as gentle as a lamb. Go thy ways, wench; serve God. What, have you dined at home?

Juliet. No, no. But all this did I know before.
What say he of our marriage? What of that?

Nurse. Lord, how my head aches! What a head have I!
It beats as it would fall in twenty pieces.
My back o' t'other side—ah, my back, my back!
Beshrew your heart for sending me about
To catch my death with jauncing up and down!

50–51 **Beshrew . . . down:** Curse you for making me endanger my health by running around.

Juliet. I' faith, I am sorry that thou art not well.
Sweet, sweet, sweet nurse, tell me, what says my love?

Nurse. Your love says, like an honest gentleman, and a courteous, and a kind, and a handsome, and, I warrant, a virtuous—Where is your mother?

Juliet. Where is my mother? Why, she is within.
Where should she be? How oddly thou repliest!

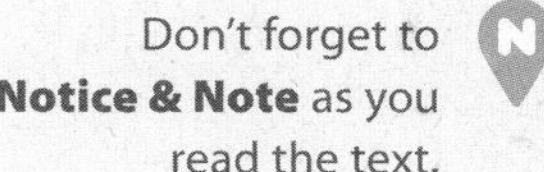

Don't forget to **Notice & Note** as you read the text.

"Your love says, like an honest gentleman,
'Where is your mother?'"

Nurse. O God's Lady dear!
Are you so hot? Marry come up, I trow.
Is this the poultice for my aching bones?
Hence forward do your messages yourself.

60–61 **Marry . . . bones:** Control yourself! Is this the treatment I get for my pain?

Juliet. Here's such a coil! Come, what says Romeo?

63 **coil:** fuss.

Nurse. Have you got leave to go to shrift today?

Juliet. I have.

Nurse. Then hie you hence to Friar Laurence' cell;
There stays a husband to make you a wife.
Now comes the wanton blood up in your cheeks:
They'll be in scarlet straight at any news.
Hie you to church; I must another way,
To fetch a ladder, by the which your love
Must climb a bird's nest soon when it is dark.
I am the drudge, and toil in your delight;
But you shall bear the burden soon at night.
Go; I'll to dinner; hie you to the cell.

70–72 The nurse will get the ladder that Romeo will use to climb to Juliet's room after they are married.

Juliet. Hie to high fortune! Honest nurse, farewell.

[*Exeunt.*]

Scene 6 *Friar Laurence's cell.*

[*Enter* Friar Laurence *and* Romeo.]

Friar Laurence. So smile the heavens upon this holy act
That after-hours with sorrow chide us not!

1–2 **So smile . . . us not:** May heaven so bless this act that we won't regret it in the future (**after-hours**).

Romeo. Amen, amen! But come what sorrow can,
It cannot countervail the exchange of joy
That one short minute gives me in her sight.
Do thou but close our hands with holy words,
Then love-devouring death do what he dare—
It is enough I may but call her mine.

4 **countervail:** outweigh.

Friar Laurence. These violent delights have violent ends
And in their triumph die, like fire and powder,
Which, as they kiss, consume. The sweetest honey
Is loathsome in his own deliciousness
And in the taste confounds the appetite.
Therefore love moderately: long love doth so;
Too swift arrives as tardy as too slow.

9–15 **These . . . slow:** The friar compares Romeo's passion to gunpowder and the fire that ignites it—both are destroyed—then to honey, whose sweetness can destroy the appetite. He reminds Romeo to practice moderation in love.

[*Enter* Juliet.]

Here comes the lady. O, so light a foot
Will ne'er wear out the everlasting flint.
A lover may bestride the gossamer
That idles in the wanton summer air,

Close Read Screencast

Listen to a modeled close read of this text.

And yet not fall; so light is vanity.

Juliet. Good even to my ghostly confessor.

Friar Laurence. Romeo shall thank thee, daughter, for us both.

23 **As much to him:** I give the same greeting to Romeo that he offers to me.

Juliet. As much to him, else is his thanks too much.

24–29 **if the measure . . . encounter:** If you are as happy as I am and have more skill to proclaim it, then sweeten the air by singing of our happiness to the world.

Romeo. Ah, Juliet, if the measure of thy joy
Be heaped like mine, and that thy skill be more
To blazon it, then sweeten with thy breath
This neighbor air, and let rich music's tongue
Unfold the imagined happiness that both
Receive in either by this dear encounter.

30–31 **Conceit . . . ornament:** True understanding (**conceit**) needs no words.

Juliet. Conceit, more rich in matter than in words,
Brags of his substance, not of ornament.
They are but beggars that can count their worth;
But my true love is grown to such excess
I cannot sum up sum of half my wealth.

Friar Laurence. Come, come with me, and we will make short work;
For, by your leaves, you shall not stay alone
Till Holy Church incorporate two in one.

[*Exeunt.*]

COLLABORATIVE DISCUSSION

Romeo and Juliet fall in love and make life-changing decisions in a matter of days. With a partner, discuss how this speed and intensity creates tension for the audience.

Assessment Practice

Answer these questions before moving on to the **Analyze the Text** questions on the following page.

1. This question has two parts. First, answer **Part A**. Then, answer **Part B**.

Part A

Why is Friar Laurence pleased that Romeo has fallen in love with Juliet?

- (A) He suspects that Rosaline only pretended to love Romeo.
- (B) He thinks marriage may end the feud between their families.
- (C) He learns that Romeo has finally made a thoughtful decision.
- (D) He hopes that marrying Juliet will make Romeo grow up.

Part B

Which statement below supports the answer to Part A?

- (A) "Virtue itself turns vice, being misapplied, / And vice sometime's by action dignified." (Scene 3, lines 21–22)
- (B) "Therefore thy earliness doth me assure / Thou art uproused with some distemp'rature" (Scene 3, lines 39–40)
- (C) "The sun not yet thy sighs from heaven clears, / Thy old groans ring yet in mine ancient ears." (Scene 3, lines 73–74)
- (D) "For this alliance may so happy prove / To turn your households' rancor to pure love." (Scene 3, lines 91–92)

2. Which sentence states a central theme in Act II?

- (A) Love can overcome the divisions between families.
- (B) Older people are always wiser than younger people.
- (C) Any serious situation can be lightened by a few jokes.
- (D) Venturing outside one's social group can be dangerous.

Ed

Test-Taking Strategies

Analyze the Text

Support your responses with evidence from the text.

NOTICE & NOTE

Review what you **noticed and noted** as you read the text. Your annotations can help you answer these questions.

1. **ANALYZE** In Act II, Scene 2, Juliet says, "What's in a name? That which we call a rose / By any other name would smell as sweet" (lines 43–44). What does she mean? How does this comparison relate to one of the conflicts in her life?

2. **CITE EVIDENCE** In Scene 3, why is Friar Laurence suspicious of Romeo's declaration of love for Juliet? What is his motivation for agreeing to marry Romeo and Juliet, despite his reservations?

3. **DRAW CONCLUSIONS** Identify at least one soliloquy and one aside in Act II. Explain what each example reveals about the character who speaks it.

4. **COMPARE** Compare Romeo's behavior before he meets Juliet with his behavior after they declare their love for each other. What do you learn about Romeo's character from the change in his behavior?

5. **IDENTIFY PATTERNS** In literature, a **motif** is a repeated image, idea, or theme. Explain the light/dark or day/night motif in Romeo's speech at the beginning of Act II, Scene 2. What does he mean when he refers to Juliet as "the sun"? Where in Act II is this motif repeated?

Choices

Here are some other ways to demonstrate your understanding of Act II.

Writing

↳ Modern Retelling

Rewrite Act II in a modern setting using today's language. Romeo's confession of his love to Juliet, his friends' mockery, the secret marriage plot: What would these events look and sound like today? Don't forget to substitute modern equivalents for those of 14th-century Italy. For example: Rather than a friar and a nurse, from whom would Romeo seek help today?

Speaking & Listening

↳ Debate

Friar Laurence and Mercutio have personal attributes that put them at odds with Romeo. Hold a debate in which characters present their points of view.

- Discuss the characteristics of Friar Laurence, Mercutio, and Romeo. What differences do these three demonstrate in Act II?
- With each person in your group taking the point of view of one of these characters, debate Romeo's plan to marry Juliet.
- Work together to write a debate summary.

Act III

Don't forget to **Notice & Note** as you read the text. 

Scene 1 *A public place.*

[*Enter* Mercutio, Benvolio, Page, *and* Servants.]

Benvolio. I pray thee, good Mercutio, let's retire.
The day is hot, the Capulets abroad,
And if we meet, we shall not scape a brawl,
For now, these hot days, is the mad blood stirring.

3–4 **we shall . . . stirring:** We shall not avoid a fight, since the heat makes people ill-tempered.

Mercutio. Thou art like one of those fellows that, when he enters the confines of a tavern, claps me his sword upon the table and says "God send me no need of thee!" and by the operation of the second cup draws him on the drawer, when indeed there is no need.

7–8 **by the . . . drawer:** feeling the effects of a second drink, is ready to fight (**draw on**) the waiter who's pouring the drinks (**drawer**).

Benvolio. Am I like such a fellow?

Mercutio. Come, come, thou art as hot a Jack in thy mood as any in Italy; and as soon moved to be moody, and as soon moody to be moved.

12–13 **as soon moved . . . to be moved:** as likely to get angry and start a fight.

Benvolio. And what to?

Mercutio. Nay an there were two such, we should have none shortly, for one would kill the other. Thou! why, thou wilt quarrel with a man that hath a hair more or a hair less in his beard than thou hast. Thou wilt quarrel with a man for cracking nuts, having no other reason but because thou hast hazel eyes. What eye but such an eye would spy out such a quarrel? Thy head is as full of quarrels as an egg is full of meat; and yet thy head hath been beaten as addle as an egg for quarreling. Thou hast quarreled with a man for coughing in the street, because he hath wakened thy dog that hath lain asleep in the sun. Didst thou not fall out with a tailor for wearing his new doublet before Easter? with another for tying his new shoes with old riband? And yet thou wilt tutor me from quarreling!

ANALYZE LITERARY DEVICES

Annotate: Mark one or more lines in which Mercutio teases his friend by insisting that Benvolio is quick to pick a fight.

Interpret: How is Mercutio's teasing an example of irony?

25 **doublet:** jacket.

26 **riband:** ribbon or laces.

Benvolio. An I were so apt to quarrel as thou art, any man should buy the fee simple of my life for an hour and a quarter.

28–29 **An I . . . quarter:** If I picked fights as quickly as you do, anybody could own me for the smallest amount of money.

Mercutio. The fee simple? O simple!

[*Enter* Tybalt *and others.*]

Benvolio. By my head, here come the Capulets.

Mercutio. By my heel, I care not.

Tybalt. Follow me close, for I will speak to them. Gentlemen, good den. A word with one of you.

Mercutio. And but one word with one of us? Couple it with something; make it a word and a blow.

Tybalt. You shall find me apt enough to that, sir, an you will give me occasion.

Mercutio. Could you not take some occasion without giving?

40–44 **consortest:** are friends with; Mercutio pretends to misunderstand him, assuming that Tybalt is insulting him by calling Romeo and him a **consort**, a group of traveling musicians. He then refers to his sword as his **fiddlestick**, the bow for a fiddle.

Tybalt. Mercutio, thou consortest with Romeo.

Mercutio. Consort? What, dost thou make us minstrels? An thou make minstrels of us, look to hear nothing but discords. Here's my fiddlestick; here's that shall make you dance. Zounds, consort!

Benvolio. We talk here in the public haunt of men.
Either withdraw unto some private place
And reason coldly of your grievances,
Or else depart. Here all eyes gaze on us.

Mercutio. Men's eyes were made to look, and let them gaze.
I will not budge for no man's pleasure, I.

[*Enter* Romeo.]

Tybalt. Well, peace be with you, sir. Here comes my man.

Mercutio. But I'll be hanged, sir, if he wear your livery.
Marry, go before to field, he'll be your follower!
Your worship in that sense may call him man.

Tybalt. Romeo, the love I bear thee can afford
No better term than this: thou art a villain.

Romeo. Tybalt, the reason that I have to love thee
Doth much excuse the appertaining rage
To such a greeting. Villain am I none.
Therefore farewell. I see thou knowst me not.

Tybalt. Boy, this shall not excuse the injuries
That thou hast done me; therefore turn and draw.

Romeo. I do protest I never injured thee,
But love thee better than thou canst devise
Till thou shalt know the reason of my love;
And so, good Capulet, which name I tender
As dearly as mine own, be satisfied.

Mercutio. O calm, dishonorable, vile submission!
Alla stoccata carries it away.

Don't forget to **Notice & Note** as you read the text.

51–54 Mercutio again pretends to misunderstand Tybalt. By **my man**, Tybalt means "the man I'm looking for." Mercutio takes it to mean "my servant." (**Livery** is a servant's uniform.)

57–59 I forgive your anger because I have reason to love you.

61 **Boy:** an insulting term of address.

66 **tender:** cherish.

68–70 Mercutio assumes that Romeo is afraid to fight. ***Alla stoccata*** is a move used in sword fighting.

[*draws*]
Tybalt, you rat-catcher, will you walk?

Tybalt. What wouldst thou have with me?

72–74 **nothing but . . . eight:** I intend to take one of your nine lives (as a cat supposedly has) and give a beating to the other eight.

Mercutio. Good King of Cats, nothing but one of your nine lives. That I mean to make bold withal, and, as you shall use me hereafter, dry-beat the rest of the eight. Will you pluck your sword out of his pilcher by the ears? Make haste, lest mine be about your ears ere it be out.

Tybalt. I am for you.

[*draws*]

Romeo. Gentle Mercutio, put thy rapier up.

79 ***passado:*** a sword fighting maneuver.

Mercutio. Come, sir, your *passado*!

[*They fight.*]

80–84 Romeo wants Benvolio to help him stop the fight. They are able to hold back Mercutio.

83 **bandying:** fighting.

Romeo. Draw, Benvolio; beat down their weapons.
Gentlemen, for shame! forbear this outrage!
Tybalt, Mercutio, the Prince expressly hath
Forbid this bandying in Verona streets.
Hold, Tybalt! Good Mercutio!

[Tybalt, *under* Romeo's *arm, thrusts* Mercutio *in, and flies with his* Men.]

85 **A plague . . . sped:** I curse both the Montagues and the Capulets. I am destroyed.

Mercutio. I am hurt.
A plague o' both your houses! I am sped.
Is he gone and hath nothing?

Benvolio. What, art thou hurt?

Mercutio. Ay, ay, a scratch, a scratch. Marry, 'tis enough.
Where is my page? Go, villain, fetch a surgeon.

[*Exit* Page.]

Romeo. Courage, man. The hurt cannot be much.

Mercutio. No, 'tis not so deep as a well, nor so wide as a church door; but 'tis enough, 'twill serve. Ask for me tomorrow, and you shall find me a grave man. I am peppered, I warrant, for this world. A plague o' both your houses! Zounds, a dog, a rat, a mouse, a cat, to scratch a man to death! A braggart, a rogue, a villain, that fights by the book of arithmetic! Why the devil came you between us? I was hurt under your arm.

Romeo. I thought all for the best.

Mercutio. Help me into some house, Benvolio,
Or I shall faint. A plague o' both your houses!
They have made worms' meat of me. I have it,
And soundly too. Your houses!

[*Exit, supported by* Benvolio.]

Close Read Screencast

Listen to a modeled close read of this text.

ANALYZE LITERARY DEVICES

Annotate: Mark the section in lines 90–96 where Mercutio uses rhythm to express his feelings.

Analyze: Why does Mercutio speak to Romeo in such a rhythmic way at this moment?

Romeo. This gentleman, the Prince's near ally,
My very friend, hath got this mortal hurt
In my behalf—my reputation stained
With Tybalt's slander—Tybalt, that an hour
Hath been my kinsman, O sweet Juliet,
Thy beauty hath made me effeminate
And in my temper softened valor's steel!

[*Reenter* Benvolio.]

Benvolio. O Romeo, Romeo, brave Mercutio's dead!
That gallant spirit hath aspired the clouds,
Which too untimely here did scorn the earth.

Romeo. This day's black fate on more days doth depend;
This but begins the woe others must end.

[*Reenter* Tybalt.]

Benvolio. Here comes the furious Tybalt back again.

Romeo. Alive in triumph, and Mercutio slain?
Away to heaven respective lenity,
And fire-eyed fury be my conduct now!
Now, Tybalt, take the "villain" back again
That late thou gavest me, for Mercutio's soul
Is but a little way above our heads,
Staying for thine to keep him company.
Either thou or I, or both, must go with him.

Tybalt. Thou, wretched boy, that didst consort him here,
Shalt with him hence.

Romeo. This shall determine that.

[*They fight.* Tybalt *falls.*]

Benvolio. Romeo, away, be gone!
The citizens are up, and Tybalt slain.
Stand not amazed. The Prince will doom thee death
If thou art taken. Hence, be gone, away!

Romeo. O, I am fortune's fool!

Benvolio. Why dost thou stay?

[*Exit* Romeo.]

[*Enter* Citizens.]

Citizen. Which way ran he that killed Mercutio?
Tybalt, that murderer, which way ran he?

Benvolio. There lies that Tybalt.

Citizen. Up, sir, go with me.
I charge thee in the Prince's name obey.

[*Enter* Prince *with his* Attendants, Montague, Capulet, *their* Wives, *and others.*]

Don't forget to **Notice & Note** as you read the text.

102–108 **This gentleman . . . valor's steel:** My friend has died protecting my reputation against a man who has been my relative for only an hour. My love for Juliet has made me less manly and brave.

110 **aspired:** soared to.

112–113 **This day's . . . must end:** This awful day will be followed by more of the same.

116 **respective lenity:** considerate mildness.

NOTICE & NOTE

CONTRASTS AND CONTRADICTIONS

When you notice that a character's behavior contradicts previous behavior, you've found a **Contrasts and Contradictions** signpost.

Notice & Note: Mark the section in lines 115–122 where Romeo says something out of character.

Analyze: What causes the sudden change in Romeo's character?

124 The sword fight probably goes on for several minutes, till Romeo runs his sword through Tybalt.

129 **I am fortune's fool:** Fate has made a fool of me.

Prince. Where are the vile beginners of this fray?

135–136 Benvolio says he can tell (**discover**) what happened.

Benvolio. O noble Prince, I can discover all
The unlucky manage of this fatal brawl.
There lies the man, slain by young Romeo,
That slew thy kinsman, brave Mercutio.

141–142 **as thou . . . Montague:** If your word is good, you will sentence Romeo to death for killing a Capulet.

Lady Capulet. Tybalt, my cousin! O my brother's child!
O Prince! O cousin! O husband! O, the blood is spilled
Of my dear kinsman! Prince, as thou art true,
For blood of ours shed blood of Montague.
O cousin, cousin!

Prince. Benvolio, who began this bloody fray?

146–147 **Romeo, that . . . was:** Romeo talked calmly (**fair**) and told Tybalt to think how trivial (**nice**) the argument was.

150–151 **could . . . peace:** could not quiet the anger of Tybalt, who would not listen to pleas for peace.

156–157 **whose dexterity retorts it:** whose skill returns it.

159–160 **his agile . . . rushes:** He rushed between them and pushed down their swords.

164 **entertained:** thought of.

Benvolio. Tybalt, here slain, whom Romeo's hand did slay.
Romeo, that spoke him fair, bid him bethink
How nice the quarrel was, and urged withal
Your high displeasure. All this—uttered
With gentle breath, calm look, knees humbly bowed—
Could not take truce with the unruly spleen
Of Tybalt deaf to peace, but that he tilts
With piercing steel at bold Mercutio's breast;
Who, all as hot, turns deadly point to point,
And, with a martial scorn, with one hand beats
Cold death aside and with the other sends
It back to Tybalt, whose dexterity
Retorts it. Romeo he cries aloud,
"Hold, friends! friends, part!" and swifter than his tongue,
His agile arm beats down their fatal points,
And 'twixt them rushes; underneath whose arm
An envious thrust from Tybalt hit the life
Of stout Mercutio, and then Tybalt fled,
But by-and-by comes back to Romeo,
Who had but newly entertained revenge,
And to't they go like lightning; for, ere I
Could draw to part them, was stout Tybalt slain;
And, as he fell, did Romeo turn and fly.
This is the truth, or let Benvolio die.

Lady Capulet. He is a kinsman to the Montague;
Affection makes him false, he speaks not true.
Some twenty of them fought in this black strife,
And all those twenty could but kill one life.
I beg for justice, which thou, Prince, must give.
Romeo slew Tybalt; Romeo must not live.

Prince. Romeo slew him; he slew Mercutio.
Who now the price of his dear blood doth owe?

178–179 Romeo is guilty only of avenging Mercutio's death, which the law would have done anyway.

Montague. Not Romeo, Prince; he was Mercutio's friend;
His fault concludes but what the law should end,
The life of Tybalt.

Don't forget to **Notice & Note** as you read the text.

Prince. And for that offense
Immediately we do exile him hence.
I have an interest in your hate's proceeding,
My blood for your rude brawls doth lie a-bleeding;
But I'll amerce you with so strong a fine
That you shall all repent the loss of mine.
I will be deaf to pleading and excuses;
Nor tears nor prayers shall purchase out abuses.
Therefore use none. Let Romeo hence in haste,
Else, when he is found, that hour is his last.
Bear hence this body, and attend our will.
Mercy but murders, pardoning those that kill.

[*Exeunt.*]

179–190 The prince banishes Romeo from Verona. He angrily points out that one of his own relatives is dead because of the feud and declares that Romeo will be put to death unless he flees immediately.

Scene 2 *Capulet's orchard.*

[*Enter* Juliet *alone.*]

Juliet. Gallop apace, you fiery-footed steeds,
Toward Phoebus' lodging! Such a wagoner
As Phaëton would whip you to the West,
And bring in cloudy night immediately.
Spread thy close curtain, love-performing night,
That runaways' eyes may wink, and Romeo
Leap to these arms, untalked of and unseen.
Lovers can see to do their amorous rites
By their own beauties; or, if love be blind,
It best agrees with night. Come, civil night,
Thou sober-suited matron, all in black,
And learn me how to lose a winning match,
Played for a pair of stainless maidenhoods.
Hood my unmanned blood bating in my cheeks
With thy black mantle; till strange love, grown bold,
Think true love acted simple modesty.
Come, night; come, Romeo, come; thou day in night;
For thou wilt lie upon the wings of night
Whiter than new snow on a raven's back.
Come, gentle night; come, loving, black-browed night;
Give me my Romeo; and, when he shall die,
Take him and cut him out in little stars,
And he will make the face of heaven so fine
That all the world will be in love with night
And pay no worship to the garish sun.
O, I have bought the mansion of a love,
But not possessed it; and though I am sold,
Not yet enjoyed. So tedious is this day
As is the night before some festival
To an impatient child that hath new robes
And may not wear them. Oh, here comes my nurse,

2–3 **Phoebus:** Apollo, the god of the sun; **Phaëton:** a mortal who lost control of the sun's chariot when he drove it too fast.

14–16 **Hood . . . modesty:** Juliet asks that the darkness hide her blushing cheeks on her wedding night.

26–27 **I have . . . possessed it:** Juliet protests that she has gone through the wedding ceremony (**bought the mansion**) but is still waiting to enjoy the rewards of marriage.

34 **the cords:** the rope ladder.

37–42 **well-a-day:** an expression used when someone has bad news. The nurse wails and moans without clearly explaining what has happened, leading Juliet to assume that Romeo is dead.

45–50 Juliet's "I" means "aye," or "yes." A **cockatrice** is a mythological beast whose glance kills its victims.

51 **my weal or woe:** my happiness or sorrow.

53–54 **God . . . mark:** an expression meant to scare off evil powers, similar to "Knock on wood"; **corse:** corpse.

56 **swounded:** fainted.

57–60 Juliet says her heart is broken and bankrupt (**bankrout**). She wants to be buried with Romeo, sharing his burial platform (**bier**).

[*Enter* Nurse, *wringing her hands, with the ladder of cords in her lap.*]

And she brings news; and every tongue that speaks
But Romeo's name speaks heavenly eloquence.
Now, nurse, what news? What hast thou there? the cords
That Romeo bid thee fetch?

Nurse. Ay, ay, the cords.

Juliet. Ay me! what news? Why dost thou wring thy hands?

Nurse. Ah, well-a-day! he's dead, he's dead, he's dead!
We are undone, lady, we are undone!
Alack the day! he's gone, he's killed, he's dead!

Juliet. Can heaven be so envious?

Nurse. Romeo can,
Though heaven cannot. O Romeo, Romeo!
Who ever would have thought it? Romeo!

Juliet. What devil art thou that dost torment me thus?
This torture should be roared in dismal hell.
Hath Romeo slain himself? Say thou but "I,"
And that bare vowel "I" shall poison more
Than the death-darting eye of a cockatrice.
I am not I, if there be such an "I,"
Or those eyes shut, that make thee answer "I."
If he be slain, say "I," or if not, "no."
Brief sounds determine of my weal or woe.

Nurse. I saw the wound, I saw it with mine eyes,
(*God save the mark!*) here on his manly breast.
A piteous corse, a bloody piteous corse;
Pale, pale as ashes, all bedaubed in blood,
All in gore blood. I swounded at the sight.

Juliet. O, break, my heart! poor bankrout, break at once!
To prison, eyes; ne'er look on liberty!
Vile earth, to earth resign; end motion here,
And thou and Romeo press one heavy bier!

Nurse. O Tybalt, Tybalt, the best friend I had!
O courteous Tybalt! honest gentleman!
That ever I should live to see thee dead!

Juliet. What storm is this that blows so contrary?
Is Romeo slaughtered, and is Tybalt dead?
My dear-loved cousin, and my dearer lord?
Then, dreadful trumpet, sound the general doom!
For who is living, if those two are gone?

Nurse. Tybalt is gone, and Romeo banished;
Romeo that killed him, he is banished.

Juliet. O God! Did Romeo's hand shed Tybalt's blood?

Nurse. It did! it did! alas the day, it did!

Juliet. O serpent heart, hid with a flow'ring face!
Did ever dragon keep so fair a cave?
Beautiful tyrant! fiend angelical!
Dove-feathered raven! wolvish-ravening lamb!
Despised substance of divinest show!
Just opposite to what thou justly seemst,
A damned saint, an honorable villain!
O nature, what hadst thou to do in hell
When thou didst bower the spirit of a fiend
In mortal paradise of such sweet flesh?
Was ever book containing such vile matter
So fairly bound? O, that deceit should dwell
In such a gorgeous palace!

Nurse. There's no trust,
No faith, no honesty in men; all perjured,
All forsworn, all naught, all dissemblers.
Ah, where's my man? Give me some aqua vitae.
These griefs, these woes, these sorrows make me old.
Shame come to Romeo!

Juliet. Blistered be thy tongue
For such a wish! He was not born to shame.
Upon his brow shame is ashamed to sit;
For 'tis a throne where honor may be crowned
Sole monarch of the universal earth.
O, what a beast was I to chide at him!

Nurse. Will you speak well of him that killed your cousin?

Juliet. Shall I speak ill of him that is my husband?
Ah, poor my lord, what tongue shall smooth thy name
When I, thy three-hours' wife, have mangled it?
But wherefore, villain, didst thou kill my cousin?
That villain cousin would have killed my husband.
Back, foolish tears, back to your native spring!
Your tributary drops belong to woe,
Which you, mistaking, offer up to joy.
My husband lives, that Tybalt would have slain;
And Tybalt's dead, that would have slain my husband.
All this is comfort; wherefore weep I then?
Some word there was, worser than Tybalt's death,
That murdered me. I would forget it fain;
But O, it presses to my memory
Like damned guilty deeds to sinners' minds!
"Tybalt is dead, and Romeo—banished."
That "banished," that one word "banished,"

ANALYZE LITERARY DEVICES

Annotate: Mark examples of oxymorons in lines 73–85.

Evaluate: How do these oxymorons help make Juliet a complex yet believable character?

81 **bower . . . fiend:** give a home to the spirit of a demon.

86–87 **all perjured . . . dissemblers:** All are liars and pretenders.

88 **aqua vitae:** brandy.

102–106 Juliet is uncertain whether her tears should be of joy or of sorrow.

114–127 If the news of Tybalt's death had been followed by the news of her parents' deaths, Juliet would have felt grief. To follow the story of Tybalt's death with the news of Romeo's banishment creates a sorrow so deep it cannot be expressed in words.

132 **beguiled:** cheated.

135–137 **I . . . maidenhead:** I will die a widow without ever really having been a wife. Death, not Romeo, will be my husband.

139 **wot:** know.

Hath slain ten thousand Tybalts. Tybalt's death
Was woe enough, if it had ended there;
Or, if sour woe delights in fellowship
And needly will be ranked with other griefs,
Why followed not, when she said "Tybalt's dead,"
Thy father, or thy mother, nay, or both,
Which modern lamentation might have moved?
But with a rearward following Tybalt's death,
"Romeo is banished"—to speak that word
Is father, mother, Tybalt, Romeo, Juliet,
All slain, all dead. "Romeo is banished"—
There is no end, no limit, measure, bound,
In that word's death; no words can that woe sound.
Where is my father and my mother, nurse?

Nurse. Weeping and wailing over Tybalt's corse.
Will you go to them? I will bring you thither.

Juliet. Wash they his wounds with tears? Mine shall be spent,
When theirs are dry, for Romeo's banishment.
Take up those cords. Poor ropes, you are beguiled,
Both you and I, for Romeo is exiled.
He made you for a highway to my bed;
But I, a maid, die maiden-widowed.
Come, cords; come, nurse. I'll to my wedding bed;
And death, not Romeo, take my maidenhead!

Nurse. Hie to your chamber. I'll find Romeo
To comfort you. I wot well where he is.
Hark ye, your Romeo will be here at night.
I'll to him; he is hid at Laurence' cell.

Juliet. O, find him! give this ring to my true knight
And bid him come to take his last farewell.

[*Exeunt.*]

Scene 3 *Friar Laurence's cell.*

2 **Affliction . . . parts:** Trouble loves you.

4 **doom:** sentence.

[*Enter* Friar Laurence.]

Friar Laurence. Romeo, come forth; come forth, thou fearful man.
Affliction is enamored of thy parts,
And thou art wedded to calamity.

[*Enter* Romeo.]

Romeo. Father, what news? What is the Prince's doom?
What sorrow craves acquaintance at my hand
That I yet know not?

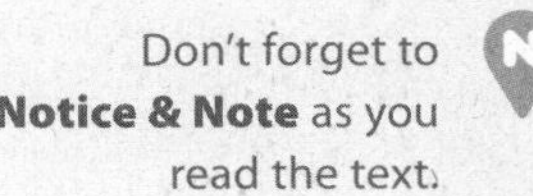
Don't forget to **Notice & Note** as you read the text.

Friar Laurence. Too familiar
Is my dear son with such sour company.
I bring thee tidings of the Prince's doom.

Romeo. What less than doomsday is the Prince's doom?

Friar Laurence. A gentler judgment vanished from his lips—
Not body's death, but body's banishment.

Romeo. Ha, banishment? Be merciful, say "death";
For exile hath more terror in his look,
Much more than death. Do not say "banishment."

Friar Laurence. Hence from Verona art thou banished.
Be patient, for the world is broad and wide.

Romeo. There is no world without Verona walls,
But purgatory, torture, hell itself.
Hence banished is banish'd from the world,
And world's exile is death. Then "banishment,"
Is death misterm'd. Calling death "banishment,"
Thou cuttst my head off with a golden axe
And smilest upon the stroke that murders me.

Friar Laurence. O deadly sin! O rude unthankfulness!
Thy fault our law calls death; but the kind Prince,
Taking thy part, hath rushed aside the law,
And turned that black word death to banishment.
This is dear mercy, and thou seest it not.

Romeo. 'Tis torture, and not mercy. Heaven is here,
Where Juliet lives; and every cat and dog
And little mouse, every unworthy thing,
Live here in heaven and may look on her;
But Romeo may not. More validity,
More honorable state, more courtship lives
In carrion flies than Romeo. They may seize
On the white wonder of dear Juliet's hand
And steal immortal blessing from her lips,
Who, even in pure and vestal modesty,
Still blush, as thinking their own kisses sin;
But Romeo may not—he is banished.
This may flies do, when I from this must fly;
They are free men, but I am banished.
And sayst thou yet that exile is not death?
Hadst thou no poison mixed, no sharp-ground knife,
No sudden mean of death, though ne'er so mean,
But "banished" to kill me—"banished"?
O friar, the damned use that word in hell;
Howling attends it! How hast thou the heart,

9 **doomsday:** death.

10 **vanished:** came.

17–23 **There is . . . murders me:** Being exiled outside Verona's walls is as bad as being dead. And yet you smile at my misfortune.

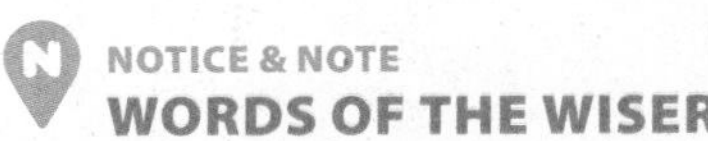
NOTICE & NOTE
WORDS OF THE WISER

Notice & Note: Mark the line(s) where Friar Laurence gives insight into Romeo's predicament.

Infer: What lesson is Friar Laurence trying to teach Romeo?

33–35 **More validity . . . than Romeo:** Even flies that live off the dead (**carrion**) will be able to get closer to Juliet than Romeo will.

44–46 **Hadst . . . to kill me:** Couldn't you have killed me with poison or a knife instead of with that awful word *banished*?

Being a divine, a ghostly confessor,
A sin-absolver, and my friend professed,
To mangle me with that word "banished"?

52 **fond:** foolish.

Friar Laurence. Thou fond mad man, hear me a little speak.

Romeo. O, thou wilt speak again of banishment.

54–56 The friar offers philosophical comfort and counseling (**adversity's sweet milk**) as a way to overcome hardship.

Friar Laurence. I'll give thee armor to keep off that word;
Adversity's sweet milk, philosophy,
To comfort thee, though thou art banished.

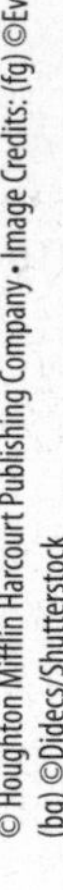

Don't forget to **Notice & Note** as you read the text.

Romeo. Yet "banished"? Hang up philosophy!
Unless philosophy can make a Juliet,
Displant a town, reverse a prince's doom,
It helps not, it prevails not. Talk no more.

Friar Laurence. O, then I see that madmen have no ears.

Romeo. How should they, when that wise men have no eyes?

Friar Laurence. Let me dispute with thee of thy estate.

63 **dispute:** discuss; **estate:** situation.

Romeo. Thou canst not speak of that thou dost not feel.
Wert thou as young as I, Juliet thy love,
An hour but married, Tybalt murdered,
Doting like me, and like me banished,
Then mightst thou speak, then mightst thou tear thy hair,
And fall upon the ground, as I do now,
Taking the measure of an unmade grave.

[Nurse *knocks within.*]

Friar Laurence. Arise; one knocks. Good Romeo, hide thyself.

Romeo. Not I; unless the breath of heartsick groans
Mist-like infold me from the search of eyes.

72–73 Romeo will hide only if his sighs create a mist and shield him from sight.

[*knock*]

Friar Laurence. Hark, how they knock! Who's there? Romeo, arise;
Thou wilt be taken.—Stay awhile!—Stand up;

[*knock*]

Run to my study.—By-and-by!—God's will,
What simpleness is this.—I come, I come!

[*knock*]

Who knocks so hard? Whence come you? What's your will?

Nurse [*within*]**.** Let me come in, and you shall know my errand.
I come from Lady Juliet.

Friar Laurence. Welcome then.

[*Enter* Nurse.]

Nurse. O holy friar, O, tell me, holy friar,
Where is my lady's lord, where's Romeo?

Friar Laurence. There on the ground, with his own tears made drunk.

Nurse. O, he is even in my mistress' case,
Just in her case! O woeful sympathy!
Piteous predicament! Even so lies she,
Blubb'ring and weeping, weeping and blubbering.
Stand up, stand up! Stand, an you be a man.

84–85 **he is even . . . her case:** He is acting the same way that Juliet is.

For Juliet's sake, for her sake, rise and stand!
Why should you fall into so deep an O?

90 **into so deep an O:** into such deep grief.

Romeo [*rises*]. Nurse—

Nurse. Ah sir! ah sir! Well, death's the end of all.

Romeo. Spakest thou of Juliet? How is it with her?
Doth not she think me an old murderer,
Now I have stained the childhood of our joy
With blood removed but little from her own?
Where is she? and how doth she? and what says
My concealed lady to our canceled love?

96 **blood . . . from her own:** the blood of a close relative of hers.

98 **concealed lady:** secret bride.

Nurse. O, she says nothing, sir, but weeps and weeps;
And now falls on her bed, and then starts up,
And Tybalt calls; and then on Romeo cries,
And then down falls again.

Romeo. As if that name,
Shot from the deadly level of a gun,
Did murder her; as that name's cursed hand
Murdered her kinsman. O tell me, friar, tell me,
In what vile part of this anatomy
Doth my name lodge? Tell me, that I may sack
The hateful mansion.

102 **that name:** the name Romeo.

106–108 **in what vile part . . . mansion:** Romeo asks where in his body (**anatomy**) his name can be found so that he can cut the name out.

[*draws his dagger*]

Friar Laurence. Hold thy desperate hand.
Art thou a man? Thy form cries out thou art;
Thy tears are womanish, thy wild acts denote
The unreasonable fury of a beast.
Unseemly woman in a seeming man!
Or ill-beseeming beast in seeming both!
Thou hast amazed me. By my holy order,
I thought thy disposition better tempered.
Hast thou slain Tybalt? Wilt thou slay thyself?
And slay thy lady too that lives in thee,
By doing damned hate upon thyself?
Why railst thou on thy birth, the heaven, and earth?
Since birth and heaven and earth, all three do meet
In thee at once; which thou at once wouldst lose.
Fie, fie, thou shamest thy shape, thy love, thy wit,
Which, like a usurer, aboundst in all,
And usest none in that true use indeed
Which should bedeck thy shape, thy love, thy wit.
Thy noble shape is but a form of wax,
Digressing from the valor of a man;
Thy dear love sworn but hollow perjury,

108–125 **Hold thy . . . bedeck thy shape, thy love, thy wit:** You're not acting like a man. Would you send your soul to hell by committing suicide (**doing damned hate upon thyself**)? Why do you curse your birth, heaven, and earth? You are refusing to make good use of your advantages, just as a miser refuses to spend his money.

126–134 The friar explains how by acting as he is, Romeo is misusing his shape (his outer form or body), his love, and his wit (his mind or intellect).

Killing that love which thou hast vowed to cherish;
Thy wit, that ornament to shape and love,
Misshapen in the conduct of them both,
Like powder in a skilless soldier's flask,
Is set afire by thine own ignorance,
And thou dismembered with thine own defense.
What, rouse thee, man! Thy Juliet is alive,
For whose dear sake thou wast but lately dead.
There art thou happy. Tybalt would kill thee,
But thou slewest Tybalt. There art thou happy.
The law, that threatened death, becomes thy friend
And turns it to exile. There art thou happy.
A pack of blessings light upon thy back;
Happiness courts thee in her best array;
But, like a misbehaved and sullen wench,
Thou poutst upon thy fortune and thy love.
Take heed, take heed, for such die miserable.
Go get thee to thy love, as was decreed,
Ascend her chamber, hence and comfort her.
But look thou stay not till the watch be set,
For then thou canst not pass to Mantua,
Where thou shalt live till we can find a time
To blaze your marriage, reconcile your friends,
Beg pardon of the Prince, and call thee back
With twenty hundred thousand times more joy
Than thou wentst forth in lamentation.
Go before, nurse. Commend me to thy lady,
And bid her hasten all the house to bed,
Which heavy sorrow makes them apt unto.

Romeo is coming.

Nurse. O Lord, I could have stayed here all the night
To hear good counsel. O, what learning is!
My lord, I'll tell my lady you will come.

Romeo. Do so, and bid my sweet prepare to chide.

[Nurse *offers to go and turns again.*]

Nurse. Here is a ring she bid me give you, sir.
Hie you, make haste, for it grows very late.

[*Exit.*]

Romeo. How well my comfort is revived by this!

Friar Laurence. Go hence; good night; and here stands all your state:
Either be gone before the watch be set,
Or by the break of day disguised from hence.
Sojourn in Mantua. I'll find out your man,

Don't forget to **Notice & Note** as you read the text.

148–149 **look . . . Mantua:** Leave before the guards take their places at the city gates; otherwise you will not be able to escape.

151 **blaze . . . friends:** announce your marriage and get the families (**friends**) to stop feuding.

162 **bid . . . chide:** Tell Juliet to get ready to scold me for the way I've behaved.

166–171 **and here . . . here:** Either leave before the night watchmen go on duty, or get out at dawn in a disguise. Stay awhile in Mantua. I'll find your servant and send messages to you about what good things are happening here.

And he shall signify from time to time
Every good hap to you that chances here.
Give me thy hand. 'Tis late. Farewell; good night.

Romeo. But that a joy past joy calls out on me,
It were a grief so brief to part with thee.
Farewell.

[*Exeunt.*]

Scene 4 *Capulet's house.*

[*Enter* Capulet, Lady Capulet, *and* Paris.]

1–2 **Things have . . . our daughter:** Such terrible things have happened that we haven't had time to persuade (**move**) Juliet to think about your marriage proposal.

Capulet. Things have fall'n out, sir, so unluckily
That we have had no time to move our daughter.
Look you, she loved her kinsman Tybalt dearly,
And so did I. Well, we were born to die.
'Tis very late; she'll not come down tonight.
I promise you, but for your company,
I would have been abed an hour ago.

8 Sad times are not good times for talking of marriage.

Paris. These times of woe afford no time to woo.
Madam, good night. Commend me to your daughter.

11 Tonight she is locked up with her sorrow.

Lady Capulet. I will, and know her mind early tomorrow;
Tonight she's mewed up to her heaviness.

[Paris *offers to go and* Capulet *calls him again.*]

12 **desperate tender:** bold offer.

Capulet. Sir Paris, I will make a desperate tender
Of my child's love. I think she will be ruled
In all respects by me; nay more, I doubt it not.
Wife, go you to her ere you go to bed;
Acquaint her here of my son Paris' love
And bid her (mark you me?) on Wednesday next—
But, soft! what day is this?

ANALYZE PARALLEL PLOTS

Annotate: In this scene, Shakespeare continues the parallel plot of Paris's marriage proposal to Juliet. Mark the spot in lines 12–21 where Lord Capulet says that he will convince Juliet to marry Paris.

Predict: How will this parallel plot affect the main plot of Romeo and Juliet's romance?

Paris. Monday, my lord.

Capulet. Monday! ha, ha! Well, Wednesday is too soon.
A Thursday let it be—a Thursday, tell her,
She shall be married to this noble earl.
Will you be ready? Do you like this haste?
We'll keep no great ado—a friend or two;
For hark you, Tybalt being slain so late,
It may be thought we held him carelessly,
Being our kinsman, if we revel much.
Therefore we'll have some half a dozen friends,
And there an end. But what say you to Thursday?

23 **no great ado:** no big festivity.

Paris. My lord, I would that Thursday were tomorrow.

Capulet. Well, get you gone. A Thursday be it then.
Go you to Juliet ere you go to bed;
Prepare her, wife, against this wedding day.
Farewell, my lord.—Light to my chamber, ho!
Afore me, it is so very very late
That we may call it early by-and-by.
Good night.

[*Exeunt.*]

Don't forget to **Notice & Note** as you read the text.

34–35 **it is . . . by-and-by:** It's so late at night that soon we'll be calling it early in the morning.

Scene 5 *Capulet's orchard.*

[*Enter* Romeo *and* Juliet *above, at the window.*]

2 **It was . . . lark:** The nightingale sings at night; the lark sings in the morning.

Juliet. Wilt thou be gone? It is not yet near day.
It was the nightingale, and not the lark,
That pierced the fearful hollow of thine ear.
Nightly she sings on yond pomegranate tree.
Believe me, love, it was the nightingale.

9 **Night's candles:** stars.

Romeo. It was the lark, the herald of the morn;
No nightingale. Look, love, what envious streaks
Do lace the severing clouds in yonder East.
Night's candles are burnt out, and jocund day
Stands tiptoe on the misty mountain tops.
I must be gone and live, or stay and die.

12–25 Juliet continues to pretend it is night to keep Romeo from leaving. Romeo says he'll stay if Juliet wishes it, even if it means death.

Juliet. Yond light is not daylight; I know it, I.
It is some meteor that the sun exhales
To be to thee this night a torchbearer

And light thee on thy way to Mantua.
Therefore stay yet; thou needst not to be gone.

Romeo. Let me be ta'en, let me be put to death.
I am content, so thou wilt have it so.
I'll say yon grey is not the morning's eye,
'Tis but the pale reflex of Cynthia's brow;
Nor that is not the lark whose notes do beat
The vaulty heaven so high above our heads.
I have more care to stay than will to go.
Come, death, and welcome! Juliet wills it so.
How is't, my soul? Let's talk; it is not day.

Juliet. It is, it is! Hie hence, be gone, away!
It is the lark that sings so out of tune,
Straining harsh discords and unpleasing sharps.

Some say the lark makes sweet division;
This doth not so, for she divideth us.
Some say the lark and loathed toad changed eyes;
O, now I would they had changed voices too,
Since arm from arm that voice doth us affray,
Hunting thee hence with hunt's-up to the day!
O, now be gone! More light and light it grows.

Romeo. More light and light—more dark and dark our woes!

[*Enter* Nurse, *hastily.*]

Nurse. Madam!

Juliet. Nurse?

Nurse. Your lady mother is coming to your chamber.
The day is broke; be wary, look about.

[*Exit.*]

Juliet. Then, window, let day in, and let life out.

Romeo. Farewell, farewell! One kiss, and I'll descend.

[*He starts down the ladder.*]

Juliet. Art thou gone so, my lord, my love, my friend?
I must hear from thee every day in the hour,
For in a minute there are many days.
O, by this count I shall be much in years
Ere I again behold my Romeo!

Romeo. Farewell!
I will omit no opportunity
That may convey my greetings, love, to thee.

Juliet. O, thinkst thou we shall ever meet again?

Romeo. I doubt it not; and all these woes shall serve
For sweet discourses in our time to come.

20 **Cynthia's brow:** Cynthia is another name for Diana, the Roman goddess of the moon. She was often pictured with a crescent moon on her forehead.

26 Romeo's mention of death frightens Juliet, and she urges him to leave quickly.

29 **division:** melody.

31–34 I wish the lark had the voice of the hated (**loathed**) toad, since its voice is frightening us apart and acting as a morning song for hunters (**hunt's-up**).

46 **much in years:** very old.

54–56 **I have . . . tomb:** Juliet sees an evil vision of the future.

59 **Dry . . . blood:** People believed that sorrow drained the blood from the heart, causing a sad person to look pale.

60–62 **fickle:** changeable in loyalty or affection. Juliet asks fickle Fortune why it has anything to do with Romeo, who is the opposite of fickle.

67 **What . . . hither:** What unusual reason brings her here?

72–73 **have . . . wit:** Stop crying (**have done**). A little grief is evidence of love, while too much grief shows a lack of good sense (**want of wit**).

81–102 In these lines Juliet's words have double meanings. To avoid lying to her mother, she chooses her words carefully. They can mean what her mother wants to hear—or what Juliet really has on her mind.

Juliet. O God, I have an ill-divining soul!
Methinks I see thee, now thou art below,
As one dead in the bottom of a tomb.
Either my eyesight fails, or thou lookst pale.

Romeo. And trust me, love, in my eye so do you.
Dry sorrow drinks our blood. Adieu! adieu!

[*Exit.*]

Juliet. O Fortune, Fortune! all men call thee fickle.
If thou art fickle, what dost thou with him
That is renowned for faith? Be fickle, Fortune,
For then I hope thou wilt not keep him long
But send him back.

Lady Capulet. [*within*]. Ho, daughter! are you up?

Juliet. Who is't that calls? It is my lady mother.
Is she not down so late, or up so early?
What unaccustomed cause procures her hither?

[*Enter* Lady Capulet.]

Lady Capulet. Why, how now, Juliet?

Juliet. Madam, I am not well.

Lady Capulet. Evermore weeping for your cousin's death?
What, wilt thou wash him from his grave with tears?
An if thou couldst, thou couldst not make him live.
Therefore have done. Some grief shows much of love;
But much of grief shows still some want of wit.

Juliet. Yet let me weep for such a feeling loss.

Lady Capulet. So shall you feel the loss, but not the friend
Which you weep for.

Juliet. Feeling so the loss,
I cannot choose but ever weep the friend.

Lady Capulet. Well, girl, thou weepst not so much for his death
As that the villain lives which slaughtered him.

Juliet. What villain, madam?

Lady Capulet. That same villain Romeo.

Juliet [*aside*]. Villain and he be many miles asunder.—
God pardon him! I do, with all my heart;
And yet no man like he doth grieve my heart.

Lady Capulet. That is because the traitor murderer lives.

Juliet. Ay, madam, from the reach of these my hands.
Would none but I might venge my cousin's death!

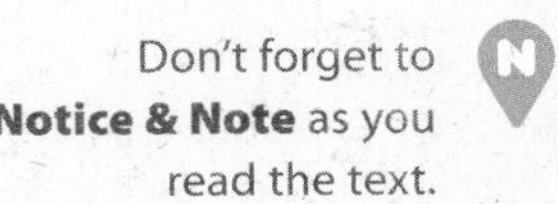

Don't forget to **Notice & Note** as you read the text.

Lady Capulet. We will have vengeance for it, fear thou not.
Then weep no more. I'll send to one in Mantua,
Where that same banished runagate doth live,
Shall give him such an unaccustomed dram
That he shall soon keep Tybalt company;
And then I hope thou wilt be satisfied.

Juliet. Indeed I never shall be satisfied
With Romeo till I behold him—dead—
Is my poor heart so for a kinsman vexed.
Madam, if you could find out but a man
To bear a poison, I would temper it;
That Romeo should, upon receipt thereof,
Soon sleep in quiet. O, how my heart abhors
To hear him named and cannot come to him,
To wreak the love I bore my cousin Tybalt
Upon his body that hath slaughtered him!

Lady Capulet. Find thou the means, and I'll find such a man.
But now I'll tell thee joyful tidings, girl.

Juliet. And joy comes well in such a needy time.
What are they, I beseech your ladyship?

Lady Capulet. Well, well, thou hast a careful father, child;
One who, to put thee from thy heaviness,
Hath sorted out a sudden day of joy
That thou expects not nor I looked not for.

Juliet. Madam, in happy time! What day is that?

Lady Capulet. Marry, my child, early next Thursday morn
The gallant, young, and noble gentleman,
The County Paris, at Saint Peter's Church,
Shall happily make thee there a joyful bride.

Juliet. Now by Saint Peter's Church, and Peter too,
He shall not make me there a joyful bride!
I wonder at this haste, that I must wed
Ere he that should be husband comes to woo.
I pray you tell my lord and father, madam,
I will not marry yet; and when I do, I swear
It shall be Romeo, whom you know I hate,
Rather than Paris. These are news indeed!

Lady Capulet. Here comes your father. Tell him so yourself,
And see how he will take it at your hands.

[*Enter* Capulet *and* Nurse.]

Capulet. When the sun sets the air doth drizzle dew,
But for the sunset of my brother's son

89 **runagate:** runaway.

90 **unaccustomed dram:** poison.

93–102 **dead:** This could refer either to Romeo or to Juliet's heart. Juliet says that if her mother could find someone to carry a poison to Romeo, she would mix (**temper**) it herself.

127 **the sunset . . . son:** the death of Tybalt.

129–137 **conduit:** fountain. Capulet compares Juliet to a boat (**bark**), an ocean, and the wind because of her excessive crying.

It rains downright.
How now? a conduit, girl? What, still in tears?
Evermore show'ring? In one little body
Thou counterfeitst a bark, a sea, a wind:
For still thy eyes, which I may call the sea,
Do ebb and flow with tears; the bark thy body is,
Sailing in this salt flood; the winds, thy sighs,
Who, raging with thy tears and they with them,
Without a sudden calm will overset
Thy tempest-tossed body. How now, wife?
Have you delivered to her our decree?

Lady Capulet. Ay, sir; but she will none, she gives you thanks.
I would the fool were married to her grave!

141 **take me with you:** let me understand you.

Capulet. Soft! take me with you, take me with you, wife.
How? Will she none? Doth she not give us thanks?
Is she not proud? Doth she not count her blest,
Unworthy as she is, that we have wrought
So worthy a gentleman to be her bridegroom?

146–148 **Not proud . . . meant love:** I'm not pleased, but I am grateful for your intentions.

Juliet. Not proud you have, but thankful that you have.
Proud can I never be of what I hate,
But thankful even for hate that is meant love.

149–157 Capulet calls Juliet a person who argues over fine points (**choplogic**) and a spoiled child (**minion**). He tells her to prepare herself (**fettle your fine joints**) for the wedding or he'll haul her there in a cart for criminals (**hurdle**). He calls her a piece of dead flesh (**green-sickness carrion**) and a coward (**tallow-face**).

Capulet. How, how, how, how, choplogic? What is this?
"Proud"—and "I thank you"—and "I thank you not"—
And yet "not proud"? Mistress minion you,
Thank me no thankings, nor proud me no prouds,
But fettle your fine joints 'gainst Thursday next
To go with Paris to Saint Peter's Church,
Or I will drag thee on a hurdle thither.
Out, you green-sickness carrion! out, you baggage!
You tallow-face!

Lady Capulet. Fie, fie; what, are you mad?

Juliet. Good father, I beseech you on my knees,

[*She kneels down.*]

Hear me with patience but to speak a word.

Capulet. Hang thee, young baggage! disobedient wretch!
I tell thee what—get thee to church a Thursday
Or never after look me in the face.
Speak not, reply not, do not answer me!
My fingers itch. Wife, we scarce thought us blest
That God had lent us but this only child;
But now I see this one is one too much,
And that we have a curse in having her.
Out on her, hilding!

164 **My fingers itch:** I feel like hitting you.

168 **hilding:** a good-for-nothing person.

Don't forget to **Notice & Note** as you read the text.

Nurse. God in heaven bless her!
You are to blame, my lord, to rate her so.

Capulet. And why, my Lady Wisdom? Hold your tongue,
Good Prudence. Smatter with your gossips, go!

Nurse. I speak no treason.

Capulet. O, God-i-god-en!

Nurse. May not one speak?

Capulet. Peace, you mumbling fool!
Utter your gravity o'er a gossip's bowl,
For here we need it not.

Lady Capulet. You are too hot.

Capulet. God's bread! it makes me mad. Day, night, late, early,
At home, abroad, alone, in company,
Waking or sleeping, still my care hath been
To have her matched; and having now provided
A gentleman of princely parentage,
Of fair demesnes, youthful, and nobly trained,
Stuffed, as they say, with honorable parts,
Proportioned as one's thought would wish a man—
And then to have a wretched puling fool,
A whining mammet, in her fortunes tender,
To answer "I'll not wed, I cannot love;
I am too young, I pray you pardon me"!
But, an you will not wed, I'll pardon you.
Graze where you will, you shall not house with me.
Look to't, think on't; I do not use to jest.
Thursday is near; lay hand on heart, advise:
An you be mine, I'll give you to my friend;
An you be not, hang, beg, starve, die in the streets,
For, by my soul, I'll ne'er acknowledge thee,
Nor what is mine shall never do thee good.
Trust to't. Bethink you. I'll not be forsworn.

[*Exit.*]

Juliet. Is there no pity sitting in the clouds
That sees into the bottom of my grief?
O sweet my mother, cast me not away!
Delay this marriage for a month, a week;
Or if you do not, make the bridal bed
In that dim monument where Tybalt lies.

171 **smatter:** chatter.

174 **Utter . . . bowl:** Save your words of wisdom for a gathering of gossips.

179 **matched:** married.

184 **puling:** crying.

185 **mammet:** doll.

189–195 Capulet swears that he'll kick Juliet out and cut her off financially if she refuses to marry.

196 **I'll not be forsworn:** I will not break my promise to Paris.

Lady Capulet. Talk not to me, for I'll not speak a word.
Do as thou wilt, for I have done with thee.

[*Exit.*]

Juliet. O God!—O nurse, how shall this be prevented?
My husband is on earth, my faith in heaven.
How shall that faith return again to earth
Unless that husband send it me from heaven
By leaving earth? Comfort me, counsel me.
Alack, alack, that heaven should practice stratagems
Upon so soft a subject as myself!
What sayst thou? Hast thou not a word of joy?
Some comfort, nurse.

207–211 Juliet is worried about the sin of being married to two men. She asks how heaven can play such tricks (**practice stratagems**) on her.

Nurse. Faith, here it is.
Romeo is banish'd; and all the world to nothing
That he dares ne'er come back to challenge you;
Or if he do, it needs must be by stealth.
Then, since the case so stands as now it doth,
I think it best you married with the County.
O, he's a lovely gentleman!
Romeo's a dishclout to him. An eagle, madam,
Hath not so green, so quick, so fair an eye
As Paris hath. Beshrew my very heart,
I think you are happy in this second match,
For it excels your first; or if it did not,
Your first is dead—or 'twere as good he were
As living here and you no use of him.

222 **beshrew:** curse.

223–225 This new marriage will be better than the first, which is as good as over.

Juliet. Speakst thou this from thy heart?

Nurse. And from my soul too; else beshrew them both.

Juliet. Amen!

229 **Amen:** I agree—that is, curse your heart and soul.

Nurse. What?

Juliet. Well, thou hast comforted me marvelous much.
Go in; and tell my lady I am gone,
Having displeased my father, to Laurence' cell,
To make confession and to be absolved.

Nurse. Marry, I will; and this is wisely done.

[*Exit.*]

Juliet. Ancient damnation! O most wicked fiend!
Is it more sin to wish me thus forsworn,
Or to dispraise my lord with that same tongue
Which she hath praised him with above compare
So many thousand times? Go, counselor!
Thou and my bosom henceforth shall be twain.
I'll to the friar to know his remedy.
If all else fail, myself have power to die.

[*Exit.*]

236–238 **Ancient damnation:** old devil; **dispraise:** criticize.

241 **Thou . . . twain:** I'll no longer tell you my secrets.

COLLABORATIVE DISCUSSION

Discuss with a partner the chain of events that begins to turn the story of Romeo and Juliet into a tragedy. Do you believe the main characters are making mistakes that will lead them down a tragic path?

Assessment Practice

Answer these questions before moving on to the **Analyze the Text** section on the following page.

1. What **two** developments in Act III suggest the story will end unhappily?

   (A) Juliet begs the nurse to tell her what happened to Romeo.

   (B) Romeo breaks his vow to love Tybalt and not to fight with him.

   (C) Friar Laurence gets frustrated with how Romeo is acting.

   (D) Juliet is distraught over Romeo's banishment.

   (E) Romeo has not left Juliet's chamber by sunrise.

2. This question has two parts. First answer **Part A**. Then, answer **Part B**.

   Part A

   In Scene 5, why does Juliet want the darkness to continue?

   (A) She is hiding from Romeo.

   (B) She and Romeo are trying to escape the city together.

   (C) She wants Romeo to stay with her a little longer.

   (D) She knows she may not live to see the morning.

   Part B

   Select the line of dialogue that best supports the answer to Part A.

   (A) "Wilt thou be gone? It is not yet near day." (Scene 5, line 1)

   (B) "Some say the lark makes sweet division." (Scene 5, line 29)

   (C) "The day is broke; be wary, look about." (Scene 5, line 40)

   (D) "What unaccustomed cause procures her hither?" (Scene 5, line 67)

Test-Taking Strategies

Analyze the Text

Support your responses with evidence from the text.

NOTICE & NOTE

Review what you **noticed and noted** as you read the text. Your annotations can help you answer these questions.

1. **INTERPRET** What is the meaning of Mercutio's repeated curse, "A plague o' both your houses!" (Scene 1, lines 85, 93, 99)? What might this curse foreshadow? What other moments in Act III have similar foreshadowing?

2. **EVALUATE** What is Romeo's motivation for killing Tybalt? Is his action justified or a mistake? Explain your response.

3. **CITE EVIDENCE** In what ways do Romeo and Juliet need the help of Friar Laurence and the Nurse in order to save their love and move forward? Support your response with evidence from the text.

4. **ANALYZE** In Scene 5, Lord Capulet becomes enraged when Juliet says she will not marry Paris. How are his words and actions in this scene like those of Romeo and Juliet? What are the likely consequences?

5. **CAUSE/EFFECT** In Scene 5, how and why does the Nurse's behavior contrast with or contradict her earlier behavior? How does this contrast or contradiction affect Juliet? Explain, citing details from the text.

Choices

Here are some other ways to demonstrate your understanding of Act III.

Media

↳ Graphic Novel

Try your hand at recreating events of Act III as a graphic-novel version. Follow these steps:

- Summarize the main action in each scene.
- If you wish, chose a different time and setting from the original play.
- Outline the images and text for each panel.
- Present your creation to a partner who focused on the same scene(s). Discuss similarities and differences in your scenes.

Writing

↳ Journal Entry

Explore the parallel feelings of despair that Romeo and Juliet feel in Act III by writing a journal entry for each character based on the text.

- Write a one-page journal entry from Juliet when she learns of Tybalt's death.
- Write a one-page journal entry from Romeo when he is awaiting exile at the friar's cell.
- If you don't know the word for something, ask for assistance from your teacher or peers.

Act IV

Don't forget to **Notice & Note** as you read the text.

Scene 1 *Friar Laurence's cell.*

[*Enter* Friar Laurence *and* Paris.]

Friar Laurence. On Thursday, sir? The time is very short.

Paris. My father Capulet will have it so,
And I am nothing slow to slack his haste.

2–3 **My . . . haste:** Capulet is eager to have the wedding on Thursday and so am I.

Friar Laurence. You say you do not know the lady's mind.
Uneven is the course; I like it not.

4–5 **You . . . course:** You don't know how Juliet feels about this. It's a very uncertain (**uneven**) plan.

Paris. Immoderately she weeps for Tybalt's death,
And therefore have I little talked of love;
For Venus smiles not in a house of tears.
Now, sir, her father counts it dangerous
That she do give her sorrow so much sway,
And in his wisdom hastes our marriage
To stop the inundation of her tears,
Which, too much minded by herself alone,
May be put from her by society.
Now do you know the reason of this haste.

13–14 **Which . . . society:** which, thought about too much by her in privacy, may be put from her mind if she is forced to be with others.

Friar Laurence [*aside*]. I would I knew not why it should be slowed.—
Look, sir, here comes the lady toward my cell.

[*Enter* Juliet.]

Paris. Happily met, my lady and my wife!

Juliet. That may be, sir, when I may be a wife.

Paris. That may be must be, love, on Thursday next.

Juliet. What must be shall be.

Friar Laurence. That's a certain text.

Paris. Come you to make confession to this father?

Juliet. To answer that, I should confess to you.

Paris. Do not deny to him that you love me.

Juliet. I will confess to you that I love him.

Paris. So will ye, I am sure, that you love me.

Juliet. If I do so, it will be of more price,
Being spoke behind your back, than to your face.

Paris. Poor soul, thy face is much abused with tears.

Juliet. The tears have got small victory by that,
For it was bad enough before their spite.

Paris. Thou wrongst it more than tears with that report.

ANALYZE LITERARY DEVICES

Annotate: Mark two instances of dramatic irony in lines 18–25.

Analyze: What information does the audience have that a character doesn't? How does this information create suspense?

Close Read Screencast

Listen to a modeled close read of this text.

30–31 **The tears . . . spite:** The tears haven't ruined my face; it wasn't all that beautiful before they did their damage.

35 Paris says he owns Juliet's face (since she will soon marry him). Insulting her face, he says, insults him, its owner.

47–48 **compass:** limit; **prorogue:** postpone.

52–53 **If in . . . wise:** If you can't find a way to help me, at least agree that my plan is wise.

56–67 **And ere this hand . . . of remedy:** Before I sign another wedding agreement (**deed**), I will use this knife to kill myself. If you, with your years of experience (**long-experienced time**), can't help me, I'll end my sufferings (**extremes**) and solve the problem myself.

71–76 **If, rather than . . . remedy:** If you are desperate enough to kill yourself, then you'll be daring enough to try the deathlike solution that I propose.

Juliet. That is no slander, sir, which is a truth;
And what I spake, I spake it to my face.

Paris. Thy face is mine, and thou hast slandered it.

Juliet. It may be so, for it is not mine own.
Are you at leisure, holy father, now,
Or shall I come to you at evening mass?

Friar Laurence. My leisure serves me, pensive daughter, now.
My lord, we must entreat the time alone.

Paris. God shield I should disturb devotion!
Juliet, on Thursday early will I rouse ye.
Till then, adieu, and keep this holy kiss.

[*Exit.*]

Juliet. O, shut the door! and when thou hast done so,
Come weep with me—past hope, past cure, past help!

Friar Laurence. Ah, Juliet, I already know thy grief;
It strains me past the compass of my wits.
I hear thou must, and nothing may prorogue it,
On Thursday next be married to this County.

Juliet. Tell me not, friar, that thou hearest of this,
Unless thou tell me how I may prevent it.
If in thy wisdom thou canst give no help,
Do thou but call my resolution wise
And with this knife I'll help it presently.
God joined my heart and Romeo's, thou our hands;
And ere this hand, by thee to Romeo's sealed,
Shall be the label to another deed,
Or my true heart with treacherous revolt
Turn to another, this shall slay them both.
Therefore, out of thy long-experienced time,
Give me some present counsel; or, behold,
'Twixt my extremes and me this bloody knife
Shall play the umpire, arbitrating that
Which the commission of thy years and art
Could to no issue of true honor bring.
Be not so long to speak. I long to die
If what thou speak'st speak not of remedy.

Friar Laurence. Hold, daughter, I do spy a kind of hope,
Which craves as desperate an execution
As that is desperate which we would prevent.
If, rather than to marry County Paris,
Thou hast the strength of will to slay thyself,
Then is it likely thou wilt undertake
A thing like death to chide away this shame,
That copest with death himself to scape from it;
And, if thou darest, I'll give thee remedy.

Juliet. O, bid me leap, rather than marry Paris,
From off the battlements of yonder tower,
Or walk in thievish ways, or bid me lurk
Where serpents are; chain me with roaring bears,
Or shut me nightly in a charnel house,
O'ercovered quite with dead men's rattling bones,
With reeky shanks and yellow chapless skulls;
Or bid me go into a new-made grave
And hide me with a dead man in his shroud—
Things that, to hear them told, have made me tremble—
And I will do it without fear or doubt,
To live an unstained wife to my sweet love.

77–88 Juliet lists the things she would do rather than marry Paris; **charnel house:** a storehouse for bones; **reeky shanks:** stinking bones; **chapless skulls:** without jaws.

Friar Laurence. Hold, then. Go home, be merry, give consent
To marry Paris. Wednesday is tomorrow.
Tomorrow night look that thou lie alone:

Let not the nurse lie with thee in thy chamber.
Take thou this vial, being then in bed,
And this distilled liquor drink thou off;
When presently through all thy veins shall run
A cold and drowsy humor; for no pulse
Shall keep his native progress, but surcease;
No warmth, no breath, shall testify thou livest;
The roses in thy lips and cheeks shall fade
To paly ashes, thy eyes' windows fall
Like death when he shuts up the day of life;

93 **vial:** small bottle.

96–106 **humor:** liquid; **no pulse . . . pleasant sleep:** Your pulse will stop (**surcease**), and you will turn cold, pale, and stiff, as if you were dead; this condition will last for 42 hours.

Each part, deprived of supple government,
Shall, stiff and stark and cold, appear like death;
And in this borrowed likeness of shrunk death
Thou shalt continue two-and-forty hours,
And then awake as from a pleasant sleep.
Now, when the bridegroom in the morning comes
To rouse thee from thy bed, there art thou dead.
Then, as the manner of our country is,
In thy best robes uncovered on the bier
Thou shalt be borne to that same ancient vault
Where all the kindred of the Capulets lie.
In the meantime, against thou shalt awake,
Shall Romeo by my letters know our drift;
And hither shall he come; and he and I
Will watch thy waking, and that very night
Shall Romeo bear thee hence to Mantua.
And this shall free thee from this present shame,
If no inconstant toy nor womanish fear
Abate thy valor in the acting it.

111–112 **same ancient vault . . . lie:** same ancient tomb where all members of the Capulet family are buried.

114 **drift:** plan.

119–120 **inconstant toy:** foolish whim; **abate thy valor:** weaken your courage.

Juliet. Give me, give me! O, tell me not of fear!

Friar Laurence. Hold! Get you gone, be strong and prosperous
In this resolve. I'll send a friar with speed
To Mantua, with my letters to thy lord.

Juliet. Love give me strength! and strength shall help afford.
Farewell, dear father.

[*Exeunt*]

Scene 2 *Capulet's house.*

[*Enter* Capulet, Lady Capulet, Nurse, *and* Servingmen.]

1–8 Capulet is having a cheerful conversation with his servants about the wedding preparations. One servant assures him that he will test (**try**) the cooks he hires by making them taste their own food (**lick their fingers**).

Capulet. So many guests invite as here are writ.

[*Exit a* Servingman.]

Sirrah, go hire me twenty cunning cooks.

Servingman. You shall have none ill, sir; for I'll try if they can
lick their fingers.

Capulet. How canst thou try them so?

Servingman. Marry, sir, 'tis an ill cook that cannot
lick his own fingers. Therefore he that cannot lick his
fingers goes not with me.

Capulet. Go, begone.

[*Exit a* Servingman.]

10 **unfurnished:** unprepared.

We shall be much unfurnished for this time.
What, is my daughter gone to Friar Laurence?

Nurse. Ay, forsooth.

Capulet. Well, he may chance to do some good on her.
A peevish self-willed harlotry it is.

[*Enter* Juliet.]

Nurse. See where she comes from shrift with merry look.

Capulet. How now, my headstrong? Where have you been gadding?

Juliet. Where I have learnt me to repent the sin
Of disobedient opposition
To you and your behests, and am enjoined
By holy Laurence to fall prostrate here
To beg your pardon. Pardon, I beseech you!
Henceforward I am ever ruled by you.

Capulet. Send for the County. Go tell him of this.
I'll have this knot knit up tomorrow morning.

Juliet. I met the youthful lord at Laurence' cell
And gave him what becomed love I might,
Not stepping o'er the bounds of modesty.

Capulet. Why, I am glad on't. This is well. Stand up.
This is as't should be. Let me see the County.
Ay, marry, go, I say, and fetch him hither.
Now, afore God, this reverend holy friar,
All our whole city is much bound to him.

Juliet. Nurse, will you go with me into my closet
To help me sort such needful ornaments
As you think fit to furnish me tomorrow?

Lady Capulet. No, not till Thursday. There is time enough.

Capulet. Go, nurse, go with her. We'll to church tomorrow.

[*Exeunt* Juliet *and* Nurse.]

Lady Capulet. We shall be short in our provision.
'Tis now near night.

Capulet. Tush, I will stir about,
And all things shall be well, I warrant thee, wife.
Go thou to Juliet, help to deck up her.
I'll not to bed tonight; let me alone.
I'll play the housewife for this once. What, ho!
They are all forth; well, I will walk myself
To County Paris, to prepare him up
Against tomorrow. My heart is wondrous light,
Since this same wayward girl is so reclaimed.

[*Exeunt.*]

Don't forget to **Notice & Note** as you read the text.

14 A silly, stubborn girl she is.

19 **behests:** orders; **enjoined:** commanded.

24 I'll have this wedding scheduled for tomorrow morning.

36–39 Lady Capulet urges her husband to wait until Thursday as originally planned. She needs time to get food (**provision**) ready for the wedding party.

39–46 Capulet is so set on Wednesday that he promises to make the arrangements himself.

ANALYZE PARALLEL PLOTS

Annotate: Mark evidence of Lord Capulet's feelings regarding Juliet's wedding to Paris.

Compare: How does Shakespeare contrast Juliet's wedding to Romeo with her upcoming wedding to Paris?

Scene 3 *Juliet's bedroom.*

[*Enter* Juliet *and* Nurse.]

Juliet. Ay, those attires are best; but, gentle nurse,
I pray thee leave me to myself tonight;
For I have need of many orisons
To move the heavens to smile upon my state,
Which, well thou knowest, is cross and full of sin.

3 **orisons:** prayers.

[*Enter* Lady Capulet.]

Lady Capulet. What, are you busy, ho? Need you my help?

Juliet. No madam; we have culled such necessaries
As are behooveful for our state tomorrow.
So please you, let me now be left alone,
And let the nurse this night sit up with you;
For I am sure you have your hands full all
In this so sudden business.

7–8 **we have . . . tomorrow:** We have picked out (**culled**) everything appropriate for the wedding tomorrow.

Lady Capulet. Good night.
Get thee to bed and rest, for thou hast need.

[*Exeunt* Lady Capulet *and* Nurse.]

Juliet. Farewell! God knows when we shall meet again.
I have a faint cold fear thrills through my veins
That almost freezes up the heat of life.
I'll call them back again to comfort me.
Nurse!—What should she do here?
My dismal scene I needs must act alone.
Come, vial.
What if this mixture do not work at all?
Shall I be married then tomorrow morning?
No, no! This shall forbid it. Lie thou there.

ANALYZE LITERARY DEVICES

Annotate: Mark an instance of foreshadowing in the text.

Analyze: What does this detail imply about how Juliet's plan will ultimately result?

23 **This shall forbid it:** A dagger will be her alternative means of keeping from marrying Paris.

[*lays down a dagger*]

What if it be a poison which the friar
Subtly hath ministered to have me dead,
Lest in this marriage he should be dishonored
Because he married me before to Romeo?

24–58 Juliet lists her various doubts and fears about what she is about to do.

I fear it is; and yet methinks it should not,
For he hath still been tried a holy man.
How if, when I am laid into the tomb,
I wake before the time that Romeo
Come to redeem me? There's a fearful point!
Shall I not then be stifled in the vault,
To whose foul mouth no healthsome air breathes in,
And there die strangled ere my Romeo comes?
Or, if I live, is it not very like
The horrible conceit of death and night,
Together with the terror of the place—

36–43 Juliet fears the vision (**conceit**) she might have on waking in the family tomb and seeing the rotting body of Tybalt.

As in a vault, an ancient receptacle
Where for this many hundred years the bones
Of all my buried ancestors are packed;
Where bloody Tybalt, yet but green in earth,
Lies fest'ring in his shroud; where, as they say,
At some hours in the night spirits resort—
Alack, alack, is it not like that I,
So early waking—what with loathsome smells,
And shrieks like mandrakes torn out of the earth,
That living mortals, hearing them, run mad—
O, if I wake, shall I not be distraught,
Environed with all these hideous fears,
And madly play with my forefathers' joints,
And pluck the mangled Tybalt from his shroud,
And, in this rage, with some great kinsman's bone
As with a club dash out my desp'rate brains?
O, look! methinks I see my cousin's ghost
Seeking out Romeo, that did spit his body
Upon a rapier's point. Stay, Tybalt, stay!
Romeo, I come! this do I drink to thee.

[*She drinks and falls upon her bed within the curtains.*]

45–54 She fears that the smells together with the sounds of ghosts screaming might make her lose her mind and commit bizarre acts. Mandrake root was thought to look like the human form and to scream when pulled from the ground.

57 **stay:** stop.

Scene 4 *Capulet's house.*

[*Enter* Lady Capulet *and* Nurse.]

Lady Capulet. Hold, take these keys and fetch more spices, nurse.

2 **pastry:** the room where baking is done.

Nurse. They call for dates and quinces in the pastry.

[*Enter* Capulet.]

Capulet. Come, stir, stir, stir! The second cock hath crowed,
The curfew bell hath rung, 'tis three o'clock.
Look to the baked meats, good Angelica;
Spare not for cost.

5 **Angelica:** In his happy mood, Capulet calls the nurse by her name.

6 **cot-quean:** a "cottage quean," or housewife. This is a joke about Capulet doing women's work (arranging the party).

Nurse. Go, you cot-quean, go,
Get you to bed! Faith, you'll be sick tomorrow
For this night's watching.

Capulet. No, not a whit. What, I have watched ere now
All night for lesser cause, and ne'er been sick.

11–13 Lord and Lady Capulet joke about his being a woman chaser (**mouse-hunt**) as a young man. He makes fun of her jealousy (**jealous hood**).

Lady Capulet. Ay, you have been a mouse-hunt in your time;
But I will watch you from such watching now.

[*Exeunt* Lady Capulet *and* Nurse.]

Capulet. A jealous hood, a jealous hood!

[*Enter three or four Servants, with spits and logs and baskets.*]

Now, fellow,
What is there?

First Servant. Things for the cook, sir; but I know not what.

Capulet. Make haste, make haste. [*Exit* Servant.] Sirrah, fetch
drier logs.
Call Peter; he will show thee where they are.

Second Servant. I have a head, sir, that will find out logs
And never trouble Peter for the matter.

20–23 The joking between Capulet and his servants includes the mild oath **Mass**, short for "by the Mass," and **loggerhead**, a word for a stupid person as well as a pun, since the servant is searching for drier logs. **straight:** right away.

Capulet. Mass, and well said, merry whoreson, ha!
Thou shalt be loggerhead. [*Exit* Servant.] Good faith, 'tis day.
The County will be here with music straight,
For so he said he would. [*music within*] I hear him near.
Nurse! Wife! What, ho! What, nurse, I say!

[*Reenter* Nurse.]

Go waken Juliet; go and trim her up.
I'll go and chat with Paris. Hie, make haste,
Make haste! The bridegroom he is come already:
Make haste, I say.

[*Exeunt.*]

Scene 5 *Juliet's bedroom.*

Don't forget to **Notice & Note** as you read the text.

[*Enter* Nurse.]

Nurse. Mistress! what, mistress! Juliet! Fast, I warrant her, she.
Why, lamb! why, lady! Fie, you slugabed!
Why, love, I say! madam! sweetheart! Why, bride!
What, not a word? You take your pennyworths now,
Sleep for a week; for the next night, I warrant,
The County Paris hath set up his rest
That you shall rest but little. God forgive me,
Marry and amen, how sound is she asleep!
I needs must wake her. Madam, madam, madam!
Aye, let the County take you in your bed,
He'll fright you up, i' faith. Will it not be?

1–11 The nurse chatters as she bustles around the room. She calls Juliet a **slugabed**, or sleepyhead, who is trying to get her **pennyworths**, or small portions, of rest now, since after the wedding Paris won't let her get much sleep.

[*opens the curtains*]

What, dressed and in your clothes and down again?
I must needs wake you. Lady! lady! lady!
Alas, alas! Help, help! my lady's dead!
O well-a-day that ever I was born!
Some aqua vitae, ho! My lord! my lady!

[*Enter* Lady Capulet.]

Lady Capulet. What noise is here?

Nurse. O lamentable day!

17 **lamentable:** filled with grief.

Lady Capulet. What is the matter?

Nurse. Look, look! O heavy day!

Lady Capulet. O me, O me! My child, my only life!
Revive, look up, or I will die with thee!
Help! help! Call help.

[*Enter* Capulet.]

Capulet. For shame, bring Juliet forth; her lord is come.

Nurse. She's dead, deceased; she's dead! Alack the day!

Lady Capulet. Alack the day, she's dead, she's dead, she's dead!

Capulet. Ha! let me see her. Out alas! she's cold,
Her blood is settled, and her joints are stiff;
Life and these lips have long been separated.
Death lies on her like an untimely frost
Upon the sweetest flower of all the field.

Nurse. O lamentable day!

Lady Capulet. O woeful time!

Capulet. Death, that hath ta'en her hence to make me wail,
Ties up my tongue and will not let me speak.

[*Enter* Friar Laurence *and* Paris, *with* Musicians.]

Friar Laurence. Come, is the bride ready to go to church?

Capulet. Ready to go, but never to return.
O son, the night before thy wedding day
Hath death lain with thy wife. See, there she lies,
Flower as she was, deflowered by him.
Death is my son-in-law, Death is my heir;
My daughter he hath wedded. I will die
And leave him all. Life, living, all is Death's.

40 **Life . . . Death's:** My life, my possessions, and everything else of mine belongs to Death.

Paris. Have I thought long to see this morning's face,
And doth it give me such a sight as this?

Lady Capulet. Accursed, unhappy, wretched, hateful day!
Most miserable hour that e'er time saw
In lasting labor of his pilgrimage!
But one, poor one, one poor and loving child,
But one thing to rejoice and solace in,
And cruel Death hath catched it from my sight!

46–48 **But one . . . my sight:** I had only one child to make me happy, and Death has taken (**catched**) her from me.

Nurse. O woe! O woeful, woeful, woeful day!
Most lamentable day, most woeful day
That ever, ever I did yet behold!
O day! O day! O day! O hateful day!
Never was seen so black a day as this.
O woeful day! O woeful day!

Paris. Beguiled, divorced, wronged, spited, slain!
Most detestable Death, by thee beguiled,
By cruel, cruel thee quite overthrown!
O love! O life! not life, but love in death!

55 **Beguiled:** tricked.

Capulet. Despised, distressed, hated, martyred, killed!
Uncomfortable time, why camest thou now
To murder, murder our solemnity?
O child! O child! my soul, and not my child!
Dead art thou, dead! alack, my child is dead,
And with my child my joys are buried!

60–61 **why . . . solemnity:** Why did Death have to come to murder our celebration?

Friar Laurence. Peace, ho, for shame! Confusion's cure lives not
In these confusions. Heaven and yourself
Had part in this fair maid! now heaven hath all,
And all the better is it for the maid.

Your part in her you could not keep from death,
But heaven keeps his part in eternal life.
The most you sought was her promotion,
For 'twas your heaven she should be advanced;
And weep ye now, seeing she is advanced
Above the clouds, as high as heaven itself?
O, in this love, you love your child so ill
That you run mad, seeing that she is well.
She's not well married that lives married long,

65–78 The friar says that the cure for disaster (**confusion**) cannot be found in cries of grief. Juliet's family and heaven once shared her; now heaven has all of her. All the family ever wanted was the best for her; now she's in heaven—what could be better than that? It is best to die young, when the soul is still pure, without sin.

But she's best married that dies married young.
Dry up your tears and stick your rosemary
On this fair corse, and, as the custom is,
In all her best array bear her to church;
For though fond nature bids us all lament,
Yet nature's tears are reason's merriment.

Capulet. All things that we ordained festival
Turn from their office to black funeral—
Our instruments to melancholy bells,
Our wedding cheer to a sad burial feast;
Our solemn hymns to sullen dirges change;
Our bridal flowers serve for a buried corse;
And all things change them to the contrary.

Friar Laurence. Sir, go you in; and, madam, go with him;
And go, Sir Paris. Every one prepare
To follow this fair corse unto her grave.
The heavens do lower upon you for some ill;
Move them no more by crossing their high will.

[*Exeunt* Capulet, Lady Capulet, Paris, *and* Friar.]

First Musician. Faith, we may put up our pipes, and be gone.

Nurse. Honest good fellows, ah, put up, put up,
For well you know this is a pitiful case.

[*Exit.*]

Second Musician. Aye, by my troth, the case may be amended.

[*Enter* Peter.]

Peter. Musicians, oh, musicians, "Heart's ease, heart's ease." Oh, an you will have me live, play "Heart's ease."

79–80 **stick . . . corse:** Put rosemary, an herb, on her corpse.

82–83 **though . . . merriment:** Though it's natural to cry, common sense tells us we should rejoice for the dead.

84 **ordained festival:** intended for the wedding.

88 **sullen dirges:** sad, mournful tunes.

94–95 **The heavens . . . will:** The fates (**heavens**) frown on you for some wrong you have done. Don't tempt them by refusing to accept their will (Juliet's death).

First Musician. Why "Heart's ease"?

Peter. Oh, musicians, because my heart itself plays "My heart is full of woe." Oh, play me some merry dump, to comfort me.

First Musician. Not a dump we, 'tis no time to play now.

Peter. You will not, then?

First Musician. No.

Peter. I will then give it you soundly.

First Musician. What will you give us?

Peter. No money, on my faith, but the gleek. I will give you the minstrel.

First Musician. Then will I give you the serving creature.

113 **pate:** top of the head.

Peter. Then will I lay the serving creature's dagger on your pate. I will carry no crotchets. I'll re you, I'll fa you, do you note me?

First Musician. An you re us and fa us, you note us.

Second Musician. Pray you put up your dagger, and put out your wit.

Peter. Then have at you with my wit! I will drybeat you with an iron wit, and put up my iron dagger. Answer me like men:

"When griping grief the heart doth wound
And doleful dumps the mind oppress,
Then music with her silver sound—

Why "silver sound"? Why "music with her silver sound"? What say you, Simon Catling?

First Musician. Marry, sir, because silver hath a sweet sound.

Peter. Pretty! What say you, Hugh Rebeck?

Second Musician. I say "silver sound" because musicians sound for silver.

Peter. Pretty too! What say you, James Soundpost?

Third Musician. Faith, I know not what to say.

Peter. Oh, I cry you mercy, you are the singer. I will say for you. It is "music with her silver sound" because musicians have no gold for sounding.

"Then music with her silver sound
With speedy help doth lend redress."

[*Exit.*]

136 **pestilent:** bothersome; irritating.

First Musician. What a pestilent knave is this same!

Second Musician. Hang him, Jack! Come, we'll in here. Tarry for the mourners, and stay dinner.

[*Exeunt.*]

COLLABORATIVE DISCUSSION

With a partner, discuss the measures taken by Juliet and Friar Laurence to fool Juliet's family. Do you agree with their plan and think there were no other options, or do you think the plan was selfish and unwise?

Assessment Practice

Answer these questions before moving on to the **Analyze the Text** section on the following page.

1. Which **two** sentences describe Juliet's fears when she goes to drink from the vial?

   (A) She will be trapped in the tomb.

   (B) The potion in the vial will do nothing.

   (C) The potion in the vial will actually kill her.

   (D) She will never see her mother or nurse again.

   (E) She will have to marry Paris.

2. This question has two parts. First answer **Part A**. Then, answer **Part B**.

   Part A

   Which statement best summarizes the interaction between Peter and the musicians?

   (A) The musicians want Peter to choose a song to play.

   (B) The musicians threaten Peter with a knife if he will not leave.

   (C) The musicians refuse to play because Peter will not pay them.

   (D) The musicians will not play because they are too overcome with grief.

   Part B

   Select the line of dialogue that best supports the answer to Part A.

   (A) "Faith, we may put up our pipes, and be gone." (Scene 5, line 96)

   (B) "Oh, play me some merry dump, to comfort me." (Scene 5, line 104)

   (C) "Then will I lay the serving creature's dagger on your pate." (Scene 5, lines 112–113)

   (D) "I say 'silver sound' because musicians sound for silver." (Scene 5, lines 127–128)

Analyze the Text

Support your responses with evidence from the text.

NOTICE & NOTE

Review what you **noticed and noted** as you read the text. Your annotations can help you answer these questions.

1. **ANALYZE** Review Juliet's dialogue with Paris in Scene 1. If Juliet had never met Romeo, might she have fallen in love with Paris? Explain.

2. **IDENTIFY** Shakespeare often employs a literary technique known as dramatic irony. **Dramatic irony** exists when the reader or viewer knows something that one or more of the characters do not. For example, when Paris asks Juliet to confess to Friar Laurence that she loves him, she carefully avoids denying it. We know that Juliet loves Romeo, not Paris. Identify two other examples of dramatic irony in Act IV. Explain how these ironic moments contribute to the building tension in the play.

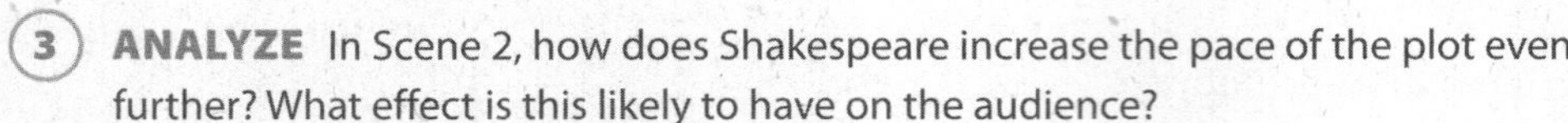

3. **ANALYZE** In Scene 2, how does Shakespeare increase the pace of the plot even further? What effect is this likely to have on the audience?

4. **COMPARE** Juliet drinks the sleeping potion, despite her fears. What does this reveal about her character? Has she changed from the beginning of the play, before she met Romeo? Explain your response.

5. **EVALUATE** Shakespeare includes **comic relief,** a humorous exchange between Peter and the musicians, at the end of Act IV—just after Juliet's family discovers her body. What message is conveyed by contrasting a humorous scene with a tragic one?

Choices

Here are some other ways to demonstrate your understanding of Act IV.

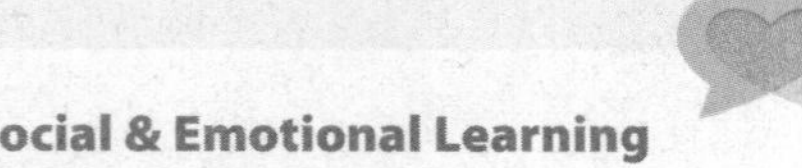

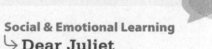

Social & Emotional Learning

↳ Dear Juliet

Consider Juliet's actions in Act IV: She lies to her family and fakes her own death. Could she have made other choices with better advice than what she received? Write a letter from Juliet to a 14th-century relationship expert in which Juliet explains her situation and seeks advice. Write a response in which the expert offers Juliet a safer solution.

Speaking & Listening

↳ Dramatic Reading

In a small group, prepare a dramatic reading of a scene from *The Tragedy of Romeo and Juliet*, Act IV.

- Choose a scene and assign roles to each member of the group. Include the role of a narrator to read the stage directions.
- Practice reading the scene as a group a few times. Then perform the dramatic reading for the rest of the class.

Act V

Don't forget to **Notice & Note** as you read the text.

Scene 1 *A street in Mantua.*

[*Enter* Romeo.]

Romeo. If I may trust the flattering truth of sleep,
My dreams presage some joyful news at hand.
My bosom's lord sits lightly in his throne,
And all this day an unaccustomed spirit
Lifts me above the ground with cheerful thoughts.
I dreamt my lady came and found me dead
(*Strange dream that gives a dead man leave to think!*)
And breathed such life with kisses in my lips
That I revived and was an emperor.
Ah me! how sweet is love itself possessed,
When but love's shadows are so rich in joy!

[*Enter Romeo's servant,* Balthasar, *booted.*]

News from Verona! How now, Balthasar?
Dost thou not bring me letters from the friar?
How doth my lady? Is my father well?
How fares my Juliet? That I ask again,
For nothing can be ill if she be well.

Balthasar. Then she is well, and nothing can be ill.
Her body sleeps in Capels' monument,
And her immortal part with angels lives.
I saw her laid low in her kindred's vault
And presently took post to tell it you.
O, pardon me for bringing these ill news,
Since you did leave it for my office, sir.

Romeo. Is it e'en so? Then I defy you, stars!
Thou knowst my lodging. Get me ink and paper
And hire posthorses. I will hence tonight.

Balthasar. I do beseech you, sir, have patience.
Your looks are pale and wild and do import
Some misadventure.

17–19 Balthasar replies that Juliet is well, since although her body lies in the Capulets' (**Capels'**) burial vault, her soul (**her immortal part**) is with the angels.

21 **presently took post:** immediately rode (to Mantua).

23 **you did . . . office:** you gave me the duty of reporting important news to you.

24 **I . . . stars:** Romeo angrily challenges fate, which has caused him so much grief.

28–29 **import some misadventure:** suggest that something bad will happen.

Romeo. Tush, thou art deceived.
Leave me and do the thing I bid thee do.
Hast thou no letters to me from the friar?

Balthasar. No, my good lord.

Romeo. No matter. Get thee gone
And hire those horses. I'll be with thee straight.

[*Exit* Balthasar.]

Well, Juliet, I will lie with thee tonight.
Let's see for means. O mischief, thou art swift
To enter in the thoughts of desperate men!
I do remember an apothecary,
And hereabouts he dwells, which late I noted
In tattered weeds, with overwhelming brows,
Culling of simples. Meager were his looks,
Sharp misery had worn him to the bones;
And in his needy shop a tortoise hung,
An alligator stuffed, and other skins
Of ill-shaped fishes; and about his shelves
A beggarly account of empty boxes,
Green earthen pots, bladders, and musty seeds,
Remnants of packthread, and old cakes of roses
Were thinly scattered, to make up a show.
Noting this penury, to myself I said,
"An if a man did need a poison now
Whose sale is present death in Mantua,
Here lives a caitiff wretch would sell it him."
O, this same thought did but forerun my need,
And this same needy man must sell it me.
As I remember, this should be the house.
Being holiday, the beggar's shop is shut.
What, ho! apothecary!

[*Enter* Apothecary.]

Apothecary. Who calls so loud?

Romeo. Come hither, man. I see that thou art poor.
Hold, there is forty ducats. Let me have
A dram of poison, such soon-speeding gear
As will disperse itself through all the veins
That the life-weary taker may fall dead,
And that the trunk may be discharged of breath
As violently as hasty powder fired
Doth hurry from the fatal cannon's womb.

35–40 **Let's . . . means:** Let me find a way (to join Juliet in death); **apothecary:** pharmacist; **tattered weeds:** ragged clothes; **culling of simples:** selecting herbs.

47 **cakes of roses:** rose petals pressed together to create a perfume.

49 **penury:** poverty.

50–52 **"An if a man . . . sell it him":** Though it is a crime to sell poison in Mantua, the apothecary is such a miserable (**caitiff**) wretch that he would probably do it for the money.

59 **ducats:** gold coins.

60–65 Romeo wants fast-acting (**soon-speeding**) poison that will work as quickly as gunpowder exploding in a cannon.

67 **any . . . them:** any person who dispenses or sells them.

72–74 Romeo urges the apothecary to improve his situation by breaking the law and selling him the poison.

75 I'm doing this for the money, not because I think it's right.

79 **dispatch you straight:** kill you instantly.

85 Romeo refers to the poison as a cordial, a drink believed to be good for the heart.

Apothecary. Such mortal drugs I have; but Mantua's law
Is death to any he that utters them.

Romeo. Art thou so bare and full of wretchedness
And fearest to die? Famine is in thy cheeks,
Need and oppression starveth in thine eyes,
Contempt and beggary hangs upon thy back;
The world is not thy friend, nor the world's law,
The world affords no law to make thee rich;
Then be not poor, but break it and take this.

Apothecary. My poverty but not my will consents.

Romeo. I pay thy poverty and not thy will.

Apothecary. Put this in any liquid thing you will
And drink it off, and if you had the strength
Of twenty men, it would dispatch you straight.

Romeo. There is thy gold—worse poison to men's souls,
Doing more murder in this loathsome world,
Than these poor compounds that thou mayst not sell.
I sell thee poison; thou hast sold me none.
Farewell. Buy food and get thyself in flesh.
Come, cordial and not poison, go with me
To Juliet's grave; for there must I use thee.

[*Exeunt.*]

Scene 2 *Friar Laurence's cell in Verona.*

[*Enter* Friar John.]

Friar John. Holy Franciscan friar, brother, ho!

[*Enter* Friar Laurence.]

Friar Laurence. This same should be the voice of Friar John.
Welcome from Mantua. What says Romeo?
Or, if his mind be writ, give me his letter.

5–12 Friar John asked another friar (**barefoot brother**) to go with him to Mantua. The health officials of the town, believing that the friars had come into contact with a deadly plague (**infectious pestilence**), locked them up to keep them from infecting others.

13 **bare:** carried (bore).

Friar John. Going to find a barefoot brother out,
One of our order to associate me,
Here in this city visiting the sick,
And finding him, the searchers of the town,
Suspecting that we both were in a house
Where the infectious pestilence did reign,
Sealed up the doors, and would not let us forth,
So that my speed to Mantua there was stayed.

Friar Laurence. Who bare my letter, then, to Romeo?

Friar John. I could not send it—here it is again—
Nor get a messenger to bring it thee,

So fearful were they of infection.

Friar Laurence. Unhappy fortune! By my brotherhood,
The letter was not nice, but full of charge,
Of dear import, and the neglecting it
May do much danger. Friar John, go hence,

Get me an iron crow and bring it straight
Unto my cell.

Friar John. Brother, I'll go and bring it thee.

[*Exit.*]

Friar Laurence. Now must I to the monument alone.
Within this three hours will fair Juliet wake.
She will beshrew me much that Romeo
Hath had no notice of these accidents;
But I will write again to Mantua,
And keep her at my cell till Romeo come—
Poor living corse, closed in a dead man's tomb!

[*Exit.*]

18–20 The letter wasn't trivial (**nice**) but contained a message of great importance (**dear import**). The fact that it wasn't sent (**neglecting it**) may cause great harm.

21 **iron crow:** crowbar.

25–26 **She . . . accidents:** She will be furious with me when she learns that Romeo doesn't know what has happened.

ANALYZE LITERARY DEVICES

Annotate: Mark the oxymoron in line 29. Note that the word *corse* means "corpse."

Analyze: What emotional effect does this create?

Scene 3 *The cemetery that contains the Capulets' tomb.*

[*Enter* Paris *and his* Page *with flowers and a torch.*]

Paris. Give me thy torch, boy. Hence, and stand aloof.
Yet put it out, for I would not be seen.
Under yond yew tree lay thee all along,
Holding thine ear close to the hollow ground.
So shall no foot upon the churchyard tread
(*Being loose, unfirm, with digging up of graves*)
But thou shalt hear it. Whistle then to me,
As signal that thou hearst something approach.
Give me those flowers. Do as I bid thee, go.

Page [*aside*]. I am almost afraid to stand alone
Here in the churchyard; yet I will adventure.

[*withdraws*]

Paris. Sweet flower, with flowers thy bridal bed I strew

[*He strews the tomb with flowers.*]

O woe! thy canopy is dust and stones
Which with sweet water nightly I will dew;
Or, wanting that, with tears distilled by moans.
The obsequies that I for thee will keep
Nightly shall be to strew thy grave and weep.

[*The* Page *whistles.*]

1 **aloof:** some distance away.

ANALYZE PARALLEL PLOTS

Annotate: Mark the transition between parallel plots that happens on this page.

Analyze: As the play comes to a close, Shakespeare brings together some parallel plots and the characters associated with them. What is the impact of Paris's entrance at this point in the play?

12–17 Paris promises to decorate Juliet's grave with flowers and sprinkle it with either perfume (**sweet water**) or his tears. He will perform these honoring rites (**obsequies**) every night.

The boy gives warning something doth approach.
What cursed foot wanders this way tonight
To cross my obsequies and true love's rite?
What, with a torch? Muffle me, night, awhile.

[*withdraws*]

[*Enter* Romeo *and* Balthasar *with a torch, a mattock, and a crow of iron.*]

Romeo. Give me that mattock and the wrenching iron.
Hold, take this letter. Early in the morning
See thou deliver it to my lord and father.
Give me the light. Upon thy life I charge thee,
Whate'er thou hearest or seest, stand all aloof
And do not interrupt me in my course.
Why I descend into this bed of death
Is partly to behold my lady's face,
But chiefly to take thence from her dead finger
A precious ring—a ring that I must use
In dear employment. Therefore hence, be gone.
But if thou, jealous, dost return to pry
In what I farther shall intend to do,
By heaven, I will tear thee joint by joint
And strew this hungry churchyard with thy limbs.
The time and my intents are savage-wild,
More fierce and more inexorable far
Than empty tigers or the roaring sea.

Balthasar. I will be gone, sir, and not trouble you.

Romeo. So shalt thou show me friendship. Take thou that.
Live, and be prosperous; and farewell, good fellow.

Balthasar [*aside*]. For all this same, I'll hide me hereabout.
His looks I fear, and his intents I doubt.

[*withdraws*]

Romeo. Thou detestable maw, thou womb of death,
Gorged with the dearest morsel of the earth,
Thus I enforce thy rotten jaws to open,
And in despite I'll cram thee with more food.

[Romeo *opens the tomb.*]

Paris. This is that banish'd haughty Montague
That murdered my love's cousin—with which grief
It is supposed the fair creature died—
And here is come to do some villainous shame
To the dead bodies. I will apprehend him.
Stop thy unhallowed toil, vile Montague!
Can vengeance be pursued further than death?

20 **cross:** interfere with.

21 **muffle:** hide.

mattock . . . iron: an ax and a crowbar.

32 **in dear employment:** for an important purpose.

33 **jealous:** curious.

37–39 Romeo's intention is more unstoppable (**inexorable**) than hungry (**empty**) tigers or the waves of an ocean.

45–48 Romeo addresses the tomb as though it were devouring people. He calls it a hateful stomach (**detestable maw**) that is filled (**gorged**) with Juliet (**the dearest morsel of the earth**).

49–53 Recognizing Romeo, Paris speaks these first few lines to himself. He is angry with Romeo, believing that Romeo's killing Tybalt caused Juliet to die of grief.

Condemned villain, I do apprehend thee.
Obey, and go with me; for thou must die.

Don't forget to **Notice & Note** as you read the text.

Romeo. I must indeed; and therefore came I hither.
Good gentle youth, tempt not a desp'rate man.
Fly hence and leave me. Think upon these gone;
Let them affright thee. I beseech thee, youth,
Put not another sin upon my head
By urging me to fury. O, be gone!
By heaven, I love thee better than myself.
For I come hither armed against myself.
Stay not, be gone. Live, and hereafter say
A madman's mercy bid thee run away.

Paris. I do defy thy conjuration
And apprehend thee for a felon here.

68 I reject your appeal.

Romeo. Wilt thou provoke me? Then have at thee, boy!

[*They fight.*]

Page. O Lord, they fight! I will go call the watch.

[*Exit.*]

Paris. O, I am slain! [*falls*] If thou be merciful,
Open the tomb, lay me with Juliet.

[*dies.*]

Romeo. In faith, I will. Let me peruse this face.
Mercutio's kinsman, noble County Paris!
What said my man when my betossed soul
Did not attend him as we rode? I think
He told me Paris should have married Juliet.
Said he not so? or did I dream it so?
Or am I mad, hearing him talk of Juliet,
To think it was so? O, give me thy hand,
One writ with me in sour misfortune's book!
I'll bury thee in a triumphant grave.
A grave? O, no, a lantern, slaughtered youth,
For here lies Juliet, and her beauty makes
This vault a feasting presence full of light.
Death, lie thou there, by a dead man interred.

82 Romeo notes that, like himself, Paris has been a victim of bad luck.

84–87 Romeo will bury Paris with Juliet, whose beauty fills the tomb with light. Paris' corpse (**Death**) is being buried (**interred**) by a dead man in that Romeo expects to be dead soon.

[*lays* Paris *in the tomb.*]

How oft when men are at the point of death
Have they been merry! which their keepers call
A lightning before death. O, how may I
Call this a lightning? O my love! my wife!

94 **ensign:** sign

98–100 **O, what . . . enemy:** I can best repay you (Tybalt) by killing your enemy (myself) with the same hand that cut your youth in two (**twain**).

102–105 Romeo can't get over how beautiful Juliet still looks. He asks whether Death is loving (**amorous**) and whether it has taken Juliet as its lover (**paramour**).

111–112 **shake . . . flesh:** rid myself of the burden of an unhappy fate (**inauspicious stars**).

115 **dateless:** eternal; never-ending. Romeo means that what he is about to do can never be undone.

117–118 Romeo compares himself to the pilot of a ship (**bark**) who is going to crash on the rocks because he is so weary and sick.

Death, that hath sucked the honey of thy breath,
Hath had no power yet upon thy beauty.
Thou art not conquered. Beauty's ensign yet
Is crimson in thy lips and in thy cheeks,
And death's pale flag is not advanced there.
Tybalt, liest thou there in thy bloody sheet?
O, what more favor can I do to thee
Than with that hand that cut thy youth in twain
To sunder his that was thine enemy?
Forgive me, cousin! Ah, dear Juliet,
Why art thou yet so fair? Shall I believe
That unsubstantial Death is amorous,
And that the lean abhorred monster keeps
Thee here in dark to be his paramour?
For fear of that I still will stay with thee
And never from this palace of dim night
Depart again. Here, here will I remain
With worms that are thy chambermaids. O, here
Will I set up my everlasting rest
And shake the yoke of inauspicious stars
From this world-wearied flesh. Eyes, look your last!
Arms, take your last embrace! and, lips, O you
The doors of breath, seal with a righteous kiss
A dateless bargain to engrossing death!
Come, bitter conduct; come, unsavory guide!
Thou desperate pilot, now at once run on
The dashing rocks thy seasick weary bark!
Here's to my love! [*drinks*] O true apothecary!
Thy drugs are quick. Thus with a kiss I die.

[*falls*]

[*Enter* Friar Laurence, *with lantern, crow, and spade.*]

Friar Laurence. Saint Francis be my speed! how oft tonight
Have my old feet stumbled at graves! Who's there?

Balthasar. Here's one, a friend, and one that knows you well.

Friar Laurence. Bliss be upon you! Tell me, good my friend,
What torch is yond that vainly lends his light
To grubs and eyeless skulls? As I discern,
It burneth in the Capels' monument.

Balthasar. It doth so, holy sir; and there's my master,
One that you love.

Friar Laurence. Who is it?

Balthasar. Romeo.

Don't forget to **Notice & Note** as you read the text.

Friar Laurence. How long hath he been there?

Balthasar. Full half an hour.

Friar Laurence. Go with me to the vault.

Balthasar. I dare not, sir.
My master knows not but I am gone hence,
And fearfully did menace me with death
If I did stay to look on his intents.

132–134 **My master . . . intents:** My master told me to go away and threatened me with death if I watched what he did.

Friar Laurence. Stay then; I'll go alone. Fear comes upon me.
O, much I fear some ill unthrifty thing.

136 **unthrifty:** unlucky.

Balthasar. As I did sleep under this yew tree here,
I dreamt my master and another fought,
And that my master slew him.

Friar Laurence. Romeo!

[*stoops and looks on the blood and weapons*]

Alack, alack, what blood is this which stains
The stony entrance of this sepulcher?
What mean these masterless and gory swords
To lie discolored by this place of peace?

140–143 **Alack . . . place of peace?** Why are these bloody swords lying here at the tomb (**sepulcher**), a place that should be peaceful? (The swords are also **masterless,** or without their owners.)

[*enters the tomb*]

Romeo! O, pale! Who else? What, Paris too?
And steeped in blood? Ah, what an unkind hour
Is guilty of this lamentable chance!
The lady stirs.

[Juliet *rises.*]

Juliet. O comfortable friar! where is my lord?
I do remember well where I should be,
And there I am. Where is my Romeo?

148 **comfortable:** comforting.

Friar Laurence. I hear some noise. Lady, come from that nest
Of death, contagion, and unnatural sleep.
A greater power than we can contradict
Hath thwarted our intents. Come, come away.
Thy husband in thy bosom there lies dead;
And Paris too. Come, I'll dispose of thee
Among a sisterhood of holy nuns.
Stay not to question, for the watch is coming.
Come, go, good Juliet. I dare no longer stay.

153–154 **A greater . . . intents:** A greater force than we can fight (**contradict**) has ruined our plans (**thwarted our intents**).

156–157 **I'll dispose . . . nuns:** I'll find a place for you in a convent of nuns.

Juliet. Go, get thee hence, for I will not away.

[*Exit* Friar Laurence.]

What's here? A cup, closed in my true love's hand?
Poison, I see, hath been his timeless end.
O churl! drunk all, and left no friendly drop
To help me after? I will kiss thy lips.
Haply some poison yet doth hang on them
To make me die with a restorative.

[*kisses him*]

Thy lips are warm!

Chief Watchman [*within*]. Lead, boy. Which way?

Juliet. Yea, noise? Then I'll be brief. O happy dagger!

[*snatches Romeo's dagger*]

This is thy sheath; there rust, and let me die.

[*She stabs herself and falls.*]

[*Enter* Watchmen *with the* Page *of Paris.*]

Page. This is the place. There, where the torch doth burn.

Chief Watchman. The ground is bloody. Search about the churchyard.

Go, some of you; whoe'er you find attach.

[*Exeunt some of the* Watch.]

Pitiful sight! here lies the County slain;
And Juliet bleeding, warm, and newly dead,
Who here hath lain this two days buried.
Go, tell the Prince; run to the Capulets;
Raise up the Montagues; some others search.

[*Exeunt others of the* Watch.]

We see the ground whereon these woes do lie,
But the true ground of all these piteous woes
We cannot without circumstance descry.

[*Reenter some of the* Watch, *with* Balthasar.]

Second Watchman. Here's Romeo's man. We found him in the churchyard.

Chief Watchman. Hold him in safety till the Prince come hither.

[*Reenter* Friar Laurence *and another* Watchman.]

Third Watchman. Here is a friar that trembles, sighs, and weeps.
We took this mattock and this spade from him
As he was coming from this churchyard side.

Chief Watchman. A great suspicion! Stay the friar too.

[*Enter the* Prince *and* Attendants.]

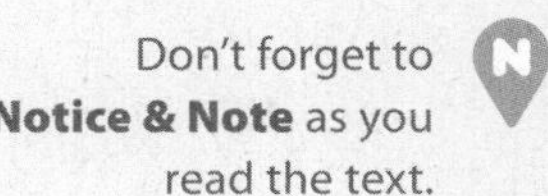
Don't forget to **Notice & Note** as you read the text.

162 **timeless:** happening before its proper time.

163 **churl:** miser.

165 **Haply:** perhaps.

173 **attach:** arrest.

178 **Raise up:** awaken.

179–181 **We see . . . descry:** We see the earth (**ground**) these bodies lie on. But the real cause (**true ground**) of these deaths is yet for us to discover (**descry**).

182–187 The guards arrest Balthasar and Friar Laurence as suspicious characters.

Prince. What misadventure is so early up,
That calls our person from our morning rest?

[*Enter* Capulet, Lady Capulet, *and others*.]

Capulet. What should it be, that they so shriek abroad?

Lady Capulet. The people in the street cry "Romeo,"
Some "Juliet," and some "Paris"; and all run,
With open outcry, toward our monument.

Prince. What fear is this which startles in our ears?

Chief Watchman. Sovereign, here lies the County Paris slain;
And Romeo dead, and Juliet, dead before,
Warm and new killed.

Prince. Search, seek, and know how this foul murder comes.

Chief Watchman. Here is a friar, and slaughtered Romeo's man,
With instruments upon them fit to open
These dead men's tombs.

Capulet. O heavens! O wife, look how our daughter bleeds!
This dagger hath mista'en, for, lo, his house
Is empty on the back of Montague,
And it missheathed in my daughter's bosom!

Lady Capulet. O me! this sight of death is as a bell
That warns my old age to a sepulcher.

[*Enter* Montague *and others*.]

Prince. Come, Montague; for thou art early up
To see thy son and heir now early down.

Montague. Alas, my liege, my wife is dead tonight!
Grief of my son's exile hath stopped her breath.
What further woe conspires against mine age?

Prince. Look, and thou shalt see.

Montague. O thou untaught! what manners is in this,
To press before thy father to a grave?

Prince. Seal up the mouth of outrage for a while,
Till we can clear these ambiguities
And know their spring, their head, their true descent;
And then will I be general of your woes
And lead you even to death. Meantime forbear,
And let mischance be slave to patience.
Bring forth the parties of suspicion.

Friar Laurence. I am the greatest, able to do least,
Yet most suspected, as the time and place
Doth make against me, of this direful murder;
And here I stand, both to impeach and purge

194 **startles:** causes alarm.

203–205 **This dagger . . . in my daughter's bosom:** This dagger has missed its target. It should rest in the sheath (**house**) that Romeo wears. Instead it is in Juliet's chest.

210 **liege:** lord.

214–215 **what manners . . . grave:** What kind of behavior is this, for a son to die before his father?

216–221 **Seal . . . patience:** Stop your emotional outbursts until we can find out the source (**spring**) of these confusing events (**ambiguities**). Wait (**forbear**) and be patient, and let's find out what happened.

223–227 Friar Laurence confesses that he is most responsible for these events. He will both accuse (**impeach**) himself and clear (**purge**) himself of guilt.

Myself condemned and myself excused.

Don't forget to **Notice & Note** as you read the text.

Prince. Then say at once what thou dost know in this.

Friar Laurence. I will be brief, for my short date of breath
Is not so long as is a tedious tale.
Romeo, there dead, was husband to that Juliet;
And she, there dead, that Romeo's faithful wife.
I married them; and their stol'n marriage day
Was Tybalt's doomsday, whose untimely death
Banish'd the new-made bridegroom from this city;
For whom, and not for Tybalt, Juliet pined.
You, to remove that siege of grief from her,
Betrothed and would have married her perforce
To County Paris. Then comes she to me
And with wild looks bid me devise some mean
To rid her from this second marriage,
Or in my cell there would she kill herself.
Then gave I her (so tutored by my art)
A sleeping potion; which so took effect
As I intended, for it wrought on her
The form of death. Meantime I writ to Romeo
That he should hither come as this dire night
To help to take her from her borrowed grave,
Being the time the potion's force should cease.
But he which bore my letter, Friar John,
Was stayed by accident, and yesternight
Returned my letter back. Then all alone
At the prefixed hour of her waking
Came I to take her from her kindred's vault;
Meaning to keep her closely at my cell
Till I conveniently could send to Romeo.
But when I came, some minute ere the time
Of her awaking, here untimely lay
The noble Paris and true Romeo dead.
She wakes; and I entreated her come forth
And bear this work of heaven with patience;
But then a noise did scare me from the tomb,
And she, too desperate, would not go with me,
But, as it seems, did violence on herself.
All this I know, and to the marriage
Her nurse is privy; and if aught in this
Miscarried by my fault, let my old life
Be sacrificed, some hour before his time,
Unto the rigor of severest law.

Prince. We still have known thee for a holy man.
Where's Romeo's man? What can he say in this?

236 It was Romeo's banishment, not Tybalt's death, that made Juliet so sad.

248 **borrowed:** temporary.

254 **kindred's:** family's.

265–269 **and to . . . law:** Her nurse can bear witness to this secret marriage. If I am responsible for any of this, let the law punish me with death.

273 **in post:** at full speed.

Balthasar. I brought my master news of Juliet's death;
And then in post he came from Mantua
To this same place, to this same monument.
This letter he early bid me give his father,
And threatened me with death, going in the vault,
If I departed not and left him there.

279–280 The Prince asks for Paris's servant, who notified the guards (**raised the watch**). Then he asks the servant why Paris was at the cemetery.

Prince. Give me the letter. I will look on it.
Where is the County's page that raised the watch?
Sirrah, what made your master in this place?

283–285 **Anon . . . call the watch:** Soon (**anon**) someone with a light came and opened the tomb. Paris drew his sword, and I ran to call the guards.

Page. He came with flowers to strew his lady's grave;
And bid me stand aloof, and so I did.
Anon comes one with light to ope the tomb;
And by-and-by my master drew on him;
And then I ran away to call the watch.

292–295 **See what . . . punished:** Look at the punishment your hatred has brought on you. Heaven has killed your children (**joys**) with love. For shutting my eyes to your arguments (**discords**), I have lost two relatives. We have all been punished.

Prince. This letter doth make good the friar's words,
Their course of love, the tidings of her death;
And here he writes that he did buy a poison
Of a poor 'pothecary, and therewithal
Came to this vault to die and lie with Juliet.
Where be these enemies? Capulet, Montague,
See what a scourge is laid upon your hate,
That heaven finds means to kill your joys with love!
And I, for winking at your discords too,
Have lost a brace of kinsmen. All are punished.

297–298 **jointure:** dowry, the payment a bride's father traditionally made to the groom. Capulet means that no one could demand more of a bride's father than he has already paid.

Capulet. O brother Montague, give me thy hand.
This is my daughter's jointure, for no more
Can I demand.

301 **at such rate be set:** be valued so highly.

Montague. But I can give thee more;
For I will raise her statue in pure gold,
That whiles Verona by that name is known,
There shall no figure at such rate be set
As that of true and faithful Juliet.

303–304 Capulet promises to do for Romeo what Montague will do for Juliet. Their children have become sacrifices to their hatred (**enmity**).

Capulet. As rich shall Romeo's by his lady's lie—
Poor sacrifices of our enmity!

Prince. A glooming peace this morning with it brings.
The sun for sorrow will not show his head.
Go hence, to have more talk of these sad things;
Some shall be pardoned, and some punished;
For never was a story of more woe
Than this of Juliet and her Romeo.

[*Exeunt.*]

COLLABORATIVE DISCUSSION

Working in a small group, review the events that lead to the tragic ending. Then discuss what makes *The Tragedy of Romeo and Juliet* still popular with today's audiences.

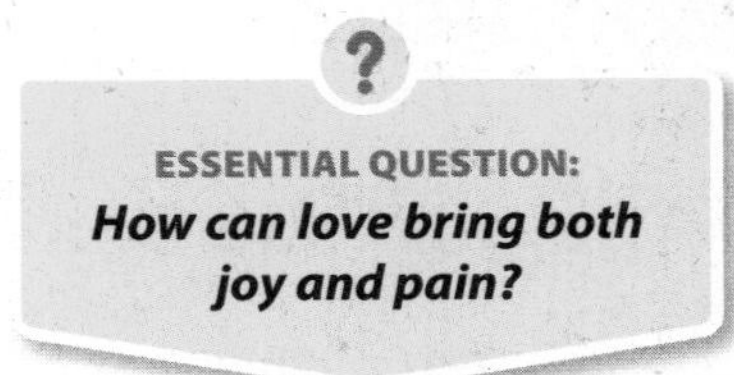
?
ESSENTIAL QUESTION:
How can love bring both joy and pain?

Review your notes and add your thoughts to your Response Log.

Assessment Practice

Answer these questions before moving on to the **Analyze the Text** section on the following page.

1. What inference can you make about Romeo's behavior when he believes that Juliet is dead in Scene 1, line 24?

   (A) He will avoid his fate and take action against being separated from Juliet.

   (B) He will get even with Juliet's family for driving her to her death.

   (C) He will do what God tells him, not what the stars in the universe command.

   (D) He will use the tragedy of Juliet's death to bring the families together forever.

2. This question has two parts. First, answer **Part A**. Then, answer **Part B**.

   Part A

   What important idea does Prince Escalus state at the end of the play?

   (A) It is dangerous to make assumptions.

   (B) A person can have only one true love.

   (C) The soul is immortal and will survive the body.

   (D) Hate between families causes sorrow and tragedy.

   Part B

   Select the **two** lines that support the answer to Part A.

   (A) "This letter doth make good the friar's words . . . And here he writes that he did buy a poison." (Scene 3, lines 286–288)

   (B) "Where be these enemies?" (Scene 3, line 291)

   (C) "Capulet, Montague / See what a scourge is laid upon your hate." (Scene 3, lines 292–293)

   (D) "And I . . . Have lost a brace of kinsmen. All are punished." (Scene 3, lines 294–295)

   (E) "A glooming peace this morning with it brings." (Scene 3, line 305)

Ed

Test-Taking Strategies

Analyze the Text

Support your responses with evidence from the text.

NOTICE & NOTE

Review what you **noticed and noted** as you read the text. Your annotations can help you answer these questions.

1. **INTERPRET** What dream does Romeo describe at the beginning of Act V, Scene 1? What part of his dream foreshadows events to come?

2. **INFER** Review the Prince's comments in Act V, Scene 3, lines 291–295. How do his **Words of the Wiser** reveal a theme, or life lesson? How might they affect the future relationship between the Montagues and Capulets?

3. **ANALYZE** Reread Friar Laurence's speech in Act V, Scene 3, lines 225–271. What various and possibly conflicting motivations does he have for making these remarks?

4. **CONNECT** Recall Juliet's response when her mother suggests the idea of marrying Paris (Act I, Scene 3, lines 98–100). What does this reveal about Juliet's character before she meets Romeo? How does this contrast with Romeo's behavior in the parallel plot involving Rosaline? By Act V, how has Juliet changed?

5. **SYNTHESIZE** *Romeo and Juliet* contains many **oxymorons,** expressions that combine contradictory terms. Choose five instances in the play; then explain how this device deepens the play's themes.

6. **EVALUATE** In a tragedy, a hero or heroine's character flaw is usually the cause of his or her downfall. Do you believe Romeo or Juliet has a character flaw that leads to his or her death? Support your response with evidence from the play.

7. **EVALUATE** Fate, or forces over which people have no control, is an important universal theme in this tragedy. Many events are blamed upon fate, starting with Shakespeare's description of Romeo and Juliet as "star-crossed lovers" in the Prologue. However, many events can also be blamed on the actions of characters. Do you believe fate or free will caused this tragic ending? Explain.

Choices

Here are some other ways to demonstrate your understanding of the ideas in this lesson.

Writing

↳ Write a Eulogy

With a partner, write a one-page collective eulogy—a tribute to one who has died—for Romeo and Juliet.

- Brainstorm important details about Romeo, Juliet, their lives, and their relationship. Think about what motivates them, how they fall in love, the challenges they face, and how they change each other. Share information from your annotations and notes on the play.
- Highlight key details about the characters of the two young people. Support your ideas with evidence from the play.
- If you have difficulty finding the right words to describe a character or express an idea, ask your peers or your teacher for help.
- Share your eulogies with another pair. Discuss the challenges of casting tragic figures in a positive light—as is necessary in a eulogy—despite the characters' flaws.

As you write and discuss, be sure to use the Academic Vocabulary words.

attribute

commit

expose

initiate

underlie

Media

↳ Analyze Media Interpretations

Countless movie and television versions of *Romeo and Juliet* have been made. Watch at least two versions and compare how each one interprets the play. Options include Baz Luhrmann's 1996 *Romeo + Juliet*, Franco Zeffirelli's 1968 *Romeo and Juliet*, and *West Side Story*, a 1961 musical based on the play and set in 1950s New York City.

As you watch, take notes on:

- Setting: time and place
- Casting, or selection of actors
- Characterization, or how the actors interpret their parts
- Effects such as lighting, music, and camera shots

Summarize your responses to the movie versions you watched. Discuss how they changed your understanding of *Romeo and Juliet* with classmates.

Research

↳ Shakespeare's Legacy

Artists in many media besides film have based works on *The Tragedy of Romeo and Juliet*. Research three of these works—songs, poems, plays, operas, or visual works of art. Use a chart to note how these adaptations remain true to Shakespeare's story and how they depart from it or put a different spin on it.

Title of Work
Genre of Work
How Is It True to Shakespeare?
How Does It Depart from Shakespeare?

Vocabulary Strategy

Shakespeare's Language

Shakespeare was a master of clever word play, including the use of **puns.** He also used many **foreign words** to add meaning and color to his writing.

A **pun** is a joke built upon multiple meanings of a word or upon two words that sound similar but have different meanings. Near the end of Act IV, Peter challenges the musicians to help him develop a pun based on a verse.

Peter. "When griping grief the heart doth wound
And doleful dumps the mind oppress,
Then music with her silver sound—
Why "silver sound"? Why "music with her silver sound"?
What say you, Simon Catling?
First Musician. Marry, sir, because silver hath a sweet sound.
Peter. Pretty! What say you, Hugh Rebeck?
Second Musician. I say "silver sound" because musicians sound for silver.
Peter. Pretty too! What say you, James Soundpost?
Third Musician. Faith, I know not what to say.
Peter. Oh, I cry you mercy, you are the singer. I will say for you. It is "music with her silver sound" because musicians have no gold for sounding.

English is filled with words of foreign origin, but Shakespeare took this a step further and included words and phrases that many English speakers do not know. These lend extra depth of meaning. Here are some examples:

- *ambuscadoes* (Spanish for "ambushes"), Act I, Scene 4
- *benedicite* (Latin for "God bless you"), Act II, Scene 3
- *passado, punto reverso, hay,* and *alla stoccata* (foreign terms for sword-fighting moves), Act II, Scene 4; Act III, Scene 1
- *aqua vitae* (Latin for "water of life," signifying brandy), Act III, Scene 2

PRACTICE AND APPLY

With a partner, explain the puns below. Brainstorm a few words that you could use in original puns. Write a brief dialogue that uses your puns.

1. "You have dancing shoes / With nimble soles; I have a soul of lead / So stakes me to the ground I cannot move." (Act I, Scene 4, lines 14–16)
2. "Ask for me tomorrow, and you / shall find me a grave man." (Act III, Scene 1, lines 91–92)

Review the word wall that you began in Act I. Which words are foreign? How do these words enhance your experience of reading Shakespeare?

Watch Your Language!

Parallel Structure

Parallel structure is the repetition of words, phrases, or grammatical structures in order to add emphasis or to improve the sound and rhythm of a piece of writing. Shakespeare regularly makes use of parallel structure to create **cadence,** or a balanced, rhythmic flow of words. Here is an example from Act II, Scene 1, lines 8–11:

> Appear thou in the likeness of a sigh;
> Speak but one rhyme, and I am satisfied!
> Cry but "Ay me!" pronounce but "love" and "dove";
> Speak to my gossip Venus one fair word . . .

Shakespeare repeats the structure of a verb followed by *but:* "Speak but . . . Cry but . . . pronounce but . . ." The parallel grammatical structures give equal weight to each phrase. Read the passage aloud to hear the cadence that the parallel structures lend to the verse.

This example from Act I, Scene 5, lines 10–11 contains a series of four past-tense verbs, each followed by the word *for.*

In this case, the speaker (a servant) sounds rather ridiculous, as if he is trying to use flowery language to deliver a simple message.

> You are looked for and called for, asked for
> and sought for, in the great chamber.

In the next example, from Act IV, Scene 1, lines 102–103, Shakespeare repeats three parallel adjectives:

Friar Laurence uses these grim adjectives to describe what Juliet's body will be like once she drinks the potion. The repetition gives his speech a somber rhythm, like a funeral march.

> Each part, deprived of supple government,
> Shall, stiff and stark and cold, appear like death;

PRACTICE AND APPLY

Write a paragraph about how the universal themes of *Romeo and Juliet* relate to your life or to the life of someone you know. Include at least two examples of parallel structure in your paragraph. Share your work with a partner and discuss how the parallel structure increases the power and clarity of your language.

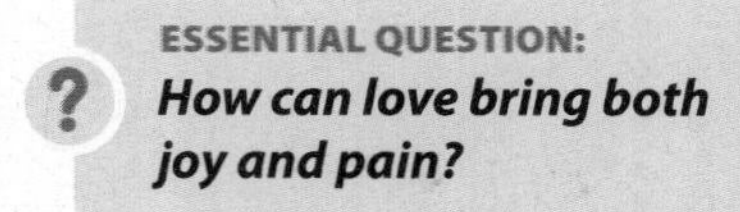
ESSENTIAL QUESTION:
How can love bring both joy and pain?

MEDIA

My Shakespeare

Video and Poem by **Kae Tempest**

Engage Your Brain

Complete this activity to start connecting with "My Shakespeare."

Role Model

Think of an artist, musician, or celebrity whose works have had an impact on you. Maybe you connect with their messages or are inspired by their actions. How do you emulate their style or ideas? Draw or list your response below.

Background

Kae Tempest (b. 1985) is a London-born poet, playwright, author, and rapper. Tempest began performing at age 16 and has performed all over the world, winning acclaim and awards at music festivals and poetry slams. The Royal Shakespeare Company commissioned Tempest to write and perform "My Shakespeare" for the World Shakespeare Festival in 2012. Since then, Tempest has written several plays and poetry collections, and recorded numerous singles and albums. Kae Tempest's latest album, *The Book of Traps and Lessons,* focuses on the importance of personal connections.

Analyze Source Material: Interpretations of Shakespeare

Kae Tempest's passionate performance of this poem shows the appeal Shakespeare has for today's youth. Shakespeare's work has been translated into more than 80 languages; it has been adapted, televised, filmed, recorded, and digitized. Shakespeare's significant presence on the Internet attests to the fact that his work has inspired the work of countless artists.

Authors often draw on historical, literary, and cultural sources for themes or topics, using their own imagination to transform the source material into their own original works of art, or **interpretations.** Just as Shakespeare drew inspiration from earlier sources, Kae Tempest credits the inspiration for "My Shakespeare" to the works of Shakespeare.

Focus on Genre
Video

- created for a specific purpose or reason
- combines visual and sound techniques
- may use film techniques such as camera shots, lighting, music, and other special effects

- In the first three stanzas, Tempest makes **allusions,** or indirect references, to the characters, themes, and scenarios in many of Shakespeare's well-known plays.
- The fourth stanza includes phrases coined by Shakespeare that are still in use today.
- In the last stanza, Tempest gets at the heart of Shakespeare's continued relevance.

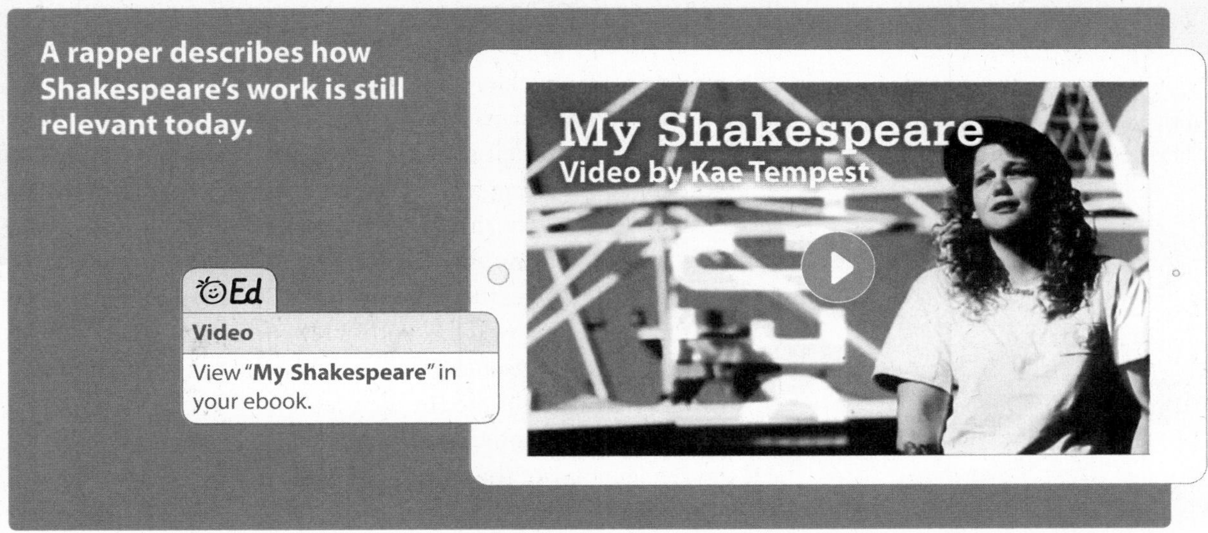

A rapper describes how Shakespeare's work is still relevant today.
My Shakespeare
Video by Kae Tempest
Ed
Video
View "My Shakespeare" in your ebook.

My Shakespeare

Poem by **Kae Tempest**

He's in every lover who ever stood alone beneath a window,
In every jealous whispered word,
in every ghost that will not rest.
He's in every father with a favorite,
Every eye that stops to linger
On what someone else has got, and feels the tightening in their chest.

He's in every young man growing boastful,
Every worn out elder, drunk all day;
muttering false prophecies and squandering their lot.
He's there—in every mix-up that spirals far out of control—and never seems to end,
even when its beginnings are forgot.

He's in every girl who ever used her wits. Who ever did her best.
In every vain admirer,
Every passionate, ambitious social climber,
And in every misheard word that ever led to tempers fraying,
Every pawn that moves exactly as the player wants it to,
And still remains convinced that it's not playing.

He's in every star crossed lover, in every thought that ever set your
teeth on edge, in every breathless hero, stepping closer to the ledge,
his is the method in our madness, as pure as the driven snow—his is
the hair standing on end, he saw that all that glittered was not gold.
He knew we hadn't slept a wink, and that our hearts were upon our
sleeves, and that the beast with two backs had us all upon our knees
as we fought fire with fire, he knew that too much of a good thing,
can leave you up in arms, the pen is mightier than the sword, still
his words seem to sing our names as they strike, and his is the milk
of human kindness, warm enough to break the ice—his, the green
eyed monster, in a pickle, still, discretion is the better part of valor,
his letters with their arms around each other's shoulders, swagger
towards the ends of their sentences, pleased with what they've done,
his words are the setting for our stories—he has become a poet who
poetics have embedded themselves deep within the fabric of our
language, he's in our mouths, his words have tangled round our own
and given rise to expressions so effective in expressing how we feel,
we can't imagine how we'd feel without them.
See—he's less the tights and garters—more the sons demanding answers from the absence of their fathers.
The hot darkness of your last embrace.
He's in the laughter of the night before, the tightened jaw of the morning after,
He's in us. Part and parcel of our Royals and our rascals.

He's more than something taught in classrooms, in language that's hard to understand,
he's more than a feeling of inadequacy when we sit for our exams,
He's in every wise woman, every pitiful villain,
Every great king, every sore loser, every fake tear.
His legacy exists in the life that lives in everything he's written,
And me, I see him everywhere, he's my Shakespeare.

ANALYZE SOURCE MATERIAL: INTERPRETATIONS OF SHAKESPEARE

Annotate: Mark phrases in lines 31–35 that describe the effect of Shakespeare's words on people today.

Analyze: How does the author support this opinion of Shakespeare's significance in the earlier lines of this stanza?

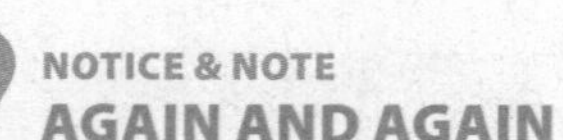

NOTICE & NOTE
AGAIN AND AGAIN

When you notice certain words and phrases recurring in the poem, you've found an **Again and Again** signpost.

Notice & Note: Mark repeated words and phrases in lines 37–45.

Analyze: Why might Kae Tempest be repeating these words?

COLLABORATIVE DISCUSSION

With a partner, discuss the overall effect of the video. Cite words and phrases in the video that depart from the text of the poem. How do these variations affect your response?

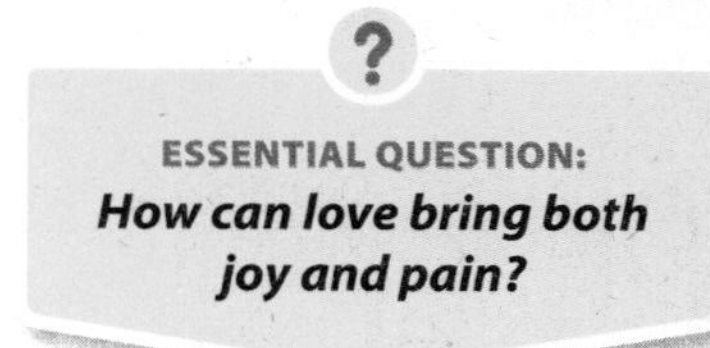
ESSENTIAL QUESTION:
How can love bring both joy and pain?

Review your notes and add your thoughts to your Response Log.

Assessment Practice

Answer these questions before moving on to the **Analyze Video and Poem** section on the following page.

1. What does the phrase "he's less the tights and garters" in line 36 suggest?

   (A) Shakespeare was a wealthy man defined by being well dressed

   (B) Shakespeare's topics and themes are relevant for all times and places.

   (C) Shakespeare did not follow the trends of other authors.

   (D) Shakespeare's work is more successful when it is performed in modern dress and adapted to modern life.

2. This question has two parts. First, answer Part A. Then, answer Part B.

   Part A

   Which sentence states a central theme of the poem?

   (A) Shakespeare's works have been internalized by each generation since his own.

   (B) Great literature is more than just ideas needed to pass a test.

   (C) The author who transforms a work owns the source material.

   (D) Shakespeare's works are more varied than many people realize.

   Part B

   Select the detail that best supports the answer to Part A.

   (A) "He's in . . . / Every eye that stops to linger / on what someone else has got . . ." (lines 4–6).

   (B) "He's in . . . / every worn out elder . . . / muttering false prophecies and squandering their lot." (lines 7–9)

   (C) " . . . we can't imagine how we'd feel without them." (line 35)

   (D) ". . . he's more than a feeling of inadequacy when we sit for our exams . . ." (line 41)

Ed

Test-Taking Strategies

Analyze Video and Poem

Support your responses with evidence from the video and text.

NOTICE & NOTE

Review what you **noticed and noted** as you read the poem. Your annotations can help you answer these questions.

1. **CITE EVIDENCE** Explain the statement that Shakespeare is "in our mouths, his words have tangled round our own . . ." What evidence does the author provide to support this idea?

2. **ANALYZE** In the last stanza, Kae Tempest acknowledges the negative ideas that today's young people might have about Shakespeare. How do the text and the video work together to refute these ideas?

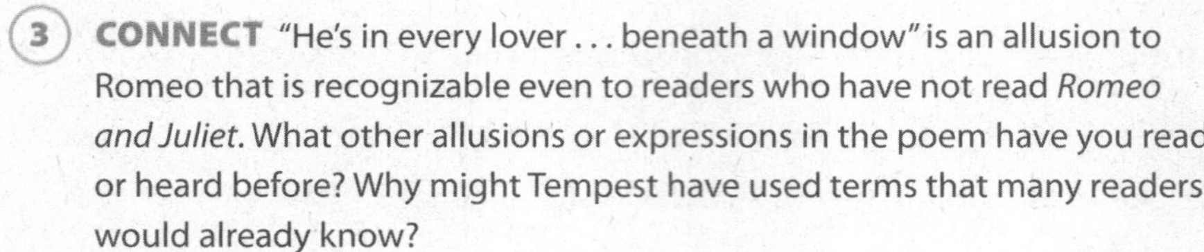

3. **CONNECT** "He's in every lover . . . beneath a window" is an allusion to Romeo that is recognizable even to readers who have not read *Romeo and Juliet*. What other allusions or expressions in the poem have you read or heard before? Why might Tempest have used terms that many readers would already know?

4. **SYNTHESIZE** Explain how the poet uses visual elements, sound elements, and speaking techniques to develop the poem's meaning through the video.

Audio-Visual Element or Technique	How It Develops the Poem's Meaning

5. **EVALUATE** What do the poem's final words, "my Shakespeare," mean? What evidence from the poem supports this meaning?

6. **INTERPRET** What does the recurrence of the words "in every" throughout the poem signal to readers? What message does Tempest convey by using these words **Again and Again**?

7. **DRAW CONCLUSIONS** How would you express the central message of the poem and video? State the theme in your own words.

Choices

Here are some other ways to demonstrate your understanding of the ideas in this lesson.

Writing

↳ Poetry

Think of something or someone that has inspired you in the way that Shakespeare's works have inspired poet and rapper Kae Tempest. (If you completed the activity on the Get Ready page, you can use your response as a starting point.) Write a three-to-four stanza poem expressing the impact the person or experience has had on your life: How has your view of the world or yourself changed as a result?

- Arrange your ideas in a logical or artistic order.
- Create a draft using literary devices such as repetition to emphasize your ideas and vivid imagery so the audience can better connect with your experience.
- Your poem does not have to rhyme, but it should have an identifiable rhythm or other sound devices.
- Ask another student to peer-review your draft; then revise and edit your poem.

When you are satisfied with your product, create a video performance of your poem like the "My Shakespeare" video. Post it online for classmates to view.

As you write and discuss, be sure to use the Academic Vocabulary words.

- **attribute**
- **commit**
- **expose**
- **initiate**
- **underlie**

Media

↳ Kae Tempest—Live!

In the years since writing and performing "My Shakespeare," Kae Tempest has recorded albums and spoken-word performances, written plays, and published prize-winning poetry collections. Watch or read at least two examples of Tempest's work. Then write a review that evaluates specific aspects. Close with a thumbs-up or down; share with friends or the class.

Social & Emotional Learning

↳ Small-Group Discussion

Kae Tempest points out that we are often unaware of how we are influenced by Shakespeare's words. Though we may not always realize it, our own words and actions have an impact on other people.

In a small group, discuss the following questions:

- When has someone's attitude positively affected you?
- When has someone's attitude negatively affected you?
- Can you think of a time when your attitude affected someone?
- People aren't happy and positive 24/7, but what can we do to ensure that our words and actions have a positive and encouraging effect?

Collaborate & Compare

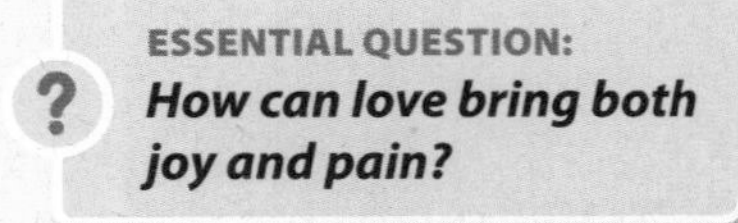

Compare Arguments

You are about to read two literary analyses about *Romeo and Juliet*. Both texts discuss the lives of Romeo and Juliet, but present different claims, or positions, about them. As you read, think about how each argument helps you understand different interpretations of characters and events in the play.

After you have read the texts, you will collaborate with a small group to analyze the literary analyses from a different perspective and then have a roundtable discussion. You will follow these steps:

- Choose one of the two literary analyses
- Find two points made in the other literary analysis that oppose or contradict points in the analysis you have chosen
- Respond to these counterclaims with relevant evidence
- Share views in a roundtable discussion

MENTOR TEXT

More than Reckless Teenagers

Literary Analysis by **Caitlin Smith**

Romeo Is a Dirtbag

Literary Analysis by **Lois Leveen**

Engage Your Brain

Choose one or both of these activities to start connecting with the literary analyses you're about to read.

Age Is Only a Number

When have you felt that someone underestimated you or dismissed your opinions because of your age? Describe a circumstance below.

Profiling Romeo and Juliet

Think about how Shakespeare characterizes Romeo and Juliet through their words, actions, motivations, and decisions. Then create a psychological profile for each of them. Assess aspects of their personality such as maturity, judgment, independence, and insight into themselves and others. Share your profiles with a partner, and discuss points of agreement and disagreement.

Compare Authors' Claims

"More than Reckless Teenagers" and "Romeo Is a Dirtbag" are both literary analyses that attempt to persuade readers to agree with specific interpretations of *Romeo and Juliet*. Literary analysis is a form of argument, in which authors state claims, or positions on topics, and support them with reasons and evidence. **Reasons** are statements authors make to explain a belief. **Evidence** includes specific facts and examples.

Take notes about the following as you read each literary analysis:

- Look for and identify the author's claim. A claim may be stated directly or implied.
- Trace the author's reasons and identify the evidence that supports each claim.
- Determine whether the author has acknowledged **counterclaims,** or opposing claims, and addressed them with reasons and evidence.

Focus on Genre
Literary Analysis

- nonfiction writing that analyzes or evaluates a literary work
- presents the writer's claim, or position, about the work
- cites reasons and textual evidence to support the writer's claim

Analyze Rhetoric

Rhetoric is the art of using words and language structures effectively, especially as a way to persuade people. **Rhetorical devices** are techniques writers use to enhance their arguments. Some rhetorical devices, such as the first three listed in the chart, are types of figurative language. Use the chart to record examples of four types of rhetorical devices the authors use in their essays.

Rhetorical Device	Example from Text	Effect
Allusion: a reference to a person, event, or text to help validate an idea		
Hyperbole: exaggerated statements not meant to be taken literally		
Meiosis: the presentation of a thing with underemphasis to make a point; understatement		
Rhetorical question: a question that is used to emphasize an idea and persuade		

Annotation in Action

Here is an example of notes a student made about these lines from "Romeo Is a Dirtbag." As you read, mark words that show the writer's use of rhetoric.

[Juliet has] a controlling father who exercises complete control over her major life decisions. How could she not be looking for a way out?	Have to agree with the author's rhetorical question!

Expand Your Vocabulary

Put a check mark next to the vocabulary words that you feel comfortable using when speaking or writing.

revere	☐
constraint	☐
condescend	☐
connive	☐
enmity	☐
sordid	☐
amenable	☐
prevaricate	☐

Turn to a partner and talk about the vocabulary words you already know. Then, write a short analysis of Romeo and Juliet's situation, using as many of the words as you can.

As you read "More than Reckless Teenagers" and "Romeo Is a Dirtbag," use the definitions in the side column to help you learn the vocabulary words you don't already know.

Background

Caitlin Mackenzie Smith, the author of "More than Reckless Teenagers," lives and works in Austin, Texas. In addition to analyzing works of literature such as Shakespeare's *Romeo and Juliet*, she does graphic design and has worked as a branding specialist. Through her work, she advances her belief that effective communication is a key component of society.

Lois Leveen is the author of works that have appeared in many newspapers, news outlets, and journals, as well as in film and performing arts venues. She has been a faculty member at UCLA and Reed College. Her experience in finding the intersection between literature and history informs her literary analysis "Romeo Is a Dirtbag." She lives in Portland, Oregon.

NOTICE & NOTE

As you read, use the side margins to make notes about the text.

More than Reckless Teenagers: In Defense of Romeo & Juliet's Love

Literary Analysis by **Caitlin Smith**

Are Romeo and Juliet foolish teenagers, or complex and self-aware characters?

COMPARE AUTHORS' CLAIMS

Annotate: In the selection title and paragraph 1, mark words and phrases that give clues to the author's claim about Romeo and Juliet.

Summarize: What is the author's position, or claim, about Romeo and Juliet as characters in Shakespeare's play?

revere
(rĭ-vîr´) *v.* to regard with devotion or awe.

constraint
(kən-strānt´) *n.* something that restricts, limits, or regulates.

1 Romeo and Juliet are complex characters thrown into a world of feuds largely against their will, looking for their own ways to survive and thrive. Whether their love is exaggerated or not, they cling to each other because they've been able to find complements in each other and chances to live their own lives instead of the lives their parents prescribe. The play isn't a caution against teenagers in love; rather, it's a caution to authority figures who reduce adolescents to children with no free will.

2 Juliet Capulet is known as one of Shakespeare's weaker female characters. She meets a boy, falls in love, and then kills herself. On the surface, she lacks the depth of some of his more **revered** heroines (Lady Macbeth, Rosalind, Beatrice, etc.). At first glance, Juliet is nothing but a stupid, rash teenage girl. However, she exists within horrifying **constraints** typical for a woman of her time. No viable options outside of marriage. A controlling father who exercises

complete control over her major life decisions. How could she not be looking for a way out? If that way out just so happened to be an attractive, sensitive boy who listened without being **condescending**? Come on, ladies.

Don't forget to **Notice & Note** as you read the text.

3 "Out, you green-sickness carrion! Out, you baggage!/You tallow face!" Juliet's father screams at her after she expresses her displeasure at the thought of marrying Paris, a man older than her, whom she does not know beyond a name and face (3.5.160–161). In her father's eyes, she is but a nuisance he no longer wants to deal with. Because Juliet doesn't want to marry the man who has imposed himself on her family, she is no longer a person.

condescending (kŏn-dĭ-sĕn´dĭng) *adj.* characterized by a patronizing or superior attitude.

4 I recently had the pleasure of studying abroad in Oxford, where we took a few trips to Stratford to see productions from the Royal Shakespeare Company (RSC), and their interpretation of this scene was striking. Juliet's father went from normal, slightly perturbed father to a towering, yelling abuser in the span of a few minutes. He slapped her, turning her next lines all the more upsetting: "Is there no pity sitting in the clouds/That sees into the bottom of my grief?—/O sweet my mother, cast me not away" (3.5.208–210). Instead of Juliet coming off as foolish or rash, her decisions make perfect sense. If her own family isn't going to respect her autonomy, does it really matter to them if she lives or dies? If Romeo is the only person who cares about her happiness, why not risk everything to see him again?

ANALYZE RHETORIC

Annotate: In paragraph 4, mark the rhetorical questions.

Analyze: What is the effect of these rhetorical questions on the reader? Do they strengthen or weaken the author's main claim?

5 Coupling specific acting choices with the words from Shakespeare's script clarifies Juliet's character beyond a lovesick thirteen-year-old to that of a constrained young woman fighting for her right to individuality.

6 Romeo as a charismatic poet-type isn't unfounded in the script at all. We're first introduced to him in a state of heartbreak, upset that the object of his affections isn't interested. At first glance, his response to Benvolio's inquiry as to what "sadness lengthens [his] hours"—"Not having that which, having, makes them short,"—is melodramatic, not endearing (1.1.168–169).

7 Furthermore, Romeo's quick turnaround to Juliet in lieu of Rosaline might be an example of fickleness. He can't have one girl, so he moves on to another without much of a thought. If that were the case, Romeo would move on once he realized Juliet is the daughter of his father's sworn enemy. He certainly wouldn't trespass on her family's grounds just to see her again.

8 In the RSC's production, Romeo was just as charismatic as he appears in the text and other interpretations. He had an almost sexual chemistry with all of his comrades on stage, but only sought to further a romantic connection with Juliet. If he was just after sex, he could have looked for it anywhere. Instead, the production claimed he wants a real connection. He finds it in Juliet.

9 In the text, Juliet is rational (to the extent that a Shakespearean tragic heroine is allowed to be) while Romeo throws himself headfirst into his emotions—an interesting reversal of gender norms, which

typically place women at the helm of emotional outbursts. This dynamic is most easily observable in the balcony scene, when Juliet begs Romeo not to swear his affections by the moon:

> 10 **ROMEO** Lady, by yonder blessèd moon I vow,
> That tips with silver all these fruit-tree tops—
>
> 11 **JULIET** O, swear not by the moon, th' inconstant moon,
> That monthly changes in her circled orb,
> Lest that thy love prove likewise variable.
>
> 12 **ROMEO** What shall I swear by?
>
> 13 **JULIET** Do not swear at all.
> Or, if thou wilt, swear by thy gracious self,
> Which is the god of my idolatry,
> And I'll believe thee (*2.2.112–121*).

14 She knows that the moon is too fleeting to be worth any oath, but Romeo is so in love he wants to swear on something. These opposing aspects of their personalities make them a great match, not just an expansion of lust at first sight or puppy love or any one of the ideas sometimes provided in defense of why Romeo and Juliet are nothing more than naive teenagers.

15 *Romeo & Juliet* is more than an unrealistic love story wherein two inexperienced teenagers believe they're in love and both directly and indirectly cause the deaths of friends and family. Juliet may be young and naive, but she's also an opportunist. She's about to be forced into marrying an older man she has no connection with. When Romeo enters her life, she sees a way out. It takes brains and guts to hitch your wagon to a guy you barely know, but Juliet has both and weighs the pros and cons herself, coming to the conclusion that this Montague boy might just be the break she's been looking for. Romeo, for his part, just wants love. His world is not the evil, **conniving** thing it is to his parents; rather, it is something to be shared with people, with a beloved.

16 If love languages existed to any extent in Verona, Romeo would know his by heart. He feels things so intensely; necessarily, he needs someone to counteract that. Juliet is perfect, not only in that she shares his affections, but she's shockingly levelheaded when the time calls for it. All in all, the tragedy of these star-crossed lovers is not their fault; it's the fault of those of us who reduce them to simple-minded adolescents who couldn't possibly know about love.

VOCABULARY

Figurative Language: Mark the phrase *hitch your wagon* in paragraph 15. Read the surrounding sentences to look for clues to its meaning.

Analyze: How does the phrase *hitch your wagon* help explain what Juliet is hoping that Romeo will do for her?

connive
(kə-nīv´) *v.* to plot or collude secretly in bad actions.

ANALYZE RHETORIC

Annotate: Mark words or phrases in paragraph 16 that describe an opposing interpretation of the characters Romeo and Juliet.

Infer: How does the author use this exaggerated, or hyperbolic, language to strengthen her argument?

Assessment Practice

Answer these questions about "More than Reckless Teenagers" before moving on to the next selection.

1. Which **two** sentences from the text support the claim that Juliet is a strong character?

   (A) "Juliet Capulet is known as one of Shakespeare's weaker female characters." (paragraph 2)

   (B) "In her father's eyes, she is but a nuisance he no longer wants to deal with." (paragraph 3)

   (C) "Instead of Juliet coming off as foolish or rash, her decisions make perfect sense." (paragraph 4)

   (D) ". . . Romeo's quick turnaround to Juliet in lieu of Rosaline might be an example of fickleness." (paragraph 7)

   (E) "Juliet may be young and naive, but she's also an opportunist." (paragraph 15)

2. In the text, the writer states that —

   (A) Juliet is passive, while Romeo is active

   (B) Romeo is emotional, while Juliet is practical

   (C) Juliet is fickle, while Romeo is loyal

   (D) Romeo is mature, while Juliet is immature

3. Which statement describes a main cause for Romeo and Juliet's situation?

   (A) Romeo and Juliet are irresponsible teenagers.

   (B) Romeo searches Verona in order to find love.

   (C) Benvolio insists that Romeo marry Rosaline.

   (D) Juliet's father tells her she must marry Paris.

Test-Taking Strategies

Romeo Is a Dirtbag. So Why Is *Romeo and Juliet* Our Favorite Love Story?

Literary Analysis by **Lois Leveen**

The author argues that Shakespeare's *Romeo and Juliet* isn't about romantic love at all.

COMPARE AUTHORS' CLAIMS

Annotate: In paragraph 2, mark one reason the author provides for her claim about *Romeo and Juliet.*

Compare: How does the tone of this claim and the reason stated in paragraph 2 differ from the tone of Caitlin Smith's claim in "More than Reckless Teenagers"?

1 Performances and adaptations of *Romeo and Juliet* can be found throughout the world and in countless languages. They are proof that *Romeo and Juliet* remains the world's favorite love story.

2 But this popularity is hardly a testament to the lasting power of Renaissance high culture. Rather, it reflects how we cling to the idea of a love story that we've collectively projected onto *Romeo and Juliet,* while ignoring the most fascinating, troubling and cautionary aspects of Shakespeare's play. Because if you believe *Romeo and Juliet* is a romantic tale about teens in true love who are kept apart by feuding parents, you've completely missed the point.

Romeo is a creep you wouldn't want dating your 13-year-old daughter.

3 Romeo meets Juliet after donning a disguise and sneaking uninvited into a party thrown by her father. This bit of trickery is necessitated by the **enmity** between their families. But our attachment to the idea of *Romeo and Juliet* as star-crossed lovers obscures the fact that Romeo sneaks in to seduce another member of the Capulet clan,

enmity
(ĕn´mĭ-tē) *n.* deep-seated, shared hatred.

Juliet's cousin Rosaline. Despite Rosaline's vow to remain chaste, Romeo confides to his buddies Benvolio and Mercutio that he even offered to "ope her lap to saint-seducing gold"—a poetic way to say he tried to pay Rosaline to let him deflower her.

Don't forget to **Notice & Note** as you read the text.

4 Upon seeing Juliet, Romeo fickly turns his attention to her. But he remains a **sordid** character. Just one hour after marrying Juliet, Romeo whines to himself that her "beauty hath made me effeminate," and proceeds to prove his manhood by stabbing her other cousin, Tybalt, to death.

sordid
(sôr´dĭd) *adj.* lacking morality.

Juliet's father isn't a cruel villain trying to force his daughter into an unhappily-ever-after marriage.

5 For much of the play, Lord Capulet is the character most in line with our modern ideas about romance. During the not-so-good-old days of the 14th century in which *Romeo and Juliet* is set, marriage was a means for wealthy Italian families to form political and business alliances. Typically, a father decided whom his daughter should marry. But Lord Capulet doesn't want to exercise this option.

COMPARE AUTHORS' CLAIMS

Annotate: Mark phrases or sentences in paragraph 5 that support the author's assertion in this section's header.

Analyze: Is the author successful in refuting the popular idea that Juliet's father is a "cruel villain"? Explain.

6 We learn this when Paris — a nephew to the city's ruling prince and thus exactly the sort of well-connected son-in-law any paterfamilias[1] should want — presses Lord Capulet to give him Juliet in marriage. Lord Capulet responds, "woo her, gentle Paris, get her heart/ My will to her consent is but a part/ An she agree, within her scope of choice / Lies my consent and fair according voice." In other words, he says Juliet should get to decide the not-so-unimportant question of whom she'll marry.

7 So why doesn't he let Juliet marry Romeo? Because she weds Romeo in secret, never giving her father a chance to accept him as a viable suitor. Which he may well have done, given that back when Romeo crashed the Capulet party, Lord Capulet protected him. Tybalt (not yet dead) recognized Romeo and was ready to show the interloper what happens when you don't RSVP properly — until Lord Capulet stopped him. An unfortunate choice for Tybalt's long-term health outcomes, but also an indication that Lord Capulet might have been **amenable** to Romeo courting his daughter.

amenable
(ə-mē´nə-bəl) *adj.* willing to accept someone or something.

Romeo and Juliet only became a teen love-story in the 20th century.

8 Although dialogue in the play reveals that Juliet is a few weeks shy of her 14th birthday, Shakespeare never tells us Romeo's age. In the era in which the play takes place, men usually married later in life, to much younger wives, making it likely that Romeo is at least twice as old as Juliet. So why do we think of Romeo and Juliet as star-crossed teenage lovers?

9 Blame an odd combination of post-WWII social science and the pool at the Beverly Hills Hotel. That's where composer Leonard

[1] **paterfamilias** (pā-tər-fə-mĭl´ē-as): man who is the head of a household.

Bernstein and playwright Arthur Laurents dreamed up a Latino-themed musical version of Shakespeare's love story, resulting in *West Side Story's* Puerto Rican Sharks and their rivals, the Jets. But the 1957 play drew as much on the sociological mindset reflected in *Rebel Without a Cause* as it did on *Romeo and Juliet*, with a libretto[2], lyrics, and even choreography[3] all influenced by then-popular social science regarding "problems" like immigration and juvenile delinquency.

ANALYZE RHETORIC

Annotate: In paragraph 10, mark the allusions the author makes to a film and a cultural movement.

Draw Conclusions: How do these allusions support the author's argument that Shakespeare's play has been misinterpreted over time?

10 A decade later, 1960s youth culture inspired Zeffirelli's Summer of Love-infused film, in which Juliet and Romeo are the ultimate teens rebelling against square parents. By the time Baz Luhrmann took up the mantle (or the doublet) in 1996, the idealization of youth culture — and the romanticizing of the doomed lovers—had become an undeniable part of the story. Luhrmann even gives the lovers one final scene together in the tomb, both awake before they die in each other's arms. If only Shakespeare had thought of that.

Double suicide is not the best basis for a rom-com.

11 It sounds a little obvious when you say it this way: A story in which a 13-year-old girl is seduced by a deceiving cad who turns out to be a killer, then is convinced by a **prevaricating** priest to fake her own death, and finally ends up taking her own life for real — this should not be a global model of a love story.

prevaricate (prĭ-văr´ĭ-kāt) *v.* to behave in an indecisive manner.

12 *Romeo and Juliet* is, after all, one of Shakespeare's tragedies (as compared to *Much Ado About Nothing*, a comedy containing a more successful scheme involving a faked death, resulting in two happily wedded couples). A convention of tragedy is that the characters who die should do so in a way that transforms the ones who live. If this were true for *Romeo and Juliet*, Lord Capulet and Lord Montague would learn their lesson by the end of the play and, moved by their children's deaths, put aside their "ancient grudge."

13 But the tragedy of this play extends beyond the title characters, in a way that suggests that misreading Romeo and Juliet, and thus *Romeo and Juliet*, is irresistible, and perhaps inevitable. Even as they stand over a pile of lifeless bodies in the final scene, Capulet and Montague revert to the same competitive behavior that prolonged their feud. Invited to take Capulet's hand to signal a newfound peace, Montague instead vows to build a gold statue of Juliet, his erstwhile enemy's daughter — a show of his own wealth that incites Capulet to say he'll erect a matching statue of Romeo. Still eager to engage in this weird one-upmanship masquerading as benevolence, they miss the potentially redemptive point of the play.

14 And so, it seems, do we. Helped along by a legacy of 20th-century pop culture, we continue to indulge our persistent desire to romanticize a play that might be Shakespeare's greatest critique of romanticizing something (and someone) that really isn't that romantic after all.

[2] **libretto** (lĭ-brĕt´ō)**:** text of a musical work.

[3] **choreography** (kôr-ē-ŏg´rə-fē)**:** a dance or ballet.

COLLABORATIVE DISCUSSION

Which argument do you think is stronger? Discuss your first thoughts with a partner, using text evidence to support your opinion.

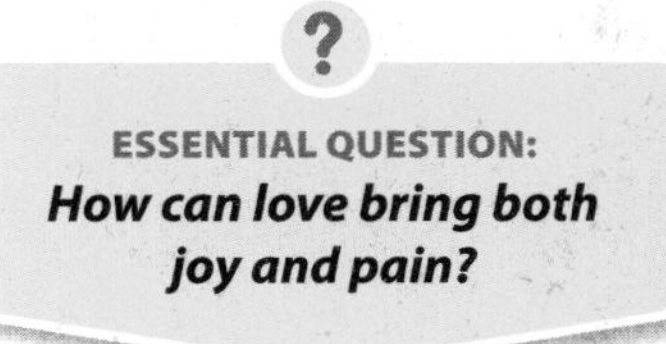
?
ESSENTIAL QUESTION:
How can love bring both joy and pain?

Review your notes and add your thoughts to your Response Log.

Assessment Practice

Answer these questions before moving on to the **Analyze the Texts** section on the following page.

1. According to the author, what is one reason that *Romeo and Juliet* began to be presented as a "teen love-story"?

- (A) Romeo and Juliet's rebellion identifies them as teenagers.
- (B) Societal changes inspired directors to present the play with young characters.
- (C) Shakespeare's dialogue gave details that showed Juliet was a teenager.
- (D) Audiences wanted performances to show the reality of young love in modern times.

2. This question has two parts. First, answer Part A. Then, answer Part B.

Part A

What is the main idea of paragraphs 11–14?

- (A) The events in *Romeo and Juliet* could have been prevented.
- (B) *Much Ado About Nothing* is a romantic play about two couples.
- (C) People want to interpret *Romeo and Juliet* as a love story.
- (D) Capulet and Montague learn from the deaths of their children.

Part B

Select the sentence that best supports the answer to Part A.

- (A) "*Romeo and Juliet* is, after all, one of Shakespeare's tragedies (as compared to *Much Ado About Nothing,* a comedy . . . resulting in two happily wedded couples)." (paragraph 12)
- (B) "A convention of tragedy is that the characters who die should do so in a way that transforms the ones who live." (paragraph 12)
- (C) "But the tragedy of this play extends beyond the title characters . . ." (paragraph 13)
- (D) ". . . we continue to indulge our persistent desire to romanticize a play that might be Shakespeare's greatest critique of romanticizing something that really isn't that romantic. . . ." (paragraph 14)

Ed

Test-Taking Strategies

Analyze the Texts

Support your responses with evidence from the texts.

NOTICE & NOTE
Review what you **noticed and noted** as you read the texts. Your annotations can help you answer these questions.

1. **DRAW CONCLUSIONS** The author of "More than Reckless Teenagers" describes a Royal Shakespeare Company performance of *Romeo and Juliet* that she attended while studying abroad. Why might she have included this **anecdote,** or story, as part of her argument?

2. **ANALYZE** Review paragraph 9 of "More than Reckless Teenagers." How does the description of Juliet's and Romeo's motivations support the author's main claim?

3. **CITE EVIDENCE** In the first sentences of "Romeo Is a Dirtbag," the author states an opposing view to her claim. What explanation does the author provide in paragraph 2 to address the opposing view and state her claim?

4. **INTERPRET** Think about the hyperbolic language the author uses in the title and the boldface headings at the beginning of each section of "Romeo Is a Dirtbag." Does this extreme or absolute language reveal the author's bias? Or, is the strong language calculated to force readers to reexamine their views of *Romeo and Juliet*?

5. **ANALYZE** What interpretation of Lord Capulet does the author argue against in paragraphs 5–7 of "Romeo Is a Dirtbag"? How is her rebuttal, or response, related to her main claim?

6. **CRITIQUE** Do the authors of "More than Reckless Teenagers" and "Romeo Is a Dirtbag" present their claims, reasons, and evidence, and responses to opposing claims effectively? Review your notes from the Get Ready page. In the chart, summarize your notes and indicate which author is more effective in each category.

	More than Reckless Teenagers	**Romeo Is a Dirtbag**
Claim		
Reasons and evidence		
Responses to opposing claims		

7. **EVALUATE** Review the chart of rhetorical devices you filled in on the Get Ready page. Which author uses rhetorical devices more effectively? Explain, using your notes as evidence.

Choices

Here are some other ways to demonstrate your understanding of the ideas in this lesson.

Writing

↳ Sketchnote

A sketchnote is a visual set of notes containing a mix of words and drawings. Create a sketchnote for one of the articles you just read. Include helpful visual cues that will help you better understand and remember the main ideas and examples in the article. Research examples of sketchnotes for guidance and inspiration.

As you write and discuss, be sure to use the Academic Vocabulary words.

- **attribute**
- **commit**
- **expose**
- **initiate**
- **underlie**

Social & Emotional Learning

↳ Relationships

Both articles in this feature discuss Romeo and Juliet's relationship and whether it is appropriate. What exactly constitutes an appropriate or healthy relationship? What makes a relationship unhealthy? Discuss your ideas with a small group. Then, work together to create a set of guidelines for establishing and maintaining healthy relationships.

Speaking & Listening

↳ Argue the Points

The arguments you have read present very different views of *Romeo and Juliet.* Form two teams—one to defend each argument—and hold a debate that covers the following points:

- interpreting the characters Romeo and Juliet. For example, are they "complex characters"? Is Romeo "a creep"?
- who or what is responsible for the play's tragic ending
- Shakespeare's underlying message
- whether later interpretations have supported or twisted Shakespeare's themes

After the debate, write an evaluation of which side's argument was more persuasive.

Expand Your Vocabulary

PRACTICE AND APPLY

Answer the questions to show your understanding of the vocabulary words. Use a dictionary or thesaurus as needed.

1. What are some common characteristics of people who are **revered**? Explain.
2. What kinds of time **constraints** do students have? Provide examples.
3. Why do people become annoyed when someone is being **condescending**?
4. How do people respond when they find that someone is **conniving** to trick them?
5. Why is it important to avoid **enmity** between groups of people?
6. Is describing someone as **sordid** a positive or negative characterization? Explain.
7. How can you show a teacher that you are **amenable** to changing the topic of a research project?
8. Would the explanation of a **prevaricating** person be firm and clear? Explain.

Vocabulary Strategy

Figurative Language

Figurative language is language that communicates meaning beyond the literal meanings of words. Writers use figurative language to make comparisons, to emphasize ideas, and to create a mood. In some cases, words are used in unusual ways to symbolize ideas or concepts. For example, the vocabulary word *connive* in paragraph 15 of "More than Reckless Teenagers" is used to personify the world. The world cannot actually "plot wrongful actions." However, the writer uses *connive* to strengthen the description of Romeo's attitude toward life.

PRACTICE AND APPLY

Explain the meaning of the figurative language marked in each example from the texts. Use a dictionary or thesaurus as necessary.

1. "In the text, Juliet is rational . . . while Romeo throws himself headfirst into his emotions."
2. "All in all, the tragedy of these star-crossed lovers is not their fault."
3. "Leonard Bernstein and playwright Arthur Laurents dreamed up a Latino-themed musical version of Shakespeare's love story."
4. "By the time Baz Luhrmann took up the mantle . . . , the idealization of youth culture . . . had become an undeniable part of the story."

Watch Your Language!

Verb Phrases

A rose by any other name **would smell** as sweet.

Verb phrases are a combination of one or more helping verbs and a main verb. In "More than Reckless Teenagers" and "Romeo Is a Dirtbag," Caitlin Smith and Lois Leveen use verb phrases to emphasize and compare Romeo's and Juliet's feelings and the actions of the people around them.

Other words can interrupt the parts of a verb phrase. In the verb phrase *doesn't want, does* and *want* are interrupted by the adverb *not*. By using the verb phrases *doesn't want* and *has imposed* in this sentence, the author of "More than Reckless Teenagers" reinforces the idea that Juliet's family wants her to marry someone against her will.

> Because Juliet doesn't want to marry the man who has imposed himself on her family, she is no longer a person.

Here the author uses the verb phrase *wouldn't trespass* to support the idea that Romeo would not enter the property of his father's enemy if he were not actually interested in Juliet. In contrast, the author of "Romeo Is a Dirtbag" uses a verb phrase to emphasize that Romeo is reckless and may not care how his actions affect people.

> He certainly wouldn't trespass on her family's grounds just to see her again.

The table shows some common helping verbs. You can use these verbs in their different forms in verb phrases.

> This bit of trickery is necessitated by the enmity between their families.

Common Helping Verbs		
be	can	am
do	have	may
might	shall	should
will	would	could

Interactive Grammar Lesson: Verbals and Verb Phrases

PRACTICE AND APPLY

Review a recent piece of your writing, noting the verb phrases you used. Exchange papers in a peer review where you discuss how to make the verb phrases more effective in showing action or state of being. Then revise the verb phrases you used, and add at least one more.

Compare Arguments

To compare arguments presented in literary analyses, you need to identify similarities and differences between the authors' claims, reasons, and evidence. Review "More than Reckless Teenagers" and "Romeo Is a Dirtbag" and identify each author's central idea and the interpretations, text evidence, and facts used to support it.

In particular, ask yourself whether the authors respond to and refute opposing arguments. Authors of strong arguments will present opposing views and objections to their arguments and address them effectively.

In a small group, record details about claims, reasons, evidence, and responses to opposing claims presented in the texts to help you examine similarities and differences between the two arguments. To prepare, refer to the chart you filled out for Analyze the Texts question 6.

Elements of an Argument and Questions	A "More than Reckless Teenagers"	B "Romeo Is a Dirtbag"
Claim: the author's main point or position. Is the claim specific? Is it reasonable?		
Reasons: logical support and explanation of why an author thinks a claim is valid. Is each reason accurate? Is it valid?		
Evidence: facts, quotations, or anecdotes, used to support reasons. Is there enough relevant evidence to support each reason?		
Responses to Opposing Claims: statements that address and refute opposing points of view. Does the argument anticipate opposing arguments and respond to them effectively?		

Analyze the Texts

Discuss these questions in your group.

1. **SYNTHESIZE** What are the main points of disagreement in the two arguments?
2. **COMPARE** How are the authors' tones, or attitudes, toward the characters of Romeo and Juliet similar and different?
3. **ANALYZE** How do the authors use rhetoric to make their arguments more persuasive? How effective is each author's use of rhetorical devices in advancing their claim?
4. **EVALUATE** Is either argument more persuasive? Why, and what text evidence can you cite to support your impression?

Compare and Present

Now your group can continue reflecting on the claims in these texts and your response to them. Use the similarities and differences that you've noticed in the authors' literary analyses to present a roundtable discussion in which the validity of the other author's argument is the topic.

1. **TURN THE IDEAS AROUND** Decide which group members will be on each side. One group will respond to the opposing views expressed in "More than Reckless Teenagers" using reasons and evidence from "Romeo Is a Dirtbag." The other will respond to the ideas in "Romeo Is A Dirtbag" using reasons and evidence from "More than Reckless Teenagers."
2. **BUILD A RESPONSE** In your group, think about how the author of your literary analysis would respond to the other author's claim, reasons, and evidence. Write two statements summarizing the other author's opposing viewpoints. Then, create responses to refute those statements. Support your rebuttal with reasons and evidence from the literary analysis your group is using.

Viewpoint the Other Author Presents	Arguments That Refute the Opposing View
"Romeo Is a Dirtbag" claims that *Romeo and Juliet* is not a love story.	The "More than Reckless Teenagers" author would say that even if *Romeo and Juliet* isn't a love story, it's important to respect characters' decisions.

3. **HOLD THE ROUNDTABLE DISCUSSION** Gather with your group to hold the discussion. Group members should listen carefully and refute or build on what they are hearing.

Reader's Choice

Continue your exploration of the Essential Question by doing some independent reading on the topic of love and loss. Read the titles and descriptions shown. Then mark the texts that interest you.

ESSENTIAL QUESTION:
How can love bring both joy and pain?

Short Reads

Available on 

These texts are available in your ebook. Choose one to read and rate. Then defend your rating to the class.

Sorry for Your Loss

Short Story by **Lisa Rubenson**

A caller struggles to find the right words in a voicemail to an ex-lover.

Rate It 

The Price of Freedom

Personal Essay by **Noreen Riols**

A former World War II secret agent recalls her passionate love affair with another agent.

Rate It 

The Bass, the River, and Sheila Mant

Short Story by **W.D. Wetherell**

What will a person sacrifice for love? Is the sacrifice always worth it?

Rate It

Sonnet 71

Sonnet by **Pablo Neruda**

The poet explores how we can't love in a vacuum. The world creeps into and affects our relationships.

Rate It 

from Why Love Literally Hurts

Science Writing by **Eric Jaffe**

Older couples who have been together for a long time frequently die within months or even days of each other. What does love have to do with that?

Rate It

Long Reads

Here are three recommended books that connect to this unit topic. For additional options, ask your teacher, school librarian, or peers. Which titles spark your interest?

Romiette and Julio

Novel by **Sharon Draper**

Romiette and Julio quickly fall for each other, but not everyone approves—including their families and a school gang.

The Fault in Our Stars

Novel by **John Green**

Hazel's lung cancer offers her little hope for the future. When she meets Augustus at a cancer support group, she is revived with the feeling of being alive and in love.

Solo

Novel in Verse by **Kwame Alexander**

Blade's life is complicated by a washed-up rock star drug addict for a father and a girl who seems unattainable. A letter containing a family secret could free him.

Extension

Connect & Create

VERSES OF LOVE This unit explores aspects of romantic love—both gaining and losing it. Compose a poem or song from the point of view of a character in one text you have read. Share your work either by performing it for the class or posting a digital version.

MOVIE POSTER Imagine that a movie has been made based on a text you have read. On your own or with a partner, design a poster that will entice audiences to see the film.

- Decide whether your poster will focus on one large image or contain several smaller images.
- Use images and artistic techniques such as color and perspective to highlight emotional aspects. Remember, romantic passion sells tickets and downloads!
- Create an engaging teaser; consider listing the movie's stars and director.

NOTICE & NOTE

- Pick one of the texts and annotate the Notice & Note signposts you find.
- Then, use the **Notice & Note Writing Frames** to help you write about the significance of the signposts.
- Compare your findings with those of other students who read the same text.

Notice & Note Writing Frames

Write a Literary Analysis

Writing Prompt

This unit includes one of the world's great plays—*The Tragedy of Romeo and Juliet*—and explores responses people have had to the play over the centuries.

Using ideas, information, and examples from multiple texts in this unit, write a literary analysis about how the ideas and themes in *Romeo and Juliet* are still relevant today.

Manage your time carefully so that you can

- review the texts in the unit;
- plan your literary analysis;
- write your analysis; and
- revise and edit your analysis.

Be sure to

- include a clear claim;
- develop the claim with reasons and evidence;
- use transitions to clarify and connect ideas; and
- end with a strong conclusion.

Review the Mentor Text

For an example of a well-written literary criticism text you can use as a mentor text, review:

- "More than Reckless Teenagers" (pages 420–423).

Review your notes and annotations about this text. Think about the techniques the author used to support her claim.

Consider Your Sources

Review the list of texts in the unit and choose at least two that you may want to use as sources for your literary analysis.

As you review potential sources, consult the notes you made on your **Response Log** and make additional notes about any ideas that might be useful as you write. Include titles and page numbers to help you provide accurate text evidence and citations when you include support from these texts.

UNIT 4 SOURCES

- [ ] **The Tragedy of Romeo and Juliet**
- [ ] **My Shakespeare** MEDIA
- [ ] **More than Reckless Teenagers**
- [ ] **Romeo Is a Dirtbag**

Analyze the Prompt

Analyze the prompt to make sure you understand the assignment.

1. Mark the phrase in the prompt that identifies the topic of your literary analysis. Restate the topic in your own words.
2. Next, look for words that suggest the purpose and audience of your literary analysis, and write a sentence describing each.

Consider Your Audience

Ask yourself:

- Who will read my analysis?
- What opinions do readers already have about my topic?
- What details will I need to include to provide context for my analysis?

What is my topic? What is my writing task?

What is my purpose?

Who is my audience?

Review the Rubric

Your literary analysis will be scored using a rubric. As you write, focus on the characteristics described in the chart. You will learn more about these characteristics as you work through the lesson.

Purpose, Focus, and Organization	Evidence and Elaboration	Conventions of Standard English
The response includes: • A strongly maintained claim • Effective responses to opposing claims • Use of transitions to connect ideas • Logical progression of ideas • Appropriate style and tone	The response includes: • Effective use of evidence and sources • Effective use of elaboration • Clear and effective expression of ideas • Appropriate vocabulary • Varied sentence structure	The response may include: • Some minor errors in usage but no patterns of errors • Correct punctuation, capitalization, sentence formation, and spelling • Command of basic conventions

1 PLAN YOUR LITERARY ANALYSIS

Develop a Claim

To draft a claim for your literary analysis, use the chart to brainstorm ideas in *Romeo and Juliet* and other texts in the unit that relate to the play's continuing relevance. Then choose one to focus on in your analysis.

Idea	Idea	Idea
My Claim:		

Determine Your Claim

A strong claim should

- clearly state an opinion about the topic
- focus on specific literary elements
- engage readers and motivate them to keep reading
- preview the direction and purpose of the analysis

Develop Reasons and Evidence

You will need to support your position with **reasons** and **evidence.** Use the chart to outline your support. Look for specific text passages that support your claim. Then explain why the evidence is important to your claim.

Help with Planning

Consult **Interactive Writing Lesson: Writing Arguments.**

Reasons for Your Position	Text Evidence	This is important because . . .

Address Opposing Views

Be prepared to address readers who might disagree with your claims about *Romeo and Juliet's* relevance. In the chart, identify an opposing claim that you anticipate, and then explain why your position is more valid.

Opposing Claim
My Response

Organize Ideas

Now decide how to structure your literary analysis. Use the table to help you organize your ideas clearly, with each idea leading logically to the next one.

Put It in Order

Here are some techniques to help you organize ideas:

- Devote a paragraph to each reason that supports your claim.
- Organize paragraphs in a logical sequence.
- Within each paragraph, order evidence to follow the plot sequence.

INTRODUCTION	• Introduce your topic in a way that grabs the reader's attention. • Clearly state your claim.
BODY PARAGRAPHS	• Present reasons and evidence that support your claim. • Use transitions to connect ideas. • Address opposing claims.
CONCLUSION	• Follow logically from the ideas presented. • Restate your claim based on the reasons and evidence you presented. • End with a new insight or final thought.

2 DEVELOP A DRAFT

Now it's time to draft your literary analysis. Examining the work of literary critics can help you apply similar techniques in your own writing.

Drafting Online

Check your assignment list for a writing task from your teacher.

Write an Effective Introduction

EXAMINE THE MENTOR TEXT

Notice how the author of **"More than Reckless Teenagers"** engages readers in her introduction.

Romeo and Juliet are complex characters thrown into a world of feuds largely against their will, looking for their own ways to survive and thrive. Whether their love is exaggerated or not, they cling to each other because they've been able to find complements in each other and chances to live their own lives instead of the lives their parents prescribe. The play isn't a caution against teenagers in love; rather, it's a caution to authority figures who reduce adolescents to children with no free will.

The author introduces the topic of Romeo and Juliet and shares insights about their characters.

She identifies an opposing claim and responds to it.

APPLY TO YOUR DRAFT

Use this chart to practice different approaches to introducing your topic in the opening of your literary analysis. As you write your draft, choose the approach that you think will best capture your readers' attention and make them want to keep reading.

Try These Suggestions:

Experiment with these approaches to appeal to your readers:

- Share a quotation.
- Pose a provocative question.
- Highlight an unusual or interesting insight.
- State a common belief about life.

QUOTATION	
QUESTION	
INSIGHT	
BELIEF	

Use Transitions

EXAMINE THE MENTOR TEXT

Notice how the author of "**More than Reckless Teenagers**" uses transitions to link ideas in her literary analysis.

> Juliet Capulet is known as one of Shakespeare's weaker female characters. She meets a boy, falls in love, and then kills herself. On the surface, she lacks the depth of some of his more revered heroines (Lady Macbeth, Rosalind, Beatrice, etc.). At first glance, Juliet is nothing but a stupid, rash teenage girl. However, she exists within horrifying constraints typical for a woman of her time. No viable options outside of marriage. A controlling father who exercises complete control over her major life decisions. How could she not be looking for a way out? If that way out just so happened to be an attractive, sensitive boy who listened without being condescending? Come on, ladies.

The author uses transitional phrases to introduce common interpretations that she views as superficial.

She uses the transition word "However" to introduce a contrasting point of view.

APPLY TO YOUR DRAFT

Transitions serve as a road map to help readers understand relationships between your claim, reasons, and evidence. Be sure to choose transitions that clearly show the links between ideas. Use the chart to guide you as you write your draft.

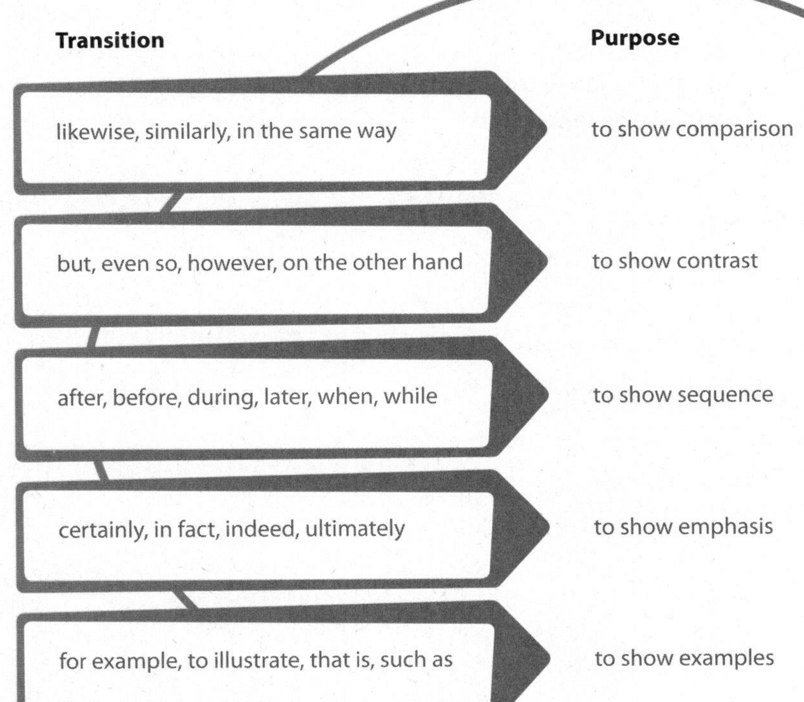

Transition	Purpose
likewise, similarly, in the same way	to show comparison
but, even so, however, on the other hand	to show contrast
after, before, during, later, when, while	to show sequence
certainly, in fact, indeed, ultimately	to show emphasis
for example, to illustrate, that is, such as	to show examples

3 REVISE YOUR LITERARY ANALYSIS

Even experienced writers rework their ideas and language as they write to make sure they are communicating their ideas effectively. Use the guide to help you revise your literary analysis.

Help with Revision

Find a **Peer Review Guide** and **Student Models** online.

REVISION GUIDE		
Ask Yourself	**Prove It**	**Revise It**
Introduction Does my introduction include a clear claim?	**Highlight** the claim.	**Add** a claim, if missing, or revise the existing one so it is clearer.
Organization Are paragraphs organized logically? Have I used transitions to connect ideas?	**Underline** the most important idea in each paragraph. **Put a star** (★) next to transitions.	**Rearrange** paragraphs or sentences. **Add** transitions to clarify and strengthen connections.
Support Do I develop my claim with reasons and evidence?	✔ **Put a check mark** next to each supporting reason or piece of evidence.	**Add** more details, examples, or quotations to strengthen ideas.
Style Have I used a formal style?	✗ **Cross out** any informal words and phrases.	**Replace** informal words and phrases with formal language.
Conclusion Does my conclusion restate my claim?	**Highlight** the part of your conclusion that restates your claim.	**Add or revise** your conclusion, if needed, to include a restatement of your claim.

APPLY TO YOUR DRAFT

Consider the following as you look for opportunities to improve your writing.

- Make sure your claim is clearly and strongly stated.
- Check that your reasons and evidence clearly connect to your claim.
- Correct any errors in grammar and punctuation.

Peer Review in Action

Once you have finished revising your literary analysis, you will exchange papers with a partner in a **peer review.** During a peer review, you will give suggestions to improve your partner's draft.

Read the introduction from a student's draft and examine the comments made by the peer reviewer to see how it's done.

Draft

Romeo and Juliet Through the Ages
By Kahlil Smith, Adams High School

Love impacts people in different ways. Some people find soul mates and live happily ever after. Some people go through life-changing transformations because of love. Shakespeare's play *Romeo and Juliet* captures these experiences, which live on today. In this essay, I will show the lessons we can learn from Romeo and Juliet's love.

Try making your opening more interesting to grab the reader's attention.

You could be more specific here. Also, your claim will sound stronger without the pronoun "I."

Now read the revised introduction below. Notice how the writer has improved the draft by making revisions based on the reviewer's comments.

Revision

The Effects of Love
By Kahlil Smith, Adams High School

"Did my heart love till now?" (1.5.50). Though a fictional character, Shakespeare's Romeo asks this question that countless people in love have asked since. Like Romeo, their experiences with love might affect them in many ways. Some people find a soul mate and live happily ever after. Others experience life-changing transformations. *The Tragedy of Romeo and Juliet* portrays experiences, emotions, and lessons of love that remain relevant today.

Much better! This quotation really gets my attention, and good job remembering to include a citation.

Nice job! Now your claim sounds more academic and makes your focus clear.

APPLY TO YOUR DRAFT

During your peer review, give each other specific suggestions for how you could make your literary analysis more effective. Use your revision guide to help you.

When receiving feedback from your partner, listen attentively and ask questions to make sure you fully understand the revision suggestions.

4 EDIT YOUR LITERARY ANALYSIS

Edit your final draft to check for proper use of standard English conventions and to correct any misspellings or grammatical errors.

Interactive Grammar Lesson: Capital Letters

Watch Your Language!

CHECK CAPITALIZATION

Capitalizing certain nouns is important to provide clarity in your writing. Take the time to check that your literary analysis follows the rules of capitalization.

Here are some examples of correct capitalization.

Capitalization Type	Example
Titles of literary works	*The Tragedy of Romeo and Juliet* "More than Reckless Teenagers"
Names with titles	Professor Susan Holmes Doctor Kim Hong Friar Laurence
Place names	Verona, Italy Stratford-upon-Avon
Proper adjectives	Shakespearean British

Correct Capitalization

Here are some types of words to check for capitalization:

- words in titles except conjunctions, articles, and prepositions shorter than five letters
- names and titles before names
- adjectives formed from proper nouns

APPLY TO YOUR DRAFT

Now apply what you've learned about capitalization to your own work.

1. Read your paper aloud and circle any titles, names, and adjectives formed from proper nouns.
2. Correct capitalization errors.
3. Exchange drafts with a peer and edit each other's work, looking for capitalization errors.

5 PUBLISH YOUR LITERARY ANALYSIS

Share It!

The prompt asks you to write a literary analysis. You may also adapt your analysis to other formats.

Ways to Share

- **Record a podcast** that discusses reasons why *Romeo and Juliet* remains popular today.
- Share ideas from your essay in an **online class discussion forum** about how love can bring both joy and pain.
- Adapt your essay as a **critical review** for a newspaper of literary magazine.

Reflect & Extend

Here are some other ways to show your understanding of the ideas in Unit 4.

Reflect on the
Essential Question

How can love bring both joy and pain?

Has your answer to the question changed after reading the texts in the unit? Discuss your ideas.

You can use these sentence starters to help you reflect on your learning.

- **Reading about . . . made me realize . . .**
- **I was surprised by . . .**
- **I still wonder about . . .**

Project-Based Learning

Create a Comic Strip

You've read about positive and negative aspects of love. Now, create a comic strip that retells one of the unit's stories or reflects on an aspect of love explored in one of the selections.

Here are some questions to ask yourself as you get started.

- What will be the overall point, joke, or message of my comic strip?
- What are my comic strip's characters, setting, and plot?
- How will I combine illustrations and text in my comic strip?

Ed

Media Project

To find help with this task online, access **Create a Comic Strip.**

Writing

Write a Short Story

Write a short story that reveals a theme about love. Develop your plot using descriptive details and other narrative techniques such as dialogue and pacing. Use the graphic organizer to plan your story.

Characters Who are the main characters? What are their traits and motivations?	
Setting Where and when will the story take place?	
Point of View Who will tell the story? How will this point of view impact the story?	
Plot What is the central conflict? How will the conflict be resolved?	
Theme What theme about love will the story reveal?	

Analyze the Image

What freedoms could these people be demanding?

Ed

Get hooked by the unit topic.

Stream to Start Video

UNIT 5

Freedom at All Costs

"If there is no struggle, there is no progress."
— Frederick Douglass

ESSENTIAL QUESTION:
Can each of us find freedom?

Spark Your Learning

Here are some opportunities to think about the topics and themes of **Unit 5: Freedom at All Costs.**

As you read, you can use the **Response Log** (page R5) to track your thinking about the Essential Question.

?

Think About the **Essential Question**

Can each of us find freedom?

One definition of *freedom* is "the power or right to act, speak, or think as one wants without restraint." What other freedoms can you think of? Can all people find some kind of freedom? Write down your thoughts.

Make the Connection

Think about groups, communities, or societies that have fought for freedom. With a partner, discuss examples of people who have fought against limits to their freedoms. What were the successes? In what instances is the struggle ongoing?

Build Academic Vocabulary

You can use these Academic Vocabulary words to write and talk about the topics and themes in this unit. Which of these words do you already feel comfortable using when speaking or writing?

	I can use it!	I understand it.	I'll look it up.
decline			
enable			
impose			
integrate			
reveal			

Prove It!

What freedoms can governments give people—or take away from them? Discuss your ideas using at least one of the Academic Vocabulary words.

Preview the Texts

Look over the images, titles, and descriptions of the texts in the unit. Mark the title of the text that interests you most.

Harrison Bergeron

Short Story by **Kurt Vonnegut Jr.**

It's a brave new world where everyone is equal, and life is better—or is it?

I Have a Dream

Speech by **Martin Luther King Jr.**

In this landmark civil rights speech, Reverend Martin Luther King Jr. shares his vision of an end to racism.

from Interview with John Lewis

Podcast from **National Public Radio**

A civil rights pioneer reflects on his lifelong fight for justice.

from Hidden Figures

History Writing by **Margot Lee Shetterly**

Female African American mathematicians shatter racial and gender barriers to make critical contributions to the Allied effort during World War II.

Booker T. and W.E.B.

Poem by **Dudley Randall**

Two prominent African American thinkers face off in this imaginary debate.

from Reading Lolita in Tehran

Memoir by **Azar Nafisi**

The author describes conditions her female students face under a repressive regime in Iran.

from Persepolis 2: The Story of a Return

Graphic Memoir by **Marjane Satrapi**

In this graphic novel, people resist harsh government repression through small acts of rebellion.

Think Outside the Box

Think about the quotation from Frederick Douglass on the second unit introduction page: "If there is no struggle, there is no progress." Douglass was at the center of a momentous struggle to free enslaved people in the United States. Do you think that overcoming oppression to find freedom always requires struggle or great effort of some kind? Why or why not? Freewrite your thoughts.

Get Ready

Harrison Bergeron

Short Story by **Kurt Vonnegut Jr.**

ESSENTIAL QUESTION:
Can each of us find freedom?

Engage Your Brain

Choose one or more of these activities to start connecting with the short story you're about to read.

We're All the Same

What would the world be like if everyone were the same—average in intelligence, talents, appearance, and strength—and no one was better than anyone else? Would people be happy and satisfied?

With a partner, brainstorm possible advantages and disadvantages of a world where everyone is the same—exactly average.

Advantages	Disadvantages

Television: Good or Bad?

Television has been a controversial technology since it became popular in the 1950s. What do you think of its impact and effects?

1. Make a list of the positive and negative aspects of TV.
2. Compare lists with a classmate.
3. Discuss points of agreement and disagreement.

World Gone Dark

Many science fiction and fantasy works describe a dystopian future, in which things go terribly wrong and life is a dark nightmare. With a partner, discuss dystopian movies, games, or books you are familiar with. What are the bleak conditions described in each work? What has caused them?

Analyze Literary Devices: Irony

Irony is a literary device that writers use to present a contrast between appearance and reality. The chart describes the two types of irony Kurt Vonnegut Jr. uses in the short story "Harrison Bergeron."

Verbal Irony	Situational Irony
• occurs when someone knowingly exaggerates, or overstates, something *Example:* "I'm the best basketball player in the whole country!" • may state the opposite of what is meant *Example:* "All the products we make here help people" (when they in fact hurt people).	• is a contrast between what a reader or character expects and what actually exists or happens *Example:* A post on social media that complains about what a waste of time social media is.

As you read, mark examples of verbal and situational irony you notice.

Focus on Genre
Short Story

- a work of fiction, typically coming from the writer's imagination
- includes the basic elements of fiction—setting, characters, plot, conflict, and theme
- focuses on one main conflict, or one specific event or moment in time
- can be read in one sitting

Analyze Point of View: Satire

Writers use **satire** to ridicule ideas, customs, behaviors, and institutions with the intent of improving them. Satire, which may reflect the author's or the narrator's perspective, can be humorous, abrasive, or angry in tone. Writers of satire often use irony and exaggeration to force readers to see something in a new way.

As you read, use the chart to analyze what the text says and what is being criticized or ridiculed.

What the Text Says	What It Criticizes or Ridicules
"All this equality was due to the 211th, 212th, and 213th Amendments to the Constitution" (paragraph 1)	It ridicules the idea of using government to make everyone the same.

Annotation in Action

Here is an example of notes a student made about a paragraph from "Harrison Bergeron." As you read the story, highlight words and phrases that show how the author uses verbal irony to create an effective satire.

"If I tried to get away with it," said George, "then other people'd get away with it—and pretty soon we'd be right back to the dark ages again, with everybody competing against everybody else. You wouldn't like that, would you?"

Their lives seem so awful! It is ironic for him to imply that the "dark ages" of the past were worse than the present.

Expand Your Vocabulary

Put a check mark next to the vocabulary words that you feel comfortable using when speaking or writing.

vigilance	☐
wince	☐
consternation	☐
cower	☐
synchronize	☐
neutralize	☐

Turn to a partner and talk about the vocabulary words you already know. Then, use as many of the vocabulary words as you can to describe what you think life will be like in 2081.

As you read "Harrison Bergeron," use the definitions in the side column to help you learn the vocabulary words you don't already know.

Background

Kurt Vonnegut Jr. (1922–2007) became one of the most acclaimed and prolific writers in America over the course of his lifetime. Like many writers of his time, Vonnegut's experiences as a soldier in World War II shaped much of his writing. During the war, Vonnegut was captured and held as a prisoner of war in Dresden, Germany, then considered one of the world's most beautiful cities. The city was leveled by a fierce firebombing in an effort to diminish the Nazis' war effort.

The destruction and horrors of the Dresden firebombing became the focus of Vonnegut's most famous novel, *Slaughterhouse-Five,* published in 1969. Vonnegut frequently wrote with dark humor and elements of fantasy and even absurdity, which has given his writing lasting appeal.

Harrison Bergeron

Short Story by **Kurt Vonnegut Jr.**

It's a brave new world where everyone is equal, and life is better—or is it?

NOTICE & NOTE
As you read, use the side margins to make notes about the text.

1 The year was 2081, and everybody was finally equal. They weren't only equal before God and the law. They were equal every which way. Nobody was smarter than anybody else. Nobody was better looking than anybody else. Nobody was stronger or quicker than anybody else. All this equality was due to the 211th, 212th, and 213th Amendments to the Constitution, and to the unceasing **vigilance** of agents of the United States Handicapper General.

vigilance
(vĭj'ə-ləns) *n.* alert attention; watchfulness.

ANALYZE POINT OF VIEW: SATIRE

Annotate: Mark the words and phrases used again and again in paragraph 1.

Analyze: What tone is the author creating through his use of repetition? How does the repetition help establish that this story is a satire?

2 Some things about living still weren't quite right, though. April, for instance, still drove people crazy by not being springtime. And it was in that clammy month that the H-G men took George and Hazel Bergeron's fourteen-year-old son, Harrison, away.

3 It was tragic, all right, but George and Hazel couldn't think about it very hard. Hazel had a perfectly average intelligence, which meant she couldn't think about anything except in short bursts. And George, while his intelligence was way above normal, had a little mental handicap radio in his ear. He was required by law to wear it at all times. It was tuned to a government transmitter. Every twenty

seconds or so, the transmitter would send out some sharp noise to keep people like George from taking unfair advantage of their brains.

4 George and Hazel were watching television. There were tears on Hazel's cheeks, but she'd forgotten for the moment what they were about.

5 On the television screen were ballerinas.

6 A buzzer sounded in George's head. His thoughts fled in panic, like bandits from a burglar alarm.

7 "That was a real pretty dance, that dance they just did," said Hazel.

8 "Huh?" said George.

9 "That dance—it was nice," said Hazel.

10 "Yup," said George. He tried to think a little about the ballerinas. They weren't really very good—no better than anybody else would have been, anyway. They were burdened with sash-weights[1] and bags of birdshot,[2] and their faces were masked, so that no one, seeing a free and graceful gesture or a pretty face, would feel like something the cat drug in. George was toying with the vague notion that maybe dancers shouldn't be handicapped. But he didn't get very far with it before another noise in his ear radio scattered his thoughts.

wince
(wĭns) *v.* to shrink or flinch involuntarily, especially in pain.

11 George **winced**. So did two out of the eight ballerinas.

12 Hazel saw him wince. Having no mental handicap herself, she had to ask George what the latest sound had been.

13 "Sounded like somebody hitting a milk bottle with a ball peen hammer,"[3] said George.

14 "I'd think it would be real interesting, hearing all the different sounds," said Hazel, a little envious. "All the things they think up."

15 "Um," said George.

16 "Only, if I was Handicapper General, you know what I would do?" said Hazel. Hazel, as a matter of fact, bore a strong resemblance to the Handicapper General, a woman named Diana Moon Glampers. "If I was Diana Moon Glampers," said Hazel, "I'd have chimes on Sunday—just chimes. Kind of in honor of religion."

VOCABULARY

Context Clues: To infer the meaning of *doozy* (paragraphs 22 and 23), look for clues in the sentences and paragraphs around it. One clue is how the author uses *doozy* to describe the sound George hears inside his head. From George's reactions to this sound—another clue—readers can infer that *doozy* means "something very extraordinary."

Analyze: Why do you think the author uses such a playful-sounding word as *doozy* to describe the sound?

17 "I could think, if it was just chimes," said George.

18 "Well—maybe make 'em real loud," said Hazel. "I think I'd make a good Handicapper General."

19 "Good as anybody else," said George.

20 "Who knows better'n I do what normal is?" said Hazel.

21 "Right," said George. He began to think glimmeringly about his abnormal son who was now in jail, about Harrison, but a twenty-one-gun salute in his head stopped that.

22 "Boy!" said Hazel, "that was a doozy, wasn't it?"

23 It was such a doozy that George was white and trembling, and tears stood on the rims of his red eyes. Two of the eight ballerinas had collapsed to the studio floor, were holding their temples.

[1] **sash-weights:** lead weights used in some windows to keep them from falling down when raised.

[2] **birdshot:** tiny lead pellets for loading in shotgun shells.

[3] **ball peen hammer:** a hammer that has a head with one flat side and one rounded side.

Don't forget to **Notice & Note** as you read the text.

24 "All of a sudden you look so tired," said Hazel. "Why don't you stretch out on the sofa, so's you can rest your handicap bag on the pillows, honeybunch." She was referring to the forty-seven pounds of birdshot in a canvas bag, which was padlocked around George's neck. "Go on and rest the bag for a little while," she said. "I don't care if you're not equal to me for a while."

25 George weighed the bag with his hands. "I don't mind it," he said. "I don't notice it any more. It's just a part of me."

26 "You been so tired lately—kind of wore out," said Hazel. "If there was just some way we could make a little hole in the bottom of the bag, and just take out a few of them lead balls. Just a few."

27 "Two years in prison and two thousand dollars fine for every ball I took out," said George. "I don't call that a bargain."

28 "If you could just take a few out when you came home from work," said Hazel. "I mean—you don't compete with anybody around here. You just set around."

29 "If I tried to get away with it," said George, "then other people'd get away with it—and pretty soon we'd be right back to the dark ages again, with everybody competing against everybody else. You wouldn't like that, would you?"

30 "I'd hate it," said Hazel.

31 "There you are," said George. "The minute people start cheating on laws, what do you think happens to society?"

32 If Hazel hadn't been able to come up with an answer to this question, George couldn't have supplied one. A siren was going off in his head.

33 "Reckon it'd fall all apart," said Hazel.

34 "What would?" said George blankly.

35 "Society," said Hazel uncertainly. "Wasn't that what you just said?"

36 "Who knows?" said George.

37 The television program was suddenly interrupted for a news bulletin. It wasn't clear at first as to what the bulletin was about, since the announcer, like all announcers, had a serious speech impediment. For about half a minute, and in a state of high excitement, the announcer tried to say, "Ladies and gentlemen—"

38 He finally gave up, handed the bulletin to a ballerina to read.

39 "That's all right—" Hazel said of the announcer, "he tried. That's the big thing. He tried to do the best he could with what God gave him. He should get a nice raise for trying so hard."

40 "Ladies and gentlemen—" said the ballerina, reading the bulletin. She must have been extraordinarily beautiful, because the mask she wore was hideous. And it was easy to see that she was the strongest and most graceful of all the dancers, for her handicap bags were as big as those worn by two-hundred-pound men.

41 And she had to apologize at once for her voice, which was a very unfair voice for a woman to use. Her voice was a warm, luminous, timeless melody. "Excuse me—" she said, and she began again, making her voice absolutely uncompetitive.

NOTICE & NOTE

AGAIN AND AGAIN

When you notice certain events, images, or words recurring over a portion of the story or poem, you've found an **Again and Again** signpost.

Notice & Note: Mark the sounds George hears in his head in paragraphs 21 and 32.

Infer: Why might the author repeatedly bring up the sounds George hears in his head?

ANALYZE POINT OF VIEW: SATIRE

Annotate: Mark the words and phrases in paragraphs 40–42 that show the kinds of qualities and abilities that are considered too competitive in 2081.

Analyze: What comment might the author be making about characteristics our society values?

42 "Harrison Bergeron, age fourteen," she said in a grackle[4] squawk, "has just escaped from jail, where he was held on suspicion of plotting to overthrow the government. He is a genius and an athlete, is under-handicapped, and should be regarded as extremely dangerous."

43 A police photograph of Harrison Bergeron was flashed on the screen—upside down, then sideways, upside down again, then right side up. The picture showed the full length of Harrison against a background calibrated in feet and inches. He was exactly seven feet tall.

44 The rest of Harrison's appearance was Halloween and hardware. Nobody had ever borne heavier handicaps. He had outgrown hindrances faster than the H-G men could think them up. Instead of a little ear radio for a mental handicap, he wore a tremendous pair of earphones, and spectacles with thick wavy lenses. The spectacles were intended to make him not only half blind, but to give him whanging headaches besides.

45 Scrap metal was hung all over him. Ordinarily, there was a certain symmetry, a military neatness to the handicaps issued to strong people, but Harrison looked like a walking junkyard. In the race of life, Harrison carried three hundred pounds.

46 And to offset his good looks, the H-G men required that he wear at all times a red rubber ball for a nose, keep his eyebrows shaved off, and cover his even white teeth with black caps at snaggle-tooth random.

47 "If you see this boy," said the ballerina, "do not—I repeat, do not—try to reason with him."

[4] **grackle:** a blackbird with a harsh, unpleasant call.

48 There was the shriek of a door being torn from its hinges.

49 Screams and barking cries of **consternation** came from the television set. The photograph of Harrison Bergeron on the screen jumped again and again, as though dancing to the tune of an earthquake.

consternation
(kŏn-stər-nā´shən) *n.* a state of great alarm, agitation, or dismay.

50 George Bergeron correctly identified the earthquake, and well he might have—for many was the time his own home had danced to the same crashing tune. "My God—" said George, "that must be Harrison!"

51 The realization was blasted from his mind instantly by the sound of an automobile collision in his head.

52 When George could open his eyes again, the photograph of Harrison was gone. A living, breathing Harrison filled the screen.

53 Clanking, clownish, and huge, Harrison stood in the center of the studio. The knob of the uprooted studio door was still in his hand. Ballerinas, technicians, musicians, and announcers **cowered** on their knees before him, expecting to die.

cower
(kou´ər) *v.* to crouch down in fear.

ANALYZE LITERARY DEVICES: IRONY

Annotate: In paragraphs 54–55, mark what titles Harrison is claiming.

Analyze: Why are Harrison's claims to these titles ironic?

54 "I am the Emperor!" cried Harrison. "Do you hear? I am the Emperor! Everybody must do what I say at once!" He stamped his foot and the studio shook.

55 "Even as I stand here—" he bellowed, "crippled, hobbled, sickened—I am a greater ruler than any man who ever lived! Now watch me become what I *can* become!"

56 Harrison tore the straps of his handicap harness like wet tissue paper, tore straps guaranteed to support five thousand pounds.

57 Harrison's scrap-iron handicaps crashed to the floor.

58 Harrison thrust his thumbs under the bar of the padlock that secured his head harness. The bar snapped like celery. Harrison smashed his headphones and spectacles against the wall.

59 He flung away his rubber-ball nose, revealed a man that would have awed Thor, the god of thunder.

60 "I shall now select my Empress!" he said, looking down on the cowering people. "Let the first woman who dares rise to her feet claim her mate and her throne!"

61 A moment passed, and then a ballerina arose, swaying like a willow.

62 Harrison plucked the mental handicap from her ear, snapped off her physical handicaps with marvellous delicacy. Last of all, he removed her mask.

63 She was blindingly beautiful.

64 "Now—" said Harrison, taking her hand, "shall we show the people the meaning of the word dance? Music!" he commanded.

65 The musicians scrambled back into their chairs, and Harrison stripped them of their handicaps, too. "Play your best," he told them, "and I'll make you barons and dukes and earls."

66 The music began. It was normal at first—cheap, silly, false. But Harrison snatched two musicians from their chairs, waved them like batons as he sang the music as he wanted it played. He slammed them back into their chairs.

synchronize
(sĭng´krə-nīz) *v.* to match the timing of.

neutralize
(no͞o´trə-līz´) *v.* to counteract or cancel the effect of.

67 The music began again and was much improved.

68 Harrison and his Empress merely listened to the music for a while—listened gravely, as though **synchronizing** their heartbeats with it.

69 They shifted their weights to their toes.

70 Harrison placed his big hands on the girl's tiny waist, letting her sense the weightlessness that would soon be hers.

71 And then, in an explosion of joy and grace, into the air they sprang!

72 Not only were the laws of the land abandoned, but the law of gravity and the laws of motion as well.

73 They reeled, whirled, swiveled, flounced, capered, gamboled, and spun.

74 They leaped like deer on the moon.

75 The studio ceiling was thirty feet high, but each leap brought the dancers nearer to it.

76 It became their obvious intention to kiss the ceiling.

77 They kissed it.

78 And then, **neutralizing** gravity with love and pure will, they remained suspended in air inches below the ceiling, and they kissed each other for a long, long time.

79 It was then that Diana Moon Glampers, the Handicapper General, came into the studio with a double-barreled ten-gauge shotgun. She fired twice, and the Emperor and the Empress were dead before they hit the floor.

80 Diana Moon Glampers loaded the gun again. She aimed it at the musicians and told them they had ten seconds to get their handicaps back on.

81 It was then that the Bergerons' television tube burned out.

82 Hazel turned to comment about the blackout to George. But George had gone out into the kitchen for a can of beer.

83 George came back in with the beer, paused while a handicap signal shook him up. And then he sat down again. "You been crying?" he said to Hazel.

84 "Yup," she said.

85 "What about?" he said.

86 "I forget," she said. "Something real sad on television."

87 "What was it?" he said.

88 "It's all kind of mixed up in my mind," said Hazel.

89 "Forget sad things," said George.

90 "I always do," said Hazel.

91 "That's my girl," said George. He winced. There was the sound of a riveting gun[5] in his head.

92 "Gee—I could tell that one was a doozy," said Hazel.

93 "You can say that again," said George.

94 "Gee—" said Hazel, "I could tell that one was a doozy."

ANALYZE LITERARY DEVICES: IRONY

Annotate: In paragraph 86, mark Hazel's reaction to the event she and George witness on television.

Analyze: How does this situational irony reinforce the author's satiric message?

[5] **riveting gun:** a power tool used to hammer rivets (bolts) that are used in construction and manufacturing to fasten metal beams or plates together.

COLLABORATIVE DISCUSSION

Is the story's ending comic, tragic—or something else? Discuss your thoughts with a partner.

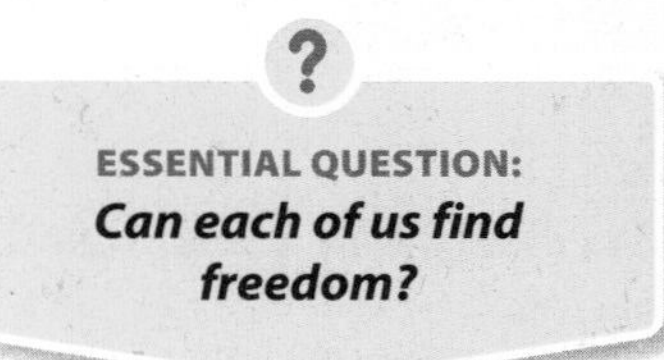

Review your notes and add your thoughts to your Response Log.

Assessment Practice

Answer these questions before moving on to the **Analyze the Text** section on the following page.

1. This question has two parts. First, answer **Part A**. Then, answer **Part B**.

Part A

At one point, Hazel suggests that George lighten the load of his handicap bag. Why does George refuse to do so?

- (A) He thinks his handicap bag should be even heavier.
- (B) He does not want to cause trouble for himself or others.
- (C) He does not want to cause trouble for Hazel or Harrison.
- (D) He enjoys having a handicap bag instead of a handicap radio.

Part B

Select **two** sentences that provide relevant support for the answer in Part A.

- (A) "George was toying with the vague notion that maybe dancers shouldn't be handicapped." (paragraph 10)
- (B) "'I could think, if it was just chimes,' said George." (paragraph 17)
- (C) "'Two years in prison and two thousand dollars fine for every ball I took out,' said George. 'I don't call that a bargain.'" (paragraph 27)
- (D) "'If you could just take a few out when you came home from work,' said Hazel." (paragraph 28)
- (E) "'If I tried to get away with it,' said George, '. . . we'd be right back to the dark ages again, with everybody competing against everybody else. . . .'" (paragraph 29)

2. Why is Harrison handicapped so much by the government?

- (A) He has many above-average skills and qualities.
- (B) He has many below-average skills and qualities.
- (C) He is being punished for breaking the law.
- (D) He is going to be the next Handicapper General.

Test-Taking Strategies

Analyze the Text

Support your responses with evidence from the text.

NOTICE & NOTE

Review what you **noticed and noted** as you read the text. Your annotations can help you answer these questions.

1. **INTERPRET** Reread paragraph 3. How does the idea of keeping people from "taking unfair advantage of their brains" demonstrate situational irony?

2. **COMPARE** Review paragraphs 27–31 and 54–66. Think about how George and Harrison respond to the handicaps imposed upon them. Why are their responses so different? Are there any similarities in their responses? Why or why not?

3. **SUMMARIZE** What is the main **conflict,** or struggle between opposing forces, in the story? How is this conflict resolved?

4. **INFER** Reread the story's ending (paragraphs 83–94). Summarize how Hazel and George react to Harrison's death. Why do they react this way?

5. **EVALUATE** Think about the impact television has in the story. Is television partly responsible for the society depicted in the story? Why or why not? Support your answer with text evidence.

6. **ANALYZE** What is the author's point of view toward society in this story? Think about elements the author points out **Again and Again.** How do these recurring events, images, and words support this point of view? Use the graphic organizer to complete your response.

Author's Point of View	Recurring Events, Images, and Words	How They Support the Author's Point of View

7. **CRITIQUE** A writer of satire aims to ridicule or criticize society in the hope of improving it. Review the examples of satire you listed on the Get Ready page. Does the story achieve the aims of satire? Could the story's insights lead to improvements in society today? Explain.

Choices

Here are some other ways to demonstrate your understanding of the ideas in this lesson.

As you write and discuss, be sure to use the **Academic Vocabulary** words.

- decline
- enable
- impose
- integrate
- reveal

Writing

Switching Perspectives

"Harrison Bergeron" is written from the third-person point of view. Rewrite or continue the story from the first-person point of view. From the perspective of one of the characters, describe what it is like to wear the handicaps described in the story.

Media

Call to Resist

You are part of an underground movement that is resisting the new Constitutional Amendments and the Handicapper General agents in the story. Create a message that describes dangers posed by the government and rallies citizens to revolt against the regime's control. Include

- a summary of threats the controls pose to citizens' physical, emotional, and intellectual health
- rhetorical appeals to logic, emotion, and/or people's ethical sense
- your group's resistance plan
- images that drive home the threats posed by the government

Deliver your message as a printed brochure, online, or using a new delivery platform people are using in 2081.

Speaking & Listening

Small-Group Discussion

"Harrison Bergeron" satirizes extreme and absurd methods used to achieve equality. Yet many groups and societies share the goal of equality under the law. Are they defining the term differently from the government's definition in the story?

Organize a group to discuss equality and how it can be achieved.

- Agree on a definition of equality the group will use.
- Cite examples of when individuals and groups have pushed governments toward greater equality.
- Acknowledge other perspectives or opinions in the group.
- Build on each other's ideas.
- Summarize your conclusions.

Expand Your Vocabulary

PRACTICE AND APPLY

Answer the questions to show your understanding of the vocabulary words. Use a dictionary or thesaurus as needed.

1. A cat keeping a close eye out for a mouse or other prey to appear is showing **vigilance.** Why?
2. If I stub my toe on that rock, I know I will **wince.** Why?
3. General **consternation** arose among the shoppers when the power went out in the store. Why?
4. When a hawk swoops down, the animal it is trying to catch is likely to **cower.** Why?
5. If the dance team does not **synchronize** all their gestures and steps, they are going to lose the dance contest. Why?
6. Our football team tried a trick play on offense, but the other team was able to **neutralize** it with a great defensive play. Why?

Vocabulary Strategy
↳ Context Clues

Interactive Vocabulary Lesson: Using Context Clues

To determine the meaning of a word or phrase you do not know, remember to look for **context clues**—punctuation marks, words, sentences, and paragraphs that can give you clues about the word's meaning. Study this example from "Harrison Bergeron" to learn more about using context clues:

Unfamiliar Word	Context	Context Clues
transmitter	And George, while his intelligence was way above normal, had a little mental handicap radio in his ear. He was required by law to wear it at all times. It was tuned to a government transmitter. Every twenty seconds or so, the transmitter would send out some sharp noise to keep people like George from taking unfair advantage of their brains. (paragraph 3)	For the radio in George's ear to work, it needs to receive a signal. The transmitter sends out a sharp noise—a signal—to George's radio. From these clues, a transmitter is probably some sort of device that sends out signals that radios can pick up, or receive.

PRACTICE AND APPLY

With a partner, locate these words and phrases in the story: ***set around*** (paragraph 28), ***speech impediment*** (paragraph 37), ***hideous*** (paragraph 40), ***calibrated*** (paragraph 43), and ***hindrances*** (paragraph 44). Use context clues to determine their meanings. Then, use each word in a complete sentence. Check your definitions in a dictionary.

Watch Your Language!

Participial Phrases

A **participle** is a verb form that acts as an adjective. It modifies, or describes, a noun or a pronoun. Most participles end in *-ing, -ed,* or *-en.*

A **participial phrase** is a group of words made up of a participle plus its modifiers and complements. To avoid confusing the reader, a participial phrase should be placed as close as possible to the word it modifies.

Writers use participial phrases to enrich their sentences with imaginative details. Study the example below from the story:

> A moment passed, and then a ballerina arose, swaying like a willow.

Notice how the participial phrase "swaying like a willow" provides a vivid image of the ballerina's gracefulness.

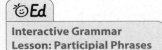

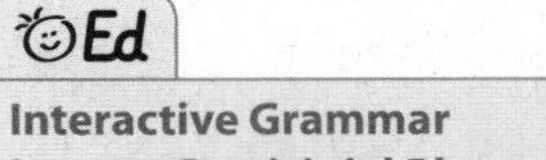
Interactive Grammar Lesson: Participial Phrases

Participial phrases are punctuated in different ways depending on their location in the sentence.

If the participial phrase is at the end of the sentence, a comma comes before it.	If the participial phrase is at the beginning of the sentence, a comma comes after it.	If the participial phrase is in the middle of the sentence, it is usually set off by two commas.
"Ladies and gentlemen—" said the ballerina, reading the bulletin. (paragraph 40)	Standing in line, they waited for the doors to open.	And then, neutralizing gravity with love and pure will, they remained suspended in air. . . . (paragraph 78)

PRACTICE AND APPLY

With a partner, review "Harrison Bergeron" and identify additional examples of participial phrases. Explain what nouns or pronouns they modify. Then, discuss how these participial phrases add to readers' understanding and enjoyment.

On your own, write two paragraphs about a future society in which everyone is forced to be average. Use participial phrases in both paragraphs and vary where they are used—at the beginning, the middle, and the end of a sentence. Make sure you punctuate correctly.

Get Ready

I Have a Dream

Speech by Martin Luther King Jr.

ESSENTIAL QUESTION:
Can each of us find freedom?

Engage Your Brain

Choose one or both of these activities to start connecting with the speech you are about to read.

Outsider

Have you ever been treated differently? How did it make you feel? Write a paragraph describing what happened and how you reacted.

You Have a Dream

Do *you* have a dream for the United States? Sketch or make a list of changes that would move the country toward your vision of a "more perfect union."

Analyze Arguments

One way to analyze Martin Luther King Jr.'s speech is to look at it as an argument. As you read, think about how each part works, noting the evidence and appeals King uses to persuade his audience.

Part of an Argument	Example from Speech
The central idea of an argument is the **claim.**	. . . the Negro still is not free; one hundred years later, the life of the Negro is still sadly crippled by the manacles of segregation and the chains of discrimination . . .
The author must support the claim with **evidence** and examples.	We can never be satisfied as long as the Negro is the victim of the unspeakable horrors of police brutality . . .
To persuade an audience of a claim, the author may make an emotional **appeal** to the audience by connecting with their experiences.	Some of you have come fresh from narrow jail cells. Some of you have come from areas where your quest for freedom left you battered by the storms of persecution and staggered by the winds of police brutality.
In the **conclusion**, the author sums up the claim with a strong statement about what the audience should believe.	I have a dream that my four little children will one day live in a nation where they will not be judged by the color of their skin, but by the content of their character.

Focus on Genre

Speech

- directly addresses and connects with audiences
- uses rhetorical devices to achieve specific purpose
- contains a clear message, stated near the beginning
- ends memorably

Analyze Rhetorical Devices

Writers use **rhetorical devices** to achieve their purposes. As you read, look for examples of these devices King uses.

Rhetorical Devices
Repetition repeats the same word(s) for emphasis.
Parallelism uses similar grammatical constructions to express related or equally important ideas. It often creates a rhythm.
An **extended metaphor** is a type of figurative language that makes a lengthy comparison between two unlike things to emphasize an important idea.

Annotation in Action

Here is an example of notes a student made about some of the first lines of "I Have a Dream." As you read the speech, highlight rhetorical devices Dr. King uses.

This momentous decree came as a great beacon light of hope to millions of Negro slaves who had been seared in the flames of withering injustice.

amazing metaphors—light and fire—in one sentence

Expand Your Vocabulary

Put a check mark next to the vocabulary words that you feel comfortable using when speaking or writing.

default	☐
desolate	☐
degenerate	☐
inextricably	☐
redemptive	☐

Turn to a partner and talk about the vocabulary words you recognize. Then, write a paragraph describing what you already know of "I Have a Dream" and Dr. King's goals using as many of the vocabulary words as you can.

As you read the speech, use the definitions in the side column to help you learn the vocabulary words you don't already know.

Background

On August 28, 1963, thousands of Americans marched on Washington, D.C., to urge Congress to pass a civil rights bill. Martin Luther King Jr. delivered his "I Have a Dream" speech on the steps of the Lincoln Memorial before more than 250,000 people. This momentous event was called the March on Washington. **Martin Luther King Jr.** (1929–1968) came from a family of preachers. As pastor of a Baptist Church in Alabama, King honed his rhetorical skills. Preaching a philosophy of nonviolence, his leadership helped bring about the passage of the Civil Rights Act of 1964. Awarded the Nobel Peace Prize, King continued his work for justice and equality until he was assassinated in 1968.

I Have a Dream

Speech by **Martin Luther King Jr.**

In this landmark civil rights speech, Reverend Martin Luther King Jr. shares his vision of an end to racism.

NOTICE & NOTE
As you read, use the side margins to make notes about the text.

1 I am happy to join with you today in what will go down in history as the greatest demonstration for freedom in the history of our nation.

2 Five score[1] years ago, a great American, in whose symbolic shadow we stand today, signed the Emancipation Proclamation.[2] This momentous decree came as a great beacon light of hope to millions of Negro slaves who had been seared in the flames of withering injustice. It came as a joyous daybreak to end the long night of their captivity.

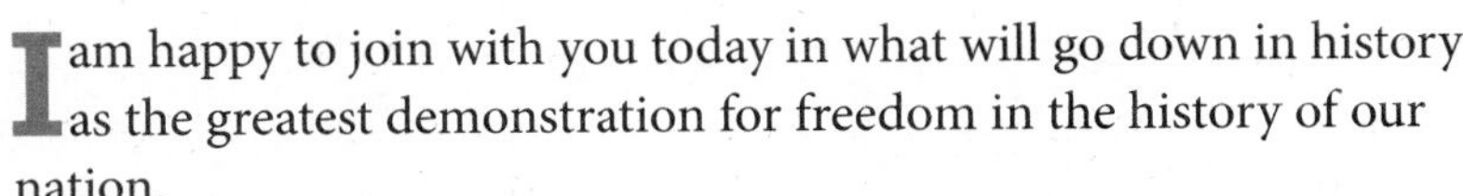

3 But one hundred years later, the Negro still is not free; one hundred years later, the life of the Negro is still sadly crippled by the manacles of segregation and the chains of discrimination; one hundred years later, the Negro lives on a lonely island of poverty in

ANALYZE ARGUMENTS

Annotate: Underline King's claim. Mark details and evidence in paragraphs 3–5 that support his claim.

Analyze: What does King believe should happen?

[1] **five score:** 100; score means "twenty." (This phrasing recalls the beginning of Abraham Lincoln's Gettysburg Address: "Four score and seven years ago . . .")

[2] **Emancipation Proclamation:** a document signed by President Lincoln in 1863, during the Civil War, that freed enslaved people who lived in states still at war with the Union.

Close Read Screencast

Listen to a modeled close read of this text.

the midst of a vast ocean of material prosperity; one hundred years later, the Negro is still languishing in the corners of American society and finds himself in exile in his own land.

4 So we've come here today to dramatize a shameful condition. In a sense we've come to our nation's capital to cash a check. When the architects of our republic wrote the magnificent words of the Constitution and the Declaration of Independence, they were signing a promissory note[3] to which every American was to fall heir. This note was the promise that all men, yes, black men as well as white men, would be guaranteed the unalienable rights of life, liberty, and the pursuit of happiness.

default
(dĭ-fôlt´) *v.* to fail to keep a promise to repay a loan.

5 It is obvious today that America has **defaulted** on this promissory note insofar as her citizens of color are concerned. Instead of honoring this sacred obligation, America has given the Negro people a bad check, a check which has come back marked "insufficient funds." But we refuse to believe that the bank of justice is bankrupt. We refuse to believe that there are insufficient funds in the great vaults of opportunity of this nation. And so we've come to cash this check, a check that will give us upon demand the riches of freedom and the security of justice.

desolate
(dĕs´ə-lĭt) *adj.* unhappy; lonely.

6 We have also come to this hallowed spot to remind America of the fierce urgency of now. This is no time to engage in the luxury of cooling off or to take the tranquilizing drug of gradualism. Now is the time to make real the promises of democracy; now is the time to rise from the dark and **desolate** valley of segregation to the sunlit path of racial justice; now is the time to lift our nation from the quicksands of racial injustice to the solid rock of brotherhood; now is the time to make justice a reality for all of God's children. It would be fatal for the nation to overlook the urgency of the moment. This sweltering summer of the Negro's legitimate discontent will not pass until there is an invigorating autumn of freedom and equality.

NOTICE & NOTE
EXTREME OR ABSOLUTE LANGUAGE

When you notice language that leaves no doubt about the author's views, you've found an **Extreme or Absolute Language** signpost.

Notice & Note: Mark examples of extreme or absolute language in paragraph 7.

Infer: Why did Dr. King use this language?

7 Nineteen sixty-three is not an end, but a beginning. And those who hope that the Negro needed to blow off steam and will now be content will have a rude awakening if the nation returns to business as usual. There will be neither rest nor tranquility in America until the Negro is granted his citizenship rights. The whirlwinds of revolt will continue to shake the foundations of our nation until the bright day of justice emerges.

degenerate
(dĭ-jĕn´ər-āt) *v.* to decline morally.

8 But there is something that I must say to my people, who stand on the worn threshold which leads into the palace of justice. In the process of gaining our rightful place, we must not be guilty of wrongful deeds. Let us not seek to satisfy our thirst for freedom by drinking from the cup of bitterness and hatred. We must forever conduct our struggle on the high plain of dignity and discipline. We must not allow our creative protests to **degenerate** into physical violence. Again and again we must rise to the majestic heights of meeting physical force with soul force. The marvelous new militancy,

[3] **promissory note:** a written promise to repay a loan.

which has engulfed the Negro community, must not lead us to a distrust of all white people. For many of our white brothers, as evidenced by their presence here today, have come to realize that their destiny is tied up with our destiny. And they have come to realize that their freedom is **inextricably** bound to our freedom. We cannot walk alone. And as we walk, we must make the pledge that we shall always march ahead. We cannot turn back.

9 There are those who are asking the devotees of civil rights, "When will you be satisfied?" We can never be satisfied as long as the Negro is the victim of the unspeakable horrors of police brutality; we can never be satisfied as long as our bodies, heavy with the fatigue of travel, cannot gain lodging in the motels of the highways and the hotels of the cities; we cannot be satisfied as long as the Negro's basic mobility is from a smaller ghetto to a larger one; we can never be satisfied as long as our children are stripped of their selfhood and robbed of their dignity by signs stating For Whites Only; we cannot be satisfied as long as the Negro in Mississippi cannot vote and a Negro in New York believes he has nothing for which to vote. No! No, we are not satisfied, and we will not be satisfied until "justice rolls down like waters and righteousness like a mighty stream."

Don't forget to **Notice & Note** as you read the text.

inextricably (ĭn-ĕk´strĭ-kə-blē) *adv.* in a way impossible to untangle.

VOCABULARY

Antonyms: To determine the antonym for *righteousness*, look the word up in an online or print thesaurus.

Analyze: How does the antonym help you understand the significance of "righteousness" in King's message?

10 I am not unmindful that some of you have come here out of great trials and tribulations. Some of you have come fresh from narrow jail cells. Some of you have come from areas where your quest for freedom left you battered by the storms of persecution and staggered by the winds of police brutality. You have been the veterans of creative suffering. Continue to work with the faith that unearned suffering is **redemptive**. Go back to Mississippi. Go back to Alabama. Go back to South Carolina. Go back to Georgia. Go back to Louisiana. Go back to the slums and ghettos of our Northern cities, knowing that somehow this situation can and will be changed. Let us not wallow in the valley of despair.

redemptive
(rĭ-dĕmp´tĭv) *adj.* causing freedom or salvation.

11 I say to you today, my friends, even though we face the difficulties of today and tomorrow, I still have a dream. It is a dream deeply rooted in the American dream. I have a dream that one day this nation will rise up and live out the true meaning of its creed, "We hold these truths to be self-evident; that all men are created equal." I have a dream that one day on the red hills of Georgia, sons of former slaves and the sons of former slave owners will be able to sit down together at the table of brotherhood. I have a dream that one day even the state of Mississippi, a state sweltering with the heat of injustice, sweltering with the heat of oppression, will be transformed into an oasis of freedom and justice. I have a dream that my four little children will one day live in a nation where they will not be judged by the color of their skin, but by the content of their character.

ANALYZE RHETORICAL DEVICES

Annotate: Mark the phrase that is repeated throughout paragraphs 11–15.

Connect: How does the meaning of this phrase change as King repeats it?

12 I have a dream today!

13 I have a dream that one day down in Alabama—with its vicious racists, with its Governor having his lips dripping with the words of interposition and nullification[4]— one day right there in Alabama, little black boys and black girls will be able to join hands with little white boys and white girls as sisters and brothers.

14 I have a dream today!

15 I have a dream that one day every valley shall be exalted, and every hill and mountain shall be made low. The rough places will be plain and the crooked places will be made straight, "and the glory of the Lord shall be revealed, and all flesh shall see it together."

NOTICE & NOTE
QUOTED WORDS

When you notice the author has quoted from a well-known text, you've found a **Quoted Words** signpost.

Notice & Note: Mark the quotation Dr. King uses in paragraph 15.

Analyze: What is he quoting from? Why is this effective?

16 This is our hope. This is the faith that I go back to the South with. With this faith we will be able to hew out of the mountain of despair a stone of hope. With this faith we will be able to transform the jangling discords of our nation into a beautiful symphony of brotherhood. With this faith we will be able to work together, to pray together, to struggle together, to go to jail together, to stand up for freedom together, knowing that we will be free one day. And this will be the day. This will be the day when all of God's children will be able to sing

[4] **Governor . . . nullification:** Rejecting a federal order to desegregate the University of Alabama, Governor George Wallace claimed that the principle of nullification (a state's alleged right to refuse a federal law) allowed him to resist federal "interposition," or interference, in state affairs.

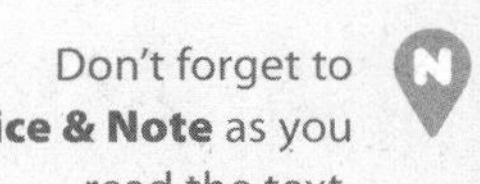

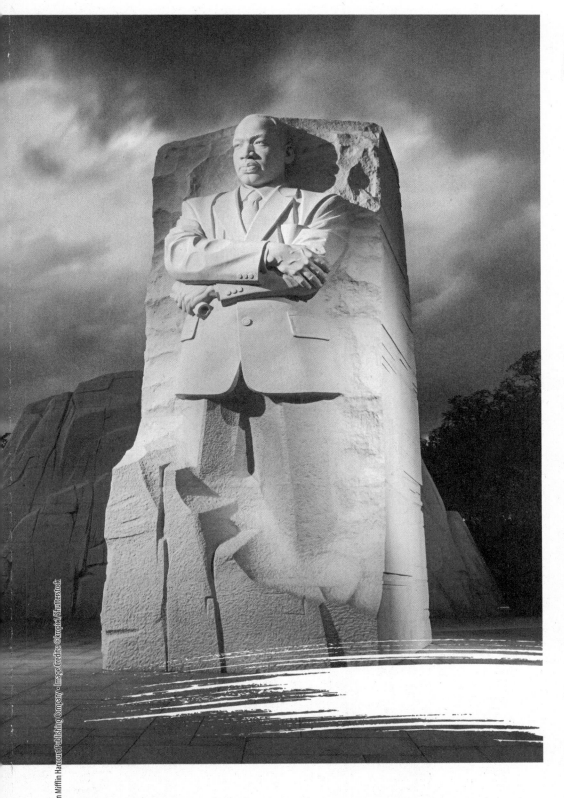

with new meaning, "My country 'tis of thee, sweet land of liberty, of thee I sing. Land where my fathers died, land of the pilgrims' pride, from every mountainside, let freedom ring." And if America is to be a great nation, this must become true.

ANALYZE RHETORICAL DEVICES

Annotate: Mark the extended metaphor King uses in paragraphs 16–17, including details that develop it.

Interpret: Explain Dr. King's vision in your own words.

17 So let freedom ring from the prodigious hilltops of New Hampshire; let freedom ring from the mighty mountains of New York; let freedom ring from the heightening Alleghenies of Pennsylvania; let freedom ring from the snowcapped Rockies of Colorado; let freedom ring from the curvaceous slopes of California. But not only that. Let freedom ring from Stone Mountain of Georgia; let freedom ring from Lookout Mountain of Tennessee; let freedom ring from every hill and molehill of Mississippi. "From every mountainside, let freedom ring."

18 And when this happens, and when we allow freedom to ring, when we let it ring from every village and every hamlet, from every state and every city, we will be able to speed up that day when all of God's children—black men and white men, Jews and Gentiles, Protestants and Catholics—will be able to join hands and sing in the words of the old Negro spiritual, "Free at last. Free at last. Thank God Almighty, we are free at last."

COLLABORATIVE DISCUSSION

Which parts of the speech did you find the most inspiring? With a partner, discuss how Dr. King uses words and phrases to support his argument. Cite specific text evidence from the speech in your discussion.

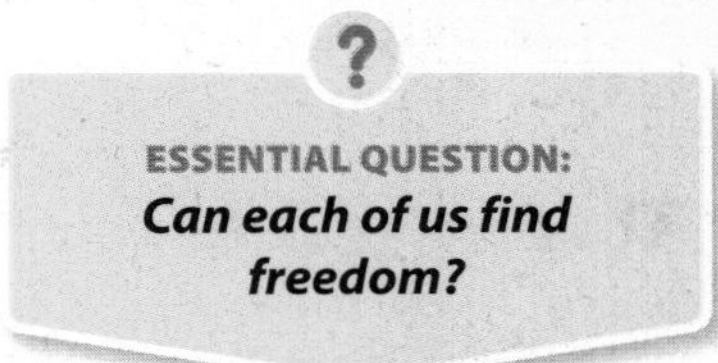

Review your notes and add your thoughts to your Response Log.

Assessment Practice

Answer these questions before moving on to the **Analyze the Text** section on the following page.

1. This question has two parts. First answer **Part A**. Then, answer **Part B**.

Part A

Which sentence states the purpose of Martin Luther King Jr.'s speech?

(A) to celebrate the end of slavery and oppression of African Americans

(B) to describe his dreams and interpret them for his audience

(C) to give a lecture about the Emancipation Proclamation

(D) to urge all people to peacefully work together for racial equality

Part B

Select the sentence that best supports the purpose in Part A.

(A) ". . . the Negro is still languishing in the corners of American society and finds himself in exile in his own land." (paragraph 3)

(B) "There will be neither rest nor tranquility in America until the Negro is granted his citizenship rights." (paragraph 7)

(C) "Let us not seek to satisfy our thirst for freedom by drinking from the cup of bitterness and hatred." (paragraph 8)

(D) "I say to you today . . . even though we face the difficulties of today and tomorrow, I still have a dream." (paragraph 11)

2. How does the metaphor of the check in paragraph 5 contribute to the development of King's ideas?

(A) by giving an example of poverty in King's community

(B) by persuading demonstrators that they should avoid banks

(C) by explaining that America must keep its promise of freedom for all people

(D) by asking the government to provide more financial assistance for African Americans

Ed

Test-Taking Strategies

Analyze the Text

Support your responses with evidence from the text.

1 **IDENTIFY** The central point of an argument is the **claim**. What is King's claim in this speech? What evidence does he cite to support his claim?

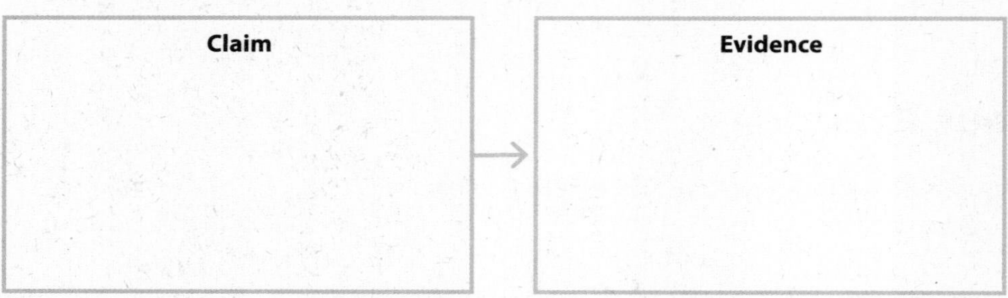

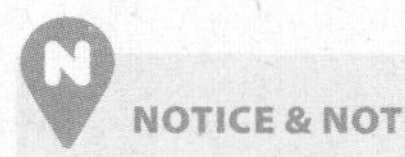

Review what you **noticed and noted** as you read the text. Your annotations can help you answer these questions.

2 **ANALYZE** How does King structure, or organize, his speech? Explain how each section integrates his ideas and advances his argument.

3 **ANALYZE** Find examples of parallelism in paragraph 6. What effect does the parallel structure create? What point is King emphasizing?

4 **ASSESS** Review the examples of repetition you noted in the chart on the Get Ready page. Explain why these words or phrases are important and how they advance King's argument.

5 **CRITIQUE** Explain how King uses **Extreme or Absolute Language** to persuade his audience. Give at least two examples. Do you think he uses this technique effectively? Explain.

6 **INTERPRET** An **allusion** is an indirect reference to something that the audience is expected to know. In his speech, King makes more than one allusion to the Declaration of Independence. Identify the allusions and explain how they advance King's argument.

7 **EVALUATE** King uses an extended metaphor to compare a familiar object—a bad check—to an abstract idea. How does King develop this figurative language? What does he believe was promised to African Americans? How has America given to African Americans "a blank check"?

8 **ANALYZE** King uses **Quoted Words** from several sources. Find at least two quotations besides the one in paragraph 15. Identify the source of each quotation and explain how it strengthens King's argument.

Choices

Here are some other ways to demonstrate your understanding of the ideas in this lesson.

Writing

↳ Current Events Blog Posts

In paragraph 9, Dr. King says that people ask civil rights activists, "When will you be satisfied?" Reread that paragraph and write a series of blog posts about how King's main idea in that paragraph applies today.

Check off each task as you complete it:

- Reread the paragraph
- Determine the main idea
- Reflect on how King's question could be answered today
- Cite real-life examples
- Build blog posts
- Cite sources you use

As you write and discuss, be sure to use the Academic Vocabulary words.

decline
enable
impose
integrate
reveal

Media

↳ Compare Accounts

It's one thing to read a speech, but it's even better to listen to it or be an audience member. Find a video or audio version of King's speech. Make a comparison chart in which you explain what you noticed about the audio or video version, and how it is different from what you noticed in the text.

Social & Emotional Learning

↳ Perspective Poll

Consider your reaction to "I Have a Dream." Now consider how others with different backgrounds and points of view have reacted to it. What do King's words mean to them? Create a poll to gauge different people's reactions. Try to get a variety of perspectives from different genders, ethnicities, and ages. Poll teachers, coaches, or family members as well! Draw conclusions about the different responses you get, and share them with classmates.

Expand Your Vocabulary

PRACTICE AND APPLY

Answer the following questions in complete sentences, incorporating the vocabulary words and their meanings.

default	desolate	degenerate	inextricably	redemptive

1. Look back at paragraph 5. Why does King say that America has **defaulted** on its promise?

2. Look back at paragraph 6. In what ways is segregation **desolate**?

3. Look back at paragraph 8. How is physical violence a good example of how protests might **degenerate**?

4. Look back at paragraph 8. How is the freedom of all people **inextricably** bound together?

5. Look back at paragraph 10. How and why does King use the word **redemptive** to link the concepts of freedom and religious faith?

Vocabulary Strategy

↳ Antonyms

Antonyms are words with opposite meanings. Recognizing antonyms can help you understand new words. For example, *cheerful* is an antonym for the vocabulary word *desolate*. Use an online or print thesaurus to find antonyms.

Interactive Vocabulary Lesson: Synonyms and Antonyms

PRACTICE AND APPLY

Use a thesaurus to find an antonym for each of the remaining vocabulary words. Then, write sentences using each antonym.

1. **default**

2. **degenerate**

3. **inextricably**

4. **redemptive**

Watch Your Language!

Repetition and Parallelism

Martin Luther King Jr. uses the techniques of repetition and parallelism to express his ideas. These patterns emphasize his important ideas and make his speech flow rhythmically.

Repetition refers to repeated words or phrases. Sometimes phrases are repeated throughout a sentence. Other times they are repeated throughout a paragraph, or between paragraphs. Writers use repetition to show how ideas are linked.

> We can never be satisfied as long as the Negro is the victim of the unspeakable horrors of police brutality; we can never be satisfied as long as our bodies, heavy with the fatigue of travel, cannot gain lodging in the motels of the highways and the hotels of the cities . . .

Here, Dr. King gives many reasons why "we can never be satisfied." He links his reasons together by repeating the same phrase again and again.

Parallelism refers to a similar sentence or phrase structure that is repeated within a sentence or paragraph. Speakers often use parallelism to highlight similarities or differences.

> I have a dream that one day every valley shall be exalted, and every hill and mountain shall be made low. The rough places will be plain and the crooked places will be made straight . . .

Here Dr. King uses parallelism to highlight the contrasts, or differences in his imagery.

PRACTICE AND APPLY

Review a piece of writing you recently submitted for class. Find two or three places where you can revise your wording to use the techniques of repetition or parallelism. Write your revised response below.

Get Ready

MEDIA

ESSENTIAL QUESTION: *Can each of us find freedom?*

from
Interview with John Lewis

Podcast from **National Public Radio**

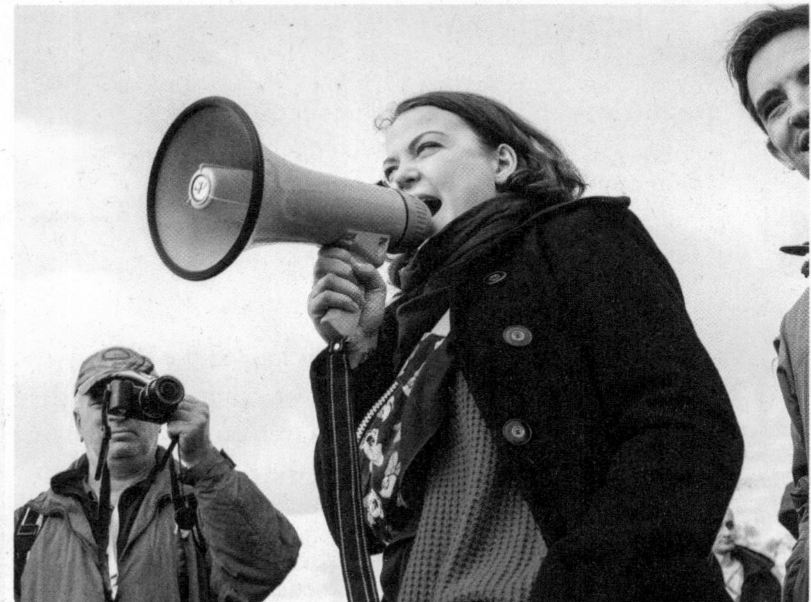

Engage Your Brain

You're about to listen to a podcast about a group of people who stood up for themselves and others in order to enact change. Think of a time you had to stand up for yourself. What fears or obstacles did you have to overcome in order to do so? Share your experience with a partner.

Background

John Lewis (1940–2020) was one of the "Big Six" civil rights activists of the 1960s Civil Rights Movement, as well as a U.S. Representative in Congress. Lewis was born in Alabama in 1940, during a time when segregation was in full force. As a teen, he was inspired by Dr. Martin Luther King Jr. and Rosa Parks. He began college in 1957 and participated in civil rights marches, helping to plan the March on Washington in 1963. In 1965, he led the march from Selma, Alabama, with Hosea Williams and was beaten so badly by state troopers that his skull was fractured. His actions helped persuade President Johnson to enact the 1965 Voting Rights Act. The Act was intended to overcome legal barriers at the state and local levels that prevented African Americans from exercising their right to vote. Lewis's life in politics was dedicated to voting rights, fighting poverty, and supporting public education. He created a graphic novel series to teach young people about the marches for civil rights.

Analyze a Podcast

The purpose of a digital media product or text is usually to inform, entertain, persuade, or express the feelings or thoughts of those who created it. Podcasts are digital audio files available on the Internet. They can be downloaded to devices, and listeners can subscribe to series of podcasts. Podcasts are especially suited for sharing personal experiences, often in the form of audio interviews.

In a podcast, sound elements and voice narration help convey information, make transitions between segments, and engage listeners' interest.

Focus on Genre
Podcast Interview

- centered on a conversation between a host or interviewer and one or more guests
- exists in a digital format, usually as a series of downloadable files
- generally intended to entertain and/or inform

Podcasts	Digital audio files that can be downloaded from the Internet
Sound Elements	Music or other sounds created by singing, playing instruments, or using computer-generated tones; creates a mood
Voice Narration	The words as well as the expression and quality of voice

Analyze Author's Purpose

An author's **purpose** is his or her reason for writing. People who participate in interviews also have a purpose. In a podcast interview, the interviewer's purpose is to elicit useful information from the interviewee. The interviewee's purpose may be to inform, entertain, express thoughts and feelings, or persuade the audience. John Lewis may have had a specific purpose in agreeing to the interview with NPR. His knowledge of critical events in American history merits analysis and preservation, and his interview with Terry Gross helps to ensure that.

A civil rights pioneer reflects on his lifelong fight for justice.
Ed
Podcast
Listen to "*from* Interview with John Lewis" in your ebook.
from Interview with John Lewis
Podcast from National Public Radio

ESSENTIAL QUESTION:
Can each of us find freedom?

Analyze the Podcast

Support your responses with evidence from the podcast.

1 **CAUSE/EFFECT** The interviewer asks John Lewis about what caused him to go against his mother's wishes and get involved in civil rights marches. What does he say inspired him to organize and march with other activists?

2 **ANALYZE** What is the interviewer's purpose as she asks questions of John Lewis? Describe the approach she takes to get Lewis to share his story.

3 **DRAW CONCLUSIONS** What factors motivated John Lewis to fight for voting rights? Explain why Lewis felt that the risks were worth taking to change the society he lived in.

4 **INTERPRET** What does John Lewis mean when he says he focused on "bringing down those signs"? How does Lewis's story about listening to Dr. King talk about activism in Montgomery help you understand his main goals?

5 **ANALYZE** John Lewis cites many numbers and statistics in the interview—estimates of protesting citizens and numbers of cities where demonstrations were held, for example. How is this information evidence for a central idea Lewis wants to convey?

6 **CITE EVIDENCE** What do you think was Lewis's purpose in agreeing to be interviewed? Cite evidence from the interview to support your answer.

Lewis's Purpose for Being Interviewed	Evidence from the Interview
	1.
	2.
	3.

Choices

Here are some other ways to demonstrate your understanding of the ideas in this lesson.

Writing
↳ Postcards from the March

Imagine you are one of the 250,000 people who participated in the 1963 March on Washington. Write three postcards to relatives or friends, describing what you are seeing, hearing, and feeling. Research images or oral histories to make your messages vivid and accurate.

Social & Emotional Learning
↳ Research & Reflect

John Lewis worked for social change using the principles of civil disobedience. Research how other civil rights leaders have used methods of nonviolent resistance. Consider your own ways of dealing with difficult or unfair situations. How can you apply the principles you researched to your own life? Capture your thoughts in a blog, a song, a poem, or a drawing.

Speaking & Listening
↳ Panel Discussion

John Lewis was a longtime member of Congress with a long list of civil rights achievements. Using reliable sources, research Lewis's many accomplishments and their impact on others. Then, organize a panel to discuss with a small group how John Lewis's contributions have had an impact on your own community's rights and freedoms.

- Gather your research and notes about the podcast in a graphic organizer.
- Choose a panel member to write and deliver an opening statement.
- Follow rules for discussion by listening attentively while others talk, building on their ideas. Support your own ideas using your notes.
- After the discussion, write a reflective paragraph about what you learned.

As you write and discuss, be sure to use the Academic Vocabulary words.

decline
enable
impose
integrate
reveal

Get Ready

MENTOR TEXT

from Hidden Figures

History Writing by **Margot Lee Shetterly**

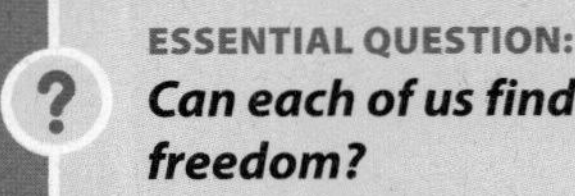

ESSENTIAL QUESTION:
Can each of us find freedom?

Engage Your Brain

Choose one or both of these activities to start connecting with the history text you're about to read.

Help Not Wanted

What do you know about opportunities that were once closed to African Americans, women, or other groups? Make a list of jobs a woman or an African American might not have been able to apply for in the past.

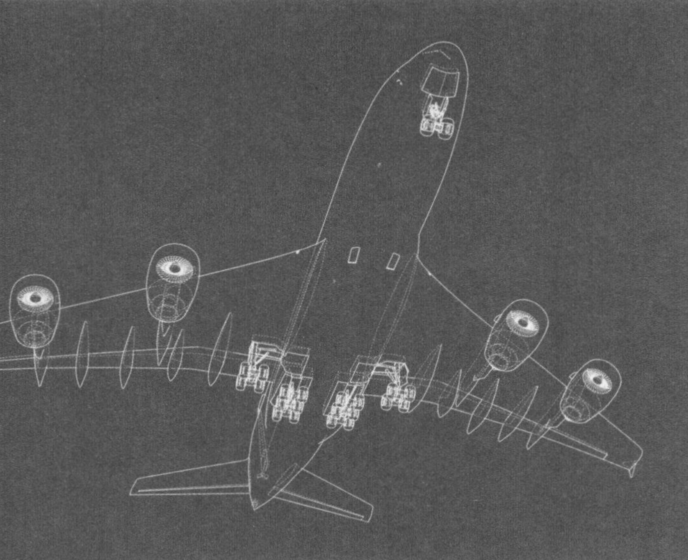

Liftoff!

What does it take to get a plane in the air? With a partner, brainstorm steps to build an airplane, including design, testing, and manufacturing. Sketch or make a list of steps.

Analyze Text Structure

Authors use a variety of **text structures.** These include thesis or main idea and details; cause and effect; problem and solution; and chronology, or time order. Most historical texts are a combination of chronology, main idea, and cause and effect.

As you read, keep track of the important events, the order in which they happen, any causal relationships, and key ideas.

Focus on Genre
↳ **History Writing**

- uses chronological order
- is a form of informational text
- includes evidence to support ideas
- contains text features to help the reader absorb and retain information

Text Structures	Examples from *Hidden Figures*
Chronological, or narration of events	By 1943, the American aircraft industry was the largest, most productive, and most sophisticated in the world, making three times more planes than the Germans, who were fighting on the other side of the war.
Cause and effect	But in the spring of 1943, with World War II in full swing and many men off serving in the military . . . employers were beginning to hire women to do jobs that had once belonged *only* to men.
Thesis/main ideas	The NACA's mission was . . . to help the United States develop the most powerful and efficient airplanes in the world. . . . World leaders felt that the country that ruled the skies would win the war.

Analyze Word Choice

Authors build meaning through word choice. **Word choice,** also known as **diction,** has a cumulative impact on the tone and meaning of a text. The author of *Hidden Figures* creates an informal tone through word choice and by addressing the audience directly. In contrast, official documents usually use formal language. Here is part of a U.S. government job offer quoted in a different part of *Hidden Figures*:

> You are hereby appointed Mathematician, Grade P-1, with pay at the rate of $2,000 per annum, for such period of time as your service may be required, but not to extend beyond the duration of the present war and for six months thereafter.

Fill in the left column of a chart like the one below with words and phrases from the example that create a particular tone. In the right column, describe that tone. As you read, continue to note words and the tone they create.

Words That Create Tone	What Is the Tone?
hereby	formal, serious

Annotation in Action

Here are one reader's notes about a part of the excerpt from *Hidden Figures.* As you read, note how text structure features make the content easier to understand.

A few years earlier, an ad like this would have been unthinkable—most employers never would have considered a woman for a job that had always been performed by a man. But in the spring of 1943, with World War II in full swing and many men off serving in the military, the country needed all the help it could get. Employers were beginning to hire women to do jobs that had once belonged *only* to men.

time clues—help show chronology

Expand Your Vocabulary

Put a check mark next to the vocabulary words that you feel comfortable using when speaking or writing.

simulate	☐
assess	☐
maneuver	☐
analytical	☐

Turn to a partner and use at least two of the words you know to talk about how aircraft are designed and tested.

As you read the selection from *Hidden Figures,* use the definitions in the side column to help you learn the vocabulary words you don't already know.

Background

Before World War II, most women did not work outside their homes. When the United States entered the war, the lack of working men created opportunities for women, including the women written about in *Hidden Figures.* **Margot Lee Shetterly** (b. 1969) grew up in Hampton, Virginia, near the Langley Research Center. As she began to learn about the history of African American women mathematicians at Langley, she researched and then wrote about them in a bestselling book, which has since been made into the movie *Hidden Figures.*

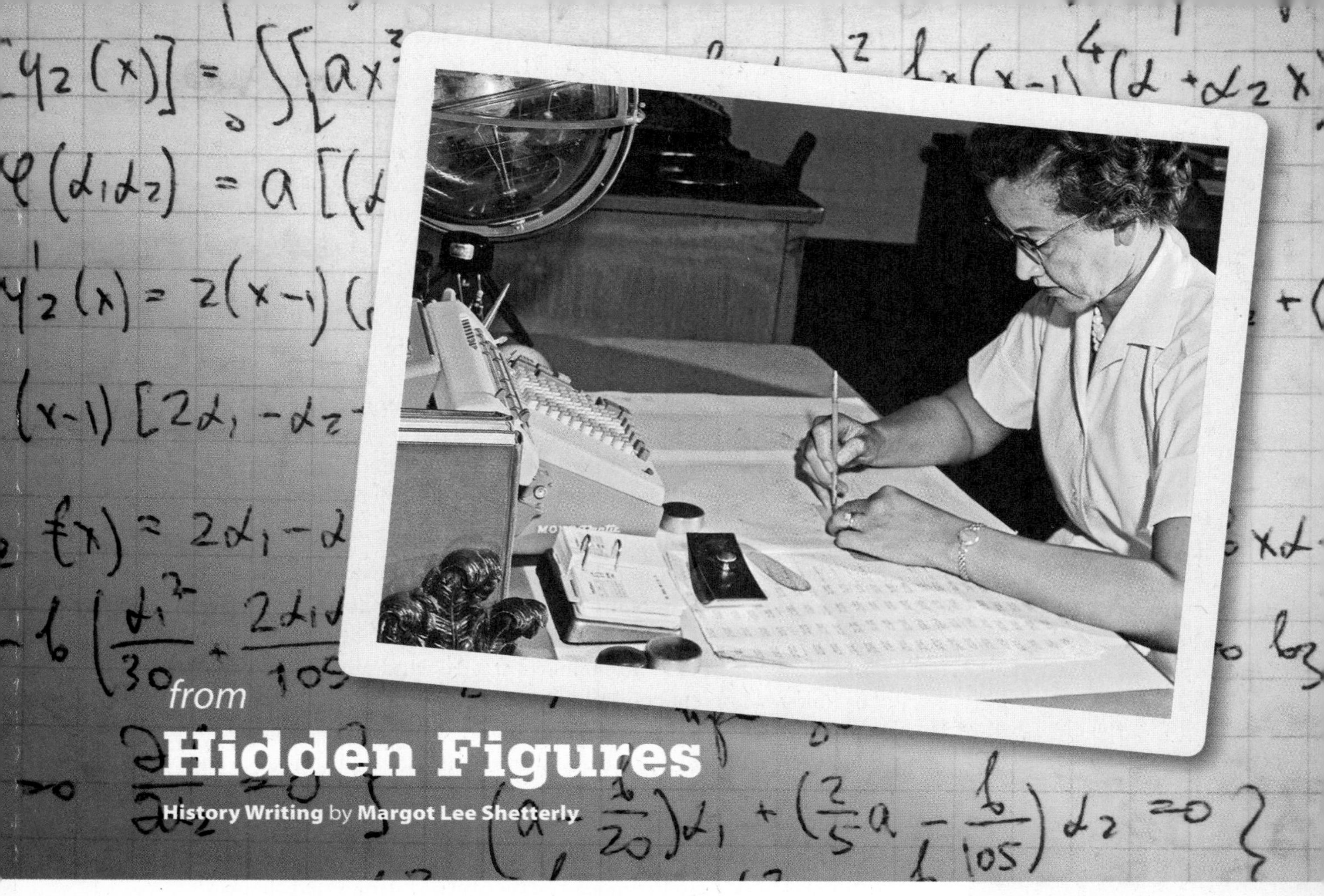

from

Hidden Figures

History Writing by Margot Lee Shetterly

Female African American mathematicians shatter racial and gender barriers to make critical contributions to the Allied effort during World War II.

NOTICE & NOTE
As you read, use the side margins to make notes about the text.

1 The newspaper ad caught the attention of many women. It read: "Reduce your household duties! Women who are not afraid to roll up their sleeves and do jobs previously filled by men should call the Langley Memorial Aeronautical Laboratory."

2 A few years earlier, an ad like this would have been unthinkable—most employers never would have considered a woman for a job that had always been performed by a man. But in the spring of 1943, with World War II in full swing and many men off serving in the military, the country needed all the help it could get. Employers were beginning to hire women to do jobs that had once belonged *only* to men.

3 This particular ad was placed by the National Advisory Committee for Aeronautics (NACA), a government agency dedicated to studying the science of flying. The NACA shared a campus with the US Army Air Corps in Hampton, Virginia, a city in the southeastern part of the state, next to the Chesapeake Bay.

ANALYZE WORD CHOICE

Annotate: Mark an informal phrase in the ad in paragraph 1.

Evaluate: How does the author's word choice affect the tone of the ad?

NOTICE & NOTE
NUMBERS AND STATS

When you notice the use of specific quantities or comparisons, you've found a **Numbers and Stats** signpost.

Notice & Note: Mark any numbers in paragraphs 4 and 5 that tell you about how the United States increased military plane production for World War II.

Interpret: Why did the author include these numbers?

4 The NACA's mission was important and unique: to help the United States develop the most powerful and efficient airplanes in the world. Airplanes moved military troops, tracked enemies, and launched bombs. World leaders felt that the country that ruled the skies would win the war. President Franklin D. Roosevelt believed in the importance of air power, so two years earlier, in 1941, he had challenged the nation to increase its production of airplanes to fifty thousand units a year. At that time, the industry had manufactured only three thousand planes a year.

5 The NACA and private industry were up for the challenge. By 1943, the American aircraft industry was the largest, most productive, and most sophisticated in the world, making three times more planes than the Germans, who were fighting on the other side of the war.

"Victory through Air Power!"

6 Before manufacturers built the airplanes, the designs were developed, tested, and refined at the Langley Memorial Aeronautical Laboratory, which was where the NACA had first begun its operations, in 1917. The engineers created wind tunnels to **simulate**, or imitate, different conditions a plane could encounter when flying. This helped the engineers to test airplane parts as well as whole aircraft, examining them for any problems, like air disturbance and uneven wing geometry.

simulate
(sĭm´yə-lāt) *v.* to create in a controlled setting conditions similar to those a person or machine might face in the real world.

7 After that testing, pilots flew the planes, trying to **assess** how the machines handled in the air. Did the aircraft roll unexpectedly? Did it stall? Was it hard to guide or **maneuver**? Making small changes to the design added up to a difference in performance. Even tiny improvements in speed and efficiency multiplied over millions of pilot miles added to a difference that could tip the balance of the war.

assess
(ə-sĕs´) *v.* to determine the qualities or abilities of something.

maneuver
(mə-nōō´ vər) *v.* to make a series of controlled movements.

8 People working at Langley knew that they were doing their part to win the war. "Victory through air power!" said Henry Reid, the engineer-in-charge of the Langley Laboratory. And the workers took their mission to heart.

WANTED: Female Mathematicians

9 Each of the engineers at the Langley Memorial Aeronautical Laboratory required the support of a number of other workers: craftsmen to build the airplane models, mechanics to maintain the test tunnels, and "number crunchers" to process the data that was collected during the tests. For the engineers, a plane was basically a complex physics experiment. Physics is the science of matter, energy, and motion. Physics meant math, and math meant mathematicians. At the Langley Laboratory, mathematicians meant women.

10 Female mathematicians had been on the job at Langley since 1935. And it didn't take long for the women to show that they were just as good or even better at computing than many of the male engineers. But few of the women were granted the title "mathematician," which would have put them on equal footing with some male employees. Instead, they were classified as "subprofessionals," a title that meant they could be paid less.

11 At Langley, the female mathematicians were called "computers." They did the computations to turn the results of the raw data gathered by the engineers into a more useful form. Today we think of computers as machines, but in the 1940s, a computer was just someone whose job it was to do computations, a flesh-and-blood woman who was very good with numbers.

12 In 1943, it was difficult for the Langley Laboratory to find as many qualified women as they needed. A recruiter from the National Advisory Committee for Aeronautics visited colleges in search of young women with **analytical** or mathematical skills.

The Human Computers

13 When the managers couldn't satisfy the demand with only white employees, the government decided to hire African Americans. A civil rights leader named A. Philip Randolph encouraged President Roosevelt to sign an executive order—a law that ordered the desegregation of the federal government and defense industry and created the Fair Employment Practices Committee. This executive order opened up new and exciting opportunities for African Americans, allowing them to work side-by-side with white people during the war.

Don't forget to **Notice & Note** as you read the text.

analytical
(ăn-ə-lĭt´ ĭ-kəl) *adj.* able to analyze, or understand something by breaking it down into parts.

ANALYZE TEXT STRUCTURE

Annotate: In paragraph 13, sentence 1, mark both the cause and the effect.

Infer: What does this cause-and-effect relationship explain about the decision to hire African American women as mathematicians at Langley?

ANALYZE WORD CHOICE

Annotate: In paragraph 14, mark the sentences that describe the result of President Roosevelt's executive order.

Evaluate: How would you describe the tone of this sentence? What words and phrases create this tone?

14 The federal government also helped create special training classes at black colleges, where people could learn the skills they would need to be successful in the war jobs. Black newspapers like the *Norfolk Journal and Guide* published articles telling their readers to apply for these new job openings. And there were many applicants! The applications were not supposed to consider race—a recent law had done away with the requirement that the application must include a photo—but it wasn't hard for employers to figure out which job candidates were black. African Americans did not have access to white colleges and universities, so black applicants came from black colleges, such as West Virginia State University, Howard University, Hampton Institute, and Arkansas Agricultural, Mechanical & Normal College. Many of the African-American candidates had years of teaching experience as well as math and science degrees.

15 Once hired, the black mathematicians were assigned to a separate work space in the Warehouse Building on the west side of the Langley campus. The East Area Computers were all white; the West Area Computers were all black, except for the supervisor and her assistant, who were white women.

16 There had always been African-American employees at Langley, but they had worked as janitors, cafeteria workers, mechanic's assistants, and groundskeepers. Hiring black mathematicians—that was something new. For the most part, the engineers welcomed extra hands, even if those hands were black. The Langley Laboratory was operating around the clock to test airplanes to be flown by American soldiers in the war: everyone had a job to do.

17 Hampton, Virginia, where the Langley campus was located, was very much a southern town. State law and Virginia custom meant that African Americans did not ride the same buses or eat in the same cafeterias or use the same bathrooms as whites. The Langley staff had to prepare for the arrival of the African-American mathematicians. One of the tasks: creating metal bathroom signs that read "Colored Girls."

18 For the black women, the experience of working at a laboratory offered the chance to do interesting work that would help support the war effort. Walking into an unfamiliar environment wasn't easy for the women of the new West Area Computing Office, but each of them was eager for the opportunity to help their country and prove that they, too, could be excellent mathematicians.

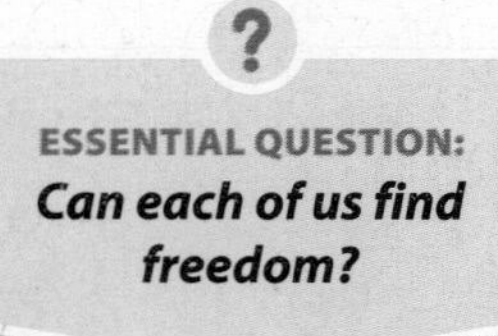

ESSENTIAL QUESTION:
Can each of us find freedom?

Review your notes and add your thoughts to your Response Log.

COLLABORATIVE DISCUSSION

If you were an African American female mathematician, would you have signed on to work at Langley Air Force Base? Discuss your views with a partner.

Assessment Practice

Answer these questions before moving on to the **Analyze the Text** section on the following page.

1. This question has two parts. First, answer Part A. Then, answer Part B.

Part A

Which sentence states the central idea of this excerpt from *Hidden Figures*?

(A) State segregation laws made hiring African American women difficult.

(B) The first female mathematicians at Langley were white and were classified as "subprofessionals."

(C) President Franklin Roosevelt believed in air power and its necessity in supporting the war effort.

(D) Government research facilities provided important opportunities for female African American mathematicians.

Part B

Select **two** sentences that support your answer choice to Part A.

(A) "President Franklin D. Roosevelt believed in the importance of air power . . . in 1941, he had challenged the nation to increase its production of airplanes to fifty thousand units a year." (paragraph 4)

(B) "But few of the women were granted the title 'mathematician,' which would have put them on equal footing with some male employees." (paragraph 10)

(C) "A civil rights leader . . . encouraged President Roosevelt to sign an executive order—a law that ordered the desegregation . . . and created the Fair Employment Practices Committee." (paragraph 13)

(D) "State law and Virginia custom meant that African Americans did not ride the same buses or eat in the same cafeterias or use the same bathrooms as whites." (paragraph 17)

(E) "For the black women, the experience of working at a laboratory offered the chance to do interesting work that would help support the war effort." (paragraph 18)

2. How did World War II affect employment opportunities for African American women?

(A) It created a push to desegregate the military and government agencies.

(B) It created a booming economy that raised wages and placed a higher value on female workers.

(C) It drove the creation of new government agencies that trained and hired African American men and women.

(D) It caused factories to move to cities with larger African American populations.

Test-Taking Strategies

Analyze the Text

Support your responses with evidence from the text.

1. **INFER** Think about the title of the text. What different meanings can you identify?

2. **CAUSE/EFFECT** During the 1940s, women were able to get jobs for the first time in many industries. What event caused that to happen?

3. **DRAW CONCLUSIONS** In paragraph 2, the author uses this extreme language: "A few years earlier, an ad like this would have been unthinkable." How does the author's choice of the word *unthinkable* convey people's attitude toward women in the workplace at the time?

4. **ANALYZE** What was NACA's mission? What details support this main idea?

5. **INFER** From the information in paragraph 10, what inferences can you draw about attitudes toward women at Langley? From the information in paragraphs 15 and 16, what inferences can you draw about attitudes toward African Americans at Langley?

My Inferences	Author's Word Choices That Support My Inferences
About attitudes at Langley toward women	
About attitudes at Langley toward African Americans	

6. **SYNTHESIZE** Review the notes you made on the Get Ready page about tone. Then choose just one or two words you would you use to summarize the overall tone of the text. Give specific examples to support your responses.

7. **CITE EVIDENCE** In paragraph 9, the author writes, "For the engineers, a plane was basically a complex physics experiment." How does the description of developing and testing aircraft support this statement?

8. **EVALUATE** Examine the photos that accompany the text. How do they contribute to your understanding of the topic?

NOTICE & NOTE

Review what you **noticed and noted** as you read the text. Your annotations can help you answer these questions.

Choices

Here are some other ways to demonstrate your understanding of the ideas in this lesson.

Writing

↳ Film Analysis

Watch the film *Hidden Figures*. As you view the movie, take notes about the differences between it and the text you read. Then write an analysis comparing the topics, ideas, and point of view. Describe how the movie enhanced your understanding of the events described in the text, citing specific examples. Compare your analysis with those of your classmates.

As you write and discuss, be sure to use the **Academic Vocabulary** words.

- decline
- enable
- impose
- integrate
- reveal

Media

↳ Social Media Profile

Create a social media profile for one of the women whose photo appears on page 487. Consult authoritative outside sources to gather information about her

- early life
- education
- contributions to science and other accomplishments

Include posts or images on your social media profile. Cite any referenced sources appropriately.

Speaking & Listening

↳ Research and Report

During World War II, more and more women were entering the workplace to replace men away at war. Research the topic, including

- jobs and industries where women most commonly took the place of men
- attitudes and reactions to women taking jobs traditionally filled by men
- how women of color were treated differently from white women

Report your findings to a small group. Discuss the similarities and differences in what each of you found.

Expand Your Vocabulary

PRACTICE AND APPLY

Work with a partner to write the dialogue for a brief scene that depicts the meaning of but does not mention each vocabulary word. Then swap your scene with another pair. Pairs will then analyze each other's scenes and identify the word that is being conveyed in each one. Here are some ideas:

- a character **simulating** something
- a character **assessing** a situation or another character
- a character **maneuvering** through a difficult space
- a situation requiring **analytical** thinking

Vocabulary Strategy

↳ Reference Sources

Interactive Vocabulary Lesson: Using Reference Sources

When you read an informational text, looking up words or terms in print and digital **reference sources** such as dictionaries, glossaries, or thesauruses can help you better understand the text. These resources help you clarify and validate your understanding of technical vocabulary.

Reference sources can be used along with context clues. Here is a sentence from the selection:

> The engineers created wind tunnels to simulate, or imitate, different conditions a plane could encounter when flying.

The word "imitate" and the context of "wind tunnels" and "different conditions" help you get the meaning of the word *simulate*. When you look the word up in a reference source to confirm the meaning, you may see a specific technical definition of the word. This will help clarify your understanding of the word's use in the text.

simulate *v.* (sĭm´yə-lāt) to produce the features of an event or process in a way that seems real but is not, usually for training or testing purposes.

PRACTICE AND APPLY

The words below are used in *Hidden Figures*. Look them up in a dictionary, glossary, or thesaurus, using context clues from the text to select the appropriate definition. Write the definition that fits the sentence.

1. refined (paragraph 6)
2. engineers (paragraph 6)
3. performance (paragraph 7)
4. process (paragraph 9)

Watch Your Language!

Pronoun-Antecedent Agreement

Pronouns take the place of nouns so that speakers and writers can avoid sounding repetitious. Pronouns can also make sentences clearer, but only if they agree with the nouns they replace—their **antecedents.**

A singular noun replaces a singular pronoun, and a plural noun replaces a plural pronoun. There are usually words, phrases, or even clauses between the antecedent and the pronoun, and those can sometimes be confusing. But you can simply look for the noun that the pronoun replaces and match the number of that noun.

Here are some examples of pronoun-antecedent agreement from *Hidden Figures:*

- These pronouns are separated from their antecedents by phrases and are in a new clause.

> People working at Langley knew that they were doing their part to win the war.

- This pronoun is in a new clause.

> President Franklin D. Roosevelt believed in the importance of air power, so two years earlier, in 1941, he had challenged the nation to increase its production of airplanes to fifty thousand units a year.

- This pronoun is in a new sentence.

> Did the aircraft roll unexpectedly? Did it stall?

Interactive Grammar Lesson: Pronoun-Antecedent Agreement

PRACTICE AND APPLY

Write a paragraph about the female mathematicians described in *Hidden Figures*. Use at least three pronouns in your paragraph. Make sure that they agree with their antecedents.

Get Ready

Booker T. and W.E.B.

Poem by Dudley Randall

ESSENTIAL QUESTION:
Can each of us find freedom?

Engage Your Brain

Choose one or both of these activities to start connecting with the poem you are about to read.

No Common Ground

The poem you are about to read depicts an imaginary conversation between Booker T. Washington (1856–1915) and W.E.B. Du Bois (1868–1963), two men who had very different ideas about what African Americans should do to improve their lives in the late 19th and early 20th centuries. How much do you already know about these men? What questions do you have about them?

Booker T. Washington	W.E.B. Du Bois
What I Know:	What I Know:
What I Want to Know:	What I Want to Know:

You Say Yes, I Say No

Have you been in a situation where you and someone else disagreed about everything you tried to talk about? Discuss with a partner, or sketch images that represent your thoughts and feelings.

Analyze Narrator Perspective

In literary works, authors use a device called a narrator. The **narrator** of a work is the character or voice that relates events or ideas to the reader. The **narrative perspective** is the point of view of that narrator.

"Booker T. and W.E.B." has two narrators, with very different perspectives. As you read, mark where the narrative perspective shifts from one man to the other.

Focus on Genre
↳ Poetry

- includes imagery that appeals to the senses
- includes sound devices such as rhyme, alliteration, assonance, consonance, and repetition
- creates a mood
- expresses a theme, or message about life

Analyze Poetic Language

"Booker T. and W.E.B." is an imaginary debate between two early leaders of the African American community. The leaders' conflicting perspectives are revealed through dialogue, as they attempt to change each other's mind. The poet employs several techniques to express how they argue their points.

Diction includes the poet's choice of words as well as **syntax**—the way of arranging words in sentences. Diction may be formal or informal. Readers should pay close attention to a poet's word choice and syntax, and notice the mood and tone they create.

An **idiom** is an expression whose meaning differs from the actual meaning of the words. For example, "bought the farm" is an idiom that means someone has died.

Understatement, or **meiosis,** is the technique of deliberately making a subject seem less important than it really is. Using understatement, a topic or idea is described with less force than expected. Understatement can allow an interaction to remain polite, despite the intensity of the disagreement.

As you read, use the chart to record examples of diction, idiom, and understatement. Think about how these techniques contribute to the **tone,** or attitude, of each speaker.

Devices	Examples and Effects
Diction	
Idiom	
Understatement (meiosis)	

Annotation in Action

Here are one reader's notes about the first stanza of "Booker T. and W.E.B." As you read, note each speaker's diction and use of idiom and understatement.

"It seems to me," said Booker T.,
"It shows a mighty lot of cheek
To study chemistry and Greek
When Mister Charlie needs a hand
To hoe the cotton on his land,
And when Miss Ann looks for a cook,
Why stick your nose inside a book?"

"mighty lot of cheek" (idiom?) makes W.E.B.'s ideas sound wrong-headed.

Background

Dudley Randall (1914–2000) grew up in Detroit, Michigan. In 1981, he was named poet laureate of Detroit. In this poem, Randall depicts the title characters' clash over the path to equality for African Americans. Booker T. Washington believed that African Americans should work hard and save money to earn the equality they deserved. W.E.B. Du Bois advocated agitation and protest to demand equal treatment. Their dispute split the Black community into a "conservative" side that supported Washington and a "radical" side that supported Du Bois.

Booker T. and W.E.B.

Poem by **Dudley Randall**

Two prominent African American thinkers face off in this imaginary debate.

NOTICE & NOTE
As you read, use the side margins to make notes about the text.

(Booker T. Washington and W.E.B. Du Bois)

"It seems to me," said Booker T.,
"It shows a mighty lot of cheek[1]
To study chemistry and Greek
When Mister Charlie needs a hand
To hoe the cotton on his land,
And when Miss Ann looks for a cook,
Why stick your nose inside a book?"

"I don't agree," said W.E.B.,
"If I should have the drive to seek
Knowledge of chemistry or Greek,
I'll do it. Charles and Miss can look
Another place for hand or cook.
Some men rejoice in skill of hand,
And some in cultivating land,

ANALYZE POETIC LANGUAGE

Annotate: In line 11, mark the way W.E.B. refers to the people Booker T. calls "Mister Charlie" and "Miss Ann" in the first stanza.

Interpret: Why do the two men refer to these people in different ways? What does this reveal about the men and the way they see themselves in relation to others?

[1] **cheek:** rude or impertinent boldness; disrespect.

Booker T. Washington

W.E.B. Du Bois

But there are others who maintain
The right to cultivate the brain."

"It seems to me," said Booker T.,
"That all you folks have missed the boat
Who shout about the right to vote,
And spend vain days and sleepless nights
In uproar over civil rights.
Just keep your mouths shut, do not grouse,
But work, and save, and buy a house."

"I don't agree," said W.E.B.,
"For what can property avail
If dignity and justice fail?
Unless you help to make the laws,
They'll steal your house with trumped-up clause.
A rope's as tight, a fire as hot,
No matter how much cash you've got.
Speak soft, and try your little plan,
But as for me, I'll be a man."

"It seems to me," said Booker T.—

"I don't agree,"
Said W.E.B.

ANALYZE NARRATOR PERSPECTIVE

Annotate: In lines 17–23, mark Booker T.'s advice to people who share W.E.B.'s perspective.

Analyze: What is Booker T.'s perspective on the path to equality for African Americans?

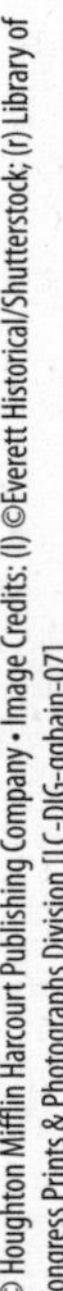

COLLABORATE AND COMPARE

Do you side with Booker T. or W.E.B.? Discuss with a partner.

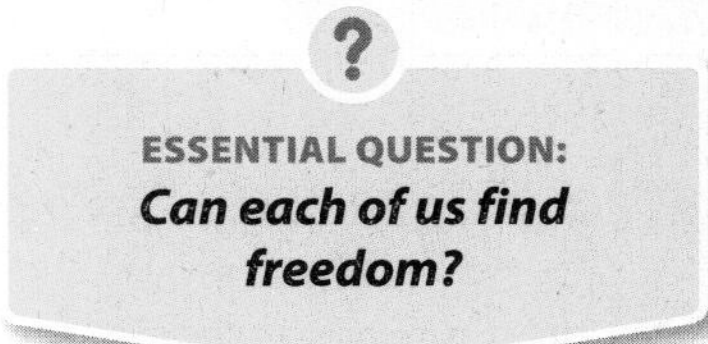

Review your notes and add your thoughts to your Response Log.

Assessment Practice

Answer these questions before moving on to the **Analyze the Text** section on the following page.

1. This question has two parts. First answer Part A. Then, answer Part B.

Part A

What opinion of civil rights protesters is expressed by Booker T. in the poem?

- (A) They are too proud to explain their views effectively.
- (B) They are not doing enough in their fight for equality.
- (C) They do not understand the civil rights laws.
- (D) They are wasting their time by protesting.

Part B

Select **two** details that support the answer to Part A.

- (A) "It shows a mighty lot of cheek / To study chemistry and Greek . . ." (lines 2–3)
- (B) "Why stick your nose inside a book?" (line 7)
- (C) "That all you folks have missed the boat / Who shout about the right to vote" (lines 18–19)
- (D) "And spend vain days and sleepless nights / In uproar over civil rights . . ." (lines 20–21)
- (E) "But work, and save, and buy a house." (line 23)

2. Which paraphrase of lines 31–32 most accurately expresses W.E.B.'s perspective?

- (A) You can be timid, but I will keep fighting for equality.
- (B) Your plan is insignificant, but mine will be famous.
- (C) You are too soft-spoken to win an argument with me.
- (D) Your quiet approach is only appropriate for children.

Test-Taking Strategies

Analyze the Text

Support your responses with evidence from the text.

NOTICE & NOTE

Review what you **noticed and noted** as you read the text. Your annotations can help you answer these questions.

1. **ANALYZE** Reread and paraphrase line 2, focusing on the word *cheek*. What does Booker T.'s choice of that word suggest to you about his opinion of W.E.B.?

2. **INFER** Reread lines 1–7. Who are "Mister Charlie" and "Miss Ann"? How does Booker T. think they should be treated? Does his attitude surprise you? Why or why not?

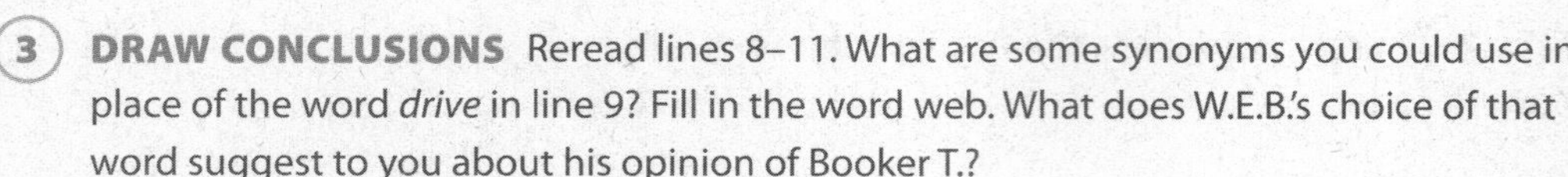

3. **DRAW CONCLUSIONS** Reread lines 8–11. What are some synonyms you could use in place of the word *drive* in line 9? Fill in the word web. What does W.E.B.'s choice of that word suggest to you about his opinion of Booker T.?

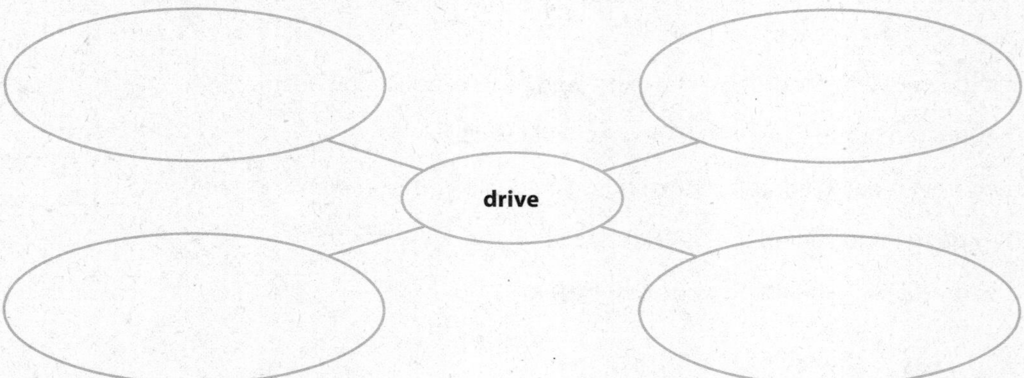

What does the word *drive* suggest about W.E.B.'s opinion of Booker T.?

4. **SYNTHESIZE** Review the third and fourth stanzas. How do Booker T's and W.E.B.'s perspectives on the fight for civil rights differ? Use evidence from the poem in your answer.

5. **INTERPRET** What is the effect of the use of rhyme and the repetition of the phrases "It seems to me" and "I don't agree"? What attitude does each phrase convey? How does this highlight the differences between the men? Use evidence from the poem in your answer.

6. **ANALYZE** Review examples of understatement, or meiosis, that you noted in the chart on the Get Ready page. Explain the effect of this device on the poem's meaning.

7. **SYNTHESIZE** Reread the poem's last two lines. How do they humorously sum up the two narrators' clashing perspectives?

Choices

Here are some other ways to demonstrate your understanding of the ideas in this lesson.

Writing

↳ Research Paper

Find out more about the lives and views of Booker T. Washington and W.E.B. Du Bois. Work with a partner to research their lives, influences, and points of view on the issues listed in the chart. Consult authoritative sources. Use a chart to organize your findings.

Issue	Booker T. Washington	W.E.B. Du Bois
Education		
Personal Achievement		
Civil Rights		

Draft and review your essay with a partner. Cite your sources appropriately.

As you write and discuss, be sure to use the **Academic Vocabulary** words.

- **decline**
- **enable**
- **impose**
- **integrate**
- **reveal**

Media

↳ Image Board

Look for other poems by Dudley Randall and consider their subject matter. How are they similar to or different from this poem? With a partner or small group, create an image board on a collaborative platform that shows the different subjects. Present your board to the class. Be sure to explain how the images connect; and share what you think was Randall's purpose for writing each poem.

Social & Emotional Learning

↳ Group Debate

Washington and Du Bois had strong views about how African Americans of their time could make social and economic progress. In the poem, they debate the value of education in bringing about social equality. Now it's your turn to participate in a class debate about the issue.

- Write down your views about whether education can be a tool for social change. List reasons and evidence for your views.
- Form debate teams. One side should argue that education is critical for our society to make progress. The other side should oppose this argument.
- During the debate, listen carefully to opposing arguments. Think about how backgrounds and cultures shape people's perspectives.
- After the debate, reflect as a group on how opinions may have changed, or new insights may have been gained as a result of hearing other perspectives.

Collaborate & Compare

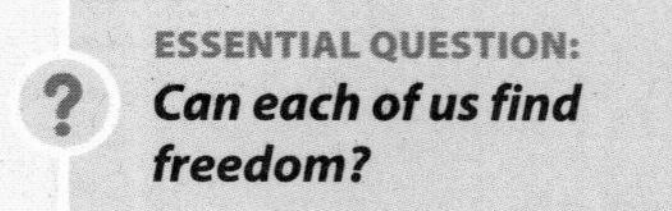

Compare Treatments of a Topic

You're about to read from a memoir and a graphic memoir about the experiences of two women in contemporary Iran. As you read, notice the presentations of the two texts, as well as how the different genres help the authors share their personal stories. Then, look for ways that the ideas in the two texts relate to each other.

A
from Reading Lolita in Tehran
Memoir by Azar Nafisi
pages 506–509
B
from Persepolis 2: The Story of a Return
Graphic Memoir by Marjane Satrapi
pages 516–517

After you have read both texts, you will collaborate with a small group to create a graphic-novel version of the excerpt from *Reading Lolita in Tehran.*

You will follow these steps:

- Brainstorm how to recast the text
- Create storyboards
- Discuss what you have learned
- Reflect on your work

from Reading Lolita in Tehran

Memoir by **Azar Nafisi**

Engage Your Brain

Choose one or both of these activities to start connecting with the memoir you're about to read.

Iran Today

The texts you are about to read are set in Iran. What do you know about the country's culture and politics? What would you like to know? With a partner, fill in the chart.

I know...	I wonder...

Men and Women: Different Rules?

Throughout history and across cultures, women have experienced different treatment and faced different social expectations than men. With a small group, discuss ways that males and females are treated differently in your culture.

Analyze Rhetorical Devices

Azar Nafisi uses rhetorical questions to engage the audience and to make a point. **Rhetorical questions** are questions that no one is required or expected to answer.

In the chart, list rhetorical questions in the text together with their purpose.

Focus on Genre
Memoir

- records actual events based on the writer's observations
- dependent on the author's point of view
- looks back at a specific event or series of events
- shares the author's feelings and what he or she has learned

Rhetorical Question Posed in Text	Purpose
How can I create this other world outside the room?	Nafisi uses the rhetorical question to explain why she creates an imaginary scene involving Sanaz.

Analyze Setting and Purpose

The setting and purpose of a text reveal important information. As you analyze the effect of setting and purpose in *Reading Lolita in Tehran*, consider the following:

- The **setting** is where a text occurs. Iran requires women to live according to a specific set of laws that govern their dress and behavior.
- The **purpose** reflects why an author wrote a text—what she hopes to communicate. In *Reading Lolita in Tehran*, Nafisi discusses how she taught a small group of women in her home in Tehran after she stopped teaching at an Iranian university.
- The **author's point of view,** or how an author thinks or feels about a subject, also helps a reader analyze the author's purpose. Azar Nafisi's point of view is shaped by her experiences as a woman and a scholar who once lived under an oppressive regime. These experiences shape her purpose in terms of the ideas she wants to communicate to the reader.

As you read the text, make notes about how the writer uses the setting and point of view to accomplish her purpose and convey her feelings about her experiences.

Annotation in Action

Here are one reader's notes about the first lines of the excerpt from *Reading Lolita in Tehran*. As you read, mark other examples of rhetorical devices the author uses.

How can I create this other world outside the room? I have no choice but to appeal once again to your imagination. Let's imagine one of the girls, say Sanaz, leaving my house and let us follow her from there to her final destination. She says her goodbyes and puts on her black robe and scarf over her orange shirt and jeans, coiling her scarf around her neck to cover her huge gold earrings.

A question right off the bat—pulls me in!

Expand Your Vocabulary

Put a check mark next to the vocabulary words that you feel comfortable using when speaking or writing.

segregate	☐
allocate	☐
convert	☐
irrelevant	☐

Turn to a partner and use the vocabulary words you already know in a short discussion about conditions for women in countries where they do not have equal rights with men.

As you read the excerpt from *Reading Lolita in Tehran*, use the definitions in the side column to learn the vocabulary words you don't already know.

Background

The Iranian Revolution in the late 1970s resulted in the overthrow of the pro-Western Shah of Iran. Iranians established a theocracy, or religious government, based on the rule of Islam. The new government passed laws that segregate men and women and that force women to adhere to an Islamic dress code. Iranian women are required to wear veils that cover their hair and neck and coats that cover their arms and legs.

Azar Nafisi (b. 1947), an Iranian, taught English literature in Tehran from 1979 until 1995. Laws passed after the revolution made Nafisi's job difficult. Her university scrutinized novels that she taught, and she was chastised for not wearing a veil. In 1995, Nafisi left the university and began teaching a small group of women in her home, where they were free to discuss books, like *Lolita*, that were considered unacceptable by Iranian authorities. In 1997, she left Iran for the United States, where she now teaches.

NOTICE & NOTE

As you read, use the side margins to make notes about the text.

from

Reading Lolita in Tehran

Memoir by **Azar Nafisi**

The author describes conditions her female students face under a repressive regime in Iran.

ANALYZE SETTING AND PURPOSE

Annotate: Mark passages in paragraphs 1 and 2 that discuss the setting.

Respond: What is the setting for this memoir? What do you think is the author's purpose for writing it?

1 How can I create this other world outside the room? I have no choice but to appeal once again to your imagination. Let's imagine one of the girls, say Sanaz, leaving my house and let us follow her from there to her final destination. She says her goodbyes and puts on her black robe and scarf over her orange shirt and jeans, coiling her scarf around her neck to cover her huge gold earrings. She directs wayward strands of hair under the scarf, puts her notes into her large bag, straps it on over her shoulder and walks out into the hall. She pauses a moment on top of the stairs to put on thin lacy black gloves to hide her nail polish.

2 We follow Sanaz down the stairs, out the door and into the street. You might notice that her gait[1] and her gestures have changed. It is in her best interest not to be seen, not be heard or noticed. She doesn't walk upright, but bends her head towards the ground and doesn't look at passersby. She walks quickly and with a sense of determination. The streets of Tehran and other Iranian cities are patrolled by militia, who ride in white Toyota patrols, four

[1] **gait:** manner of walking.

gun-carrying men and women, sometimes followed by a minibus. They are called the Blood of God. They patrol the streets to make sure that women like Sanaz wear their veils properly, do not wear makeup, do not walk in public with men who are not their fathers, brothers or husbands. She will pass slogans on the walls, quotations from Khomeini[2] and a group called the Party of God: MEN WHO WEAR TIES ARE U.S. LACKEYS.[3] VEILING IS A WOMAN'S PROTECTION. Beside the slogan is a charcoal drawing of a woman: her face is featureless and framed by a dark chador.[4] MY SISTER, GUARD YOUR VEIL. MY BROTHER, GUARD YOUR EYES.

3 If she gets on a bus, the seating is **segregated**. She must enter through the rear door and sit in the back seats, **allocated** to women. Yet in taxis, which accept as many as five passengers, men and women are squeezed together like sardines, as the saying goes, and the same goes with minibuses, where so many of my students complain of being harassed by bearded and God-fearing men.

4 You might well ask, What is Sanaz thinking as she walks the streets of Tehran? How much does this experience affect her? Most probably, she tries to distance her mind as much as possible from her surroundings. Perhaps she is thinking of her brother, or of her distant boyfriend and the time when she will meet him in Turkey. Does she compare her own situation with her mother's when she was the same age? Is she angry that women of her mother's generation could walk the streets freely, enjoy the company of the opposite sex, join the police force, become pilots, live under laws that were among the most progressive in the world regarding women? Does she feel humiliated by the new laws, by the fact that after the revolution, the age of marriage was lowered from eighteen to nine, that stoning became once more the punishment for adultery and prostitution?

5 In the course of nearly two decades, the streets have been turned into a war zone, where young women who disobey the rules are hurled into patrol cars, taken to jail, flogged, fined, forced to wash the toilets and humiliated, and as soon as they leave, they go back and do the same thing. Is she aware, Sanaz, of her own power? Does she realize how dangerous she can be when her every stray gesture is a disturbance to public safety? Does she think how vulnerable the Revolutionary Guards are who for over eighteen years have patrolled the streets of Tehran and have had to endure young women like herself, and those of other generations, walking, talking, showing a strand of hair just to remind them that they have not **converted**?

Don't forget to **Notice & Note** as you read the text.

segregate
(sĕg´rĭ-gāt) *v.* to cause people to be separated based on gender, race, or other factors.

allocate
(ăl´ə-kāt) *v.* to set apart or designate for a special purpose.

ANALYZE RHETORICAL DEVICES

Annotate: Mark the rhetorical questions in paragraph 5.

Respond: What is the effect of these questions?

NOTICE & NOTE
EXTREME OR ABSOLUTE LANGUAGE

When you notice language that leaves no doubt about a situation, you've found an **Extreme or Absolute Language** signpost.

Notice & Note: Mark examples in paragraph 5 of absolute or extreme language.

Analyze: Why did the author use this language?

convert
(kən-vûrt´) *v.* to change one's system of beliefs.

[2] **Khomeini** (kō-mā´ nē)**:** Ruhollah Khomeini (1902–1989), religious and political leader of Iran after the 1979 revolution.

[3] **U.S. lackeys:** people who serve United States policies. The Iranian government is hostile to the U.S. because it supported the former Shah of Iran.

[4] **chador** (chə´dər)**:** a long scarf that covers a Muslim woman's hair, neck, and shoulders.

6 We have reached Sanaz's house, where we will leave her on her doorstep, perhaps to confront her brother on the other side and to think in her heart of her boyfriend.

7 These girls, my girls, had both a real history and a fabricated one. Although they came from very different backgrounds, the regime that ruled them had tried to make their personal identities and histories **irrelevant**. They were never free of the regime's definition of them as Muslim women.

irrelevant
(ĭr-rĕl´ə-vənt) *adj.* unrelated to the matter being considered.

COLLABORATIVE DISCUSSION

Do you think Sanaz has power, as the author states, or is she powerless because of government repression? Discuss with a partner.

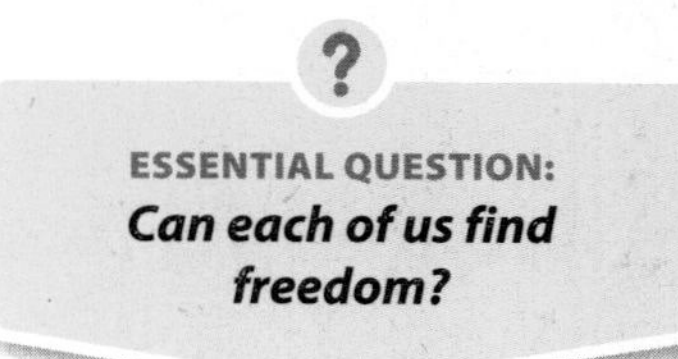

Review your notes and add your thoughts to your Response Log.

Assessment Practice

Answer these questions before moving on to the **Analyze the Text** section on the following page.

1. In the first paragraph, what does the description of Sanaz tell you?

- (A) She openly disobeys laws governing how women in Iran must dress.
- (B) She has more freedom in how she dresses than other women in Iran.
- (C) She is interested in fashion even though she has to cover herself.
- (D) She is more concerned with what people think of her than she is with following the laws governing women.

2. This question has two parts. First, answer Part A. Then, answer Part B.

Part A

What is meant by the author's statement in paragraph 7 that "These girls, my girls, had both a real history and a fabricated one"?

- (A) Young women in Iran are taught a version of history in school that omits any details of government wrongdoing.
- (B) Women in Iran daydream about doing as they please.
- (C) The regime views them as rule-obeying Muslims, not individuals.
- (D) They read about other cultures to prepare to escape Iran.

Part B

Select the quotation that best supports the answer to Part A.

- (A) "You might notice that her gait and her gestures have changed." (paragraph 2)
- (B) "Most probably, she tries to distance her mind as much as possible from her surroundings." (paragraph 4)
- (C) "In the course of nearly two decades, the streets have been turned into a war zone . . ." (paragraph 5)
- (D) ". . . the regime that ruled them had tried to make their personal identities and histories irrelevant." (paragraph 7)

Ed

Test-Taking Strategies

Analyze the Text

Support your responses with evidence from the text.

NOTICE & NOTE

Review what you **noticed and noted** as you read the text. Your annotations can help you answer these questions.

1. **ANALYZE** This excerpt opens with a clue to the author's purpose. What is it? How does she use details of setting to achieve her purpose? Cite evidence from notes you took as you read the text.

2. **INFER** Identify details the author uses to describe Sanaz. Why might the author have included these details?

3. **ANALYZE** Why might Iranian authorities have imposed such stringent laws on women?

4. **CITE EVIDENCE** Review the notes you took on the Get Ready page about rhetorical questions. In the chart, cite two examples and explain the author's purpose in using them.

Rhetorical Question	Author's Purpose

5. **DRAW CONCLUSIONS** Review the slogans that Sanaz passes. How does the fact that the author quotes this **Extreme or Absolute Language** reveal her point of view?

6. **SYNTHESIZE** What can you determine about how Sanaz and the other women in the literature group cope with the laws about their behavior and appearance?

7. **INTERPRET** In the last paragraph, the author writes, "These girls, my girls, had both a real history and a fabricated one." What does she mean by this? Cite examples from the text.

Choices

Here are some other ways to demonstrate your understanding of the ideas in this lesson.

Social & Emotional Learning

↳ Journal Entry

Reflect on the restrictions placed on women in Iran. From this perspective, think about conditions in the United States. Are there liberties that Americans sometimes take for granted? Write your thoughts in the form of a journal entry. Share with the class if you feel comfortable doing so. How are other class members' reflections similar to or different from your own? Add your observations as another journal entry.

As you write and discuss, be sure to use the Academic Vocabulary words.

- **decline**
- **enable**
- **impose**
- **integrate**
- **reveal**

Media

↳ Timeline

Using authoritative sources, research how Iranian politics, society, and culture has changed since 2003, when Nafisi's memoir was written. Create a digital or hand-crafted timeline showing these changes, with images or other graphics to illustrate your points. Publish your timeline, or present it to a small group. Cite any referenced sources appropriately.

Speaking & Listening

↳ Podcast

With a partner, record a podcast in which you discuss the following questions:

- In what ways do Iranian women today respond to the restrictions put on them?
- How do you think you would respond if the United States experienced societal change as dramatic as Iran's?

Provide examples to support your ideas during the discussion, including evidence from the text. Once finished, take turns listening to other groups' podcasts. What similarities and differences do you notice between podcasts? Discuss conclusions as a whole class.

Expand Your Vocabulary

PRACTICE AND APPLY

Use your understanding of the vocabulary words to answer the following questions.

segregate **allocate** **convert** **irrelevant**

1. Are your friends' opinions ever **irrelevant**? Explain.
2. If your job were to **allocate** money to the clubs or sports teams at school, how would you do it?
3. Why might you **segregate** children according to age?
4. Is someone who believes fiercely in something likely to **convert**? Explain.

Vocabulary Strategy

Denotative and Connotative Meanings

Ed
Interactive Vocabulary Lesson: Denotation and Connotation

A word's **denotation** is its strict dictionary definition. But many words have slight nuances or differences in meaning. These nuances, or **connotations,** have associated meanings and emotions. Nafisi explains that in Iran, the buses are segregated. The vocabulary word *segregate* has a similar denotation to the word *separate*. They both mean "to set apart." But the word *segregate* has an altogether different connotation. To segregate suggests separating people or things forcefully, often in an unfair way.

PRACTICE AND APPLY

For each vocabulary word below, write the word's denotation. Then write the connotation of the word as it appears in the selection.

Vocabulary Word	Denotation	Connotation
allocate		
irrelevant		
convert		

Watch Your Language!

Verb Tense

In her memoir, Nafisi alternates between past and present tense, using each tense in a consistent way. When she uses **present tense,** Nafisi refers the reader to the actions taking place in the women's literature group, as if they are currently taking place. When the author uses **past tense,** she reflects on her time with the women, as well as on the events and atmosphere of Iran.

She doesn't walk upright, but bends her head towards the ground and doesn't look at passersby.	By using present tense as if the actions are currently taking place, the author creates a more immediate picture of her students.

These girls, my girls, had both a real history and a fabricated one.	By using past tense, the author reflects on the women in the group.

Interactive Grammar Lesson: Verb Tense

PRACTICE AND APPLY

Locate two additional sentences that use present-tense verbs and two additional sentences that use past-tense verbs. Write the sentences and describe how the author uses the verb tenses to make her point.

Present Tense	Effect of the Verb Tense
1.	
2.	

Past Tense	Effect of the Verb Tense
3.	
4.	

from Persepolis 2: The Story of a Return

Graphic Memoir by **Marjane Satrapi**

Engage Your Brain

Choose one or more of these activities to start connecting with the graphic memoir you are about to read.

Change Now!

Throughout history, people have found ways to advocate for change. Whether it is students hoping to see change in their schools or citizens protesting against their governments, people possess the capability to make changes. With a partner, discuss ways that people have protested against injustice throughout history.

Thinking About Words

What comes to mind when you hear the words *repression* and *dictator*? Make a sketch or freewrite your thoughts.

Banned!

Make a list of things you value that a dictatorship or repressive government could ban, or take away. Your list can include items like clothing or digital technology, certain kinds of music, or liberties such as freedom of speech. Compare your list with a partner's and discuss why you included the items you did.

Background

Since the Iranian Revolution of the late 1970s, "morality police" ensure that people comply with the laws in Iran. Those who do not comply may be taken to the morality police headquarters to be questioned, beaten, or jailed.

Marjane Satrapi (b. 1969) was born in Iran. After the revolution, her parents sent her to school in Europe. Later, she studied illustration. The first volume of *Persepolis* tells the story of Satrapi's childhood in Iran, and *Persepolis 2* tells the story of her adolescence in Europe and Iran and of her struggle to fit in. *Persepolis,* a movie based on both books, has won many awards. Satrapi lives in Paris.

Determine Author's Point of View

Point of view refers to how an author thinks or feels about a subject. In a memoir, an author uses rhetoric, choosing words carefully to advance a point of view. Graphic novelists, however, use both graphics and rhetoric to advance their points of view.

Title	How Point of View Is Conveyed	Examples
Reading Lolita in Tehran	The author's **perspective** as a woman and scholar living under a repressive regime is shown in the rhetoric she uses.	• phrases such as, "flogged, fined, forced to wash the toilets and humiliated"
Persepolis 2	The author tells the story through words and stark black-and-white images. Readers must study details in the drawings, as well as read captions and thought bubbles, to understand the author's point of view.	• the way the main character's face is drawn • the way the panels are sequenced, which reflects a point of view

Focus on Genre
Graphic Novel

- uses sequential art to tell a story in different panels
- content can be fiction or nonfiction
- contains text features
- text appears in captions and in dialogue and thought balloons

Analyze Accounts in Different Mediums

A personal story can be told using different **mediums,** or ways of communicating. Examples of mediums include memoirs, graphic novels, plays, and films. Each format allows the author to emphasize details that help to tell his or her story.

Read this sentence from *Reading Lolita in Tehran:*

> They patrol the streets to make sure women like Sanaz wear their veils properly, do not wear makeup, do not walk in public with men who are not their fathers, brothers or husbands.

Notice how this memoir is a personal account written from memory or firsthand knowledge. The writer uses concrete details and sensory words to help the reader visualize events and people.

In contrast, the middle panel in the second row of *Persepolis 2* provides visuals for the reader to understand the same situation. Readers must pay attention to the visual details in the drawings and the sequence of the panels as well as the text to understand the author's message.

As you read the excerpt from *Persepolis 2,* make notes about how the author conveys information through both images and words.

from

Persepolis 2: The Story of a Return

Graphic Memoir by **Marjane Satrapi**

In this graphic novel, people resist harsh government repression through small acts of rebellion.

DETERMINE AUTHOR'S POINT OF VIEW

Annotate: Mark a panel in which emotion is shown.

Interpret: How does the image pair with the words to show the author's point of view about her experiences?

ANALYZE ACCOUNTS IN DIFFERENT MEDIUMS

Annotate: Mark a speech bubble, a caption, and a thought bubble.

Analyze: Why might the author have chosen to tell this story using speech bubbles and captions—that is, in graphic form?

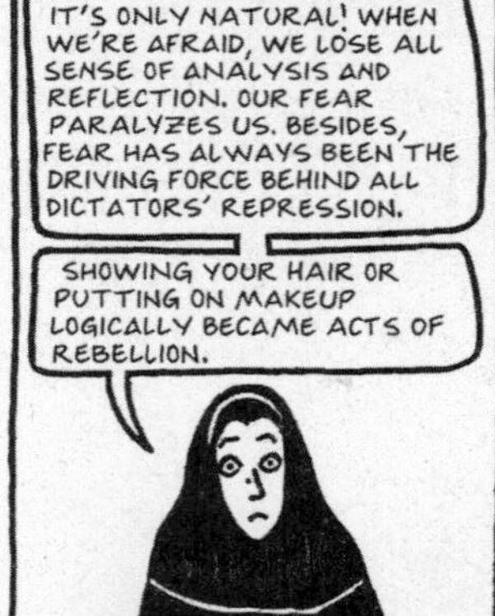

COLLABORATIVE DISCUSSION

What details in this excerpt surprised you? Discuss with a partner.

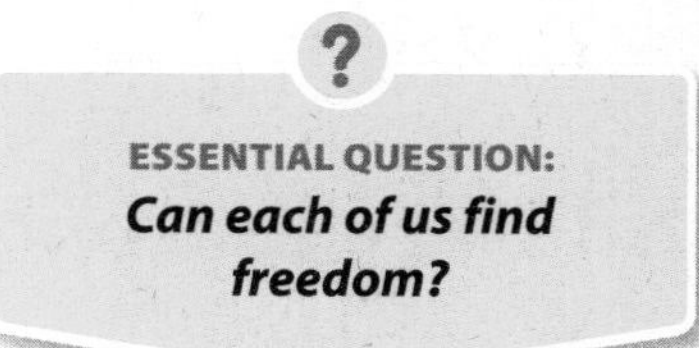

Review your notes and add your thoughts to your Response Log.

Assessment Practice

Answer these questions before moving on to the **Analyze the Text** section on the following page.

1. This question has two parts. First, answer **Part A**. Then, answer **Part B**.

Part A

What is this passage mostly about?

Ⓐ how the narrator's mother tried to escape from Iran

Ⓑ how women tried to educate themselves in Iran

Ⓒ how women rebelled against oppression in Iran

Ⓓ how the narrator's mother is brave even in the face of danger

Part B

Select the sentence that supports the answer to Part A.

Ⓐ "Between 1980 and 1983, the government had imprisoned and executed so many high-school and college students that we no longer dared to talk politics." (panel 2)

Ⓑ "To our leaders, the smallest thing could be a subject of subversion." (panel 4)

Ⓒ "What's going on in the political prisons?" (panel 7)

Ⓓ "Showing your hair or putting on makeup logically became acts of rebellion." (panel 8)

2. How does the caption in the second panel add to the reader's understanding of the text?

Ⓐ The factual information explains why the revolution occurred.

Ⓑ The factual information provides historical background for the text.

Ⓒ The opinions help explain the author's point of view.

Ⓓ The opinions help explain why people demonstrated against the government.

Test-Taking Strategies

Analyze the Text

Support your responses with evidence from the text.

NOTICE & NOTE

Review what you **noticed and noted** as you read the text. Your annotations can help you answer these questions.

1. **INFER** How does the main character in the graphic memoir feel about any power she may possess? Does she feel powerful or powerless? Why?

2. **ANALYZE** Look at the second and third panels in the excerpt. How does the author use both words and graphics to make a point about how the people's struggle has changed?

3. **INFER** The narrator says that she spent an entire day at the committee because of a pair of red socks. What might red socks have **symbolized,** or represented, to the committee?

4. **INTERPRET** The narrator's facial expression remains the same in each of the panels. How would you describe it? How does this visual consistency help reveal the author's point of view?

5. **DRAW CONCLUSIONS** Reread the last row of panels. What is the contrast between what you would expect the character to focus on, and what she actually pays attention to? How does this contrast point to the author's larger message?

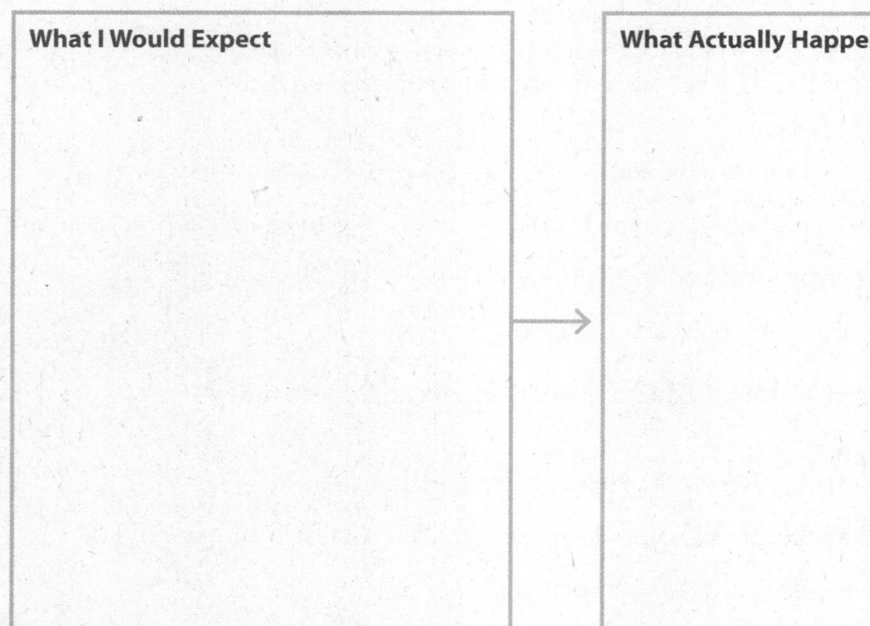

Choices

Here are some other ways to demonstrate your understanding of the ideas in this lesson.

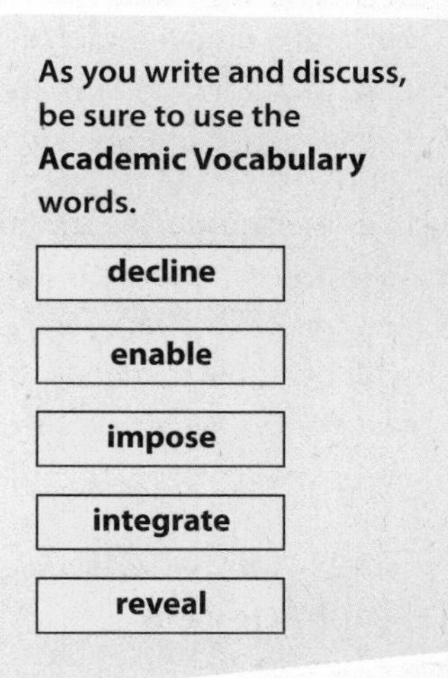

As you write and discuss, be sure to use the **Academic Vocabulary** words.
decline
enable
impose
integrate
reveal

Writing
Analysis

The images in graphic novels can convey information that traditional novels communicate in words. For example, graphic-novel images can communicate information about characters' emotions, attitudes, and points of view in addition to what characters look like. Review at least two graphic novels, paying attention to what is conveyed by the images alone. Then write an analysis in which you discuss what kinds of information the images communicate, and how that information is conveyed.

Media
Graphic Short

Create a graphic short that focuses on one of these ideas developed in the *Persepolis 2* excerpt:

- being subjected to scrutiny
- doubting oneself
- questioning rules or authority
- participating in small acts of rebellion

Draft a short plot and develop a storyboard that showcases setting, character emotions, and theme. Have a partner review your work and make necessary adjustments before creating your final draft. Once finished, present your graphic short to the class.

Speaking & Listening
Small-Group Debate

With a small group, debate the merits of graphic novels.

- Should they be considered as important as text-only works?
- Are they an effective way of communicating information?

Take a stand, supporting your argument with evidence from novels you have read. Consider other perspectives—making sure everyone is given an opportunity to speak—and build on each other's ideas.

Compare Treatments of a Topic

Both *Reading Lolita in Tehran* and *Persepolis 2* discuss life in Iran following the Iranian Revolution of the 1970s. Even though the texts address a similar topic, they do so using different genres. Both prose and graphic novel formats allow the author to communicate her story to the reader, but only one uses illustrations integrated with text.

In a small group, discuss the common elements in the two selections. Take notes in the chart below about each author's purpose, message, and use of language. On your own, write a few sentences describing your personal reactions to reading about the same general topic in two genres. Which genre did you prefer? Why?

Elements	A *Reading Lolita in Tehran*	B *Persepolis 2*
Author's purpose		
Author's message		
Use of language		
Notes about my reactions to the two selections:		

Analyze the Texts

Discuss these questions in your group.

1. **CONNECT** How is the way the authors communicate with readers similar and different in the two texts?
2. **COMPARE** What information is presented in both texts? What details are emphasized in each account?
3. **ANALYZE** What is the effect of using language only, as opposed to combining language and images? Are any aspects of the story gained by using images and/or lost by using fewer words in a graphic memoir?
4. **SYNTHESIZE** What have you learned from these two sources about the status of women in Iran since the Iranian Revolution?

Collaborate and Present

Now your group can continue exploring the ideas in these texts by collaborating to create a graphic-novel version of the excerpt from *Reading Lolita in Tehran*. Follow these steps, using an online collaborative platform if possible.

1. **BRAINSTORM** Imagine that Nafisi had written her memoir in the form of a graphic novel. Brainstorm how to recast the selection into a graphic novel. Think about how to create panels to convey the story.
2. **CREATE YOUR STORYBOARDS** Create sequential panels to tell Nafisi's story.
   - Illustrate the panels with hand-drawn or computer-generated images.
   - Decide how to use speech bubbles, thought bubbles, and captions to convey the specific activities of the women's literature group and captions to describe the setting in Iran.
   - Use details from the memoir that you think advance the story.
3. **DISCUSS WHAT YOU HAVE LEARNED** After partners or groups present their graphic novels to the class, discuss how effectively they convey Nafisi's message. Communicate and accept suggestions for improvement in a constructive manner. Think about what aspects of the excerpt from *Reading Lolita in Tehran* are emphasized in your graphic novel. How has the medium shaped the message in each case?
4. **REFLECT ON YOUR WORK** Evaluate your role in creating the graphic novel and in the group discussion. Jot down notes about your preparation for and participation in this activity. What were your main contributions?

Reader's Choice

Continue your exploration of the Essential Question by doing some independent reading about struggles for freedom. Read the titles and descriptions shown. Then mark the texts that interest you.

ESSENTIAL QUESTION:
Can each of us find freedom?

Short Reads

Available on Ed

These texts are available in your ebook. Choose one to read and rate. Then defend your rating to the class.

We Wear the Mask

Poem by **Paul Laurence Dunbar**

The poem's speaker conceals great pain under "the mask" that "lies."

Rate It 

The Prisoner Who Wore Glasses

Short Story by **Bessie Head**

A political prisoner combines cleverness and courage to get the best of a brutal overseer.

Rate It 

Reforming the World *from* America's Women

History Writing by **Gail Collins**

Middle-class women become radicalized as they fight for equality and the right to vote.

Rate It 

from Long Walk to Freedom

Memoir by **Nelson Mandela**

Nelson Mandela shows fearlessness and humility as he devotes his life to ending apartheid in South Africa.

Rate It 

Eulogy for Martin Luther King Jr.

Speech by **Robert F. Kennedy**

Robert F. Kennedy, as presidential candidate, delivers news that shocks the world.

Rate It 

Long Reads

Here are three recommended books that connect to this unit topic. For additional options, ask your teacher, school librarian, or peers. Which titles spark your interest?

Long Walk to Freedom

Memoir by **Nelson Mandela**

Nelson Mandela recounts his lifelong fight for human rights and racial equality in South Africa. Jailed for decades because of his efforts to free others from oppression, Mandela was eventually released and awarded the Nobel Peace Prize.

Goodbye, Vietnam

Novel by **Gloria Whelan**

When Vietnamese government soldiers start apprehending citizens, Mai's family decides to flee to Hong Kong. They endure harsh conditions on crowded boats to escape the brutality of their home country.

March

Graphic Memoir by **John Lewis**

In this graphic memoir, see how Congressional Representative John Lewis's life as a civil rights activist started. Protesting beside Martin Luther King Jr., Lewis helped change our nation, facing dangers and oppression while doing so.

Extension

↳ Connect & Create

TALKING ABOUT FREEDOM The title of this unit, Freedom at All Costs, suggests that sacrifice or hardship may be necessary to win liberty. Is this true? If so, what are the sacrifices? Write three or four journal entries where a character in one of the texts reflects on this question.

IMAGE BOARD Create an image board that reflects the subject, characters, or theme of the text you read.

1. Decide what images you want to include.
2. Include photos and/or illustrations that show settings, characters, events, or situations described in the text. If you like, include your own artwork.
3. Write captions describing how each image connects to the text.

Share your finished product with the class.

NOTICE & NOTE

- Pick one of the texts and annotate the Notice & Note signposts you find.
- Then, use the **Notice & Note Writing Frames** to help you write about the significance of the signposts.
- Compare your findings with those of other students who read the same text.

Notice & Note Writing Frames

Write a Research Report

Writing Prompt

Using ideas, information, and examples from multiple texts in this unit, write a research report about how a person or group of people overcame oppression by fighting for change.

Manage your time carefully so that you can

- review the texts in the unit;
- plan your report;
- write your report;
- revise and edit your report.

Be sure to

- organize your ideas clearly;
- use evidence from multiple sources;
- write with a formal, objective tone;
- end with a strong conclusion.

Review the Mentor Texts

For an example of a well-written research report you can use as a mentor text and source for your essay, review:

- *from* **Hidden Figures** (pages 485–489).

Make sure to carefully review your notes and annotations about this text. Think about the techniques the author used to present information in an interesting way.

Consider Your Sources

Review your list of texts in the unit and choose at least three that you may want to use as a source of ideas or evidence for your report.

As you review sources, consult the notes you made on your **Response Log.** Make additional notes about any ideas or facts that might be useful to use in your research report. Include source titles and page numbers in your notes to help you provide accurate citations when you include facts or ideas from these texts.

UNIT 5 SOURCES

- ☐ **Harrison Bergeron**
- ☐ **I Have a Dream**
- ☐ *from* **Interview with John Lewis** MEDIA
- ☐ *from* **Hidden Figures**
- ☐ **Booker T. and W.E.B.**
- ☐ *from* **Reading Lolita in Tehran**
- ☐ *from* **Persepolis 2: The Story of a Return**

Analyze the Prompt

Review the prompt to make sure you understand the assignment.

1. Mark the sentence in the prompt that identifies the topic of your research report. Rephrase this sentence in your own words.
2. Next, look for words that indicate the audience and purpose of your essay, and write a sentence describing each.

Consider Your Audience

Think about the following:

- Who will read my report?
- What do my readers already know about the topic?
- What facts will interest my audience most?

What is my writing task?

What topics might work?

What is my purpose?

Who is my audience?

Review the Rubric

Your research report will be scored using a rubric. As you write, focus on the characteristics as described in the chart. You will learn more about these characteristics as you work through the lesson.

Purpose, Focus, and Organization	Evidence and Elaboration	Conventions of Standard English
The response includes: • A strongly maintained controlling idea • Use of transitions to connect ideas • Logical progression of ideas • Appropriate style and tone	The response includes: • Effective use of evidence and sources • Effective use of elaboration • Clear and effective expression of ideas • Appropriate vocabulary • Varied sentence structure	The response may include: • Some minor errors in usage but no patterns of errors • Correct punctuation, capitalization, sentence formation, and spelling • Command of basic conventions

1 PLAN YOUR RESEARCH REPORT

Help with Planning

Consult **Interactive Writing Lesson: Conducting Research.**

Research Your Topic

As you research, narrow the topic to focus on one specific person or group in the struggle for freedom. Your topic should be developed with well-chosen, relevant, and interesting support. This support may take many forms:

- quotations from well-known people
- stories or anecdotes
- concrete details, such as numbers, years, or descriptions
- definitions, including explanations of key vocabulary terms

Use the chart to gather information about your topic.

- Keep track of your sources, including page numbers, so you can cite them in your report.
- Choose reliable and credible sources. If possible, confirm facts in more than one source.
- Use the advanced search function in search engines to obtain specific research.

Consider Your Topics

Potential topics might include:

- **African Americans living in the Jim Crow South**
- **Female mathematicians or scientists at NASA or other workplaces**
- **The U.S. Civil Rights Movement**
- **Racial segregation in U.S. schools**
- **Women in Iran**
- **Booker T. Washington**
- **W.E.B. Du Bois**
- **Dr. Martin Luther King Jr.**
- **Groups affected by censorship**

My Topic:		
Quotation, Concrete Detail, Fact, Story, or Definition	**Relevance to My Topic**	**Source**

Write a Thesis Statement

A strong thesis statement clearly expresses, in one or two sentences, the main idea of your report. Make sure your thesis statement mentions the group or person you are focusing on, how they were oppressed, and how they fought back.

My Thesis Statement:

Develop Ideas and Support

After you research your topic, you will identify and organize information that supports your thesis.

Develop three main ideas in the chart below. Each main idea will become a body paragraph that includes details, quotations, stories, or definitions. Add notes on any support that you will include in each body paragraph.

Main Idea 1:
Main Idea 2:
Main Idea 3:

Conduct Effective Research

- Consider using advanced search functions on search engines to identify specific research.
- Remember that you do not need to include in your report all of the information you learned in your research. Instead, choose the most significant facts and examples that support your thesis.
- Think about how you will integrate information from your research into your report so that one idea flows smoothly to the next.

Organize Ideas

Decide how to structure your report.

INTRODUCTION	• Catch the attention of your audience and show them why they should care about the topic. • Start with a question, quote, story, or detail about your topic. • Clearly state your thesis at the end of your introduction.
BODY PARAGRAPHS	• Present main ideas that support your thesis. • Write a paragraph about each main idea. • Use supporting details to develop each main idea. • Use transitions to show relationships between ideas. • Include vivid words, facts, and descriptions to make your report interesting. • Cite your sources to avoid plagiarism.
CONCLUSION	• Restate your thesis and tell why it is significant or meaningful. • Add something new for the reader to think about, such as a quote or a story.

Create Structure

Organize the facts and ideas in your body paragraphs so that they are not repetitive. Each body paragraph should focus on a separate idea and include details, stories, or quotations that support that idea. Make sure each idea leads logically to the next.

2 DEVELOP A DRAFT

Now it is time to draft your research report. Examine how professional authors organize their research into an interesting, coherent report. You may use similar techniques in your own writing.

Ed

Drafting Online

Check your assignment list for a writing task from your teacher.

Explain a Main Idea

EXAMINE THE MENTOR TEXT

Notice how Margot Lee Shetterly, the author of *Hidden Figures*, explains why World War II created a need for female scientists and engineers.

The author introduces the **main idea.**

She explains a **cause-and-effect** relationship. Women were needed at NACA because many men were at war.

A few years earlier, an ad like this would have been unthinkable —most employers never would have considered a woman for a job that had always been performed by a man. But in the spring of 1943, with World War II in full swing and many men off serving in the military, the country needed all the help it could get. Employers were beginning to hire women to do jobs that had once belonged only to men.

She includes specific **details** to help the reader to understand the timeline.

She **restates** the main idea and explains the implications.

APPLY TO YOUR DRAFT

Use this chart to practice writing a body paragraph.

Use Transitions

Transitions show the reader how ideas are related. Examples are: *so, in fact, but, however, in addition to, after, before.*

Topic Sentence Use your topic sentence to introduce the main idea.	
Sentences with Supporting Details Your details may include facts, quotations, or definitions that add depth to your main idea.	
Concluding Sentence Restate your main idea and tell about its significance.	

Use Precise Language and Tone

EXAMINE THE MENTOR TEXT

In *Hidden Figures*, Margot Lee Shetterly uses precise language and scientific vocabulary, helping her create an authoritative tone.

The author uses **language** from the time to explain why airplanes were so important during the war.

She uses **technical and scientific words** to discuss airplane production.

World leaders felt that the country that ruled the skies would win the war. President Franklin D. Roosevelt believed in the importance of air power, so two years earlier, in 1941, he had challenged the nation to increase its production of airplanes to fifty thousand units a year....

The NACA and private industry were up for the challenge. By 1943, the American aircraft industry was the largest, most productive, and most sophisticated in the world....

The author states her idea with a **confident, precise** tone and uses specific, descriptive words.

APPLY TO YOUR DRAFT

Review your research plan. Identify a portion of your report that will require using scientific or technical language or language specific to a time period. Use the chart below to note explanations of terms that may be unfamiliar to your readers.

Technical, Scientific, or Time Period-Specific Words	Definition or Explanation

3 REVISE YOUR RESEARCH REPORT

Even professional writers need to revise their work. Use the guide below to help you as you revise your research report.

Help with Revision

Find a **Peer Review Guide** and **Student Models** online.

REVISION GUIDE		
Ask Yourself	**Prove It**	**Revise It**
Introduction Does my research report start in an interesting way? Does it include a thesis statement?	**Draw** a box around your introduction. **Highlight** your thesis statement.	**Add** a question, anecdote, or quotation to your introduction to catch your reader's attention. **Revise** your thesis until it sounds strong, clear, and confident.
Body Does each body paragraph include a main idea to support my thesis? Do relevant details support my ideas?	**Highlight** the main ideas that support your thesis. **Star** (★) any information that does not relate to the main ideas or your thesis. **Underline** relevant details that support your thesis and main ideas.	**Revise** the body paragraphs to focus on the main ideas. **Delete** any extraneous information. **Add** specific details and facts to strengthen your ideas.
Sources Did I cite my sources?	**Put a check mark** (✔) by each of your sources.	**Add** citation information.
Transitions Do my ideas progress logically throughout the report? Did I use transitions to link ideas?	Reread your report. **Put a check mark** (✔) by anything that doesn't flow logically. **Circle** the transitions between ideas.	**Revise** any parts that are unclear. **Add** transitions to link ideas together.
Style and Tone Did I write with an appropriate style and tone for my audience?	**Circle** language that is too casual or words your audience may not know.	**Revise** for a formal tone. **Define** any unfamiliar words.
Conclusion Did I end with a satisfying conclusion that relates to my introduction?	**Highlight** your concluding statement.	**Revise** your conclusion for clarity. Connect it to the introduction.

APPLY TO YOUR DRAFT

Consider the following as you look for opportunities to improve your writing.

- Make sure your work conforms to the guidelines in a style manual provided by your teacher.
- Check that your main ideas and conclusion are clear and focused.
- Avoid using informal language.

Peer Review in Action

Once you have finished revising you report, you will exchange papers with a partner in a **peer review.** During a peer review, you will give suggestions to improve your partner's draft.

Read the introduction from a student's draft, and examine the comments made by his peer reviewer.

Draft

Dr. King: Leader of the Civil Rights Movement
By Landon Hunter, Oak River High School

I think Martin Luther King Jr. was a very important person in the Civil Rights Movement. He fought for equal rights and gave a speech that is still important today, the "I Have a Dream" speech. He was very influential, and he helped people fight for equal rights and an end to segregation. We remember him today with respect and admiration.

Avoid using first person in a formal essay. Look for a better way to grab the reader's attention, such as with a quote or a story.

Your thesis should include main ideas that tell how Dr. King achieved his goals.

Now read the revised introduction below. Notice how the writer has improved his draft by making revisions based on his peer reviewer's comments.

Revision

Dr. King: Leader of the Civil Rights Movement
By Landon Hunter, Oak River High School

At the March on Washington 50 years ago, Martin Luther King Jr. stirred his audience with a powerful vision of racial equality in the United States. The words of his dream still echo in our heads many years later, but his influence reaches far beyond one speech. Dr. King was an important voice of the Civil Rights Movement because he used religion, peaceful protest, and powerful words to motivate people to fight for equal rights and an end to segregation.

Much better! Your opening catches the reader's attention right away.

Good job adding a transition to link your thoughts.

This thesis is a lot stronger—it's more specific and it references the main ideas the report will explore.

APPLY TO YOUR DRAFT

During your peer review, give each other specific suggestions for how you could make your reports more detailed, relevant, and engaging. Use your revision guide to help you.

When receiving feedback from your partner, listen attentively and ask questions to make sure you fully understand the revision suggestions.

4 EDIT YOUR RESEARCH REPORT

Edit your final draft to check for proper use of standard English conventions and to correct any misspellings or grammatical errors.

Interactive Grammar Lesson: Pronoun-Antecedent Agreement

Watch Your Language!

CHECK FOR PRONOUN-ANTECEDENT AGREEMENT

The noun that a pronoun replaces is called its *antecedent*. The pronoun should agree with, or match, the noun that it replaces.

- A **singular pronoun** replaces a singular noun.
- A **plural pronoun** replaces a plural noun.

Below are examples of pronoun-antecedent agreement from *Hidden Figures*.

Pronoun Type	Example
Singular Pronouns	**President Franklin D. Roosevelt believed in the importance of air power, so two years earlier, in 1941, he had challenged the nation to increase its production of airplanes to fifty thousand units a year.**
Plural Pronouns	**People working at Langley knew that they were doing their part to win the war.**

Choose Pronouns Correctly

- The pronoun *it* should replace something that is not a person.
- Pay attention to whether the pronoun is a subject or an object pronoun.
- Some pronouns are possessive, meaning they show ownership.
- For more information on pronouns, reference the guidelines in a style manual provided by your teacher.

APPLY TO YOUR DRAFT

Now apply what you've learned about pronouns to your own work.

1. **Read your paper aloud.** Underline the pronouns in one paragraph, such as the first paragraph.
2. **Highlight the nouns, or antecedents.** Check that the pronouns match the antecedents. Continue as time allows.
3. **Exchange** drafts with a peer and review pronoun-antecedent agreement in each other's work.

5 PUBLISH YOUR RESEARCH REPORT

Share It!

Finalize your report for your writing portfolio. You may also use your report as inspiration for other projects.

Ways to Share

- **Create a multimedia presentation** for your class.
- **Create a poster** that visually presents the information in your report.
- **Record a podcast.**

Reflect & Extend

Here are some other ways to show your understanding of the ideas in Unit 5.

Reflect on the **Essential Question**

Can each of us find freedom?

Has your answer to the question changed after reading the texts in the unit? Discuss your ideas.

You can use these sentence starters to help you reflect on your learning.

- **I'm still considering . . .**
- **I wasn't expecting to realize . . .**
- **I still believe . . .**

Project-Based Learning

Create a Protest Song

With a group of classmates, write and record a protest song addressing an injustice that concerns you. Here are some questions to ask yourself to get started:

- What injustice is our song going to address? Why is this issue important to us?
- Who is the target audience of our song?
- What themes do we want to express in our song?

Media Projects

To find help with this task online, access **Create a Protest Song.**

Writing

Write a Poem

Write a poem that explores the idea of freedom or oppression. Use the chart to jot down ideas. Then, write your poem.

Ask Yourself	My Notes
How will I **structure** my poem?	
Who will the **speaker** be?	
What **message** will my poem express?	

Analyze the Image
What threats or challenges does this person face?
Ed
Get hooked by the unit topic.
Stream to Start Video

Epic Journeys

"If a journey doesn't have something to teach you about yourself, then what kind of journey is it?"

— Kira Salak

ESSENTIAL QUESTION:

What drives us to take on a challenge?

Spark Your Learning

Here are some opportunities to think about the topics and themes of **Unit 6: Epic Journeys.**

As you read, you can use the **Response Log** (page R6) to track your thinking about the Essential Question.

?

Think About the **Essential Question**

What drives us to take on a challenge?

What motivates people to take on a challenge? The hope of a reward? The feeling of personal accomplishment? Something else? Make a list of reasons. Then compare lists with a partner, noting similarities and differences.

Make the Connection

Epic journeys take many forms, from traveling through forbidding places to exploring the mind. What journeys can you think of that have changed you or people you know? Discuss your ideas with a partner.

Build Academic Vocabulary

You can use these Academic Vocabulary words to write and talk about the topics and themes in this unit. Which of these words do you already feel comfortable using when speaking or writing?

	I can use it!	I understand it.	I'll look it up.
motivate			
objective			
pursuit			
subsequent			
undertake			

Prove It!

What does it take to successfully meet a challenging goal? Discuss your ideas using at least two of the academic vocabulary words.

Preview the Texts

Look over the images, titles, and descriptions of the texts in the unit. Mark the title of the text that interests you most.

from The Odyssey

Epic Poem by **Homer**

Odysseus and his fellow sailors encounter epic, life-threatening adventures as they make their way home to Ithaca.

Archaeology's Tech Revolution

Informational Text by **Jeremy Hsu**

New technologies are helping archaeologists learn more about lost worlds.

from The Cruelest Journey: 600 Miles to Timbuktu

Travel Writing by **Kira Salak**

The author achieves the unthinkable—a solo 600-mile kayak trip on the Niger River.

The Journey

Poem by **Mary Oliver**

The narrator describes the moment when she realizes that she can, and must, change her life.

Think Outside the Box

Think about the quotation from Kira Salak on page 535: "If a journey doesn't have something to teach you about yourself, then what kind of journey is it?"

What could we learn about ourselves from taking on a challenge or setting out on a journey of some kind? Jot down your ideas.

The Epic

Extraordinary heroes in pursuit of hideous monsters. Brutal battles fought and perilous quests undertaken. Spectacular triumphs and crushing defeats. The epic, still very much alive in today's novels and movies, began thousands of years ago in the oral tradition of ancient Greece. There, listeners gathered around poet-storytellers to hear the daring exploits of the hero Odysseus. Across storm-tossed seas, through wild forests, amid countless dangers and subsequent narrow escapes, the hero, motivated by a singular focus on his objective, prevails against all odds. It's no wonder that Homer's Odyssey *remains one of the most beloved epics in Western literature. It captivates us and carries us off into a time and place quite different from—yet somehow similar to—our own.*

Characteristics of the Epic

An **epic** is a long narrative poem. It recounts the adventures of an **epic hero,** a larger-than-life figure who undertakes great journeys and performs deeds requiring remarkable bravery and cunning. As you begin your own journey through Homer's epic, you can expect to encounter the following elements.

<table>
<tr><th colspan="2">Elements of the Epic</th></tr>
<tr><td>Epic Hero
• possesses superhuman strength, craftiness, and confidence
• helped or harmed by gods or fate
• embodies qualities valued by the culture
• overcomes perilous situations</td><td>Archetypes
Characters and situations recognizable across times and cultures
• brave hero
• sea monster
• suitors' contest
• evil temptress
• loyal servant
• buried treasure</td></tr>
<tr><td>Epic Plot
Depicts a long, strange journey filled with such complications as
• strange creatures
• treacherous weather
• divine intervention
• large-scale events</td><td>Epic Themes
Reflect universal concerns, such as
• courage
• loyalty
• beauty
• the fate of a nation
• life and death
• a homecoming</td></tr>
<tr><td colspan="2">Epic Setting
• includes fantastic or exotic lands
• involves more than one nation or culture</td></tr>
</table>

The Language of Homer

The people of ancient Greece who first experienced *The Odyssey* heard it sung in a live performance. The poet, or another performer, used epic similes, epithets, and allusions to help keep the audience enthralled.

- A **simile** is a comparison between two unlike things, using the word *like* or *as*. Homer often employs the **epic simile,** a comparison developed over several lines. For example, the epic simile in this passage compares an angry Odysseus to a sausage.

> His rage
> held hard in leash, submitted to his mind,
> while he himself rocked, rolling from side to side,
> as a cook turns a sausage, big with blood
> and fat, at a scorching blaze, without a pause,
> to broil it quick: so he rolled left and right, . . .

- An **epithet** renames a person or thing with a descriptive phrase. To maintain the meter of the poem or complete a line of verse, the poet would often use an epithet containing the necessary number of syllables. For example, Homer often refers to Odysseus by such epithets as "son of Laertes" and "raider of cities."
- An **allusion** is a reference to a literary or historical person, place, event, or composition. For example, when Telemachus, Odysseus' son, beholds the palace of Menelaus, he exclaims, "This is the way the court of Zeus must be." Every listener in Greece immediately understood the allusion to Zeus, the ruler of the gods.

Examining the Homeric Epics

Considered the greatest masterpieces of the epic form, *The Iliad* and *The Odyssey* present high drama and intense emotions. In both books, important plot elements include the interference of gods in human affairs, the epic heroism of the central characters, and the saga and aftermath of the Trojan War. As sources for his epics, Homer drew on stories and legends that had been passed down orally by bards for centuries.

The Trojan War The legendary conflict between Greece (or Achaea) and Troy began around 1200 BCE. Paris, a Trojan prince, kidnapped Helen, the wife of Menelaus, king of Sparta. Menelaus recruited the armies of allied kingdoms to attack Troy and recover his wife. For ten years the Greek forces held Troy under siege, but they could not breach the city walls.

Finally, Odysseus, king of Ithaca, planned a way to break the stalemate. He ordered his men to build a giant wooden horse. The people of Troy awoke the next day to find that horse outside the city gates—and no Greeks in sight. Assuming the Greeks had retreated, leaving the horse as a peace offering, they brought it inside the gates. They discovered too late that the horse was filled with Greek soldiers and their city was doomed.

Heroism *The Odyssey* recounts Odysseus' adventures and struggles as he returns home from post-war Troy, along with the conflicts that arise in Ithaca before and after his return. He prevails against gruesome monsters, enchanting women, and greedy rivals intent on preventing him from reaching his objective. Odysseus employs cleverness and guile to overcome his trials.

Get Ready

from The Odyssey

Epic Poem by **Homer**

Translated by **Robert Fitzgerald**

ESSENTIAL QUESTION:
What drives us to take on a challenge?

Engage Your Brain

Choose one or more of these activities to start connecting with the poem you're about to read.

That's Epic!

What does the word *epic* mean to you? With a partner, brainstorm people, events, or situations you would call epic. Then look the word up in a dictionary. How close is the dictionary definition to the way you use the word?

My Hero

Think about someone you consider a hero. What qualities or characteristics do you admire in this person? Brainstorm a list of up to 10 heroic traits. Exchange lists with a partner, and note any overlapping traits.

The Hero's Journey

The term "hero's journey" refers to an individual who goes on an adventure and returns transformed in some way. Think about films, video games, or books that describe this kind of epic adventure. Choose one, and then draw or describe the specifics of the journey and how it changed the individual.

Analyze Character: Epic Hero

Odysseus is an **epic hero**—a larger-than-life character who embodies the ideals of a nation or culture. Epic heroes take part in long, dangerous adventures and accomplish great deeds. They are considered **archetypes** because they can be found in many works from different cultures throughout the ages. Often their character traits provide clues to the epic's **themes.** In addition, the form, style, and point of view of epics provides insight into the historical time in which they were written.

Although epic heroes may have superhuman abilities, they still have human flaws. These flaws make them more complex and also more believable. For example, Odysseus demonstrates extraordinary strength and courage, but his overconfidence results in a tendency to dismiss warnings. His imperfections help make him more human, so that the audience can relate to his mistakes.

As you read, take notes in the chart to help you analyze how the complex character of Odysseus develops over the course of the epic.

Question about Odysseus	Notes from the Epic
What do you learn about Odysseus' character through the way he faces various conflicts?	
What traits, or qualities, does Odysseus show through his interactions with other characters?	
What do Odysseus' character traits tell you about what the ancient Greeks found admirable? What themes do you predict Homer might develop?	

Analyze Epic Poetry

An **epic** is a long narrative poem, usually an adventure story. An epic plot spans many years and involves a long journey. Often, the fate of an entire nation is at stake. An epic **setting** spans great distances and foreign lands. Epic **themes** reflect universal concerns, such as courage, honor, life, and death. To appreciate *The Odyssey* as poetry, follow these steps:

- Read the epic aloud. Listen for sound devices, such as alliteration, meter, and rhyme, and notice how they reflect and enhance meaning.
- Pay attention to structure by following punctuation closely. Remember that the end of a line does not indicate the end of a thought.
- Consider how imagery and figurative language, including epic similes, develop characters, create a mood, and reveal plot events. Note allusions and epithets.

Focus on Genre
↳ Epic Poem

- **a long, narrative poem on a serious subject in an elevated or formal style**
- **tells adventures of a hero whose traits reflect the ideals of a nation or culture**
- **addresses universal themes**
- **occurs across cultures and time periods**

As you read, make notes in the chart about poetic elements you notice.

Poetic Device	Example
Sound devices	
Imagery and figurative language	
Allusions and epithets	
Other poetic elements	

Annotation in Action

Here are one reader's notes about a passage in *The Odyssey*. As you read, note characteristics of epic poetry.

He saw the townlands
and learned the minds of many distant men,
and weathered many bitter nights and days
in his deep heart at sea, while he fought only
to save his life, to bring his shipmates home.

epic poem setting—
a wanderer who
sees many lands

Background

Homer may have lived sometime between 900 and 800 BCE—if he ever lived at all. Although the ancient Greeks credited him with composing *The Iliad* and *The Odyssey*, people have long argued about whether he really existed. Many theorists speculate on who Homer may have been and where he may have lived. Details in the stories suggest that he was born and lived in the area of the eastern Aegean Sea, either on the island of Chios or in Smyrna, and that he was blind.

Whatever position modern scholars take on the debate, most believe that one or two exceptionally talented individuals created the Homeric epics. *The Iliad* and *The Odyssey* each contain 24 books of verse, but they probably predate the development of writing in Greece. The verses, which were originally sung, gradually became part of an important oral tradition. Generations of professional reciters memorized and performed the poems at festivals throughout Greece. By 300 BCE, several versions of the books existed, and scholars undertook the job of standardizing the texts.

Homer's poems profoundly influenced Greek culture and, as a result, contributed to the subsequent development of Western literature, ideas, and values. The Roman poet Virgil wrote a related poem, the *Aeneid*, in Latin, and Odysseus appears in Dante's *Inferno*. Poets throughout English literature, from Geoffrey Chaucer in the Middle Ages to William Shakespeare in the Renaissance to John Keats in the Romantic era, have found inspiration in Homer. James Joyce's 1922 novel *Ulysses* (the Latin form of Odysseus' name) transforms one ordinary Dublin day into an Odyssean journey. Dozens of movies have retold the saga of the Trojan War and the long journey home, both directly and symbolically. For thousands of years people have taken the tales of a wandering Greek bard and made them their own.

from

The Odyssey

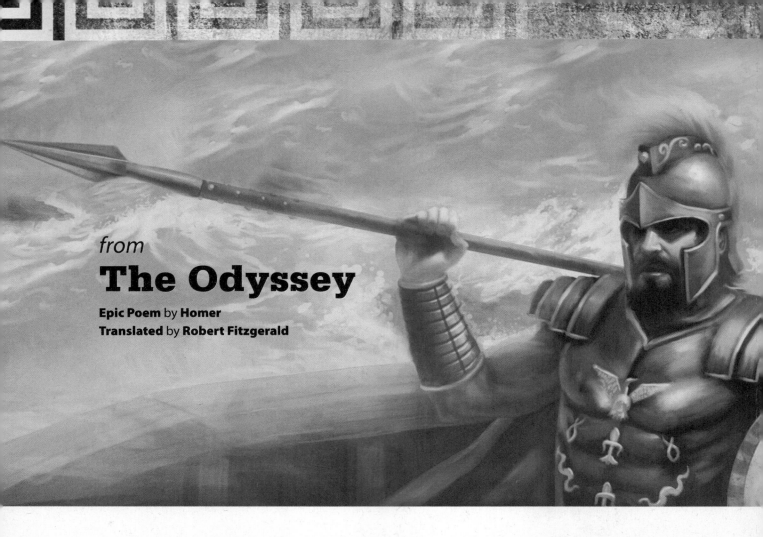

Epic Poem by **Homer**
Translated by **Robert Fitzgerald**

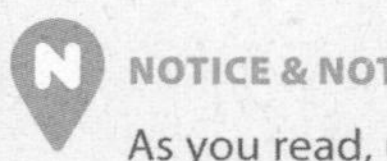

NOTICE & NOTE

As you read, use the side margins to make notes about the text.

Odysseus and his fellow sailors encounter epic and life-threatening adventures as they make their way home to Ithaca.

Important Characters in *The Odyssey* (in order of mention)

Book 1

Helios (hē´lē-ŏs), the sun god, who raises his cattle on the island of Thrinacia (thrĭ-nā´shə)

Zeus (zo͞os), the ruler of the Greek gods and goddesses; father of Athena and Apollo

Telemachus (tə-lĕm´ə-kəs), Odysseus' son

Penelope (pə-nĕl´ə-pē), Odysseus' wife

Book 9

Alcinous (ăl-sĭn´ō-əs), the king of the Phaeacians (fē-ā´shənz)

Cyclopes (sī-klō´pēz), a race of one-eyed giants; an individual member of the race is a Cyclops (sī´klŏps)

Apollo (ə-pŏl´ō), the god of music, poetry, prophecy, and medicine

Poseidon (pō-sīd´n), the god of the seas, earthquakes, and horses; father of the Cyclops who battles Odysseus

Athena (ə-thē´nə), the goddess of war, wisdom, and cleverness; goddess of crafts

Book 12

Circe (sûr´sē), a goddess and enchantress who lives on the island of Aeaea (ē-ē´ə)

Sirens (sī´rənz), creatures, part woman and part bird, whose songs lure sailors to their death

Don't forget to **Notice & Note** as you read the text.

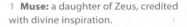

BOOK 1
A Goddess Intervenes

Sing in me, Muse, and through me tell the story
of that man skilled in all ways of contending,
the wanderer, harried for years on end,
after he plundered the stronghold
on the proud height of Troy.

He saw the townlands
and learned the minds of many distant men,
and weathered many bitter nights and days
in his deep heart at sea, while he fought only
to save his life, to bring his shipmates home.
But not by will nor valor could he save them,
for their own recklessness destroyed them all—
children and fools, they killed and feasted on
the cattle of Lord Helios, the Sun,
and he who moves all day through heaven
took from their eyes the dawn of their return.

Of these adventures, Muse, daughter of Zeus,
tell us in our time, lift the great song again. . . .

The story of Odysseus begins with the goddess Athena appealing to Zeus to help Odysseus, who has been wandering for ten years on the seas, to find his way home to his family on Ithaca. While Odysseus has been gone, his son, Telemachus, has grown to manhood and Odysseus' wife, Penelope, has been besieged by suitors wishing to marry her and gain Odysseus' wealth. The suitors have taken up residence in her home and are constantly feasting on the family's cattle, sheep, and goats. They dishonor Odysseus and his family. Taking Athena's advice, Telemachus travels to Pylos for word of his father. Meanwhile, on Ithaca, the evil suitors plot to kill Telemachus when he returns.

1 **Muse:** a daughter of Zeus, credited with divine inspiration.

3 **harried:** tormented; harassed.

Close Read Screencast

Listen to a modeled close read of this text.

11–13 **their own recklessness . . . the Sun:** a reference to an event occurring later in the poem—an event that causes the death of Odysseus' entire crew.

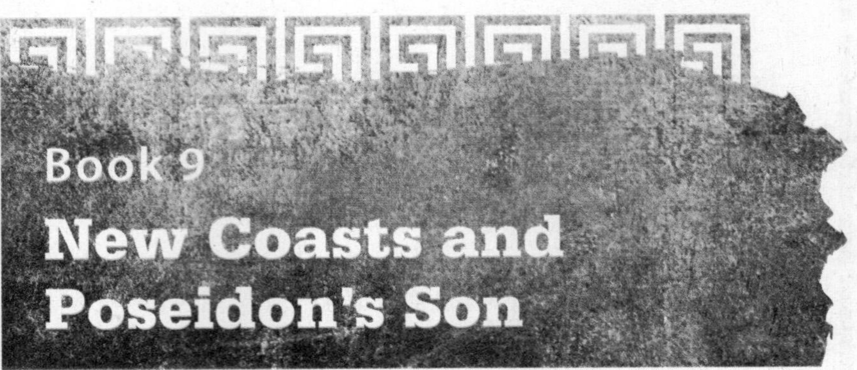

Book 9
New Coasts and Poseidon's Son

The Cyclops

Odysseus has spent ten years wandering the Mediterranean Sea. By Book 9, he has reached the island of Scheria, where King Alcinous has welcomed him with a banquet. Odysseus agrees to tell King Alcinous stories about his adventures, including the following story about a race of creatures called the Cyclopes.

"In the next land we found were Cyclopes,
giants, louts, without a law to bless them.
In ignorance leaving the fruitage of the earth in mystery
to the immortal gods, they neither plow
nor sow by hand, nor till the ground, though grain—
wild wheat and barley—grows untended, and
wine-grapes, in clusters, ripen in heaven's rain.
Cyclopes have no muster and no meeting,
no consultation or old tribal ways,
but each one dwells in his own mountain cave
dealing out rough justice to wife and child,
indifferent to what the others do. . . ."

VOCABULARY

Words from Latin: The word *indifferent* in line 12 contains the Latin root *differens,* meaning "to quarrel or dispute." The prefix *in-* means "not."

Analyze: Based on the information above and the word's context, what do you think *indifferent* means? Look the word up in a dictionary to confirm its meaning.

Across the bay from the land of the Cyclopes is a lush, deserted island. Odysseus and his crew land on the island in a dense fog and spend days feasting on wine and wild goats and observing the mainland, where the Cyclopes live. On the third day, Odysseus and his company of men set out to learn if the Cyclopes are friends or foes.

"When the young Dawn with finger tips of rose
came in the east, I called my men together
and made a speech to them:

'Old shipmates, friends,
the rest of you stand by; I'll make the crossing
in my own ship, with my own company,
and find out what the mainland natives are—
for they may be wild savages, and lawless,
or hospitable and god fearing men.'
At this I went aboard, and gave the word
to cast off by the stern. My oarsmen followed,
filing in to their benches by the rowlocks,
and all in line dipped oars in the gray sea.

22 **stern:** the rear end of a ship.

As we rowed on, and nearer to the mainland,
at one end of the bay, we saw a cavern
yawning above the water, screened with laurel,
and many rams and goats about the place
inside a sheepfold—made from slabs of stone
earthfast between tall trunks of pine and rugged
towering oak trees.

A prodigious man

slept in this cave alone, and took his flocks
to graze afield—remote from all companions,
knowing none but savage ways, a brute
so huge, he seemed no man at all of those
who eat good wheaten bread; but he seemed rather
a shaggy mountain reared in solitude.
We beached there, and I told the crew
to stand by and keep watch over the ship;
as for myself I took my twelve best fighters
and went ahead. I had a goatskin full
of that sweet liquor that Euanthes' son,
Maron, had given me. He kept Apollo's
holy grove at Ismarus; for kindness
we showed him there, and showed his wife and child,
he gave me seven shining golden talents
perfectly formed, a solid silver winebowl,
and then this liquor—twelve two-handled jars
of brandy, pure and fiery. Not a slave
in Maron's household knew this drink; only
he, his wife and the storeroom mistress knew;
and they would put one cupful—ruby-colored,
honey-smooth—in twenty more of water,
but still the sweet scent hovered like a fume
over the winebowl. No man turned away
when cups of this came round.

A wineskin full

I brought along, and victuals in a bag,
for in my bones I knew some towering brute
would be upon us soon—all outward power,
a wild man, ignorant of civility.

We climbed, then, briskly to the cave. But Cyclops
had gone afield, to pasture his fat sheep,
so we looked round at everything inside:
a drying rack that sagged with cheeses, pens
crowded with lambs and kids, each in its class:
firstlings apart from middlings, and the 'dewdrops,'

Don't forget to **Notice & Note** as you read the text.

27 **screened with laurel:** partially hidden by laurel trees.

42–43 **Euanthes** (yo͞o-ăn´thēz); **Maron** (mâr´ŏn).

46 **talents:** bars of gold or silver of a specified weight, used as money in ancient Greece.

57 **victuals** (vĭt´lz)**:** food.

66–67 The Cyclops has separated his lambs into three age groups.

or newborn lambkins, penned apart from both.
And vessels full of whey were brimming there—
bowls of earthenware and pails for milking.
My men came pressing round me, pleading:
                                                  'Why not
take these cheeses, get them stowed, come back,
throw open all the pens, and make a run for it?
We'll drive the kids and lambs aboard. We say
put out again on good salt water!'

how sound that was! Yet I refused. I wished
to see the caveman, what he had to offer—
no pretty sight, it turned out, for my friends.
We lit a fire, burnt an offering,
and took some cheese to eat; then sat in silence
around the embers, waiting. When he came
he had a load of dry boughs on his shoulder
to stoke his fire at suppertime. He dumped it
with a great crash into that hollow cave,
and we all scattered fast to the far wall.
Then over the broad cavern floor he ushered
the ewes he meant to milk. He left his rams

68 **whey:** the watery part of milk, which separates from the curds, or solid part, during the making of cheese.

74 **good salt water:** the open sea.

78 **burnt an offering:** burned a portion of the food as an offering to secure the gods' goodwill. (Such offerings were frequently performed by Greek sailors during difficult journeys.)

ANALYZE CHARACTER: EPIC HERO

Annotate: Mark foreshadowing in lines 75–77 suggesting that Odysseus has a weakness that may bring trouble.

Evaluate: What flaws might be revealed in these lines?

Don't forget to **Notice & Note** as you read the text.

and he-goats in the yard outside, and swung
high overhead a slab of solid rock
to close the cave. Two dozen four-wheeled wagons,
with heaving wagon teams, could not have stirred
the tonnage of that rock from where he wedged it
over the doorsill. Next he took his seat
and milked his bleating ewes. A practiced job
he made of it, giving each ewe her suckling;
thickened his milk, then, into curds and whey,
sieved out the curds to drip in withy baskets,
and poured the whey to stand in bowls
cooling until he drank it for his supper.
When all these chores were done, he poked the fire,
heaping on brushwood. In the glare he saw us.

'Strangers,' he said, 'who are you? And where from?
What brings you here by sea ways—a fair traffic?
Or are you wandering rogues, who cast your lives
like dice, and ravage other folk by sea?'

We felt a pressure on our hearts, in dread
of that deep rumble and that mighty man.
But all the same I spoke up in reply:

'We are from Troy, Achaeans, blown off course
by shifting gales on the Great South Sea;
homeward bound, but taking routes and ways
uncommon; so the will of Zeus would have it.
We served under Agamemnon, son of Atreus—
the whole world knows what city
he laid waste, what armies he destroyed.
It was our luck to come here; here we stand,
beholden for your help, or any gifts
you give—as custom is to honor strangers.
We would entreat you, great Sir, have a care
for the gods' courtesy; Zeus will avenge
the unoffending guest.'

He answered this

from his brute chest, unmoved:

'You are a ninny,

or else you come from the other end of nowhere,
telling me, mind the gods! We Cyclopes
care not a whistle for your thundering Zeus
or all the gods in bliss; we have more force by far.
I would not let you go for fear of Zeus—
you or your friends—unless I had a whim to.
Tell me, where was it, now, you left your ship—
around the point, or down the shore, I wonder?'

He thought he'd find out, but I saw through this,
and answered with a ready lie:

96 **withy baskets:** baskets made from twigs.

102 **fair traffic:** honest trading.

117–120 It was a sacred Greek custom to honor strangers with food and gifts. Odysseus is reminding the Cyclops that Zeus will punish anyone who mistreats a guest.

'My ship?
Poseidon Lord, who sets the earth a-tremble,
broke it up on the rocks at your land's end.
A wind from seaward served him, drove us there.
We are survivors, these good men and I.'

Neither reply nor pity came from him,
but in one stride he clutched at my companions
and caught two in his hands like squirming puppies
to beat their brains out, spattering the floor.
Then he dismembered them and made his meal,
gaping and crunching like a mountain lion—
everything: innards, flesh, and marrow bones.
We cried aloud, lifting our hands to Zeus,
powerless, looking on at this, appalled;
but Cyclops went on filling up his belly
with manflesh and great gulps of whey,
then lay down like a mast among his sheep.
My heart beat high now at the chance of action,
and drawing the sharp sword from my hip I went
along his flank to stab him where the midriff
holds the liver. I had touched the spot
when sudden fear stayed me: if I killed him
we perished there as well, for we could never
move his ponderous doorway slab aside.
So we were left to groan and wait for morning.

154 ponderous: heavy in a clumsy way; bulky.

When the young Dawn with fingertips of rose
lit up the world, the Cyclops built a fire
and milked his handsome ewes, all in due order,
putting the sucklings to the mothers. Then,
his chores being all dispatched, he caught
another brace of men to make his breakfast,
and whisked away his great door slab
to let his sheep go through—but he, behind,
reset the stone as one would cap a quiver.
There was a din of whistling as the Cyclops
rounded his flock to higher ground, then stillness.
And now I pondered how to hurt him worst,
if but Athena granted what I prayed for.
Here are the means I thought would serve my turn:

161 brace: pair.

163–164 The Cyclops reseals the cave with the massive rock as easily as an ordinary human places the cap on a container of arrows.

a club, or staff, lay there along the fold—
an olive tree, felled green and left to season
for Cyclops' hand. And it was like a mast
a lugger of twenty oars, broad in the beam—
a deep-sea-going craft—might carry:

171 left to season: left to dry out and harden.

173 lugger: a small, wide sailing ship.

so long, so big around, it seemed. Now I
chopped out a six foot section of this pole
and set it down before my men, who scraped it;
and when they had it smooth, I hewed again
to make a stake with pointed end. I held this
in the fire's heart and turned it, toughening it,
then hid it, well back in the cavern, under
one of the dung piles in profusion there.
Now came the time to toss for it: who ventured
along with me? whose hand could bear to thrust
and grind that spike in Cyclops' eye, when mild
sleep had mastered him? As luck would have it,
the men I would have chosen won the toss—
four strong men, and I made five as captain.

At evening came the shepherd with his flock,
his woolly flock. The rams as well, this time,
entered the cave: by some sheep-herding whim—
or a god's bidding—none were left outside.
He hefted his great boulder into place
and sat him down to milk the bleating ewes
in proper order, put the lambs to suck,
and swiftly ran through all his evening chores.
Then he caught two more men and feasted on them.
My moment was at hand, and I went forward
holding an ivy bowl of my dark drink,
looking up, saying:

'Cyclops, try some wine.

Here's liquor to wash down your scraps of men.
Taste it, and see the kind of drink we carried
under our planks. I meant it for an offering
if you would help us home. But you are mad,
unbearable, a bloody monster! After this,
will any other traveller come to see you?'

He seized and drained the bowl, and it went down
so fiery and smooth he called for more:

'Give me another, thank you kindly. Tell me,
how are you called? I'll make a gift will please you.
Even Cyclopes know the wine-grapes grow
out of grassland and loam in heaven's rain,
but here's a bit of nectar and ambrosia!'

Three bowls I brought him, and he poured them down.
I saw the fuddle and flush come over him,
then I sang out in cordial tones:

Don't forget to **Notice & Note** as you read the text.

182 **profusion:** abundance.

ANALYZE EPIC POETRY

Annotate: In lines 198–208, mark a passage indicating one of Odysseus' character traits.

Analyze: How does Odysseus' behavior in this passage reflect Greek ideas and values and suggest a theme?

213 **nectar** (nĕk´tər) **and ambrosia** (ăm-brō´zhə)**:** the drink and food of the gods.

215 **fuddle and flush:** the state of confusion and redness of the face caused by drinking alcohol.

'Cyclops
you ask my honorable name? Remember
the gift you promised me, and I shall tell you.
My name is Nohbdy: mother, father, and friends,
everyone calls me Nohbdy.'

And he said:

'Nohbdy's my meat, then, after I eat his friends.
Others come first. There's a noble gift, now.'

Even as he spoke, he reeled and tumbled backward,
his great head lolling to one side: and sleep
took him like any creature. Drunk, hiccupping,
he dribbled streams of liquor and bits of men.

Now, by the gods, I drove my big hand spike
deep in the embers, charring it again,
and cheered my men along with battle talk
to keep their courage up: no quitting now.
The pike of olive, green though it had been,
reddened and glowed as if about to catch.
I drew it from the coals and my four fellows
gave me a hand, lugging it near the Cyclops
as more than natural force nerved them; straight
forward they sprinted, lifted it, and rammed it
deep in his crater eye, and I leaned on it
turning it as a shipwright turns a drill
in planking, having men below to swing
the two-handled strap that spins it in the groove.
So with our brand we bored that great eye socket
while blood ran out around the red hot bar.
Eyelid and lash were seared; the pierced ball
hissed broiling, and the roots popped.

231 the pike: the pointed stake.

In a smithy
one sees a white-hot axehead or an adze
plunged and wrung in a cold tub, screeching steam—
the way they make soft iron hale and hard—:
just so that eyeball hissed around the spike.
The Cyclops bellowed and the rock roared round him,
and we fell back in fear. Clawing his face
he tugged the bloody spike out of his eye,
threw it away, and his wild hands went groping;
then he set up a howl for Cyclopes
who lived in caves on windy peaks nearby.
Some heard him; and they came by divers ways
to clump around outside and call:

244 smithy: blacksmith's shop.

245 adze (ădz)**:** an axelike tool with a curved blade.

255 divers: various.

'What ails you,
Polyphemus? Why do you cry so sore
in the starry night? You will not let us sleep.

257 Polyphemus (pŏl-ə-fē´məs)**:** the name of the Cyclops.

Sure no man's driving off your flock? No man
has tricked you, ruined you?'

Out of the cave
the mammoth Polyphemus roared in answer:
'Nohbdy, Nohbdy's tricked me, Nohbdy's ruined me!'
To this rough shout they made a sage reply:
'Ah well, if nobody has played you foul
there in your lonely bed, we are no use in pain
given by great Zeus. Let it be your father,
Poseidon Lord, to whom you pray.'

So saying
they trailed away. And I was filled with laughter
to see how like a charm the name deceived them.
Now Cyclops, wheezing as the pain came on him,
fumbled to wrench away the great doorstone
and squatted in the breach with arms thrown wide
for any silly beast or man who bolted—
hoping somehow I might be such a fool.
But I kept thinking how to win the game:
death sat there huge; how could we slip away?
I drew on all my wits, and ran through tactics,
reasoning as a man will for dear life,
until a trick came—and it pleased me well.
The Cyclops' rams were handsome, fat, with heavy
fleeces, a dark violet.

Three abreast
I tied them silently together, twining
cords of willow from the ogre's bed;
then slung a man under each middle one
to ride there safely, shielded left and right.
So three sheep could convey each man. I took
the woolliest ram, the choicest of the flock,
and hung myself under his kinky belly,
pulled up tight, with fingers twisted deep
in sheepskin ringlets for an iron grip.
So, breathing hard, we waited until morning.
When Dawn spread out her finger tips of rose
the rams began to stir, moving for pasture,
and peals of bleating echoed round the pens
where dams with udders full called for a milking.
Blinded, and sick with pain from his head wound,
the master stroked each ram, then let it pass,
but my men riding on the pectoral fleece
the giant's blind hands blundering never found.
Last of them all my ram, the leader, came,
weighted by wool and me with my meditations.
The Cyclops patted him, and then he said:

Don't forget to **Notice & Note** as you read the text.

263 **sage:** wise.

264–267 Odysseus' lie about his name has paid off.

272 **breach:** opening.

298 **pectoral fleece:** the wool covering a sheep's chest.

'Sweet cousin ram, why lag behind the rest
in the night cave? You never linger so,
but graze before them all, and go afar
to crop sweet grass, and take your stately way
leading along the streams, until at evening
you run to be the first one in the fold.
Why, now, so far behind? Can you be grieving
over your Master's eye? That carrion rogue
and his accurst companions burnt it out
when he had conquered all my wits with wine.
Nohbdy will not get out alive, I swear.
Oh, had you brain and voice to tell
where he may be now, dodging all my fury!
Bashed by this hand and bashed on this rock wall
his brains would strew the floor, and I should have
rest from the outrage Nohbdy worked upon me.'

He sent us into the open, then. Close by,
I dropped and rolled clear of the ram's belly,
going this way and that to untie the men.
With many glances back, we rounded up
his fat, stiff-legged sheep to take aboard,
and drove them down to where the good ship lay.
We saw, as we came near, our fellows' faces
shining; then we saw them turn to grief
tallying those who had not fled from death.
I hushed them, jerking head and eyebrows up,

Don't forget to **Notice & Note** as you read the text.

and in a low voice told them: 'Load this herd;
move fast, and put the ship's head toward the breakers.'
They all pitched in at loading, then embarked
and struck their oars into the sea. Far out,
as far off shore as shouted words would carry,
I sent a few back to the adversary:

'O Cyclops! Would you feast on my companions?
Puny, am I, in a Caveman's hands?
How do you like the beating that we gave you,
you damned cannibal? Eater of guests
under your roof! Zeus and the gods have paid you!'

The blind thing in his doubled fury broke
a hilltop in his hands and heaved it after us.
Ahead of our black prow it struck and sank
whelmed in a spuming geyser, a giant wave
that washed the ship stern foremost back to shore.
I got the longest boathook out and stood
fending us off, with furious nods to all
to put their backs into a racing stroke—
row, row, or perish. So the long oars bent
kicking the foam sternward, making head
until we drew away, and twice as far.
Now when I cupped my hands I heard the crew
in low voices protesting:

'Godsake, Captain!

330 **put . . . the breakers:** turn the ship around so that it is heading toward the open sea.

334 **adversary:** opponent; enemy.

335–339 Odysseus assumes that the gods are on his side.

340–348 The hilltop thrown by Polyphemus lands in front of the ship, causing a huge wave that carries the ship back to the shore. Odysseus uses a long pole to push the boat away from the land.

351 **cupped my hands:** put his hands on either side of his mouth in order to magnify his voice.

Why bait the beast again? Let him alone!'
'That tidal wave he made on the first throw
all but beached us.'

'All but stove us in!'

'Give him our bearing with your trumpeting,
he'll get the range and lob a boulder.'

'Aye

He'll smash our timbers and our heads together!'

I would not heed them in my glorying spirit,
but let my anger flare and yelled:

'Cyclops,

if ever mortal man inquire
how you were put to shame and blinded, tell him
Odysseus, raider of cities, took your eye:
Laertes' son, whose home's on Ithaca!'

At this he gave a mighty sob and rumbled:

'Now comes the weird upon me, spoken of old.
A wizard, grand and wondrous, lived here—Telemus,
a son of Eurymus; great length of days
he had in wizardry among the Cyclopes,
and these things he foretold for time to come:
my great eye lost, and at Odysseus' hands.
Always I had in mind some giant, armed
in giant force, would come against me here.
But this, but you—small, pitiful and twiggy—
you put me down with wine, you blinded me.
Come back, Odysseus, and I'll treat you well,
praying the god of earthquake to befriend you—
his son I am, for he by his avowal
fathered me, and, if he will, he may
heal me of this black wound—he and no other
of all the happy gods or mortal men.'

Few words I shouted in reply to him:
'If I could take your life I would and take
your time away, and hurl you down to hell!
The god of earthquake could not heal you there!'

At this he stretched his hands out in his darkness
toward the sky of stars, and prayed Poseidon:
'O hear me, lord, blue girdler of the islands,
if I am thine indeed, and thou art father:

366 **Now comes . . . of old:** Now I recall the destiny predicted long ago.

367–375 **A wizard . . . you blinded me:** Polyphemus tells of a prophecy made long ago by Telemus, a prophet who predicted that Polyphemus would lose his eye at the hands of Odysseus.

377 **the god of earthquake:** Poseidon.

378 **avowal:** honest admission.

grant that Odysseus, raider of cities, never
see his home: Laertes' son, I mean,
who kept his hall on Ithaca. Should destiny
intend that he shall see his roof again
among his family in his father land,
far be that day, and dark the years between.
Let him lose all companions, and return
under strange sail to bitter days at home.'

In these words he prayed, and the god heard him.
Now he laid hands upon a bigger stone
and wheeled around, titanic for the cast,
to let it fly in the black-prowed vessel's track.

But it fell short, just aft the steering oar,
and whelming seas rose giant above the stone
to bear us onward toward the island.

There

as we ran in we saw the squadron waiting,
the trim ships drawn up side by side, and all
our troubled friends who waited, looking seaward.
We beached her, grinding keel in the soft sand,
and waded in, ourselves, on the sandy beach.
Then we unloaded all the Cyclops' flock
to make division, share and share alike,
only my fighters voted that my ram,
the prize of all, should go to me. I slew him
by the sea side and burnt his long thighbones
to Zeus beyond the stormcloud, Cronus' son,
who rules the world. But Zeus disdained my offering;
destruction for my ships he had in store
and death for those who sailed them, my companions.

Now all day long until the sun went down
we made our feast on mutton and sweet wine,
till after sunset in the gathering dark
we went to sleep above the wash of ripples.

When the young Dawn with finger tips of rose
touched the world, I roused the men, gave orders
to man the ships, cast off the mooring lines;
and filing in to sit beside the rowlocks
oarsmen in line dipped oars in the gray sea.
So we moved out, sad in the vast offing,
having our precious lives, but not our friends."

NOTICE & NOTE
CONTRASTS AND CONTRADICTIONS

When you notice a sharp contrast between what you would expect and what a character actually does, you've found a **Contrasts and Contradictions** signpost.

Notice & Note: How does the Cyclops' behavior in lines 386–397 contrast with his previous behavior? Mark key details.

Infer: Why do you think the Cyclops acted this way?

400 **titanic for the cast:** drawing on all his enormous strength in preparing to throw.

402 **aft:** behind.

404 **the island:** the deserted island where most of Odysseus' men had stayed behind.

415 **Cronus' son:** Zeus' father, Cronus, was a Titan, one of an earlier race of gods.

428 **offing:** the part of the deep sea visible from the shore.

Book 12
Sea Perils and Defeat

The Sirens

Odysseus and his men continue their journey home toward Ithaca. They spend a year with the goddess Circe on the island of Aeaea. Circe sends Odysseus and his crew to the Land of the Dead (the underworld), after which they return to Circe's island. While the men sleep, Circe takes Odysseus aside to hear about the underworld and to offer advice.

"Then said the Lady Circe:
'So: all those trials are over.
Listen with care
to this, now, and a god will arm your mind.
Square in your ship's path are Sirens, crying
beauty to bewitch men coasting by;
woe to the innocent who hears that sound!
He will not see his lady nor his children
in joy, crowding about him, home from sea;
the Sirens will sing his mind away
on their sweet meadow lolling. There are bones
of dead men rotting in a pile beside them
and flayed skins shrivel around the spot.
Steer wide;
keep well to seaward; plug your oarsmen's ears
with beeswax kneaded soft; none of the rest
should hear that song.
But if you wish to listen,
let the men tie you in the lugger, hand
and foot, back to the mast, lashed to the mast,
so you may hear those harpies' thrilling voices;
shout as you will, begging to be untied,
your crew must only twist more line around you
and keep their stroke up, till the singers fade.'

2–3 In Circe, Odysseus has found a valuable ally. In this section, she describes in detail the dangers that he and his men will meet on their way home.

18 those harpies' thrilling voices: the delightful voices of those horrible female creatures.

At dawn, Odysseus and his men continue their journey. Odysseus decides to tell the men of Circe's warnings about the Sirens, whom they will soon encounter. He is fairly sure that they can survive this peril if he keeps their spirits up. Suddenly, the wind stops.

"The crew were on their feet
briskly, to furl the sail, and stow it; then,
each in place, they poised the smooth oar blades
and sent the white foam scudding by. I carved
a massive cake of beeswax into bits
and rolled them in my hands until they softened—
no long task, for a burning heat came down
from Helios, lord of high noon. Going forward
I carried wax along the line, and laid it
thick on their ears. They tied me up, then, plumb

Don't forget to **Notice & Note** as you read the text.

30–31 plumb amidships: exactly in the center of the ship.

39 **Perimedes** (pĕr-ĭ-mē´dēz).

amidships, back to the mast, lashed to the mast,
and took themselves again to rowing. Soon,
as we came smartly within hailing distance,
the two Sirens, noting our fast ship
off their point, made ready, and they sang. . . .

The lovely voices in ardor appealing over the water
made me crave to listen, and I tried to say
'Untie me!' to the crew, jerking my brows;
but they bent steady to the oars. Then Perimedes
got to his feet, he and Eurylochus,
and passed more line about, to hold me still.
So all rowed on, until the Sirens
dropped under the sea rim, and their singing
dwindled away.

My faithful company
rested on their oars now, peeling off
the wax that I had laid thick on their ears;
then set me free."

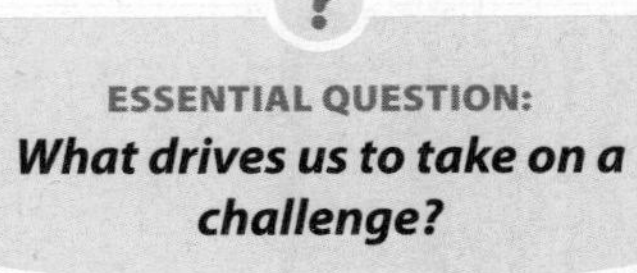
?
ESSENTIAL QUESTION:
What drives us to take on a challenge?

Review your notes and add your thoughts to your Response Log.

COLLABORATIVE DISCUSSION

In what instances does Odysseus demonstrate his greatest acts of heroism? Discuss your ideas with a partner, citing text evidence to support your ideas.

Assessment Practice

Answer these questions before moving on to the **Analyze the Text** section on the following page.

1. This question has two parts. First, answer **Part A**. Then, answer **Part B**.

Part A

What character trait of Odysseus is revealed when he escapes the Cyclops?

(A) cruelty

(B) cunning

(C) curiosity

(D) charm

Part B

In which line does Odysseus exhibit the trait in Part A?

(A) "'Why not / take these cheeses, get them stowed . . .'" (Book 9, lines 70–71)

(B) "'Poseidon Lord, who sets the earth a-tremble, / broke it up on the rocks at your land's end.'" (Book 9, lines 132–133)

(C) "'If I could take your life I would and take / your time away . . .'" (Book 9, lines 383–384)

(D) "'Plug your oarsmen's ears / with beeswax kneaded soft.'" (Book 12, lines 13–14)

2. Which **two** lines from Book 9, "The Cyclops," reveal Odysseus' pridefulness?

(A) "'. . . the rest of you stand by; I'll make the crossing / in my own ship . . .'" (Book 9, line 16–17)

(B) "I saw the fuddle and flush come over him . . ." (Book 9, line 215)

(C) "So, breathing hard, we waited until morning." (Book 9, line 291)

(D) "I would not heed them in my glorying spirit . . ." (Book 9, line 359)

(E) "In these words he prayed, and the god heard him." (Book 9, line 398)

Ed

Test-Taking Strategies

Analyze the Text

Support your responses with evidence from the text.

NOTICE & NOTE

Review what you **noticed and noted** as you read the text. Your annotations can help you answer these questions.

1. **INTERPRET** In the opening lines of Book 1, the poet calls upon Muse, a daughter of Zeus often credited with inspiration. Why would he open the epic in this way?

2. **ANALYZE** How does Odysseus regard the Cyclops, based on the description in lines 1–12 of Book 9? What does this description reveal about Odysseus' values as well as the values of the ancient Greeks?

3. **ANALYZE** Why does Odysseus continue to taunt the Cyclops as he pulls away from the shore? What traits does he demonstrate through this behavior, and what are the consequences?

4. **DRAW CONCLUSIONS** The author uses many epithets for Odysseus, such as "carrion rogue" and "raider of cities." What effect does the repetition of these epithets have on your understanding of the character of Odysseus?

5. **INTERPRET** Review the chart of poetic devices you filled in on the Get Ready page. Use the graphic organizer to identify three examples, and describe their effect on the reader.

Poetic Device	Example	Effect

6. **INFER** In Book 12, Odysseus takes the advice Circe offers about protection against the Sirens' song. Does Odysseus' behavior contradict what you would expect him to do, or is it consistent with his behavior?

7. **SYNTHESIZE** What universal themes does Homer explore in *The Odyssey*? Choose two events and explain how in each one Homer conveys a universal theme, or message that applies to all people across time.

8. **EVALUATE** In what ways does the role of the gods reflect characteristics of an epic?

Choices

Here are some other ways to demonstrate your understanding of the ideas in this lesson.

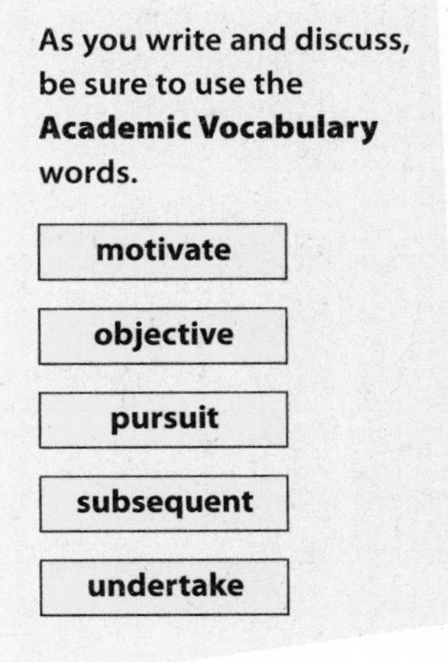
As you write and discuss, be sure to use the **Academic Vocabulary** words.

motivate

objective

pursuit

subsequent

undertake

Writing

↳ Switching Perspectives

The point of view in *The Odyssey* rarely wavers from that of Odysseus. Nevertheless, other characters' words and actions hint at what they are thinking. Write a one-page narrative of an event from *The Odyssey* from the point of view of a character or creature other than Odysseus.

- Review Odysseus' adventures in the poem.
- Choose an event and a point of view you want to write from.
- Outline the event from your new perspective.
- Draft your narrative. Include
    - dialogue
    - descriptions
    - sensory language

Exchange drafts with another student. Review each other's work, focusing on word choice and details. Share tips for improvement. Then revise and edit your narrative. Consider reading your narrative to the class, or recording it.

Speaking & Listening

↳ Research and Record

Find two audio recordings of *The Odyssey* and listen to the parts you have read in this unit. Pay attention to each reader's timing, phrasing, emphasis, and intonation. Create a chart, noting how each version makes action and characters more vivid, as well as how each helps you better understand the poem.

Next, organize a group to create your own recording of a scene from *The Odyssey.* Integrate the qualities you liked most from the two recordings.

Media

↳ Graphic Adaptation

Choose one scene from *The Odyssey* that you want to adapt as a graphic story.

Follow these steps:

- Summarize the main action in the scene.
- Create a storyboard, assigning images that will go in each panel.
- Create the panels, either by sketching or with digital tools.
- Don't rely too heavily on text. Let the characters' facial expressions, interactions, and the setting communicate as much of the plot as possible.
- Compare graphic adaptations with a partner. Discuss similarities and differences you see in your stylistic choices.

Vocabulary Strategy

↳ Words from Latin

Recognizing **word roots** can help you determine the meanings of unfamiliar words. For example, the word *desolation,* meaning "a feeling of loneliness," contains the Latin root *sol,* which means "alone." This root is found in numerous other English words. Study the Latin roots and their meanings in the chart, along with example words that contain each root.

Latin Root	Meaning	Examples
sol	"alone"	soliloquy, solo
trem	"tremble"	tremor, tremulous
plac	"calm"	implacable, placate
vers	"turn"	adversity, versatile

PRACTICE AND APPLY

For each Latin root in the chart, follow these steps:

1. Look online or in print resources for one additional example of a word that uses the Latin root.
2. Use your knowledge of the root's meaning to write a definition for each example word.
3. Consult a dictionary to confirm each example word's meaning.
4. Use each example word in a sentence.

Interactive Vocabulary Lesson: Understanding Word Origins

Watch Your Language!

Absolute Phrases

An **absolute phrase** consists of a noun and a participle, a verb form usually ending in *-ed* or *-ing* that acts as an adjective. Absolute phrases must be set off with commas and may also contain objects of the participle and any modifiers. Rather than modifying a specific word in a sentence, absolute phrases describe the main clause of a sentence. Absolute phrases are a helpful way to add information to a sentence.

It was then, my deadline approaching, that I realized I could sleep with my eyes open.

Look at this example of an absolute phrase from *The Odyssey.*

> There
> as we ran in we saw the squadron waiting,
> the trim ships drawn up side by side, and all
> our troubled friends who waited, looking seaward.

In this sentence, the absolute phrase *the trim ships drawn up side by side* is a description. The phrase adds information and helps explain how the waiting squadron looked. The noun *ships* is modified by the adjective *trim,* the participle *drawn*, and the additional modifiers *up side by side.* The absolute phrase modifies the first part of the sentence: *There as we ran in we saw the squadron waiting.*

PRACTICE AND APPLY

Write a paragraph about a theme in *The Odyssey,* including one or two absolute phrases. Share your writing with a partner and discuss how absolute phrases add variety and interest.

Get Ready

MENTOR TEXT

Archaeology's Tech Revolution

Informational Text by **Jeremy Hsu**

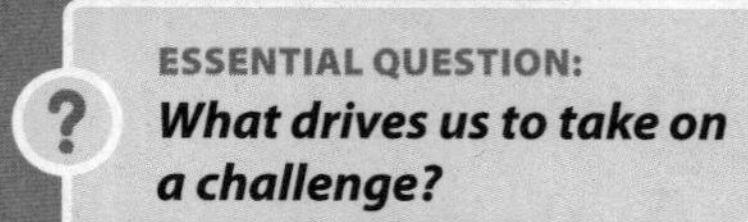

Engage Your Brain

Choose one or both of these activities to start connecting with the text you're about to read.

What's the Subject?

Look at the title, headings, and images in this article. What do you predict it will be about? Discuss your prediction with a partner.

Old and New Tech

How much do you rely on technology? From the time you wake up (to a digital alarm?), through how you get around, use tools to learn, communicate with others, prepare food, find entertainment: Old and new technology is baked into our everyday lives. With a partner, list the technology tools and inventions you use in a typical day.

Make Predictions

We make predictions every day—about our lives, about current events, and about texts we are reading. When we **predict** while reading, we make a reasonable guess about what is likely to happen next in a text.

Predictions are inferences about the future. We may base predictions on:

- prior knowledge—what we already know about a situation or subject
- information gleaned from scanning a text to preview titles, headings, and photos or illustrations
- details from the text

As we gather more information, our predictions may change. Before you read the article, make a prediction about the topic based on the title. As you read, revisit your prediction to correct or confirm it.

Focus on Genre
↳ Informational Text

- **provides factual information**
- **includes evidence to support ideas**
- **may contain text features to organize and clarify ideas**
- **includes domain-specific vocabulary**

Determine Central Idea

Authors of informational texts often present one central idea as their main claim, or thesis. They can't, however, just make their claim or present an idea. They must provide relevant examples and evidence to support those claims.

As you read, note the central ideas the author presents and the evidence and relevant examples that support those ideas. Use a chart to help you analyze the central ideas in the article.

Introduction: What is this article mostly about? What is the central thesis?	
Central Ideas	**Supporting Evidence and Relevant Examples**
1.	
2.	
3.	
4.	
Conclusion: How does the author pull it all together?	

Annotation in Action

Here are one reader's notes about the author's central idea. As you read, make notes about examples and details that support key ideas in the article.

> Those modern archaeologists whom "Raiders" inspired luckily learned from the mistakes of Dr. Jones, and use advanced technology such as satellite imaging, airborne laser mapping, robots and full-body medical scanners instead of a scientifically useless whip.
>
> *tools modern archaeologists use*

Expand Your Vocabulary

Put a check mark next to the vocabulary words that you feel comfortable using when speaking or writing.

Word	
innovation	☐
GPS	☐
artifact	☐
forensic analysis	☐

Turn to a partner and talk about the vocabulary words you already know. Then discuss technology tools you know about, using as many of the vocabulary words as you can.

As you read the informational text, use the definitions in the side column to help you learn the vocabulary words you don't already know.

Background

Jeremy Hsu has been working as a science and technology journalist since 2008 and has written on subjects as diverse as supercomputing and wearable electronics. He contributes to a variety of publications, including *Scientific American, Discover*, and *Popular Science*. In this article, Hsu uses Indiana Jones, the iconic archaeologist of a series of popular movies, to introduce how the field of archaeology has changed with advancements in technology.

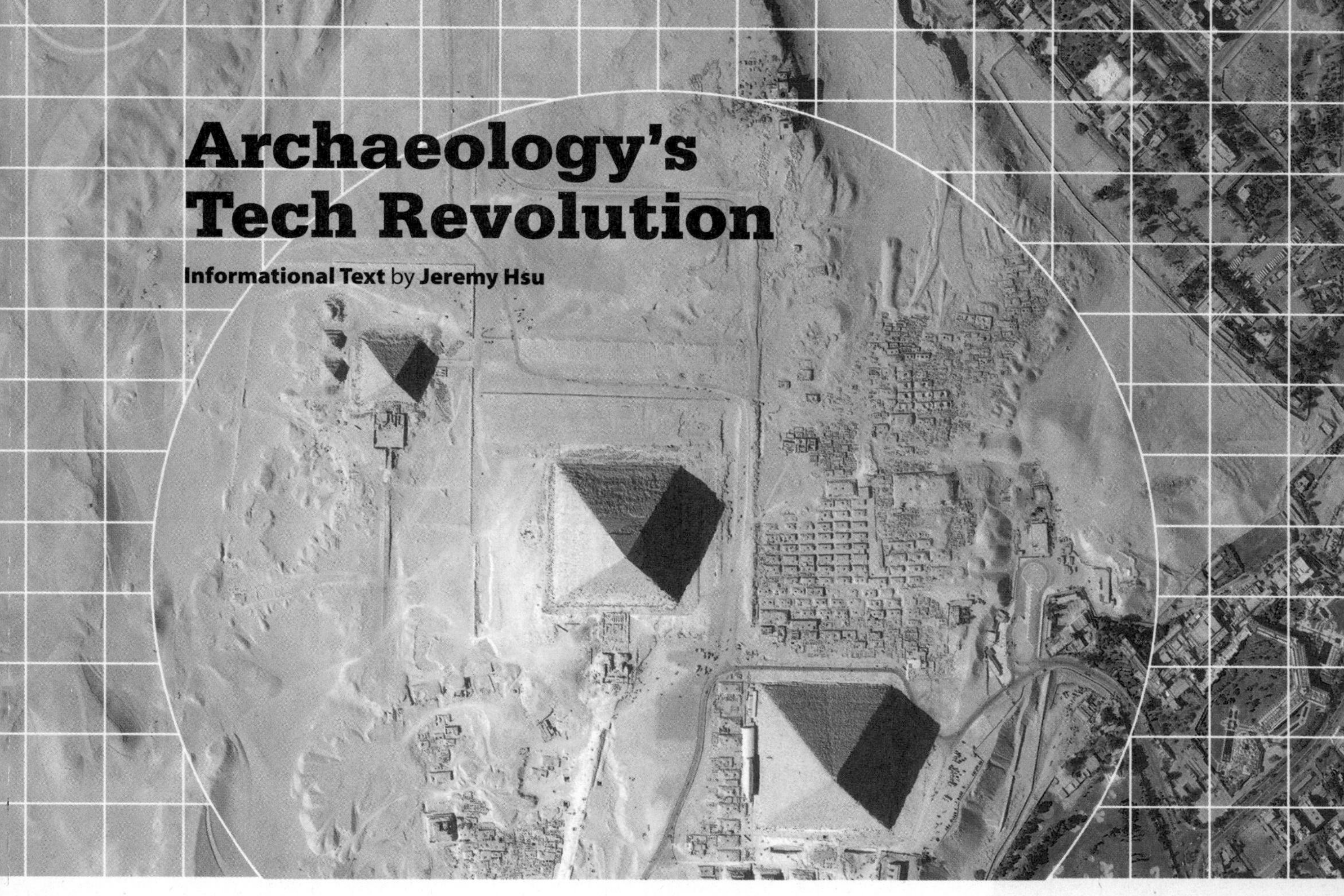

Archaeology's Tech Revolution

Informational Text by **Jeremy Hsu**

New technologies are helping archaeologists learn more about lost worlds.

NOTICE & NOTE
As you read, use the side margins to make notes about the text.

1 Let's face it, Indiana Jones was a pretty lousy archaeologist. He destroyed his sites, used a bullwhip instead of a trowel[1] and was more likely to kill his peers than co-author a paper with them. Regardless, "Raiders of the Lost Ark," which celebrates its 30th anniversary on June 12, did make studying the past cool for an entire generation of scientists. Those modern archaeologists whom "Raiders" inspired luckily learned from the mistakes of Dr. Jones, and use advanced technology such as satellite imaging,[2] airborne laser mapping, robots and full-body medical scanners instead of a scientifically useless whip.

MAKE PREDICTIONS

Annotate: Mark words or phrases in the title and paragraph 1 that help you predict what this article is about.

Predict: What do you expect to learn from reading this article?

2 Such **innovations** have allowed archaeologists to spot buried pyramids from space, create 3-D maps of ancient Mayan ruins from the air, explore the sunken wrecks of Roman ships and find evidence of heart disease in 3,000-year-old mummies. Most of the new toolkit

innovation
(ĭn-ə-vā´shən) *n.* something newly introduced.

[1] **trowel** (trou´əl)**:** a small implement with a pointed, scoop-shaped blade used for digging.
[2] **satellite imaging:** the scanning of the earth by satellite or high-flying aircraft to obtain information about it.

A LIDAR (Light Detection and Ranging) image created with data from the National Oceanic and Atmospheric Administration's National Geodetic Survey.

comes from fields such as biology, chemistry, physics or engineering, as well as commercial gadgets that include **GPS,** laptops and smartphones.

GPS
n. Global Positioning System, a utility that provides positioning, navigation, and timing services.

3 "If we dig part of a site, we destroy it," said David Hurst Thomas, a curator in anthropology at the American Museum of Natural History in New York. "Technology lets us find out a lot more about it before we go in, like surgeons who use CT and MRI scans."[3]

4 Archaeologists have harnessed such tools to find ancient sites of interest more easily than ever before. They can dig with greater confidence and less collateral damage,[4] apply the latest lab techniques to ancient human **artifacts** or remains, and better pinpoint when people or objects existed in time.

artifact
(är´tə-făkt) *n.* an object produced or shaped by human workmanship.

NOTICE & NOTE
WORD GAPS

When you notice unfamiliar vocabulary, such as a technical word, you've found a **Word Gaps** signpost.

Notice & Note: Mark the word in paragraph 5 that describes what kind of satellite imaging the team uses.

Analyze: Do you know this term from someplace else?

Satellites mark the spot

5 One of the current revolutions in archaeology relies upon satellites floating in orbit above the Earth. Sarah Parcak, an Egyptologist at the University of Alabama in Birmingham, and an international team recently used infrared satellite imaging to peer as far down as 33 feet (10 meters) below the Egyptian desert. They found 17 undiscovered pyramids and more than 1,000 tombs.

6 The images also revealed buried city streets and houses at the ancient Egyptian city of Tanis, a well-known archaeological site that was featured in "Raiders of the Lost Ark" three decades ago.

7 Even ordinary satellite images used by Google Earth have helped. Many of the old Egyptian sites have buried mud brick architecture that crumbles over time and mixes with the sand or silt above them.

[3] **CT and MRI scans:** special X-ray tests that produce cross-sectional images.
[4] **collateral damage** (kə-lăt´ər-əl dăm´-ĭj): unintended injury or damage.

Don't forget to **Notice & Note** as you read the text.

Satellite imagery of the Giza pyramid complex on the outskirts of Cairo, Egypt.

When it rains, soils with mud brick hold moisture longer and appear discolored in satellite photos.

8 "In the old days, I'd jump into the Land Rover and go look at a possible site," said Tony Pollard, director of the Centre for Battlefield Archaeology at the University of Glasgow in Scotland. "Now, before that, I go to Google Earth."

Digging with less damage

9 Tools such as ground-penetrating radar can also help archaeologists avoid destroying precious data when they excavate ancient sites, Thomas said.

10 "Many Native American tribes are very interested in remote sensing that is noninvasive and nondestructive, because many don't like the idea of disturbing the dead or buried remains," Thomas explained.

11 Magnetometers[5] can distinguish between buried metals, rocks and other materials based on differences in the Earth's magnetic field. Soil resistivity surveys detect objects based on changes in electrical current speed.

DETERMINE CENTRAL IDEA

Annotate: Mark words and phrases in paragraph 11 that explain magnetometers.

Analyze: How could the use of a magnetometer help preserve Native American sites?

Dusting off old bones

12 Once objects or bones have surfaced, archaeologists can return them to the lab for **forensic analysis** that would impress any CSI[6] agent. Computed tomography (CT) scanners commonly used in medicine have revealed blocked arteries in an ancient Egyptian princess who ended up mummified 3,500 years ago.

forensic analysis (fə-rĕn´sĭk ə-năl´ĭ-sĭs) *n.* the scientific collection and analysis of physical evidence in criminal cases.

[5] **magnetometers** (măg-nĭ-tom´ĭ-tərz): instruments for comparing the intensity and direction of magnetic fields.

[6] **CSI:** crime scene investigator.

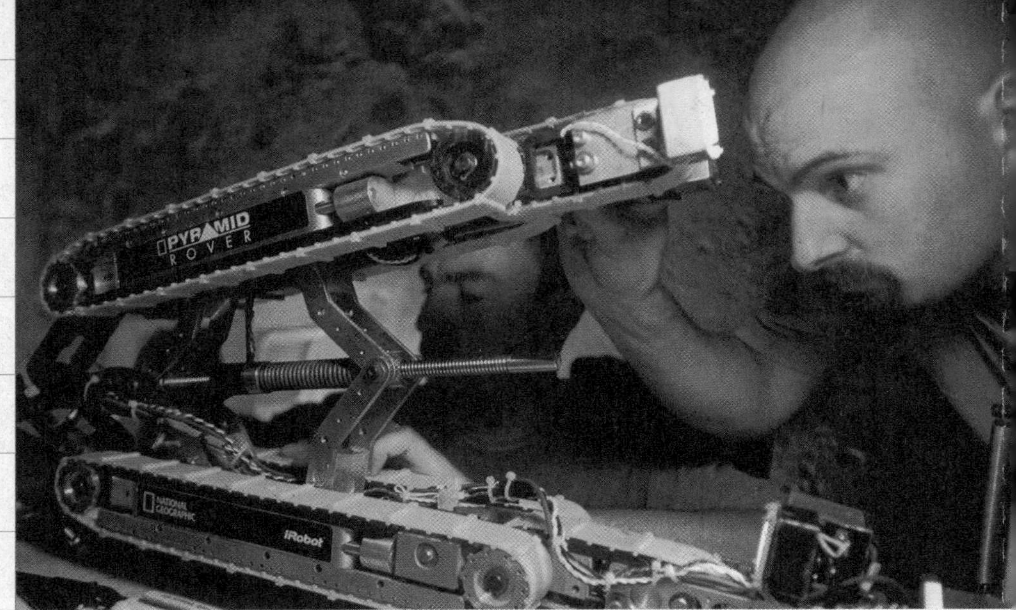

A rover robot to be sent into an air shaft of the Pyramid of Khufu in Giza, Egypt.

DETERMINE CENTRAL IDEA

Annotate: Mark text in paragraphs 13–15 that describes the kinds of information archaeologists can obtain from bones.

Analyze: What does this text reveal about the use of technology in archaeology?

13 Looking at the ratios of different forms of elements, called isotopes, in the bones of ancient people may reveal what they ate. The dietary details can include whether they favored foods such as corn or potatoes, or if they were strictly hunters.

14 A similar chemical signature[7] based on the isotope ratio of different geographical locations can reveal where humans originally grew up. Archaeologists used it to identify the origins of dozens of soldiers found in a 375-year-old mass grave in Germany.

15 "Once they excavated them, they did analysis on bones and identified in most cases where individual soldiers came from," Pollard said. "Some came from Finland, some came from Scotland."

Back to the future

16 Archaeologists have many other new tools in the toolkit. The laser mapping technique used on the Mayan ruins, called LIDAR (Light Detection And Ranging), has become a norm for archaeology in just a few years. Robots have begun exploring pyramids and caves as well as underwater shipwrecks.

17 "When I was a bad boy and went into archaeology instead of med school, my mother thought I'd spent all my time in the past," Thomas said. "It couldn't be further from the truth; we do all we can to keep up technologically."

18 Technology won't eliminate the need to dig anytime soon, archaeologists say. But if that day comes, "archaeology will get a lot more boring," Pollard said. He wasn't alone with that sentiment.

19 "It's all very well to use satellite imaging, but until you get out into the field, you're stuck in your lab," Parcak said. "It's a constant in archaeology; you've got to dig and explore."

[7] **chemical signature:** a unique pattern, produced by an analytical instrument, indicating the presence of a particular molecule.

COLLABORATIVE DISCUSSION

Do you think new technology has made archaeology a more interesting career choice, or not? Discuss with a partner.

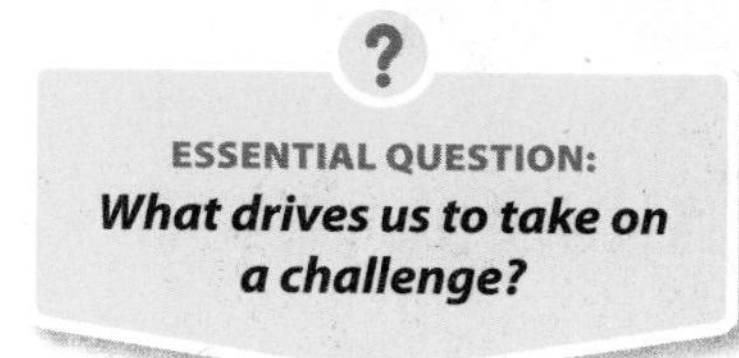
?
ESSENTIAL QUESTION:
What drives us to take on a challenge?

Review your notes and add your thoughts to your Response Log.

Assessment Practice

Answer these questions before moving on to the **Analyze the Text** section on the next page.

1. This question has two parts. First, answer **Part A**. Then, answer **Part B**.

Part A

What is the author's central idea about modern archaeologists?

- (A) They use the tools first advanced by Indiana Jones.
- (B) They use sophisticated technology that has made onsite fieldwork unnecessary.
- (C) They are historians whose main goal is to find artifacts and place them in museums.
- (D) They are technologically savvy and work to minimize damage to sites and artifacts.

Part B

Which quotation supports the answer to Part A?

- (A) "Regardless, 'Raiders of the Lost Ark,' which celebrates its 30th anniversary on June 12, did make studying the past cool for an entire generation of scientists." (paragraph 1)
- (B) "Most of the new toolkit comes from fields such as biology, chemistry, physics or engineering. . . ." (paragraph 2)
- (C) "They can dig with greater confidence and less collateral damage. . . ." (paragraph 4)
- (D) "Technology won't eliminate the need to dig anytime soon, archaeologists say." (paragraph 18)

2. How are robots useful to archaeologists?

- (A) They date human remains by detecting chemical signatures in bones.
- (B) They can explore sites that are inaccessible or dangerous.
- (C) They coordinate with satellites to scan large underground areas.
- (D) They reveal discoloration that shows mud brick architecture.

Ed

Test-Taking Strategies

Analyze the Text

Support your responses with evidence from the text.

1. **PREDICT** Recall the predictions you made before reading the article. Which ones can you confirm? Which do you need to correct?

2. **DRAW CONCLUSIONS** What is the author's central idea about the technology revolution in archaeology?

3. **SUMMARIZE** What would you say is the most significant result of the technology revolution in archaeology?

4. **CITE EVIDENCE** Describe one of the images in the article. How does it help support the author's claims?

5. **ANALYZE** The author uses many technical and discipline-specific words to explain his subject. What **Word Gaps,** or unfamiliar terms, did you identify? If a definition was not provided, how did you figure out the meaning of each?

6. **EVALUATE** The article includes a number of graphic features to help readers understand the technologies being discussed. Identify at least two, and describe how they enhance the text narrative.

7. **CRITIQUE** When you read informational texts, you should take a **Questioning Stance,** which means you think more deeply about the information the author provides. How would you answer this **Big Question:** What did the author think I already knew? Did you feel you had adequate background knowledge to understand the new technology in the archaeological "toolkit"? Why or why not?

NOTICE & NOTE

Review what you **noticed and noted** as you read the text. Your annotations can help you answer these questions.

Choices

Here are some other ways to demonstrate your understanding of the ideas in this lesson.

Writing

↳ Research and Report

Jeremy Hsu mentions a variety of technologies that are available to archaeologists today that weren't in the past. Research how the tools and technologies available to archaeologists have changed over the past 100 years, and improvements the new tools have brought. Record your findings in the chart, and draft a report to share with a small group. Cite your sources appropriately.

Purpose or Task	Old Tool	New Tool	How New Tool Has Improved Research
Locating a site			
Field work			
Lab work			

As you write and discuss, be sure to use the **Academic Vocabulary** words.

- motivate
- objective
- pursuit
- subsequent
- undertake

Media

↳ Virtual Tour

Briefly research active archaeological sites that have footage of the excavation process available online. Create a presentation in which you provide a virtual tour of one of these sites:

- Explain researchers' purpose for digging there.
- Describe the progress that has been made.
- Identify tools or processes being used.
- Summarize discoveries and the significance of the work being done.

Include video clips and images that show viewers the site and excavations. Cite referenced sources appropriately. Present to the class, and post to a site where others can view your presentation.

Social & Emotional Learning

↳ Small-Group Discussion

In a small group, consider why studying the past is so important. Reflect on and discuss the following questions:

- What can we learn from people who lived before us?
- What can we learn about ourselves from examining the past?

Provide specific examples and consider multiple perspectives to enhance your discussion. Summarize your group's conclusions.

Expand Your Vocabulary

PRACTICE AND APPLY

Answer each question to demonstrate your understanding of the vocabulary words. Then, explain your responses.

innovation	GPS	artifact	forensic analysis

1. The automobile was once an **innovation.** Is it still?
2. Why is **GPS** a popular utility?
3. Imagine your class is gathering **artifacts** for a time capsule. What will you contribute?
4. **Forensic analysis** is used in criminal cases. Why do archaeologists use it?

Vocabulary Strategy

↳ Use References

Interactive Vocabulary Lesson: Using Reference Sources

The author of the article you have just read incorporates popular, historical, and technical references into the text. Though you may be able to understand the author's central idea without knowing what these references are, knowing them will enhance your comprehension and make the article more interesting to you.

PRACTICE AND APPLY

Use print or digital resource materials, including glossaries, dictionaries, and encyclopedias, to define or explain each reference from the article.

1. *Raiders of the Lost Ark*
2. curator
3. Google Earth
4. isotopes
5. Mayan ruins
6. LIDAR (Light Detection and Ranging)

Watch Your Language!

Use Appositives Effectively

An **appositive** is a noun or pronoun that identifies or renames another noun or pronoun. An **appositive phrase** includes an appositive and its modifiers.

An appositive can be either essential or nonessential. An essential appositive provides information that is needed to identify what is referred to by the preceding noun or pronoun.

> The author Jeremy Hsu has written several articles about technology.

A nonessential appositive adds extra information about a noun or pronoun whose meaning is already clear.

> Indiana Jones, played by Harrison Ford, was a popular movie character.

In "Archaeology's Tech Revolution," the author uses appositives in the following ways.

- To name or identify

> Looking at the ratios of different forms of elements, called isotopes, in the bones of ancient people may reveal what they ate.
>
> "If we dig part of a site, we destroy it," said David Hurst Thomas, a curator in anthropology at the American Museum of Natural History in New York.

- To describe or explain

> The images also revealed buried city streets and houses at the ancient Egyptian city of Tanis, a well-known archaeological site that was featured in "Raiders of the Lost Ark" three decades ago.

Ed

Interactive Grammar Lesson: Appositives and Appositive Phrases

PRACTICE AND APPLY

Write your own sentences with appositives, using the examples from "Archaeology's Tech Revolution" as models. Your sentences can be about your own experiences with technology. When you have finished, share your sentences with a partner and compare your use of appositives.

Collaborate & Compare

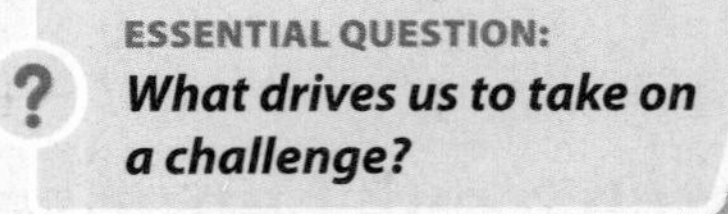

Compare Messages Across Genres

You're about to read an excerpt from a travel book and a poem describing two kinds of journeys. As you read, notice how the ideas in both texts relate to the topic of a personal quest. Then, pay attention to how these ideas are presented in two different genres—travel writing and poetry.

A
from The Cruelest Journey: 600 Miles to Timbuktu
Travel Writing by Kira Salak
pages 582–589
B
The Journey
Poem by Mary Oliver
pages 597–599

After you have read both texts, you will collaborate with a small group on a response to both texts. You will follow these steps:

- Discuss the nature of each journey, using text evidence
- Offer your own and listen to others' points of view
- Take notes on the discussion
- Reflect on your work

from The Cruelest Journey: 600 Miles to Timbuktu

Travel Writing by **Kira Salak**

Engage Your Brain

Choose one or both of these activities to start connecting with the text you're about to read.

Trips Terrible or Terrific

Traveling provides us with enduring memories, but it can also lead to some uncomfortable experiences and feelings. With a group, discuss your most memorable travel experiences—good or bad!

From Here to Timbuktu

People sometimes refer to "Timbuktu" to mean a hard-to-find or even imaginary place. But Timbuktu is a real place! With a partner or in a group, research its location, history, and culture. Then create a short travelogue with photos, maps, or illustrations of the city. Post online or present to the rest of the class.

Analyze Ideas and Events

Travel writing is a type of nonfiction that records an author's experiences exploring new places. Travel writers don't just present a series of facts; they present a narrative that describes a setting, reflects a purpose, and communicates messages about life. In this excerpt, Kira Salak uses narrative techniques to reveal her reflections about her journey.

The chart describes three literary techniques Salak uses in her narrative. As you read, respond to the questions in the third column.

Focus on Genre
Travel Writing

- **type of narrative nonfiction**
- **usually illustrated with photographs, maps, or other visuals that help the reader visualize the places being described**
- **provides author's impressions about places visited**
- **includes vivid details and imagery to describe people, places, and events**

Technique	What It Is	Questions to Ask as You Read
Imagery	descriptive words and phrases that re-create sensory experiences for the reader	What images create a vivid picture of Salak's journey?
Mood	the emotional response a work creates in readers	What details create mood?
Pacing	the speed at which events unfold. Short sentences speed up the pace, while longer sentences slow it down. Present tense adds a sense of immediacy.	Where in the narrative does the author vary the pacing?

Evaluate Graphic Features

Authors use graphic features to help convey their message. These may include diagrams, charts, tables, timelines, illustrations, photographs, and maps. In particular, maps that accompany travel writing help the reader better understand where the narrative occurs geographically.

As you read the excerpt from *The Cruelest Journey: 600 Miles to Timbuktu*, take notes about how the graphic features help the author achieve her purpose.

Annotation in Action

Here are one reader's notes about the beginning of *The Cruelest Journey: 600 Miles to Timbuktu.* As you read, note how the writer uses images and details to create a vivid picture of her journey.

The idea is to paddle nearly 600 miles on the Niger River in a kayak, alone, from the Malian town of Old Ségou to Timbuktu. And now, at the very hour when I have decided to leave, a thunderstorm bursts open the skies, sending down apocalyptic rain, washing away the very ground beneath my feet.

major thunderstorm sets up seriously tense mood

Expand Your Vocabulary

Put a check mark next to the vocabulary words that you feel comfortable using when speaking or writing.

Word	
circuitously	☐
disingenuous	☐
integrity	☐
embark	☐
stagnant	☐

Using the vocabulary words you already know, write a short narrative about a risky mission or trip.

As you read *The Cruelest Journey,* use the definitions in the side column to learn the vocabulary words you don't already know.

Background

Kira Salak (b. 1971) is an adventurer, an explorer, and a journalist. Her book *The Cruelest Journey: 600 Miles to Timbuktu* documents her 600-mile solo kayak trip on the Niger River. As the first person ever to achieve this feat, she traveled through a remote and dangerous region in Africa. Salak also is one of few people to have completed Bhutan's "Snowman Trek" across 216 mountainous miles through the Himalayas. Salak has received awards for her fiction and nonfiction books. This selection is an excerpt from *The Cruelest Journey.*

from The Cruelest Journey: 600 Miles to Timbuktu

Travel Writing by **Kira Salak**

NOTICE & NOTE

As you read, use the side margins to make notes about the text.

The author achieves the unthinkable—a solo 600-mile kayak trip on the Niger River.

ANALYZE IDEAS AND EVENTS

Annotate: Mark the author's description of the rainstorm.

Analyze: How does she use details to create a mood?

1 In the beginning, my journeys feel at best ludicrous, at worst insane. This one is no exception. The idea is to paddle nearly 600 miles on the Niger River in a kayak, alone, from the Malian town of Old Ségou to Timbuktu. And now, at the very hour when I have decided to leave, a thunderstorm bursts open the skies, sending down apocalyptic rain, washing away the very ground beneath my feet. It is the rainy season in Mali, for which there can be no comparison in the world. Lightning pierces trees, slices across houses. Thunder racks the skies and pounds the earth like mortar fire, and every living thing huddles in tenuous shelter, expecting the world to end. Which it doesn't. At least not this time. So that we all give a collective sigh to the salvation of the passing storm as it rumbles its way east, and I survey the river I'm to leave on this morning. Rain or no rain, today is the day for the journey to begin. And no one, not even the oldest in the village, can say for certain whether I'll get to the end.

2 "Let's do it," I say, leaving the shelter of an adobe hut. My guide from town, Modibo, points to the north, to further storms. He says he will pray for me. It's the best he can do. To his knowledge, no man has ever completed such a trip, though a few have tried. And certainly no woman has done such a thing. This morning he took me aside

and told me he thinks I'm crazy, which I understood as concern and thanked him. He told me that the people of Old Ségou think I'm crazy too, and that only uncanny good luck will keep me safe.

3 Still, when a person tells me I can't do something, I'll want to do it all the more. It may be a failing of mine. I carry my inflatable kayak through the narrow passageways of Old Ségou, past the small adobe huts melting in the rains, past the huddling goats and smoke of cooking fires, people peering out at me from the dark entranceways. It is a labyrinth[1] of ancient homes, built and rebuilt after each storm, plastered with the very earth people walk upon. Old Ségou must look much the same as it did in Scottish explorer Mungo Park's time when, exactly 206 years ago to the day, he left on the first of his two river journeys down the Niger to Timbuktu, the first such attempt by a Westerner. It is no coincidence that I've planned to leave on the same day and from the same spot. Park is my benefactor of sorts, my guarantee. If he could travel down the Niger, then so can I. And it is all the guarantee I have for this trip—that an obsessed 19th-century adventurer did what I would like to do. Of course Park also died on this river, but I've so far managed to overlook that.

4 I gaze at the Niger through the adobe passageways, staring at waters that began in the mountainous rain forests of Guinea and traveled all this way to central Mali—waters that will journey northeast with me to Timbuktu before cutting a great circular swath through the Sahara and retreating south, through Niger, on to Nigeria, passing **circuitously** through mangrove swamps and jungle, resting at last in the Atlantic in the Bight of Benin.[2] But the Niger is more than a river; it is a kind of faith. Bent and plied by Saharan sands, it perseveres more than 2,600 miles from beginning to end through one of the hottest, most desolate regions of the world. And

VOCABULARY

Word Roots: The word *uncanny* (paragraph 2) contains the Middle English root *can*, meaning "to know how." The prefix *un-* means "not."

Analyze: Based on the information above and the word's context, what do you think *uncanny* means? Look the word up in a dictionary to confirm its meaning.

circuitously
(sər-kyo͞o′ĭ-təs-lē) *adv.* in an indirect and lengthy manner.

[1] **labyrinth:** a complex collection of paths, such as a maze.
[2] **Bight of Benin:** a bay on Africa's west coast between Ghana and Nigeria.

when the rains come each year, it finds new strength of purpose, surging through the sunbaked lands, giving people the boons of crops and livestock and fish, taking nothing, asking nothing. It humbles all who see it.

ANALYZE IDEAS AND EVENTS

Annotate: In paragraph 5, mark the author's strongest belief about travel.

Infer: Why do you think she chose to make this trip?

disingenuous
(dĭs-ĭn-jĕn´yo͞o-əs) *adj.* insincere, deceitful.

5 If I were to try to explain why I'm here, why I chose Mali and the Niger for this journey—now that is a different matter. I can already feel the resistance in my gut, the familiar clutch of fear. I used to avoid stripping myself down in search of motivation, scared of what I might uncover, scared of anything that might suggest a taint of the pathological.[3] And would it be enough to say that I admire Park's own trip on the river and want to try a similar challenge? That answer carries a whiff of the **disingenuous**; it sounds too easy to me. Human motivation, itself, is a complicated thing. If only it was simple enough to say, "Here is the Niger, and I want to paddle it." But I'm not that kind of traveler, and this isn't that kind of trip. If a journey doesn't have something to teach you about yourself, then what kind of journey is it? There is one thing I'm already certain of: Though we may think we choose our journeys, they choose us.

6 Hobbled donkeys cower under a new onslaught of rain, ears back, necks craned. Little children dare each other to touch me, and I make it easy for them, stopping and holding out my arm. They stroke my white skin as if it were velvet, using only the pads of their fingers, then stare at their hands to check for wet paint.

integrity
(ĭn-tĕg´rĭ-tē) *n.* consistency and strength of purpose.

7 Thunder again. More rain falls. I stop on the shore, near a centuries-old kapok tree under which I imagine Park once took shade. I open my bag, spread out my little red kayak, and start to pump it up. I'm doing this trip under the sponsorship of *National Geographic Adventure*, which hopes to run a magazine story about it. This means that they need photos, lots of photos, and so a French photographer named Rémi Bénali feverishly snaps pictures of me. I don't know what I hate more—river storms or photo shoots. I value the privacy and **integrity** of my trips, and I don't want my journey turning into a circus. The magazine presented the best compromise it could: Rémi, renting a motor-driven pirogue,[4] was given instructions to find me on the river every few days to do his thing.

8 My kayak is nearly inflated. A couple of women nearby, with colorful cloth wraps called *pagnes* tied tightly about their breasts, gaze at me cryptically, as if to ask: *Who are you and what do you think you're doing?* The Niger churns and slaps the shore, in a surly mood. I don't pretend to know what I'm doing. Just one thing at a time now, kayak inflated, kayak loaded with my gear. Paddles fitted together and ready. Modibo is standing on the shore, watching me.

9 "I'll pray for you," he reminds me.

10 I balance my gear, adjust the straps, get in. And, finally, irrevocably, I paddle away. . . .

[3] **taint of the pathological:** trace of mental illness.
[4] **pirogue** (pĭ-rōg´): a canoe made from a hollowed tree trunk.

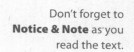

11 The storm erupts into a new overture. Torrential rains. Waves higher than my kayak, trying to capsize me. But my boat is self-bailing[5] and I stay afloat. The wind drives the current in reverse, tearing and ripping at the shores, sending spray into my face. I paddle madly, crashing and driving forward. I travel inch by inch, or so it seems, arm muscles smarting and rebelling against this journey. I crawl past New Ségou, fighting the Niger for more distance. Large river steamers rest in jumbled rows before cement docks, the town itself looking dark and deserted in the downpour. No one is out in their boats. The people know something I don't: that the river dictates all travel.

12 A popping feeling now and a screech of pain. My right arm lurches from a ripped muscle. But this is no time and place for such an injury, and I won't tolerate it, stuck as I am in a storm. I try to get used to the pulses of pain as I fight the river. There is only one direction to go: forward. Stopping has become anathema.[6]

13 I wonder what we look for when we **embark** on these kinds of trips. There is the pat answer that you tell the people you don't know: that you're interested in seeing a place, learning about its people. But then the trip begins and the hardship comes, and hardship is more honest: it tells us that we don't have enough patience yet, nor humility, nor gratitude. And we thought that we did. Hardship brings us closer to truth, and thus is more difficult to bear, but from it alone comes compassion. And so I've told the world that it can do what it wants with me during this trip if only, by the end, I have learned something more. A bargain, then. The journey, my teacher.

14 And where is the river of just this morning, with its whitecaps that would have liked to drown me, with its current flowing backward against the wind? Gone to this: a river of smoothest glass, a placidity unbroken by wave or eddy, with islands of lush greenery awaiting me like distant Xanadus.[7] The Niger is like a mercurial god, meting

Don't forget to **Notice & Note** as you read the text.

ANALYZE IDEAS AND EVENTS

Annotate: Mark the short sentences in paragraph 11.

Evaluate: How do these sentences affect the pacing in this part of the narrative?

embark
(ĕm-bärk´) *v.* to set out on a course or a journey, often aboard a boat.

[5] **self-bailing:** the boat has holes, or scuppers, that allow water to drain from the cockpit.
[6] **anathema:** something hated or despised.
[7] **Xanadus** (zăn´ə-do͞oz): Xanadu, the summer palace of Kublai Khan; connotes an elaborate, ideal paradise.

EVALUATE GRAPHIC FEATURES

Annotate: Examine the photograph.

Connect: What does this image tell you about the geography and culture of the setting?

out punishment and benediction on a whim. And perhaps the god of the river sleeps now, returning matters to the mortals who ply its waters? The Bozo and Somono[8] fishermen in their pointy canoes. The long passenger pirogues, overloaded with people and merchandise, rumbling past, leaving diesel fumes in their wake. And now, inexplicably, the white woman in a little red boat, paddling through waters that flawlessly mirror the cumulus clouds above. We all belong here, in our way. It is as if I've entered a very lucid dream, continually surprised to find myself here on this river—I've become a hapless actor in a mysterious play, not yet knowing what my part is, left to gape at the wonder of what I have set in motion. Somehow: I'm in a kayak, on the Niger River, paddling very slowly but very surely to Timbuktu.

15 *As Salak continues on her journey—including a side trip on a tributary of the Niger—she encounters raging storms, dangerous hippos, and unrelenting heat. Because she is traveling in a small kayak and unable to carry many supplies, she comes ashore each night, seeking shelter and food from the locals, who live along the banks of the river. The locals are very curious about a woman undertaking such a dangerous journey alone. Some of them greet her warmly and generously; others with hostility. Finally, weak from dysentery, she approaches her final destination—Timbuktu.*

from Chapter Thirteen

16 "This river will never end," I say out loud, over and over again, like a mantra. My map shows an obvious change to the northeast, but that turn hasn't come for hours, may never come at all. To be so close to Timbuktu, and yet so immeasurably far away. All I know is that I must keep paddling. I *have* to be close. Determined still to get to Timbuktu's port of Korioumé by nightfall, I shed the protection of my long-sleeved shirt, pull the kayak's thigh straps in tight, and prepare for the hardest bout of paddling yet.

[8] **Bozo and Somono:** ethnic groups native to Mali and the Niger River delta.

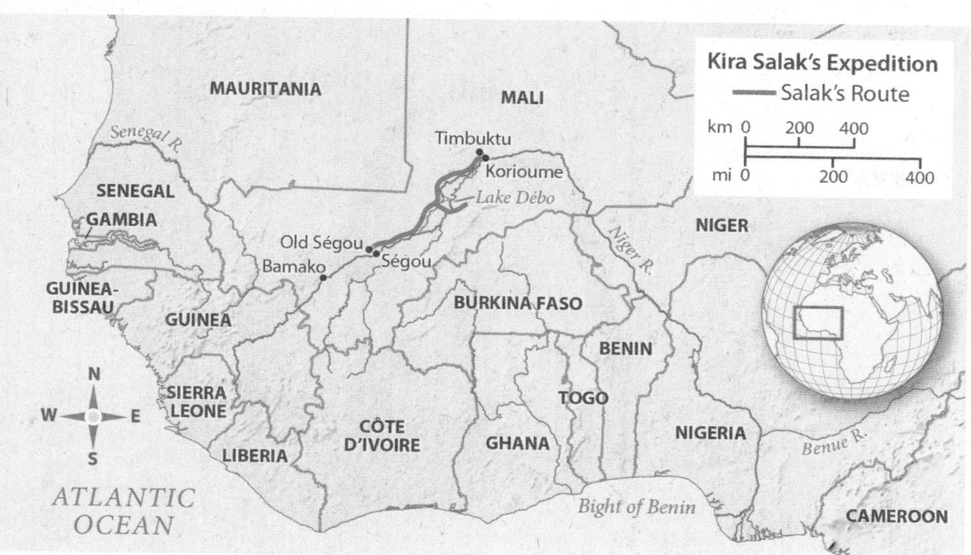

EVALUATE GRAPHIC FEATURES

Annotate: Trace the route of the Niger River on the map.

Evaluate: How does the map help you better understand the author's journey?

17 I paddle like a person possessed. I paddle the hours away, the sun falling aside to the west but still keeping its heat on me. I keep up a cadence in my head, keep my breaths regular and deep, in synch with my arm movements. The shore passes by slowly, but it passes. As the sun gets ominously low, burning a flaming orange, the river turns almost due north and I can see a distant, square-shaped building made of cement: the harbinger of what can only be Korioumé. Hardly a tower of gold, hardly an El Dorado, but I'll take it. I paddle straight toward it, ignoring the pains in my body, my raging headache. *Timbuktu, Timbuktu!* Bozo fishermen ply the river out here, and they stare at me as I pass. They don't ask for money or cadeaux[9]—can they see the determination in my face, sense my fatigue? All they say is, *"Ça va, madame?"*[10] with obvious concern. One man actually stands and raises his hands in a cheer, urging me on. I take his kindness with me into the final stretch, rounding the river's sharp curve to the port of Korioumé. . . .

18 Just as the last rays of the sun color the Niger, I pull up beside a great white river steamer, named, appropriately, the *Tombouctou*. Rémi's boat is directly behind me, the flash from his camera lighting up the throng of people gathering on shore. There is no more paddling to be done. I've made it. I can stop now. I stare up at the familiar crowd waiting in the darkness. West African pop music blares from a party on the *Tombouctou*.

19 Slowly, I undo my thigh straps and get out of my kayak, hauling it from the river and dropping it onshore for the last time. A huge crowd has gathered around me, children squeezing in to stroke my kayak. People ask where I have come from and I tell them, "Old Ségou." They can't seem to believe it.

20 "Ségou?" one man asks. He points down the Niger. His hand waves and curves as he follows the course of the river in his mind.

21 "Oui," I say.

NOTICE & NOTE
WORD GAPS

When you notice vocabulary that is unfamiliar, you've found a **Word Gaps** signpost.

Notice & Note: Mark the footnote for "cadeaux."

Draw Conclusions: Why do you think the author chose to use the French word for "gifts" instead of the English one?

[9] **cadeaux** (kə-dō´): French word meaning "gifts."
[10] **Ça va, madame?** (sä vä, mä-däm´): French for "How are you, madam?"

22 "Ehh!" he exclaims.

23 "Ségou, Ségou, Ségou?" a woman asks.

24 I nod. She runs off to tell other people, and I can see passersby rushing over to take a look at me. What does a person look like who has come all the way from Ségou? They stare down at me in my sweat-stained tank top, my clay-smeared skirt, my sandals both held together with plastic ties.

25 I unload my things to the clamor of their questions, but even speaking seems to pain me now. Such a long time getting here. And was the journey worth it? Or is it blasphemy to ask that now? I can barely walk, have a high fever. I haven't eaten anything for more than a day. How do you know if the journey is worth it? I would give a great deal right now for silence. For stillness.

26 My exhaustion and sickness begin to alter this arrival, numbing the sense of finish and self-congratulation and replacing it with only the most important of questions. I've found that illness does this to me, quiets the busy thoughts of the mind, gives me a rare clarity that I don't usually have. I see the weeks on the river, the changing tribal groups, the lush shores down by Old Ségou metamorphosing[11] slowly into the treeless, sandy spread near Timbuktu. I'm wishing I could explain it to people—the subtle yet certain way the world has altered over these past few weeks. The inevitability of it. The grace of it. Grace, because in my life back home every day had appeared the same as the one before. Nothing seemed to change; nothing took on new variety. It had felt like a **stagnant** life.

stagnant (stăg´nənt) *adj.* unchanging; without activity or development.

27 I know now, with the utter conviction of my heart, that I want to avoid that stagnant life. I want the world to always be offering me the new, the grace of the unfamiliar. Which means—and I pause with the thought—a path that will only lead through my fears. Where there are certainty and guarantees, I will never be able to meet that unknown world.

[11] **metamorphosing:** completely changing into another form.

COLLABORATIVE DISCUSSION

What do you think about the author's solution for avoiding a "stagnant life"? Discuss your thoughts with a partner.

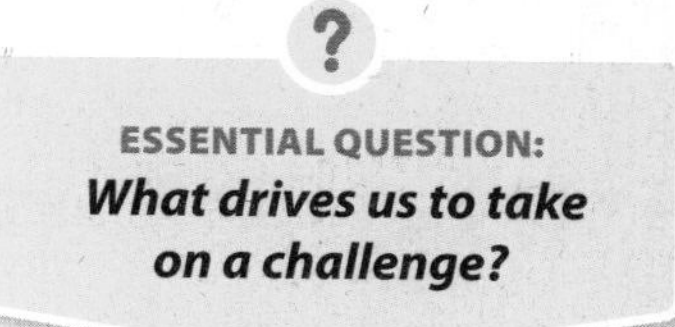
?
ESSENTIAL QUESTION:
What drives us to take on a challenge?

Review your notes and add your thoughts to your Response Log.

Assessment Practice

Answer these questions before moving on to the **Analyze the Text** section on the following page.

1. Which statement best captures Salak's thoughts as her journey ends?
   - (A) triumphant and energized at the end of the journey
   - (B) disappointed in the journey because she has ended up ill and hurt
   - (C) longing for something safe and familiar after surviving her journey
   - (D) grateful at having experienced so many new people and places

2. This question has two parts. First, answer **Part A**. Then, answer **Part B**.

   Part A

   What does *mercurial* mean in paragraph 14?
   - (A) unnecessary
   - (B) unknowable
   - (C) changeable
   - (D) furious

   Part B

   Select **two** text excerpts that support the answer in Part A.
   - (A) ". . . [the river's] whitecaps that would have liked to drown me. . . . Gone to this: a river of smoothest glass . . ." (paragraph 14)
   - (B) ". . . meting out punishment and benediction on a whim." (paragraph 14)
   - (C) "And perhaps the god of the river sleeps now, returning matters to the mortals who ply its waters?" (paragraph 14)
   - (D) "And now, inexplicably, the white woman in a little red boat, paddling through waters that flawlessly mirror the cumulus clouds above." (paragraph 14)
   - (E) ". . . hapless actor in a mysterious play, not yet knowing what my part is, left to gape at the wonder of what I have set in motion." (paragraph 14)

Ed

Test-Taking Strategies

Analyze the Text

Support your responses with evidence from the text.

NOTICE & NOTE

Review what you **noticed and noted** as you read the text. Your annotations can help you answer these questions.

1. **ANALYZE** In paragraph 2, why does the author mention a statistic—the number of people who have completed the journey?

2. **INTERPRET** Reread paragraphs 5 and 6. What reasons does Salak give for making this trip? Why does she really undertake this journey? What does she expect to learn from the experience?

3. **COMPARE** Compare the pacing in paragraphs 11–12 to that in paragraphs 13–14. Which section seems to move faster, and why? How does the pacing help convey what the author says in each passage?

4. **ANALYZE** What does the dialogue in paragraphs 19–23 add to the narrative? How does it contribute to the central idea of the selection?

5. **CRITIQUE** The text includes a map showing Salak's journey. What other visual aids would you have found helpful in visualizing her journey?

6. **CITE EVIDENCE** Review the notes you took about imagery, based on the question on the Get Ready page. In the chart, cite two examples and explain how each helps the reader picture people and events.

Imagery	Effect on Reader

7. **INFER** The author uses several French words and phrases. Why did she think it was important to create this **Word Gap** by introducing a foreign language?

8. **INTERPRET** Look back at the notes you took about mood, based on the question on the Get Ready page. What words would you use to describe the mood of Kira Salak's narrative?

Choices

Here are some other ways to demonstrate your understanding of the ideas in this lesson.

Writing

↳ Blog Posts

In a series of blog posts, reflect on Kira's journey to Timbuktu.

- Post 1: Summarize Kira's journey using your own words.
- Post 2: Highlight an aspect of Kira's narrative that especially interests you, and explain why.
- Post 3: Describe somewhere you would like to visit and why.

Publish your posts for other students to view. Visit other students' blogs, and note the similarities and differences in what they had to say about Kira's journey and their own dreams of traveling.

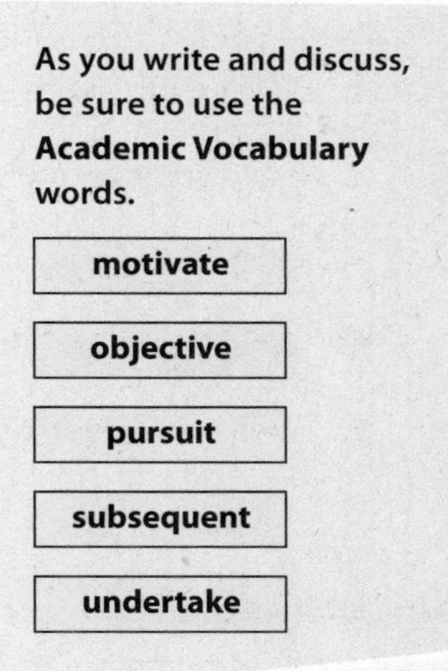

As you write and discuss, be sure to use the **Academic Vocabulary** words.
motivate
objective
pursuit
subsequent
undertake

Media

↳ Community Tour

Consider the different places students can go in your community. Try to think of places that others might not know about but would enjoy! How can they get there? Does it cost anything to visit? Develop a map of places to visit within your community. Consider places like museums, theaters, shops, or parks.

- Mark different routes to get to each one. Can students walk, bike, bus, or drive there?
- List limitations such as cost, large crowds, distance, or unpredictable weather. What should students consider when planning a trip to each place?

Present your community tour to a small group. Did others map the same places you did? Why is it important for us to be connected to our communities?

Speaking & Listening

↳ Maze Challenge

As a class, create a (safe) maze for students to navigate through with various obstacles. Use desks, backpacks, books, or whatever else is available in your classroom. Then, study the maze. Write detailed instructions for how to navigate it successfully.

- Now, put your directions to the test. Pair up with a classmate willing to go through the maze…blindfolded!
- Take turns observing different pairs of students giving and receiving directions.
- Revise your set of instructions to be more helpful as you witness each pair's attempt.

As a class, discuss what made each student's attempt successful or unsuccessful. How does this activity connect to the unit's essential question: What drives us to take on a challenge?

Expand Your Vocabulary

PRACTICE AND APPLY

Answer each question in a way that demonstrates your comprehension of the vocabulary word.

circuitously	disingenuous	integrity	embark	stagnant

1. What might be the benefits of traveling **circuitously** to an unfamiliar destination?
2. Have you ever given a **disingenuous** answer? Explain.
3. When have you acted with **integrity**? Explain.
4. What would you do to get ready to **embark** on a trip around the world?
5. What would you do if you felt your life was **stagnant**?

Vocabulary Strategy

Word Roots

Interactive Vocabulary Lesson: Common Roots, Prefixes, and Suffixes

A root is a word part that contains the core meaning of the word. Many English words contain roots that come from older languages such as Greek, Latin, Old English (Anglo-Saxon), and Norse. For example, the vocabulary word *salvation* comes from the Latin *salvare*, meaning "to save." The root gives you a clue to the word's meaning, which is "deliverance from sin or destruction."

Knowing the meaning of a word's root can help you determine its meaning. In addition, knowing the meanings of roots will help you guess the meanings of other words with the same root.

PRACTICE AND APPLY

Look up the words in the chart in a dictionary. Write the meaning of the root in the third column. In the fourth column, write down at least two other words with the same root.

Word	Root	Meaning of Root	Two Other Words with Root
ludicrous (paragraph 1)	*ludus*		
persevere (paragraph 4)	*severus*		
desolate (paragraph 4)	*solus*		
mantra (paragraph 16)	*men-*		

Watch Your Language!

Sentence Variety

Authors vary **sentence length and style** to keep a piece from becoming monotonous. Authors also use sentence length to achieve a specific effect. For example, long sentences tend to slow readers down. A series of short, choppy sentences can add tension.

Read this sentence from the selection:

> I gaze at the Niger through the adobe passageways, staring at waters that began in the mountainous rain forests of Guinea and traveled all this way to central Mali—waters that will journey northeast with me to Timbuktu before cutting a great circular swath through the Sahara and retreating south, through Niger, on to Nigeria, passing circuitously through mangrove swamps and jungle, resting at last in the Atlantic in the Bight of Benin.

Salak could have written the passage this way:

> I gaze at the Niger through the adobe passageways. I stare at waters that began in the mountainous rain forests of Guinea and traveled all this way to central Mali. These waters will journey northeast with me to Timbuktu. Then they will cut a great circular swath through the Sahara and retreat south, through Niger, on to Nigeria. Along the way, they will pass circuitously through mangrove swamps and jungle. They will rest at last in the Atlantic in the Bight of Benin.

By using a long, winding sentence, the author mirrors the flow of the Niger river.

Later, Salak changes her sentence style as shown in this example:

> Just one thing at a time now, kayak inflated, kayak loaded with my gear. Paddles fitted together and ready.

Here, Salak uses shorter phrases and sentences to mirror the sequence of quick actions she performs.

PRACTICE AND APPLY

Write a short narrative about a trip or meaningful experience. Use a variety of sentence lengths to mirror what you describe.

The Journey

Poem by **Mary Oliver**

Engage Your Brain

Choose one or both of these activities to start connecting with the poem you're about to read.

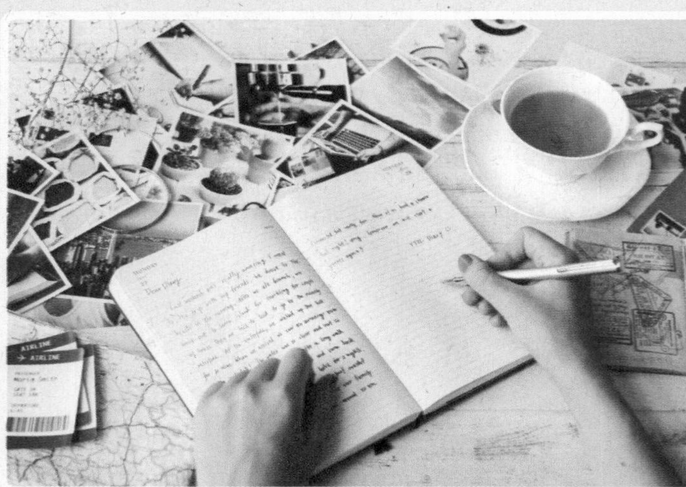

Life Changes

Journeys can involve physical travel, or they can be more metaphorical. During the course of their lives, many people pursue emotional journeys that lead to great change in their lives. Think about a period of time when you have changed. In a small group, describe your journey.

A Fresh Path

Imagine you write an advice column for your school newspaper. What advice would you give to readers who want to make a change in their lives, but don't know how to start? Write a response with advice and support to help your readers start the process.

Interpret Figurative Language

Figurative language is language that communicates meaning beyond the literal meanings of words. In figurative language, words are often used to represent ideas and concepts they would not otherwise be associated with. Poets use figurative language to make revealing comparisons and to create mood.

In "The Journey," Mary Oliver uses two types of figurative language: personification and metaphor.

Personification	Metaphor
Authors use **personification** to give human qualities to an object, animal, or idea. For example, Oliver describes the wind as having stiff fingers, like a human.	Authors use **metaphor** to compare two things that are basically unlike but have something in common. Unlike similes, metaphors do not use the word *like* or *as*. In "The Journey," Oliver compares the subject's emotional state to a trembling house. An **extended metaphor** is a longer metaphor that continues the comparison at length, even throughout an entire poem or literary work.

As you read "The Journey," make notes about the figurative language in the poem.

Focus on Genre

Poetry

- uses figurative language
- uses structure to communicate ideas
- expresses a theme, or message about life
- uses imagery, rhythm, and word choice to elicit emotion from readers

Make Connections

As a good reader, you make connections between the text and issues outside of the text. Doing so broadens your understanding of the text and helps you identify universal themes that comment on what it means to be human.

- **Personal experiences:** Think about whether the text reminds you of anything you have personally experienced in your life. Consider how your experiences influence your understanding or impressions of the text.
- **Other texts:** Notice if the text reminds you of something else you have read. Perhaps it is similar in genre, or maybe the theme reminds you of another text you have read.
- **Society at large:** Consider whether the text comments on or relates to issues in society at large. Remember that while the text may not seem to resonate with one particular group, people in another group may strongly identify with the same text.

As you read "The Journey," take notes about connections you make with the poem's ideas.

Annotation in Action

Here are one reader's notes about "The Journey." As you read, make notes about the poem's figurative language, and how its ideas relate to your personal experiences.

the stars began to burn through the sheets of clouds, and there was a new voice	metaphor about the speaker's mind clearing?

Background

Mary Oliver (1935–2019) was known for observing the natural world in a way that was both romantic and unflinchingly honest. Oliver's poems often draw attention to small details—a bird calling, a still pond, a grasshopper. Her vivid imagery of the natural world opened a window for her to explore larger issues, such as love, loss, wonder, and grief. Oliver published numerous poetry collections, along with many essays and two books about the craft of writing poetry. She won the Pulitzer Prize for Poetry and a National Book Award.

The Journey

Poem by **Mary Oliver**

The speaker describes the moment when she realizes that she can, and must, change her life.

NOTICE & NOTE
As you read, use the side margins to make notes about the text.

One day you finally knew
what you had to do, and began,
though the voices around you
kept shouting
their bad advice—
though the whole house
began to tremble
and you felt the old tug
at your ankles.
"Mend my life!"
each voice cried.
But you didn't stop.

NOTICE & NOTE

AHA MOMENT

When you notice a sudden realization that shifts a character's understanding, you've found an **Aha Moment** signpost.

Notice & Note: Mark the moment when the speaker begins to come to a new realization.

Infer: How might this change things?

INTERPRET FIGURATIVE LANGUAGE

Annotate: Mark the metaphor in lines 19–22.

Infer: What is the speaker comparing in this metaphor?

You knew what you had to do,
though the wind pried
with its stiff fingers
at the very foundations—
though their melancholy
was terrible.
It was already late
enough, and a wild night,
and the road full of fallen
branches and stones.
But little by little,
as you left their voices behind,
the stars began to burn
through the sheets of clouds,
and there was a new voice,
which was slowly
recognized as your own,
that kept you company
as you strode deeper and deeper
into the world,
determined to do
the only thing you could do—
determined to save
the only life you could save.

COLLABORATIVE DISCUSSION

Reread the last two lines of the poem. Whose life is the speaker referring to? Do you agree that it's the only life she can save? Discuss with a partner.

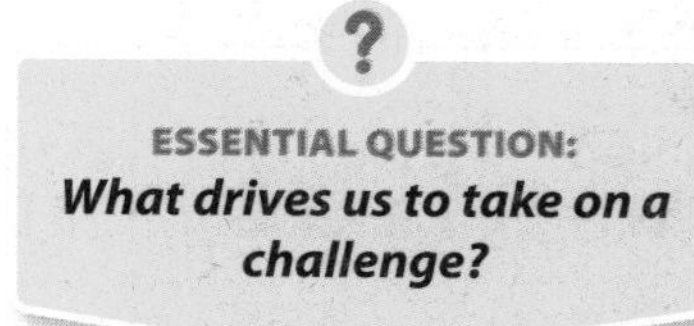

?
ESSENTIAL QUESTION:
What drives us to take on a challenge?

Review your notes and add your thoughts to your Response Log.

Assessment Practice

Answer these questions before moving on to the **Analyze the Text** section on the following page.

1. This question has two parts. First, answer **Part A**. Then, answer **Part B**.

Part A

What is a central theme of "The Journey"?

Ⓐ Each person must chart his or her own path through life.

Ⓑ People should take advice from those around them or they will regret it.

Ⓒ It is better to be alone than to be in a crowd full of selfish people.

Ⓓ Ignoring the needs of others may lead to a dark and stormy life.

Part B

Which excerpt from the poem best supports the theme in Part A?

Ⓐ "... though the voices around you / kept shouting / their bad advice ..." (lines 3–5)

Ⓑ "It was already late / enough, and a wild night, / and the road full of fallen / branches and stones." (lines 19–22)

Ⓒ "... the stars began to burn / through the sheets of clouds ..." (lines 25–26)

Ⓓ "... and there was a new voice, / which was slowly / recognized as your own ..." (lines 27–29)

2. Which of the following is an example of personification?

Ⓐ "One day you finally knew / what you had to do" (lines 1–2)

Ⓑ "though the wind pried / with its stiff fingers / at the very foundations" (lines 14–16)

Ⓒ "But little by little, / as you left their voices behind" (lines 23–24)

Ⓓ "as you strode deeper and deeper / into the world" (lines 31–32)

Ed

Test-Taking Strategies

Analyze the Text

Support your responses with evidence from the text.

NOTICE & NOTE

Review what you **noticed and noted** as you read the text. Your annotations can help you answer these questions.

1. **INFER** In line 3, who are "the voices around you"? What might the voices represent?

2. **INTERPRET** How does Oliver personify the wind? What is the figurative meaning of this strong wind outside the home of a person who is undertaking a journey?

3. **ANALYZE** Notice that the poem is written in one long stanza, not broken into smaller stanzas. How does Oliver use this structure to develop an extended metaphor?

4. **SYNTHESIZE** Trace the nature images that occur throughout the poem. How does Oliver use each image to develop the extended metaphor in the poem?

5. **INFER** What universal themes does the poem reveal? How do the title and structure of the poem help convey these themes?

6. **ANALYZE** Choose two examples of figurative language. Explain how each one contributes to the poem's mood.

7. **INTERPRET** In the last line, the speaker expresses determination to "save / the only life you could save." How does this expand on the speaker's **Aha Moment** that a change had to be made?

8. **CONNECT** Review the notes you took about making connections with the poem. Fill out the graphic organizer to show the connections you made to yourself, other texts, and society—the world around you.

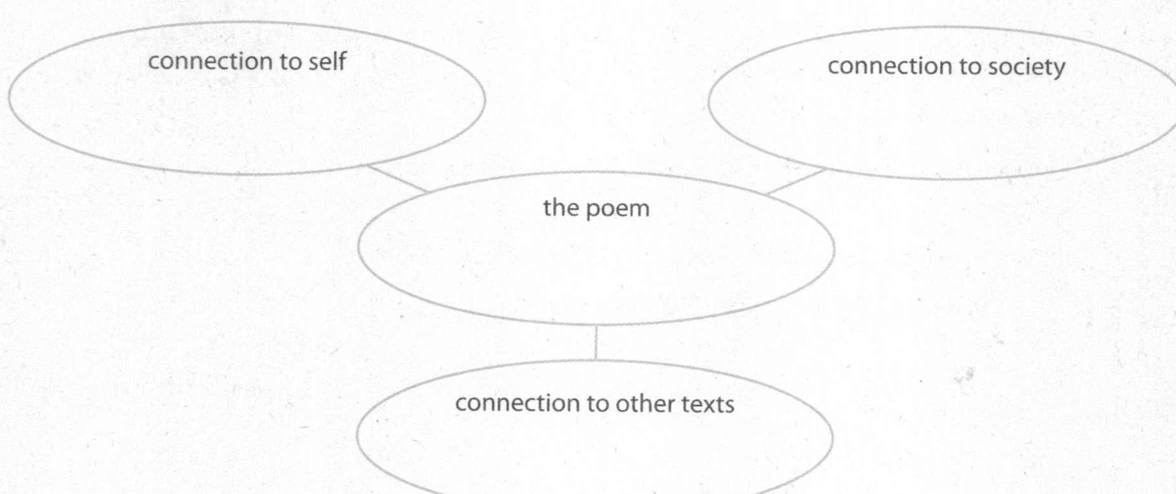

Choices

Here are some other ways to demonstrate your understanding of the ideas in this lesson.

Writing

↳ Music Connection

Think about the main messages, or themes, in the poem. What is the speaker saying about life's journey? Create a brief presentation in which you

- paraphrase the poem using your own words
- share a clip from a song you think best expresses one of the poem's messages
- describe the connection between the song and the poem

As other students present, note the similarities and differences in your analyses.

As you write and discuss, be sure to use the Academic Vocabulary words.

motivate

objective

pursuit

subsequent

undertake

Media

↳ Image Board

Think about how the poem "The Journey" connects to your life as well as society at large. What experiences or lessons about life does it make readers consider?

Arrange 4–5 images as a visual response to the poem. These can be images you've drawn or taken yourself, clipped from magazines, or found online. Present your image board to a small group and describe how each one connects to the themes found within the poem.

Social & Emotional Learning

↳ Journal Entry

Think of an emotional or physical journey you have taken in your life. Maybe you had to move to a new school, went through a breakup, joined a team, or went on a trip. In a journal entry, describe the following:

- What obstacles did you have to overcome?
- How did others help or hinder your progress?
- What strengths did you discover in yourself? Did you learn things about yourself that you want to work on?

Compare Messages Across Genres

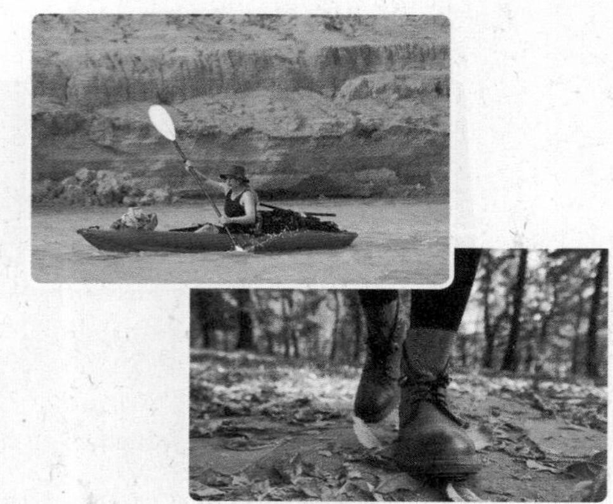

Both *The Cruelest Journey* and "The Journey" are about making a journey. Although the texts explore a similar topic, they use different genres to do so. One uses the prose genre of travel writing; the other uses the genre of poetry.

In a small group, discuss the similarities and differences between the prose and the poetic treatments. Use the graphic organizer to develop your response.

	A *The Cruelest Journey*	B "The Journey"
Purpose		
Message		
Language		
Personal Connection		

Analyze the Texts

Discuss these questions in your group.

1. **CONNECT** What similarities do you see between the journey described by Salak and the journey discussed in the poem?
2. **COMPARE AND CONTRAST** How would you state the overall theme of each text? Is either a universal theme, that is, a theme that applies to all people across cultures and time periods? Explain.
3. **CRITIQUE** Kira Salak's *The Cruelest Journey* describes a physical journey. Mary Oliver's poem "The Journey" describes a psychological and emotional journey. Why do you think each author chose the genre she did to convey her subject and message? Was each author's choice effective? Explain.
4. **SYNTHESIZE** What have you learned from these sources together about how to take on a challenge?

Collaborate and Reflect

Now your group can continue exploring the ideas in these texts by collaborating on a response to the texts. Follow these steps:

1. **DISCUSS** In your group, discuss which journey you identify with more closely. Think about how these and similar journeys can apply to the broader human experience.
2. **USE TEXT EVIDENCE** Support your response with evidence from the texts. Refer to your notes in the graphic organizer on the previous page.
3. **LISTEN** Consider your group members' points of view. Think about how personal experiences have shaped each person's point of view. Adjust your own response as you reflect on your classmates' comments.
4. **ASK QUESTIONS** Ask questions for clarification or to gain information.
5. **WRITE** In the chart below, take notes on the discussion. Then, compose a brief summary of your group's discussion. Include what you have learned and what insights you have gained.

Interactive Speaking & Listening Lesson: Participating in Collaborative Discussions

Notes from the Discussion

Summary

Reader's Choice

Continue your exploration of the Essential Question by doing some independent reading on journeys and challenges. Read the titles and descriptions shown. Then mark the texts that interest you.

ESSENTIAL QUESTION:
What drives us to take on a challenge?

Short Reads

Available on 

These texts are available in your ebook. Choose one to read and rate. Then defend your rating to the class.

from The Odyssey

Books 9, 10, 11, 12, 17, 21, 22, 23

Epic Poem by **Homer**

Odysseus faces daunting challenges as he tries to return home to Ithaca after the Trojan War.

Rate It 

Siren Song

Poem by **Margaret Atwood**

What is it really like to be a Siren stuck on an island? Not as glamorous as it might seem.

Rate It 

from The Odyssey: A Dramatic Retelling of Homer's Epic

Drama by **Simon Armitage**

What's the best path between two evils? Odysseus orders his crew to sail straight between an abyss and a monster.

Rate It 

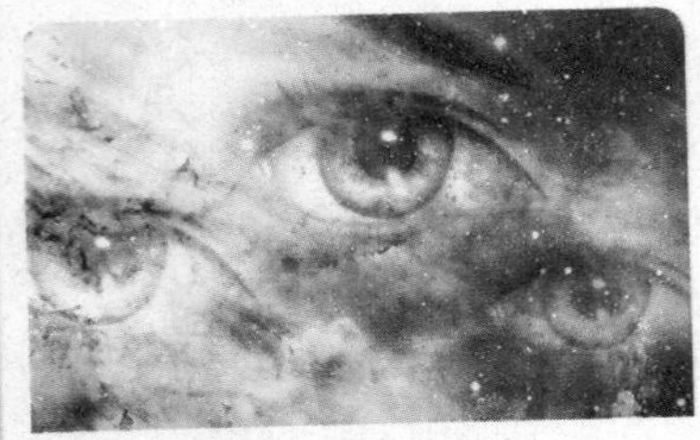

Ilse, Who Saw Clearly

Short Story by **E. Lily Yu**

A traveling magician steals the eyes from everyone in Ilse's village, so Ilse goes on a quest to get them back.

Rate It 

The Real Reasons We Explore Space

Argument by **Michael Griffin**

What is it about space that challenges us to go there?

Rate It 

Long Reads

Here are three recommended books that connect to this unit topic. For additional options, ask your teacher, school librarian, or peers. Which titles spark your interest?

The Thief

Novel by **Megan Whalen Turner**

The king's scholar is in search of an ancient treasure. He enlists the help of Gen, a well-known thief. Can Gen be trusted on this perilous journey, or does he have plans of his own?

Finding Miracles

Novel by **Julia Alvarez**

Milly is self-conscious about the fact that she is adopted. When Pablo—a refugee from the country where Milly was born—starts attending her school, she is forced to face who she is and where she came from.

The Marrow Thieves

Science Fiction by **Cheri Dimaline**

In future North America, indigenous people are hunted and harvested for their bone marrow because of its remedial powers. A group of friends struggles to survive and figure out how to defeat the marrow thieves.

Extension

↳ Connect & Create

ADVICE FROM A PRO As an epic hero, Odysseus knows all about epic challenges. With a partner, write a text message exchange between Odysseus and a character from a text you have both read. Odysseus is giving advice about how to meet challenges and overcome obstacles the character is facing—and he may be receiving advice, too.

DIFFERENT QUESTS The individuals in this unit are all engaged in some kind of quest—some for adventure, others to gain knowledge or to right wrongs. In the text you read, what was the quest or journey? Write a review of the text in which you describe the quest and how it made you think differently about what an epic journey can be.

NOTICE & NOTE

- Pick one of the texts and annotate the Notice & Note signposts you find.
- Then, use the **Notice & Note Writing Frames** to help you write about the significance of the signposts.
- Compare your findings with those of other students who read the same text.

Notice & Note Writing Frames

Write an Expository Essay

Writing Prompt

Using ideas, information, and examples from the texts in this unit, write an expository essay that answers the Essential Question—what drives people to take on a challenge.

Manage your time carefully so that you can

- review the texts in the unit;
- plan your essay;
- write your essay; and
- revise and edit your essay.

Be sure to

- begin with a clear thesis, or controlling idea, that responds to the Essential Question;
- include in your introduction an engaging quotation, anecdote, or detail;
- organize supporting ideas in a logically structured body that clearly develops the thesis;
- use domain-specific vocabulary, an appropriately formal tone, and logical transitions that clarify and connect ideas; and
- end with a logical conclusion that sums up your main ideas.

Review the Mentor Text

For an example of a well-written expository essay you can use as a mentor text, review:

- **"Archaeology's Tech Revolution"** (pages 569–573).

Be sure to review your notes and annotations about this text. Note the techniques the author uses to make his essay compelling and effective.

Consider Your Sources

Review the list of texts in the unit and choose at least three that you may want to use as a source of ideas or evidence for your essay.

As you review potential sources, consult the notes you made on your **Response Log** and make additional notes about any ideas that might be useful as you write. Note page and line or paragraph numbers so you can cite text evidence accurately when you include support from these texts.

UNIT 6 SOURCES

- ☐ **The Epic**
- ☐ *from* **The Odyssey**
- ☐ **Archaeology's Tech Revolution**
- ☐ *from* **The Cruelest Journey: 600 Miles to Timbuktu**
- ☐ **The Journey**

Analyze the Prompt

Review the prompt to make sure you understand the assignment.

1. Mark the sentence in the prompt paragraph that identifies the topic of your essay. Rewrite this sentence in your own words.
2. Look for words that indicate the purpose and audience for your essay and write a sentence describing each.

Find a Purpose

Two common purposes of an expository essay are

- **to explain a complex idea**
- **to describe causes or effects of an event or phenomenon**

What is my topic? What is my writing task?

What is my purpose?

Who is my audience?

Review the Rubric

Your essay will be scored using a rubric. As you write, focus on the characteristics of a high-scoring essay as described in the chart. You will learn more about these characteristics as you work through the lesson.

Purpose, Focus, and Organization	Evidence and Elaboration	Conventions of Standard English
The response includes: • A strongly maintained controlling idea, or thesis • Use of transitions to connect ideas • Logical progression of ideas • Appropriate style and tone	The response includes: • Effective use of evidence and sources • Effective use of elaboration • Clear and effective expression of ideas • Appropriate vocabulary • Varied sentence structure	The response may include: • Some minor errors in usage but no patterns of errors • Correct punctuation, capitalization, sentence formation, and spelling • Command of basic conventions

1 PLAN YOUR EXPOSITORY ESSAY

Develop a Thesis

To develop your thesis, first consider your response to the Essential Question.

We often take on a challenge because

____

Plan Your Thesis

A thesis, or controlling idea, expresses in one or two sentences the central idea of the essay.

Then, review the notes you took about the texts in the unit. Write a thesis statement that expresses your position.

Sample thesis:	Mary Oliver's poem "The Journey" reflects the drive to take on a challenge in pursuit of emotional growth.
My thesis:	

Identify Support

Now consider how you will support your thesis. Choose three points, or **main ideas,** to write about and identify **evidence** that supports those ideas. Remember to include the title, author, page number, and other relevant information for your **sources**.

Help with Planning

Consult **Interactive Writing Lesson: Writing Informative Texts.**

Main Idea:	Evidence:	Source:
Main Idea:	Evidence:	Source:
Main Idea:	Evidence:	Source:

Research and Refine

No matter your level of experience with your topic, at this point your essay will benefit from a bit of research.

- Choose at least one of your points to investigate further.
- Look for examples, statistics, or quotations from experts that can strengthen one of your points, perhaps the point that has the weakest support so far.
- Don't forget to record source information so you can cite what you find.

Key point:	
Evidence:	Source:

Organize Ideas

Organize your ideas so that your first draft will progress logically from introduction through body paragraphs to the conclusion.

INTRODUCTION	• Consider beginning with a question, quotation, or statistic to grab your readers' attention. • State your thesis clearly.
BODY PARAGRAPHS	• Present key ideas and supporting evidence for your thesis with one main idea per paragraph. • Use transitions to show how each paragraph is related to the next.
CONCLUSION	• Restate your claim and its significance. • You may choose to include an idea related to your thesis to give readers something new to think about, or use that great quotation that didn't quite fit into your introduction.

Create Structure

Here are some options for structuring your essay:

- **Start with general or familiar ideas, then move to ideas that might be new to readers.**
- **Explore causes and effects of this aspect of human behavior.**
- **Explain your topic spatially (by location) or chronologically.**

2 DEVELOP A DRAFT

Now it is time to draft your essay. What do you write to motivate your readers to keep reading? For ideas, examine how professional authors craft effective essays. Then, use similar techniques in your own writing.

Ed

Drafting Online

Check your assignment list for a writing task from your teacher.

Introduce the Topic

EXAMINE THE MENTOR TEXT

In "Archaeology's Tech Revolution," Jeremy Hsu opens with a colorful description of Indiana Jones's approach to archaeology. To contrast, he lists several technologies used by today's scientists and uses a vivid quotation that lends credibility to his thesis.

This transition connects innovations already mentioned with accomplishments the author is about to list.

Such innovations have allowed archaeologists to spot buried pyramids from space, create 3-D maps of ancient Mayan ruins from the air, explore the sunken wrecks of Roman ships and find evidence of heart disease in 3,000-year-old mummies. Most of the new toolkit comes from fields such as biology, chemistry, physics or engineering, as well as commercial gadgets that include GPS, laptops and smartphones.

"If we dig part of a site, we destroy it," said David Hurst Thomas, a curator in anthropology at the American Museum of Natural History in New York. "Technology lets us find out a lot more about [a site] before we go in, like surgeons who use CT and MRI scans."

These facts come from research and the author's personal knowledge. Their rapid-fire presentation makes them all the more impressive.

A quotation from an expert supports the author's overall thesis and provides additional explanation.

APPLY TO YOUR DRAFT

Use the chart to generate ideas about how you might begin your essay. Remember, you want to use a piece of information that is on topic and that also grabs your reader's attention.

How will I begin?	
A surprising fact	
A relevant anecdote	
A quotation	
An intriguing question	

Preview the Main Points in the Introduction

EXAMINE THE MENTOR TEXT

Jeremy Hsu transitions neatly into the fourth paragraph of his introduction to "Archaeology's Tech Revolution," connecting the paragraph with the mention of tools in the previous paragraphs. Then he mentions the main points the body of his article will cover.

The first sentence previews the author's first point: technology makes it easier to locate a good archaeological site.

Archaeologists have harnessed such tools to find ancient sites of interest more easily than ever before. They can dig with greater confidence and less collateral damage, apply the latest lab techniques to ancient human artifacts or remains, and better pinpoint when people or objects existed in time.

The author previews the rest of his main points in the order he will address them later in the text.

APPLY TO YOUR DRAFT

Your introduction should briefly mention, in a concise summary, the main points the body of your essay will explain and elaborate on.

Review your notes for your body paragraphs. Then try drafting two different ways your introduction can preview your main points. Which is most effective?

Mind Your Tone

As you write, remember to use a **formal voice,** or **tone.** Avoid slang and informal language. Look for opportunities to use **academic language** and **domain-specific vocabulary.**

Preview Main Points	
Option #1	**Option #2**

3 REVISE YOUR ESSAY

Experienced writers know the importance of revision. Review your essay and consider how it can be improved. Use the guide to help you revise.

Ed

Help with Revision

Find a **Peer Review Guide** and **Student Models** online.

REVISION GUIDE		
Ask Yourself	**Prove It**	**Revise It**
Introduction Does my introduction engage readers and state a clear thesis?	**Highlight** the thesis statement and **circle** an engaging idea in the introduction.	**Add to** or revise your thesis to clarify or strengthen your position. **Add** an attention-getting question, detail, or quotation.
Transitions Are ideas organized logically and linked with transitions?	**Highlight** the main idea in each body paragraph and **note** the order of those ideas. **Circle** transitional words and phrases.	**Reorder** paragraphs. **Add** transitions to connect ideas and clarify the organization.
Evidence Does text evidence support the ideas in each body paragraph?	**Underline** each supporting fact, definition, example, description, statistic, or quotation.	**Add** facts, details, examples, or quotations to support ideas.
Conclusion Does my conclusion effectively summarize ideas?	**Highlight** the restated thesis or summary idea of the conclusion.	**Add** a restatement of the thesis or summary of the essay's main points.
Style Is the style appropriately formal, including domain-specific vocabulary?	**Note** the use of "I" or any slang or informal word choices. **Underline** domain-specific terms.	**Replace** informal language. **Add** precise technical or academic language as appropriate.

APPLY TO YOUR DRAFT

Consider the following as you look for opportunities to improve your writing.

- Consider whether your introduction grabs the reader's attention.
- Make sure your thesis is clearly and strongly stated.
- Check that you have adequate reasons, each supported with relevant facts and examples.

Peer Review in Action

Once you have finished revising your essay, you will exchange papers with a partner in a **peer review.** During a peer review, you will give suggestions to improve your partner's draft.

Read the introduction from a student's draft and examine the comments from her peer reviewer. This student chose to focus her essay on one of the selections in the unit.

Draft

Include the Essential Question for readers who don't know it.

Change Is Hard
By Grace Chen, Springfield High School

One answer to the Essential Question is that we can become better by facing a challenge and meeting its demands. Mary Oliver's poem "The Journey" reflects this universal human drive to take on a challenge in the pursuit of emotional growth. "The Journey" tells us that this kind of change is hard, that it is worth the struggle, and that one's own life is all that a person can truly change.

I think you need to say more about the poem. Expand this into two paragraphs?

This is a solid thesis, but the connection between challenge and change isn't clear.

Now read the revised introduction below. Notice how the writer has improved her draft by following her reviewer's comments.

Revision

Change Is Hard
By Grace Chen, Springfield High School

What drives us—all of us—to take on a challenge? Deep inside, each of us wants to grow, to improve, to become a better version of who we are. We are driven to take on challenges because challenges pull growth out of us; they demand change. Whether a particular challenge is physical, emotional, intellectual, spiritual, or all of these, when you meet it, you're a better version of you than you were before.

Nice way to explain the link between challenge and change.

Mary Oliver's poem "The Journey" describes this universal human need to face what challenges us so that we can grow. On the surface, the poem is a description of a house in a storm. On a deeper level, it's about a person beginning to stand up for herself, acknowledging her own truth and deciding, finally, to pursue that truth, whatever it may be. In the process, "The Journey" tells us three things: change is hard, change is worth the struggle, and one's own life is all that a person can truly expect to change.

Great overview of the literal and metaphorical meaning in the poem. I think this will help readers understand your ideas.

I like how you preview your three main points!

APPLY TO YOUR DRAFT

During your peer review, give each other specific suggestions for how you could make your essay more effective.

When receiving feedback from your partner, listen attentively and ask questions to make sure you fully understand the revision suggestions.

4 EDIT YOUR ESSAY

Edit your draft to make sure your essay reflects standard English conventions and spelling.

Ed
Interactive Grammar Lesson: Spelling

Watch Your Language!

SPELL COMMONLY CONFUSED WORDS CORRECTLY

Many pairs of English words are **homophones:** They are pronounced the same way but are spelled differently and have different meanings, like *your* and *you're* and *principal* and *principle*. There are other words that are close in pronunciation but different in spelling and meaning, like *accept* and *except*. This chart includes a few commonly confused words that might appear in an expository essay.

Words	Definitions	Examples
affect/effect	As a verb, ***affect*** generally means "to influence," but it can also mean "to pretend; to put on falsely." ***Effect*** is usually used as a noun that means "result or consequence."	Thinking it would **affect** (influence) her audience's impression of her, Chloe **affected** (faked) a British accent. The **effect** (result) was a roar of laughter.
than/then	Use ***than*** in making comparisons. On all other occasions, use ***then***.	I enjoyed this story more **than** that one. **Then**, I read a third one and liked it most of all.
there/their/ they're	***There*** is the opposite of *here*. ***Their*** is possessive and means "belonging to them." ***They're*** is a contraction for "they are."	**There** you are! Will you help Carmen and Melissa get **their** groceries inside? It's pouring rain and **they're** getting soaked!

APPLY TO YOUR DRAFT

Now apply what you've learned to your own work.

1. **Find a list** of commonly confused words. Print or copy it, read it, and circle words to watch for in your writing. Pro tip: many writers have a short list of confusing or hard-to-spell words they always double-check.
2. **Check your essay** against your list and make appropriate corrections.
3. **Exchange drafts** with a peer and review spelling in each other's work.

5 PUBLISH YOUR ESSAY

Share It!

Finalize your essay for your writing portfolio. You may also use your essay as inspiration for other projects

Ways to Share

- **Write an article** for your school's blog.
- **Create an infographic** that explains your thesis and supporting points.
- **Record a podcast** that summarizes your essay.

Speaking & Listening

Participate in a Collaborative Discussion

Throughout this unit, you have considered what drives—or inspires—people to take on a challenge. Now you will synthesize your ideas by participating in a collaborative discussion on the topic of how different people meet the need for challenges in life.

Use Your Essay as the Basis for Participation

Review your essay, and use the chart below to guide you as you make notes for the collaborative discussion.

Notes for Collaborative Discussion	
Key Point	Evidence
Key Point	Evidence
Key Point	Evidence

Get Organized and Practice

- Join classmates to make groups of four. Try to include students who have different perspectives on the Essential Question.
- Present your ideas to the group, using content and academic vocabulary that is appropriate to your topic.
- Encourage classmates to ask questions about your ideas and examples so that you will be prepared to "think on your feet" during the whole-class discussion.
- As a group, choose one or two questions you would like to pose to the class for further discussion.

Practice Effective Discussion Techniques

- Listen closely to one another.
- Don't interrupt.
- Stay on topic.
- Ask helpful, relevant questions.
- Provide clear, thoughtful, relevant answers and feedback.

Participate in the Collaborative Discussion

Present your group's discussion questions to the class. Help make the questions clear to other students and participate actively in the discussion that follows. Refer to your notes as needed.

An effective participant in a collaborative discussion:

- makes a clear, logical, and well-defended generalization about the challenges people seek and meet
- uses relevant quotations and specific examples to illustrate ideas
- listens actively and responds thoughtfully and politely to the ideas of other speakers
- builds on the ideas of other speakers' contributions
- helps to ensure that everyone takes part in the discussion
- uses academic language for an appropriate voice and tone
- summarizes the discussion by synthesizing ideas from multiple participants

Share It!

- **Create a podcast** by recording your discussion and the audience interaction. Review and edit the recording to share the most effective parts of the discussion.
- **Create a blog post** for a school or class website that summarizes and reflects on discussion highlights.

Interactive Speaking & Listening Lesson: Participating in a Collaborative Discussion

Reflect & Extend

Here are some other ways to show your understanding of the ideas in Unit 6.

Reflect on the
Essential Question

What drives us to take on a challenge?

Has your answer to the question changed after reading the texts in the unit? Discuss your ideas.

You can use these sentence starters to help you reflect on your learning:

- **I've changed my mind about . . .**
- **I'm still considering . . .**
- **I have new ideas about . . .**

Project-Based Learning

Create a Movie Trailer

With a group, choose a movie you enjoy about characters who take on a challenge. Then create a movie trailer for the movie. Here are some questions to ask yourself as you get started.

- What is going to be our **hook**? How can we make sure the **audience** will want to see the movie?
- How much about the movie will we reveal in the trailer?
- How will we **edit** clips to make the trailer engaging?

Media Projects

To find help with this task online, access **Create a Movie Trailer.**

Writing

Write a Play

Write a play about someone who decides to take on a major challenge that will likely change his or her life. Use the chart to jot down your ideas. Then, write your play.

Ask Yourself	My Notes
Who are the **major and minor characters** in my play?	
How will I use dialogue to move the **plot** along?	
What is the **setting**?	

Resources

HMH *Into Literature* Resources

For more instruction and practice, access the *Into Literature* Resources and Interactive Lessons.

UNIT 1

Response Log

Use this Response Log to record your ideas about how each of the texts in Unit 1 relates to or comments on the **Essential Question.**

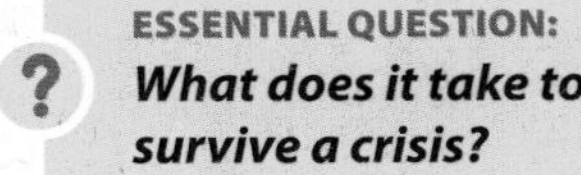
ESSENTIAL QUESTION:
What does it take to survive a crisis?

from A Chance in the World	
Is Survival Selfish?	
The Leap	
The End and the Beginning	
from Night	
from Maus	

UNIT 2

Response Log

Use this Response Log to record your ideas about how each of the texts in Unit 2 relates to or comments on the **Essential Question.**

ESSENTIAL QUESTION:
Are some differences too great to overcome?

The Power of a Dinner Table	
Unusual Normality	
Once Upon a Time	
Theme for English B	
The Vietnam Wall	
Views of the Wall	
The Gettysburg Address	
from Saving Lincoln	

UNIT 3

Response Log

Use this Response Log to record your ideas about how each of the texts in Unit 3 relates to or comments on the **Essential Question.**

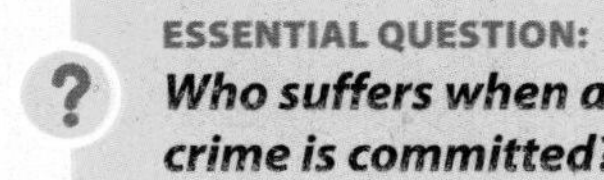
ESSENTIAL QUESTION:
Who suffers when a crime is committed?

Entwined	
Why Are We Obsessed with True Crime?	
from The 57 Bus	
Gift-Wrapped Fathers	
Bully	
Unsolved "Vigilante" Murder in the Heartland	

UNIT 4

Response Log

Use this Response Log to record your ideas about how each of the texts in Unit 4 relates to or comments on the **Essential Question.**

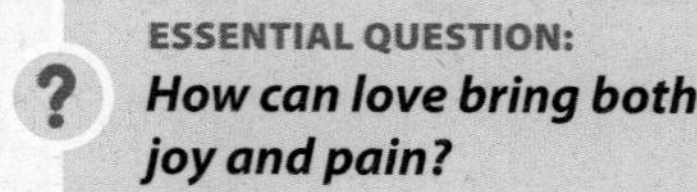
ESSENTIAL QUESTION:
How can love bring both joy and pain?

The Tragedy of Romeo and Juliet	
My Shakespeare	
More than Reckless Teenagers	
Romeo Is a Dirtbag	

UNIT 5

Response Log

Use this Response Log to record your ideas about how each of the texts in Unit 5 relates to or comments on the **Essential Question.**

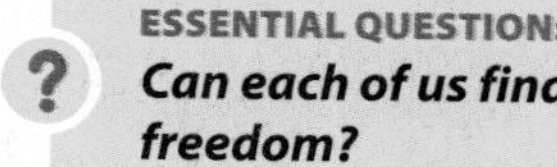

ESSENTIAL QUESTION:
Can each of us find freedom?

Harrison Bergeron	
I Have a Dream	
from Interview with John Lewis	
from Hidden Figures	
Booker T. and W.E.B.	
from Reading Lolita in Tehran	
from Persepolis 2: The Story of a Return	

UNIT 6

Response Log

Use this Response Log to record your ideas about how each of the texts in Unit 6 relates to or comments on the **Essential Question.**

ESSENTIAL QUESTION:
What drives us to take on a challenge?

from The Odyssey	
Archaeology's Tech Revolution	
from The Cruelest Journey: 600 Miles to Timbuktu	
The Journey	

NOTICE & NOTE Handbook

Get More Out of What You Read

Answer your own questions!

Two educators spent years working with students and reading and rereading the books that students read most. They identified a handful of common things authors include in fiction and nonfiction texts that signal the reader to pay attention. They call them **signposts**. When you notice a signpost and think about it, you can take control of your own reading.

Learn more about the signposts below.

SIGNPOSTS FOR LITERARY TEXTS
(such as poetry, plays, and fiction)

SIGNPOSTS FOR INFORMATIONAL TEXTS
(such as articles and arguments)

Contrasts and Contradictions

LITERARY ANALYSIS CONNECTION

Paying attention to Contrasts and Contradictions can help you analyze

- character development
- conflict
- theme
- relationship between setting and plot
- mood

Contrasts and Contradictions occur either when there is a sharp contrast between what we would expect and what we observe the character doing, or when the character behaves in a way that contradicts previous behavior or well-established patterns. Contrasts and Contradictions can also occur within or between settings, especially when the setting is very different from the everyday world we live in.

Read carefully and be alert for moments when a character begins acting or thinking in a new way, or in a way that surprises you because it's not how most people would react. Words like *but* or *despite* can provide clues to these differences.

When you notice Contrasts and Contradictions, pause. Think about what this unexpected or unusual behavior tells you about the character or the setting.

A good question to ask is . . .

I didn't see her leap through the air, only heard the sudden thump and looked out my window. She was hanging by the backs of her heels from the new gutter we had put in that year, and she was smiling. I was not surprised to see her, she was so matter-of-fact. She tapped on the window. I remember how she did it, too. It was the friendliest tap, a bit tentative, as if she was afraid she had arrived too early at a friend's house. Then she gestured at the latch, and when I opened the window she told me to raise it wider and prop it up with the stick so it wouldn't crush her fingers. She swung down, caught the ledge, and crawled through the opening. . . .

—from "The Leap," p. 42

Why would the character act (feel) this way?

Aha Moment

An **Aha Moment** occurs when characters realize something that shifts the way they act or what they understand about themselves, others, or the world.

These moments can be quite subtle and require close reading to identify. Other times, it's more obvious that a change in thinking has occurred. Be alert for these realizations, because they often mark an important turning point.

Some phrases that can signal an Aha Moment are:

It occurred to me . . .

His face grew pale . . .

For the first time . . .

She suddenly recognized . . .

When you notice an Aha Moment, pause. Think about what effect the character's new knowledge might have on the story.

A good question to ask is . . .

How might this change things?

LITERARY ANALYSIS CONNECTION

Paying attention to Aha Moments can help you analyze

- character development
- internal conflict
- plot

Pyramus had left
a little later than his Thisbe had,
and he could see what surely were the tracks
of a wild beast left clearly on deep dust.
His face grew ashen. And when he had found
the bloodstained shawl, he cried: "Now this same night
will see two lovers lose their lives: she was
the one more worthy of long life: it's I
who bear the guilt for this. O my poor girl,
it's I who led you to your death; I said
you were to reach this fearful place by night;
I let you be the first who would arrive.

—from "Pyramus and Thisbe," Digital Lesson

Tough Questions

LITERARY ANALYSIS CONNECTION

Paying attention to Tough Questions can help you analyze

- internal conflict
- theme
- character development

Tough Questions are questions characters raise that reveal their inner struggles. Characters might ask these questions of themselves, in their heads, or they might voice them out loud and ask other characters.

Be alert to the times when characters ask themselves difficult questions, or when others ask questions that make a character think hard or feel deeply. At these moments, you can learn about characters' internal conflicts and gain insight into the theme of the story.

Some phrases that can signal Tough Questions are:

Why couldn't I . . .

How was she supposed to . . .

Could he forgive himself if . . .

I didn't know . . .

When you notice Tough Questions, pause. Think about what the questions suggest about the character or the theme and how these struggles might affect the rest of the story.

A good question to ask is . . .

What does this question make me wonder about?

Thus began my two years of high school and making other teenagers confused about who I was. You see, I didn't fit into any box. I didn't have the same worries about what shoes or clothes I wore. And so my teenage counterparts always wanted to find out why I was like that. Why I didn't worry about my essays or exams or things.

And of course I couldn't tell them, because I felt that they were not ready to hear the truth. What was I going to say?

During a break from class, "Hey, you know, I was a child soldier at thirteen. Let's go back to class now."

—from "Unusual Normality," p. 117

Words of the Wiser

Notice & Note Peer Coach Videos

Words of the Wiser are pieces of advice or insights about life that a wiser character, who is usually older, offers to the main character.

Look for moments when a character is receiving advice or wisdom about how to deal with a difficult problem or decision. These moments often occur when a character is wrestling with an inner conflict, and the advice can offer clues to the theme of the story.

When you notice Words of the Wiser, pause. Think about what the advice or insight suggests about the story's theme and how it is likely to affect how the characters deal with their problems or decisions.

A good question to ask is . . .

What's the life lesson and how might it affect the character?

LITERARY ANALYSIS CONNECTION

Paying attention to Words of the Wiser can help you analyze

- theme
- internal conflict
- relationship between character and plot

Friar Laurence. Hence from Verona art thou banished.
Be patient, for the world is broad and wide.

Romeo. There is no world without Verona walls,
But purgatory, torture, hell itself.
Hence banished is banish'd from the world,
And world's exile is death. Then "banishment,"
Is death misterm'd. Calling death "banishment,"
Thou cuttst my head off with a golden axe
And smilest upon the stroke that murders me.

Friar Laurence. O deadly sin! O rude unthankfulness!
Thy fault our law calls death; but the kind Prince,
Taking thy part, hath rushed aside the law,
And turned that black word death to banishment.
This is dear mercy, and thou seest it not.

—from *The Tragedy of Romeo and Juliet:* Act III, Scene 3, p. 361

Again and Again

LITERARY ANALYSIS CONNECTION

Paying attention to Again and Again can help you analyze

- plot
- setting
- symbolism
- theme
- character development
- conflict
- mood

Again and Again occurs when events, images, or particular words recur over a portion of the story or novel.

Authors repeat certain words, images, or events Again and Again to

- reveal things about character motivation
- offer insight into the story's theme
- make connections between elements of the plot
- help create the story's mood

When you notice the Again and Again signpost, pause. Think about the meaning the repeated words, images, or events might have and how it relates to the setting, plot, theme, or character development.

A good question to ask is . . .

Why might the author bring this up again and again?

In a house, in a suburb, in a city, there were a man and his wife who loved each other very much and were living happily ever after. They had a little boy, and they loved him very much. They had a cat and a dog that the little boy loved very much. They had a car and a caravan trailer for the holidays, and a swimming pool which was fenced so that the little boy and his playmates would not fall in and drown. They had a housemaid who was absolutely trustworthy and an itinerant gardener who was highly recommended by the neighbors. . . .

—from "Once Upon a Time," p. 132

Memory Moment

Notice & Note Peer Coach Videos

A **Memory Moment** occurs when a character has a recollection that interrupts the forward progress of the story.

Be alert for places where the character is thinking about something that occurred at an earlier time. These moments can

- provide insight into the current situation
- explain character motivation
- offer insight into the theme of the story

Some phrases that can signal a Memory Moment are:

I hadn't seen her since . . .

When he was growing up . . .

My father used to tell me . . .

My mother once said . . .

When you notice a Memory Moment, pause. Think about why the author included this detail from the past, and continue to think about it as you keep reading.

A good question to ask is . . .

Why might this memory be important?

. . .With a start, I realized I knew Chris; I had played baseball against him. Which meant I knew the victim as well.

Russell Gramercy was the coach of the Verplanck American Legion League baseball team of which his son, Chris, was the star pitcher. Russell Gramercy was also a chemistry professor at Howland College, the school I had just started two weeks earlier, though I wasn't in any of his classes. The previous year, the American Legion team I was on had played against Verplanck. Chris had been pitching, and he struck me out twice. He was by far the best player in our area, and scouts from the majors as well as LSU and Arizona State had shown interest in him. His father coached him that day, and I remembered Russell Gramercy putting his arm around Chris's shoulder with pride as he came off the field with another victory.

"Are you okay?" the paramedic asked me at one point. "Are you injured?"

—from "Entwined," p. 204

LITERARY ANALYSIS CONNECTION

Paying attention to Memory Moments can help you analyze

- character development
- theme
- plot
- relationship between character and plot

Big Questions

When you read any informational text or argument, it's important to remember that the author is asserting a version of the truth. This version may be factual and mostly free of bias, or it may include slanted, overstated, or even untrue claims or descriptions. You have to remain slightly skeptical in order to determine the truth. That's why it's important to approach these texts from a **Questioning Stance,** or position. As you read, keep these three **Big Questions** in mind:

What surprised me?

What did the author think I already knew?

What changed, challenged, or confirmed what I already knew?

These questions will not only help you evaluate what you read with a critical eye and keep you from being misled, they will also help make the things you read more interesting. In addition, they can help you get to the root of things that might confuse you. The chart below gives more detail about each of the Big Questions.

What surprised me?	What did the author think I already knew?	What changed, challenged, or confirmed what I already knew?
Look for parts of the text that make you think "really!?", and put an exclamation point there. !	Look for places where the language is tough or where the author is writing about things you don't know much about, and put a question mark there. ?	Look for ideas that change your thinking. Put a *C* by those places. C
You might think . . . "I didn't know that!" "Really? Is that true?" "Oh! Now I get it." "How could anyone think that way?" "I hadn't thought of it that way."	**You might think . . .** "The author thought I'd know what this word means." "The author thought I could picture this." "The author thought I'd know something about this." "The author thought I'd get how this happens."	**You might think . . .** "I realize now . . ." "This makes me rethink my opinion about . . ." "That affirms what I already thought."

Contrasts and Contradictions

Notice & Note Peer Coach Videos

Contrasts and Contradictions occur either when the author presents ideas, things, or people that are very different from one another, or when you come across something that opposes what you know or would expect.

Signal words and phrases that can indicate a Contrast and Contradiction within the text include

- however
- conversely
- nevertheless
- instead
- as opposed to
- on the contrary

To find Contrasts and Contradictions between the text and your own expectations, take note of things that surprise you as you read.

When you notice Contrasts and Contradictions, pause. Think about why the author may have chosen to focus on these differences or to challenge your assumptions.

Depending on the context, good questions to ask yourself are . . .

How does this differ from what I know or expect?

Under what condition is this true?

Why did the author point this out?

RELATED READING SKILLS

- Compare and contrast
- Generalize
- Identify main idea
- Infer
- Identify cause and effect
- Identify details
- Understand author's purpose or bias

What is the difference and why does it matter?

. . . In July 2007, I was having a drink with a friend in Grand Central Station when an underground steam pipe exploded just outside. From where we sat, we heard a dull "boom!" and then suddenly, people were running, streaming out of the tunnels and out the doors.

My friend and I walked quickly and calmly outside, but to get any further, we had to push our way through a crowd of people who were staring, transfixed, at the column of smoke rising from the front of the station. Some people were crying, others were screaming, others were on their cell phones . . . but the crowd, for the most part, was *not* doing the one thing that would increase everyone's chances of survival, if in fact a terrorist bomb with god knows what inside it had just gone off—namely, moving away from the area.

—from "Is Survival Selfish?," p. 24

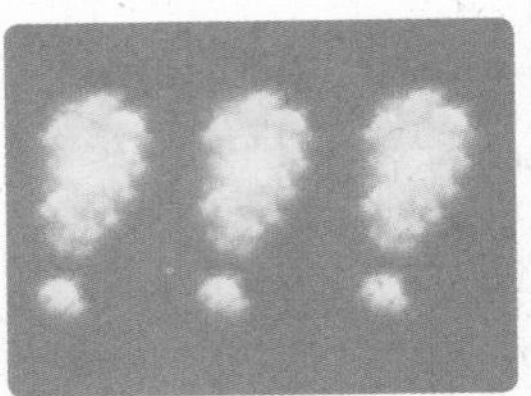

Extreme or Absolute Language

RELATED READING SKILLS

- Draw conclusions
- Generalize
- Identify author's point of view
- Identify main idea
- Infer
- Recognize hyperbole
- Identify cause and effect
- Understand author's purpose or bias

Extreme or Absolute Language occurs when the author uses language that leaves no doubt. It allows for no exceptions and may seem to exaggerate or overstate a claim.

This language includes words such as

- every
- always
- indisputably
- unarguably
- perfectly
- apocalyptic
- miraculous
- unconditionally

It can also include dramatic words and phrases intended to cause a strong reaction, such as "despicable creature," "breathtakingly beautiful," or "contradicts our highest values."

When you notice Extreme or Absolute Language, pause and think. The author might be expressing strong feelings or may be exaggerating or even trying to mislead readers.

Some good questions to ask are . . .

What does this reveal about the author's biases or purpose?

Is this language appropriate?

In the beginning, my journeys feel at best ludicrous, at worst insane. This one is no exception. The idea is to paddle nearly 600 miles on the Niger River in a kayak, alone, from the Malian town of Old Ségou to Timbuktu. And now, at the very hour when I have decided to leave, a thunderstorm bursts open the skies, sending down apocalyptic rain, washing away the very ground beneath my feet. It is the rainy season in Mali, for which there can be no comparison in the world. . . .

—from *The Cruelest Journey: 600 Miles to Timbuktu*, p. 582

Why would the author use this language?

Numbers and Stats

Notice & Note Peer Coach Videos

Numbers and Stats occur either when authors use specific figures to show amounts, size, or scale, or when they are vague when you would have expected more details.

Some key words that may show when an author is being vague include

- several
- few
- a majority
- an average amount
- more significant
- a minimal difference

When you notice Numbers and Stats, pause. Think about why the author may have chosen to use or leave out specific figures in describing something.

Some good questions to ask are . . .

What do these numbers help me see?

What purpose do these numbers serve in this context?

Do these numbers help prove a point?

RELATED READING SKILLS

- Draw conclusions
- Find facts
- Generalize
- Identify details
- Infer
- Make comparisons
- Recognize evidence
- Understand author's purpose or bias

Why did the author use these numbers or amounts?

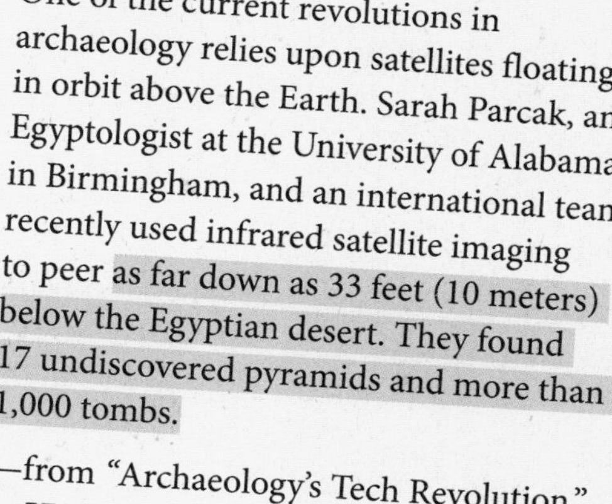
One of the current revolutions in archaeology relies upon satellites floating in orbit above the Earth. Sarah Parcak, an Egyptologist at the University of Alabama in Birmingham, and an international team recently used infrared satellite imaging to peer as far down as 33 feet (10 meters) below the Egyptian desert. They found 17 undiscovered pyramids and more than 1,000 tombs.

—from "Archaeology's Tech Revolution," p. 570

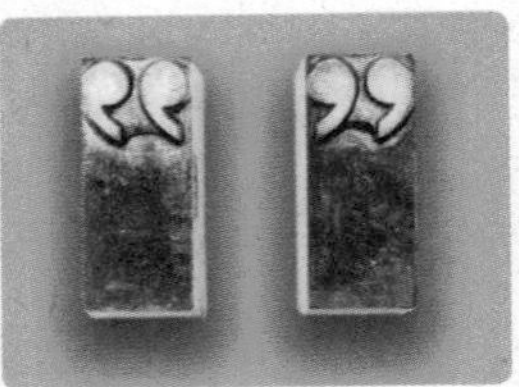

Quoted Words

RELATED READING SKILLS

- Compare and contrast
- Draw conclusions
- Identify author's point of view
- Infer
- Identify cause and effect
- Separate fact from opinion
- Understand author's purpose or bias

Quoted Words occur when the author cites or quotes the opinions or conclusions of a person or group to provide support for a point. Authors often include words from people who are experts on a topic or from people who were participants in or witnesses to events.

When you notice Quoted Words, pause. Think about why the author may have chosen to quote this particular person or group.

Some good questions to ask are . . .

What is this person's perspective?

What are the qualifications of this person?

But before you devour the latest crime shows, you might want to consider how consuming hours of disturbing content is affecting you—and why you can't stop watching it.

"Bingeing true crime is not that much different from people watching a 24-hour news cycle covering a killing spree or a terrorist attack," said Jooyoung Lee, an associate professor of sociology at the University of Toronto.

"I think human beings, in general, are just drawn to extreme cases of violence. And when I say drawn to them, I don't mean that they watch something and hope to emulate it; there's just this fascination."

—from "Why Are We Obsessed with True Crime?," p. 221

Why was this person quoted or cited and what did this add?

Word Gaps

Notice & Note Peer Coach Videos

Word Gaps occur either when authors use vocabulary that is unfamiliar, or when they use familiar words in unexpected ways. Authors of informational texts often use words with multiple meanings, technical or scientific words, or words that are unique to specific subjects.

Sometimes authors provide clues to these words, such as putting them in boldfaced or italic font or highlighting them. Other times, authors follow a less-known word with the phrase *is like* to help explain it. Many times, however, the way you identify a Word Gap is simply by noticing that you've come across a word that you don't understand.

When you notice Word Gaps, pause. Ask yourself the following questions. The answers will help you decide if you need to look the word up or keep reading for more information.

Do I know this word from someplace else?

Does this seem like technical talk for experts on this topic?

RELATED READING SKILLS

- Generalize
- Identify details
- Infer
- Make comparisons
- Understand author's purpose or bias
- Use context clues

Can I find clues in the text to help me understand the word?

"Nobody wanted to talk to us," retired Missouri State Highway Patrol Trooper Dan Boyer tells *A&E Real Crime*. Boyer was among the first responders to arrive outside the D&G tavern where McElroy was ambushed.

A reported crowd of up to 60 men had largely dispersed, but some onlookers remained, staring at the pickup. Those who spoke out were taciturn. "'I didn't see anything. I don't know what happened,'" Boyer recalls witnesses saying.

—from "Unsolved 'Vigilante' Murder in the Heartland," p. 267

Using a Glossary

A glossary is an alphabetical list of vocabulary words. Use a glossary just as you would a dictionary—to determine the meanings, parts of speech, pronunciation, and syllabification of words. (Some technical, foreign, and more obscure words in this book are defined for you in the footnotes that accompany many of the selections.)

Many words in the English language have more than one meaning. This glossary gives the meanings that apply to the words as they are used in the selections in this book.

The following abbreviations are used to identify parts of speech of words:

adj. adjective *adv.* adverb *n.* noun *v.* verb

Each word's pronunciation is given in parentheses. A guide to the pronunciation symbols appears in the Pronunciation Key below. The stress marks in the Pronunciation Key are used to indicate the force given to each syllable in a word. They can also help you determine where words are divided into syllables.

For more information about the words in this glossary or for information about words not listed here, consult a dictionary.

Pronunciation Key

Symbol	Examples
ă	**pat**
ā	**pay**
ä	f**a**ther, h**a**rd
âr	**care**
b	**bib**
ch	**church**
d	**deed**, mill**ed**
ĕ	**pet**
ē	**bee**
f	**fife**, **ph**ase, rou**gh**
g	**gag**
h	**hat**
hw	**wh**ich
ĭ	**pit**
ī	**pie**, **by**
îr	**pier**
j	**judge**
k	**kick**, **c**at, pi**que**
l	**lid**, nee**dle*** (nēd′l)
m	**mum**
n	**no**, sudde**n*** (sŭd′n)
ng	thi**ng**
ŏ	**pot**
ō	**toe**
ô	c**augh**t, p**aw**
oi	**noise**
o͝o	**took**
o͞o	**boot**
o͝or	**lure**
ôr	**core**
ou	**out**
p	**pop**
r	**roar**
s	**sauce**
sh	**sh**ip, di**sh**
t	**tight**, s**t**opp**ed**
th	**th**in
th	**th**is
ŭ	**cut**
ûr	**ur**ge, t**er**m, f**ir**m, w**or**d, h**ear**d
v	**valve**
w	**w**ith
y	**y**es
z	**z**ebra, **x**ylem
zh	vi**s**ion, plea**s**ure, gara**ge**
ə	**a**bout, it**e**m, ed**i**ble, gall**o**p, circ**u**s
ər	butt**er**

Sounds in Foreign Words

Symbol	Examples
KH	*German* i**ch**, a**ch**; *Scottish* lo**ch**
N	*French*, bo**n** (bôN)
œ	*French* **feu**, **œuf**; *German* sch**ö**n
ü	*French* **tu**; *German* **ü**ber

*In English the consonants *l* and *n* often constitute complete syllables by themselves.

Stress Marks

The strongest, or primary, stress of a word is indicated by a mark (′). Words of one syllable show no stress mark.

Glossary of Academic Vocabulary

attribute (ăt´rə-byo͞ot) *n.* a characteristic, quality, or trait.

capacity (kə-păs´ĭ-tē) *n.* the ability to contain, hold, produce, or understand.

commit (kə-mĭt´) *v.* to carry out, engage in, or perform.

confer (kən-fûr´) *v.* to grant or give to.

decline (dĭ-klīn´) *v.* to fall apart or deteriorate slowly.

dimension (dĭ-mĕn´shən) *n.* a feature, scale, or measurement of something.

emerge (ĭ-mûrj´) *v.* to come forth, out of, or away from.

enable (ĕ-nā´bəl) *v.* to give the means or opportunity.

enforce (ĕn-fôrs´) *v.* to compel observance of or obedience to.

entity (ĕn´tĭ-tē) *n.* a thing that exists as a unit.

expose (ĭk-spōz´) *v.* to make visible or reveal.

external (ĭk-stûr´nəl) *adj.* related to, part of, or from the outside.

generate (jĕn´ə-rāt) *v.* to produce or cause something to happen or exist.

impose (ĭm-pōz´) *v.* to bring about by force.

initiate (ĭ-nĭsh´ē-āt) *v.* to start or cause to begin.

integrate (ĭn´tĭ-grāt) *v.* to pull together into a whole; unify.

internal (ĭn-tûr´nəl) *adj.* inner; located within something or someone.

motivate (mō´tə-vāt) *v.* to provide a cause for doing something.

objective (əb-jĕk´tĭv) *n.* an intention, purpose, or goal.

presume (prĭ-zo͞om´) *v.* to take for granted as being true; to assume something is true.

pursuit (pər-so͞ot´) *n.* the action of chasing or following something.

resolve (rĭ-zŏlv´) *v.* to decide or become determined.

reveal (rĭ-vēl´) *v.* to show or make known.

statistic (stə-tĭs´tĭk) *n.* a piece of numerical data.

subsequent (sŭb´sĭ-kwĕnt) *adj.* coming after or following.

sustain (sə-stān´) *v.* to support or cause to continue.

trace (trās) *v.* to discover or determine the origins or developmental stages of something.

underlie (ŭn-dər-lī´) *v.* to be the cause or support of.

undertake (ŭn-dər-tāk´) *v.* to assume responsibility for or take on a job or course of action.

utilize (yo͞ot´l-īz) *v.* to make use of.

Glossary of Critical Vocabulary

allocate (ăl´ə-kāt) *v.* to assign or designate for.

amenable (ə-mē´nə-bəl) *adj.* willing to accept someone or something.

analytical (ăn-ə-lĭt´ĭ-kəl) *adj.* able to analyze, or understand something by breaking it down into parts.

anomalous (ə-nŏm´ə-ləs) *adj.* unusual or uncommon; out of the ordinary.

artifact (är´tə-făkt) *n.* an object produced or shaped by human workmanship.

audacious (ô-dā´shəs) *adj.* bold, rebellious.

baffle (băf´əl) *v.* to confuse or perplex.

berate (bĭ-rāt´) *v.* to criticize or scold.

cacophony (kə-kŏf´ə-nē) *n.* jarring, discordant sound.

callous (kăl´əs) *adj.* emotionally hardened; unfeeling.

charismatic (kăr-ĭz-măt´ĭk) *adj.* magnetic; captivating; having the qualities of a leader who is popular and enthusiastic.

circuitously (sər-kyōō´ĭ-təs-lē) *adv.* in an indirect and lengthy manner.

comply (kəm-plī´) *v.* to obey an instruction or command.

conceive (kən-sēv´) *v.* to form or develop in the mind; devise.

condescending (kŏn-dĭ-sĕn´dĭng) *adj.* characterized by a patronizing or superior attitude.

condolence (kən-dō´ləns) *n.* sympathy with a person who has experienced pain, grief, or misfortune.

connive (kə-nīv´) *v.* to plot or collude secretly in bad actions.

consternation (kŏn-stər-nā´shən) *n.* a state of great alarm, agitation, or dismay.

constraint (kən-strānt´) *n.* something that restricts, limits, or regulates.

constrict (kən-strĭkt´) *v.* to limit or impede growth.

consume (kən-sōōm´) *v.* to completely destroy or eradicate.

convert (kən-vûrt´) *v.* to change one's system of beliefs.

counterparts (koun´tər-pärts) *n.* people or things that have the same characteristics and function.

cower (kou´ər) *v.* to crouch down in fear.

decisive (dĭ-sīs´ĭv) *adj.* final or concluding.

default (dĭ-fôlt´) *v.* to fail to keep a promise to repay a loan.

degenerate (dĭ-jĕn´ər-āt) *v.* to decline morally.

desolate (dĕs´ə-lĭt) *adj.* unhappy; lonely.

detract (dĭ-trăkt´) *v.* to take away from.

din (dĭn) *n.* loud noise.

disingenuous (dĭs-ĭn-jĕn´yōō-əs) *adj.* insincere, deceitful.

distend (dĭ-stĕnd´) *v.* to bulge or expand.

divert (dĭ-vûrt´) *v.* to turn aside from a course.

edict (ē´dĭkt) *n.* an official rule or proclamation.

emaciated (ĭ-mā´shē-āt-id) *adj.* made extremely thin and weak.

embark (ĕm-bärk´) *v.* to set out on a course or a journey (often aboard a boat).

empathy (ĕm´pə-thē) *n.* the ability to identify with or understand the perspective, experiences, or motivations of another individual and to comprehend and share another individual's emotional state.

emulate (ĕm´yə-lāt) *v.* to imitate in order to equal or to excel.

encroach (ĕn-krōch´) *v.* to gradually intrude upon or invade.

enmity (ĕn´mĭ-tē) *n.* deep-seated, shared hatred.

execute (ĕk´sĭ-kyo͞ot) *v.* to carry out or accomplish.

exonerate (ĭg-zŏn´ə-rāt) *v.* to free from blame.

extricate (ĕk´strĭ-kāt) *v.* to release or disentangle from.

fathom (făth´əm) *v.* to comprehend.

forensic analysis (fə-rĕn´sĭk ə-năl´ĭ-sĭs) *n.* the scientific collection and analysis of physical evidence in criminal cases.

GPS *n.* Global Positioning System, a utility that provides positioning, navigation, and timing services.

ineffably (ĭn-ĕf´ə-blē) *adv.* in a way that cannot be expressed; indescribably or unutterably.

inextricably (ĭn-ĕk´strĭ-kə-blē) *adv.* in a way impossible to untangle.

infrared (ĭn´frə-rĕd) *adj.* pertaining to electromagnetic radiation having wavelengths greater than those of visible light and shorter than those of microwaves.

innovation (ĭn-ə-vā´shən) *n.* something newly introduced.

integrity (ĭn-tĕg´rĭ-tē) *n.* consistency and strength of purpose.

intention (ĭn-tĕn´shən) *n.* purpose or plan.

intricate (ĭn´trĭ-kĭt) *adj.* complicated or elaborate.

intrusion (ĭn-tro͞o´zhən) *n.* act of trespass or invasion.

ire (īr) *n.* anger; fury; wrath.

irrelevant (ĭr-rĕl´ə-vənt) *adj.* insignificant, unimportant.

irrevocably (ĭ-rĕv´ə-kə-blē) *adv.* in a way that is impossible to retract or revoke.

laud (lôd) *v.* to praise.

liability (lī-ə-bĭl´ĭ-tē) *n.* the state of being legally obligated or responsible.

macabre (mə-kä´brə) *adj.* upsetting or horrifying in connection with death or injury; gruesome; ghastly.

maneuver (mə-no͞o´vər) *v.* to make a series of controlled movements.

negligent (nĕg´lĭ-jənt) *adj.* characterized by paying little attention to or failing to care for properly.

neutralize (no͞o´trə-līz) *v.* to counteract or cancel the effect of.

normalize (nôr´mə-līz) *v.* to cause something previously regarded as abnormal to be accepted as normal.

perish (pĕr´ĭsh) *v.* to die or come to an end.

petition (pə-tĭsh´ən) *v.* to make a formal request, usually in writing.

prevaricate (prĭ-văr´ĭ-kāt) *v.* to behave in an indecisive manner.

redemptive (rĭ-dĕmp´tĭv) *adj.* causing freedom or salvation.

rehabilitation (rē-hə-bĭl-ĭ-tā´shən) *n.* the act of being restored to good health or condition.

reprieve (rĭ-prēv´) *n.* the cancellation or postponement of punishment.

reputable (rĕp´yə-tə-bəl) *adj.* having a good reputation; honorable.

resolve (rĭ-zŏlv´) *v.* to decide or become determined.

retribution (rĕt-rə-byo͞o´shən) *n.* punishment given in response to a wrongdoing.

revere (rĭ-vîr´) *v.* to regard with devotion or awe.

sanctuary (săngk´cho͞o-ĕr-ē) *n.* a sacred place.

segregate (sĕg´rĭ-gāt) *v.* to cause people to be separated based on gender, race, or other factors.

serrated (sĕr´ā-tĭd) *adj.* having a jagged, saw-toothed edge.

sibling (sĭb´lĭng) *n.* a brother or a sister; a person with one or both parents in common with another person.

simulate (sĭm´yə-lāt) *v.* to create in a controlled setting conditions similar to those a person or machine might face in the real world.

sordid (sôr´dĭd) *adj.* lacking morality.

stagnant (stăg´nənt) *adj.* unchanging; without activity or development.

stereotype (stĕr´ē-ə-tīp) *n.* one that is thought of as conforming to a set type or image.

surreptitiously (sûr-əp-tĭsh´əs-lē) *adv.* done by stealthy or secret means.

synchronize (sĭng´krə-nīz) *v.* to match the timing of.

taciturn (tăs´ĭ-tûrn) *adj.* untalkative; reserved.

tentative (tĕn´tə-tĭv) *adj.* with caution and without confidence.

thwart (thwôrt) *v.* to prevent the occurrence of.

transfix (trans-fĭks´) *v.* to captivate or make motionless with awe.

transpire (trăn-spīr´) *v.* to come about or happen.

vantage point (văn´tĭj point) *n.* a position that allows for a good view of something.

vigilance (vĭj´ə-ləns) *n.* alert attention; watchfulness.

vigilante (vĭj-ə-lăn´tē) *n.* a person who is not a law officer, but who pursues and punishes people suspected of wrongdoing.

visceral (vĭs´ər-əl) *adj.* arising from sudden emotion rather than from thought.

wince (wĭns) *v.* to shrink or flinch involuntarily, especially in pain.

Index of Skills

B

C

D

J

K

L

Index of Titles and Authors

Acknowledgments

Excerpt from *The 57 Bus* by Dashka Slater. Text copyright © 2017 by Dashka Slater. Reprinted by permission of Macmillan Publishing Group.

Excerpts from *The American Heritage Dictionary of The English Language, Fifth Edition.* Text copyright © 2016 by Houghton Mifflin Harcourt Publishing Company. Reprinted by permission of Houghton Mifflin Harcourt Publishing Company.

Excerpt from "Archaeology's Tech Revolution Since Indiana Jones" from *Live Science* by Jeremy Hsu. Text copyright © 2011 by Purch. Reprinted by permission of Wright's Media on behalf of Purch.

"Booker T. and W.E.B." from *Roses and Revolutions: The Selected Writings of Dudley Randall.* Text copyright © 1969 by Dudley Randall. Reprinted by permission of the Estate of Dudley Randall.

Excerpt from *A Chance in the World* by Steve Pemberton. Text copyright © 2012 by Steve Pemberton. Reprinted by permission of HarperCollins Christian Publishers.

Graphic Novel excerpt from *The Complete Maus: A Survivor's Tale* by Art Spiegelman. *Maus, Volume I* copyright © 1973, 1980, 1981, 1982, 1983, 1984, 1985, 1986 by Art Spiegelman; *Maus, Volume II* copyright © 1986, 1989, 1990, 1991 by Art Spiegelman. Reprinted by permission of The Wylie Agency LLC, and Pantheon Books, an imprint of the Knopf Doubleday Publishing Group, a division of Penguin Random House LLC. All rights reserved.

Excerpt from *The Cruelest Journey: 600 Miles to Timbuktu* by Kira Salak. Text copyright © 2005 by Kira Salak. Adapted and reprinted by permission of the author and National Geographic Society.

"The End and the Beginning" from *Miracle Fair* by Wisława Szymborska, translated by Joanna Trzeciak. Text copyright © 2001 by Joanna Trzeciak. Used by permission of W. W. Norton & Company, Inc.

"Entwined" by Brian Tobin. Text copyright © 2015 by Brian Tobin. Reprinted by permission of Brian Tobin.

"Gift-Wrapped Fathers" by Eduardo (Echo) Martinez. Text copyright © 2019 by Eduardo Martinez. Reprinted by permission of the author.

"Harrison Bergeron" from *Welcome to the Monkey House: Stories* by Kurt Vonnegut. Text copyright © 1961 by Kurt Vonnegut, copyright renewed © 1989 by Kurt Vonnegut. Reprinted by permission of Wylie Agency, Inc., and Dell Publishing, an imprint of Random House, a division of Penguin Random House LLC. All rights reserved.

Excerpt from *Hidden Figures Young Readers' Edition* by Margot Lee Shetterly. Text copyright © 2016 by Margot Lee Shetterly. Reprinted by permission of Margot Lee Shetterly, and HarperCollins Publishers.

"I Have a Dream" speech by Martin Luther King, Jr. Text copyright © 1963 by Martin Luther King, Jr., renewed © 1991 by Coretta Scott King. Reprinted by permission of Writers House LLC on behalf of the Heirs of the Estate of Martin Luther King, Jr.

Adaptation of "Is Survival Selfish?" by Lane Wallace from *The Atlantic*, January 29, 2010. Text copyright © 2010 Lane Wallace (LaneWallace.com). Adapted and reprinted by permission of Lane Wallace.

"The Journey" from *Dream Work* by Mary Oliver. Text copyright © 1986 by Mary Oliver. Reprinted by permission of Charlotte Sheedy Literary Agency, and Grove Atlantic, Inc.

"The Leap" by Louise Erdrich from *Harper's Magazine*, March 1990. Text copyright © 1990 by Harper's Magazine. Reprinted by permission of Harper's Magazine. All rights reserved.

"More than Reckless Teenagers" by Caitlin Smith, from *Hothouse Literary Journal*, October 23, 2018. Text copyright © 2018 by Caitlin Smith. Reprinted by permission of the author.

"My Shakespeare" by Kae Tempest. Text copyright © 2012 by Kae Tempest. Reprinted by permission of Johnson & Alcock on behalf of the author.

Excerpt from *Night* by Elie Wiesel. Translated by Marion Wiesel. Text copyright © 1972, 1985, 2006 by Elie Wiesel. Translation copyright © 2006 by Marion Wiesel. Preface to the new translation and Nobel Peace Prize Acceptance Speech copyright © 2006 by Elie Wiesel. Reprinted by permission of Georges Borchardt, Inc., Recorded Books, and Hill and Wang, a division of Farrar, Straus and Giroux.

Excerpts from *The Odyssey* by Homer and translated by Robert Fitzgerald. Translation copyright © 1961, 1963 and copyright © renewed 1989 by Benedict R.C. Fitzgerald on behalf of the Fitzgerald children. This edition copyright © 1998 by Farrar, Straus and Giroux, LLC. Reprinted by permission of Farrar, Straus and Giroux, LLC.

"Once Upon a Time" excerpted from *Jump and Other Stories* by Nadine Gordimer. Text copyright © 1991 by Felix Licensing, B.V. Reprinted by permission of United Agents LLP on behalf of Felix Licensing, B.V., Farrar, Straus and Giroux, LLC, Penguin Canada, a division of Penguin Random House Canada Limited, and Russell & Volkening as agents for the author.

Excerpt from *Persepolis 2: The Story of a Return* by Marjane Satrapi, translated by Anjali Singh. Translation copyright © 2004 by Anjali Singh. Published by Jonathan Cape. Reprinted by permission of the author, The Random House Group Limited, and Pantheon Books, an imprint of the Knopf Doubleday Publishing Group, a division of Penguin Random House LLC. All rights reserved. Any third-party use of this material, outside of this publication, is prohibited. Interested parties must apply directly to Penguin Random House LLC for permission.

"The Power of a Dinner Table" by David Brooks, from *The New York Times*, October 18, 2016. Text copyright © 2016 by The New York Times. Reprinted by permission of PARS International Corp on behalf of The New York Times. All rights reserved. Protected by the Copyright Laws of the United States. The printing, copying, redistribution, or retransmission of this Content without express written permission is prohibited. www.nytimes.com

Excerpt from *Reading Lolita in Tehran: A Memoir in Books* by Azar Nafisi. Text copyright © 2002 and 2015 by Azar Nafisi. Reprinted by permission of Penguin Books Ltd. and Random House, an imprint and division of Penguin Random House LLC. Any third-party use of this material, outside of this publication, is prohibited. Interested parties must apply directly to Penguin Random House LLC for permission.

"Romeo Is a Dirtbag" by Lois Leveen from *Huffington Post,* December 6th, 2017. Text copyright © 2017 by Lois Leveen. Reprinted by permission of the author, Lois Leveen.

"Theme for English B" from *The Collected Poems of Langston Hughes* by Langston Hughes, edited by Arnold Rampersad with David Roessel, Associate Editor. Text copyright © 1994 by the Estate of Langston Hughes. Reprinted by permission of Harold Ober Associates, and Alfred A. Knopf, an imprint of Knopf Doubleday Publishing Group, a division of Penguin Random House LLC. All rights reserved.

"Unsolved 'Vigilante' Murder in the Heartland" (retitled from "Unsolved 'Vigilante' Murder in the Heartland: Missouri Town Goes Quiet After Bully Shot") by C. M. Frankie. Text copyright © 2019 by A&E Television Networks, LLC, www.aetv.com. Reprinted by permission of A&E Television Networks, LLC. All rights reserved.

"Unusual Normality" by Ishmael Beah from *All These Wonders,* edited by Catherine Burns. Text copyright © 2017 by Ishmael Beah. Reprinted by permission of SLL/Sterling Lord Literistic, Inc.

"The Vietnam Wall" from *The Lime Orchard Woman* by Alberto Ríos. Text copyright ©1988 by Alberto Ríos. Reprinted by permission of the author.

"Why Are We Obsessed with True Crime?" by Laura Hensley. Text copyright © 2017 by Corus Television Limited Partnership. Reprinted by permission of the Corus Television Limited Partnership.